Communications
in Computer and Information Science   **544**

More information about this series at http://www.springer.com/series/7899

Emmanouel Garoufallou · Richard J. Hartley
Panorea Gaitanou (Eds.)

Metadata and Semantics Research

9th Research Conference, MTSR 2015
Manchester, UK, September 9–11, 2015
Proceedings

 Springer

Editors

Emmanouel Garoufallou
Institute of Thessaloniki
Alexander Technological Educational
Thessaloniki
Greece

Panorea Gaitanou
Ionian University
Corfu
Greece

Richard J. Hartley
Manchester Metropolitan University
Manchester
UK

ISSN 1865-0929   ISSN 1865-0937 (electronic)
Communications in Computer and Information Science
ISBN 978-3-319-24128-9   ISBN 978-3-319-24129-6 (eBook)
DOI 10.1007/978-3-319-24129-6

Library of Congress Control Number: 2015947955

Springer Cham Heidelberg New York Dordrecht London
© Springer International Publishing Switzerland 2015

Printed on acid-free paper

Springer International Publishing AG Switzerland is part of Springer Science+Business Media
(www.springer.com)

Preface

Metadata and semantics are integral to any information system and significant to the sphere of Web data. Research and development focusing on metadata and semantics are crucial to advancing our understanding and knowledge of metadata; and, more profoundly, for being able to effectively discover, use, archive, and repurpose information. In response to this need, researchers are actively examining methods for generating, reusing, and interchanging metadata. Integrated with these developments is research on the application of computational methods, linked data, and data analytics. A growing body of work also targets conceptual and theoretical designs providing foundational frameworks for metadata and semantic applications. There is no doubt that metadata weaves its way through nearly every aspect of our information ecosystem, and there is great motivation for advancing the current state of understanding in the fields of metadata and semantics. To this end, it is vital that scholars and practitioners convene and share their work.

Since 2005, the Metadata and Semantics Research Conference (MTSR) has served as a significant venue for dissemination and sharing of metadata and semantic-driven research and practices. This year, 2015, marked the ninth MTSR—Metadata and Semantics Research Conference, drawing scholars, researchers and practitioners investigating and advancing our knowledge on a wide range of metadata and semantic-driven topics. MTSR has grown in numbers and submission rates over the last decade, marking it as a leading, international research conference. Continuing the successful mission of previous MTSR conferences (MTSR 2005, MTSR 2007, MTSR 2009, MTSR 2010, MTSR 2011, MTSR 2012, MTSR 2013, and MTSR 2014), MTSR 2015 sought to bring together scholars and practitioners that share a common interest in the interdisciplinary field of metadata, linked data, and ontologies.

The MTSR 2015 program and the contents of these proceedings show a rich diversity of research and practices from metadata and semantically focused tools and technologies, linked data, cross language semantics, ontologies, metadata models, semantic systems, and metadata standards. The general session of the conference included 12 papers covering a broad spectrum of topics, proving the interdisciplinary field of metadata, and was divided into three main themes: Ontology Evolution, Engineering, and Frameworks; Semantic Web and Metadata Extraction, Modeling, Interoperability and Exploratory Search; and Data Analysis, Reuse and Visualization. Metadata as a research topic is maturing, and the conference also supported the following five tracks: Digital Libraries, Information Retrieval, Linked and Social Data; Metadata and Semantics for Open Repositories, Research Information Systems and Data Infrastructures; Metadata and Semantics for Agriculture, Food, and Environment; Metadata and Semantics for Cultural Collections and Applications; and European and National Projects. Each of these tracks had a rich selection of papers, in total 26, giving broader diversity to MTSR, and enabling deeper exploration of significant topics.

All the papers underwent a thorough and rigorous peer-review process. The review and selection this year were highly competitive and only papers containing significant research results, innovative methods, or novel and best practices were accepted for publication. From the general session, only 11 submissions were accepted as full research papers, representing 36.6 % of the total number of submissions. Additional contributions from tracks covering noteworthy and important results were accepted, totaling 38 accepted contributions for MTSR 2015.

Manchester has been the scene of many significant contributions to the development of computers. The School of Computer Science at the University of Manchester is one of the oldest in the UK. The University of Manchester has made a considerable contribution to the development of computing. This includes many firsts including the first stored program computer, the first floating point machine, the first transistor computer, and the first computer to use virtual memory. Thus we were delighted to secure as this year's keynote speaker Professor Carole Goble. Professor Goble leads a large team of researchers and developers working in e-Science, building e-infrastructure for researchers working at the lab, national, and pan-national level. She is heavily involved in European cyber infrastructures for the Life Sciences and is currently active in linking these with the NIH BD2K Commons initiative. She applies technical advances in knowledge technologies, distributed computing, workflows and social computing to solve information management problems for life scientists, especially systems biology, and other scientific disciplines, including biodiversity, chemistry, health informatics and astronomy. Her current research interests are in reproducible research, asset curation and preservation, semantic interoperability, knowledge exchange between scientists and new models of scholarly communication. She has recently been advocating the releasing of research as Research Objects (www.researchobject.org) and is a long-established leading figure in the Semantic Web and Linked Data, chairing the International Semantic Web Conference in 2014 and co-founding the leading journal in the field. The title of her outstanding keynote presentation was "Research Objects: the why, what, and how".

We conclude this preface by thanking the many people who contributed their time and energy to MTSR 2015, and made possible this year's conference. We thank, also, all the organizations that supported the conference.

We extend a sincere thank you to members of the Program Committees (track committees included), the Steering Committee and the Organizing Committees (both general and local), and the conference reviewers. A special thank you to our colleague D. Koutsomiha, who assisted us with the proceedings; and to Stavroula, Vasiliki, and Nikoleta for their endless support and patience.

July 2015

Emmanouel Garoufallou
R.J. Hartley
Panorea Gaitanou

Organization

General Chairs

R.J. Hartley	Manchester Metropolitan University, UK
Emmanouel Garoufallou	Alexander Technological Educational Institute (ATEI) of Thessaloniki, Greece

Program Chairs

Panorea Gaitanou	Ionian University and Benaki Museum, Greece
Imma Subirats	Food and Agriculture Organization (FAO) of the United Nations, Italy

Special Track Chairs

Nikos Houssos	National Documentation Centre, Greece
Imma Subirats	Food and Agriculture Organization (FAO) of the United Nations, Italy
Juliette Dibie	AgroParisTech and INRA, France
Liliana Ibanescu	AgroParisTech and INRA, France
Miguel-Ángel Sicilia	University of Alcalá, Spain
Michalis Sfakakis	Ionian University, Greece
Lina Bountouri	Ionian University and EU Publications Office, Luxembourg
Emmanouel Garoufallou	Alexander Technological Educational Institute (ATEI) of Thessaloniki, Greece
Rania Siatri	Alexander Technological Educational Institute (ATEI) of Thessaloniki, Greece
Stavroula Antonopoulou	American Farm School, Greece

Steering Committee

Juan Manuel Dodero	University of Cádiz, Spain
Emmanouel Garoufallou	Alexander Technological Educational Institute (ATEI) of Thessaloniki, Greece
Nikos Manouselis	Agro-Know Technologies, Greece
Fabio Sartori	Università degli Studi di Milano-Bicocca, Italy
Miguel-Angel Sicilia	University of Alcalá, Spain

Organizing Committee

Jill Griffiths	Manchester Metropolitan University, UK
Frances Johnson	Manchester Metropolitan University, UK
Damiana Koutsomiha	American Farm School, Greece
Anxhela Dani	Alexander Technological Educational Institute (ATEI) of Thessaloniki, Greece
Chrysanthi Chatzopoulou	Alexander Technological Educational Institute (ATEI) of Thessaloniki, Greece

Technical Support Staff

Dimitris Spanoudakis	National Kapodistrian University of Athens, Greece

Program Committee

Rajendra Akerkar	Western Norway Research Institute, Norway
Arif Altun	Hacetepe University, Turkey
Ioannis N. Athanasiadis	Democritus University of Thrace, Greece
Panos Balatsoukas	University of Manchester, UK
Tomaz Bartol	University of Ljubljana, Slovenia
Ina Bluemel	German National Library of Science and Technology TIBm, Germany
Derek Bousfield	Manchester Metropolitan University, UK
Caterina Caracciolo	Food and Agriculture Organization (FAO) of the United Nations, Italy
Ozgu Can	Ege University, Turkey
Christian Cechinel	Federal University of Pampa, Brazil
Artem Chebotko	University of Texas - Pan American, USA
Sissi Closs	Karlsruhe University of Applied Sciences, Germany
Ricardo Colomo-Palacios	Universidad Carlos III, Spain
Constantina Costopoulou	Agricultural University of Athens, Greece
Sally Jo Cunningham	Waikato University, New Zealand
Sándor Darányi	University of Borås, Sweden
Milena Dobreva	University of Malta, Malta
Juan Manuel Dodero	University of Cádiz, Spain
Erdogan Dogdu	TOBB Teknoloji ve Ekonomi University, Turkey
Juan José Escribano Otero	Universidad Europea de Madrid, Spain
Muriel Foulonneau	Tudor Public Research Centre, Luxembourg
Panorea Gaitanou	Ionian University and Benaki Museum, Greece
Emmanouel Garoufallou	Alexander Technological Educational Institute (ATEI) of Thessaloniki, Greece
Manolis Gergatsoulis	Ionian University, Greece
Jane Greenberg	Drexel University, USA
Jill Griffiths	Manchester Metropolitan University, UK
R.J. Hartley	Manchester Metropolitan University, UK

Nikos Houssos	National Documentation Centre, Greece
Carlos A. Iglesias	Universidad Politecnica de Madrid, Spain
Frances Johnson	Manchester Metropolitan University, UK
Brigitte Jörg	Thomson Reuters, UK
Dimitris Kanellopoulos	University of Patras, Greece
Sarantos Kapidakis	Ionian University, Greece
Brian Kelly	CETIS, University of Bolton, UK
Christian Kop	University of Klagenfurt, Austria
Rebecca Koskela	University of New Mexico, USA
Daniela Luzi	National Research Council, Italy
Paolo Manghi	Institute of Information Science and Technologies (ISTI), National Research Council (CNR), Italy
Xavier Ochoa	Centro de Tecnologias de Informacion Guayaquil, Ecuador
Mehmet C. Okur	Yaşar University, Turkey
Matteo Palmonari	University of Milano-Bicocca, Italy
Manuel Palomo Duarte	University of Cádiz, Spain
Laura Papaleo	University of Genoa, Italy
Christos Papatheodorou	Ionian University, Greece
Marios Poulos	Ionian University, Greece
T.V. Prabhakar	Indian Institute of Technology Kanpur, India
Athena Salaba	Kent State University, USA
Salvador Sanchez	University of Alcalá, Spain
Fabio Sartori	Università degli Studi di Milano-Bicocca, Italy
Pinar Senkul	METU, Turkey
Cleo Sgouropoulou	Technological Educational Institute of Athens, Greece
Rania Siatri	Alexander Technological Educational Institute (ATEI) of Thessaloniki, Greece
Miguel-Ángel Sicilia	University of Alcalá, Spain
Imma Subirats	Food and Agriculture Organization (FAO) of the United Nations, Italy
Shigeo Sugimoto	University of Tsukuba, Japan
Stefaan Ternier	Open University of The Netherlands, The Netherlands
Emma Tonkin	King's College London, UK
Effie Tsiflidou	Agro-Know, Greece
Thomas Zschocke	United Nations University, Germany

Additional Reviewers

Stavroula Antonopoulou	American Farm School, Greece
Massimiliano Assante	Istituto di Scienza e Tecnologie dell' Informazione "A. Faedo" - CNR, Italy
Alessia Bardi	Istituto di Scienza e Tecnologie dell' Informazione "A. Faedo" - CNR, Italy

Pablo Delatorre	Universidad de Cádiz, Spain
Sotiris Karetsos	Agricultural University of Athens, Greece
Damiana Koutsomiha	American Farm School, Greece
Chris Munro	University of Manchester, UK
Alev Mutlu	Koceli University, Turkey
Fabrizio Pecoraro	Istituto di Ricerche sulla Popolazione e le Politiche Sociali, Italy
Riccardo Porrini	Università degli Studi di Milano-Bicocca, Italy
Dimitris Rousidis	University of Alcalá, Spain
Emine Sezer	Ege University, Turkey
Richard Williams	University of Manchester, UK
Georgia Zafeiriou	University of Macedonia, Greece
Burley Zhong Wang	Sun Yat-Sen University, China

Track on Digital Libraries, Information Retrieval, Linked and Social Data

Special Track Chairs

Emmanouel Garoufallou	Alexander Technological Educational Institute (ATEI) of Thessaloniki, Greece
Rania Siatri	Alexander Technological Educational Institute (ATEI) of Thessaloniki, Greece

Program Committee

Panos Balatsoukas	University of Manchester, UK
Ozgu Can	Ege University, Turkey
Sissi Closs	Karlsruhe University of Applied Sciences, Germany
Mike Conway	University of North Carolina at Chapel Hill, USA
Phil Couch	University of Manchester, UK
Milena Dobreva	University of Malta, Malta
Ali Emrouznejad	Aston University, UK
Panorea Gaitanou	Ionian University and Benaki Museum, Greece
Jane Greenberg	Drexel University, USA
Jill Griffiths	Manchester Metropolitan University, UK
R.J. Hartley	Manchester Metropolitan University, UK
Frances Johnson	Manchester Metropolitan University, UK
Nikos Korfiatis	University of East Anglia, UK
Rebecca Koskela	University of New Mexico, USA
Valentini Moniarou-Papaconstantinou	Technological Educational Institute of Athens, Greece
Dimitris Rousidis	University of Alcalá, Spain
Athena Salaba	Kent State University, USA
Miguel-Angel Sicilia	University of Alcalá, Spain
Christine Urquhart	Aberystwyth University, UK

Evgenia Vassilakaki	Technological Educational Institute of Athens, Greece
Sirje Virkus	Tallinn University, Estonia
Georgia Zafeiriou	University of Macedonia, Greece

Track on Metadata and Semantics for Open Repositories, Research Information Systems, and Data Infrastructures

Special Track Chairs

| Imma Subirats | Food and Agriculture Organization (FAO) of the United Nations, Italy |
| Nikos Houssos | National Documentation Centre, Greece |

Program Committee

Sophie Aubin	Institut National de la Recherche Agronomique, France
Daniele Bailo	Istituto Nazionale di Geofisica e Vulcanologia, Italy
Thomas Baker	Sungkyunkwan University, Korea
Hugo Besemer	Wageningen UR Library, The Netherlands
Gordon Dunshire	University of Strathclyde, UK
Jan Dvorak	Charles University of Prague, Czech Republic
Jane Greenberg	Drexel University, USA
Siddeswara Guru	University of Queensland, Australia
Kris Jack	Mendeley, UK
Keith Jeffery	Keith G. Jeffery Consultants, UK
Rebecca Koskela	University of New Mexico, USA
Jessica Lindholm	Malmö University, Sweden
Daniela Luzi	Institute for Research on Population and Social Policies - Italian National Research Council (IRPPS-CNR), Italy
Devika P. Madalli	Indian Statistical Institute, India
Paolo Manghi	Institute of Information Science and Technologies - Italian National Research Council (ISTI-CNR), Italy
Natalia Manola	University of Athens, Greece
Brian Matthews	Science and Technology Facilities Council, UK
Eva Mendez	Carlos III University, Spain
Jochen Schirrwagen	University of Bielefeld, Germany
Birgit Schmidt	University of Göttingen, Germany
Joachim Schöpfel	University of Lille, France
Chrisa Tsinaraki	European Commission, Joint Research Centre, Italy
Yannis Tzitzikas	University of Crete and ICS-FORTH, Greece
Daniel Vila	Polytechnic University of Madrid, Spain
Zhong Wang	Sun-Yat-Sen University, China

Peter Wittenburg	Max Planck Institute for Psycholinguistics, The Netherlands
Zhang Xuefu	Agricultural Information Institute, Chinese Academy of Agricultural Sciences (CAAS), China
Marcia Zeng	Kent State University, USA

Track on Metadata and Semantics for Agriculture, Food, and Environment

Special Track Chairs

Juliette Dibie	AgroParisTech and INRA, France
Liliana Ibanescu	AgroParisTech and INRA, France
Miguel-Ángel Sicilia	University of Alcalá, Spain

Program Committee

Christopher Brewster	Aston Business School, Aston University, UK
Patrice Buche	INRA, France
Caterina Caracciolo	Food and Agriculture Organization (FAO) of the United Nations, Italy
Sander Janssen	Alterra, Wageningen UR, The Netherlands
Stasinos Konstantopoulos	NCSR Demokritos, Greece
Claire Nedellec	INRA, France
Ivo Jr. Pierozzi	Embrapa Agricultural Informatics, Brazil
Vassilis Protonotarios	Agro-Know, Greece
Mathieu Roche	CIRAD, France
Catherine Roussey	IRSTEA, France
Effie Tsiflidou	Agro-Know, Greece
Jan Top	Vrije Universiteit, The Netherlands

Track on Metadata and Semantics for Cultural Collections and Applications

Special Track Chairs

| Michalis Sfakakis | Ionian University, Greece |
| Lina Bountouri | Ionian University, Greece and EU Publications Office, Luxembourg |

Program Committee

Trond Aalberg	Norwegian University of Science and Technology (NTNU), Norway
Karin Bredenberg	The National Archives of Sweden, Sweden
Costis Dallas	University of Toronto, Canada

Enrico Fransesconi EU Publications Office, Luxembourg,
  and Consiglio Nazionale delle Ricerche,
  Florence, Italy
Manolis Gergatsoulis Ionian University, Greece
Antoine Isaac Vrije Universiteit Amsterdam, The Netherlands
Sarantos Kapidakis Ionian University, Greece
Irene Lourdi National and Kapodistrian University of Athens,
  Greece
Christos Papatheodorou Ionian University and Digital Curation Unit, IMIS,
  Athena RC, Greece
Stephen Stead Paveprime Ltd., UK
Chrisa Tsinaraki Joint Research Centre, European Commission, Italy
Andreas Vlachidis University of South Wales, UK
Katherine Wisser Graduate School of Library and Information
  Science, Simmons College, USA
Maja Žumer University of Ljubljana, Slovenia

Track on European and National Projects

Special Track Chairs

Emmanouel Garoufallou Alexander Technological Educational Institute
  (ATEI) of Thessaloniki, Greece
Rania Siatri Alexander Technological Educational Institute
  (ATEI) of Thessaloniki, Greece
Stavroula Antonopoulou American Farm School, Greece

Program Committee

Panos Balatsoukas University of Manchester, UK
Mike Conway University of North Carolina at Chapel Hill, USA
Panorea Gaitanou Ionian University and Benaki Museum, Greece
Jane Greenberg Drexel University, USA
R.J. Hartley Manchester Metropolitan University, UK
Nikos Houssos National Documentation Center (EKT), Greece
Damiana Koutsomiha American Farm School, Greece
Paolo Manghi Institute of Information Science and Technologies
  (ISTI), National Research Council, Italy
Dimitris Rousidis University of Alcalá, Spain
Dimitris Spanoudakis National and Kapodistrian University of Athens,
  Greece
Miguel-Angel Sicilia University of Alcalá, Spain
Sirje Virkus Tallinn University, Estonia

Contents

Data Analysis, Reuse and Visualization

**Track on Digital Libraries, Information Retrieval, Linked and Social Data
Models, Frameworks and Applications**

Data Quality and Evaluation Studies

**Track on Metadata and Semantics for Open Repositories, Research
Information Systems and Data Infrastructure**

Track on Metadata and Semantics for Agriculture, Food and Environment

Track on Metadata and Semantics for Cultural Collections and Applications

Track on European and National Projects

Poster Papers

Ontology Evolution, Engineering, and Frameworks

An Orchestration Framework for Linguistic Task Ontologies

Catherine Chavula and C. Maria Keet[✉]

Department of Computer Science, University of Cape Town, Cape Town, South Africa
{cchavula,mkeet}@cs.uct.ac.za

Abstract. Ontologies provide knowledge representation formalism for expressing linguistic knowledge for computational tasks. However, natural language is complex and flexible, demanding fine-grained ontologies tailored to facilitate solving specific problems. Moreover, extant linguistic ontological resources ignore mechanisms for systematic modularisation to ensure semantic interoperability with task ontologies. This paper presents an orchestration framework to organise and control the inheritance of ontological elements in the development of linguistic task ontologies. The framework is illustrated in the design of new task ontologies for the Bantu noun classification system. Specific use is demonstrated with annotation of lexical items connected to ontology elements terms and with the classification of nouns in the ABox into noun classes.

1 Introduction

Ontologies are increasingly being used to provide computationally ready data for Natural Language Processing (NLP) tasks in a uniform standard. Ontologies are being used to publish language resources and annotation schemes for different application scenarios on the Semantic Web. For example, natural language features are encoded in an ontology to document linguistics domain knowledge as well as to provide terminology for annotating machine readable language data in [8]. Another recent growing application for linguistic metadata frameworks or ontologies, is annotating lexicalisations of ontology elements terms with linguistic features specified in linguistic ontologies [14]. The ontology lexicalisations are used to facilitate ontology-based NLP tasks such as generating natural language descriptions of Semantic Web documents [5] and to build multilingual resources for world internationalisation (e.g. AGROVOC in many languages).

Natural language is complex and fluid, and demands modular ontologies to capture linguistic knowledge at the required level of specificity. For example, some features vary across languages and other features exist only in specific languages. However, ontological axioms are based on intensional definitions [10]; this is a problem when capturing language-specific features, which require instance level definitions. Additionally, lack of principled methodologies to link or align generic linguistic ontologies has led to isolated ontologies which can not be integrated due to conflicting representations of the domain knowledge, or not used

© Springer International Publishing Switzerland 2015
E. Garoufallou et al. (Eds.): MTSR 2015, CCIS 544, pp. 3–14, 2015.
DOI: 10.1007/978-3-319-24129-6_1

with existing resources due to formats. Generic linguistic ontologies or frameworks attempt to address these problems by creating resources that capture all linguistic features [9,13]. However, these linguistic resources do not capture language specific features at the desired level of granularity. Task ontologies provide a means of bridging general language knowledge with fine-grained language specific knowledge which may be tailored for specific computational tasks such as Natural Language Generation (NLG). However, the same challenges of alignment and intensional specification resurfaces.

Given the challenges for modelling language specific task oriented ontologies, the paper makes three contributions. Firstly, we present an orchestration architecture for facilitating systematic modular design and interoperability of linguistic task ontologies. Our approach merges ideas from BioTop, a domain ontology for the life sciences [2], and the DOGMA approach [11], an ontology engineering methodology. Secondly, we present Noun Class System (NCS) for Bantu languages specification in OWL ontologies based on the orchestration architecture, and thirdly, we present the classification of Bantu nouns into their noun class based on the ontology of the linguistic noun classification, therewith satisfying one of the competency questions.

The remainder of the paper is structured as follows. Section 2 describes the framework for the orchestration of linguistic task ontologies. Section 3 summarises the NCS in Bantu languages and describes the ontology development process for the Bantu noun class system ontology, and its use cases. Section 4 compares our approach with related work, and we conclude in Section 5.

2   Orchestration Framework Architecture

Human natural languages are complex and dynamic. For example, some features are universal to all languages while others exist in only specific languages. Ontologies provide an approach for specifying this complex linguistic knowledge. However, the differences in features for different languages, necessitate specialised ontology modules. Unfortunately, there is lack of principled methods for aligning fine grained conceptualisation with other high level domain conceptualisations. The orchestration framework has been developed to be used in the design of task specific linguistic ontologies to achieve semantic interoperability with the existing linguistic ontologies. The approach adopted in the architecture of the framework is inspired by ideas from BioTop, a top-domain ontology for the life sciences [2], and the DOGMA approach [11] to ontology engineering and conceptual model development. The architecture of the framework provides a systematic modular design for aligning foundational ontologies, linguistic description ontologies, and task specific linguistic ontologies.

One of the challenges for aligning task ontologies with domain ontologies is to specify the alignment mechanism between task ontologies, domain ontologies and foundational ontologies. BioTop uses a 'pyramid' of one foundational ontology–Basic Formal Ontology (BFO), several top-domain ontologies (BioTop), and multiple domain ontologies (such as Cell Ontology (CL) and Gene Ontology

(GO) [2]). BioTop is a top-level domain ontology that is used to create new domain ontologies which are semantically interoperable with existing ontologies as well as to improve or align existing ontologies in the life sciences domain. Our framework adopts the BioTop architecture to provide an alignment mechanism between task ontologies and domain ontologies and, within the framework, we have defined a Top-domain ontology layer that consists of generic ontologies.

DOGMA is an ontology engineering methodological framework for guiding ontology engineers to build ontological resources which are usable and reusable [11]. The DOGMA approach aims to build ontologies independent of the application requirements whilst ensuring that the specified knowledge can be reused by other applications and meet their specific requirements. DOGMA uses the *principle of double articulation* to axiomatize knowledge: domain knowledge is specified to capture the intended meaning of the vocabulary, and is reused to add application-specific constraints in order to meet application requirements or to handle highly specialised differences. Natural language is highly flexible and same concepts may vary across languages. Expressing specialised linguistic knowledge in an ontology for a single natural language is challenging because knowledge captured in ontologies is based on *intensional semantic structure* [10]. Thus, we adopted the DOGMA approach in order to accommodate the diversity of languages: an ontological conceptualization and a specific knowledge axomitization with added constraints.

The proposed approach defines four linked ontological layers: top-level, top-domain and domain ontologies,task ontologies and a fifth layer for added precision for each language:

- **Top level ontologies**, which represent high level categories of things in the world independent of a subject domain;
- **Top-domain ontologies**, which contain linguistic knowledge independent of linguistic theories and languages, and provide conceptual interlinkages with domain ontologies, task specific and domain independent knowledge; **domain ontologies** concepts can also be covered at this level, if the ontology covers sub-domain knowledge.
- **Domain ontologies**, which contain specialised knowledge of a particular sub-domain.
- **Task ontologies**, which specify language-specific scenario oriented knowledge to enhance specific computational tasks (e.g. the classification of nouns into their classes, see Section 3.6);
- **Logic-based conceptual models/axiomatizations**, which contain more precise knowledge for a specific 'application', in our case with natural language specific idiosyncrasies and additional constraints.

Fig. 1 shows the general idea of our modular architecture, which will be instantiated for linguistics knowledge and the Bantu noun class system in Section 3. The arrows in the diagram show the alignments, which can be equivalence and/or subsumption alignments between the entities in the ontologies. The purpose of the framework is to ensure that task specific ontologies can be developed in a

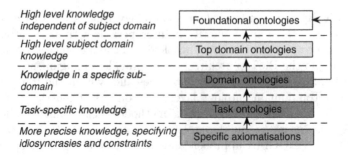

Fig. 1. Framework ontological layers

modular and systematic fashion and that the resulting ontologies are interoperable with other ontological resources in the linguistics domain. For example, the Bantu noun classification system has different singular/plural mapping schemes across languages and it is impossible to capture this knowledge in a single conceptualisation. Modular design is suitable for this scenario but lacks mechanism for linking and aligning these modules with extant linguistic ontological resources. In the DOGMA approach, application knowledge specification uses agreed terms or vocabulary defined in the domain knowledge. Similarly, task ontologies can be defined at two levels, a task ontology and language specific task ontologies. The proposed framework has been applied in the design and implementation of Bantu NCS ontologies, which is described in the next section.

3 Applying the Framework to Bantu Noun Class System Ontologies

Bantu languages are a major language family on the African continent, with over 220 Million speakers across Sub-Saharan Africa. Bantu languages are largely agglutinative with complex structural and syntactic features [12] (as are, e.g., Finnish and Quechua). Bantu languages have several structural similarities that enable some of computational solutions to be adapted across the family. For example, noun classification is one of those pervasive features [12]. Nouns are categorized into classes to a large extent by the prefixes the nouns take. Formalising the Bantu NCS into a computational artefact is one of the requirements identified for Semantic Web NLP based applications for Bantu languages [3].

The Bantu NCS ontologies seek to provide fine-grained specification of entities and relationships for the NCS of Bantu Languages; this level of specification is necessary for deep morphological analysis of nominal phrases [7]. Further, the ontologies will serve as a computational model for the analysis of Bantu nouns and documentation of complex relationships, which may lead to further linguistic research. Also, NCS ontology can be used for annotation of nouns with their noun classes which is a necessary component in multilingual ontology-driven information systems. Clearly, the purposes of the NCS ontology require that the ontology be interoperable with existing ontological resources and the proposed framework enables Bantu NCS ontologies have been applied to achieve this. We describe basics aspects of the noun class system first, and then the ontology development methodology, design, its contents, and how the framework is applied.

3.1 Overview of Bantu Noun Class System

Nominal classification is a common feature in many languages. For instance, those in romance languages category (e.g., French and Italian), have a gender category, which classifies nouns into types such as feminine and masculine [6]. Although the Bantu noun classification has been given the treatment of gender category, Bantu classification exhibit attributes that need to be considered in its own category. The Bantu noun classification is largely based on semantics and morphological marking of nominal prefixes or word structure of a noun [12]. Early studies of Bantu nominal morphology identified individual prefixes on nouns and labelled the prefixes with Arabic numerals which were then proposed as Bantu noun classes [12]. Plural and singular forms of Bantu nouns take different prefixes. Thus, using this classification, each class can have a corresponding singular or plural form, i.e., the classes are categorised into singular and plural forms with each marked by a corresponding prefix; e.g., a pairing of noun stems and prefixes in Chichewa (in Guthrie zone (N31)) for class7/class8 are *chi-/zi-* and for class12/class13 they are *ka-/ti-*; e.g. *chi*patso ('fruit') and *zi*patso ('fruits'). These prefixes are added to other morphemes or words to create singular or plural nouns, e.g., *ka*chipatso ('small fruit'). The collection of prefixes contributes to the construction of the traditional Bantu NCS. The class of a noun determines the markers on syntactic elements in a phrase or sentence (e.g., verbs and adjectives) and contributes to their inflectional behaviour; e.g., *chi*patso *cho*koma ('tasty fruit').

The number of classes varies in different languages but the majority of the languages exhibit some similarities in the semantics of the classes, prefixing and the pairing of the classes into singular and plural forms. In the community of Bantu linguists, the Bleek-Meinhof classification is widely used [12]. The Bleek-Meinhof classification uses the prefixes as indicators of classes and the NCS is built by listing all the prefixes available in a language with Arabic Numerals prefixes. Thus, singular and plural forms of a word belong to two separate classes. In order to maintain the relationship between the singular and plural classes, linguists use the Bleek-Meinhof numbering system and may group the plural and its singular classes as one class, e.g., class1 and class2 becomes class1/2 [6].

3.2 Methodology for NCS Ontologies Development

The development of the ontologies followed a bottom-up approach [16]. In particular, this involved i) a preliminary domain analysis to establish the technical feasibility of having an NCS ontology; ii) assessment of relevant existing ontologies and non-ontological resources (databases and documentation of linguistic resources), including those described in Section 4 below; iii) identification of the concepts and relationships in Bantu noun classification, including adopting concepts from the GOLD ontology; iv) develop a first version of the ontology, based on knowledge of Chichewa and isiZulu using Meinhof's classification, for community evaluation [3].

Experiences with this NCS ontology induced a scope and structural change from the aim to lexicalise an ontology in Chichewa and isiZulu with the *lemon* model, to that it should cater for the whole Bantu language family, and more generally, be an extensible system. The bottom-up approach was followed and more resources consulted, such as [12], consulting domain experts (linguists) and Bantu language speakers and presenting (verbalised and visualised) drafts of the ontology, and competency questions formulated, including:

CQ1: Is the nominal classification feature in the ontology capturing the taxonomic structure for Bantu noun class system?

CQ2: Do the corresponding relationships capture the constraints in the relationship of nominal concepts in Bantu languages?

CQ3: Can it infer the class of a noun based on either knowing the singular or plural or noun class of a noun word?

For purposes of interoperability and extensibility, a comprehensive alignment to GOLD was carried out (GOLD was chosen, since the initial motivation for the ontology was for linguistic annotation) and a modular architecture was devised. Thereafter, the ontologies were evaluated in the tasks of noun classification into their classes and annotation of nominal lexical items (class labels in an ontology) with their noun classes.

3.3   NCS Ontologies Design and Implementation

The design of NCS ontologies captures the noun classification concepts and relationships within Bantu Languages spectrum. The current release of the ontology uses the proposed orchestration framework and has been re-engineered (cf. [3]) in the following way:

- The major improvement is the use of an orchestration framework to cater for the differences in the noun classes across Bantu languages, rather than only Chichewa and isiZulu: the use of a double articulation principle [11] to capture these differences and alignment with GOLD by applying its principles in the ontology.
- Multiple classification schemes of Bantu noun system have been used (cf. only Meinhof's).
- New concepts, relationships, and constraints to capture fine-grained linguistic domain knowledge to obtain desired inferences.

Practically, the ontologies have been represented in OWL, and are available from http://meteck.org/files/ontologies/ in NCS1.zip. This contains a GOLD module (with a SUMO module), the NCS ontology, and, at the time of writing, language-specific axiomatisations for Chichewa, Xhosa, and Zulu.

3.4   Overview of the NCS Ontology

The NCS ontology design is based on the classification of Bantu nouns at fine-grained morphemic units, and the structural and lexical relationships among these units. The taxonomic structure has two main parts: the first part provide the morphological structure of Bantu nouns and the second part provides the hierarchy of concepts for properties of Bantu nouns including the NCS based on Bleek-Meinhof [6,12]. The first part allows the labelling of Bantu nouns beyond the part-of-speech category and captures the lexical units of the nouns and how they are structured in relation to the NCS. The second component models the grammatical features of the nouns and captures the Bantu NCS concepts. The gender and grammatical number linguistic categories are included to avoid confusion with the noun classification feature. Fig. 2 shows the taxonomy of concepts in the ontology (only a subset of the noun classes are shown). Traditional Bleek-Meinhof classes and modern paired labelling schemes were used to specify the ontologies classes drawn from Bantu Languages studies [12].

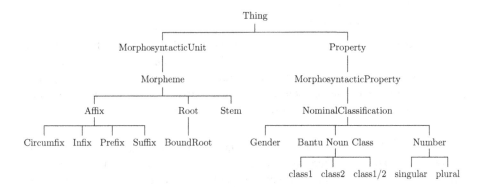

Fig. 2. Section of the class hierarchy of the Bantu NCS.

3.5   Application of the Framework

The design of the NCS ontologies follow the proposed architecture, and is depicted schematically in Fig. 5. At the bottom we have the logic-based conceptual models—also called 'application ontologies' or structured metadata—that capture concepts and relationships in Bantu NCS domain for a specific language. These language-specific ontologies are specialisations of the general NCS ontology as 'task ontology', following the double articulation principle. The resulting ontologies are aligned with a relevant module of GOLD, which was already aligned to the SUMO foundational ontology. The NCS ontologies are therefore linked to these resources by following these principles and the proposed framework. Conceptual models for noun classes of other Bantu Languages can easily be 'plugged in', starting from the NCS ontology as its top ontology. The framework can also be extended 'horizontally' to cater for other languages; e.g., a task ontology about verb conjugation in the Romance languages with specifics for Spanish and Italian each in its OWL file, yet remaining interoperable.

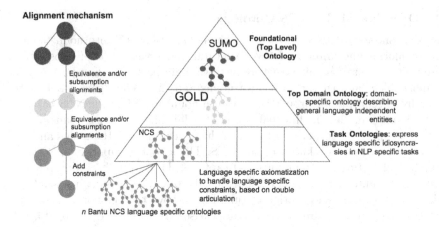

Fig. 3. GOLD and Noun Class System alignment using the proposed framework

3.6   Using the Ontologies

The NCS ontologies provide language-specific linguistic properties that are useful in language studies and in language engineering tasks. One of the foreseen usage scenarios is in the annotation of text for computational language processing such as morphological analysis as well as annotating lexical items in computational lexicons. We describe two use cases.

Use Case I: Linguistic Annotation. Data on the Semantic Web consists of language independent factual knowledge which is based on formal vocabularies specified in ontologies. Unfortunately, this enormous amount of data is inaccessible to many potential human users because of the complexity of the logic-based knowledge representation model. Expressing or accessing this knowledge using natural language ensures that the knowledge is accessible to end-users. However, such interaction methods need Natural Language Processing (NLP) tasks to be incorporated into Semantic Web applications or tools. Evidently, these NLP tasks require ontologies that are grounded with rich linguistic data in multiple languages, i.e., lexical knowledge specifying how ontology elements are expressed in multiple languages and their associated linguistic properties [14].

Ontology lexicalisation provides a means of enriching ontologies with linguistic knowledge [14]. Several models have been proposed to express how ontology elements are linguistically realised. For example, the lexicon model for ontologies, *lemon*, is a descriptive model for structuring and publishing ontology lexicalisations on the Semantic Web [14]. *lemon* defines the structure for lexical entries and how the entries interface with ontology elements terms. Externally defined linguistic properties, e.g., linguistic annotation ontologies, are used to describe the entries in the lexicons. In the context of NCS ontology, Bantu noun entries in *lemon* format can be annotated with their noun classes. Linguistic properties defined in the upper layers of the orchestration framework can be used with

```
@prefix dcterms: <http://purl.org/dc/terms/>.
@prefix rdfs: <http://www.w3.org/2001/02/rdf-schema#>.
@prefix ncsNY: <http://www.meteck.org/files/ontologies/ncsNY/>.
@prefix lemon: <http://www.lemon-model.net/>.
@prefix gold: <http://purl.org/linguistics/gold/>.
@prefix : <http://www.mteck.org/id/dcterms/lexiconNY>.
:myDCLexicon a lemon:Lexicon ;
lemon:language "ny" ;
lemon:entry :chiyankhulo.
:chiyankhulo a lemon:LexicalEntry ;
ncsNY:BantuNounClass ncsNY:class7;
gold:PartOfSpeechProperty gold:noun;
lemon:canonicalForm [lemon:writtenRep "chiyankhulo"@ny];
lemon:sense [lemon:reference dcterms:language] .
ncs:BantuNounClass rdfs:subPropertyOf lemon:property.
gold:PartOfSpeechProperty rdfs:subPropertyOf lemon:property.
```

Fig. 4. Chichewa dcterms:language entry.

properties defined in the NCS ontology consistently. For instance, Fig. 4 shows the lexical entry for the property dcterms:language (http://purl.org/dc/terms/language) from the Dublin Core Metadata Initiative (DCMI), and the entry uses NCS ontology elements to specify a noun class of a Chichewa lexicon.

Use Case II : ABox Classification. Modelling linguistic properties in ontologies provide more expressiveness to specify the complex relationships that exist among concepts. Using the proposed orchestration framework, language specific idiosyncrasies can be captured and formalised in a generic paradigm without interfering language universals. Positively, the combined knowledge from all the framework layers can be used to infer new relationships not explicitly specified; this is useful in language processing because automatic individual classification may compensate incomplete linguistic annotation especially for under-resourced languages. One of the requirements (CQ3) of the NCS ontologies is to be able to infer the class of a noun (ABox individual) with a singular or plural relationship to another annotated noun (see Section 3.2). A task-based evaluation of this requirement requires that the reasoner returns correct ABox classification or accurate responses to DL queries concerning ABox classification. For example, the NCS ontology of Chichewa specifies the relationship between classes 7 and 8 using ncs:hasPlural and ncs:hasSingular, so that with the singular asserted, it can deduce the plural (where the plural relationship has been specified), or vv, which is illustrated in Fig. 5 for *chiyankhulo*.

4 Related Work

Ontologies have been widely used by researchers to formalise linguistic knowledge for use in ontology driven information systems and the Semantic Web. For example, GOLD is a linguistic ontology that documents expert linguistic

Fig. 5. Example of deductions for *chiyankhulo*, given *ziyankhulo* is in class 8.

knowledge in an ontology. GOLD is aligned with Suggested Upper Merged Ontology (SUMO), a foundational ontology, to ensure semantic interoperability with other ontologies. GOLD captures linguistic properties independent of any linguistic theory and the ontology contains general and language specific linguistic properties. Due to these attributes, we used GOLD as a Top Domain Ontology for our instantiated framework. However, GOLD encodes the Bantu noun classes as a type of gender by defining a Roman numeral based gender concept. We capture the classification in a different way as noun classes are mostly based on the underlying meaning, e.g., humans are in classes 1 and 2, and other morphological aspects (recall Section 3.1).

Ontologies have also been used to mediate between domain ontologies and natural language realisations of ontological entities. For example, General Upper Model (GUM) ontology implements an interface for the interaction of domain-specific knowledge and general linguistic resources [1]. Thus, GUM provides an abstraction between surface realization and domain specific knowledge. Although, GUM can be categorised as a task ontology targeting NLP tasks such as NLG, the ontology does not provide any means for linking with other linguistic ontologies. Our work is different as the proposed orchestration framework provide a method for linking linguistic ontologies to task linguistic ontologies to ensure interoperability.

Due to the heterogeneity of terminology for annotating linguistic properties, different data models have been proposed to make language data and metadata interoperable. The ISO TC37/SC4 Data Category Registry (DCR) is a community maintained repository for linguistics concepts and metadata categories [13]. The terminologies or data categories can be imported for use in applications on the Semantic Web; the categories have been used to create LexInfo ontology, which is used in annotating ontology-lexicons in *lemon* format [5]. Still, the available categories are limited, lacking complete noun class information. For example, only Zulu noun classes have been proposed for DCR categories [15] and that consists of a subset of the noun classes identified for all Bantu languages. We have demonstrated how our framework can be used to accommodate Bantu noun classes for all languages in its family. Additionally, we have proposed a framework for linguistic task ontologies but DCR only focuses on terminologies for linguistic annotation.

Similar to DCR, Ontologies of Linguistic Annotation (OLiA) is a repository of linguistic data categories. OLiA formalises the semantics of linguistic annotation terminologies as OWL2/DL ontologies to achieve both structural and conceptual interoperability between different annotation schemes in the extant repositories such as GOLD and ISOcat [4]. However, Bantu languages being under-resourced, are not covered to an adequate level of detail. The NCS ontology focuses on language specific attributes of nouns which can be applied to NLP applications within Bantu languages and this sets it apart from resources such as OLiA, which attempt to align general linguistic ontologies to ensure interoperability. Furthermore, the orchestration framework adds a modular design architecture at a lower level, allowing language-specific idiosyncrasies to be accommodated.

A repository for PartOfSpeech features for tagging two South African Languages is proposed in [7]. The repository is designed to have a taxonomic representation of linguistic categories for Bantu languages and the design of the repository is to be implemented in a relational database. This work is similar to our NCS ontologies, but the representation of the NCS is not considered as part of the ontology. Additionally, the repository does not consider the formalisation of the linguistic properties into a formal ontology.

5   Discussion and Conclusions

The representation issue of the tension between genericity and specificity of representing domain knowledge, has been solved by merging into a single framework, a pyramidal modular architecture with the *double articulation principle*. The proposed framework can be applied in developing task-oriented ontologies whose conceptualisation does not match any of the existing (linguistic) ontologies but has to be used with the existing resources and refine existing ones. This framework was applied to linguistic ontologies so as to control the development of task specific linguistic ontologies to ensure that concepts are aligned with extant domain and foundational ontologies, with as finer-grained instantiation the design of noun class ontologies. Multiple noun class ontologies (conceptual models/structured metadata) have been developed for different Bantu language using the proposed framework. Thanks to alignment with GOLD and SUMO, the NCS ontologies can be used with other linguistic ontologies to annotate text and other structured linguistic resources. In addition, the NCS ontologies can be used to classify nouns of a specific Bantu language using a specific Bantu NCS ontology. This can be used as pre-processing stage of language resources and can reduce the cost of developing such resources and improve the performance of NLP tasks such as morphological processing. We have also illustrated how the ontology can be used in the classification of nouns where the nouns are individuals in the ontology and annotation of lexical entries with linguistic properties. The ontologies may be used with other community-maintained terminology repositories that capture other linguistic properties. Our future direction of this work includes using the framework to further align other task ontologies and building a library of ontologies which have been aligned using this approach, and use this repository to conduct an empirical evaluation of the framework. We are currently adding the NCS ontologies to the linguistic Linked Open Data (LOD) cloud so that it also can be used for ontology-driven multilingual information systems.

Acknowledgments. We thank Dr Langa Khumalo and Atikonda Mtenje for their input and feedback. This work is based upon research supported by the National Research Foundation of South Africa (Project UID: 93397).

References

1. Bateman, J.A.: Upper modeling: organizing knowledge for natural language processing. In: Proc. of the 5th INLG Workshop, Pittsburgh, PA, pp. 54–60 (June 1990)
2. Beisswanger, E., Schulz, S., Stenzhorn, H., Hahn, U.: Biotop: An upper domain ontology for the life sciences: A description of its current structure, contents and interfaces to obo ontologies. Applied Ontology **3**(4), 205–212 (2008)
3. Chavula, C., Keet, C.: Is lemon sufficient for building multilingual ontologies for bantu languages? In: Proc. of OWLED 2014, Riva del Garda, Italy, October 17–18. CEUR-WS, vol. 1265, pp. 61–72 (2014)
4. Chiarcos, C.: Ontologies of linguistic annotation: survey and perspectives. In: Proc. of LREC 2012. ELRA Proceedings, Istanbul, Turkey (May 2012)
5. Cimiano, P., Nagel, D., Unger, C.: Exploiting ontology lexica for generating natural language texts from RDF data. In: Proc. of 14th European Workshop on NLG, Sofia, Bulgaria, pp. 10–19 (August 2013)
6. Corbett, G.G.: Gender. Cambridge University Press, Cambridge (1991)
7. Faass, G., Bosch, S., Taljard, E.: Towards a Part-of-Speech Ontology; Encoding Morphemic Units of Two South African Languages. Nordic Journal of African Studies **21**(3), 118–140 (2012)
8. Farrar, S., Langendoen, D.: Markup and the GOLD ontology. In: Proc. of Ws. on Digitizing and Annotating Text and Field Recordings (2003)
9. Farrar, S., Langendoen, D.T.: A linguistic ontology for the semantic web. GLOT International **7**(3), 97–100 (2003)
10. Guarino, N.: Formal ontology and information systems. In: Proc. of FOIS 1998, Trento, Italy, pp. 3–15. IOS Press (1998)
11. Jarrar, M., Meersman, R.: Ontology engineering – the DOGMA approach. In: Dillon, T.S., Chang, E., Meersman, R., Sycara, K. (eds.) Advances in Web Semantics I. LNCS, vol. 4891, pp. 7–34. Springer, Heidelberg (2008)
12. Katamba, F.: Bantu Nominal Morphology. In: Nurse, D., Phillippson, G. (eds.) The Bantu Languages. Curzon Press, London (2003)
13. Kemps-Snijders, M., Windhouwer, M., Wittenburg, P., Wright, S.: ISOcat: Remodelling metadata for language resources. International Journal of Metadata, Semantics and Ontologies **4**(4), 261–276 (2009)
14. McCrae, J., Aguado-de Cea, G., Buitelaar, P., Cimiano, P., Declerck, T., Gómez-Pérez, A., Gracia, J., Hollink, L., Montiel-Ponsoda, E., Spohr, D., Wunner, T.: Interchanging lexical resources on the Semantic Web. LRE **46**(4), 701–719 (2012)
15. Pretorius, L., Bosch, S.E.: Towards extending the isocat data category registry with zulu morphosyntax. In: Proceedings of the 10th Joint ACL - ISO Workshop on Interoperable Semantic Annotation (2014)
16. Suárez-Figueroa, M., Gómez-Pérez, A., Fernández-López, M.: Exploiting ontology lexica for generating natural language texts from RDF data. In: Ontology Engineering in a Networked World, pp. 9–34. Springer (2012)

On the Preservation of Evolving Digital Content – The Continuum Approach and Relevant Metadata Models

Nikolaos Lagos[1(✉)], Simon Waddington[2], and Jean-Yves Vion-Dury[1]

[1] Xerox Research Centre Europe (XRCE), 38240 Meylan, France
{Nikolaos.Lagos,Jean-Yves.Vion-Dury}@xrce.xerox.com
[2] Centre for e-Research Department of Digital Humanities,
King's College London, London, UK
simon.waddington@kcl.ac.uk

Abstract. We consider the preservation of digital objects in continually evolving ecosystems, for which traditional lifecycle approaches are less appropriate. Motivated by the Records Continuum theory, we define an approach that combines active life with preservation and is non-custodial, which we refer to as the continuum approach. Preserving objects and their associated environment introduces high level of complexity. We therefore describe a model-driven approach, termed the Continuum approach, in which models rather than the digital objects themselves can be analysed. In such setting, the use of appropriate metadata is very important, we therefore outline the PERICLES Linked Resource Model, an upper ontology for modelling digital ecosystems, and compare and contrast it to the Australian Government Recordkeeping Metadata Standard, developed within the record keeping community.

Keywords: Preservation · Dependency management · Ontology · LRM · Evolving content · Continuum approach

1 Introduction

In this paper, we consider the preservation of digital objects comprising a number of interdependent digital entities. Such objects are assumed to exist within a continually changing environment, which may result in them becoming unusable over time. Traditional approaches to digital preservation (e.g. OAIS [1]) are based on lifecycle models where digital objects are submitted to an archive or repository at the end of their active life. The objects are then maintained as far as possible in a reusable form, aiming to preserve both the content and state. We present two examples from media and science which illustrate when separation of preservation from active life is not feasible or desirable, and where it is required to preserve digital objects within their existing environment. We term this a continuum approach, motivated by the Record Continuum theory in the related field of record keeping [2].

In order to maintain the reusability of complex digital objects and their associated environment, it is necessary to consider risks that can occur due to changes in the environment and to determine and perform mitigating actions. In previous

E. Garoufallou et al. (Eds.): MTSR 2015, CCIS 544, pp. 15–26, 2015.
DOI: 10.1007/978-3-319-24129-6_2

approaches, experiments are performed on representations of the digital ecosystem itself such as a sandbox. However when considering complex interdependent ecosystems, in which change can propagate across multiple entities, this approach becomes impractical. We therefore adopt a model-driven approach, where the models provide an abstract representation of essential features of the ecosystem, which can then be analysed and manipulated independently of the ecosystem itself. In such an approach, the use and organization of appropriate metadata to represent relevant information is crucial.

We introduce the PERICLES Linked Resource Model (LRM) as an abstract tool for modelling digital ecosystems. PERICLES is a four-year Integrated Project (2013-2017) funded by the European Union under its Seventh Framework Programme (ICT Call 9), which aims to address the challenge of ensuring that digital content remains accessible in an environment that is subject to continual change. We then compare and contrast the LRM with the Australian Government Recordkeeping Metadata Standard Version 2.0 [3] (AGRkMS), which has been developed based on the Records Continuum approach by the record keeping community, particularly in relation to describing digital ecosystems.

The paper is organised as follows. In section two we describe our model-driven continuum approach to preservation, and compare this to traditional lifecycle approaches. In section three we introduce, compare, and contrast the two metadata models that can be used to support this model-driven approach to preservation, namely the LRM and AGRkMS models. We present the conclusions in section four.

2   Continuum Versus Lifecycle Approaches to Digital Preservation

2.1   Lifecycle Models

Lifecycle models are a point of reference for many approaches to digital preservation. They provide a framework for describing a sequence of actions or phases such as creation, productive use, modification and disposal for the management of digital objects throughout their existence. These models suggest a linear sequence of distinct phases and activities which in practice might be non-linear or even chaotic. Lifecycle models provide an idealised abstraction of reality, and might typically be used in higher-level organisational planning and for detecting gaps in procedures. This approach has provided a basis for much research and practice in digital preservation.

The DCC lifecycle model [4] is one of the most well-known preservation-related lifecycle models. It provides a graphical, high-level overview of the stages required for successful curation and preservation of data from initial conceptualisation or receipt through the iterative curation cycle.

The UK Data Archive describes a research data lifecycle [5]. It comprises six sequential activities and, unlike the DCC model, it is more focused on the data user's perspective. Overviews of lifecycle models for research data are provided by Ball [6] and the CEOS Working Group on Data Life Cycle Models and Concepts [7].

So-called lifecycle approaches typically envisage a clear distinction between active life and end-of-active life. The Open Archival Information System (OAIS) [1] is a commonly adopted reference model for an archive, consisting of an organisation of people and systems that has accepted the responsibility to preserve information and make it available for a designated community. The focus of OAIS is therefore on "long term", being also concerned with the impacts of changing technologies, including support for new media and data formats, but also changing user communities.

The PLANETS project developed a functional model [8] and an associated test bed that demonstrate how certain types of external change can be managed within the setting of an OAIS compliant archive. The basic principle is to monitor and detect external change, to conduct experiments on a representative sample of the entities within a sandbox to determine the impact of potential mitigating actions (e.g. migration or emulation), and to implement the proposed actions. Such actions should preserve a pre-defined set of properties considered important by user communities in characterising the content (often termed significant properties [9]). A major focus in PLANETS and in related projects was on document formats. This overall approach has been extended by many other projects such as SCAPE[1]and CASPAR[2]. We will refer to the principle of adapting content in a changing environment to enable future reuse as "dynamic" preservation.

2.2 Continuum Approaches

Continuum approaches combine two main aspects. Firstly, there is no distinction made between active life and end-of-active life; that is, preservation is fully integrated into the active life of the digital objects. A second aspect is that preservation is non-custodial, that is we do not aim to remove entities from their environment, both physical and organisational and place them in the custody of a third party.

Continuum approaches have been proposed in the related field of record keeping. A record is defined as something that represents proof of existence[3]. Records can either be created or received by an organisation in pursuance of or compliance with legal obligations, or in the transaction of business [10]. An essential aspect is that the content and structure of a record are fixed, but the surrounding context can change over time. Thus a record is "always in a state of becoming" [2]. This is in marked contrast to archival theory, which aims to preserve not only content but also state.

The Records Continuum (RC) was originally proposed by Upward in 1996 [11]. Despite this, it is only relatively recently that attempts have been made at practical implementation of these ideas. This has occurred primarily at institutions in Australia. The Australian Government Recordkeeping Metadata Standard Version 2.0 [3] (AGRkMS) adopts a number of RC concepts. The corresponding metadata model represents "information about records and the contexts in which they are captured and used". This is a static representation that cannot adapt to changing context.

---

[1] http://www.scape-project.eu/

[2] http://cordis.europa.eu/project/rcn/92920_en.html

[3] http://en.wikipedia.org/wiki/Records_management

2.3   Example: Software -Based Art

In this sub-section, we provide a concrete example to illustrate the applicability of the continuum approach from the PERICLES Media case study, provided by Tate. Software-based art (SBA) includes self-contained or networked systems, where the functionality depends on external data or services. Works can be written in different programming languages with different configurations of hardware and proprietary and open source software.

SBAs are often based on emerging computing technology, with which artists explore the potential for creating new and innovative works. Due to the rapid pace of technological advances, the hardware and software platforms on which these works are constructed rapidly become obsolete, which poses a major challenge for longer term preservation. The artist's intent is often a major factor in determining the conservation strategy for SBAs. In some cases, artists will specify for instance a specific type of display technology for viewing the artwork, such as a CRT device. In other cases, the artist provides no specification of their intent, and in such cases it is left to the discretion of the conservator to determine the most appropriate form of display.

There is often a requirement to display artworks in different exhibitions, which have varying physical and technical constraints. For instance some artworks make use of an internet connection to display live data from the internet. However, it may be desirable in some cases to operate an artwork from locally cached data. This would require modification to the underlying software. Unlike traditional artworks, there is not one definitive physical object to preserve. SBAs can exist in multiple versions, with varying claims of authenticity. Indeed without appropriate provenance information or information about the artist intent, it is often difficult to determine which versions can be considered as the most faithful representation.

To summarise, when considering SBAs, there is no clear final state of the data. Indeed the works are in a state of continuous evolution as changing technology requires updates to be made to deal with technological obsolescence, both to allow continuing access (e.g. by scholars) as well as display at public exhibitions. If these works are viewed as sufficiently valuable to be retained for long timeframes, and resources allow, then they will need to be updated indefinitely. Despite the need for preserving and conserving a large number of digital artefacts, it is not clear that a repository or archive in the traditional sense is the most appropriate solution. An organisation such as a gallery or a museum is involved both in acquiring and conserving artworks, whilst at the same time supporting their active use.

3   Metadata Models for the Continuum Approach

3.1   PERICLES Linked Resource Model

The Linked Resource Model (LRM) is an upper level ontology designed to provide a principled way to modelling evolving ecosystems, focusing on aspects related to the changes taking place. At its core the LRM defines the ecosystem by means of participating entities and dependencies between them. A set of other properties and specialised entity types are also provided but they are all conditioned on what is allowed/required by the *change management* policy. The main concepts of the LRM are illustrated in Fig. 1 (the prefix `pk` refers to the LRM namespace) and discussed below.

Resource. Represents any physical, digital, conceptual, or other kind of entity and in general comprises all things in the universe of discourse of the LRM Model[4]. A resource can be *Abstract* (c.f. `AbstractResource` in Fig. 1), representing the abstract part of a resource, for instance the idea or concept of an artwork, or *Concrete* (c.f. `ConcreteResource` in Fig. 1), representing the part of an entity that has a physical extension and can therefore be accessed at a specific location (a corresponding attribute called location is used to specify spatial information; for instance for a `Digital-Resource`, which represents objects with a digital extension, this information can be the URL required to retrieve and download the corresponding bit stream). The above two concepts can be used together to describe a resource; for example, both the very idea of an artwork, as referred by papers talking about the artist's intention behind the created object, and the corresponding video stream that one can load and play in order to manifest and perceive the artwork. To achieve that, the abstract and concrete resources can be related through a specific `realizedAs` predicate, which in the above example could be used to express that the video file is a concrete realization of the abstract art piece.

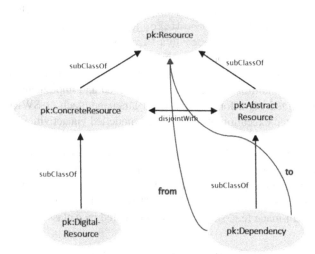

Fig. 1. Part of the core LRM ontology.

Dependency. The core concept of the static LRM is that of *dependency*. An LRM `Dependency` describes the context under which change to one or more entities has an impact on other entities of the ecosystem. The description of a dependency minimally includes the intent or purpose related to the corresponding usage of the involved

---

4 This definition is close to CIDOC CRM's Entity [12] – we are also exploring other possible mappings [13].

entities. The topology of a dependency is potentially higher than a binary relation, as it can relate several dependees to several dependent resources. From a functional perspective, we expect that dedicated policies/rules will further refine the context (e.g. conditions, time constraints, impact) under which change is to be interpreted for a given type of dependency.

To enable recording the intent of a dependency, we can relate in the LRM the Dependency entity with an entity that describes the intent formally or informally via a property that we name "intention", as illustrated in Fig. 2. In Fig. 2 the "from" and "to" properties indicate the directionality of the dependency.

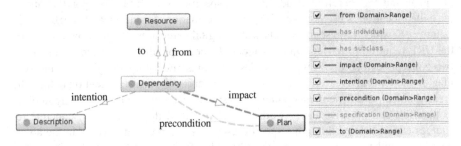

Fig. 2. A view of the Dependency concept in LRM

Plan. The condition(s) and impact(s) of a change operation are connected to the Dependency concept in LRM via precondition and impact properties as illustrated in Fig. 2. These connect a Dependency to a Plan, which represents a set of actions or steps to be executed by someone/something (either human or software). The Plan can be used, thus, as a means of giving operational semantics to dependencies. Plans can describe how preconditions and impacts are checked and implemented (this could be for example defined via a formal rule-based language, such as SWRL [14]. The temporally coordinated execution of plans can be modelled via activities.

Activity. The Activity class has a start and/or end time, or a duration. An Event class is used to situate events in terms of activities. An activity is something that occurs over a period of time and, via events, acts upon or influences entities. Finally, a resource that performs an activity, i.e. is the "bearer" of change in the ecosystem, either human or man-made (e.g. software), is represented by a class called Agent.

3.2   Australian Government Recordkeeping Metadata Standard

The AGRkMS is designed to provide the necessary metadata that will help ensuring that records remain accessible and usable over time. The AGRkMS standard defines five different entity types, Record (e.g. electronic documents), Agent (e.g. people), Business (e.g. the functions and activities of what an organisation does), Mandate (e.g. policies), and Relationship (e.g. information about the relationship between a record and an agent) [15]. Definitions and detailed description of all entity types can be found in [3], [15].

3.3   On the Relation of the AGRkMS to the PERICLES LRM

As mentioned in the previous paragraphs, the AGRkMS focuses on the accessibility and utility of records over time, while the LRM aims at modelling how changes to the ecosystem, and their impact, can be captured. The above difference is also reflected in the models themselves: while the AGRkMS meta-model introduces a number of constructs for recording provenance, current and past relationships among specific types of entities, and a number of metadata to describe security, authentication, and licensing related aspects, the LRM concentrates on notions that can help in characterising change. Naturally, therefore, the LRM does not define in great detail the metadata required for domain-specific purposes but rather focuses on the main concepts and structures that allow change to be recorded and acted upon, including operational notions.

Another important aspect of the LRM stems from the nature of the relation that it has to the notion of policy (which seems to correspond in some aspects to the notion of Mandate in AGRkMS). A policy governs at all times the dynamic aspects related to changes (e.g. conditions required for a change to happen and/or impact of changes). As a consequence, the properties of the LRM are dependent on the policy being applied, and therefore most of the defined concepts are related to what the policy expects. The LRM therefore at its core is only assuming the ecosystem is described by means of entities and dependencies between these. A set of other properties and specialised entity types are also provided but they are all conditioned on what is allowed/required by the policy.

Entities and Implementation Approaches. The AGRkMS supports two different approaches to instantiating its core entities (c.f. 3.2).

- Single-entity implementation: Only records are modelled as entities (typed using the Record class), while the rest are modelled as properties of a record.
- Multiple-entity implementation: More than one of the core types is modelled as an entity. For example specific instances can use two entities (Record and Agent), three entities (e.g. Record, Agent, and Relationship), or all five entities.

As mentioned in [15] a multiple-entity implementation is recommended. That is because, among other reasons, a single-entity approach implies significant simplification of metadata for all other entities except for Record and has limited ability to record and trace changes to the rest of the entities (more detailed comparison between the two approaches can be found in [15]).

On the other hand, the LRM is mainly centered to the notion of dependency and domain-specific entity types can be represented by domain-specific LRM instantiations that specialise the core entities presented in section 3.1. For instance, the physical extension of a record can be represented as an instance of the ConcreteResource class (or DigitalResource class if the record is in digital form) in the LRM, while the AGkRMS Agent concept can be mapped to the LRM Agent class enabling explicit representation of the activities that the agent carries out. When compared to the two implementations of the AGRkMS standard, an approach implementing the LRM is closer to the multiple-entity implementation. Single-entity implementations are not supported, as change is modelled in term of the relations between different entities.

On the Notions of Relationship and Dependency. In AGRkMS a Relationship is defined as an entity that "provides the means of linking records to their business context, not only at creation, but also with continued use and management of the records over time" [15].

The Relationship entity, we believe, is therefore extremely useful as it links two or more entities together in time and context. The following example extracted from [15, pp. 52-53] illustrates how this can be done (Fig. 3).

"Consider a digital record item — a document containing a set of diagrams — that has been created using the Microsoft Visio 2000 drawing application. The organisation is about to implement a new corporate drawing package to replace MS Visio 2000. The work group who created the set of diagrams wants to be able to continue accessing (but not editing) the diagrams created using MS Visio 2000. Therefore, the work group has decided to convert these diagrams to JPEG format. Example 15 shows the metadata required to describe this conversion using the Relationship entity: the Agent entity A (a 'Person' — someone from the work group) 'Converts' (Relationship — entity B) the Record entity C (an 'Item' — the Microsoft Visio 2000 drawing) to the new format." [15, pp. 52-53].

Example 15   Relationship entity with Category 'Recordkeeping Event' and Name Scheme 'Converts' — Part 1

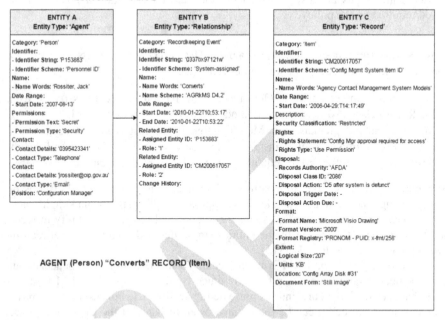

Fig. 3. Example from the Records Continuum meta-model documentation

The Relationship entity, as presented above, shares a number of similarities to the notion of Dependency as defined by the LRM model (c.f. 3.1). Take for instance the same example described above but with the assumption that MS Visio is not about to be replaced by another tool but that a corresponding policy defines that MS Visio drawings should be periodically backed up as JPEG objects by the specific work group. The Relationship entity contains a number of important metadata already describing each Conversion in terms of its temporal information and the entities it involves along with their roles in the relationship (i.e. Person making the conversion and object being converted). The same information can be expressed also by LRM dependencies. The main difference is that the LRM dependency is strictly connected to the intention underlying a specific change.

In the case described here the intent may be described as "The work group who created the set of diagrams wants to be able to access (but not edit) the diagrams created using MS Visio 2000. Therefore, the work group has decided to convert these diagrams to JPEG format" and it implies the following.

- There is an explicit dependency between the MS Visio and the JPEG objects. More specifically, the JPEG objects are depending on the MS Visio ones. This means that if an MS Visio object MS1 is converted to a JPEG object JPEG1 and the MS1 is edited before the transfer to the new drawing package then JPEG1 should either be updated accordingly or another JPEG object JPEG2 should be generated and JPEG1 optionally deleted (the description is not explicit enough here to decide which of the two actions should be performed). This dependency would be especially useful in a scenario where MS Visio keeps on being used for some time in parallel to the JPEG entities being used as back up.
- The dependency between MS1 and JPEG1 is unidirectional. Actually JPEG objects are not allowed to be edited and if they are, no change to the corresponding MS Visio objects should apply.
- The dependency applies to the specific work group, which means that if a Person from another work group modifies one of the MS Visio objects, no specific conversion action has to be taken (the action should be defined by the corresponding Policy). This is partly captured by the Permissions, Rights, and Security Classification related properties of the Agent and Record entities.

Operational Aspects. The AGRkMS metamodel via the Relationship concept, in addition to information we saw above, allows information about who or what carried out the change (viewed as an "event" in AGRkMS), but also who or what authorised it, the effects it had, and any resulting actions.

The LRM model aims in addition to such descriptive information to also provide concepts that will allow to record operational information such as what are the conditions under which a change is triggered and what is the possible impact of this change on other entities. Let us take once more the example above: we need to be able to express the fact that a transformation to the JPEG is possible only if the corresponding MS Visio object exists (which corresponds to an existential constraint) and if the Human that triggers the Conversion has the required Permissions to do that (e.g. belongs to the specific workgroup). The impact of the Conversion (generating a new JPEG object) could also be conditioned on the existence of a corresponding JPEG object containing an older version of the MS Visio object. The actions to be undertaken in that case, would be decided based on the policy governing the specific operation. Assuming that only the most recent JPEG object must be archived, the old one must be deleted and replaced by the new one (conversely deciding to keep the old JPEG object as well may imply having to archive the old version of the corresponding old MS Visio object as well).

As explained in section 3.1 the condition(s) and impact(s) of a change operation are connected to the Dependency concept in LRM via "precondition" and "impact" properties (Fig. 2) and can be used to give operational semantics to dependencies.

Events. The Relationship entity in the AGRkMS meta-model describes events that take place and/or provenance relationships. According to [15], recordkeeping event relationships can also be scheduled for the future, providing a way of triggering these events automatically something that is delegated to the specific infrastructure of the organization/company adopting the AGRkMS meta-model.

Events in LRM have a different status. They are the concepts that allow the LRM to record and plan how stimuli received from the external world and/or from the system itself should be interpreted. Events in the LRM are like instantaneous messages that trigger a change to the system. Events can trigger activities. An activity is something that occurs over a period of time and, via events, acts upon or influences entities. Using this model, the LRM makes a fine-grained separation of the entities involved in the triggering of a change. For example, being able to record external events that led to a change in regulations and consequently to the policies governing the set of entities.

4   Conclusions

We have defined a continuum approach to preservation that integrates preservation processes into the active life of content to deal with digital objects within continually evolving environments. We have also provided examples where this approach is more appropriate than traditional lifecycle approaches. Dealing with the environment on which digital objects are dependent introduces additional complexity. Following a model-driven approach, we have defined an ontology termed the Linked Resource Model to model evolving ecosystems that aim to deal with this issue by providing an abstract representation.

Continuum approaches have been proposed in the parallel field of record keeping. The AGRkMS meta-model provides a static representation of ecosystems, but we conclude that it is not sufficient for modelling evolving ecosystems, the primary purpose of the LRM. Indeed the models are complementary in several important aspects.

The AGRkMS meta-model describes in detail a large set of metadata that can be useful for the LRM. (For now we have identified the notions of Roles, Identifier Schemes and Security and Permissions-related properties as candidates for integration). When designing the LRM we decided to delegate the definition of domain-specific properties and metadata to domain-specific instantiations/specialisations. The RC meta-model can be used to enrich the LRM ontology in that vain.

The LRM treats in detail the notions related to change and its propagation. We believe that the LRM could extend relevant aspects of the RC meta-model related to how change is not only recorded but also acted upon. The LRM concepts related to operational aspects of change could be of interest for the AGRkMS meta-model.

The study presented in this paper is based on a limited number of examples. We plan to further validate our conclusions in the context of PERICLES, based on use cases of real-world complexity, and explore other aspects related to the LRM, such as how much overhead is required for the continuum approach and the LRM model to be implemented. We believe though that the benefits of a principled approach to metadata modelling, as proposed by the LRM model, could lead to a number of useful functionalities, at least in the setting considered here, such as risk analysis, certified information integrity (via provenance recording), and impact-based recommendations.

Acknowledgements. This work was supported by the European Commission Seventh Framework Programme under Grant Agreement Number FP7-601138 PERICLES.

References

1. CCSDS - Consultative Committee for Space Data Systems: Reference Model for an Open Archival Information System (OAIS), Recommended Practice, CCSDS 650.0-M-2 (Magenta Book) (2) (2012)
2. McKemmish, S.: Placing records continuum theory and practice. Archival Science 1(4), 333–359 (2001)
3. National Archives of Australia: Australian Government Recordkeeping Metadata Standard Version 2.0 (2008). http://www.naa.gov.au/Images/AGRkMS_tcm16-47131.pdf (accessed on May 28, 2015)
4. Higgins, S.: The DCC Curation Lifecycle Model. International Journal of Digital Curation 3(1), 134–40 (2008). http://ijdc.net/index.php/ijdc/article/view/69 (accessed on May 28, 2015)
5. UK Data Archive. Research Data Lifecycle. http://www.data-archive.ac.uk/create-manage/life-cycle (accessed on May 28, 2015)
6. Ball, A.: Review of Data Management Lifecycle Models (version 1.0). REDm-MED Project Document redm1rep120110ab10. Bath, UK: University of Bath (2012). http://opus.bath.ac.uk/28587/1/redm1rep120110ab10.pdf (accessed on May 28, 2015)
7. Committee on Earth Observation Satellites Working Group on Information systems and Services (WGISS): Data Life Cycle Models and Concepts CEOS 1.2 (2012). http://ceos.org/document_management/Working_Groups/WGISS/Interest_Groups/Data_Stewardship/White_Papers/WGISS_DSIG_Data-Lifecycle-Models-And-Concepts-v13-1_Apr2012.docx (accessed on May 28, 2015)
8. Sierman, B., Wheatley, P.: PLANETS. D3-4 Report on the Planets Functional Model (2009). http://www.planets-project.eu/docs/reports/Planets_PP7-D3-4_ReportOnThePlanetsFunctional Model.pdf (accessed on May 28, 2015)
9. Wilson, A.: Significant Properties Report (2007). http://www.significantproperties.org.uk/wp22_significant_properties.pdf (accessed on May 28, 2015)
10. ARMA International: Glossary of Records and Information Management Terms, 4th edn. ARMA International. ISBN: 978-1-933654-15-4

11. Upward, F.: Structuring the records continuum (Series of two parts) Part 1: post custodial principles and properties. Archives and Manuscripts **24**(2), 268–285 (1996). http://www.infotech.monash.edu.au/research/groups/rcrg/publications/recordscontinuum-fupp1.html (accessed on May 28, 2015)

12. Doerr, M.: The CIDOC CRM, an ontological approach to schema heterogeneity. In: Semantic Interoperability and Integration, vol. 4391 (2005)

13. Vion-Dury, J.-Y., Lagos, N., Kontopoulos, E., Riga, M., Mitzias, P., Meditskos, G., Waddington, S., Laurenson, P., Kompatsiaris, Y.: Designing for inconsistency – the dependency-based PERICLES approach. In: Proceedings of SW4CH Workshop in Advances in Intelligent Systems and Computing (to appear, 2015)

14. Horrocks, I., Patel-Schneider, P.F., Boley, H., Tabet, S., Grosof, B., Dean, M.: SWRL: A Semantic Web Rule Language Combining OWL and RuleML. W3C Member Submission (2004). http://www.w3.org/Submission/SWRL/ (accessed on May 28, 2015)

15. National Archives of Australia: Australian Government Recordkeeping Metadata Standard Version 2.0 Implementation Guidelines: Exposure Draft (2010). http://www.naa.gov.au/Images/AGRkMS-guidelines_tcm16-47133.pdf (accessed on May 28, 2015)

Challenges for Ontological Engineering in the Humanities – A Case Study of Philosophy

Pawel Garbacz[✉]

Department of Philosophy,
The John Paul II Catholic University of Lublin, Lublin, Poland
`garbacz@kul.pl`

Abstract. The paper develops an idea of an engineering ontology whose purpose is to represent philosophy as a research discipline in the humanities. I discuss a three recent attempts in this respect with the aim to identify their modelling potential. The upshot of this analysis leads to a new conceptual framework for ontological engineering for philosophy. I show how this framework can be implemented in the form of a simple OWL ontology.

1 Introduction

Representation of knowledge in the humanities poses a number of specific challenges for symbolic Artificial Intelligence. They are mainly due to the idiosyncratic nature of this type of intellectual activity and the features of informational artefacts it provides. Any formal representation thereof needs to account for different, often conflicting, world views adopted by the humanities scholars, the pervasive use of ethnic languages, the instability the technical terminology, in particular the variability of meanings [13]. In addition, the very notion of the humanities, which is to cover all humanistic disciplines, seems to be a grab bag category ([2, p.222]), which collects rather heterogeneous disciplines like archaeology and performance studies. Thus, despite a number of recent unification initiatives (like NeDiMAH Methods Ontology [4] or Scholarly Domain Model [7]), the prospects of arriving at one common symbolic framework for symbolic knowledge representation are still dim.

Some humanistic disciplines seem to have fared better than the others in this respect. For example, there are various formal reference models for library science (Dublin Core, FBFR, etc.) or for cultural heritage (e.g., CIDOC CRM Reference Model – see [6]). Other, like philosophy or musicology, are neglected. In this paper I discuss the challenges for symbolic knowledge representation in philosophy. More specifically speaking, I will investigate the issues and requirements relevant for the ontological engineering paradigm. Section 2 identifies a three recent attempts to representing philosophical knowledge as specimens of the typical solutions to these issues. Section 3 outlines a different type of solution, which aims to overcome some shortcomings of these previous attempts. The implementation of this solution is described in Sect. 4.

© Springer International Publishing Switzerland 2015
E. Garoufallou et al. (Eds.): MTSR 2015, CCIS 544, pp. 27–38, 2015.
DOI: 10.1007/978-3-319-24129-6_3

2 Main Paradigms in Ontological Engineering for Philosophy

Research in knowledge representation for philosophy is scarce and uncoordinated. This section reports three major attempts at providing an informational artefact to store and reason over the data that come from the philosophical resources. The three specimen in question reveal two key paradigm typologies in ontology development.

The first typology concerns the level of detail on which a given ontology represents its domain. One type groups ontologies whose categories grasp only the main differences between the entities they refer to. They make as few distinctions as possible and exhibit a relatively small number of categories, which are usually organised in shallow taxonomies. The other type in this typology collects highly discriminative ontologies with numerous categories and distinctions, which usually involve many layers of logical divisions.

The second typology concerns the amount of the domain knowledge that a given ontology encodes in its structure, which is defined by its set of terminological axioms (in the sense of Description Logic). So there are ontologies designed to include as much of the respective domain knowledge as possible within a given set of expressivity constraints that are imposed by the formal language employed. On the other end of this spectrum there are ontologies that minimise this domain knowledge import.

Although in principle the two typologies are orthogonal, a discriminative ontology usually involves more domain knowledge than a non-discriminative one.[1]

2.1 Indiana Philosophy Ontology Project

Indiana Philosophy Ontology (aka: InPhO) project [2] was developed as a support tool for the Stanford Encyclopedia of Philosophy (http://plato.stanford.edu/), which is one of the most comprehensive, informative and popular online, open access, and dynamic reference dataset in philosophy.[2]

The InPhO is published as an OWL ontology (of the AL(D) expressivity). The top-most layer is rather sparse – it contains six main categories: Human, Idea, Nationality, Organization, Profession, and Publication. The ontology development focused on the category of ideas, which breaks down into a classification that contains more than 200 subcategories. [2] claims this to be the most noteworthy aspect of this ontology. Its main tenet is "semantic inheritance relationships holding between the contents of ideas rather than more formal inheritance relationships observed in their types (e.g. social or structural roles)." [2, p.213].

---

[1] Obviously, the above characterisation is in the need of refinement because one ontology may be more discriminative (or knowledge-laden) than another ontology *with respect to* one group of its categories and less discriminative (knowledge-laden) with respect to another group.

[2] All URLs mentioned in this paper were accessed on May 19, 2015.

So, for example, the concept "philosophical idea" is not broken down into kinds of philosophical ideas like concepts, positions, statements, etc., but it is split into philosophical ideas about epistemology, philosophical ideas about logic, etc. Another crucial aspect of InPhO is its approach towards the distinction between (abstract) classes and (concrete) individuals. The InPhO developers chose a pragmatic approach, where a philosophical idea was, as a rule, classified as an individual when it corresponds to an individual entry in the Stanford Encyclopedia of Philosophy.

The InPhO ontology was populated in a semi-automated way, where the initial text mining techniques were audited by the domain experts (i.e., SEP authors) by means of the in-house three-step feedback-harnessing strategy:

1. an expert assesses whether a term found by the standard statistical methods (the tf-idf algorithm, n-gram models, etc.) is relevant for his or her entry;
2. the experts evaluates the level of relatedness of the term for the entry;
3. the expert evaluates the non-taxonomic relationships found in the unvalidated sources (e.g., in Wikipedia).

At the time of writing this paper the Indiana Philosophy Ontology project was still maintained at https://inpho.cogs.indiana.edu/.

2.2 PhiloSurfical Ontology

The PhiloSurfical ontology [9] was a data component of the PhiloSurfical annotation tool, which was used to contextually navigate a classic work in twentieth century philosophy, L. Wittgenstein's *Tractatus Logico-Philosophicus*.

The developers of the PhiloSurfical ontology focused on the following aspects of the study of philosophy: (i) historical events (ii) generic uncertainty (iii) information objects (iv) interpretation events (v) contradictory information (vi) viewpoints (vii) varying granularity

As opposed to the InPhO project the PhiloSurfical ontology is built upon CIDOC CRM Reference Model, which is an upper-level ontology used in the cultural heritage systems. The former ontology was extended in a number of directions, including specific types of events related to the philosophical activity. For example, the CIDOC CRM category 'E28 - Conceptual-Object' was extended with a number of subcategories, one of which is the category of philosophical ideas that is defined in terms of the following eight main subcategories: (i) argument-entity, (ii) problem area, (iii) problem, (iv) method, (v) view, (vi) rhetorical figure, (v) concept, and (vi) distinction. Each of these categories is further specialised into subcategories, e.g., the category of problems is split into 23 subcategories. Therefore, the PhiloSurfical ontology is relatively detailed description of the discipline of philosophy. The OWL ontology available from contains almost 400 OWL classes and more than 300 object properties.

The categories of the PhiloSurfical ontology were used to annotate Wittgenstein's *Tractatus Logico-Philosophicus*, but the results are no longer available at the project's website: http://philosurfical.open.ac.uk/.

2.3   Philospace Ontology

The Discovery project was aimed at developing personal desktop applications used to enrich the content of Philosource, which is a federation of semantic digital libraries in the field of philosophy [5]. One of the ontologies developed for the sake of this project is the Philospace ontology, developed as an annotation schema to be used within the Philospace annotation tool.[3]

Fig. 1. The class hierarchy in the Philospace ontology

The Philospace ontology is a relatively small artefact. Extending another ontology built in this project, the Scholarship ontology, it contains 21 classes and 20 object properties – see figure 2. All these categories are not specific to philosophy, but appear to be tailored for the needs of representing any humanistic discipline.

2.4   A Faceted Typology of Engineering Ontologies for Philosophy

Despite a huge number of classes and their instances the InPhO ontology represents the non-discriminative approach in ontology development. The Idea category contains (as subclasses) philosophical subdisciplines (e.g., logic, ethics, etc.), theories (e.g., bayesianism, connectionism, etc.), arguments (e.g., arguments for the existence of God), and concepts (e.g., mind, causation, etc.). Also within a single category one can find heterogeneous conceptual structures. For example,

---

[3] See: http://www.dbin.org/brainlets/discovery/ontologies/philospace_0.1.owl. Another ontology developed for the Discovery project, Wittgenstein ontology [10], is currently inaccessible since the two versions of this ontology available at http://wab.uib.no/wab_philospace.page contain ill-formed IRIs.

the category of relations has three instances: medieval theories of relations, relative identity, and logical atomism, where the first is a collection of theories, the second is a concept, and the third is a theory. At the same time it is an example of those ontologies that involve a significant portion of the domain knowledge in its terminology. The PhiloSurfical ontology exemplifies the discriminative paradigm

	non-discriminative	discriminative
knowledge-free	Philospace	
knowledge-laden	InPhO	PhiloSurfical

Fig. 2. A facet typology of engineering ontologies for philosophy

in ontology development. The categories it contains are extremely detailed. For example, there is a class of philosophical problems and its subclass focussed on the problems with relations. The latter is further split into four subclasses, where each covers one specific relation: dependence, independence, identity, and difference. The numerous distinctions defined in this ontology involve a significant portion of philosophical knowledge. Some of these distinctions presuppose also the *validity* of certain specific philosophical views. For example, the class GOD is a subclass of the class SUPERNATURAL-ENTITY – this subsumption is not compatible with those views that see gods as natural objects. Therefore, the PhiloSurfical ontology also involves a significant portion of the domain knowledge.

On the other hand, the Philospace ontology assumes no philosophical knowledge and at the same time belongs to the group of non-discriminative ontologies.

3   Towards A New Paradigm

It seems to me that the discriminative ontologies are likely to be conceptually inflexible and may need to be adapted for new datasets more often. This is due to the high level of detail at which they capture their respective domains. This level of detail may also hinder their reuse as certain conceptual choices made by their developers may be unacceptable to their potential re-users. At the same time it is this level of detail that results in a more adequate structurisation of the domain knowledge. At the other end of this spectrum we find non-discriminative ontologies. The ontologies of this type are highly flexible and are unlikely to be in the need to adaptation for new datasets. The downsize is now a certain sloppiness in the way they represent their domains. The "one-size fits all" principle seems to be at odds with the aims usually set forth for symbolic knowledge representation. Given these very aims one could expect that an engineering ontology for a given domain should involve, *ceteris paribus*, as much domain knowledge as possible (given the expressivity constraints in question). The reason is that the ontology is, after all, a formal representation of the domain knowledge. Nonetheless, in the case of the humanities, in particular in the case of the discipline of philosophy, this rule needs to be revised. The philosophical research has *not* produced a homogeneous body of consistent knowledge. This field of study is all about controversies, interpretations, and viewpoints. In fact the scope and depth of disagreement is so significant that even the term "philosophical knowledge" looks like an oxymoron. Therefore if we want to maximise the scope of the philosophical research to be represented by an engineering ontology, we need to minimise the impact of particular philosophical assumptions we make building the ontology. Otherwise, we might find ourselves in a position of not being able to express certain views or claims.

For these reasons in what follows I will suggest a conceptual framework for an engineering ontology for the domain philosophy, which is to (i) maximise the discriminative power of the ontology (ii) while minimising the domain knowledge import. Incidentally, note that any ontology of such kind can fill the empty slot in fig. 2.

The main philosophical assumption is the distinction between knowledge resources and their contents, which distinction refines a more familiar distinction between information carriers and information. The notion of *knowledge resource* (aka: *resource*) is understood here as equivalent to the notion of information content entity from the Information Artefact Ontology (https://code.google.com/p/information-artifact-ontology/). So a resource is an entity that conveys a certain piece of information. Note that in this sense a resource is not a (printed or written) piece of paper, but a certain abstraction of over a collection of such pieces of papers. For example, suppose that each copy of a certain journal paper is a single piece of printed paper. The sense of "resource" I use is then that there is just one resource (of this journal paper) with multiple copies. The resource that these pieces contain is a kind of abstraction over them.

A *resource content* is an entity that is existentially dependent on a resource in the following sense: when the former exists, then there exists at least one resource that expresses the resource content. So resource contents constitute another layer of abstraction over the pieces of paper we usually refer to as texts. The notion of resource content is equivalent to the notion of work in the Functional Requirements for Bibliographic Records standard [8]. The role of resource contents is to collect texts that convey the same conceptual content, e.g., when one paper contains a text "Endurants exist." and the other paper contains a text "Continuants exist.", then one can arguably claim that these two texts convey the same content.

In order to represent philosophical information I will use three basic types of resource contents:

1. categories
2. propositions
3. propositional structures

A *category* is a resource content whose role is to represent (i.e., stand for) a collection of entities. Usually categories are rendered in ethnic languages by means of common nouns. The notion of category is understood here rather broadly as it includes also relations (of any arity). So there exists a category of human beings as well as the category of parenthood, the latter representing the particular relations that hold between parents and their children (by means of ordered couples).

A *proposition* is a resource content whose role is to represent atomic situations (or, in the philosophical jargon, states of affairs). Examples of situations include that John is a human being, that endurants exist, that no cause follows its effect, etc. A situation is atomic if no part of it is a situation. Usually propositions are rendered in ethnic languages by means of simple sentences. Therefore, propositions are understood as carriers of truth values and objects of the so-called propositional attitudes. So they can be either true or false, accepted or rejected, stipulated or inferred, etc.

Propositions are mereologically complex entities. In particular each proposition contains (as its part) at least one category.

A *propositional structure* is a mereological sum (fusion) of more than one proposition. Usually propositional structures are expressed in ethnic languages by means of complex sentences or sentences concatenations (e.g., as paragraphs, articles' sections and whole articles, books' chapters, etc.). The basic types of propositional structures include arguments and theories. Note that although propositions and propositional structures are mereologically complex, a category may also contain other categories as parts. For example, the category "vague identity" contains two categories (as its parts): "identity" and "vagueness".

In the humanities resource contents are subject to interpretation. The ontology presented in this paper defines the notion of interpretation applicable to categories – interpretation of propositions and propositional structures is a topic of a further study. On the first approximation, an interpretation of a category is a proposition that relates this category to its extension. Different interpretations of a category will then define its different extensions. The notion of category extension is systematically ambiguous. For certain (philosophical) categories their extensions are just classes of entities that fall under these categories. Thus, for instance, the category of abstract objects is simply the class of all abstract objects. This group contains those categories whose membership is modally rigid, i.e., it does not depend on temporal indices, possible worlds, contexts, etc. That whether x is an abstract object or not has this characteristics. There is another group of categories whose extensions are modally sensitive. Take any role as an example, e.g., take the category of students. Although John is now a student, he might not be, e.g., he was not and he will not be a student. For such categories the extensions need to be parametrised, either with the temporal or modal aspect (or both). Such extensions may be represented as mappings from these parameters to classes of entities, e.g., the extension of the category of students may be a mapping f_1 from temporal indices to classes of human beings – $f_1(t)$ will be a class of those human beings that are students at time t. Note that in certain research contexts we may need to represent this extension by means of a double parametrisation, e.g., as a mapping f_2, where $f_2(t, w)$ is a class of those human beings that are students at time t and in a possible situation (world) w. The latter may be needed, for example, when one takes into account counterfactual situations in formal models of planning activities. Now the problem with such categories is that although we can enumerate some basic types of extensions, we cannot list all of them as the number and the type of parameters depends on the domain of interest. For example, representing concepts from the psychological point of view we may need take conceptual frames as parameters – cf. [1]. Fortunately, in the case of philosophy most of the categories are modally rigid, so if x is a process, then it is a process in all circumstances.

There is an additional aspect of interpretation for those categories that are relations. Namely, philosophical interpretations of some basic relations as dependence or causality may differ in the arities assigned to these relations. For example, the standard account of the grounding takes it to be a binary relation (e.g., a certain legal fact is grounded in a social fact). But [12] argues for the quaternary account of grounding, where the grounding pattern reads "fact f_1 rather than fact f_2 is grounded in fact f_3 rather than f_4. Even given a fixed arity one interpretation of a relation may differ from the other in the categorical conditions imposed on its arguments. For example, there are two competing accounts of the grounding relation. One imposes no constraints as to what may ground what [11]. The other interprets it as a relation between facts or situations [3]. In order to account for these possibilities my notion of interpretation of relations will take into account (also) the number of arguments for a relation and the categorical restrictions of each argument.

One category may have multiple interpretations which specify the category's different extensions. This implies that we need to construe the former as individual entities, on a par with categories, propositions, and propositional structures. Consequently, the interpretation-sensitivity of categories may be represented by means of the *ternary* relationship that binds category interpretations, interpreted categories, and categories' extensions. In the case of relations it may be handy to be able to employ the quaternary relationship that binds relation interpretations, interpreted relations, relation arguments' indices, and their categories.

4   Implementation

The above ideas were materialised in the form of an OWL ontology, by the name of OntOfOnt. The ontology is scoped to only one philosophical discipline: metaphysics (ontology). In other words, it is designed as an engineering ontology for philosophical ontology. This scope restriction implied a number of minor extensions to the above design, e.g., adding the ontological_mode_of_representation class.

The ontology contains 40 classes, which are related by 41 object properties. The ontology's axiomatisation attempts to employ the full expressive power available in OWL 2 DL (ALCRIQ(D)). Still, a more adequate formal characterisation of the notions discussed in the previous section would require the full strength of the first order logic. The class hierarchy is shown in Fig. 3.

Since OntOfOnt is not a foundational ontology, for the sake of ontological clarity its upper level categories were "stitched" up to the categories of two

Table 1. OntOfOnt upper level categories characterisation

OntOfOnt	CIDOC CRM	IAO
agent	owl:equivalentClass E39_Actor	rdfs:subClassOf BFO_0000030
category_extension	rdfs:subClassOf E70_Thing	rdfs:subClassOf BFO_0000141
membership	rdfs:subClassOf E70_Thing	rdfs:subClassOf BFO_0000141
resource_content	owl:equivalentClass E73_Information_Object	rdfs:subClassOf BFO_0000031
knowledge_resource	rdfs:subClassOf E84_Information_Carrier	owl:equivalentClass IAO_0000030

Table 2. OntOfOnt versions

OntOfOnt version	URL
base ontology	http://www.metaontology.pl/metaontology.owl
base ontology embedded in IAO ontology	http://www.metaontology.pl/iao_metaontology.owl
base ontology embedded in CIDOC-CRM ontology	http://www.metaontology.pl/cidoc-crm_metaontology.owl
base ontology populated with http://philpapers.org data	http://www.metaontology.pl/metaontology_populated.owl

foundational ontologies: CIDOC CRM and Information Artefact Ontology – see Table 1. The various versions of the ontology are available from the URLs specified in table 2.

In order to illustrate its modelling potential the ontology was populated with the data available from the http://philpapers.org website. This website organises the scholarly papers in philosophy with respect to a number of keywords. In particular it specifies a set of keywords relevant for philosophical ontology. A close look at http://philpapers.org revealed that its keywords include all three types of resource contents defined above. In the first run I selected among them those that correspond to OntOfOnt's categories. These categories and the papers assigned thereof were loaded to OntOfOnt accordingly. In addition during the load a number of additional categories were identified on the basis of the papers' abstracts. The identification process was semi-automated by the user's selection of the keywords with the highest tf-idf ranks. The whole load process was supported by a purpose-specific JAVA application. Note that this process did not involve any philosophical analysis, so it assumed, among other things, that each category has the same interpretation throughout the papers assigned to it.

The relationships that support the representation of category interpretations cannot be directly expressed in OWL languages, which are restricted to binary relations. In order to overcome this restriction I employed the standard procedure of reification, whose results are shown in Fig. 4.

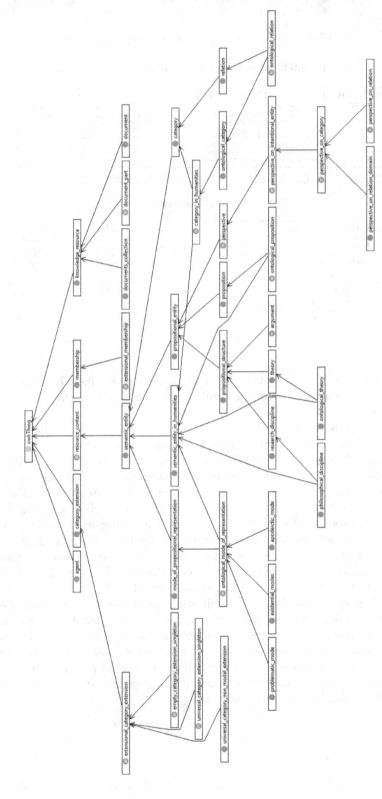

Fig. 3. OntOfOnt class hierarchy

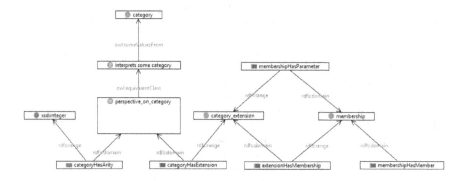

Fig. 4. OntOfOnt reifications

5   Further Work

The main theoretical issue to be resolved has to do with the impoverished notion of category interpretation assumed in this paper. The notion described above grasps only the extensional aspect of categories, ignoring their intentional dimension. In a sense all categories with the same extensions are equivalent. So, for example, the category of equilateral triangles will be characterised exactly in the same way as the category of equiangular triangles despite the fact that these categories are different because they are defined in different ways. A more comprehensive notion of category interpretation needs to take this essential aspect of categories into account.

As far as the applicative issues are concerned the main obstacle again hinges upon the notion of interpretation. This time the task is to specify for each resource content the interpretations involved in this content and identify the same interpretations across different contents. To this end we need laborious philosophical analysis of the respective resources. As a rule, this process cannot be automated or even computer-aided, but it needs to be done by a human user who is sufficiently conversant in the domain at stake so that he or she could identify and distinguish between different interpretations of thereof. Only then the full expressive potential of OntOfOnt can be employed and the specific nature of philosophy as a discipline in the humanities can be established.

Acknowledgments.   This research has been supported by the DEC-2012/07/B/HS1/01938 grant funded by National Science Centre (Poland).

References

1. Barsalou, L.W.: Frames, concepts, and conceptual fields. In: Lehrer, A., Kittay, E.F. (eds.) Frames, Fields, and Contrasts, pp. 21–74. Lawrence Erlbaum Associates (1992)

2. Buckner, C., Niepert, M., Allen, C.: From encyclopedia to ontology: Toward dynamic representation of the discipline of philosophy. Synthese **182**(2), 205–233 (2011)
3. Correia, F., Schnieder, B.: Grounding: an opinionated introduction. In: Metaphysical Grounding, pp. 1–36. Cambridge University Press (2012)
4. DCU Ontology Team: NeMO - NeDiMAH Methods Ontology. NeMO Entity Class Definitions. Tech. Rep. 0.1, Digital Curation Unit (2015). http://www.nedimah.eu/reports/developing-nemo-nedimah-methods-ontology
5. DIorio, P.: Discovery. D1.8 Final Report. Tech. rep. (2009). http://www.discovery-project.eu/reports/discovery-final-report.pdf
6. Doerr, M.: The CIDOC Conceptual Reference Module: An Ontological Approach to Semantic Interoperability of Metadata. AI Magazine **24**(3), 75–92 (2003)
7. Hennicke, S., Gradmann, S., Dill, K., Tschumpel, G., Thoden, K., Morbindoni, C., Pichler, A.: D3.4 Research Report on DH Scholarly Primitives. Tech. rep. (2015). http://dm2e.eu/files/D3.4_1.0_Research_Report_on_DH_Scholarly_Primitives_150210.pdf
8. IFLA: Functional Requirements for Bibliographic Records: Final Report. K. G. Saur (1998)
9. Pasin, M., Motta, E.: Ontological requirements for annotation and navigation of philosophical resources. Synthese **182**(2), 235–267 (2011)
10. Pichler, A., Zöllner-Weber, A.: Sharing and debating Wittgenstein by using an ontology. Literary and Linguistic Computing **28**(4), 700–707 (2013)
11. Schaffer, J.: On what grounds what. In: Metametaphysics: new essays on the foundations of ontology, pp. 347–383. Oxford University Press (2009)
12. Schaffer, J.: Grounding, transitivity, and contrastivity. In: Metaphysical Grounding: Understanding the Structure of Reality, pp. 122–38 (2012)
13. Veltman, K.H.: Towards a Semantic Web for Culture. Journal of Digital Information **4**(4) (2006)

Threshold Determination and Engaging Materials Scientists in Ontology Design

Jane Greenberg[1(✉)], Yue Zhang[1], Adrian Ogletree[1], Garritt J. Tucker[2], and Daniel Foley[2]

[1] Metadata Research Center (MRC), College of Computing & Informatics (CCI), Drexel University, Philadelphia, PA, USA
{janeg,yue.zhang,aogletree}@drexel.edu
[2] Computational Materials Science and Design (CMSD), Materials Science and Engineering Department, College of Engineering, Drexel University, Philadelphia, PA, USA
gtucker@coe.drexel.edu, df92@drexel.edu

Abstract. This paper reports on research exploring a threshold for engaging scientists in semantic ontology development. The domain application, *nanocrystalline metals*, was pursued using a multi-method approach involving algorithm comparison, semantic concept/term evaluation, and term sorting. Algorithms from four open source term extraction applications (RAKE, Tagger, Kea, and Maui) were applied to a test corpus of preprint abstracts from the arXiv repository. Materials scientists identified 92 terms for ontology inclusion from a combined set of 228 unique terms, and the term sorting activity resulted in 9 top nodes. The combined methods were successful in engaging domain scientists in ontology design, and give a threshold capacity measure (*threshold acceptability*) to aid future work. This paper presents the research background and motivation, reviews the methods and procedures, and summarizes the initial results. A discussion explores term sorting approaches and mechanisms for determining thresholds for engaging scientist in semantically-driven ontology design and the concept of ontological empowerment.

Keywords: Nanocrystalline metals · Materials science · Semantic terminology · Ontology design · Ontological empowerment · Threshold determination · Helping Interdisciplinary Vocabulary Engineering (HIVE)

1 Introduction

Vocabularies, taxonomies, and semantic ontological systems have been a mainstay of scientific endeavors from earliest times. Aristotle's *History of Animals* (*Historia Animalium*) [1] is among the most recognized examples. In this seminal work, animals are classified by observable properties, such as having blood or being bloodless, their living habitat, and movement processes (walking, flying, or swimming). Aristotle further introduced binomial naming; that is, the classing and naming of organisms by their genus and what we today identify as species. During the nineteenth century, Carl Linnaeus, the 'father of modern taxonomy,' advanced binomial nomenclature for plant specimens by

© Springer International Publishing Switzerland 2015
E. Garoufallou et al. (Eds.): MTSR 2015, CCIS 544, pp. 39–50, 2015.
DOI: 10.1007/978-3-319-24129-6_4

introducing facets, hierarchies (genus/species, supra- and sub- categories), associations, and other types of relationships that are integral components of many contemporary semantic ontologies [2].

Fast forward to today, where semantic ontologies are being integrated into our digital data infrastructure. Ontologies have a crucial role to play in aiding data discovery, reuse, and interoperability; and, most significantly, they can facilitate *new science* [3]. Development of ontology encoding standards, such as the Web Ontology Language (OWL)[4] and the Simple Knowledge Organizing System (SKOS)[5], are interconnected with the growth of Big Data and the desire to advance data science activity. Additionally, the 'open data movement' has motivated various communities to generate and share ontologies; there have been numerous collaborations to this end in biology, medicine and health sciences, ecology, and geology.

Materials science, as an interdisciplinary field of study, has been able to benefit from ontology work in these other disciplines; however, documented efforts targeting materials science are limited to a few examples [6]. Researchers associated with the Materials Metadata Infrastructure Initiative (M^2I^2) [7] at the Metadata Research Center, Drexel University, are addressing this shortcoming by exploring means for advancing ontological practices in the field of materials science. As part of this effort, an interdisciplinary research team of information and materials scientists are studying ways to engage domain scientists in ontology development while extending the Helping Interdisciplinary Vocabulary Engineering (HIVE) technology [8, 9, 10].

This paper reports on the M^2I^2 effort, and specifically the development of an ontology for nanocrystalline metals. The chief goal was to explore a threshold for engaging scientists in semantic ontology development.   To further explain, we seek baseline data on the engagement capacities of scientists (domain experts) for aiding ontology development. More precisely, how much time and effort can we anticipate of scientists, without them feeling like ontology work is an intellectual drain.

A secondary goal was to identify means by which information scientists/non-domain experts can easily facilitate ontology design processes., To this end, we identified fairly generic, domain agnostic technologies that can be applied across various materials science sectors as well as other disciplines. We explain these technologies in our methods and reporting. The unified goal is to establish an ontology design framework that can be used across a range of disciplines and sub-disciplines.

The remainder of this paper reports on this research and is organized as follows. Section 2 presents background information on materials science and nanocrystalline metals; Section 3 provides the case for shared semantics in materials science; Sections 4-6 cover the research objectives, methods, and procedures; Section 7 presents the results; Section 8 includes a contextual discussion of the results and examines challenges and opportunities for determining thresholds for engaging materials scientists in ontology design. Section 9, the last section of this paper, presents several conclusions, notes research limitations, and identifies next steps for future research.

2   Materials Science and Engineering: Nanocrystalline Materials

Materials Science and Engineering (MSE) is the study of the intersection of materials' processing, structure, properties, and performance [11]. The goal is to improve existing materials and develop new materials for a myriad of scientific and technological applications. The origins of MSE lie within the overlapping interests of chemistry, physics, and engineering. MSE research is relevant to other engineering and scientific disciplines, as the impact of advanced materials has shown to be universally beneficial. Over the past few decades, one significant driving force behind materials research has been the emergence of nanotechnology and nanoscience [12], where both science and engineering at the atomic/molecular level are investigated. Advancements in structural, electronic, magnetic, optical, and other functional properties of materials have correlated well with advancements in nanotechnology research.

Engineering or manipulating the nanostructure of a material enables enhancement for a wide array of physical properties (e.g., mechanical, electrical, optical, etc. [13]. Nanostructured materials are characterized by the fundamental structure or building block of the *material being* on the order of *nanometers*. Nanocrystalline (NC) metals, a type of nanostructured material, has received noticeable interest due to improvements in its mechanical properties. In NC metals, the length-scale of the fundamental unit (i.e., grain or crystal) is on the order of 1-100 nanometers [14].

NC metals have been the subject of numerous studies, as their mechanical strength has been recorded in early efforts to exceed that of traditional metals with larger grains or crystals. A growing body of research confirms that additional property enhancements in NC metals show promise in more common products and applications. Specific examples demonstrate how NC metals incorporated into artificial limbs may improve human health [15]. Innovative NC driven capacities, the open data movement, and calls to accelerate materials science R&D provoke the development of shared semantics.

3   The Materials Genome Initiative and the Case for Shared Semantics

Materials are integral to our daily lives; and global efforts along with industry/academic partnerships seek to advance MSE R&D. In the United States, the Obama Administration has launched the Materials Genome Initiative (MGI) [16] to accelerate the development of new materials in areas impacting human health, energy and the environment, and social welfare. The MGI 2014 Strategic Plan [17] recognizes the significance of data in 'Objective 3, Facilitate Access to Materials Data;' and Section 3.2 specifically calls for semantics to aid discovery across data repositories.

Semantic ontologies are important for this objective; they aid scientists and data managers in discovering, using, and repurposing research data together with additional components of the research enterprise (e.g., data, models, simulations, instrumentation, software, code, etc.).

Biology, geology, medicine, and environmental science have extensive disciplinary networks of shared semantics ontologies. Two examples include the Biosharing portal [18] in the United Kingdom, which provides links to a vast collection standards including scientific ontologies; and the National Center for Biological Ontologies (NCBO) bioportal [19], which houses 441 ontologies covering scientific and medical topics. Federal agencies are also responsible for maintaining terminologies that equate with semantic ontologies. A case in point is the United States Geological Survey (USGS), which maintains the Integrated Taxonomic Information System [20] and other terminologies in the geological and biological sciences. All of these facilities allow scientists to access and use semantics on a global scale. More significantly, sharing semantics supports data discovery, use, integration, and other functionalities that can promote new science.

Shared semantic ontologies have flourished in various scientific domains, although efforts in materials science and engineering (MSE) are limited. One reason for the slow uptake in this area may be that materials science and engineering research endeavors are able to leverage ontologies developed in other noted areas. Another reason is that scientist may not see the value of ontologies or a direct impact or value, making their engagement difficult. Ontology creation is a time-consuming, intellectually demanding undertaking; and scientists have limited time to devote to such efforts. To this end, ontology R&D needs to educate scientists/domain specialists as to the value of ontologies and provide mechanisms so that involvement in the ontology creation process is not too labor intensive.

Ontology work for Chronic Obstruction Pulmonary Disease (COPD) provides one example addressing these goals, driven by the practice of *ontological empowerment* [21]. User-friendly open source thesaurus software (TemaTres) was used to engage domain experts (medical researchers) in ontology design and maintenance work. In this case the domain experts had a sense empowerment by contributing to and maintaining the ontology. Moreover, the COPD ontology was seen as a valuable tool. The MSE predicament might be addressed in a similar way by facilitating domain expert engagement and leveraging the information scientist's expertise to provide a user-friendly development environment. Specific research objectives guiding the research presented in this paper are outlined in the next section.

4   Research Objectives

The objectives of this research were to:

- Explore an approach for engaging materials scientists in ontology development, including means by which information scientists may aid the process.
- Gather a threshold capacity measure, consisting of engagement time and number of terms, for domain scientists' engagement in the development of semantic ontologies.
- Develop a base-level ontology for nanocrystalline metals.
- Consider implications of this research for other areas in materials science and engineering (MSE) and other disciplines.

5   Methods

The posited research objectives were addressed using a multi-method approach involving algorithm comparison, semantic concept/term evaluation, and term sorting.

- The algorithm comparison combined term extraction results of four natural language processing open source applications. (*The phrase 'algorithm comparison' is used hereafter to reference this method.*) RAKE and Tagger support unsupervised algorithms, and Kea and Maui support supervised methods. Supervised methods involve training the models with documents that have been indexed by a person, indicating a gold standard.
- The semantic concept/term evaluation method followed general relevance evaluation processes, with a three tier scale of 'valuable', 'not sure', or 'not valuable'. (*Concepts are intellectual ideas represented by single and bound terms as well as phrases. This paper generally uses "term/s," although the discussion of algorithms uses the phrase 'keyphrases', consistent with broader Kea and Maui reporting in the scientific literature.*)
- The term-sorting activity was a basic clustering process, asking participants to separate and group concepts in preparation for establishing hierarchies and associations.

More details on method execution are presented in Section 6, Sample and Procedures.

6   Sample and Procedures

The research was conducted using a test corpus of 10 abstracts drawn from the arXiv repository. We generated our test corpus by searching the repository for the phrase "nanocystalline", selecting the 10 most recent preprints (as of May 2015), and collecting their abstracts for analysis. The following steps document the research design for the three methods.

6.1   Algorithm Implementation

To obtain our sample of terms, we needed to understand how to implement each of the algorithms and their operations.

- **RAKE** parses text into phrases (terms, bound terms, or term strings) based on given stop lists and desired keyphrase length and frequency. A candidate score is calculated for each phrase based on co-occurrence [22]. Finally, RAKE returns a list of keyphrases ranked by their scores. In this research, we generated word groups with the following constraints: each word had at least 4 characters, each phrase had at most 3 words, and each keyword appeared in the text at least once. We then selected phrases with scores higher than 5.0 as our keyphrases.

- **Tagger** is also an open source tool used for unsupervised automatic indexing [23]. Like RAKE, Tagger cleans the input text, splits it into words, rates the word according to relevance, and returns the top five candidates as keyphrases.

- **Kea** creates a model for keyphrase extraction using training files with manual indexing tags [24], and differs from RAKE and Tagger. The algorithm first splits text into sequences and calculates feature scores for all candidate phrases. A secondary step involves generating a model from keyphrases that are manually indexed and identified in the files. When extracting keyphrases from a new document, Kea parses text for candidate phrases, calculates feature values, and applies the training model to generate the keyphrases. In this research, we applied the default model in Kea package to use free indexing on our documents.

- **Maui** is similar to Kea. This algorithm first trains selected documents and keyphrases to build a model, and then uses the model to test on new data [25]. Maui selects candidate phrases by parsing sentences into textual sequences as tokens and extracting tokens based on given stop lists. For each candidate term, Maui calculates a score based on several features and put the scores into a machine learning model to learn the probability of real candidates. Compared to the Kea system, Maui only includes three basic Kea features and adds six new features. In our research, we used the Maui model created with the SemEval-2010 keyphrase set [26] for free indexing.

6.2   Term Evaluation

The terms extracted from each of the algorithms were combined into a single alphabetical list, and duplicate terms were removed. The list was distributed to three participants: one professor and two doctoral students working in the area of nanocrystalline metals. These domain experts were asked evaluate 'if the term was valuable as a vocabulary word for disciplinary study of nanocrystalline metals.' The following three indicators were used in the evaluation: valuable (v), not sure (ns), and not valuable (nv) for disciplinary study. These results were combined into a single set. Cases where all three ratings for a term were "v" or "nv" were easily determined as "v" and "nv." There were no cases where all three ratings were "ns". Table 1 shows our methodology for combining mixed ratings.

Table 1. Rating Synthesis.

Mixed ratings	Overall rating
v, v, nv	v
v, ns, nv	v
v, nv, nv	nv

6.3   Term Sorting

The sorting activity involved further clustering of terms under higher-level concepts for the development of hierarchies. This activity was supported by ConceptCodify

[27], which allows users to create groups with group names (functioning a top nodes or facets), and put cards into each groups (instances).

7   Results

The results of this study are helpful in understanding how selected technologies can help information scientists work with domain experts, and for obtaining a measure of domain scientists' capacities for ontology design engagement. The results of this study are presented below under the designated methodological sub-headings.

7.1   Algorithm Comparison

In this research, different algorithms extracted different numbers of key phrases. RAKE generated terms ranked by their scores for each document, and we chose terms with a score higher or equal to 5.0. Therefore, we had 7 key phrases for each document, and in total we had 70 key phrases. Tagger extracted the top 5 terms with highest relevance for each document, and we have 50 key phrases from all the files. Kea indexed each document by 10 key phrases with each phrases less or equal to 5 words. Similarly, Maui indexed each file by 10 key phrases with each phrases less or equal to 3 words. Thus, Kea and Maui each generated 100 key phrases from all the files. Table 1 summarizes the outputs form each algorithm and Table 2 gives an example of key phrase extraction for each application.

Table 2. Algorithm comparison.

Application/algorithm	RAKE	Tagger	Kea	Maui
Algorithm	Unsupervised	Unsupervised	Supervised	Supervised
Training files	N/A	N/A	Default	SemEval-2010
Maximum word length of phrases	3	3	5	3
Number of terms	70	50	100	100

The outputs from this activity were combined into a single dataset for the term evaluation activity.

7.2   Term Extraction and Evaluation

The term evaluation process allowed domain experts to identify terms, representing concepts, for ontology inclusion. Table 3 presents the total number of phrases extracted by different algorithms and the total number of unique phrases. Keyphrases extracted by different algorithms were saved as four independent files; we then tallied the number of keyphrases in each file, and removed duplicated keyphrases.

Table 3. Example of keyphrase extraction from one document.

Application/ algorithm	Example of keyphrase extraction for one document
RAKE	local temperature rise, grain structure stabilized, average grain sizes, nanoscale grain structure, 8.8, significant plastic deformation, stable nanocrystalline alloy, driven grain growth, intense strain localization, grain growth
Tagger	nanocrystalline, shear bands, evolution, strain localization, formation
Kea	shear bands, Grain Structures, Nanocrystalline, shear, Strain Localization, Thermally-Stable, Nanoscale, Nanoscale Grain, Nanoscale Grain Structures, Grain growth
Maui	thermally stable, grain structure, strain localization, nanoscale grain, shear bands, nanoscale grain structure, Thermally, Stable, nanocrystalline, localization

Table 4. Total number of terms extracted and total number unique terms.

Algorithm	Total number of terms/phrases extracted	Total number of unique terms
RAKE	70	69
Tagger	50	50
Kea	100	96
Maui	100	96
Combination of all data	320	311

Table 4, column two presents the number of terms generated by each algorithm, and column 3 presents the number of unique terms per individual algorithm. The unique terms per individual algorithm execution were combined into a single set (311 terms); and close to 27% (83) of these terms were duplicative. That is, the term (which can include a keyphrase as abound term/s) was extracted via more than one of the algorithms. The 83 terms were removed, resulting a set of 228 unique terms for evaluation as candidate ontology terms.

The evaluation activity targeted the 228 terms and resulted in a corpus of 92 terms deemed valuable for ontology inclusion. The rating, noted above in the methods section, required at least rating of 'v/ (valuable) with a second rating of 'v' or 'ns; (valuable and not-sure). As reported above, there were no cases that had all three cases as 'ns' (not sure). The 92 terms deemed valuable were the corpus for the terms sorting activity, and serves as the nanocrystalline ontology source.

7.3   Term Sorting

The initial term sorting activity resulted in the identification of 9 top nodes listed on the left-hand of Table 5. Instances per node ranged from 2 to 11 for the initial ontology rendering, with an average of 6 instances per node. The right hand side presents two of the top nodes and associated instances.

Table 5. Nanocrystalline metals--ontology

Top Nodes (Facets)	Nodes and Instances	
1. materials 2. structures 3. processes 4. material classes: 5. properties 6. techniques 7. descriptors 8. devices 9. physical objects	**materials**	**structures**
	nanocrystalline graphene	nanoparticles
	nanocrystalline aluminum studied	nanosheet
	substrate	vacancy
	graphene	grain structures
		shear bands...

The initial sorting activity reported on here is being reviewed among the three participants. The scientist overseeing the initial activity responded to two survey prompts, and indicated that the term sorting/grouping task too roughly 20 minutes. The scientist also noted that the sorting activity was a "very straightforward task. The only factor that gave me [him] pause was the occurrence of phrases containing redundant terms (i.e. nano crystalline alumina alongside nano crystalline and alumina)." This example points to syntagmatic and paradigmatic relationships--a very common ontology design challenge. As part of next steps, the research team plans address orphaned terms, and provide a mechanism for adding and tracking missing nodes and instances to complete the ontology, and move forward to creating SKOS encoded instance of this ontology.

8   Discussion: Threshold Determination

This research provides insight into what is a acceptable capacity for engaging scientists in ontology development. The algorithm preparation time was, as anticipated, fairly reasonable (approximately 4 work days of an information scientists time). The selected methods and unifying framework, merging outputs and eliminating duplicate terms, was an easy way to produce a corpus.

The term selection results were straight forward, taking each scientist roughly 10 minutes to evaluate the collection of 228 unique terms, resulting in a unified list 92 terms for ontology inclusion. An unexpected aspect of the term evaluation activity was that the two doctoral students were more direct using either 'v' (valuable) or 'nv' (not valuable), but neither used the 'ns' (not sure) criteria. It is difficult to gauge why they did not use this third indicator; it could be that the evaluation instructions were not clear, although all three indicators were evident on the scoring sheet. It is also possible that the doctoral students had great comfort with this activity or have been engaged in database work, and their evaluation patterns are reflective of Gruber's classic notion of concepts (represented by terms) being either *in a world* or *outside*, with no ambiguity [28]. Follow-up is needed here to learn more about this result.

The second domain scientist task involved working with the ConceptCodify application and establishing group names (top nodes) and instances, drawing from the set of 92 terms. The scientist championing this work reported that it was relatively simple and took roughly 20 minutes. While some aspect of pause was noted, the scientist showed no frustration or sign cognitive overload, indicating that the method, number of terms, and time demand were suitable. These results point to an initial measure of *threshold acceptability*, and more data is needed to indicate where a time increase or more terms to evaluate or sort would indicate a threshold capacity.

This study is not without limitations. The nanocrystalline metals ontology, while robust with examples, is limited is scope. The sample was generated from a set of 10 of the most recent articles on nanocrystalline metals deposited in arXiv. A more extensive sample will very likely result in more terms requiring evaluation, and a larger corpus for the sorting activity. The time and intellectual demand from domain scientists will increase with a larger sample. To this end, the ontology research team is rethinking the sorting exercise and how to efficiently gather valid terms for completing the ontology. In closing, it's likely that social networking technology, as demonstrated by YAMZ (formerly SeaIce) [29], with the thumbs up/down to garner team agreement, may offer an approach.

9   Conclusion

This study investigated a means for determining a threshold for engaging scientists in semantic ontology development. The research was conducted in the area of nanocrystalline metals, where there is limited evidence of a shared ontology. Materials scientists identified 105 terms for ontology inclusion; and an exploratory sorting activity resulted in 9 top nodes.

In reviewing the study's objectives, the results present confirm an approach for engaging materials scientists in ontology development. The method pursued also demonstrates a way that information scientists may aid the process by generating a corpus of term. The resulting base-level ontology indicates a measure of threshold capacity for domain scientist engagement of approximately 10 minutes for evaluation, and 20 minutes for terms sorting and grouping.

Development and maintenance of semantic ontologies is crucial for advancing and accelerating MSE research. Semantic ontologies help provide insight into the full scope of a domain and enable discovery, sharing, and interoperability. In closing, ontologies, as intellectual maps, provide valued intelligence where they are applied. The M^2I^2 will translate lessons learned here into our next stage of research, and will continue to advance ontology R&D in MSE.

Acknowledgements. We would like to acknowledge the National Consortium for Data Science (NCDS), 2014 Data Science Fellows Program; the National Science Foundation under Grant Number OCI 0940841; and thank you also to the participating scientists.

References

1. Aristotle: The History of Animals (350 B.C.E.) Translated by D'Arcy Wentworth Thompson. The Internet Classics Archive. http://classics.mit.edu/Aristotle/history_anim.html
2. Heuer, P., Hennig, B.: The classification of living beings. In: Munn, K., Smith, B. (eds.) Applied Ontology: An Introduction, vol. 9, pp. 197–217. Walter de Gruyter (2008)
3. Greenberg, J.: Philosophical foundations and motivation via scientific inquiry. In: Smiraglia, R., Lee, H.L. (eds.) Ontology for Knowledge Organization, pp. 5–12. Ergon-Verlag (2015)
4. Web Ontology Language. http://www.w3.org/standards/techs/owl#w3c_all
5. Simple Knowledge Organization System. http://www.w3.org/standards/techs/skos#w3c_all
6. Cheung, K., Drennan, J., Hunter, J.: Towards an ontology for data-driven discovery of new materials. In: AAAI Spring Symposium: Semantic Scientific Knowledge Integration, pp. 9–14, March 2008
7. Materials Metadata Infrastructure Initiative (M^2I^2). https://cci.drexel.edu/MRC/projects/materials-metadata-infrastructure-initiative/
8. Helping Interdisciplinary Vocabulary Engineering. https://cci.drexel.edu/hivewiki/index.php/Main_Page
9. Conway, M.C., Greenberg, J., Moore, R., Whitton, M., Zhang, L.: Advancing the DFC semantic technology platform via HIVE innovation. In: Garoufallou, E., Greenberg, J. (eds.) MTSR 2013. CCIS, vol. 390, pp. 14–21. Springer, Heidelberg (2013)
10. Zhang, Y., Greenberg, J., Tucker, G.T., Ogletree, A.: Advancing materials science semantic metadata via HIVE. In: International Conference on Dublin Core and Metadata Applications, São Paulo, Brazil, September 1–4, 2015
11. Callister, W.D., Jr.: Materials Science and Engineering—An Introduction, 5th edn. John Wiley and Sons (2000) (ISBN 0-471-32013-7)
12. Nano work - Nanotechnology Reports. http://www.nanowerk.com/nanotechnology/reports/reports.php
13. Tucker, G.J., Tiwari, S., Zimmerman, J.A., McDowell, D.L.: Investigating the Deformation of Nanocrystalline Copper with Microscale Kinematic Metrics and Molecular dynamics. Journal of the Mechanics and Physics of Solids **60**, 471–486 (2012)
14. Tucker, G.J., McDowell, D.L.: Non-equilibrium Grain Boundary Structure and Inelastic Deformation Using Atomistic Simulations. International Journal of Plasticity **27**, 841–857 (2011)

15. Affatato, S.: Ceramic-On-Metal for Total Hip Replacement: Mixing and Matching Can Lead to High Wear. Artificial Organs **34**(4), 319–323 (2010)
16. Materials Genome Initiative. https://www.whitehouse.gov/mgi
17. Materials Genome Initiative Strategic Plan: National Science and Technology Council Committee on Technology Subcommittee on the Materials Genome Initiative, December 2014. https://www.whitehouse.gov/sites/default/files/microsites/ostp/NSTC/mgi_strategic_plan_-_dec_2014.pdf
18. Biosharing. https://www.biosharing.org/
19. National Center for Biological Ontologies—bioportal. bioportal.bioontology.org/
20. Integrated Taxonomic Information System (ITIS). www.itis.gov
21. Greenberg, J., Deshmukh, R., Huang, L., Mostafa, J., La Vange, L., Carretta, E., O'Neal, W.: The COPD Ontology and Toward Empowering Clinical Scientists as Ontology Engineers. Journal of Library Metadata **10**(2–3), 173–187 (2010)
22. Rose, S., Engel, D., Cramer, N., Cowley, W.: Automatic Keyword Extraction from Individual Documents (2010)
23. Presta, A.: Tagger. GitHub. https://github.com/apresta/tagger
24. Witten, I.H., Paynter, G.W., Frank, E., Gutwin, C., Nevill-Manning, C.G.: KEA: practical automatic keyphrase extraction. In: Proceedings of the Fourth ACM Conference on Digital Libraries, pp. 254–255. ACM (1999)
25. Frank, E., Paynter, G.W., Witten, I.H., Gutwin, C., Nevill-Manning, C.G.: Domain-specific keyphrase extraction. In: Proc. of the 16th International Joint Conference on Artificial Intelligence, Stockholm, Sweden, pp. 668–673. Morgan Kaufmann Publishers, San Francisco (1999)
26. Kim, S.N., Medelyan, O., Kan, M.Y., Baldwin, T.: Semeval-2010 task 5: automatic keyphrase extraction from scientific articles. In: Proceedings of the 5th International Workshop on Semantic Evaluation, pp. 21–26. Association for Computational Linguistics (2010)
27. ConceptCodify. https://conceptcodify.com/
28. Gruber, T.: What is an Ontology (1993)
29. Greenberg, J., Murillo, A., Kunze, J., Callaghan, S., Guralnick, R., Nassar, N., Ram, K., Janee, G., Patton, C.: Metadictionary: advocating for a community-driven metadata vocabulary application. In: DC-2013: CAMP-4-DATA Workshop: Proceedings of the International Conference on Dublin Core and Metadata Applications, Lisbon, Portugal, September 2–6, 2013

What are Information Security Ontologies Useful for?

Miguel-Angel Sicilia[1(✉)], Elena García-Barriocanal[1], Javier Bermejo-Higuera[2],
and Salvador Sánchez-Alonso[1]

[1] Computer Science Department, University of Alcalá, Ctra. Barcelona,
km. 336, 28871 Alcalá de Henares, Madrid, Spain
{msicilia,elena.garciab,salvador.sanchez}@uah.es
[2] Automation Department, University of Alcalá, Alcalá de Henares, Spain
javier.bermejo@uah.es

Abstract. The engineering of ontologies in the information security domain have received some degree of attention in past years. Concretely, the use of ontologies has been proposed as a solution for a diversity of tasks related to that domain, from the modelling of cyber-attacks to easing the work of auditors or analysts. This has resulted in ontology artefacts, degrees of representation and ontological commitments of a diverse nature. In this paper, a selection of recent research in the area is categorized according to their purpose or application, highlighting their main commonalities. Then, an assessment of the current status of development in the area is provided, in an attempt to sketch a future roadmap for further research. The literature surveyed shows different levels of analysis, from the more conceptual to the more low-level, protocol-oriented, and also diverse levels of readiness for practice. Further, several of the works found use existing standardized, community-curated databases as sources for ontology population, which points out to a need to use these as a baseline for future research, adding ontology-based functionalities for those capabilities not directly supported by them.

1 Introduction

The field of information security is concerned with preserving the confidentiality, integrity and availability of information assets of any kind. With the widespread use of the Internet and more recently, mobile technologies, security has emerged as a global concern due to the increase in the frequency, impact and sophistication of threats that serve different malicious purposes or are the vehicle of activist protest. While it is difficult to precisely measure the impact and increase of cybercrime for several reasons (Hyman, 2013) the trends and the potential for disrupting business and public administration activities has raised concern for organizations but also for policy makers (Wall & Williams, 2013).

Specifically, the fight against the abovementioned growth of cybercrime requires a significant amount of resources. And this makes specially appealing those techniques or methods that could complement current security technology and practice with a higher degree of automation for some controls (Montesino and Fenz, 2011) or with some form of intelligence. Approaches for using some kind of intelligence for information security

© Springer International Publishing Switzerland 2015
E. Garoufallou et al. (Eds.): MTSR 2015, CCIS 544, pp. 51–61, 2015.
DOI: 10.1007/978-3-319-24129-6_5

tasks can be roughly categorized in two groups. On the one hand, we have those related to machine learning models that essentially operate on numerical or categorical data. These have been used for a range of diverse applications, e.g. detection of malicious code (Shabtai et al., 2009). And on the other hand, we have those approaches exploiting formal logics and symbolic representations of different kinds (including those making use of terminologies for extracting such representations from text). In this paper, we focus on the second category, as it has the potential to complement the first one in giving computational semantics to data and thus eventually make it better suited for building machine learning models on top. Further, it also opens different possibilities for tasks that are not based on learning from data as done in machine learning, but on the codification of expert or technical knowledge, which is known to play an important role nowadays in information security (Fenz & Ekelhart, 2009). For example, Atymtayeva et al. (2014) focuses on formalizing expert knowledge on the field, as expressed in standards or other guidance documents. This interest is a due to the fact that in this domain, a considerable part of the knowledge applied by practitioners is codified in the form of best practice guidelines or knowledge bases, some of them openly shared in communities or Web sites. For example, the major vulnerability databases are nowadays widely used, and standardization efforts have progressed in the last decade resulting on schemas and coding systems as the *Common Vulnerability Enumeration* dictionary[1] (Mann & Christey, 1999) and related databases that support by themselves some basic form of computational semantics.

Focusing on the second category just mentioned, the domain of information security is no exception in the interest of using ontologies as a way of providing computational semantics to different tools and techniques that are of potential utility in the domain – and some authors consider that nowadays we are in an adequate moment to pursue the use of ontologies in the field (Elçi, 2004). There have been several papers surveying the use of ontologies in this domain for particular applications, e.g. (Souag et al., 2015b), but there is a lack of a clear overall view of the aspects that each of the proposals for information security ontologies capture and their intended practical applicability. Further, there are no assessments of the degree to which these ontologies are mature and complete enough to fulfil their intended use to an extent that makes them applicable in real world scenarios. Also, it is important to assess the extent to which ontologies may supplement current databases as the *National Vulnerability Database* (NVD)[2] to support additional automation capabilities, and not simply re-stating schemas that are already widely used through them.

In this paper, we attempt to contribute to the understanding of the value and potential of ontology-based applications in the domain of information security. Concretely, we report the analysis of a sample of recent research in the topic in an attempt to provide a picture of the active research directions and some of the main issues that need to be addressed to cope with the practical application needs of information security professionals. We do not attempt to provide a systematic or comprehensive review, but a portray of developed concrete application areas and the extent to which research outcomes are prepared for facing adoption by a wider community of practitioners. Concretely, the analysis shows that there are diverse levels of abstraction in the ontologies, from

---

[1] https://cve.mitre.org

[2] https://nvd.nist.gov/

conceptual, requirements-oriented models to formalizations of network protocols or implementation specifications, so that there is a need to categorize them and to layer them to reflect that separation of concerns. Also, the level of direct applicability is disparate, as some of the examples reported in the papers are really simple ones and do not justify by themselves the use of a formal representation, while others do, but it may be argued that other languages as regular expressions could also serve as a proper representation for the task. Finally, it becomes evident that ontology population is an issue, and several authors revert to curated knowledge bases as the NVD or OWASP. In these cases, the question is the extent to which the ontologies are complementing these knowledge bases with some extra, logics-based capabilities that cannot be made actionable with the original languages used in these databases. In summary, the topic is nowadays receiving a considerable degree of attention, but arguably more effort is needed in justifying the extra burden of the logics-based languages provided by ontologies, and thus comparison with other formalisms or with existing databases should become a priority.

The rest of this paper is structured as follows. Section 2 describes the main categories found in the analysis and discusses some of the representative proposals in each of those categories. Then, Section 3 provides an assessment of different issues that arise when trying to compare, use together or apply to practical work the different ontologies reviewed. Finally, conclusions and outlook are provided in Section 4.

2   Main Categories

We have surveyed recent literature in English in the topic only from 2014 to the time of last update of this paper in June 2015. We used Google Scholar for the task, selecting studies in international scholarly journals or conferences that directly addressed the topic. We used as query search the following:

ontology AND "information security OR cybersecurity"

While this query may not cover all the results, it is broad enough to have a representative sample, and we leave a more exhaustive search to a future systematic review. Google Scholar gave an estimation of 1,590 results, but only 997 results actually returned[3]. We evaluated here only the first 40 results (four pages of results) according to the search engine's relevance measures.

Only papers reporting some ontology, and at least detailing some part of its structure were included. And only ontologies that had information security or some aspect of information security as main concern have been included. It should be noted that there are other related papers that are not directly reporting ontologies but methodological aspects of the formalization of knowledge, e.g. Atymtayeva et al. (2014) proposes such a methodology. The categorization presented here provides an interpretation of the main aims and application purposes of the ontologies, however some of them may be used also for other purposes. The aim of the categorization was that of identifying current areas of research that may have an impact in practice, so that

---

[3] Note that Google Scholar countings are only estimations, usually exceeding by far the number of results actually available.

future studies could assess in detail the extent to which ontologies currently contribute in each of these practical applications.

2.1 Security Requirement Engineering

This category encompasses ontology proposals that have as objective the modelling of the information security context or requirements. They provide a view of security that is related to the assets to be protected and its value, and reflect the viewpoint of auditors or analysts. Automation is targeted to correctly trace requirements, assess management strategies or aid in the development process, but not in the technical implementation of actual controls, alerting, countermeasures or configuration checks.

Souag et al. (2015) describe a generic security ontology implemented using OWL 1.0, covering core concepts related to security (threats, vulnerabilities, countermeasures, requirements and the like) with the explicit aim of supporting requirements engineering. Their work is based on standards as ISO 27001 and an analysis of previous ontological efforts that were systematically reviewed by the same authors (Souag et al., 2015b). The ontology is structured around several dimensions: *organization* (organization, asset, location, person), *risk* (risk, threat, vulnerability, impact, attack method, etc.) and *treatment* (security goal, control, security criterion, etc.). The authors provide a completeness analysis with regards to other previously reported ontologies, as a proof that theirs was inclusive of all the features present in previous work. This is a representative paper of the viewpoint of security analysts or management staff, that following standards as the ISO 27001 focus on risk assessment ant the establishment of a management system with a number of auditable controls.

Schiavone et al. (2014) report a conceptual model for "enterprise security" that could also be categorized as focused on requirements, in this case with a particular emphasis on quality assurance. They describe an "enterprise ontology" using concepts as *enterprise capability*, *enterprise value* or *enterprise reference architecture* that serve as a conceptual model linked with security-oriented concepts as *threat, countermeasure* or *vulnerability*. However, the ontology stays at the level of business understanding, i.e. an overall view of the system and the implementation details are apparently portrayed in Fig.1 as references to some "external security ontology".

In a related but different direction, Gyrard et al (2014) present an ontology to help developers and project managers to secure the IoT-based applications to ensure 'security by design' from the beginning of the project. In this case, the ontology is used in an interactive application as a structured information source for developers, which can be regarded as a way to add in the requirements analysis process.

2.2 Reference Ontologies

This is a special case, as it concerns ontologies described without a concrete application purpose, but targeted to a generic conceptualization of the domain. Takahashi and Kadobayashi (2014) report a kind of "reference ontology", with the broad goal of "building a basis for cybersecurity information exchange on a global scale". There are no specific functions in the design of this ontology, even though it relies heavily in existing standards and specifications, from industry or from institutions as the NVD. Basically, their proposal is a re-structuring of those previous specifications. Yao et al (2014) report a similar approach of creating the ontology methodically, but in this case, the sources of the experiment of population reported are not specified.

2.3   Specification and Matching of Security Policies and Access Control

Access control at several levels is another area of active application of ontologies, following the idea that access control roles, privileges and profiles are essentially a matter of matching entities. Actually, standard RBAC (*Role-Based Access Control*) by itself is a mechanism that includes ontology-related concepts in the definition of roles as inheritance and role hierarchies (understood as privilege modularization), and has been expressed in OWL in the past (Finin et al., 2008).

In a more specific direction, Di Modica and Tomarchio (2015) present an architecture for the matchmaking and mapping of Web service security policies. However, these policies are low-level, technical policies as those that can be expressed using the *WS-SecurityPolicy* specification. The main concepts thus include *protocol*, *algorithm* and *credential*, as they are targeting the description of software services. Bennamar et al (2005) for example also use a *policy* concept, but referring to the specifics of access control policies and breaking down the policies into elements specific to those. A literature search in this topic reveals that access control and ontologies has been subject to studies

Access control mechanisms can be considered also in this category. For example, Dasgupta et al. (2015) describe a core ontology for access control in digital libraries. Tong et al. (2015) apply rules to Network Access Control (NAC) policies.

2.4   Vulnerability Analysis

Salini and Shembagan (2015) use ontologies and SWRL rules to predict attacks based on vulnerability assessment information. The approach is based on using well-known and properly curated databases of vulnerabilities to derive ontology models from them. Concretely, they use the National Vulnerability Database (NVD) and the Open Web Application Security Project (OWASP) databases. The approach basically leverages the data of collections as CVE, CWE and scoring systems for impact as the CVSS. While this approach is of direct application to systems, it is only a change in formalism from sound databases, so that the main merits of the approach rely on the quality of the resources used to populate the ontology.

Vulnerability or threat assessment usually relies on the CVSS scoring mechanism, for example, the VULCAN security ontology also uses CVSS as the base element for assessing threats in complex cloud systems (Kamongi et al., 2015).

2.5   Attack Detection

Razzaq et al. (2014) provide an example of ontologies and rules for attack detection. Concretely, they formalize HTTP concepts and provide an evaluation based on the

OWASP[4] knowledge base. Sharma et al. (2015) describe an ontology to model attacks in mobile ad-hoc networks that may be used for similar purposes, even though no relevant evaluation is reported. Shenbagam & Salini (2014) report another proposal for the prediction and classification of attacks in the context of Web applications.

2.6   Information Extraction

In every domain, ontologies provide a way to drive and enrich information extraction from documents. An example of such use in the cybersecurity domain is described by Balducinni et al (2015). They present an architecture and cases of the use of an ontology that models hardware and operating system events and objects that are particularly useful when analysing log information. For example, an instance of a `DNSQueryRecord` is sable to structure log information including IP addresses, DNS queries or domain names. This use of ontologies is particularly useful in the phases of analysing masses of unstructured information. Takahashi and Kadobayashi (2014b) report a related way of using ontologies to integrate disparate information formats and schemas.

2.7   Preparation for Machine Learning

Kumar et al. (2015) describe the use of ontologies to categorize intrusion data for the use of a machine learning approach that uses K-means clustering. The paper does not provide the details of the data used for the evaluation, so there is not enough information to assess the contribution of ontologies to the process with respect to using direct intrusion records with not formal logics support. Zhang et al. (2014) use the CWE[5] (*Common Weakness Enumeration*) standardized list of weaknessess to mine relations among vulnerabilities using association rules (concretely, the *APriori* algorithm). Again, the contribution of using the ontology beyond the use of a formal language is not independently evaluated.

3   Assessment of Current Practice

The studies referenced here are diverse in scope and coverage of the different concerns of information security practice. In some cases, the authors themselves declare the need for further research. For example, the use of ontologies for security requirements engineering remains controversial, as Souag et al. (2015) conclude "the goal of constructing this kind of security ontologies remains ambitious and was found to be more complex than expected. [...] A truly complete security ontology remains a utopian goal." None of the studies attempt to evaluate against some existing technology or practice, i.e. experimentally or empirically assessing why the use of ontologies brings some clear

---

[4] https://www.owasp.org/
[5] https://cwe.mitre.org/

benefit with respect to current practice. This should in our opinion be addressed in future studies for a better justification of ontologies in the field.

In addition to that, there are a number of aspects described below that in our opinion should be addressed in future research in the topic to make studies easier to evaluate, and to better contrast existing standard practices with the proposed novel uses of ontologies.

3.1   Levels of Analysis

An important concern in these ontologies is the level of analysis, which is determined by the aims of the ontology. As an example, Souag et al. (2015) include the concept of Security policy defined as follows: "expresses the defense strategy or strategic directions of the information security board of an organization". In the work of Di Modica and Tomarchio (2015) the concept of policy is oriented to express system or service capabilities, e.g. a LoginProtocol that supports one-time passwords. Clearly, these are classes that represent different accounts of the protocol concept that cannot be directly matched. In a similar direction, these authors include the concept of security Objective as "a high level abstraction by which we mean a particular security service offered by the system. The following services can be offered: authentication, authorization, confidentiality, integrity and non-repudiation". This is of a different nature from Souag et al. concept of Security goal. Benammar et al (2015) also include the policy concept but in this case for the matchmaking of a particular kind of system policy, that of access control policies. This represents an additional level of concreteness in the entities considered under the term "policy".

These and many other differences of similar concepts respond to the different entities being modelled. In one case, objectives and policies are related to a software artefact (a service) while in other case, they are relative to a socio-technical construct, i.e. an organization. This is calling for some sort of explicit categorization of the level of analysis of different security ontologies. Such clear categorization would allow for using them together but with a clear understanding of the entities being referred to.

Reference ontologies as that of Takahashi and Kadobayashi (2014) should thus provide a modular structure in different levels of abstraction, to make clear the levels in which they can be mapped to other application-specific ontologies.

3.2   Readiness for Practice

The conclusions of Souag et al. (2015) clearly point out to a lack of maturity or a need for new tools or approaches to effectively support practice in the realm of security requirements, which covers a broad spectrum of activities from project requirement analysis to auditing of information security management systems.

In other cases, the ontologies are directly applicable to carry out particular automated tasks, as the policy mapping and matchmaking described by Modica and Tomarchio (2015). In this case, the value provided basically relies in the extent to which the catalogue of protocols, algorithms and other service capabilities is complete and up to date with the state of the art. In the case of other access control policies as

RBAC, it is not clear the extent to which ontology languages may provide practical benefits beyond the existing standardized applications.

3.3   Ontology Population

One of the main problems with ontologies in general is that of the lack of a developed and up-to-date instance base. In this aspect, some ontologies are more of a challenge to be maintained than others. It is important to highlight that without a complete developed instance base, most ontologies are simply useless. For example, matching Web service policies can only be useful if the catalogue of instances representing protocols and algorithms is complete with regards to current practice and it is maintained up-to-date.

Some cases simply leverage existing databases as the NVD that are yet in a level of formality that requires few actions to make them applicable in a practical context. Actually, there are non-ontological languages as the *Open Vulnerability and Assessment Language* (OVAL)[6] that most likely resolves most of the vulnerability assessment needs, and there are on-going community efforts as STIX[7] to standardize threat information. For example, Razzaq et al. (2014) formalize the contents of the detailed, community curated OWASP knowledge base, but it is not clear if many or most of the rules on HTTP that can be formalized with ontology languages could not have been encoded in other formalisms as regular expressions with similar detection power.

Also in this direction, some authors present ontologies that aim at integrating together several of these data sources. For example, Iannacone et al. (2015) reported the integration of 13 structured sources. Others also mention diverse data sources, but there is no currently a community-curated ontology resource that can be directly downloaded and used and that integrates the diverse databases and knowledge bases curated by professional and practitioner's communities.

4   Conclusions and outlook

While the use of ontologies in the domain of information security has received considerable attention in the last years, its readiness for application and level of maturity is still far from completely achieved. We have identified several particular application areas for which ontologies have been proposed as useful tools recently, and also identified existing databases as the main potential baseline for further research. We hope this paper contributes to strengthening research in the area, and fostering debate on the concrete role and value provided by ontologies in this domain.

Existing curated databases and community standardization efforts as the NVD or OWASP represent the main value behind many of the proposals reviewed, which suggests that research in the field should be targeted to identify and fill the gap left by these for clear application cases, or bridge and map them to allow for combined use of these resources. For example, an interesting way of testing the benefits of ontologies

---

[6] https://oval.mitre.org/
[7] https://stix.mitre.org/

might be that of comparing the automation capabilities provided by them with the established specifications and tools collected in the *Security Content Automation Protocol* (SCAP)[8] suite for vulnerability or exposure analysis. Also, proposals of reference ontologies should similarly start from a deep modelling of such type of community-sourced resources, so that they convey current practice in a more faithful way.

The use of information security ontologies to support subsequent machine learning tasks is raised in several studies. However, there is not a clear evaluation of the extent to which the later really benefit from the formal logics representation for the learning task itself, beyond the eventual achievement of more standardized data schemas.

Future work should address a comprehensive, systematic review of the use of ontologies in information security that provides the complete picture of the state of the art in the area that has only been succinctly depicted here. That would provide the required roadmap to a more systematic exploration of the potential of ontologies in the field.

Acknowledgements. The research presented in this paper is part of project PREDECIBLE ("Sistema de analítica predictiva para defensa en el ciberespacio basada en escenarios reproducibles") selected for funding by the Spanish Ministry of Defence.

References

Atymtayeva, L., Kozhakhmet, K., Bortsova, G.: Building a knowledge base for expert system in information security. In: Cho, Y.I., Matson, E.T. (eds.) Soft Computing in Artificial Intelligence. AISC, vol. 270, pp. 57–76. Springer, Heidelberg (2014)

Balduccini, M., Kushner, S., Speck, J.: Ontology-driven data semantics discovery for cybersecurity. In: Pontelli, E., Son, T.C. (eds.) PADL 2015. LNCS, vol. 9131, pp. 1–16. Springer, Heidelberg (2015)

Benammar, O., Elasri, H., Jebbar, M., Sekkaki, A.: Security Policies Matching Through Ontologies Alignment To Support Security Experts. Journal of Theoretical & Applied Information Technology 71(1) (2015)

Di Modica, G., Tomarchio, O.: Matchmaking semantic security policies in heterogeneous clouds. Future Generation Computer Systems (in press, 2015)

Elçi, A.: Isn't the time ripe for a standard ontology on security of information and networks? In: Proceedings of the 7th International Conference on Security of Information and Networks, p. 1. ACM (2014)

Fenz, S., Ekelhart, A.: Formalizing information security knowledge. In: Proceedings of the 4th ACM International Symposium on Information, Computer, and Communications Security, pp. 183–194 (2009)

Finin, T., Joshi, A., Kagal, L., Niu, J., Sandhu, R., Winsborough, W., Thuraisingham, B.: R OWL BAC: representing role based access control in OWL. In: Proceedings of the 13th ACM Symposium on Access Control Models and Technologies, pp. 73–82, June 2008

---

[8] http://scap.nist.gov/

Gyrard, A., Bonnet, C., Boudaoud, K.: An ontology-based approach for helping to secure the ETSI machine-to-machine architecture. In: Proc. of the 2014 IEEE International Conference on Internet of Things (iThings) and Green Computing and Communications (GreenCom), IEEE and Cyber, Physical and Social Computing (CPSCom), pp. 109–116 (2014)

Hyman, P.: Cybercrime: it's serious, but exactly how serious? Communications of the ACM **56**(3), 18–20 (2013)

Iannacone, M., Bohn, S., Nakamura, G., Gerth, J., Huffer, K., Bridges, R., Ferragut, E., Goodall, J.: Developing an ontology for cyber security knowledge graphs. In: Proc. of the 10th Annual Cyber and Information Security Research Conference, p. 12. ACM, April 2015

Kamongi, P., Gomathisankaran, M., Kavi, K.: Nemesis: automated architecture for threat modeling and risk assessment for cloud computing. In: Proc. of the 6th ASE International Conference on Privacy, Security, Risk and Trust (PASSAT), Cambridge, MA, USA (2015)

Kumar, K., Vijayalakshmi, K., Bharathi, R.: Semantic Intrusion Detection for the Application Layer-Service Level Attack Detection. Journal of Convergence Information Technology **10**(3), 1–8 (2015)

Mann, D.E., Christey, S.M.: Towards a common enumeration of vulnerabilities. In: Proc. of the 2nd Workshop on Research with Security Vulnerability Databases, Purdue University, West Lafayette, Indiana (1999)

Montesino, R., Fenz, S.: Information security automation: how far can we go? In: Proc. of the Sixth IEEE International Conference on Availability, Reliability and Security (ARES), pp. 280–285 (2011)

Razzaq, A., Anwar, Z., Ahmad, H.F., Latif, K., Munir, F.: Ontology for attack detection: An intelligent approach to web application security. Computers & Security **45**, 124–146 (2014)

Shabtai, A., Moskovitch, R., Elovici, Y., Glezer, C.: Detection of malicious code by applying machine learning classifiers on static features: A state-of-the-art survey. Information Security Tech. Report **14**(1), 16–29 (2009)

Salini, P., Shenbagam, J.: Prediction and Classification of Web Application Attacks using Vulnerability Ontology. International Journal of Computer Applications **116**(21) (2015)

Schiavone, S., Garg, L., Summers, K.: Ontology of Information Security in Enterprises. Electronic Journal Information Systems Evaluation **17**(1) (2014)

Sharma, S., Trivedi, M., Kurup, L.: Using Ontologies to Model Attacks in an Internet based Mobile Ad-hoc Network (iMANET). International Journal of Computer Applications **110**(2) (2015)

Shenbagam, J., Salini, P.: Vulnerability ontology for web applications to predict and classify attacks. In: Proc. of the 2014 International Conference on Electronics, Communication and Computational Engineering (ICECCE), pp. 268–272. IEEE (2014)

Souag, A., Salinesi, C., Mazo, R., Comyn-Wattiau, I.: A security ontology for security requirements elicitation. In: Piessens, F., Caballero, J., Bielova, N. (eds.) ESSoS 2015. LNCS, vol. 8978, pp. 157–177. Springer, Heidelberg (2015)

Souag, A., Mazo, R., Salinesi, C., Comyn-Wattiau, I.: Reusable knowledge in security requirements engineering: a systematic mapping study. Requirements Engineering, 1–33 (2015)

Takahashi, T., Kadobayashi, Y.: Reference Ontology for Cybersecurity Operational Information. The Computer Journal, bxu101 (2014)

Takahashi, T., Kadobayashi, Y.: Mechanism for linking and discovering structured cybersecurity information over networks. In: Proc. of the 2014 IEEE International Conference on Semantic Computing (ICSC), pp. 279–284 (2014)

Tong, W., Liang, X., Li, X., Zhao, J., Liang, X.: An analysis method of NAC configuration conflict based on ontology. In: Proc. of the 3rd International Conference on Digital Enterprise and Information Systems (DEIS2015), p. 46 (2015)

Wall, D.S., Williams, M.L.: Policing cybercrime: networked and social media technologies and the challenges for policing. Policing and Society **23**(4), 409–412 (2013)

Yao, Y., Ma, X., Liu, H., Yi, J., Zhao, X., Liu, L.: A semantic knowledge base construction method for information security. In: Proc. of the 2014 IEEE 13th International Conference on Trust, Security and Privacy in Computing and Communications (TrustCom), pp. 803–808 (2014)

Zhang, X.Q., Xu, J.Y., Gu, C.H.: Information Security Vulnerability Association Analysis Based on Ontology Technology. Journal of East China University of Science and Technology (Natural Science Edition) **1**, 022 (2014)

Semantic Web and Metadata Extraction, Modelling, Interoperability and Exploratory Search

Interoperable Multimedia Annotation and Retrieval for the Tourism Sector

Antonios Chatzitoulousis, Pavlos S. Efraimidis, and Ioannis N. Athanasiadis(✉)

Electrical and Computer Engineering Department,
Democritus University of Thrace, Xanthi, Greece
achatzit@ee.duth.gr, pefraimi@ee.duth.gr, ioannis@athanasiadis.info

Abstract. The Atlas Metadata System (AMS) employs semantic web annotation techniques in order to create an interoperable information annotation and retrieval platform for the tourism sector. AMS adopts state-of-the-art metadata vocabularies, annotation techniques and semantic web technologies. Interoperability is achieved by reusing several vocabularies and ontologies, including Dublin Core, PROV-O, FOAF, Geonames, Creative commons, SKOS, and CiTO, each of which provides with orthogonal views for annotating different aspects of digital assets. Our system invests a great deal in managing geospatial and temporal metadata, as they are extremely relevant for tourism-related applications. AMS has been implemented as a graph database using Neo4j, and is demonstrated with a dataset of more than 160000 images downloaded from Flickr. The system provides with online recommendations, via queries that exploit social networks, spatiotemporal references, and user rankings. AMS is offered via service-oriented endpoints using public vocabularies to ensure reusability.

1 Introduction

Data shared on the Internet are typically not accompanied with useful metadata to enable efficient search and discovery. Even in the cases meta-information is present, it comes in custom formats, not using standard dictionaries, nomenclatures or organization. Semantic Web [9] and Linked Data [10] attempt to resolve such problems by adding rich meta information for both machines and humans, while creating and adopting standards and organization in sharing data on the Web. In the past years we have observed the creation and adoption of several templates for sharing data that include dictionaries and ontologies for describing information about data, along with semantic services that allow for the search and discovery of data on the web, such as DAML-S/UDDI Matchmaker [20], KIM [12], or OWLS-MX [13].

This work contributes to the realization of the Semantic Web by designing and implementing a metadata annotation system for tourism-related applications, called Atlas Metadata System (AMS for short), which consists of an metadata schema for multimedia content, that reuses common terms from existing vocabularies and ontologies. The system deployed enables interoperability not

© Springer International Publishing Switzerland 2015
E. Garoufallou et al. (Eds.): MTSR 2015, CCIS 544, pp. 65–76, 2015.
DOI: 10.1007/978-3-319-24129-6_6

only by reusing existing terminology, but also by adopting services for search and discovery on the Semantic Web. On top of that, we demonstrate that by the annotation of user network and preferences, we can exploit *social network* dynamics for improved recommendations. This work aims to investigate interoperability in sharing multimedia content in the case of tourism-related applications, but also contributes to the demonstration of systems for open, reusable data on the web.

1.1 Problem Definition and Challenges

With this work, we try to overcome several general open issues in sharing content online along with particular shortfalls related to the tourism sector. Below we outline those issues in brief.

Lost in the Data Ocean: We are overflown with an abundance of data that do not come together with useful meta-information. There so many photographs and videos on the Web that could be potentially interesting for tourism related applications. However, most of the time they come along with low-level metadata that are concerned with the file name, size or the date of creation. They lack information about the content itself, as a title, a description, or any kind of classification or tags. There are several tools developed to automatically tagging multimedia content related to tourism, as in [15]. At the same time, information about the creator, licensing and sharing principles are also typically absent. Geospatial information is sometimes available, but not always in ways that makes the content reusable. For example, to make multimedia content directly relevant to tourism applications, relationships to *Points of Interest* are needed.

Limited Standard Adoption: There is an anarchy on which metadata dictionaries to adopt. It is common practice to develop new metadata schemas in isolation, instead of looking for relevant existing nomenclatures. This is not just a matter of bad practice that which results into problems of ontology alignment. It involves several difficulties in drawing boundaries between sectors, and lots of community work to reach consensus. W3C and OCG communities have produced relevant dictionaries and practices for sharing Web and Geospatial Information, but there are several other overlapping domain specific efforts.

Discovery for Machines, not Humans: Still most search and discovery tools are made for humans and require interpretation. Service oriented technologies allow for machine to machine transactions that together with public Application Programming Interfaces (API) may enable for advanced tourism contextual recommendations.

In this work we address those challenges in the context of tourism recommendation systems. The Atlas Metadata System (AMS) aims to be an interoperable platform that reuses standard vocabularies for annotating multimedia metadata and allow for search and discovery via open services.

1.2 Related Work

There have been several metadata models proposed for annotating multimedia content related to mobile photography and video, or more specifically tourism related applications. Already in 2002, Maedche and Staab envisioned scenarios on how Semantic Web technologies can be used for next-generation tourism information systems [14]. The issue of designing an appropriate metadata schema for tourism related applications is recurring. A straightforward schema has been proposed in [18], which consists of three main entities people, events, and places. In the same work, annotation is considered a side product of some other user activity, with her mobile device, like photo sharing or social discourse. In 2006, Torniai *et al.* presented a system which employs RDF for the description of photographs, including location and compass heading information, and is used to discover geo-related pictures from other users [22]. Most of the metadata schema follows Dublin Core. PhotoMap [23] focuses on tours/itineraries and encompasses five context dimensions for a metatada schema in OWL-DL: spatial, temporal, social, computational and spatiotemporal. These concepts correspond to the major elements for describing a photo (i.e., where, when, who, with what). Kanellopoulos and Panagopoulos in [11] propose a metadata model in RDF to annotate information about tourist destinations and peers. Last, but not least, a methodology that allows for the automatic population of ontologies on the basis of natural language processing is proposed in [17]. In particular, with their approach, a given ontology can be enriched by adding instances gathered from natural language texts.

Here we build upon previous work, while concentrating mostly on existing image repositories and how their metadata can be exploited for tourism related applications. Our results show that reuse of existing vocabularies together with service oriented technologies are the key for interoperability.

2 Atlas Metadata System

2.1 Goals and Systems Specification

The Atlas Metadata System (AMS) employs semantic web annotation techniques in order to create an interoperable information annotation and retrieval platform for the tourism sector. The Atlas Metadata System is equipped with a metadata schema that combines both anagraphic user information and tourism related classifications, spatial and temporal references, social networks and user preferences. More importantly, the schema adopted in AMS reuses to the greatest extend existing vocabularies for expressing such relationships.

Specifically, the proposed system aims to:

– Fuse existing content from public repositories, as Flickr and Panoramio, and enhance their metadata, with data from other sources, to become more relevant and useful for tourism recommendations.

- Allow for improved recommendations by exploiting social networks and spatial and temporal relationships.
- Make multimedia metadata available as web services using standard protocols and vocabularies.

Using AMS services, users (either machines or humans) can search and discover for tourism-related metadata by employing appropriate ontologies; e.g. Geonames dictionary for spatial information, Dublin Core for general information, FOAF for social relationships, etc.

AMS is structured in two modules. The first module operates offline and is responsible to extract data from existing APIs and databases to populate AMS repository. This involves scripting against legacy systems or popular services such as Flickr. At the end of this step, nodes have been created in the graph database; identities of content, users and Points of Interest have been resolved; and spatial indexes have been encoded.

The second component is the online system that serves the metadata through various interfaces, such as SPARQL, RESTfull services, etc. Users (humans or machines) though the online component ask for recommendations on tourism-related multimedia, either based on their profiles, history, current or intended location.

Both components share a common metadata schema that has been designed with reusing existing vocabularies.

2.2   AMS Metadata Schema

We identify three main entities in our system:

- **Image:** These are photographs taken by users. It is the main entity we want to annotate.
- **Agent:** An entity that owns, created, likes or published an Image. An agent may be a person, an organization, or even an artifact. Points of Interests may be agents too.
- **Location:** This is the place where a photograph was taken, or an agent resides. It is related with other geographical entities through spatial relations.

Relations between those entities and their attributes are expressed using existing vocabularies, as discussed below. An overview of the attributes of each entity is illustrated in Figure 1.

2.3   Vocabularies Reused

In order to maximize the potential for interoperability, we reused several existing terms for designing the AMS schema. Below we introduce the various dictionaries employed, and list some of the terms we reused from each one.

Dublin Core is a generic purpose metadata schema for annotating digital artifacts [2]. We employed several terms from this scheme to represent the

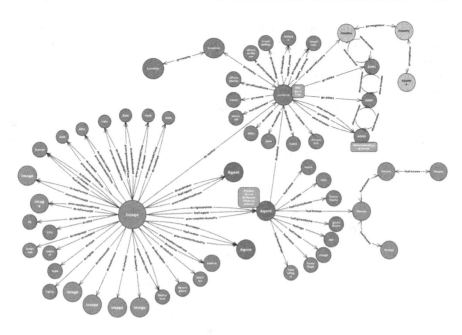

Fig. 1. The metadata schema proposed. The main entities and their attributes are shown.

information about our items, their creation history, licensing, versions spatiotemporal coverage and theme classifications, using `dc:abstract`, `dc:created`, `dc:creator`, `dc:dateAccepted`, `dc:dateCopyrighted`, `dc:dateSubmitted`, `dc:description`, `dc:format`, `dc:hasFormat`, `dc:hasPart`, `dc:hasVersion`, `dc:identifier`, `dc:isFormatOf`, `dc:isPartOf`, `dc:isVersionOf`, `dc:issued`, `dc:language`, `dc:license`, `dc:modified`, `dc:publisher`, `dc:rights`, `dc:rightsHolder`, `dc:source`, `dc:spatial`, `dc:subject`, `dc:temporal`, `dc:title`, `dc:type`.

PROV-O is a W3C recommendation [7] for representing and interchanging provenance information generated in different systems and under different contexts. We reused the following terms `prov:generatedAtTime`, `prov:wasAttributedTo`, `prov:alternateOf`, and `prov:wasDerivedFrom`.

FOAF is vocabulary for describing and linking persons and their relations [3]. We used it to represent the social relationships between our users, with `foaf:agent`, `foaf:person`, `foaf:knows`.

Geonames [4] is an ontology that provides unique identifiers for over 8.3 million toponyms listed in geonames.org database and their spatial relations. In Atlas we employed Geonames to attribute geographical entities to our media using: `gn:name`, `gn:alternateName`, `gn:officialName`, `gn:parentCountry`, `gn:ADM1`, `gn:ADM2`, `gn:ADM3`, `gn:locationMap`, `gn:latitude`, `gn:longitude`.

SKOS, the Simple Knowledge Organization System, is a W3C recommended common data schema for knowledge organization systems such as thesauri, classification schemes, subject heading systems and taxonomies [6]. We employed SKOS for representing the narrower/broader relationships of classification terms, with `skos:narrower`, `skos:broader`, `skos:prefferedLabel`

CiTO, originally an ontology for scholar citations [19], has been reused in our work for its capacity to express *like* relationships, via the property `cito:likes`.

Creative Commons [8] also maintains a machine readable dictionary for content licensing which we adopted, via `cc:license`.

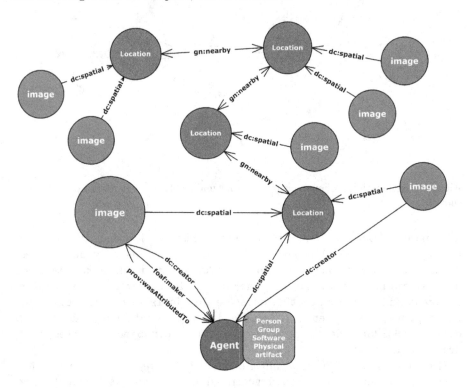

Fig. 2. Relations between entities from various dictionaries

Table 1 illustrates the synonym relations that are provided by different vocabularies for the image nodes, and Figure 2 illustrates some of those relations as a graph. Several different public dictionaries can be used to traverse the graph and find relationships in Atlas.

2.4   Graph Relationships

A feature of the AMS is that entities may be related to entities of the same class, creating linked graphs. This is the case of *Locations* that are linked to each other with the **gn:nearby** property, creating a spatial graph. The same

Table 1. Some of the synonym relations for `Image` nodes.

Domain	Properties	Range
`Image`	`dc:creator`, `prov:wasAttributedTo`, `foaf:maker`	`Person`
`Image`	`dc:created`, `prov:generatedAtTime`	`date`
`Image`	`dc:license`, `cc:license`	`license`

holds for Agent nodes that are linked via `foaf:knows` to other agents. These relations eventually create a social graph that can be exploited in our prototype for retrieving higher order relationships between locations or agents, by using graph databases principles [16].

2.5 Implementation

AMS is implemented with several state-of-the-art semantic web technologies. Specifically, we employed Neo4j [5] to deploy AMS metadata storage. Neo4j allows for rapid traversals of the AMS metadata registry, and supports for RDF/SPARQL endpoints. This seems as a natural choice for tourism systems where recommendations will come from spatial or social graphs via a graph querying language as Cypher, rather than ontological reasoning or geoprocessing computations. At the same time, AMS metadata can become available as REST-full web services using various end points of Neo4j, including Cypher query language, SPARQL, and Neo4j spatial plugin.

3 Demonstration

3.1 Experimental Setup

To demonstrate AMS we used the Image Collection used in the ATLAS project [1]. The collection consists of 162'583 images geolocated in Greece, originally published on Flickr. Through the Flickr API we extracted metadata about the images and their 28'358 contributors, including their social network on flickr. We enhanced Flickr metadata by developing and applying some scripts which identified entities, added extra relationships from tags, created spatial and temporal relationships, resolved toponyms with Geonames, and added Creative Commons licenses. The AMS graph database is powered with Neo4j, occupies more than 600 MB of metadata, includes enhanced features, and publishes metadata using standard vocabularies.

3.2 Simple Queries with Cypher

Using the Cypher query language we can express queries using alternative, equivalent vocabularies, to demonstrate the AMS capacity for interoperability. In the example below we retrieve ten images of a certain user, using the `dc:creator` relationship. The same query could be expressed via the FOAF ontology using `foaf:maker`.

```
START n=node:owner(owner_id = "10179878@N03")
MATCH (n)<-[r:'dc:creator']-(m) RETURN n,r,m LIMIT 10
```

Graph databases are best suited for graph traversals. In the following example, the indirect connections are extracted from a social graph. Specifically, we ask for higher order friends-of-a-friend of a certain user, and sort them by the number of the different paths between them.

```
START n=node:owner(owner_id = "10179878@N03")
MATCH (n)-[:'foaf:knows'*2..2]-(friend_of_friend)
WHERE  (NOT (n)-[]-(friend_of_friend))
RETURN friend_of_friend, COUNT(*)
ORDER BY COUNT(*) DESC
```

"Like" relationships may be exploited for discovering users with similar interests. In the example below we ask for users that share similar ratings in common photographs. Here we exploit cito:likes and foaf:knows semantics to represent the underlying relationships.

```
MATCH (me:Owner { owner_id: '12337376@N03' }) -
    [ml:'cito:likes']->(image:Image)<-[pl:'cito:likes']
    - (person:Owner)
WHERE NOT (me)-[:'foaf:knows']->(person) and
      abs(pl.rating - ml.rating) < 2
RETURN person.username,image.title,ml.rating,pl.rating
```

3.3   Open Querying Endpoints via Plugins

An important features of Neo4j is that is comes with a handful set of plugins, that support for machine interoperability with several protocols, which maximize our system capacity for reuse. First is the Neo4j REST-full API that allows to directly interact with the database via the http protocol. All the example queries of the previous section may be directly executed via the transactional Neo4j API. A simple query to retrieve all properties of a certain node may look like this:

```
GET http://ams.example.org/db/data/node/415508
```

The SPARQL plugin allows for semantic web interoperability. SPARQL is a W3C standardized RDF query language, and is recognized as one of the key technologies for Linked Data and the Semantic Web. A sample query in AMS is the following one that requests for subjects and objects of the relations foaf:knows, as:

```
POST http://ams.example.org/db/data/ext/SPARQLPlugin/graphdb/
                                            execute_sparql
{
  "query" : "SELECT ?x ?y
      WHERE { ?x <http://xmlns.com/foaf/spec/#term_knows> ?y . }"
}
```

Last but not least, the Spatial plugin allows for geospatial queries. For example, one may retrieve all images within a distance of 0.5km around a certain coordinate via the http protocol, as:

```
POST http://ams.example.org/db/data/ext/SpatialPlugin/graphdb/
                                findGeometriesWithinDistance
Content-Type: application/json
{
  "layer" : "images",
  "pointY" : 40.626340,
  "pointX" : 22.948362,
  "distanceInKm" : 0.5
}
```

3.4 Advanced Recommendations

AMS is capable to respond efficiently to more advanced queries, which can be used for contextual suggestions to its users. For example, we want to make image suggestions based on the ratings of users with similar interests. For this we employ the cosine similarity measure [21] with the k-nearest neighbors algorithm to make image recommendations, similar to [24]. Cosine similarity is a distance measure for estimating the similarities in image ratings, and with the k-nearest neighbors algorithm, the k closest images are selected according to this distance. An implementation in AMS system would look like:

```
MATCH  (b:Owner)-[r:'cito:likes']->(i:Image), (b)-[s:SIMILARITY]
       -(a:Owner {username:'Antonis  Chatzitoulousis'})
WHERE  NOT((a)-[:'cito:likes']->(i))
WITH   i, s.similarity AS similarity, r.rating AS rating
ORDER BY i.title, similarity DESC
WITH   i.title AS image, COLLECT(rating)[0..3] AS ratings
WITH   image, REDUCE(s = 0, j IN ratings | s + j)*1.0 /
       LENGTH(ratings) AS reco
ORDER BY reco DESC
RETURN   image AS Image, reco AS Recommendation
```

The corresponding results screen of Neo4j graph database is shown in Figure 3. The same method could be followed for suggestions on various Points of Interests, including attractions, cities, categories, etc, by recommending POIs that have been rated by users with similar profiles and have not been visited yet, by exploiting user profiles. Recommendations can be improved by including the spatiotemporal aspects, by considering the locations where images have been taken, or periods of time. For example, search for photographs of POIs close to Parthenon in December based on the ratings of users with similar interests. Temporal aspects may consider museum/office hours, weekends, periods of festivities etc. Spatial aspects may consider geographical regions for focal search. The social network can be explored further for giving suggestions by limiting the k-nearest neighbors algorithm to the friends-of-a-friend network.

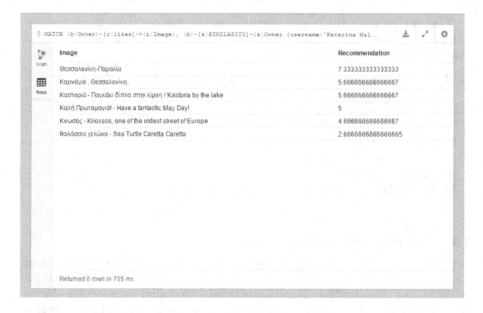

Fig. 3. Image suggestions that were highly-rated from users with similar interests

4   Conclusions and Future Work

This work illustrated how AMS, an advanced metadata system for the tourism sector may be implemented to overcome common problems in sharing Open Linked Data on the Semantic Web. Interoperability is achieved through multiple technologies and interfaces deployed, allowing for option in both human and machine interaction. Reuse of common dictionaries and ontologies ensures that a set of options are available to the various clients, that do not need to be adapted to a custom metadata schema. Finally, the use of social network metadata enables advanced recommendations that exploit user profiles and preference. Another lesson learned by this exercise in that graph databases are both mature and rodust technology that can be used effectively for metadata management, esp in the case of larger repositories. Semantic Web technologies are adequately supported and the service-oriented paradigm allows for easy integration, adaptive management and fast responses.

Future extensions for this work may exploit geospatial services for visualizing results using Google Earth, OpenLayers, and similar tools. Another line of action could consider matching user profiles with other social platforms, through Twitter or Facebook social graphs.

Acknowledgments. Research in this study has received funding by European and national funds from NSRF 2007-2013, OP Competitiveness and Entrepreneurship, Cooperation 2011, in the context of the *Advanced Tourism Planning System* (ATLAS) project, grant number 11SYN-10-1730.

References

1. Advanced tourism planning system (ATLAS). http://atlas.web.auth.gr/
2. Dublin Core Metadata Initiative (DCMI) Metadata Terms. http://dublincore.org/documents/dcmi-terms/
3. FOAF Vocabulary Specification. http://xmlns.com/foaf/spec/20140114.html
4. GeoNames Ontology. http://www.geonames.org/ontology/
5. Neo4j, the World's Leading Graph Database. http://neo4j.com/
6. SKOS Simple Knowledge Organization System Reference. W3C Recommendation (2009). http://www.w3.org/TR/2009/REC-skos-reference-20090818/
7. PROV-O: The PROV Ontology. W3C Recommendation (2013). http://www.w3.org/TR/prov-o/
8. Abelson, H., Adida, B., Linksvayer, M., Yergler, N.: CC REL: the creative commons rights expression language. In: de Rosnay, M.D., Martin, J.C.D. (eds.) The Digital Public Domain - Foundations for an Open Culture, pp. 149–187. OpenBook Publishers (2012)
9. Berners-Lee, T., Hendler, J., Lassila, O., et al.: The semantic web. Scientific American **284**(5), 28–37 (2001)
10. Bizer, C., Heath, T., Idehen, K., Berners-Lee, T.: Linked data on the web (LDOW2008). In: Proceedings of the 17th International Conference on World Wide Web, pp. 1265–1266. ACM (2008)
11. Kanellopoulos, D.N., Panagopoulos, A.A.: Exploiting tourism destinations' knowledge in an RDF-based P2P network. Journal of Network and Computer Applications **31**(2), 179–200 (2008)
12. Kiryakov, A., Popov, B., Terziev, I., Manov, D., Ognyanoff, D.: Semantic annotation, indexing, and retrieval. Web Semantics: Science, Services and Agents on the World Wide Web **2**(1), 49–79 (2004)
13. Klusch, M., Fries, B., Sycara, K.: OWLS-MX: A hybrid semantic web service matchmaker for OWL-S services. Web Semantics: Science, Services and Agents on the World Wide Web **7**(2), 121–133 (2009)
14. Maedche, A., Staab, S.: Applying semantic web technologies for tourism information systems. In: Information and Communication Technologies in Tourism (ENTER 2002). Springer (2002)
15. Pliakos, K., Kotropoulos, C.: PLSA-driven image annotation, classification, and tourism recommendations. In: Proceedings of IEEE International Conference on Image Processing (ICIP), Paris, France, October 2014
16. Robinson, I., Webber, J., Eifrem, E.: Graph Databases. O'Reilly (2013)
17. Ruiz-Martinez, J.M., Minarro-Gimenez, J.A., Castellanos-Nieves, D., Garcia-Sanchez, F., Valencia-Garcia, R.: Ontology population: an application for the e-tourism domain. International Journal of Innovative Computing, Information and Control **7**(11), 6115–6134 (2011)
18. Sarvas, R.: User-centric metadata for mobile photos. In: Pervasive Image Capture and Sharing Workshop at Ubicomp 2005. Citeseer (2005)
19. Shotton, D.: CiTO, the citation typing ontology. J. Biomedical Semantics **1**(S–1), S6 (2010). http://vocab.ox.ac.uk/cito
20. Sycara, K., Paolucci, M., Ankolekar, A., Srinivasan, N.: Automated discovery, interaction and composition of semantic web services. Web Semantics: Science, Services and Agents on the World Wide Web **1**(1), 27–46 (2003)
21. Tan, P.N., Steinbach, M., Kumar, V.: Introduction to Data Mining. Addison-Wesley (2005)

22. Torniai, C., Battle, S., Cayzer, S.: Sharing, discovering and browsing photo collections through RDF geo-metadata. In: Proceedings of the 3rd Italian Semantic Web Workshop, SWAP 2006. CEUR Workshop Proceedings, vol. 201 (2006)
23. Viana, W., Filho, J.B., Gensel, J., Villanova Oliver, M., Martin, H.: PhotoMap – automatic spatiotemporal annotation for mobile photos. In: Ware, J.M., Taylor, G.E. (eds.) W2GIS 2007. LNCS, vol. 4857, pp. 187–201. Springer, Heidelberg (2007)
24. White, N.: Movie recommendations with k-nearest neighbors and cosine similarity, Graph Gist winter challenge winners. http://gist.neo4j.org/?8173017

Species Identification Through Preference-Enriched Faceted Search

Yannis Tzitzikas[1,2], Nicolas Bailly[3], Panagiotis Papadakos[1(✉)], Nikos Minadakis[1], and George Nikitakis[2]

[1] Institute of Computer Science, FORTH-ICS, Heraklion, Greece
{tzitzik,papadako,minadak}@ics.forth.gr
[2] Computer Science Department, University of Crete, Heraklion, Rethymno
nikitak@csd.uoc.gr
[3] Hellenic Centre for Marine Research LifeWatchGreece, Heraklion, Greece
nbailly@hcmr.gr

Abstract. There are various ways and corresponding tools that the marine biologist community uses for identifying one species. Species identification is essentially a decision making process comprising steps in which the user makes a selection of characters, figures or photographs, or provides an input that restricts other choices, and so on, until reaching one species. In many cases such decisions should have a specific order, as in the textual dichotomous identification keys. Consequently, if a wrong decision is made at the beginning of the process, it could exclude a big list of options. To make this process more flexible (i.e. independent of the order of selections) and less vulnerable to wrong decisions, in this paper we investigate how an exploratory search process, specifically a *Preference-enriched Faceted Search* (PFS) process, can be used to aid the identification of species. We show how the proposed process covers and advances the existing methods. Finally, we report our experience from applying this process over data taken from FishBase, the most popular source for marine resources. The proposed approach can be applied over any kind of objects described by a number of attributes.

1 Introduction

Correct identification of fish species is important in the fisheries domain for a sustainable management of stocks, balancing exploitation and conservation of biodiversity [10]. Species identification is actually a decision making process comprising steps in which the user makes a selection that restricts subsequent choices. The decisions are actually selections of characters, figures or photographs. The European Project Key2Nature[1] (2007-2010) reviewed a number of identification systems used in biodiversity works and education, and published proceedings of a conference on the state of the art in collaboration with two other projects, EDIT and STERNA [1]. Up to the development of informatics, the steps in the classic textual dichotomous identification

---

[1] Key2Nature website http://www.keytonature.eu

E. Garoufallou et al. (Eds.): MTSR 2015, CCIS 544, pp. 77–88, 2015.
DOI: 10.1007/978-3-319-24129-6_7

keys were constrained by a fixed order. Consequently, if a wrong decision is made at the beginning of the identification process, the final identification is wrong.

Here we investigate how a particular exploratory search process, specifically the *Preference-enriched Faceted Search* (for short PFS) introduced in [6] and implemented by the system *Hippalus* [3], can be used for supporting the identification process in a way that is more flexible and less prone to errors. We show how the proposed process, which is based on methodologies and tools developed for *exploratory search*, covers and advances the existing methods for species identification (including the current computer-aided identification systems). The main idea is that species are modeled as objects characterized by a number of attributes. The user explores the information space by issuing two main kinds of actions: (a) the classical left-clicks of faceted search that *change* the focus (i.e. change the viewed set of objects), and (b) right-clicks that express *preference* which *rank* the focus. The order by which users issue such actions does not affect the outcome, enabling in this way the user to decide what is more convenient to him/her at each step during the interaction. We demonstrate how we have applied this approach over the data of FishBase[2]. However, the approach is generic, i.e. it can be applied over any kind of objects described by a number of attributes (or metadata), and it could be exploited for identifying a phenomenon in general; identification tasks are important in many domains, e.g. in patent search (for investigating whether an idea is already covered by existing patents) [3], for identifying a rare disease [7], for diagnostics of car breakdowns, and others.

2   Related Work and Background

Section 2.1 describes in brief the current species identification methods, Section 2.2 introduces the basics of Preference-enriched Faceted Search, and Section 2.3 introduces the system Hippalus.

2.1   Species Identification

There are various ways for identifying one species. According to [8, 10] the following four methods[3] can be identified (see [9] for a more detailed overview):

1. 'Eye-balling' drawings and key features by decreasing taxonomic level from class downward;
2. Display of all pictures available for a given geographic area and/or a given family with possible restriction on fin ray meristics;
3. Dichotomous keys; these keys can be classically implemented as in printed textual documents; however, computer-aided identification systems such as XPER[4], LucId[5] and others allow users to select steps in the order they prefer, which is a first step for the process we describe below; and

---

[2] FishBase website http://www.fishbase.org
[3] excluding DNA barcode identification
[4] XPER website http://*www.xper3.fr/*
[5] LucId website http://www.lucidcentral.com

4. Polythetic keys, such as simple morphometric ratios measured on the body of individuals (e.g., fishes), or biochemistry results as in bacteria identification.

In the identification through outlines (corresponding to category 1 above) the user restricts the search space gradually by selecting drawings in each step. Figure 1 shows the first step, where the user can select 1 out of 6 highly distinctive outlines representing different classes of fishes. After his first selection, he continues in the same manner, by selecting another figure from a set of figures with more refined groupings (decreasing taxonomic level), and so on.

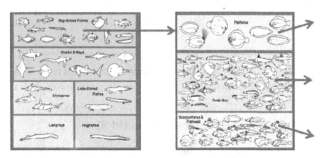

Fig. 1. Example of the 'Eye-balling' drawings by decreasing taxonomic level from class downwards.

In the identification through *pictures* the user selects a taxonomic group (from class down to genus), and/or a geographic area, and eye-balls the corresponding displayed pictures on one web page. Other criteria like the number of dorsal and anal spines can be used to restrict choices. In the identification through *dichotomous keys* (corresponding to category 3 above), the user answers successive questions like in a decision-tree, usually about the morphology of the species. The principle, established at the end of the 17th century [11], but popularized only 100 years later, is the following: (a) the user has to answer a first question that has 2 possible answers (hence the qualification of dichotomous), and (b) each of the possible two answers leads via a number either to a new question, or to a species, which then finishes the identification. An example of a dichotomous key implemented in simple HTML in FishBase is given in [http://www.fishbase.org/keys/description.php?keycode=2] [12].

Finally, in the identification through *morphometric ratios* (e.g. the Morphometrics Tool of FishBase) ratios are computed from body measurements provided by the user, e.g. Total Length (TL), Head Length (HL), Eye Diameter (ED), Body Depth (BD), etc., and other information about the area and family for reducing the number or possible species. Figure 2 shows the form for identification through morphometric ratios.

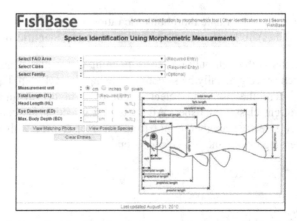

Fig. 2. Form for identification through morphometric ratios in FishBase.
http://www.fishbase.org/Identification/Morphometrics/centimeters/Index.php

2.2   The Preference-Enriched Faceted Search (PFS)

A highly prevalent model for *exploratory search* is the interaction of *Faceted and Dynamic Taxonomies* (FDT) [5], usually called *Faceted Search*, which allows the user to get an *overview* of the information space (e.g. search results) and offers him various groupings of the results (based on their attributes, metadata, or other dynamically mined information). These groupings enable the user to restrict his focus *gradually* and in a simple way (through clicks, i.e. without having to formulate queries), enabling him to locate resources that would be difficult to locate otherwise (especially the low ranked ones). This model is currently the de facto standard in various domains: e-commerce (e.g. eBay), booking applications (e.g. booking.com), library and bibliographic portals (e.g. ACM Digital Library), museum portals (e.g. Europeana), mobile phone browsers, and many others.

The enrichment of search mechanisms with *preferences*, hereafter *Preference-enriched Faceted Search* [6, 4], for short *PFS*, has been proven useful for recall-oriented information needs, because such needs involve decision making that can benefit from the gradual interaction and expression of preferences [5]. The distinctive features of PFS is the ability to express preferences over attributes whose values can be hierarchically organized, and/or multi-valued, while scope-based rules resolve automatically the conflicts. As a result the user is able to restrict his current focus by using the faceted interaction scheme (hard restrictions) that lead to non-empty results, and rank according to preference the objects of his focus.

A relevant work to the suggested approach is discussed in [13]. This work ranks the results based on a probabilistic framework that does not consider explicit users' preferences and assumes a data model that on contrast to our approach, does not exploit hierarchically organized and/or set-valued attributes.

2.3 The Hippalus System

Hippalus [3] is a publicly accessible web system that implements the PFS interaction model [6]. It offers actions that allow the user to order facets, values, and objects using *best, worst, prefer to* actions (i.e. relative preferences), *around to* actions (over a specific value), or actions that order them lexicographically, or based on their values or count values. Furthermore, the user is able to *compose* object related preference actions, using *Priority, Pareto, Pareto Optimal* (i.e. skyline) and other.

The information base that feeds Hippalus is represented in RDF/S[6] (using a schema adequate for representing objects described according to dimensions with hierarchically organized values). For loading and querying such information, Hippalus uses Jena[7], a Java framework for building Semantic Web applications. Hippalus offers a web interface for Faceted Search enriched with preference actions. The latter are offered through HTML 5 context menus[8]. The performed actions are internally translated to statements of the preference language described in [6], and are then sent to the server through HTTP requests. The server analyzes them, using the language's parser, and checks their validity. If valid, they are passed to the appropriate preference algorithm. Finally, the respective preference bucket order is computed and the ranked list of objects according to preference, is sent to the user's browser.

Hippalus displays the preference ranked list of objects in the central part of the screen, while the right part is occupied by information that relates to the information thinning (object restrictions), preference actions history and preference composition. The preference related actions are offered through right-click activated pop-up menus (through HTML5 context menus). The interaction is demonstrated in the next section.

3 A PFS-Based Approach for Species Identification

Section 3.1 describes the PFS-based fish identification process through an example. Section 3.2 provides details about the final dataset, while Section 3.3 compares the identification approaches.

3.1 The Interaction By Example

We shall describe the PFS-based fish identification process through an example. We use the dataset of the pilot phase containing only 720 species (mainly coming from Greece) where each species is described by six (6) attributes: *Body Shape, Country, Genus, Length, Maximum Depth, and Weight*. We used the Hippalus Data Translator (HDT) tool for transforming the original FishBase data to the corresponding RDFS multi-dimensional schema that is supported by Hippalus. This resulted to 3,254 RDF triples. The system with those 720 species is Web accessible[9].

---

[6] http://www.w3.org/TR/rdf-schema/
[7] http://jena.apache.org/
[8] Available only to firefox 8 and up.
[9] http://www.ics.forth.gr/isl/Hippalus/examples (requires Firefox version 8 or higher)

Scenario: Suppose that someone catches a fish while fishing in a boat close to a coach of Cephalonia (a Greek island in the Ionian Sea). The caught fish is a rather flattened fish of around 3 kilograms and its length is between 60-65 cm. The fish looks like the one in Figure 3. Below we discuss how that fisherman could use the system Hippalus for the identification of that particular fish.

Fig. 3. The caught fish.

The first screen of Hippalus is shown in Figure 4. The left frame shows the facets and the middle frame shows the list of species names that the system is aware of. The right frames show the history of user in terms of focus restriction actions, preference expression actions, and also allows the user to prioritize his/her preferences.

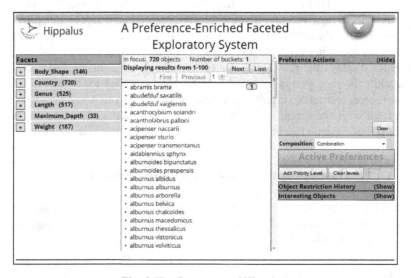

Fig. 4. The first screen of Hippalus.

Since the caught fish is a rather flattened fish, the user expands the facet **Body Shape** and on the value **flattened** he selects through right-click the value **Best**. We can see (in Figure 5) that now the list of species has been divided into two blocks: the first contains the flattened fishes, while the second those having a different shape.

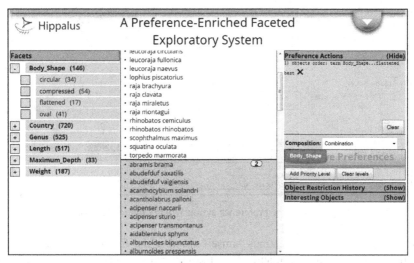

Fig. 5. After the preference action *Best(BodyShape:Flattened)*.

Since the weight of the fish is around 3 kilograms the user expands the facet Weight and on the value 3000g he selects through right-click the value *Around*. We can see (in Figure 6) that now the two blocks have been refined and a series or smaller blocks are shown. The first block contains a single species, namely *Torpedo marmorata*, meaning that this is the more probable one.

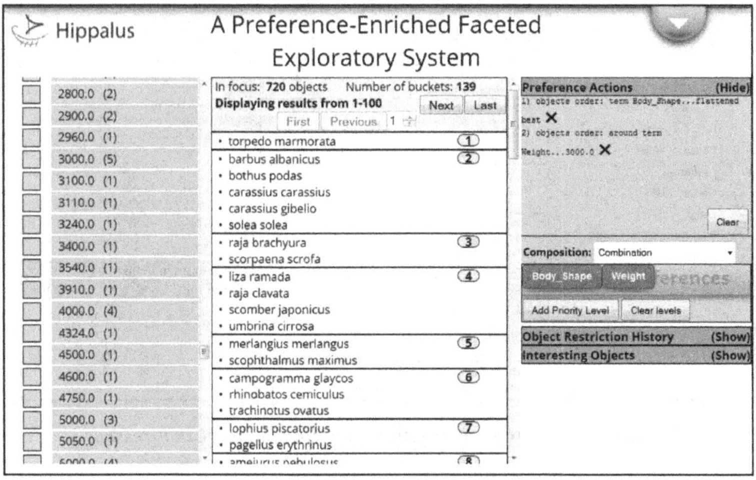

Fig. 6. After the preference action *Around(Weight:3000)*

The user now expands the facet Country and since Greece is close to Italy, and therefore it could be a species native in either Greece or Italy, or both, he selects Spain and through right-click he selects the value *Worst*, for expressing that Spain is the worst option, i.e. the less probable. We observe (in Figure 7) that the first block did not change.

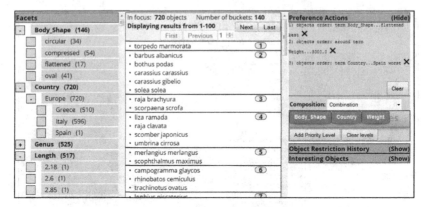

Fig. 7. After the preference action *Worst(Country:Spain)*.

At that point the user questions himself whether the fish is indeed flattened or compressed, because he is not sure about the semantics of this terminology. For this reason he goes again to the facet `Body Shape` he finds the value `compressed` and through right-click he selects the value ***Best***. Now the first block contains two species (Figure 8): *Torpedo marmorata* and *Solea solea* (the former due to its past ***Best*** action on flattened, the latter due to the current Best action on compressed).

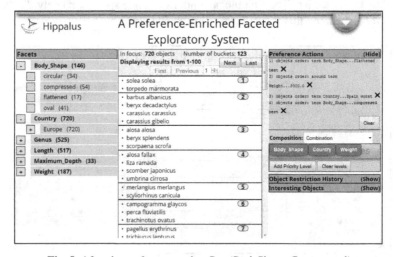

Fig. 8. After the preference action *Best(BodyShape:Compressed)*

The user now expands the facet `Length` and selects the value ***Around*** over the value 63. Now the first block contains 3 species, namely *Solea solea, Scomber colias,* and *Carassius carassius* (Figure 9).

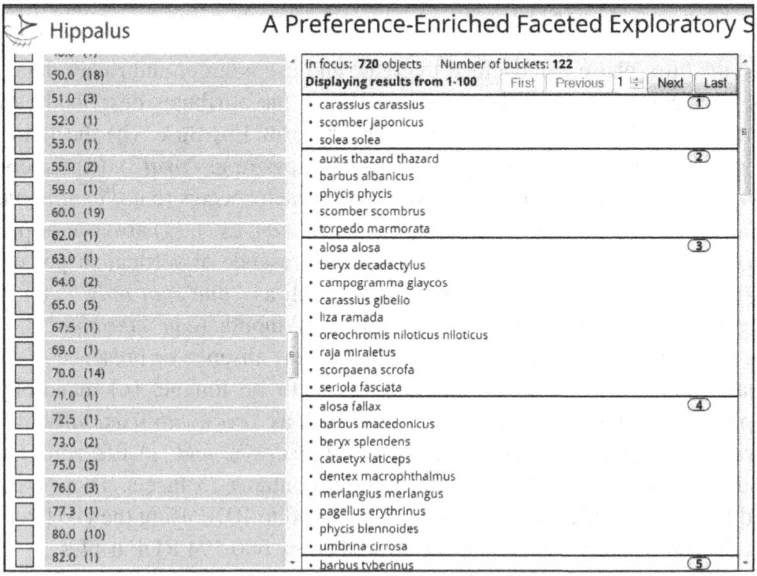

Fig. 9. After the preference action *Around(Length:63)*.

Since the user is more certain about the body shape of the fish, in comparison to weight and length, he decides to express, through the *Priorities* frame (middle right of the screen), that his preferences on Body Shape should have more priority than his preferences over the other facets. Figure 10 shows the new result. The first block contains one species, **Scomber colias**. This is probably the right species. To confirm, the user should check the species account in FishBase[10], and compare the various characteristics he can observe on the individual with those reported in Fish-Base.

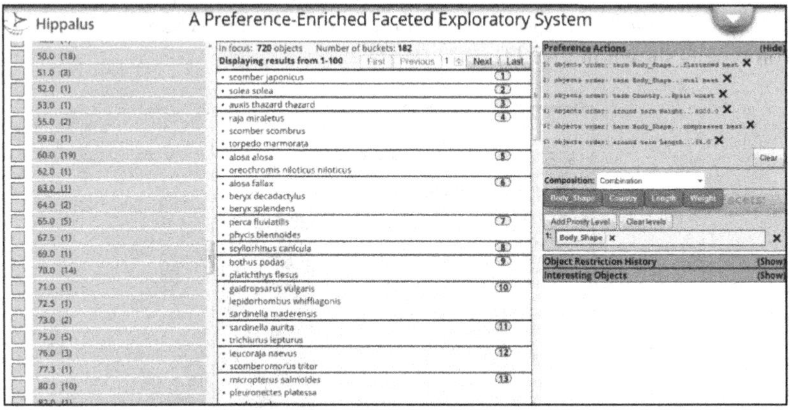

Fig. 10. After prioritizing first the preferences about Body Shape.

[10] http://www.fishbase.org/summary/Scomber-colias.html

3.2   Larger and Richer Dataset

Based on the pilot phase, we decided to create and use a larger and richer dataset that contains all species from FishBase and apart from the attributes described earlier, it also contains: (a) the *"preferred picture"* attribute of FishBase, (b) the family that each species belongs to, (c) more types of body shapes (e.g. *"oval"*), (d) the common names of each species, (e) dorsal fin attributes for each species (e.g. *"continuous with caudal fin"*), (f) forehead information (e.g. *"clearly convex"*), (g) absence or presence of horizontal stripes on body side, (h) absence or presence of vertical stripes on body side, (i) information about spots on body side, such as *"one spot only"* , (j) type of mouth (e.g. *"clearly protrusible"*), (k) position of mouth (e.g. *"terminal"*), (l) absence or presence of mandible (lower jaw) teeth, (m) absence or presence of maxilla (upper jaw) teeth, (n) absence or presence of teeth on tongue, (o) mandible teeth shape, (p) maxilla teeth shape, (q) type of eyes such as *"eyes with fixed fatty (adipose) tissue/eyelids"*, (r) type of scales (e.g. *"ctenoid scales"*), and (s) life zone (type of water) such as *"saltwater"*. In total, this dataset contains 23 facets. These data were extracted from a CSV file and were then transformed to RDF using the HDT tool. The resulting dataset contains 32,471 species described by 600,194 RDF triples.

Various optimizations of Hippalus were developed (specifically those described in [6]) for offering efficient interaction over this dataset which is the biggest real dataset that Hippalus has ever loaded. In brief it takes 5.7 seconds to load the dataset, while actions that restrict the focus of the user are almost instant (e.g. restriction to species that belong to the Myctophidae family takes only 93ms). On the other hand the computation of preference actions is more expensive, but can take advantage of the almost instant focus restriction actions. For example lexicographically ordering species according to family (i.e. an expensive preference action due to the large number of preference relations), takes 17 seconds for 10,000 species, while it takes only 438ms in the restricted focus of 720 species.

Moreover, and for supporting the identification through pictures, we have extended Hippalus with images, i.e. if one attribute value is a URL corresponding to an image, that image is displayed in the object list in the middle frame. A screenshot of the current prototype is shown in Fig. 11.

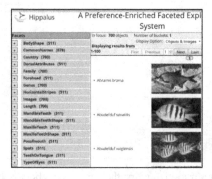

Fig. 11. Screenshot from the new (ongoing) version of Hippalus

3.3   Comparison of Species Identification Methods

To summarize, Table 1 describes the current fish species identification methods and the proposed PFS one, according to various criteria. We should also mention that some other computer-aided information system, such as XPER3[11] and LucId[12] among others, also offer the no predefined-order and they may also provide weighing about easiness of observation for each characters, or guide the process by attributing frequency of occurrence in species in a given geographic area, but it has to be predefined by the creator of the knowledge database. Rather, PFS allows the user to express his confidence in his own decision, which is a noticeable progress. We conclude that PFS is a promising method for aiding species identification .Moreover the PFS method is a generic method that can be directly applied over any dataset expressed in CSV.

Table 1. Features of each Identification Method

Features \ Identification Method	Morphometric Ratios	Dichotomous Keys	Eye Balling	PFS-based method
Support of images	No	No	Yes	Yes
Existence of gradual Process	No	Yes	Yes	Yes
Flexibility of the process (order independent)	Non applicable (no process)	No	No	Yes
Soft Constraints / Preferences	No	No	No	Yes
Hard Constraints / Restrictions	Yes	Yes	Yes	Yes

4   Concluding Remarks

We have investigated how a rather strict decision making process comprising a strictly ordered set of decisions, can be treated as a series of soft constraints (preferences) which can be expressed by simple clicks, without any predefined order. The interaction model, called PFS (Preference-enriched Faceted Search), not only offers processes that are more flexible (the user can start from the easy decisions, or whatever decision seems easier) but also allows the decisions to be treated as preferences (i.e., not as hard constraints), therefore the outcome of the process is less vulnerable to errors. Moreover by selecting values from facets corresponding to physical dimensions, the user can obtain what he could obtain with the Simple Morphometric Ratios-based identification approach. The experimental investigation performed using data from FishBase has demonstrated the feasibility of the approach and allowed us to identify, and subsequently implement, useful extensions of the system Hippalus. In future we plan to release an operational version of the system (available to all) for further evaluation, and to investigate the usefulness of preference-aware exploration in other identification tasks. The current deployments are already web accessible[9].

---

[11] XPER website http://*www.xper3.fr/*
[12] LucId website http://www.lucidcentral.com

Acknowledgements. Work partially supported by LifeWatchGreece ("Construction and Operation of the National Lifewatch Research Infrastructure", 2012-2015, MIS 384676). Many thanks also to Angelos Mavroulakis for developing the converter that was used for loading the data to Hippalus.

References

1. Nimis, P.L., Vignes-Lebbe, R. (eds): Tools for identifying biodiversity: progress and problems. In: Proceedings of the International Congress, Paris, September 20–22, x+455 p. EUT Edizioni Università di Trieste, Trieste (2010)
2. Fafalios, P., Salampasis, M., Tzitzikas, Y.: Exploratory patent search with faceted search and configurable entity mining. In: Proceedings of the 1st International Workshop on Integrating IR Technologies for Professional Search, in Conjunction with the 35th European Conference on Information Retrieval (ECIR 2013), Moscow, Russia, March 2013
3. Papadakos, P., Tzitzikas, Y.: Hippalus: preference-enriched faceted exploration. In: ExploreDB 2014 Proceedings of the 1st International Workshop on Exploratory Search in Databases and the Web Co-located with EDBT/ICDT 2014, Athens, Greece, March 2014
4. Papadakos, P., Tzitzikas, Y.: Comparing the Effectiveness of Intentional Preferences Versus Preferences Over Specific Choices: A User Study. International Journal of Information and Decision Sciences, Interscience Publishers (to appear)
5. Saco, G.M., Tzitzikas, Y. (eds.) Dynamic Taxonomies and Faceted Search: Theory, Practice and Experience. Springer (2009)
6. Tzitzikas, Y., Papadakos, P.: Interactive Exploration of Multidimensional and Hierarchical Information Spaces with Real-Time Preference Elicitation. Journal Fundamenta Informaticae **122**(4), 357–399 (2013)
7. Sacco, G.M.: E-Rare: Interactive diagnostic assistance for rare diseases through dynamic taxonomies. In: Database and Expert Systems Application, DEXA 2008 Workshops. IEEE (2008)
8. Bailly, N., Reyes, R., Atanacio, R., Froese, R.: Simple identification tools in fishbase. In: Nimis, P.L., Vignes-Lebbe, R. (eds.): Tools for Identifying Biodiversity: Progress and Problems. Proceedings of the International Congress, Paris, September 20-22. EUT Edizioni Università di Trieste, Trieste, pp. 31–36 (2010)
9. Pankhurst, R.J.: Practical Taxonomic Computing, xi + 202 p. Cambridge University Press (1991)
10. Fischer, J. (ed.): Fish Identification Tools for Biodiversity and Fisheries Assessments: Review and Guidance for Decision-makers. Fisheries and Aquaculture Technical Paper No. 585, Rome: FAO, 107 p. (2013)
11. Griffing, L.R.: Who Invented The Dichotomous Key? Richard Waller's Watercolors of the Herbs of Britain. Am. J. Bot. **98**(12), 1911–1923 (2011)
12. Renaud, C.B.: Lampreys of the world. An Annotated and Illustrated Catalogue of Lamprey Species Known to Date. FAO Species Catalogue for Fishery Purposes No. 5. FAO, Rome, 109 p. (2011)
13. Qarabaqi, B., Riedewald, M.: User-driven refinement of imprecise queries. In: Proceedings of 30th International Conference of Data Engineering ICDE 2014, Chicago, U.S.A., pp. 916–927, March 2014

An Expert System for Water Quality Monitoring Based on Ontology

Edmond Jajaga[1(✉)], Lule Ahmedi[2], and Figene Ahmedi[3]

[1] Department of Computer Science, South East European University,
Ilindenska n. 335 1200, Tetovë, Macedonia
e.jajaga@seeu.edu.mk
[2] Department of Computer Engineering, University of Prishtina,
Kodra e diellit pn 10000, Prishtinë, Kosova
lule.ahmedi@uni-pr.edu
[3] Department of Hydro-Technic, University of Prishtina,
Kodra e diellit pn 10000, Prishtinë, Kosova
figene.ahmedi@uni-pr.edu

Abstract. Semantic technologies have proved to be a suitable foundation for integrating Big Data applications. Wireless Sensor Networks (WSNs) represent a common domain which knowledge bases are naturally modeled through ontologies. In our previous works we have built domain ontology of WSN for water quality monitoring. The SSN ontology was extended to meet the requirements for classifying water bodies into appropriate statuses based on different regulation authorities. In this paper we extend this ontology with a module for identifying the possible sources of pollution. To infer new implicit knowledge from the knowledge bases different rule systems have been layered over ontologies by state-of-the-art WSN systems. A production rules system was developed to demonstrate how our ontology can be used to enable water quality monitoring. The paper presents an example of system validation with simulated data, but it is developed for use within the InWaterSense project with real data. It demonstrates how Biochemical Oxygen Demand observations are classified based on Water Framework Directive regulation standard and provide its eventual sources of pollution. The system features and challenges are discussed by also suggesting the potential directions of Semantic Web rule layer developments for reasoning with stream data.

Keywords: Expert system · Semantic Web · Ontology · Metadata · SSN · Big Data · Stream data

1 Introduction

Social networks, logging systems, sensor networks etc. are delivering huge amount of continuous flow of data also known as stream data. More data are produced more machine intelligence is required to deal with them. Streaming technologies like Complex Event Processing (CEP), Data Stream Management Systems, and Stream Reasoning (SR) are supporting Big Data applications development. According to a survey

© Springer International Publishing Switzerland 2015
E. Garoufallou et al. (Eds.): MTSR 2015, CCIS 544, pp. 89–100, 2015.
DOI: 10.1007/978-3-319-24129-6_8

conducted by Gartner Inc. 22% of the 218 respondents with active or planned big data initiatives said they were using stream or CEP technologies or had plans to do so [7]. In particular, SR provides a high impact area for developing powerful applications for analyzing stream data. State-of-the-art stream data knowledge bases are merely modeled through ontologies. Ontologies, in particular OWL ontologies, are mainly modeled in Description Logic (DL). Reasoning in ontological terms is not enough to express real-world application scenarios. For example, deriving new and implicit knowledge from ontologies is efficiently done through rule-based reasoning. However, layering Semantic Web rule-based DL systems, such as SWRL, over DL ontologies lacks the expressivity to handle some reasoning tasks, especially for the domain of SR e.g. finding average values [1]. A lot of research has been taken by the SR community to address data management and query processing on streaming data [4], while little efforts have been taken to address the stream reasoning inference problems [14]. In absence of a proper Semantic Web rule system different ones have been layered over stream data ontology bases. In our previous works in [1, 2], we have discussed about pros and cons for approaching hybrid and homogeny solutions. Mainly, the reasons for passing to hybrid solutions include non-monotonicity issues and solving complex reasoning tasks.

InWaterSense[1] is a R&D project for developing intelligent WSNs for WQM which objectives include:

- Build a Wireless Sensor Networks (WSN) infrastructure in the river Sitnica for monitoring water quality with the aim of providing a best practice scenario for expanding it to other surface water resources as well in the Republic of Kosovo.
- Monitor water quality in the river Sitnica supported by the WSN in order to make the quality data available to the community and the decision makers for determining the current health of the river.
- Transform the existing WSN for WQM into an intelligent platform to operate almost autonomously, and support more functionality as envisioned by the future Internet and intelligent systems.

In line with our project objectives, especially the later one, we have built INWATERSENSE (INWS) ontology framework [2], a SSN[2]-based ontology for modeling WQM domain. An extension of this ontology is developed for enabling identification of the potential polluter. Moreover, an expert system, using the Java Expert System Shell (Jess) [11], was developed to reason over INWS ontology. Jess is a rule engine and scripting environment written in Java. The contribution illustrates the main characteristics of an expert system for WQM. Namely, it classifies water bodies based on observed water quality values and investigates eventual sources of water quality degradation. We discuss the features and challenges of this system while also addressing its potential improvements. Since we plan in the future to build a pure Semantic Web framework for WQM, we also discuss the main challenges expected for building such system. The Jess expert system described in this paper will then be compared with this system.

---

[1] http://inwatersense.uni-pr.edu/
[2] Semantic Sensor Network Ontology, http://purl.oclc.org/NET/ssnx/ssn

The paper is organized as follows. We begin in the following section with description of INWS ontology model and the requirements for rule-based stream data reasoning. Section 3 describes the conceptual architecture of our SR framework for WQM. The expert system implementation is described in Section 4, while its challenges and discussions together with the pure Semantic Web approach are presented in Section 5. The paper ends with the concluding notes and future plans.

2   Background

The INWS ontology framework [2] models the WSN for WQM into three modules: core[3], regulations[4] and pollutants[5]. The core ontology extends the SSN ontology to meet the requirements for a WSN for WQM. It models WSN infrastructure entities, observations, observation time and location and water quality parameters. The regulations ontology models classification of water bodies based on different regulation authorities such as Water Framework Directive (WFD) [17]. And finally, the pollutants ontology models the entities for investigating sources of pollution.

A typical scenario for WQM in a WSN platform is as below:

Scenario 1. Water quality sensor probes are deployed in different measurement sites of a river. A sensor probe emits water quality values. We want to (1) classify the water body into the appropriate status according to WFD regulations and (2) identify the possible polluter if the values are below the allowed standard.

In order to handle the requirements of this scenario, a SR system should support reasoning over both streaming information and background data [19]. In particular, to enable efficient rule-based reasoning over stream data we address some specific requirements about this property which are already mentioned in state-of-the-art systems e. g. StreamRule [25]. Namely, a SR rule systems need to support a combination of reasoning features like: closed-world, non-monotonic, incremental and time-aware reasoning.

Since the Web is open and accessible by everyone, Semantic Web recommended standards (OWL and SWRL) manage knowledge bases in terms of open world assumption (OWA). In OWA, if some knowledge is missing it is classified as undefined as opposed to the closed-world assumption (CWA) which classifies the missing information as false. In the Web, addition of new information does not change any previously asserted information which is known as monotonic reasoning. This is not the case with non-monotonic reasoning during which addition of new information implies eventual modifications in the knowledge base. In SR application domains, OWL and SWRL's OWA and monotonic reasoning do not offer the desired expressivity level. For example, modifying the river pollution status is not allowed through SWRL rules. Following the SWRL's monotonic nature a river instance firstly asserted as "clean" cannot be later modified as "polluted".

---

[3] http://inwatersense.uni-pr.edu/ontologies/inws-core.owl

[4] http://inwatersense.uni-pr.edu/ontologies/inws-regulations.owl

[5] http://inwatersense.uni-pr.edu/ontologies/inws-pollutants.owl

Inferring new implicit data from stream data will result in multiple CRUD operations, which in SR is known as incremental reasoning. In our case study, new coming sensor observation data need to be consumed quickly and together with previously inferred data will serve as for inferring new implicit data.

SR systems should also include time-annotated data i.e. the time model, and like CEP should offer explicit operators for capturing temporal patterns over streaming information [19]. The INWS ontology layer implements the time model through OWL Time ontology[6]. Supporting temporal operators (serial, sequence, etc.) means the system can express the following example rule: *Enhanced phosphorus levels in surface waters (that contain adequate nitrogen) can stimulate excessive algal growth* [18]. If before excessive algal growth, enhanced phosphorus level has been observed then more probably the change of phosphorus levels has caused the algal growth. Thus, a sequence of these events needs to be tracked to detect the occurrence of this complex event.

Moreover, in order to enable reasoning in terms of time and quantity intervals of continuous and possibly infinite streams the SR notion of windows need to be adopted for rules [13]. For example, a rule to assert which sensors provided measurements that are above allowed average threshold the last 30 minutes sliding the window every 5 minutes, will be easily expressible with the help of the window concept. This has raised the need for a specific kind of rules in SR, namely continuous rules. Rather than evaluating rules against almost static ABox knowledge base as in traditional Semantic Web rule systems, continuous rule-based reasoning must run over dynamic stream data instead. With the set of new-coming data streams new logical decisions will arise: new information need to be published on the knowledge base or a fact modification/retraction need to be performed.

3   System Architecture

As depicted in Fig. 1, our system's architecture consists of three layers: *data, INWS ontology* and *rules layer*. The RDF data (up left) and RDF streams (up right) constitute the *data layer* (grey track). Arrows describe data flow direction. Domain specific ABox knowledge which does not change or changes "slowly" is formulated in the form of RDF data e.g. river names. RDF streams are defined as a sequence of RDF triples that are continuously produced and annotated with a timestamp [9]. Water quality measured values, annotated as RDF streams, will continuously populate the core ontology. In particular, a single RDF stream will hold information of observed water quality value, timestamp and location. The middle part of Fig. 1 represents the *INWS ontology* (green track) described in the previous section. The *rule layer* (yellow track) consists of common rules (bottom left) and continuous rules (bottom right). In the previous section we mentioned the concept of continuous rules which should infer new implicit knowledge from RDF streams.

---

[6] http://www.w3.org/TR/owl-time/

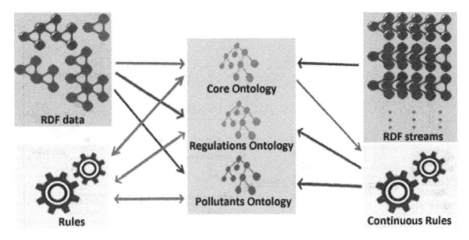

Fig. 1. InWaterSense conceptual framework: *data layer* (grey track), *ontology layer* (green track) and *rules layer* (yellow track)

4 Implementation

We decided to use Jess as a platform for implementing our system of reasoning over the INWS ontology framework. As a production rule system, Jess supports closed-world and non-monotonic reasoning. Moreover, it has a tight integration with Java through Jess's Java API and Protégé through JessTab[7] plugin. JessTab is a plug-in for the Protégé[8] ontology editor and knowledge-engineering framework that allows one to use Jess and Protégé together. The system is validated with simulated data, but it is developed for use within the InWaterSense project with real data.

The Jess implemented architecture of our system and its related components for reasoning over the INWS ontology are presented in Fig. 2. Namely, input data in their available format, say SQL, are transformed into RDF streams using D2RQ[9] tool. SWOOP [12] is used to load the D2RQ generated RDF data and produce the abbreviated RDF/XML syntax for object property instances to be readable by Protégé [2]. RDF data streams are next imported into the core ontology. The set of rules for water quality classification based on WFD regulations are defined and may run against the knowledge base. Moreover, a set of rules for investigating sources of pollution by observing if eventual critical events appear are defined and may be activated. A simple user interface was developed using Java Swing[10], which offers a user to monitor water quality based on the WFD regulations and to eventually find the possible sources of pollution.

---

[7] http://www.jessrules.com/jesswiki/view?JessTab

[8] Protégé ontology editor, http://protege.stanford.edu/

[9] D2RQ Accessing Relational Databases as Virtual RDF Graphs, http://d2rq.org/

[10] http://openjdk.java.net/groups/swing/

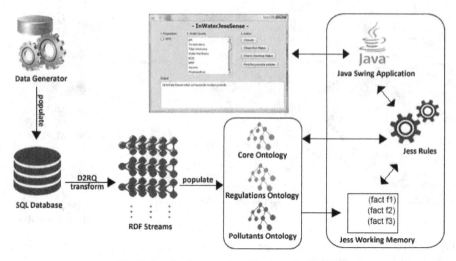

Fig. 2. Jess implemented architecture for WQM

4.1   The Pollutants Ontology

The INWS pollutants ontology was designed based on examples of sources of pollution and the potential pollutant discharges which could arise described in [18]. Two
classes are added: `PollutionSources`, describing the sources of pollution e.g.
urban storm water discharges, and `Pollutants`, representing contaminants present
in the environment or which might enter the environment which, due to its properties
or amount or concentration, causes harm e.g. heavy metals. A property `potential-
Pollutant` links individuals of `PollutionSources` and `Pollutants` (based
on the Table on page 3 in [18]). `PollutionSources` class is also linked with a
string through two properties: `pollutionSourceName`, representing the name of
the pollution source, and `pollutionType`, representing the type of the pollution
source which can be point, diffuse or both of them. Moreover, a property `hasSour-
cesOfPollution` was added to relate the rivers with the sources of pollution.

4.2   Implementation of the Scenario

To implement the *Scenario 1* using our system interface, as depicted in Fig. 3, one
should select the regulation authority i.e. WFD, select the water quality parameters
which are to be monitored and press the button "Classify". The JTextArea below the
"Output" label serves for printing rules messages.

The system offers multiple selections of water quality parameters. A simple rule is
fired at application startup to set up the observations interval beginning time from the
earliest time of observations streams and end time from the latest one. For brevity and
clarity, we will demonstrate Biochemical Oxygen Demand (*BOD5*) observations
WFD classification. According to WFD regulations: *if BOD$_5$ observations' average
value is between 1.3 and 1.5 mg O$_2$/l then river belongs to "Good" status of oxygen*

condition, if the average is below 1.3 then river belongs to "High" status, else the river belongs to "Moderate" status. Expressing this rationale with Jess rules was done through a number of rules. Namely, a rule of primer priority creates auxiliary Jess facts holding BOD$_5$ measurement values coming from the RDF streams. We should have used observation values directly from the ontology mappings but the Jess rule which calculates the average value constrains the usage of Jess facts.

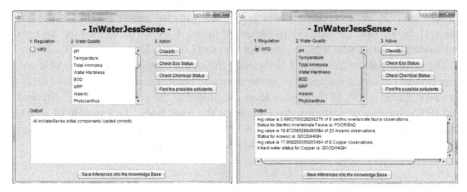

Fig. 3. The Jess system interface: initial view (left) and after WFD classification view (right)

After finding the average value it is asserted as a fact into the WM. Finally, another rule WFDclassifyWaterBOD does the WFD classification based on the previously asserted average value. This rule is illustrates below:

```
1  (defrule WFDclassifyWaterBOD
2  (BODaverage (v ?x)) (CurrentInterval (v ?i)) =>
3  (if (and (< ?x 1.5) (> ?x 1.3)) then (and
4  (printout t "Status for BOD is: GOOD" crlf)
5  (make-instance (str-cat "GoodBODStatus" ?*r*) of http://.../inws-
       regulations.owl#GoodBODMeasurement map)
6  (make-instance (str-cat "ObservationInstantBOD" ?*r*) of
       http://.../inws-regulations.owl#ObservationInstant map)
7  (slot-insert$ (str-cat "ObservationInstantBOD" ?*r*)
8  http://www.w3.org/2006/time#inXSDDateTime 1 ((new Date) toString))
9  (slot-insert$ (str-cat "ObservationInstantBOD" ?*r*)
10   http://.../inws-regulations.owl#hasStatus 1
11   (str-cat "http://.../inws-core.owl#GoodBODStatus" ?*r*))
12 (slot-insert$ (str-cat "http://.../inws-core.owl#" ?i)
13   http://.../inws-regulations.owl#hasStatus 1
14   (str-cat "http://.../inws-core.owl#GoodBODStatus" ?*r*))))
15 (if (< ?x 1.3) then <HIGH status classification code here>)
16 (if (> ?x 1.5) then <MODERATE status classification code here>))
```

Code in Line 1 serves for declaring a rule definition and its name. Line 2 represent the left hand side of the rule while lines 3-16 the right hand side of the rule. The previously calculated average value is assigned to variable ?x while the current interval of observations present in the WM is assigned to ?i (Line 2). If ?x is between 1.5 and 1.3 begin assertions for good status (Line 4-14). Namely, a message is printed out (Line 4); a new instance of regulations ontology class GoodBODMeasurement is created (Line 5) (?*r* is a global variable holding random integer numbers); a new instance of ObservationInstant class is created (Line 6) associated with current date and time through inXSDateTime property (Line 7-8). This instance is also related with the instance created in Line 5 through hasStatus property (Line 9-11). Current interval instance (Line 12) is associated with the newly asserted status instance (Line 13-14). The same steps presented in line 4-14 are performed for the high and moderate status, which are omitted for brevity (Line 15-16).

The second part of *Scenario 1* is encoded through a couple of rules. The first one detects newly asserted instances of moderate status i.e. instances of ModerateBOD-Measurement class. If there is at least one instance the second rule will fire and find BOD_5 sources of pollution discharging in the river body. An example of BOD_5 observations status is illustrated in Fig. 4. BOD_5 sources of pollution are also listed after the user has clicked the "Find possible pollutants" button.

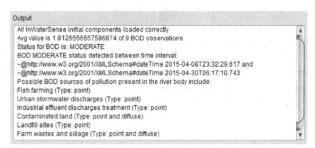

Fig. 4. *Scenario 1* example output for BOD_5 observations WFD classification and sources of pollution

5   Challenges and Discussion

In this section will be discussed the features of the Jess system and the challenges to be addressed for its further improvements. Meanwhile, potential future directions for building a pure Semantic Web rule system, such as SWRL, for WQM also take place in the discussion. This system is planned to support time-aware, closed-world, non-monotonic and incremental reasoning to enable stream data reasoning.

5.1   Continuous Rules

The Jess system effectively identifies water quality status for the set of input RDF streams. Upcoming RDF streams are collected into another set of streams which in turn are imported into INWS ontology for rule-based reasoning. As per future works we plan to automate this process. Namely, RDF streams coming from SQL through D2RQ translation will continually populate the ontology and be automatically mapped into Jess's WM. Meanwhile, with the time passing old facts will be discarded from the WM and be deployed into the knowledge base for future reasoning. If a class is mapped through JessTab command `mapclass` then it will place all its instances into the WM. This is not practical with stream data as data flow is massive and rules will consider a specific set (time or quantity constrained window) of RDF streams. A workaround solution would be to create Jess facts out of window's selected Protégé instances. But this way the WM will hold Protégé instances and their one or many Jess facts copies. Moreover, instead of producing a query output results like in C-SPARQL, the continuous firing of rules will continually modify the knowledge base i. e. do incremental reasoning. This is efficiently done through JessTab functions for manipulation of ontology classes and instances. However, using inferred knowledge between observation RDF streams sets is planned for future system improvements.

5.2   Logic Foundation

The core issue for building a pure Semantic Web system for stream data from which follow the respective expressivity constrains is the system's underlying logic foundation. Production rules and LP implementations has shown great success in the domain of SR. Different Semantic Web applications fall into different logic domains and possibly in a mixture of them [6]. The authors of [6] conclude that the Description Logic Programs (DLP) fragment should offer extension for both LP and DL. In the area of SR, DL reasoning fulfills the requirements for modeling the knowledge bases. When it comes to rule-based reasoning DL's OWA limits the expressivity power for even simple reasoning tasks (e.g. counting class instances). Since LP adopts CWA approach together with non-monotonicity an LP extension of DLP, would be ideal for the WQM case study and stream data in general.

5.3   Forward/Backward-Chaining and Rete Algorithm

Inferring new knowledge in rule systems can be done in two methods: deriving conclusions from facts, known as forward-chaining or starting from conclusion (goal) by matching facts also known as backward-chaining.

In production rule systems, matching rules with relevant facts is efficiently done with the Rete algorithm [9]. Executing rules through Rete algorithm means all relevant facts must be loaded into the WM [3]. Considering the massive flow of stream data the WM will become overwhelmed. Adding here the amount of the inferred facts, the memory will become exhausted. With the introduction of the continuous rules this issue will be resolved by capturing only snapshots (time-based or count-based windows) of streams and thus facts will enter and leave WM as needed.

In SR applications facts are changing very often, while rules change "slowly". Newly inserted facts in WM will cause rule firing. This intuitively indicates the forward-chaining nature of stream data applications. Rete algorithm natively adopts forward-chaining approach. However, the traditional Rete algorithm does not support aggregation of values in time-based windows [20]. Authors in [20] present a CEP system which extends Rete algorithm for supporting time-aware reasoning by leveraging the time-based windows and enabling calculation of complex events e.g.

finding average value. They have added a time enabled beta-node to restrict event detection to a certain time-frame. On the other side, Semantic Streams [21], prove that backward-chaining can also be enabled on stream data even though its slight modification has been needed to produce the legal flow of data.

5.4   Hybrid and Homogeny Stream Data Approaches

State-of-the-art rule-based systems for reasoning over stream data mainly fall into two broad categories: hybrid and pure Semantic Web approaches [1].

Hybrid approaches layer different rule systems over ontologies like: production rules, CEP, LP, Answer Set Programming etc. In our previous work [1] we described in more detail about each approach and their pros and cons. In general, hybrid ones have achieved the desired system behavior by translating the ontology into the corresponding formalisms of the overlaying rule system. A drawback of this translation is that a possible loss of information may occur. For example, translating complex subclass statements consisting of disjunction of classes or expressed with existential quantification are not possible into Plausible Logic [5]. Moreover, when adding a rule a possible side-effect may occur. For example, in production rule systems adding a rule may require extra work because of the algorithm used for executing the rules as depicted in [3]. This makes it harder for domain experts to write rules without IT support. In some cases (as shown in [3]) development layers are conflate to each other making rules maintenance more laborious. SWRL on the other side is declarative rule language not bound to any particular execution algorithm [3]. However, equipping SWRL with non-monotonic reasoning means the order of rules should be taken into account [24]. StreamRule demonstrates how non-monotonic, incremental and time-aware reasoning can be integrated into a unique platform for stream data reasoning. However, the continuous rule feature is implemented through separate steps. Namely, stream filtering and aggregation is done through a stream query processor such as CQELS [26] while OClingo [27] is used to enable non-monotonic reasoning.

Pure Semantic Web approaches like [22] and [23] do not make any distinction between stream and random data and lack implementation. These approaches prove that SWRL can be used to infer new and approximate knowledge in stream data domains. The work presented in [16] describes a Rete-based approach of RIF rules for producing data in a continuous manner. Although supporting time-aware and incremental reasoning, the approach does not deal with non-monotonic and closed-world reasoning. Rscale [8] is another industrially-approved reasoning system which leverages OWL 2 RL language profile to infer new knowledge. It enables incremental reasoning, non-monotonic and closed-world reasoning through translation of facts and rules into SQL tables and queries respectively. However, it does not support time-aware reasoning, and as a non-Semantic Web approach follows the hybrid approach disadvantages. JNOMO [24] shows how SWRL can be extended to embrace non-monotonicity and CWA. However, inclusion of temporal reasoning is envisioned as per future works.

6   Conclusion and Future Work

The main contributions of this paper include an extension of INWS ontology with metadata descriptions for water quality pollution sources and an expert system that uses INWS ontology to enable WQM. The system efficiently classifies water bodies based on WFD standards encoded into Jess rules running over the set of observations RDF streams. Moreover, a set of Jess rules are used to detect the eventual sources of pollution. However, the notion of windows needs to be adopted for Jess rules to enable continuous rules feature. The system's features and challenges were also discussed as lessons learned for future plans of building Semantic Web homogeny solution for reasoning over stream data. Forward-chaining reasoning method is a natural approach for stream data while an LP extension to DLP was also identified as a suitable underlying logic for the rule system reasoning over stream data. Our future works also include the evaluation of the expert system described in this paper and comparing it with the pure Semantic Web system.

Acknowledgements. The work described in this paper was supported by "InWaterSense: Intelligent Wireless Sensor Networks for Monitoring Surface Water Quality", an EU funded project managed by European Union Office in Kosovo, implemented by University of Prishtina.

References

1. Jajaga, E., Ahmedi, L., Abazi-Bexheti, L.: Semantic Web trends on reasoning over sensor data. In: 8th South East European Doctoral Student Conference, Greece (2013)
2. Ahmedi, L., Jajaga, E., Ahmedi, F.: An ontology framework for water quality management. In: Corcho, Ó., Henson, C.A., Barnaghi, P.M. (eds.) SSN@ISWC, Sydney, pp. 35–50 (2013)
3. MacLarty, I., Langevine, L., Bossche, M.V., Ross, P.: Using SWRL for Rule Driven Applications. Technical report (2009)
4. Unel, G., Roman, D.: Stream reasoning: a survey and further research directions. In: Andreasen, T., Yager, R.R., Bulskov, H., Christiansen, H., Larsen, H.L. (eds.) FQAS 2009. LNCS, vol. 5822, pp. 653–662. Springer, Heidelberg (2009)
5. Groza, A., Letia, I.A.: Plausible description logic programs for stream reasoning. Future Internet **4**, 865–881 (2001)
6. de Bruijn, J., Polleres, A., Lara, R., Fensel, D.: OWL DL vs. OWL flight: conceptual modeling and reasoning for the semantic web. In: Fourteenth International World Wide Web Conference, pp. 623–632. ACM, Chiba (2005)
7. Report Highlight for Survey Analysis: Big Data Investment Grows but Deployments Remain Scarce in 2014, http://www.gartner.com/newsroom/id/2848718
8. Liebig, T., Opitz, M.: Reasoning over dynamic data in expressive knowledge bases with rscale. In: The 10th International Semantic Web Conference, Bonn, Germany (2011)
9. Forgy, C.L.: Rete: A fast algorithm for the many pattern/many object pattern match problem. Artificial Intelligence **19**(1), 17–37 (1982)
10. Barbieri, D.F.: C-SPARQL: SPARQL for continuous querying. In: Proceedings of the 18th International World Wide Web Conf. (WWW 2009), pp. 1061–1062 (2009)

11. Hill, E.F.: Jess in action: java rule-based systems. Manning Publications Co., Greenwich (2003)
12. Horrocks, I., Patel-Schneider, P.F., Boley, H., Tabet, S., Grosof, B., Dean, M.: SWRL: A Semantic Web Rule Language Combining OWL and RuleML (2004)
13. Stuckenschmidt, H., Ceri, S., Della Valle, E., van Harmelen, F.: Towards expressive stream reasoning. In: Proceedings of the Dagstuhl Seminar on Semantic Aspects of Sensor Networks (2010)
14. Della Valle, E., Schlobach, S., Krötzsch, M., Bozzon, A., Ceri, S., Horrocks, I.: Order matters! harnessing a world of orderings for reasoning over massive data. Semantic Web Journal 4(2), 219–231 (2013)
15. Sheth, A., Henson, C., Sahoo, S.S.: Semantic sensor web. IEEE Internet Computing 12(4), 78–83 (2008)
16. Albeladi, R., Martinez, K., Gibbins, N.: Incremental rule-based reasoning over RDF streams: an expression of interest. In: RDF Stream Processing Workshop at the 12th Extended Semantic Web Conference, Portoroz, Slovenia (2015)
17. Directive 2000/60/EC of the European Parliament and of the Council of Europe of 23 October 2000 establishing a framework for Community action in the Field of water quality O.J. L327/1 (2000)
18. Sources of Pollution, Foundation for Water Research, Information Note FWR-WFD16 (2005)
19. Margara, A., Urbani, J., van Harmelen, F., Bal, H.: Streaming the web: reasoning over dynamic data. Web Semantics: Science, Services and Agents on the World Wide Web 25, 24–44 (2014)
20. Walzer, K., Groch, M., Breddin, T.: Time to the rescue - supporting temporal reasoning in the rete algorithm for complex event processing. In: Bhowmick, S.S., Küng, J., Wagner, R. (eds.) DEXA 2008. LNCS, vol. 5181, pp. 635–642. Springer, Heidelberg (2008)
21. Whitehouse, K., Zhao, F., Liu, J.: Semantic streams: a framework for composable semantic interpretation of sensor data. In: Römer, K., Karl, H., Mattern, F. (eds.) EWSN 2006. LNCS, vol. 3868, pp. 5–20. Springer, Heidelberg (2006)
22. Wei, W., Barnaghi, P.: Semantic annotation and reasoning for sensor data. In: Barnaghi, P., Moessner, K., Presser, M., Meissner, S. (eds.) EuroSSC 2009. LNCS, vol. 5741, pp. 66–76. Springer, Heidelberg (2009)
23. Keßler, C., Raubal, M., Wosniok, C.: Semantic rules for context-aware geographical information retrieval. In: Barnaghi, P., Moessner, K., Presser, M., Meissner, S. (eds.) EuroSSC 2009. LNCS, vol. 5741, pp. 77–92. Springer, Heidelberg (2009)
24. Calero, J.M.A., Ortega, A.M., Perez, G.M., Blaya, J.A.B., Skarmeta, A.F.G.: A nonmonotonic expressiveness extension on the semantic web rule language. J. Web Eng. 11(2), 93–118 (2012)
25. Mileo, A., Abdelrahman, A., Policarpio, S., Hauswirth, M.: StreamRule: a nonmonotonic stream reasoning system for the semantic web. In: Faber, W., Lembo, D. (eds.) RR 2013. LNCS, vol. 7994, pp. 247–252. Springer, Heidelberg (2013)
26. Le-Phuoc, D., Dao-Tran, M., Xavier Parreira, J., Hauswirth, M.: A native and adaptive approach for unified processing of linked streams and linked data. In: Aroyo, L., Welty, C., Alani, H., Taylor, J., Bernstein, A., Kagal, L., Noy, N., Blomqvist, E. (eds.) ISWC 2011, Part I. LNCS, vol. 7031, pp. 370–388. Springer, Heidelberg (2011)
27. Gebser, M., Grote, T., Kaminski, R., Obermeier, P., Sabuncu, O., Schaub. T.: Answer set programming for stream reasoning. In: CoRR (2013)

Discovering the Topical Evolution of the Digital Library Evaluation Community

Leonidas Papachristopoulos[1,4]([✉]), Nikos Kleidis[2], Michalis Sfakakis[1], Giannis Tsakonas[3], and Christos Papatheodorou[1,4]

[1] Department of Archives, Library Science and Museology, Ionian University, Corfu, Greece
{l11papa,sfakakis,papatheodor}@ionio.gr
[2] Department of Informatics, Athens University of Economics and Business, Athens, Greece
klidisnik@aueb.gr
[3] Library & Information Center, University of Patras, Patras, Greece
john@lis.upatras.gr
[4] Digital Curation Unit, IMIS, 'Athena' Research Centre, Athens, Greece

Abstract. The successful management of textual information is a rising challenge for all the researchers' communities, in order firstly to assess its current and previous statuses and secondly to enrich the level of their metadata description. The huge amount of unstructured data that is produced has consequently populated text mining techniques for its interpretation, selection and metadata enrichment opportunities that provides. Scientific production regarding Digital Libraries (DLs) evaluation has been grown in size and has broaden the scope of coverage as it consists a complex and multidimensional field. The current study proposes a probabilistic topic modeling implemented on a domain corpus from the JCDL, ECDL/TDPL and ICADL conferences proceedings in the period 2001-2013, aiming at the unveiling of its topics and subject temporal analysis, for exploiting and extracting semantic metadata from large corpora in an automatic way.

Keywords: Research trends discovery · Digital library evaluation · Topic modeling · Metadata extraction · Latent Dirichlet Allocation

1 Introduction

The advent of digital libraries (DLs) overstated the problem of subject classification as they accommodate large amount of textual information, which is not adequately organized. Manual classification can work only for finite collections. The use of text mining techniques is proposed as an effective way for the encountering of that information overflow. Automated or semi-automated methods can play significant role in knowledge management, setting limits to the chaotic ecosystem on which have been imposed to. The various uses of text mining have been intensively highlighted by scientific literature, focusing on the fact that such applications can ameliorate text categorization, information retrieval and textual information modification into numeric in order to be submitted in a secondary analysis [1].

© Springer International Publishing Switzerland 2015
E. Garoufallou et al. (Eds.): MTSR 2015, CCIS 544, pp. 101–112, 2015.
DOI: 10.1007/978-3-319-24129-6_9

Topic modeling consist a form of text mining aiming at the meaningful summarization of corpora into sets of words, called 'topics'. The whole process narrows human intervention on the setting of the parameters of the specific algorithm implemented each time and, accordingly, mandates a high level of participation on the stage of interpretation of the results. One of the most basic and popular models, which is applied in the specific study, is Latent Dirichlet Allocation (LDA), introduced by [2]. LDA can identify the topics that compose a collection and offers a probabilistic assumption for the existence of these topics in each document. The extracted topics can help researchers clarify issues over the nature of the corpus and the interlinking between the documents. A full explanation of LDA algorithm is beyond the scope of this paper.

The DL evaluation domain emerged in parallel with the older DL subdomains, such as metadata, architectures, indexing/retrieval mechanisms, etc. and it accounts for a rich literature. Every DL is evaluated under a variety of criteria and uses different methods that origin from different domains. DL evaluation is a multifaceted domain and therefore its topical extent should be explored.

This paper continues the efforts aiming to the exploration of the DL evaluation domain [3][4] and its objective is twofold: firstly, we attempt to identify the topics emerged in a representative corpus on the domain, aspiring to their usage as subject descriptors of its documents and secondly, to reformulate field evolution through the temporal analysis of its subjects appearance. We specify these goals to the following research questions:

1. Which are the most prominent topics emerged in DL evaluation? We investigate this sub-goal applying the LDA algorithm on a domain specific corpus.
2. How these topics evolved temporally within the period 2001-2013? For this purpose we study the evolution of its topics laying them on a timeline.
3. Can we specify content orientation of each conference in our corpus? We segment our analysis to the constituent conferences of the corpus.

The paper is structured as follows. Section 2 describes related work on topic modeling implementation and the adoption of a technique in the field of DLs and on the temporal analysis of topics of the existing scientific production; Section 3 provides an overview of the methodological steps for corpus selection and preparation for analysis. Section 4 presents, justifies and interprets research results and finally, Section 5 concludes the paper and underlines possible directions for further research.

2   Literature Review

The literature has been hyperactive in the study of the role of topic modeling within the operation of DLs. The role of topics extracted from topic modeling has been assessed as an alternative to subject descriptors in digital libraries [5]. Implementing a user study, authors juxtaposed topic modeling results and Library of Congress Subject Headings (LCSH) and gave clear answer to the interrogative form of their research entitled "Are Learned Topics More Useful Than Subject Headings?". Indeed, topic modeling can be a reliable tool assisting any cataloguer to extract semantics and assign metadata, as in many cases the description of the material originated from topic modeling processes was more meaningful to user's eyes. However, the use of topic modeling in DL shouldn't be considered as the 'divine law'. The level of usefulness of topic modeling results should be examined by users via a scoring process, which will limit the existence of 'junk' topics [6].

In [7] topic modeling was implemented on records harvested from 668 repositories in order to prove that heterogeneous metadata can be enriched automatically. Each record was attributed to a specific topic creating better searching conditions for the users of a prototype portal developed for the needs of the research. Furthermore, LDA algorithm has been used to extract topics in order to compute topic-based document similarity for automatic annotation of poorly annotate metadata records harvested on behalf of ONEMercury search service [8].

Topic modeling can have multiple dimensions. Although it demands human effort in the part of interpretation, it has been used as an interpretive tool as well. LDA has been applied in MEDLINE's articles to improve the understanding of MeSH subject headings attached to them [9]. Additionally, [10] proved that LDA can be a useful tool for measuring item to item similarity and organizing DL content. For [11] the use of automatically generated information for the improvement of the retrieval of documents of a DL is self-evident. However, a rising issue is the representation of the discovered topics to the end user.

The multidisciplinarity of the DL field imposes the need for the analysis of the emerged topics. An expanded analysis on CiteSeer documents has been conducted for the period 1990-2004 using a probabilistic model called 'Segmented Author-Topic Model' (S-ATM). The research proved that the application of topic modeling algorithms can lead to the effective temporal tracing of subjects that concerned the DL community [12].

Two crucial issues concerning the application of topic modeling algorithms are the pre-selection of (i) the number of topics that describe thematically a corpus, as well as (ii) the number of iterations so that to ensure the algorithm convergence. Regarding the investigation of these issues in the studied DL evaluation corpus the number of the manually extracted topics in the wider area of the DL was considered. More specifically, [13] accomplished a research using traditional content analysis aiming at the identification of the core topics and subtopics for the period 1990-2010. The authors used a corpus, analogous with the current study (JCDL, ECDL/TPDL, ICADL proceedings), and -based on the keywords of the publications- created a knowledge map of 21 core topics and 1015 subtopics, which were considered as relevant topics nested in the core topics. The authors acknowledged that they had not integrated in their study the temporal evolution of the DL field. Aiming at the development of a curriculum for DLs [14], they manually created a corpus of JCDL proceedings, D-Lib Magazine papers and panel sessions at the aforementioned conferences, which was then analyzed based upon word frequency. The results showed that DLs' core topics are eight and can be clustered into two main categories: DL collections (development/creation) and DL services and sustainability. As far as we concern, the current study is the first one that implements a topic modeling method in the field of DL evaluation offering a high level of granularity in such a fuzzy environment.

3   Methodology

3.1   Corpus Selection and Preparation

Due to the significance of conference proceedings in the evolution of the DL domain, the current research is based on a data set consisted of evaluation studies published in the proceedings of the most significant conferences of the domain, namely JCDL,[1] ICADL[2] and ECDL/TPDL,[3] during the period 2001-2013[4] The corpus was selected from the whole set of the conferences' accepted papers by three domain experts followed the procedure described in [15] and it was validated by the application of Naïve Bayes classifier as described in [4]. Totally 395 short and full-length evaluation-oriented papers were selected, which 147 were from ECDL/TPDL, 123 from JCDL and 125 from ICADL.

Following to the selection stage, a preprocessing phase was necessary to create the necessary 'bag of words', which would be used as an input to the topic modeling tool. PDF documents were transformed into text format and were tokenized. The following step was to remove the most frequent and rare words (above 2,100 or under 5 appearances) as those which appear in Fox's list [16]. Reduced-vocabulary topic modeling can increase the number of interpretable and useful topics [7].

The resulting data set is consisted of 742,224 tokens and the corresponding dictionary has 38,298 unique terms. Token is a word which is meaningful on a linguistic and methodological level. The average number of tokens per year is 57,094, while each paper averagely contributes 1,879 tokens. Although the majority of papers derived from ECDL/TPDL conference (p=147), JCDL's tokens are dominant in the data set (t=299,957).

3.2   Implementation Tools and Processes

The aforementioned preprocessed corpus was used as an input in Mimno's jsLDA (javascript LDA) web tool [17]. jsLDA is a user friendly web-based implementation of LDA in javascript language, which offers instant presentation of the results accompanied by a graphical view, giving the opportunity to the user to have a clear overview of the experiment. The data set was converted to CSV format and was uploaded to the application.[5] The parameters for the Dirichlet term and topic smoothing were set to 0.01 and 0.1 respectively. As already mentioned, using as starting point the numbers of the manually extracted topics from [13, 14], finally, the application was run to learn 13 topics as other experiments with higher or lower number of topics were offer low interpretability. For this purpose three domain experts were

---

[1] ACM/IEEE Joint Conference on Digital Libraries
[2] International Conference on Asian Digital Libraries
[3] European Conference on Digital Libraries (TPDL), formerly known as International Conference on Theory and Practice of Digital Libraries (ECDL)
[4] ICADL proceedings are available since 2002.
[5] http://snf-623861.vm.okeanos.grnet.gr/leo-tools/jsLDA-master/jslda.html

monitoring the whole experimental results to identify the optimal number of topics. Additionally, we decided to set a threshold of ten words for each topic. According to [6] the choice of ten *"is arbitrary, but it balances between having enough words to convey the meaning of a topic, but not too many words to complicate human judgments or our scoring models"*. For model training, the number of sampling iterations was set to 1,000. It was observed that approaching the number of iterations to 1,000, the topic structure was made more stable and interpretable, while further increments of the number of iterations left the topic structure unchanged.

4   Results and Analysis

4.1   Topics' Rationale and Interpretation

Current research ended up that 13 were the most meaningful set of topics after an iterative run of experiments (Table 1). Through topic modeling each topic was represented by a distribution of words from the corpus, while each document is considered as a random mixture of these topics. Therefore, running jsLDA to our corpus, each paper was assigned to a ranked list of topics. The most representative paper of each topic was used by the experts as the most appropriate way for interpreting it [18]. In particular the experts considered the distribution of the words as well as the most representative paper for each topic aiming to interpret the topics and also to assign an appropriate textual label to each of them. For example, the label 'Reading behavior' was assigned to the topic represented by the work of [19], which is a typical research on the reading behavior of users regarding a specific device. Papers classified in the specific topic use as sample students, who express their experience on reading or annotating through a specific device, aiming at the evaluation of its effectiveness.

On the other hand, the papers in the 'Similarity performance' topic present new approaches for data access and retrieval. Researchers that apply such experiments implement various algorithms on datasets assessing their performance and aspiring to ameliorate them. The dimension of content is crucial for the DL evaluation field [20]. The educational sector uses DLs as a mean of an alternative and informal channel of knowledge dissemination. Many works in DL conferences focus on the functionality and usefulness of application with educational content, gathering student attitudes and behavioral intentions through quantitative methods, such as questionnaires.

The topic on 'Distributed services' affirms the fact that DLs are not secluded. Large amount of data are transferred within a network of numerous nodes. The systems that accommodate all this workload should be assessed regarding their efficiency (response time, etc.). According to the 'Interaction Triptych Model', system technology, *"which is placed between the 'Content' and the 'System'"* [20], can be evaluated through performance measures. Additionally, the evaluation of recommender systems aims at the improvement of the performance of the respective algorithms. The latter use as input tags that are provided by users and propose relevant results to searches conducted by other. The specific kind of studies can be characterized as user-centered, as they need users' contribution in two phases of the experiments: the modulation of the algorithm and its evaluation upon the provided recommendations.

Table 1. Emerged Topics

Label	Topic
1 **Reading behavior**	participants study text book students books reading paper page notes
2 **Similarity performance**	similarity entities entity name names set data features quality blocks
3 **Educational content**	students resources learning design resource project educational teachers knowledge questions
4 **Distributed services**	data system server content service distributed node network nodes file
5 **Recommending systems**	user users paper papers algorithm citation set recommendation cluster tags
6 **Metadata quality**	metadata data records resources content services objects elements language quality
7 **Multimedia**	video image images videos task topics topic performance surrogates text
8 **Text classification**	text words word performance method table classification data using results
9 **Search engines**	search web results page pages users relevance google engines relevant
10 **Information seeking**	information users system evaluation user research process analysis specific systems
11 **Preservation cost**	music preservation file data cluster sentiment files cost musical analysis
12 **Information retrieval**	query terms queries term retrieval search using results relevant set
13 **Interface usability**	user search users interface task system tasks participants browsing interfaces

The dimension of quality is tightly connected with the issue of metadata. The content accommodated in DLs should be appropriately described to be retrieved. Metadata quality evaluation is based on the measure of specific criteria such as accuracy, completeness, timeliness, accessibility provenance, etc. [21]. The metadata evaluation field can be distinguished in two subtopics: (i) the proposed metadata evaluation metrics are assessed regarding their effectiveness and the set of criteria they adopt, and (ii) records and entities are set on the center of evaluation activity in order to identify weakness in collections' descriptors.

The content of DL is not restricted to textual material. Video and image items have gained their role in the DLs' ecosystem and have attracted the attention of research community. In general, 'Multimedia evaluation' focuses on specific features that affect their effectiveness. Usually a set of measures is implemented to assess user performance while interacting with them.

'Text classification' papers can be characterized as performance-centered, because text-trained algorithms are applied to cluster datasets. Algorithm results are collated with gold standard corpora in order to specify their classification performance. Search engine results have concern the DL evaluation community, as Google, Yahoo and other engines provide results, which are evaluated regarding their relevancy. Researchers usually compare the search engine results and their interface appeal and make the appropriate suggestions. Information seeking patterns can lead to the development of the analogous systems for the fulfillment of users information needs. The 'Information seeking' topic is a user-oriented topic, as researchers focus on users' habits and patterns to discover a specific resource. Methodologically, the specific evaluation initiatives are 'interpretation intensive', as the researcher has to identify the state of the user and discover his interaction style with the system.

Another topic that emerged was 'Preservation'. Data and files should be carefully managed to be available for future access. Apart from technical issues, preservation is a matter of economic resources and the viability of any preservation action should be based on cost assessment. On the other hand, 'Information retrieval' papers attempt to exploit any possible method in order to improve users' abilities for discovering content. Researchers perform searches using specific queries and terms and assess the performance of the results. Finally, the 'Interface usability' topic reflects those works, which are trying to identify how much enjoyable and efficient is the DL environment. The words that appear in the topic, such as 'users', 'participants' and 'tasks', describe the methodological processes of interface evaluation. Users are asked to perform some tasks and browse. The expressed comments about 'look and feel' and their experience will lead to design recommendations.

4.2   Topic Relations

The adjacency matrix provided by jsLDA tool for the representation of the relations between the topics was visualized to identify latent relationships between the topics. Figure 1 presents the positive relationship weights among topics provided by the adjacency matrix. The network shows a significant relation between 'information retrieval' and 'search engine' topics. In fact, queries -that are the major component of information retrieval field- are those which are implemented in search engine evaluations. On the other hand, the graph presents a reasonable relationship between 'reading behavior', 'educational content', 'interface usability' and 'multimedia'. The aforementioned topics have in common 'user experience', which is attempted to be evaluated in all of them. The assessment of browsing video or reading text on the screen is vital for interface design.

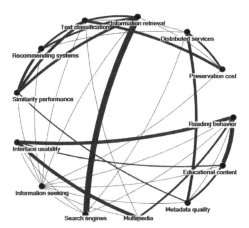

Fig. 1. Topic correlations

We ought to highlight also the relationship between 'distributed services' and 'metadata quality'. DLs often attempt to harvest metadata from different resources without knowing their descriptive value. The harvested records are evaluated in relation to their quality and the added value that provide to the DL. Additionally, 'Reading behavior' and 'Educational content' depict the experience that students build, when they consume educational content. Both employ user-centered methodologies, as they use students as research subjects. Moreover, service and system performance topics ('Recommending systems', 'Information retrieval', 'Text classification' and 'Similarity performance') constitute a coherent part of the graph.

4.3   Topic Trends

The study of topic evolution on the whole corpus reflects the scientific interests of the specific community on the temporal axis, while a specific view of each conference contributes to the identification of its profile. Corpus temporal analysis (Fig. 2) indicates that 'Information seeking' behavior is one of the community's constant concerns. On the other hand, issues that are related to 'Educational content' flourish for a short period (2002-2004), but since then they have a limited, but consistent, appearance. Recently, in the period 2011-2013, the DL evaluation field shows an increase of its interest on 'Similarity performance' and 'Text classification'. That point insinuates an intention for adopting automatic procedures and performance measures in DL operations regarding indexing and retrieval. The other topics, such as 'Distributed services', 'Reading behavior', 'Search engines' and 'Multimedia features', seem to have a moderate temporal evolution in our corpus.

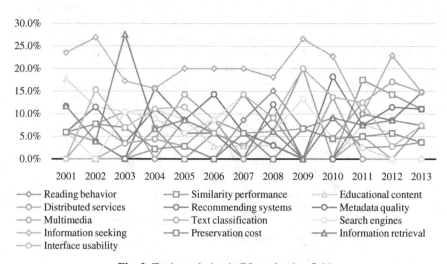

Fig. 2. Topic evolution in DL evaluation field

Each paper of the corpus was categorized according to the highest ranked topic from the list that was assigned to. Then, the corpus' papers were clustered by year and by conference to facilitate a segmented analysis of our corpus. We created three different tables –as many as our conferences– having two dimensions (years and topics), which are visualized bellow.

Specifically, the ICADL evaluation papers tend to study 'Information seeking', as the topic appears regularly during 2002-2013 (Fig. 3). At the same time 'Information retrieval' and 'Metadata quality' present an analogous track having specific peak years (2003 and 2010 respectively). Since 2010 the aforementioned topics seem to monopolize the thematic preferences of the community. It is worth mentioning that for the ICADL conference there are no available proceedings for the year 2001, while it was co-organized with the JCDL conference in 2010.

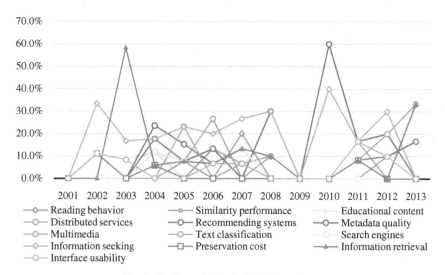

Fig. 3. Topic evolution in ICADL conference

On the other hand, JCDL captures the pulse of community; it isn't monopolized by specific topics in the DL evaluation area (Fig. 4). It stands as a multi-topic conference, which redirects yearly its focus. 'Metadata quality' and 'Text classification' seem to be the most recent trends appearing constantly the last three years.

Finally, concerning the DL evaluation area, ECDL/TPDL can be safely characterized as an 'Information seeking' conference as the topic has –apart from 2007– a high yearly representation (Fig. 5). A contiguous pattern is followed by 'Distributed services' and 'Interface usability' evaluations. Although 'Search engine' evaluation attracted a lot of attention during the period 2003–2010, since then the topic have ceased, while 'Similarity performance' papers gained its place within the specific conference since 2011 and after some sparse appearances on 2001, 2004 and 2008.

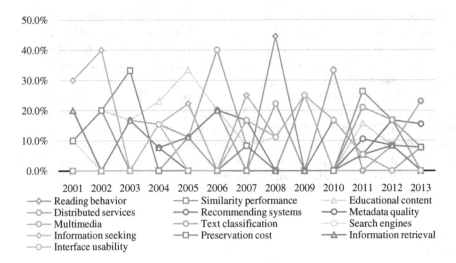

Fig. 4. Topic evolution in JCDL conference

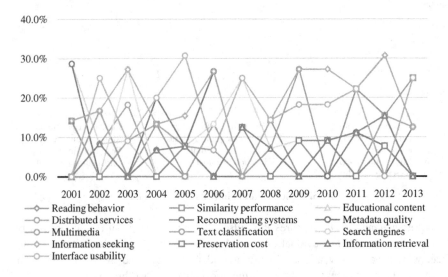

Fig. 5. Topic evolution in ECDL/TPDL conference

5   Conclusions

Topic modeling techniques provide an efficient method for exploiting and extracting semantic metadata from large corpora in an automatic way. In this work, the LDA algorithm was utilized for the extraction of the topics of DL evaluation literature as published in three of the most valuable conferences of the domain.

Our analysis offered an insight into the range of topics, while a network graph indicated the connections among them. Considering previous manual attempts on DLs' topic decomposition [13][14], we can notice that the number of the extracted topics of the present research is close to theirs, given the size of the DL evaluation field.

The segmented topical analysis of each conference indicates that JCDL is constantly reorienting its topical focus, attracting papers which are in the forefront of research agenda. On the other hand ECDL/TPDL and ICADL have a more specific topic identity. ECDL/TPDL, with respect to the DL evaluation, is a purely 'Information seeking' venue giving a constant opportunity for such publications. Additionally, the popularity of 'Interface usability' papers within the specific conference in conjunction with 'Information seeking' indicates an inclination to user-centered methodologies.

ICADL seem to have a limited research agenda, as the topics appeared yearly are few. Furthermore, 'Similarity performance' and 'Text classification' are considered as the DL community's hot topics. Both of the aforementioned topics are system-centered affecting accordingly the methodological trends of DL community as quantitative methods will be mostly used. Any attempt of predicting future topical trends will be very useful for the re-synthesis of DL curricula, as the latter will form the new generation of DL researchers.

Future research includes a bibliometric analysis of the papers belonging to each topic to identify important entities of the community, such as authors or publication venues. Having matched entities to topics, we would have shape a recommendation tool for any researcher who wishes to scientifically contribute to the DL domain.

Acknowledgements. We want to express our deepest thanks to our colleague Vangelis Nomikos, who technically supported the implementation of jsLDA.

References

1. Delen, D., Crossland, M.D.: Seeding the survey and analysis of research literature with text mining. Expert Syst. Appl. **34**, 1707–1720 (2008)
2. Blei, D.M., Ng, A.Y., Jordan, M.I.: Latent dirichlet allocation. J. Mach. Learn. Res. **3**, 993–1022 (2003)
3. Tsakonas, G., Mitrelis, A., Papachristopoulos, L., Papatheodorou, C.: An exploration of the digital library evaluation literature based on an ontological representation. J. Am. Soc. Inf. Sci. Technol. **64**, 1914–1926 (2013)
4. Afiontzi, E., Kazadeis, G., Papachristopoulos, L., Sfakakis, M., Tsakonas, G., Papatheodorou, C.: Charting the digital library evaluation domain with a semantically enhanced mining methodology. In: Proceedings of the 13th ACM/IEEE-CS Joint Conference on Digital Libraries, Indianapolis, IN, USA, pp. 125–134 (2013)
5. Noh, Y., Hagedorn, K., Newman, D.: Are learned topics more useful than subject headings. In: Proceedings of the 11th Annual International ACM/IEEE Joint Conference on Digital Libraries, pp. 411–412. ACM, New York (2011)
6. Newman, D., Noh, Y., Talley, E., Karimi, S., Baldwin, T.: Evaluating topic models for digital libraries. In: Proceedings of the 10th ACM/IEEE-CS Joint Conference on Digital Libraries, pp. 215–224. ACM Press (2010)

7. Newman, D., Hagedorn, K., Chemudugunta, C., Smyth, P.: Subject metadata enrichment using statistical topic models. In: Proceedings of the 7th ACM/IEEE-CS Joint Conference on Digital Libraries, pp. 366–375. ACM, New York (2007)
8. Tuarob, S., Pouchard, L.C., Mitra, P., Giles, C.L.: A generalized topic modeling approach for automatic document annotation. Int. J. Digit. Libr. **16**, 111–128 (2015)
9. Newman, D., Karimi, S., Cavedon, L.: Using topic models to interpret MEDLINE's medical subject headings. In: Nicholson, A., Li, X. (eds.) AI 2009. LNCS (LNAI), vol. 5866, pp. 270–279. Springer, Heidelberg (2009)
10. Aletras, N., Stevenson, M., Clough, P.: Computing Similarity Between Items in a Digital Library of Cultural Heritage. J. Comput. Cult. Herit. **5**, 16:1–16:19 (2013)
11. Aletras, N., Baldwin, T., Lau, J.H., Stevenson, M.: Representing topics labels for exploring digital libraries. In: ACM/IEEE Joint Conference on Digital Libraries (JCDL 2014) International Conference on Theory and Practice of Digital Libraries (TPDL 2014), London, September 8–12 (2014)
12. Bolelli, L., Ertekin, S., Zhou, D., Giles, C.L.: Finding topic trends in digital libraries. In: Proc. 2009 Jt. Int. Conf. Digit. Libr., JCDL 2009, p. 69 (2009)
13. Nguyen, S.H., Chowdhury, G.: Digital library research (1990-2010): a knowledge map of core topics and subtopics. In: Airong, J. (ed.) ICADL 2011. LNCS, vol. 7008, pp. 368–372. Springer, Heidelberg (2011)
14. Pomerantz, J., Wildemuth, B.M., Yang, S., Fox, E.A.: Curriculum development for digital libraries. In: Proceedings of the 6th ACM/IEEE-CS Joint Conference on Digital Libraries, pp. 175–184. ACM, New York (2006)
15. Tsakonas, G., Mitrelis, A., Papachristopoulos, L., Papatheodorou C.: An exploration of the research trends in the digital library evaluation domain. In: 12th ACM/IEEE-CS Joint Conference on Digital Libraries, pp. 347–348. ACM, New York (2012)
16. Fox, C.: A Stop List for General Text. SIGIR Forum **24**, 19–21 (1989)
17. Mimno, D.: jsLDA: An implementation of latent Dirichlet allocation in javascript. https://github.com/mimno/jsLDA
18. Moro, S., Cortez, P., Rita, P.: Business intelligence in banking: A literature analysis from 2002 to 2013 using text mining and latent Dirichlet allocation. Expert Syst. Appl. **42**, 1314–1324 (2015)
19. Marshall, C.C., Ruotolo, C.: Reading-in-the-small: a study of reading on small form factor devices. In: Proceedings of the 2nd ACM/IEEE-CS Joint Conference on Digital Libraries, pp. 56–64. ACM Press, New York (2002)
20. Fuhr, N., Tsakonas, G., Aalberg, T., Agosti, M., Hansen, P., Kapidakis, S., Klas, C.-P., Kovaks, L., Landoni, M., Micsik, A., Papatheodorou, C., Peters, C., Solvberg, I.: Evaluation of Digital Libraries. Int. J. Digit. Libr. **8**, 21–38 (2007)
21. Bruce, T.R., Hillmann, D.I.: The continuum of metadata quality: defining, expressing, exploiting. In: Hillman, D., Westbrooks, E. (eds.) Metadata in practice. ALA Editions, Chicago (2004)

Application of Metadata Standards for Interoperability Between Species Distribution Models

Cleverton Borba[1,2(✉)] and Pedro Luiz Pizzigatti Correa[1]

[1] Computer Engineering Department, University of Sao Paulo (USP), São Paulo, Brazil
{cleverton.borba,pedro.correa}@usp.br,
cleverton.borba@unasp.edu.br
[2] Computer Science Department, Centro Universitário Adventista
de São Paulo (UNASP), São Paulo, Brazil

Abstract. This paper presents a study about the use of metadata standards for the area of Biodiversity Informatics. Species Distribution Modeling tools generated models that offer information about species distribution and allow scientists, researchers, environmentalists, companies and govern to make decisions to protect and preserve biodiversity. Studies reveal that this area require new technologies and this include the interoperability between models generated by Species Distribution Tools. To ensure interoperability, we present a schema that use metadata standards to generate XML archives that contain all information necessary to reuse models of species distribution. This paper is part of a major study that claims for the use of a metadata standards as a fundamental way to provide structured biodiversity information.

Keywords: Species distribution modeling · Metadata · Biodiversity informatics · Ecological informatics · Interoperability

1   Introduction

In the last two decades, support technologies to biodiversity conservation has been developed and enhanced. The responsible area for studies and research for the use of technology to biodiversity conservation is called Biodiversity Informatics, or Ecological Informatics [5], [13], [17], and according Peterson [11] this area has the objective to meet the demand for technology to support the conservation and preservation of biodiversity.

Michener and Jones in [10] declare that the Ecological Informatics offers tools and approaches to ecological data management and transform data into information and knowledge. Recognized as a new area of study, and in an early stage of development, new tools and technologies are still in progress. Among these developments, we can mention the Species Distribution Modeling (SDM) tools, that according Elith [2] has as main objectives: (1) the prediction of the current species distribution, (2) understand environmental related factors, and (3) perform prediction of species abundance.

E. Garoufallou et al. (Eds.): MTSR 2015, CCIS 544, pp. 113–118, 2015.
DOI: 10.1007/978-3-319-24129-6_10

However, studies have shown that the species distribution modeling has become more complex [14] and [7], and equally the SDM tools require application of new techniques and improvements of modeling strategies [12] as interoperability of data between the available tools.

Among the most serious problems in scientific biodiversity projects is the necessity to "integrate data from different sources, software applications and services for analysis, visualization and publication, attempting to offer interoperability of data, information, applications and tools" [1].

Berendsohn and the other authors said in [1] that the lack of shared vocabularies and the diversity of data structures used avoids data sharing. Biodiversity data is derived from many sources, different formats, and available on various hardware and software platforms. An essential step to understand the global biodiversity patterns is to provide a standardized view of these heterogeneous data sources to improve interoperability, and is the key to the advance of common terms [15].

In this context metadata is the information that describes "who, what, where, when, why and how" a set of ecological data was collected [3]. In other words, metadata is data explaining about data. Therefore, the use of metadata standard helps the interoperability between biodiversity data, and consequently support the connection between SDM tools.

The objective of this paper is to show how metadata standards can aid the interoperability between models generated by SDM tools, and ensure the reusability of models and data in the same tool or another one.

The methodology used in this research is first, show the contribution of metadata standards for the species distribution modeling and for the Biodiversity Informatics area, after that study the metadata standard that more could help the object of this research to make interoperable, parameters, algorithms, species occurrence data, and all information used to generate model of SDM. This paper is part of a major research about interoperability.

2   Metadata Standards for Species Distribution Modeling

Michener et al. in [9] affirm that three factors are fundamental and depend on the availability of suitable and appropriate metadata: (1) the value of the biodiversity data in long term, (2) the use of environmental data for the ecological advancing understanding, and (3) significant environmental problem solving. This metadata present descriptive information, the context, quality, and structure accessibility of ecological information.

For technological and computational tools in Biodiversity Informatics, metadata standards are important to understand, process, and share ecological information. Then below are presented some metadata standards used at some stage of biodiversity information lifecycle.

Dublin Core is defined by [6] as a simplest set of elements but effective to describe a wide range of features, and it has a model that allows different communities to use their elements allowing specific domain extensions that make sense in a more limited area of operation. As the definition implies, this metadata standard is not specific to biodiversity data, however it offered basis for other standards were created for specific ecological information.

Based on the standard Dublin Core, Wieczorek [16] defines Darwin Core standard as a manual of norms that includes a glossary of terms, concepts, attributes or properties that is designed to facilitate the sharing of information on biodiversity. Darwin Core is used in many tools and portals that have the objective to process and turn available biodiversity information.

Darwin Core Archive, was presented by [4] to support the Biodiversity Informatics area, is internationally recognized, simplifying the biodiversity data sharing, and was developed based on the Darwin Core standard. The main idea of this standard is that their archives are logically organized in a way that the authors call "star", with one data archive surrounded by a number of extension files [4].

Other metadata standard is the EML (Ecological Metadata Language) that has emerged as a metadata language to ecological information and biodiversity, and according Fegraus et al. [3] EML is a method for formalizing and standardizing the set of concepts that are essential for the description of environmental data.

EML is presented as a implementation of a set of XML archives that can be used in a modular and extensible way to document ecological data. Each EML module is designed to describe a logical part of the total metadata that must be included in any set of ecological data [8].

Exist other metadata standards, but in this research we decide to use this four metadata because they are related each other, as presented in the Figure 1, and they are used for famous portals of biodiversity data, as GBIF (http://www.gbif.com), SpeciesLink (http://splink.cria.org.br/), ALA (www.ala.org.au), among others.

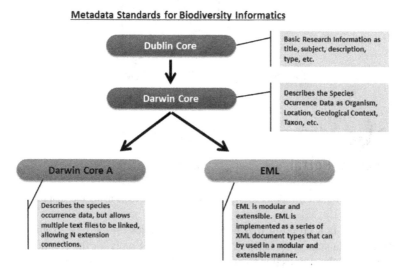

Fig. 1. "Genealogy" of metadata standards used in the Biodiversity Informatics and were used in this research.

3   Application of Metadata Standard for Interoperability Between SDM Tools.

The use of metadata standard is necessary to ensure interoperability between models generated by SDM tools. A metadata standard presents a pattern vocabulary to communicate biodiversity data through SDM tools, portals and researchers.

For this initial research, two metadata standards were chose, the Darwin Core Archive (DwA) and EML. One of the features of DwA, is that to produce a file in this format, is not necessary to install any data editing software, making it an option of easy usability. To produce a EML metadata format, is available two tools, Metacat, Morpho, and also in a R package to access biodiversity repositories [8].

The Fig. 2 shows a scheme for reusing models generated by SDM tools that use metadata standards to ensure interoperability between these models. The necessary information to make a species distribution model available for reuse are, occurrence data used on the modeling, the algorithm used, the parameter defined for the algorithm, the "n" layers used, and the map generated by the SDM tool.

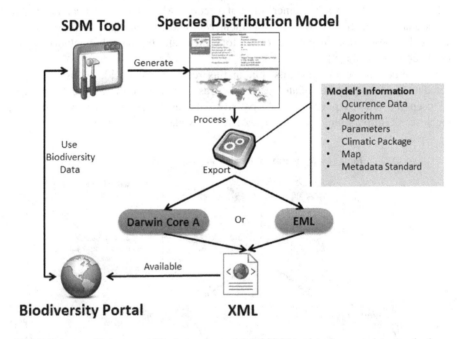

Fig. 2. Scheme of interoperability between models of SDM tools using metadata standards.

This architecture is a proposal that needs further studies on the best usability of the available metadata standards. Despite the availability of tools for the creation of EML files in this work, the proposal is to use only the definition of the standard EML.

4   Conclusion

In conclusion, through this research it was possible to realize the importance of technological and computational studies for the conservation and preservation of biodiversity. Increasingly, decision makers need tools that provide relevant information and easy access. Among these studies, computational interoperability has been mentioned by authors of the area as an important aspect to SDM tools.

In this context, this paper presented some metadata standards that have been used in the area of Biodiversity Informatics and more specifically in Species Distribution Modeling. Metadata standards offered for biodiversity area are at an advanced stage of development and use. For this reason, the use of metadata standards already well defined has been chosen for this work proposal.

Therefore, this article presents a framework for the development of an interoperable connector that will abstract the information of species distribution models generated by the tools and make these data available on a biodiversity standard metadata. The abstracted data models are the algorithms, parameters, occurrence data, environmental layers, and the generated map. With all the information at hand, it is possible to generate a set of files to be reused, thus producing a computing interoperability of species distribution models.

Future Research: As future work, metadata standards studies on biodiversity area will be improved. It will also be developed computational connector in the Java programming language and also studies related to export of metadata archives on Jason format for mobile devices.

References

1. Berendsohn, W.G., Güntsch, A., Hoffmann, N., Kohlbecker, A., Luther, K., Müller, A.: Biodiversity information platforms: From standards to interoperability. ZooKeys **150**, 71–87 (2011)
2. Elith, J., Philips, S.J., Hastie, T., Dudik, M., Chee, Y.E., Yates, C.J.: A statistical explanation of maxent for ecologists. Diversity and Distributions **17**, 43–57 (2011)
3. Fegraus, E.H., Andelman, S., Jones, M.B., Schildhauer, M.: Maximizing the Value of Ecological Data with Structured Metadata: An Introduction to Ecological Metadata Language (EML) and Principles for Metadata Creation. Bulletin of the Ecological Society of America, 158–168 (2005)
4. GBIF: Darwin Core Archives – How-to Guide. Copenhagen: Global Biodiversity Information Facility (2010)
5. Goethals, P.L.M., Chon, T.S.: Special issue of the 7th International Conference on Ecological Informatics, December 13-16, Ghent, Belgium: 'Unravelling complexity and supporting sustainability' (2010). Ecological Informatics **17**, 1–2 (2013)
6. Hillmann, D.: Using Dublin Core (2015). http://www.dublincore.org/documents/usageguide/ (retrieved March 04, 2015)
7. Hortal, J., Roura-Pascual, N., Sanders, N.J., Rahbek, C.: Understanding (insect) species distributions across spatial scales. Ecography **33**, 51–53 (2010)

8. KNB: Ecological Metadata Language (EML) Specification: The Knowledge Network for Biocomplexity (2015)
9. Michener, W.K., Brunt, J.W., Helly, J.J., Kirchner, T.B., Stafford, S.G.: Nongeospatial Metadata For The Ecological Sciences. Ecological Applications **7**, 330–342 (1997)
10. Michener, W.K., Jones, M.B.: Ecoinformatics: supporting ecology as a data-intensive science. Trends in Ecology & Evolution **27**, 85–93 (2012)
11. Peterson, A.T., Knapp, S., Guralnick, R., Soberón, J., Holder, M.T.: The big questions for biodiversity informatics. Systematics & Biodiversity **8**(2), 159–168 (2010)
12. Peterson, A.T., Soberón, J., Pearson, R.G., Anderson, R.P., Martínez-Meyer, E., Nakamura, M., Araújo, M.B.: Ecological Niches and Geographic Distributions. Princeton University Press, UK (2011)
13. Recknagel, F.: Ecological informatics: A discipline in the making. Ecological Informatics **6**(1), 1–3 (2011)
14. Soberón, J., Nakamura, M.: Niches and distributional areas: concepts, methods, and assumptions. Paper presented at the PNAS Proceedings of the National Academy of Sciences of the United States of America (2009)
15. Wieczorek, J., Bloom, D., Guralnick, R., Blum, S., Döring, M., Giovanni, R., Vieglais, D.: Darwin Core: An Evolving Community-Developed Biodiversity Data Standard. PLoS ONE **7** (2012)
16. Wieczorek, J., Döring, M., De Giovanni, R., Robertson, T., Vieglais, D.: Darwin Core (2009). http://rs.tdwg.org/dwc/index.htm (retrieved April 15, 2015)
17. Yang, Z.F.: Ecological informatics for ecosystem conservation in view of environmental risk assessment and management. Stochastic Environmental Research and Risk Assessment **25**(5), 641–642 (2011)

Data Analysis, Reuse and Visualization

Majority Voting Re-ranking Algorithm for Content Based-Image Retrieval

Mawloud Mosbah[(⊠)] and Bachir Boucheham

University 20 Août 1955 of Skikda, Skikda, Algeria
mos_nasa@hotmail.fr, boucheham_bachir@yahoo.fr

Abstract. We propose a new algorithm, known as Majority Voting Re-ranking Algorithm (MVRA), which re-ranks the first returned images answered by an image retrieval system. Since this algorithm proceeds to change the images rate before any visualizing to the user, it does not require any assistance. The algorithm has been experimented using the Wang database and the Google image engine and has been compared to other methods based on two clustering algorithms namely: HACM and K-means. The obtained results indicate the clear superiority of the proposed algorithm.

Keywords: Image retrieval · Re-ranking · Majority voting re-ranking · HACM · K-means · Precision · Recall

1 Introduction

Since its appearance as a research field, image retrieval area has received great interest. Indeed, a lot of work has been done in this domain and many advances have been made ranging from utilizing textual annotation [7], adapting some techniques coming from documentary research to making use of image features such as color [1, 2], [14], [29], [30, 31, 32,], texture [17],[19] and shape [20]. The textual search paradigm suffers from the subjectivity problem when the latter, based on visual features, has the semantic gap as an obstacle. Attempts to attenuate the semantic gap between the low level features and the high level concepts within images include features fusion [25]. However this approach induces some problems, such as: (i) the curse of dimensionality and the heterogeneous representation of features if the combination is performed during the indexation stage [6], (ii) how to weight the scores of the different used features if the fusion is done only on the scores [12]. Even with features conjunction, the effectiveness remains far from satisfying the user. For this purpose, another solution has been proposed known as relevance feedback mechanism [24], [11], [23], [35]. According to this mechanism, the system exploits additional information provided by the user with his/her relevance judgment of the first returned images. This additional information allows the system to more understand the user need through learning. The results of this learning will be applied later in order to re-rank the other images of the asked database. A large spectrum of learning algorithms, coming from pattern recognition field, have been employed: SVM [16], the genetic programming [13], fuzzy sets [3]..Etc.

© Springer International Publishing Switzerland 2015
E. Garoufallou et al. (Eds.): MTSR 2015, CCIS 544, pp. 121–131, 2015.
DOI: 10.1007/978-3-319-24129-6_11

Unfortunately, besides the burden posed on the user, there are many obstacles during learning that hinder producing a good predictor or classification model, among of them are: (i) the set of images labelled by the user and being utilized during learning process remains not sufficient, (ii) occurrences of images visualized to be annotated as non-relevant by the user do not reflect the real distribution or all the entities of non-relevant images available within the asked database [36].

As an alternative falling between the two cited strategies (fusion and re-ranking based on learning) is the automatic re-ranking without any learning and without any feedback. The only difference between the ranking and re-ranking adopting this alternative is that the signature and similarity formulas can be changed, in addition to the second implicit difference that of the initial ranking is conducted over all the database images while the re-ranking is applied only on the first subset image. Our paper falls then into this category.

The remainder of this paper is organized as follows: in section 2, we give a survey on the systems adopting fusion and re-ranking without relevance feedback mechanism, section 3 is devoted to explain our proposed algorithm, the experimental results have been shown on section 4. Discussion, future perspectives and some drawn conclusions have been given in section 5.

2   Related Works

 Review of literature shows that only few works are related to the re-ranking without relevance feedback or without user assistance. We can also remark that most systems belonging to this class are based on the clustering algorithms and the majority of them have been constructed to work on the web. In [5] for instance, the authors have proposed ReS-PEC system (Re-ranking sets of Pictures by Exploiting Consistency). This system has several integral components. First, each image is segmented into similar regions or blobs. The set of feature vectors retrieved from the top image search results is then clustered using the mean shift algorithm. They then posit the cluster that corresponds to the largest number of parent images to be the object of interest, and they refer to this as the significant cluster. Lastly, a larger set of images from the image search is re-ranked based on similarity to this significant cluster. Other work in this context is [28], in which the authors have given a new approach to improve also the results answered by a web retrieval engine using a keywords query. This approach uses the visual features of majority of images to determine the new rank of images. For finding the visual features of majority of images, they define two different concepts: one is using of clustering, the other is using of average of image features (computational average values of image features). They have proposed two methods for the both concepts. In [27], images are first retrieved using visual features such as colour histogram. Next, the retrieved images are analysed using hierarchical agglomerative clustering method (HACM) and the rank of the results is adjusted according to the distance of a cluster from a query.

A fundamental problem that frequently arises in a great variety of fields such as pattern recognition, image processing, machine learning and statistics is the clustering problem [18], in its basic form the clustering problem is defined as the problem of finding groups of data points in a given data set. Each of these groups is called a cluster and can be defined as a region in which the density of objects is locally higher than in other regions [22].

The clustering operation aims to classify elements within its classes automatically. It is then unsupervised classification that does not require any additional information of adjustment neither at the beginning nor during the classification operation.

Clustering techniques for improving retrieval performance have been proposed in the literature on information retrieval [21], [33], and also proposed in CBIR [7, 8, 9], [26]. Classifying the answered images within two classes (relevant and non-relevant) helps to find another rank for these images susceptible to be better than the initial ranking. This new ranking imposed implicitly by the clustering operation consists of ranking the images belonging to the relevant class first followed by the images belonging to the non-relevant class. The class of high number of images is considered as the relevant class while the other which contains the fewer number of images is qualified as non-relevant class.

3   The Proposed Algorithm

Our proposed algorithm (Majority Voting Re-ranking Algorithm: MVRA) aims to rerank the first returned images in order to eliminate noise returned within results. It proceeds to organize a vote between the first returned images. As any vote operation, there are Candidates and Electors. The candidates are initially the last subset images while the electors are the rest of the set (The first subset). During every iteration, the containing of these two subsets has to be changed. For the Candidates set, the last two images after re-ranking (after voting operation) should be discarded and the last two images of the Electors set should be added. This gives the sense that the Candidates set is a window which moves towards the somet during each iteration until reach it during the last one. The algorithm is then as follows:

```
The MVRA Algorithm
Let N: the number of the first returned images.
Initialization :
Re-ranking_set= Φ.
Images= {Im1,Im2, …, ImN}    (The First Returned Images)
Candidates= {Im(N-4), Im(N-3), Im(N-2), Im(N-1), ImN}
Electors=Images minus Candidates= {Im1, Im2,…, Im(N-5)}

1. Calculate the distance matrix : Electors*Candidates
WHILE (Electors ≠ Φ) do
2. Organizing a vote: Each elector from Electors gives one point for one
image of the Candidates who's the distance is the smallest.
3. Re-ranking the Candidates based on the points collected during the vote
process.
4.
Re_ranking_set=re-ranking_set plus the last both images within the Candi-
dates.
Candidates=candidates minus the last two images within the Candidates.
Candidates=the last both images within the Electors plus Candidates.
Electors= Electors minus the last two images within the Electors.
END WHILE
Inversing the re-ranking set before visualizing it to the user.
END.
```

4   Experimental Results

In order to test the plus added by the proposed algorithm and its effectiveness with respect to HACM and K-means, we have used the first set images returned by a CBIR system working on the Wang repository [34]. This base includes 1000 heterogeneous images distributed over 10 semantic classes. We have also used the first set of images answered by the Google Image engine [15]. Either with The employed CBIR system which achieves the initial research or during the re-ranking, we use the color moments in the HSV color space as an indexing signature and the Euclidean distance as a matching measure. Note that The Google Image engine utilizes an index based on textual annotation. Using color moments is an alternative aiming to capture quickly the global information in the image which helps to obtain an interactive system with reasonable response time and reduce data stored during the indexation stage [32] by computing only some dominant attributes such as: the first order moment (the Mean), the second order moment (the Variance) and the third order moment (Skewness). These three low order moments are given respectively by the following formulas:

- The Mean

$$\grave{u}_i = \frac{1}{N} \sum_{j=1}^{N} f_{ij} \tag{1}$$

- The Variance

$$\sigma_i = \sqrt{\frac{1}{N} \sum_{j=1}^{N} \left(f_{ij} - \grave{u}_i \right)^2} \tag{2}$$

- The Skewness

$$\pounds_i = \left(\frac{1}{N} \sum_{j=1}^{N} \left(f_{ij} - \grave{u}_i \right)^3 \right)^{\frac{1}{3}} \tag{3}$$

As a matching measure, we have utilized the Euclidean distance given by the following formula:

$$L_2(V, V') = \left(\sum_{m=1}^{M} \left(V_m - V'_m \right)^2 \right)^{\frac{1}{2}} \tag{4}$$

To compare results in the case of a local database such as Wang database, we construct the Precision/Recall curves as shown in the following figures. The precision and Recall values have been obtained using the following formulas [4]:

$$\mathrm{Pr}\,ecision = \frac{Number \text{ of relevant images retrieved}}{Total \text{ number of images retrieved}} \tag{5}$$

$$\mathrm{Re}\,call = \frac{Number \text{ of relevant images retrieved}}{Total \text{ number of images in the database}} \tag{6}$$

Note that, we cannot compute the recall values in the case of results answered by Google image engine because the interrogated database is on line and we cannot know, by consequence, the value of the denominator that of the total number of relevant images in the database. For this purpose, rather than recall, we utilize the number of returned images.

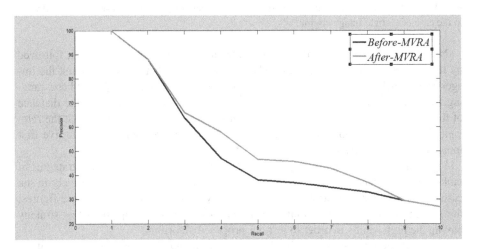

Fig. 1. The Average Precision/Recall curves before and after re-ranking by MVRA in the case of CBIR system.

Note that the blue curve represents the case without applying MVRA algorithm and the red curve is related to the case after utilizing the MVRA algorithm.

According to the results shown in Fig.1 and Fig. 2, a significant improvement is obtained when applying the new proposed algorithm.

We also compare our algorithm to other methods based on HACM and K-means clustering algorithms. The purpose of the clustering algorithm is to distinguish the relevant images from the non-relevant ones. We consider here only the binary unsupervised classification. The application of the clustering algorithm then produces two classes, since the images input of the cluster operation are the results returned by another image retrieval system either based text or based on visual descriptors, the majority of them are then relevant. This remark is important to designate the relevant class from the non-relevant one. In light of this remark, the class with the high number of images constitutes the relevant class and vice versa.

Fig. 2. The Precision/Number of returned images curves before and after re-ranking by MVRA in the case of Google Image engine.

Naturally the images belonging to the relevant-class will be ranked first, followed by the images of non-relevant class. The question to rise here is how to rank the images inside each class. Many strategies, introduced in [28], can be applied here, ranging from keeping the initial rank until computing another rank based on the distance of the image with the centroid of its class, of the large class (that means that the relevant class), the centroid of all the images clustered, and the centroid of the five first images of the initial research.

Fig. 3 and Fig. 4 depict respectively the comparison between the five strategies of ranking images inside each class and so for HACM and K-means respectively in the case of re-ranking results answered by a CBIR system. As described by these figures, the strategy that keeps the initial rank is the best one. We adopt then this strategy having the high results in order to test our proposed algorithm.

Note that the curves within Fig. 3, Fig. 4, Fig. 6 and Fig. 7 represent cases of re-ranking elements within clusters in this respect: keeping initial rate, utilizing the centroid of the cluster, utilizing the centroid of the large cluster, utilizing the centroid of all images and utilizing the centroid of the 5 first images.

According to Fig. 3 and Fig. 4 keeping the initial rank where re-ranking images within its clusters is the best case in terms of effectiveness and so over the both clustering algorithms either based on HACM or k-means.

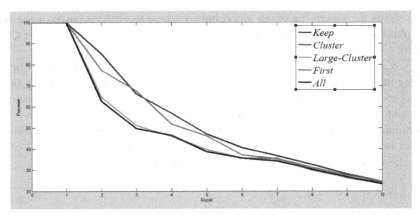

Fig. 3. The Precision/Recall curves after re-ranking with methods based on HACM in the case of CBIR system.

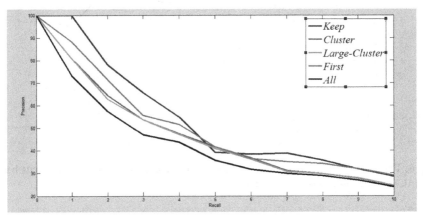

Fig. 4. The Precision/Recall curves after re-ranking with methods based on K-means in the case of CBIR system.

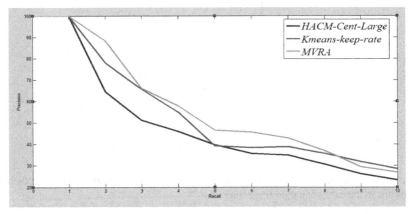

Fig. 5. The comparison in terms of Precision/Recall between the three strategies in the case of CBIR system.

Fig. 5 shows the superiority of our algorithm compared to methods based on the both algorithms HACM and K-means in the case of re-ranking results returned by a CBIR system.

Fig. 6 and Fig. 7 depict respectively the comparison between the five strategies of ranking images inside each class and so for HACM and K-means respectively in the case of re-ranking results answered by Google Image engine in order to designate the best one for comparing it with our proposed algorithm.

Keeping the initial rank is the best strategy when using K-means while attributing another rank for images based on the distance of the image with the centroid of the large cluster seems to be the best in the case of HACM algorithm.

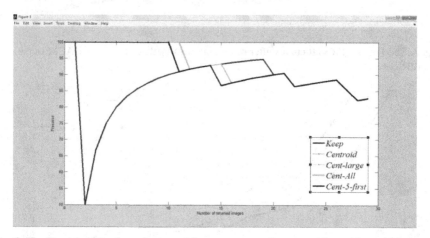

Fig. 6. The Precision/Number of returned Images curves after re-ranking with methods based on HACM in the case of Google Image engine.

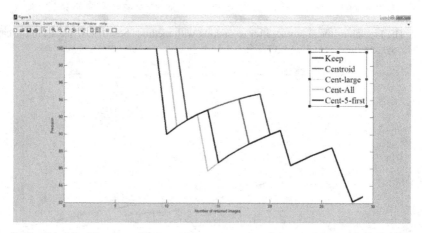

Fig. 7. The Precision/Number of Returned images curves after re-ranking with methods based on K-means in the case of Google Image engine.

According to Fig. 6, there are two strategies that can be considered the best in the case of using HACM: based on the centroid of the large cluster and the centroid of all images. Fig. 7, describing strategies of re-ranking in the case of k-means, indicates that keeping the initial ranking of images when re-ranking images in the cluster remains the best case in terms of performance.

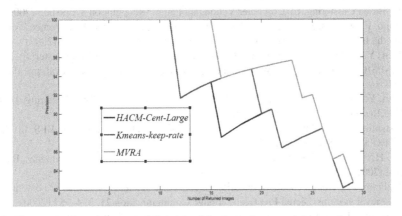

Fig. 8. The comparison in terms of Precision/Number of returned Images between the three strategies in the case of Google Image engine.

Results shown in Fig. 8 indicate the clear superiority of our algorithm over the other methods based on the HACM and K-means cluster algorithms in the case of re-ranking results answered by the Google Image engine.

5   Conclusion

We have proposed a new algorithm for re-ranking results answered by an image re-search system. This algorithm, experimented on a CBIR system working on the Wang database and Google image engine, has improved the results in terms of precision and it outperforms methods based on HACM and K-means clustering algorithms. As a perspective, we plan to consider the proposed algorithm as a ranking method rather than re-ranking one. In other words, we plan to apply the algorithm on all database images. Other alternative consists of combining the proposed algorithm with other re-ranking algorithms, which hopefully will yield better results.

References

1. Abdesselam, A., Wang, H., Kulathuramaiyer, N.: Spiral Bit-string Representation of Color for Image Retrieval. The International Arab Journal of Information Technology **7**(3), 223–230 (2010)
2. Al-Hamami, A., Al-Rashdan, H.: Improving the Effectiveness of the Color Coherence Vector. The International Arab Journal of Information Technology **7**(3), 324–332 (2010)

3. Arevalillo-Herràez, M., Zacarés, M., Benavent, X., Esther, D.: A relevance feedback CBIR algorithm based on fuzzy sets. Signal Processing: Image Communication **23**, 490–504 (2008)
4. Babu, G.P., Mehre, B.M., Kanhalli, M.S.: Color Indexing for Efficient Image Retrieval. Multimedia Tools Application **1**, 327–348 (1995)
5. Ben-Haim, N., Babenko, B., Belongie, S.: Improving Web-based Image Search via Content Based Clustering. In: Computer Vision and Pattern Recognition Workshop (2006)
6. Bruno, E., Kludas, J., Marchand-Maillet, S.: Combining Multimodal Preferences for Multimedia Information Retrieval. In: *MIR 2007* Augsburg, Bavaria, Germany (2007)
7. Chen, Y., Wang, J.Z., Krovetz, R.: Content-Based Image Retrieval by Clustering. In: 5th ACM SIGMM International Workshop on Multimedia Information Retrieval, pp. 193–200 (2003)
8. Chen, Y., Wang, J.Z., Krovetz, R.: Content-Based Image Retrieval by Clustering. In: *MIR 2003* Berkeley, California, USA (2003)
9. Costantini, L., Nicolussi, R.: Image Clustering Fusion Technique Based on BFS. In: CIKM 2011 Glasgow, Scotland, UK (2011)
10. Dai, H.V.: Association texte + images pour l'indexation et la recherche d'images. Rapport final (2009)
11. Doulamis, N., Doulamis, A.: Evaluation of relevance feedback schemes in content-based in retrieval systems. Signal Processing: Image Communication **21**, 334–357 (2006)
12. Escalante, H.J., Hérnadez, C.A., Sucar, L.E., Montes, M.: Late Fusion of Heterogenous Methods for Multimedia Image Retrieval. In: MIR 2008 Vancouver, British Columbia, Canada (2008)
13. Ferreira, C.D., Santos, J.A., da Torres, R.S., Gonçalves, M.A., Rezende, R.C., Fan, W.: Relevance Feedback based on genetic programming for Image Retrieval. Pattern Recognition Letters **32**, 27–37 (2011)
14. Gong, Y., Chuan, C.H., Xiaoyi, G.: Image Indexing and Retrieval Using Color Histograms. Multimedia Tools and Applications **2**, 133–156 (1996)
15. Google Image Engine, December 5 2013. http://www.google.com/imghp
16. Hoi, C., Lyu, M.R.: A Novel Log-based Relevance Feedback Technique in Content-based Image Retrieval. In: MM 2004, New York, USA (2004)
17. Huang, P.W., Dai, S.K., Lin, P.L.: Texture image retrieval and image segmentation using composite sub-band gradient vectors. Journal of Visual Communication and Image Representation **17**(5), 947–957 (2006)
18. Ain, A.K., Murty, M.N., Flynn, P.J.: Data clustering: A review. ACM Computing Surveys **31**(3), 264–323 (1999)
19. Jhanwar, N., Chaudhuri, S., Seetharaman, G., Zavidovique, B.: Content based image retrieval using motif co-occurrence matrix. Image and Vision Computing **22**(14), 1211–1220 (2004)
20. Ko, B.C., Byun, H.: FRIP: A region-based image retrieval tool using automatic image segmentation and stepwise boolean and matching. IEEE Transactions on Multimedia **7**(1), 105–113 (2005)
21. Lee, K.S., Park, Y.C., Choi, K.S.: Re-ranking model based on document clusters. Inf. Process. Manag. **37**(1), 1–14 (2001)
22. Likas, A., Vlassis, N., Verbeek, J.: The Global K-means Clustering Algorithm. IAS technical report series, nr. IAS-UVA-01-02 (2003)
23. MacArthur, S., Brodley, C.E., Kak, A.C.: Interactive Content-Based Image Retrieval Using Relevance Feedback. Computer Vision and Image Understanding **88**, 55–75 (2002)

24. Mosbah, M., Boucheham, B.: Relevance Feedback within CBIR Systems. International Journal of Computer, Information Science and Engineering **8**(4), 19–23 (2014)
25. Ngu, A., Sheng, Q., Huynh, D., Lei, R.: Combining multi-visual features for efficient indexing in a large image database. The VLDB Journal **9**, 279–293 (2001)
26. Park, G., Baek, Y., Lee, H.-K.: A ranking algorithm using dynamic clustering for content-based image retrieval. In: Lew, M., Sebe, N., Eakins, J.P. (eds.) CIVR 2002. LNCS, vol. 2383, pp. 328–337. Springer, Heidelberg (2002)
27. Park, G., Baek, Y., Lee, H.K.: Re-ranking Algorithm Using Post-Retrieval Clustering for Content-based Image Retrieval. Information Processing and Management (2003)
28. Park, G., Baek, Y., Lee, H.K.: Web Image Retrieval Using Majority-based Ranking Approach Mltimedia Tools Application **31**, 195–219 (2006)
29. Pass, G., Zabith, R.: Histogramme Refinement for Content based Image Retrieval. In: IEEE Workshop on Applications of Computer Vision, pp. 96–102 (1996)
30. Qiu, G.: Embedded colour image coding for content-based retrieval. Journal of Visual Communication and Image Representation **15**(4), 507–521 (2004)
31. Swain, M.J., Ballard, D.H.: Color Indexing International Journal of Computer Vision **7**, 11–32 (1991)
32. Strieker, M.A., Orengo, M.: Similarity of color images. In: Proceedings of SPIE Storage and Retrieval for Image and Video Databases III, vol. 2185, pp. 381–392, San Jose, CA (1995)
33. Tombros, A., Villa, R., Van Rijsbegen, C.J.: The Effectiveness of query-specific hierarchic clustering in information retrieval. Inf. Process. Manag. **38**(4), 559–582 (2002)
34. Wang Images Database, December 5 2013. http://Wang.ist.psu.edu/docs/related.shtml
35. Zhou, X.S., Huang, T.S.: Relevance Feedback in image retrieval A comprehensive review. Multimedia Systems **8**, 536–544 (2003)
36. Zhou, X.S., Huang, T.S.: Small Sample Learning during Multimedia Retrieval using BiasMap. In: IEEE Int'1 Conf Computer Vision and Pattern Recognition, Hawaii (2001)

Narrative Analysis for HyperGraph Ontology of Movies Using Plot Units

Sandeep Reddy Biddala$^{(\boxtimes)}$ and Navjyoti Singh

Center for Exact Humanities, IIIT Hyderabad, Hyderabad, India
bs.reddy@research.iiit.ac.in, navjyoti@iiit.ac.in

Abstract. We give a initial report on the potential of narrative theory driven graph based representations of movies for narrative analysis and summarization. This is done using automatic generation of Plot Units and determination of affect states for characters. Given the power of theory driven graph representations of movies based on these initial experiments, we present a graph ontology for movies based on hypergraphs. An example as to how graph representations for narrative analysis fit into this ontology is also presented. We thus argue that a graph data model for the content of movies could better capture its underlying semantics.

Keywords: Plot units · Ontology · Hypergraphs · Movies · Narrative analysis

1 Introduction and Related Work

Researches on narrative analysis for movies have been attempting to bridge the semantic gap between the data representations and narrative content of the movies. But many of the techniques and applications for semantic processing of films uses audio and video signal processing techniques which either deal with the analysis of movie at frame level [1,2] or event level [3,4]. Depending on the system, the segments of a movie are annotated with audio visual features (such as the dominant color of a shot), structural features or semantic features [5]. Many times these low level features undermine the importance of story and other narrative features.

There have also been attempts to index, summarize and classify movies with supporting files like subtitles and movie scripts like in [6,7,8]. Some attempts have also been made to analyze movies from the perspective of social relationships of characters line [9,10,11]. These proposed methods aim to capture the semantic relations between various entities in a movie in the form of a graph. However, the semantics they generate are very restrictive, because they are not based on well defined and acceptable theories for story representation. They do not fully expose the power of graph based representations for narrative analysis.

There are many theories on the representation of story. Plot Units is one such theory developed to primarily summarize a story. It was introduced by Lehnert[12] in 1980 as a conceptual knowledge structure to represent a story. Plot units is a technique which aims to capture the memory representations of a story. Plot units are

© Springer International Publishing Switzerland 2015
E. Garoufallou et al. (Eds.): MTSR 2015, CCIS 544, pp. 132–144, 2015.
DOI: 10.1007/978-3-319-24129-6_12

conceptual structures that overlap with each other when a narrative is cohesive. When overlapping intersections between plot units are interpreted as arcs in a graph of plot units, the resulting graph encodes the plot of the story. Structural features of the graph then reveal which concepts are central to the story, and which concepts are peripheral. Plot unit structures consist of affect states for each character, and links defining the relationships between them. Plot units include three types of affect states: positive (+), negative (-), and mental (M). Affect states can be connected by causal links and cross-character links, which explain how the narrative hangs together. Causal links exist between affect states for the same character and have four types: motivation (m), actualization (a), termination (t) and equivalence (e). m and a links are forward links, while t and e links are backward. In total, there are 15 possible primitive plot unit configurations. Cross-character links indicate that a single event affects multiple characters.

Plot units kind of graph representation is particularly useful for computation of stories. Even though plot units were developed for textual stories, research[13] has shown that movies represented using plot units using manual annotation has helped users in better browsing and understanding the contents of a movie. In this paper we present a model for generating automatic plot units for movies from screenplays or movie scripts using NLP techniques based on the works of [14]. We present the results of automatic plot unit generation for two movies we experimented with and also give a preliminary report and ideas as to how they could be used for short video generation and other analyses and information extraction purposes.

The use of graph based theories for representing the content of movies brings about the need for a proper upper level ontology which can be used to model those theories and used for the annotation of a movie. There have been several movie and narrative annotation projects in the past based on different ontologies and theories. The EU funded ANSWER project [15] aimed at providing a formal language for script and movie notation, with the goal of pre-visualization. The OntoMedia project[16] uses an ontology which mainly focuses on the events and their organization into a timeline undermining other important aspects and entities of a story like characters and settings and relations which also constitute a cinematic narrative. Knowledge Intensive Interactive Story Design (KIIDS) employs KIIDSOnto[17] which incorporates Propp's model of tale[18]. The Character Based Annotation of Dramatic Media Objects (CADMOS)[19] was designed for the representation of dramatic features in audio visuals. The ontology of CADMOS which is referred as Drammar focuses on the character's motivated actions and tagging editor has been built based on Drammar called Cinematic[20].

The ontologies and annotation schema of movies described so far in these projects are descriptive. They are not well suited for graph based representations of a movie and are very restrictive. In this paper we also describe an upper level ontology for describing the narrative content of a movie. This ontology reduces a movie into hypergraph of tags which describe the content and semantics in it and is called the

HyperGraph based ontology of movie. The ontology can be used to model other graph based representations of narratives like that of plot units.

The paper is divided into the following sections. The second section explains the method of generation of plot units for movies from scripts. The third section deals with the analyses and short video generation from movie using the automatically generated plot units. The fourth section explains the HyperGraph ontology and gives an example as to how plot units could be modeled using it. The fifth section concludes the paper.

2   Automatic Generation of Plot Units for Movies

In this section we describe the procedure for the automatic generation of plot units from movie scripts. There are two main stages in our approach:
1.   Movie Script Parsing
2.   Plot Unit Creation

2.1   Movie Script Parsing

Scripts for many popular movies can be found online. Movie script is an organized description of the movement, actions, expression, and dialogs of the characters. The organization of those components in a particular script is embodied by a set of typographic and stylistic rules. The actual content of the screenplay generally follows a (semi) regular format. Fig 1. shows a small snippet of the script from the film The Godfather. In order to parse the movie script, it is modeled using regular expressions. The movie script is parsed scene wise and each scene is reconstructed in a more readable fashion which makes it easy to be able to use NLP tools on it.

2.2   Automatic Plot Unit Generation

The system we developed creates plot units considering the entire movie as one whole. The identification and creation of the plot units can be broken down to several steps as done in AESOP, a system described in [14]. The first step, character identification is done by first making a list of characters and all its referenced names and then used in conjunction with the Stanford Named Entity Recognizer and the Stanford Deterministic Coreference Resolution System. For affect state recognition we used the MPQA lexicon[21] in which a WordNet synset is assigned one of the three labels: +Effect, -Effect and Null which we assumed to correspond to positive (+), negative (-) and Mental (M) affect states respectively. The sense of a word is determined using Lesk Word Sense Disambiguation algorithm and the corresponding affect is determined using the lexicon.

Fig. 1. Snippet of a movie script

The next step, affect state projection, is done using Stanford Dependency parser based on the verb argument structure method, described in [14], which projects affect states assigned to a verb phrase (VP) onto characters based on 4 simple rules. The rules are based on the structuring of AGENT(the subject of VP), VP and PATIENT(direct object of VP).

The final step involves the creation of causal and cross-character links, which is done using some simple heuristics. For forward links (m and a-links), only 5 configurations (M $\overleftarrow{m}$ M, + $\overleftarrow{m}$ M, - $\overleftarrow{m}$ M, M $\overrightarrow{a}$ +, M $\overrightarrow{a}$ +) produce acceptable plot unit structures. So when a forward causal link is added, the types and ordering of the two affect states uniquely determine which label it should get (m or a). We used another heuristic for determining t-links, which are backward causal links (e-links are ignored because they form a very small part of the causal links). This heuristic is based on the observation that forward links connect affect states which are close by(chronologically) and backward links usually connect affect states which are far apart. A t-link is made between affect states which are farthest when the verbs associated with them are conceptually similar which is determined using Verb Ocean[22].

In addition to the heuristic used in AESOP for cross-character links(a cross-character link is added when two characters in a clause have affect states that originated from the same word), a cross character link is added between affect states of different characters if they occur closely in the movie script i.e. they appear in the same scene and they are at most two sentences away from each other, because the former heuristic adds very few cross-character links owing to the language in scripts.

3 Results and Analysis of Automatically Generated Plot Units

We applied the proposed method on two movie scripts, the results of which are presented in this section. The two movies chosen were The Godfather, which is a crime drama and The Avengers, which is a superhero action movie. The number of affect states, links and basic plot units for both the movies are presented in Table 1.

Table 1. The results of automatically generated plot units

Movie Name	Number of Characters	Number of Affect States	m-links	a-links	t-links	Cross-links
The Avengers	24	1043	329	166	127	283
The Godfather	31	806	221	123	133	237

3.1 Character Analysis Using Automatically Generated Plot Units

The number of affect states for a character suggests the importance of the character. For example, in The Godfather, the character Michael Corleone has the highest number of affect states, who happens to be protagonist of the movie. Fig 2. shows the scene wise variation of the affect states for the main character Michael Corleone of The Godfather. The activity variation and the presence of the character can be understood from the graph. The character was relatively inactive during the first 25-30 scenes, after which the character becomes more prominent in the film. The scene number 39, where Michael goes to the hospital to meet his father, is one of the pivotal scenes of the movie and it can be observed that the character has mixed emotions in this scene. Michael is worried about his father but is relieved after saving him and his own actions surprise him. Also the distribution of affect states shows that the affect states for this character are concentrated more in the middle scenes than in the establishing scenes or climax scenes. This is in accordance with the 3 act structure for screenplays where the majority of the story gets into motion in the middle scenes which fall under the confrontation act.

3.2 Related Events Detection Using Automatically Generated Plot Units

Automatically generated plot units graph could be used to find other details regarding the movie under consideration. By finding the tree using Breadth First Search(BFS) algorithm from a node of interest as root we could get the plot units which are related to it. For example, traversing the node which relates to Michael shooting Virgil Sollozzo, gave nodes relating to the assassination attempt on Vito Corleone, the kidnapping of Tom Hagen, the killing of Luca Brasi and the meeting with Michael Corleone all of which partly explain his death. For evaluation purposes, we took some affect states which represent some events in the movie The Godfather and manually identified events which are related to it. We then ran BFS from the affect state to get the events related to it. We compared them against the manually identified events, the results of which can be checked in Table 2.

Table 2. Results of Related Events Detection for The Godfather

Affect State Number	Event Being Represented	Number of Manually Identified Related Events	Number of Events Identified Through Plot Units	Number of Events Correctly Matched
398	Killing of Virgil Sollozzo	7	8	5
722	Tessio's Betrayal	5	11	4
587	Don's meeting with the heads of the five families	3	5	2

3.3   Video Summarization Using Automatically Generated Plot Units

We worked on a basic version of a summarization system using the automatically generated plot units graph. Our idea is that the articulation points of the undirected, unlabeled plot units graph can capture all the important elements of the story. Firstly we found strongly connected components (SCC) for the graph and found the articulation points for each of the SCC. Most of the SCCs contained only a small number of the nodes and articulation points. We took the largest SCC (the largest SCC in our experiments contained the about 80-85% of the nodes and therefore contained the largest number of articulation points as well) and then found out the sentences in the movie script associated with the nodes of articulation points of the SCC. One sentence before and after from the script were added to the final set of sentences. This is done in order to capture the context of the sentence in the script. Thus the short video $S = \{s_1, s_2, s_3 \ldots \ldots s_m\}$ where s_i is the sequence of the video containing the ith articulation point in chronological order of the largest SCC.

To find the sequences from the movie video which are associated with the sentences extracted from sentences of articulation points, we aligned the movie script with the corresponding subtitles file as they have time stamps for the dialogs in the movie. We used the method described in [23] which uses dynamic programming to solve the longest matching subsequence problem. We developed the short version of the movie from the original video using the sentences of articulation points and their corresponding time stamps. Table 3. gives the results for the short video generation for 2 films, The Godfather and The Avengers.

We used content attention value described in [9] for evaluating the generated short video. We compared the content attention value of the short video to the content attention value of the entire movie. Mathematically, the content attention value is

$$CA = \lambda_{ci} A_{ci} + \lambda_{lco} A_{lco} + \lambda_{lcc} A_{lcc} \tag{1}$$

where λ_{ci}, λ_{lco}, $\lambda_{lcc} \geq 0$ and $\lambda_{ci} + \lambda_{lco} + \lambda_{lcc} = 1$ are normalized combination coefficients and A_{ci}, A_{lco}, A_{lcc} are number of involved characters, leading character occurrence frequency and number of dialogues between leading characters, respectively. For video segments Seg_i, the character related features are defined as:

$$A_{ci}(Seg_i) = \sum_{m=1}^{N_c} I(f_{mi}) \tag{2}$$

$$A_{lco}(Seg_i) = \sum_{m \in L} f_{mi} \tag{3}$$

$$A_{lcc}(Seg_i) = \sum_{m \in L} \sum_{n \in L} Dia(i, m, n) \tag{4}$$

where N_c is the total number of characters involved in the movie, f_{mi} is the occurrence frequency of the mth character in segment i, $I(.) \in \{1, 0\}$ is an indication function of a boolean condition, L is the leading character set, $Dia(i, m, n)$ records the dialog counts between the mth and n^{th} leading characters in the ith movie segment.

Even though the system cannot be adjusted for the length of the generated video, the generated short video seems to be promising based on content attention values. This method can be further expanded and improved to adjust the length of the videos and used for sub story generation.

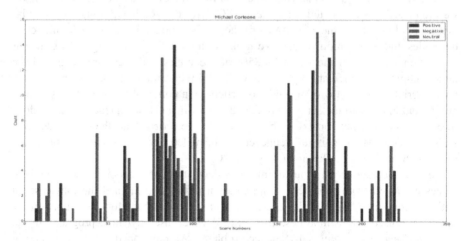

Fig. 2. Scene wise variation of affect states for Michael Corleone of The Godfather.

Table 3. Automatic Short Video Generation results.

Movie Name	Actual Runtime (in seconds)	Number of scenes	Runtime of Generated Video (in seconds)	Number of scenes in Generated Video	Number of nodes in the biggest SCC	Content Attention Value Ratio
The Avengers	8534	190	3614	83	1043	0.75
The Godfather	10629	140	5374	69	641	0.69

4   HyperGraph Based Ontology for Movies

The work presented so far gives an idea into the power of graph based representations (plot units in this case) for narrative multimedia content like movies. Narratives often require linked data kind of representation to model them rather than a structural point of view. Plot units is one such representation in addition to other representations of narratives like that of [10], [13], [24]. An ontology for a movie based on graph representations should be able to preserve the macroscopic vision that allows a quick and simultaneous understanding of various important elements of the story. It should capture all the elements of the movie; content as well as the expressive part of it. Also the ontological model should be computationally feasible and should be able to provide a tag set which can be efficiently stored in a database and retrieved for various applications. The annotation schema described by the ontology should be easy enough to be able automate the tagging process as much as possible. In this section we propose an upper level ontology upon which these graph based representations of movies can be modeled.

Movie as a narrative constitutes a flow in which various elements of its content, both aesthetic and thematic are embedded. These categories of embedded entities, culled from memory, go in building up the plot and the theme of the movies. Ontologically, there are six categories of discrete contents which are embedded in the flow as described in [25,26]. The typology of entities embedded in cinema are:

1. Setting - The locations, the settings and their nature , the time periods of the happenings in the movie
2. Characters - The characters in the movie through which the story is conveyed.
3. Significant Things - Objects which form important part of the story. Eg. like a clock.
4. Phenomenal States - States which set the base for the progress of the story in a movie like death, murder, chase etc.
5. Significant Events and Actions - These form the important actions, including the dialogues and other events which happen as part of the story.
6. Relation between the above ontological categories - For example, relations between characters, relation between character and the locale, relation between events, etc.

These ontological entities are embedded in structured units of flow like shots, scenes and episodes which need to modeled as well. Apart from these ontological categories there are many other characteristics specific to a movie like cinematography, lighting, editing, background music, special effects, etc. which form the expressive and aesthetic content of a movie. But all these expressive elements are manifested through the six basic ontological categories described and can be modeled as their attributes. More attributes may be added depending on the theory under consideration but eventually they will be expressed and manifested through the basic categories. Thus, the ontology being discussed is modeled on the six categories of entities without paying much heed to other entities of a movie which can modeled as attributes of these categories, therefore granting flexibility in terms of mapping of other graph based representations onto this ontology.

In [27,28], the structural and behavioral aspects of data that form multimedia information systems have been modeled as a graph based object oriented model. In [29,30], a data model called Directed Recursive Hypergraph Data Model (DRHM) has been described in which the content of multimedia is reduced to nodes and edges of a hypergraph. Although directed labeled graphs are frequently used in the research of content retrieval, conceptual graphs, which are used for the knowledge representation, often require to be recursive graphs – the nodes of which may recursively be graphs. Hypergraphs, which are generalisation of graphs can be used better to represent multimedia content and their relations and links because of their better expressive capabilities. Hypergraphs also have the capabilities of modeling hierarchical and structural form of data through labeled hyperedges. Graphs having the characteristics of recursive graphs and hypergraphs as well as directed ones will be required in the representation of the contents of movies. The ontology we present for movies is based on hypergraphs and is called HyperGraph Based Ontology for Movie.

This ontology reduces all the entities and elements of a movie to the hypernodes and hyperedges with attributes of a labeled recursive hypergraph. The overview of the ontology is given in Table 4.

Nodes which are essentially same but with different attributes become two different nodes and are linked together through a relation or hyperedge. For example, in the movie "The Avengers", Bruce Banner and The Hulk are the same person but with different characteristics and hence this calls for different hypernode representations for the characters and these hypernode representations are related using a hyperedge.

Table 4. Overview of HyperGraph Model of Movie

Types of Nodes	Entity Representing	Description
Basic nodes	Time	These are basic hypernodes which represent the time-line. This is the materialization of the temporal flow in the movie.
1st level nodes	Structural and Hierarchical entities like shots, scenes and episodes	They are hypernodes with properties. They are embedded in the temporal flow of movie. They are connected to the time-line nodes only once (through a start time and end time relation using a hyperedge)
2nd level nodes	Ontological categories except relations	They are hypernodes with properties. They can be connected to the basic time-line nodes through hyperedges more than once
3rd level nodes	Relations of the ontological categories	They are labled hyperedges with properties. Depending on the type and context they may or may not be connected to the basic time-line nodes. They can inturn be treated as hypernodes for a different relation.

4.1   Formal Representation of HyperGraph Based Ontology of Movies

Formally, the Movie HyperGraph H can be represented as:

$$H = Tn \cup Sh \cup Sc \cup Ep \cup S \cup C \cup T \cup E \cup P \cup R \cup St \cup Et \tag{5}$$

where Tn are the basic set of time nodes, over which all other nodes are overlaid. Sh is the set of shots, Sc is the set of scenes, Ep is the set of episodes forming the first level of hypernodes. Similarly S is the set of settings in the movie, C is the set of characters in the movie, T is the set of significant things, E is the set of events and actions and P is the set of phenomenal states. These five constitute the second level of nodes discussed previously. R is the set of relations, which are technically hyperedges, between the nodes corresponding to the ontological categories. R is a subset of the power set of all the union of the ontological categories and R itself. Formally,

$$R \subseteq \Delta (S \cup T \cup C \cup P \cup E \cup R) \tag{6}$$

$\Delta(.)$ is the power set and R is thus a recursive set of nodes. St is the set of hyper-edges which connect the first set of hypernodes (Sh,Sc,Ep), which are structural in nature, to the time nodes and, like discussed, they can appear only once on the time-line.

$$X=\{\{s,t_1,t_2\}:s\in(Sh\cup Sc\cup Ep),t_1\in Tn,t_2\in Tn\} \tag{7}$$

$$St\in\{x\in\Delta(X):\forall(s,t_1,t_2)\in x,t_1>t_2\wedge(((s,t_1,t_2),(s^{'},t_1^{'},t_2^{'})\in St\wedge s=s^{'})\Rightarrow(t_1=t_1^{'}\wedge t_2=t_2^{'}))\} \tag{8}$$

Similarly, Et is the set of hyperedges which connect the second and third set of nodes. These can appear multiple times on the timeline.

$$Y=\{\{e,t_1,t_2\}:e\in(S\cup C\cup T\cup P\cup E\cup R),t_1\in Tn,t_2\in Tn\} \tag{9}$$

$$Et\subseteq\{y\in Y:\forall(e,t_1,t_2)\in Et,t_1>t_2\} \tag{10}$$

4.2   Modeling of Plot Units Using the HyperGraph Ontology

The upper level ontology presented in the previous section can be used to model graph representations of movies. In this section, we discuss the modeling of plot units of movie using the HyperGraph ontology. The main components of the plot units representation are Characters and Events and therefore the focus has been only on the modeling of these entities and the links between them.

Hypergraph for plot units is

$$H=C\cup E\cup A\cup L \tag{11}$$

where C is the set of characters, E is the set of events, A is the set of affect states and L is the set of links between affect states. While C and E are hypernodes, A and L are hyperedges. These hyperedges can be mathematically described as follows:

$$A\subseteq\{(c,e,i):c\in C,e\in E,i\in\{-1,0,1\}\} \tag{12}$$

$$L\subseteq\{(a_1,a_2,l):a_1,a_2\in A,l\in\{motivation,actualisation,termination,equivalence,cross\}\} \tag{13}$$

Thus, literally A is the subset of the set consisting of all possible tuples of charac-ters, events and one of the affects. Similarly L is the subset of the set consisting of all possible tuples of two affect states and one of the possible links which connect two affect states (though a much more finer distinction can be made on the basis of causal links and cross character links). Finally a plot unit P is a subgraph of the hypergraph consisting of A and L which are connected and follow the grammar of plot units. Mathematically,

$$P\subseteq H \tag{14}$$

$$P = \{(L' \subseteq L, A' \subseteq A): L' \wedge A' \text{ are connected and follow the grammar of plot units}\} \quad (15)$$

It can thus be observed that HyperGraph ontology works well for plot representations of movies involving graphs.

4.3   CinemaScope

A browser based annotation tool for movies called *CinemaScope* based on Hyper-Graph ontology is being developed. The tool is being designed to model graph based representations for movies. It uses HypergraphDB[1], a hypergraph based database at the back end to store the data models and tags. The tool is equipped with other functionalities like shot segmentation, script parsing, script-subtitle alignment and basic searching of the hypergraph.

5   Conclusions

In this paper, we demonstrated the power of theory based graph representations for movies through the automatic generation of plot units from movie scripts. We developed some basic methods for character analysis, information extraction and summarization using the generated plot units, the results of which seem promising. We proposed an ontology called HyperGraph based ontology for movies for theory driven graph representations of movies based on these preliminary results. Much more refined methods can be used both for the generation of plot units as well as for the usage of them. The CinemaScope tool can be added with provisions for handling graph representations of data like GraphML. In the future it can be extended to be an semantic archive of movies and be released as an API for modeling graph representations of movies based on HyperGraph ontology.

References

1. Zhang, H.J., Low, C.Y., Smoliar, S.W., Wu, J.H.: Video parsing, retrieval and browsing: an integrated and content-based solution. In: Proc. ACM Multimedia Conf., pp. 15–24 (1995)
2. Lienhart, R., Comparison of automatic shot boundary detection algorithms. In: Proc. SPIE, vol. 3656, pp. 290–301 (1999)
3. Li, Y., Narayanan, S., Kuo, C.-C.J.: Content-based movie analysis and indexing based on audiovisual cues. IEEE Trans. Circuits Syst. Video Technol. 14(8), 1073–1085 (2004)
4. Chu, W.-T., Cheng, W.-H., Hsu, J.Y.-J., Wu, J.-L.: Towards semantic indexing and retrieval using hierarchical audio models. ACM Multimedia Syst. J. 10(6), 570–583 (2005)
5. Bocconi, S., Nack, F.: VOX POPULI: automatic generation of biased video sequences. In: SRMC 2004 Proceedings of the 1st ACM Workshop on Story Representation, Mechanism and Context, pp. 9–16 (2004)

---

[1] http://www.hypergraphdb.org/index

6. Yi, H., Rajan, D., Chia, L.-T.: Semantic video indexing and summarization using subtitles. In: PCM 2004 Proceedings of the 5th Pacific Rim Conference on Advances in Multimedia Information Processing, vol. 1, pp. 634–641 (2004)
7. Katsiouli, P., Tsetsos, V., Hadjiefthymiades, S.: Semantic video classification based on subtitles and domain terminologies. In: KAMC 2007 1st International Workshop on Knowledge Acquisition from Multimedia (2007)
8. Tsoneva, T., Eindhoven Philips Res. Eur, Barbieri, M., Weda, H.: Automated summarization of narrative video on a semantic level. In: ICSC 2007, International Conference on Semantic Computing, pp. 169–176, September 2007
9. Sang, J., Xu, C.: Character-based movie summarization. In: MM 2010 Proceedings of the International Conference on Multimedia, pp. 855–858 (2010)
10. Weng, C.-Y., Chu, W.-T., Ja-Ling, W.: RoleNet: movie analysis from the perspective of social networks. IEEE Transactions on Multimedia 11(2), 256–271 (2009)
11. Park, S.-B., Kyeong-Jin, O., Jo, G.-S.: Social network analysis in a movie using character-net. Multimedia Tools and Applications 59(2), 601–627 (2012)
12. Lehnert, W.G.: Plot units and narrative summarization. Cognitive Science 5(4), 293–331 (1981)
13. Xu, Y.: Representation of Story Structures for Browsing Digital Video. Ph.D. Thesis, University of Surrey: U.K
14. Goyal, A., Riloff, E., Daumé III, H.: A Computational Model for Plot Units. Computational Intelligence Journal (2013)
15. "ANSWER Annual Report". http://cordis.europa.eu/fp7/ict/content-knowledge/docs/answer-annual-report-2009.pdf
16. Jewell, M., Lawrence, K., Tuffield, M., Prugel-Bennett, A., Millard, D., Nixon, M., Shadbolt, N.: OntoMedia: an ontology for the representation of heterogeneous media. In: Proceeding of SIGIR Workshop on Mutlimedia Information Retrieval, ACM SIGIR (2005)
17. Peinado, F., Gervs, P.: Evaluation of Automatic Generation of Basic Stories. New Generation Computing 24(3), 289–302 (2006)
18. Propp, V.: Morphology of the Folktale. University of Texas Press (1968)
19. Cataldi, M., Damiano, R., Lombardo, V., Pizzo, A.: Representing dramatic features of stories through an ontological model. In: Si, M., Thue, D., André, E., Lester, J., Tanenbaum, J., Zammitto, V. (eds.) ICIDS 2011. LNCS, vol. 7069, pp. 122–127. Springer, Heidelberg (2011)
20. Lombardo, V., Damiano, R.: Narrative annotation and editing of video. In: Aylett, R., Lim, M.Y., Louchart, S., Petta, P., Riedl, M. (eds.) ICIDS 2010. LNCS, vol. 6432, pp. 62–73. Springer, Heidelberg (2010)
21. Yoonjung, C., Lingjia, D., Janyce, W.: Lexical acquisition for opinion inference: a sense-level lexicon of benefactive and malefactive events. In: Proceedings of the 5th Workshop on Computational Approaches to Subjectivity, Sentiment and Social Media Analysis, pp. 107–112, June 2014
22. Chklovski, T., Pantel, P.: VerbOcean: mining the web for fine-grained semantic verb relations. In: Proceedings of Conference on Empirical Methods in Natural Language Processing (EMNLP 2004). Barcelona, Spain (2004)
23. Ronfard, R., Thuong, T.T., Alpes, I.R.: A framework for aligning and indexing movies with their script. In: IEEE Int. Conf. on Multimedia and Expo (2003)
24. Schärfe, H., Øhrstrøm, P.: Representing time and modality in narratives with conceptual graphs. In: Ganter, B., de Moor, A., Lex, W. (eds.) ICCS 2003. LNCS, vol. 2746. Springer, Heidelberg (2003)

25. Muni, B. (300 BC).: Nāṭya śāstra, with Abhinavagupta's commentary, with Hindi Commentary by Dwivedi Parasnath, 1996, Varanasi: Sampurnanand Sankrit Mahavidyalaya
26. Chatman, S.: Story and Discourse: Narrative Structure in Fictionand Film (1978)
27. Radev, I., Pissinou, N., Makki, K., Park, E.K.: Graph-based object-oriented approach for structural and behavioral representation of multimedia data. In: CIKM 1999 Proceedings of the eighth International Conference on Information and Knowledge Management, pp. 522–530 (1999)
28. Radev, I., Pissinou, N., Makki, K.: Film video modeling. In: Proceedings of IEEE Workshop on Knowledge and Data Engineering Exchange, KDEX 1999, Chicago, Illinois, November 1999
29. Hochin, T.: Graph-Based Data Model for the Content Representation of Multimedia Data. In: Gabrys, B., Howlett, R.J., Jain, L.C. (eds.) KES 2006. LNCS (LNAI), vol. 4252, pp. 1182–1190. Springer, Heidelberg (2006)
30. Hochin, T., Tatsuo, T.: A Directed Recursive Hypergraph Data Model for Representing the Contents of Multimedia Data. Mem. Fac. Eng. Fukui Univ. **48**, 343–360 (2000)

Track on Digital Libraries, Information Retrieval, Linked and Social Data Models, Frameworks and Applications

RDA Element Sets and RDA Value Vocabularies: Vocabularies for Resource Description in the Semantic Web

Fabrício Silva Assumpção[1(✉)], José Eduardo Santarem Segundo[1,2],
and Plácida Leopoldina Ventura Amorim da Costa Santos[1]

[1] Graduate Program in Information Science,
UNESP – Universidade Estadual Paulista, Marília, Brazil
{fsassumpcao,placida}@marilia.unesp.br, santarem@usp.br
[2] Department of Education, Information and Communication,
Universidade de São Paulo (USP), Ribeirão Preto, Brazil
santarem@usp.br

Abstract. Considering the need for metadata standards suitable for the Semantic Web, this paper describes the RDA Element Sets and the RDA Value Vocabularies that were created from attributes and relationships defined in Resource Description and Access (RDA). First, we present the vocabularies included in RDA Element Sets: the vocabularies of classes, of properties and of properties unconstrained by FRBR entities; and then we present the RDA Value Vocabularies, which are under development. As a conclusion, we highlight that these vocabularies can be used to meet the needs of different contexts due to the unconstrained properties and to the independence of the vocabularies of properties from the vocabularies of values and vice versa.

Keywords: Resource Description and Access (RDA) · Resource Description Framework (RDF) · Functional Requirements for Bibliographic Records (FRBR) · Vocabularies

1 Introduction

In Information Science, the representation of resources has been based on several instruments, including metadata standards, which are created for specific contexts and focused on specific technological environments. With the Semantic Web initiative, there is an attempt to develop and implement technologies that allow the creation of descriptions of resources accessible and processable not only by its syntax, but also by its semantics.

In this sense, Information Science needs metadata standards suitable for the Semantic Web, that is, metadata standards appropriated for the creation of representations accessible by applications that use Semantic Web technologies. Based on this need, some initiatives arise in descriptive cataloging in order to create suitable metadata standards and/or to adapt those already existing.

© Springer International Publishing Switzerland 2015
E. Garoufallou et al. (Eds.): MTSR 2015, CCIS 544, pp. 147–158, 2015.
DOI: 10.1007/978-3-319-24129-6_13

One of these initiatives occurs in parallel with the development and implementation of Resource Description and Access (RDA) [17] and it has as its main goal the creation of vocabularies of properties and vocabularies of values based on RDA. The results of this initiative have been released under the names RDA Element Sets and RDA Value Vocabularies.

Considering the contributions of this initiative, in this paper we aim to present the RDA Element Sets and the RDA Value Vocabularies, describing their development, classes, properties and values.

2   RDF Data Model in Resource Description

Descriptive cataloging deals with the description of formal aspects of information resources and establishes names and titles to provide access to these resources. In order to do it, descriptive cataloging comprises instruments for description that were created over the course of time; some of these instruments are the metadata standards and the content standards.

Over the past decades, we have faced changes in descriptive cataloging as a result of the development of information and communication technologies. Such changes require different views of the treatment of information resources and the use of practices for information organizations on the Web [2].

One of these changes involves the traditional approach that has defined catalogs' structures since the 19th century, when cataloging practices and instruments began to be formalized. The traditional catalog record, which "is composed of the values of multiple properties associated with a bibliographic entity, for example its title and physical description" [7], results from this approach.

Revision of this approach is necessary because in the Resource Description Framework (RDF) data model [16] – one of the base technologies for the Semantic Web – "the focus is on individual metadata statements represented by three-part data triples in the form subject-predicate-object" [6]. RDF is a data model that allows us to describe any kind of resources using triples composed by subject-predicate-object or, as we prefer to use in this paper, resource-property-value [2] [8].

With the focus changing, we will have individual statements, each one describing a property of the resource; for example, "The book has the title The Lord of the Rings", "The book was published in 2005" and "The book was written by J. R. R. Tolkien", rather than a single record with all the properties together, as we can see in Machine Readable Cataloging (MARC) 21 Format for Bibliographic Data. "The RDF approach is very different from the traditional library catalog record exemplified by MARC21, where descriptions of multiple aspects of a resource are bound together by a specific syntax of tags, indicators, and subfields as a single identifiable stream of data that is manipulated as a whole. In RDF, the data must be separated out into single statements that can then be processed independently from one another; processing includes the aggregation of statements into a record-based view, but is not confined to any specific record schema or source for the data. Statements or triples can be mixed and matched from many different sources to form many different kinds of user-friendly displays." [6]

We can see the record-based approach not only in catalogs' structures but also in metadata and content standards used in descriptive cataloging, such as the MARC 21 Format for Bibliographic Data and Anglo-American Cataloguing Rules 2nd edition (AACR2), respectively. Thus, as the approach changes, we will need metadata and content standards suitable for RDF data model.

Considering this necessity, some initiatives have been undertaken for the following purposes: (1) creating metadata standards suitable for RDF, for instance, the Bibliographic Framework Initiative (BIBFRAME) and the vocabularies created from Functional Requirements for Bibliographic Records (FRBR), Functional Requirements for Authority Data (FRAD), Functional Requirements for Subject Authority Data (FRSAD), International Standard Bibliographic Description (ISBD), and RDA, and (2) adapting the standards already existent such that they can be used in RDF, for instance, Metadata Object Description Schema (MODS) RDF Ontology, Metadata Authority Description Schema (MADS)/RDF, and the vocabularies created from MARC 21 and Universal MARC format (UNIMARC).

These initiatives apply the concepts of "vocabulary", "vocabularies of properties", and "vocabularies of values". To provide a better understanding of RDA Element Sets and RDA Value Vocabularies, in the next section we briefly discuss such concepts and their relationships to descriptive cataloging.

3   Vocabularies

In RDF descriptions, each statement is composed of a resource, a property and a value; this later may be literally described (a literal value) or ascribed to another resource [8]. Following the previous examples, the resource is "the book", the properties are "has the title", "was published in" and "was written by", and the values are "The Lord of the Rings" and "2005" (literal values) and "J. R. R. Tolkien" (a resource). In this case, "J. R. R. Tolkien" is considered a resource because we may continue to describe it; for example, "J. R. R. Tolkien was born in 1892".

The properties should be from vocabularies and the values may be taken from the vocabularies. By vocabulary, we mean a set of terms. So, a set of terms used as properties is a vocabulary of properties and a set of terms used as values is a vocabulary of values.

These kinds of vocabularies are familiar to those within Information Science. Vocabularies of properties may be understood as metadata standards [8]: predetermined sets of methodologically constructed and standardized metadata (descriptive elements or attributes that represent characteristics of a resource or that are assigned to it) [1]. Dublin Core, for example, is a vocabulary of properties because it provides a set of properties (terms) to describe resources.

Vocabularies of values are similar to subject headings lists and authority files; these well-known instruments of Information Science provide sets of terms (topical and chronological terms, personal, corporate and geographic names, etc.) to be used as values. In addition, there are vocabularies used to represent languages, countries, document and content types, etc. Some examples of these vocabularies are the lists of languages and country codes used in MARC 21 Formats, the list of terms used as general material designation in AACR2, and the lists of codes for illustrations, target audience, form of item, nature of content and literary form in 008 field of MARC 21 Format for Bibliographic Data.

In RDF statements, resources and properties should be identified by Uniform Resource Identifiers (URIs), while values should be identified by a URI only if they are resources, that is, when they are not literal values [8]. So, vocabularies, in the semantic Web context, define URIs for their properties and values.

4   Vocabularies Created from RDA

RDA was published in 2010 as result of the AACR foundation's revision that began in 1997. "RDA essentially standardizes how metadata content is identified, transcribed and generally structured, although it is independent of any specific metadata encoding. RDA also identifies a general set of metadata elements, and in many cases provides a controlled vocabulary for use as the content of an element." [9]

One of the bases of the RDA is the conceptual model Functional Requirements for Bibliographic Records (FRBR) that, expanded by Functional Requirements for Authority Data (FRAD), provides a set of entities, attributes and relationships for RDA.

In a meeting held in 2007, representatives of RDA developers and the Dublin Core Metadata Initiative (DCMI) recommended some activities in order to create a "metadata standard that is compatible with the Web Architecture and that is fully interoperable with other Semantic Web initiatives" [4]. The activities recommended were: "development of an RDA Element Vocabulary; development of an RDA DC Application Profile based on FRBR and FRAD; and disclosure of RDA Value Vocabularies using RDF/RDFS/SKOS." [4]

Starting from these recommendations, the DCMI RDA Task Group was established in 2007 with the objective "To define components of the draft standard RDA - Resource Description and Access as an RDF vocabulary for use in developing a Dublin Core application profile" [5].

In 2011, based on a review of its goals and activities, the group changed its name to the Bibliographic Metadata Task Group. In January 2014, the vocabularies of properties created from attributes and relationships defined in RDA were published on the Open Metadata Registry under the name RDA Element Sets and, in June of the same year, they were also released on the RDA Registry platform [13,14,15]. Some vocabularies of values are already published in RDA Registry under the name RDA Value Vocabularies, while some remain under development in the Open Metadata Registry [12].

The platforms used for publishing these vocabularies, Open Metadata Registry [15] and RDA Registry [10], provide "information about the metadata standard in a machine-actionable format, capable of integration into applications" [9]. In these platforms, the statements about classes, properties and values are available for humans (in a HTML interface) and for machines (in Turtle, Notation 3, N-Triples, RDF/XML, RDFa, Microdata, JSON-LD and RDF/JSON) [15].

5   RDA Element Sets

RDA Element Sets comprise seven vocabularies: one with classes, five with properties used for each class, and one with properties unconstrained by FRBR classes.

5.1   Vocabularies of Classes

In the Semantic Web, a class is defined as a set of individuals or even "an abstraction mechanism for grouping resources with similar characteristics" [11]. "A class is much like a class in a scientific taxonomic sense: it is a grouping of like resources that all belong together based on some common characteristics that make them members of the same set." [3]

We recognize the concept of class used in the Semantic Web as being similar to the concept of entity used in FRBR and RDA. For instance, intellectual creations may be gathered into a class "Work" and its creators may be gathered into classes like "Person", "Family" and "Corporate body". Based on this similarity, a vocabulary of classes from RDA entities was defined. This vocabulary comprises the following terms: Work, Expression, Manifestation, Item, Agent, Person, Family, and Corporate Body.

The classes corresponding to the entities person, family and corporate body are subclasses of the Agent class, since these entities share attributes and relationships between them. Agent is not a class present in FRBR, but it was defined in FRBR-object oriented (FRBRoo) [9]. By defining Person, Family and Corporate Body as subclasses of Agent, it became unnecessary to duplicate statements about the properties, as we see in section 5.2.

The terms of the vocabulary of classes are used to describe to which class the resource belongs. To describe it we might use the property *type*, provided by RDF language [16], and the URI representing the class:

- Work: http://www.rdaregistry.info/Elements/c#C10001
- Expression: http://www.rdaregistry.info/Elements/c#C10006
- Manifestation: http://www.rdaregistry.info/Elements/c#C10007
- Item: http://www.rdaregistry.info/Elements/c#C10003
- Agent: http://www.rdaregistry.info/Elements/c#C10002
- Person: http://www.rdaregistry.info/Elements/c#C10004
- Family: http://www.rdaregistry.info/Elements/c#C10008
- Corporate Body: http://www.rdaregistry.info/Elements/c#C10005.

The vocabulary of classes is identified by http://www.rdaregistry.info/Elements/c/. In RDA Registry, this namespace is represented by the prefix *rdac*.

5.2   Vocabularies of Properties Restricted to FRBR

There are different vocabularies of properties and different namespaces for each class (Work, Expression, Manifestation, Item and Agent). These five vocabularies contain properties created from attributes and relationships defined in RDA.

The property *has title proper* (Fig. 1), for example, was created from the attribute *Title proper* defined in RDA, rule 2.3.2. This property should be applied to manifestations, so it belongs to Manifestation vocabulary, which is identified by the namespace http://rdaregistry.info/Elements/m/ (prefix: *rdam*). We can use the property *has title proper* in a RDF statement by applying one of its URIs:

- http://www.rdaregistry.info/Elements/m/#P30156 (*rdam:P30156*): "Abstract or numeric URIs that don't contain a language-specific label can help maintain the language-neutral sense of the element or concept." [9];
- http://www.rdaregistry.info/Elements/m/#titleProper.en (*rdam:titleProper.en*): lexical URI with an English label; this URI redirect to numeric URI and might be modified over the time; URIs with labels in other languages might be created, as well.

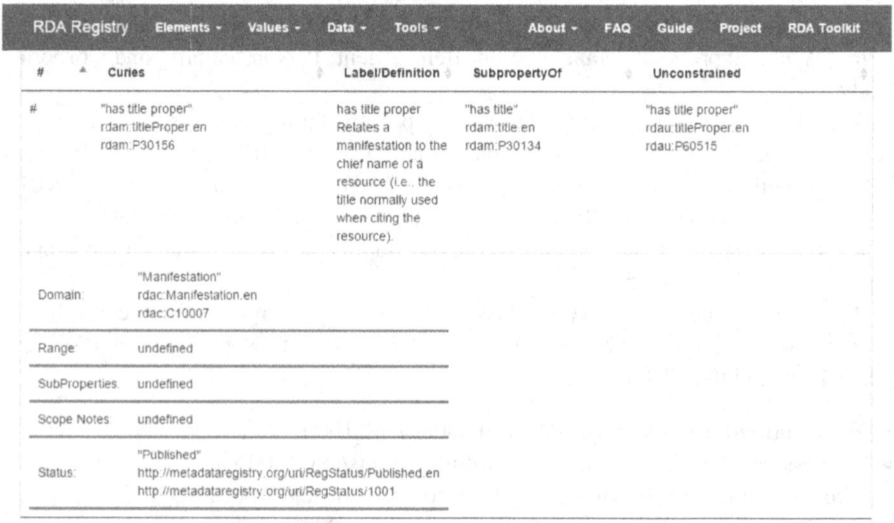

# ▲	Curies	Label/Definition	SubpropertyOf	Unconstrained
#	"has title proper" rdam:titleProper.en rdam:P30156	has title proper Relates a manifestation to the chief name of a resource (i.e., the title normally used when citing the resource).	"has title" rdam:title.en rdam:P30134	"has title proper" rdau:titleProper.en rdau:P60515
Domain:	"Manifestation" rdac:Manifestation.en rdac:C10007			
Range:	undefined			
SubProperties:	undefined			
Scope Notes:	undefined			
Status:	"Published" http://metadataregistry.org/uri/RegStatus/Published.en http://metadataregistry.org/uri/RegStatus/1001			

Fig. 1. The property *has title proper* in RDA Registry

Some properties are defined as sub-properties. This relation of sub-property occurs when we have a property with a broader meaning and another with a narrower meaning. The property *has title proper* (Fig. 1) is a sub-property of the property *has title* (http://www.rdaregistry.info/Elements/m/#P30134 or *rdam:P30134*).

The domain of each property is defined in these five vocabularies. The domain specifies in which classes a property can be used. The property *has title proper*, for example, is intended to be used for resources belonging to the Manifestation class, so the domain of this property is this class. In Fig. 1, the domain of the property *has title proper* is identified by *rdac:C10007* (abbreviated form of http://www.rdaregistry. info/Elements/c/#C10007).

The range specifies which values can be used for the property or the class to which the values should belong. The range is defined for some of the properties of the five vocabularies. For instance, the range of the property *has title proper* (Fig. 1) is undefined, so this property can accept any kind of value, whether a literal or a resource, while the values of the property *has author* (Fig. 2) should be an individual of the class Agent.

RDA Registry	Elements ▾	Values ▾	Data ▾	Tools ▾	About ▾	FAQ	Guide	Project	RDA Toolkit
# ▲	Curies		Label/Definition	Subproperty Of		Unconstrained			
#	"has author" rdaw:author.en rdaw:P10061		has author Relates a work to a person, family, or corporate body responsible for creating a work that is primarily textual in content, regardless of media type (e.g., printed text, spoken word, electronic text, tactile text) or genre (e.g., poems, novels, screenplays, blogs).	"has creator" rdaw:creator.en rdaw:P10065		"has author" rdau:author.en rdau:P60434			
Domain:	"Work" rdac:Work.en rdac:C10001								
Range:	"Agent" rdac:Agent.en rdac:C10002								

Fig. 2. The property *has author* in RDA Registry

Here we present an example of some properties used for works, expressions, manifestations, and item descriptions.

```
<?xml version="1.0" encoding="UTF-8"?>
<rdf:RDF xmlns:rdaw="http://rdaregistry.info/Elements/w/"
xmlns:rdae="http://rdaregistry.info/Elements/e/"
xmlns:rdam="http://rdaregistry.info/Elements/m/"
xmlns:rdai="http://rdaregistry.info/Elements/i/"
xmlns:rdf="http://www.w3.org/1999/02/22-rdf-syntax-ns# " >
    <rdf:Description rdf:about="http://example.com/work-1">
      <rdf:type
rdf:resource="http://rdaregistry.info/Elements/c/C10001"/
>
      <rdaw:P10088>The lord of the rings</rdaw:P10088>
      <rdaw:P10061 rdf:resource="http://example.com/person-
1"/>
```

```
  </rdf:Description>
  <rdf:Description
rdf:about="http://example.com/expression-1">
  <rdf:type
rdf:resource="http://rdaregistry.info/Elements/c/C10006"/
>
  <rdae:P20001>text</rdae:P20001>
  <rdae:P20006>English</rdae:P20006>
  <rdae:P20037 rdf:resource="http://example.com/person-
2"/>
  <rdae:P20231 rdf:resource="http://example.com/work-1"/>
</rdf:Description>
<rdf:Description
rdf:about="http://example.com/manifestation-1">
  <rdf:type
rdf:resource="http://rdaregistry.info/Elements/c/C10007"/
>
  <rdam:P30156>The lord of the rings</rdam:P30156>
  <rdam:P30088>Boston</rdam:P30088>
  <rdam:P30176>Houghton Mifflin Company</rdam:P30176>
  <rdam:P30011>2005</rdam:P30011>
  <rdam:P30181>1178 pages</rdam:P30181>
  <rdam:P30002>unmediated</rdam:P30002>
  <rdam:P30001>volume</rdam:P30001>
  <rdam:P30004>ISBN 978-0-618-64015-7</rdam:P30004>
  <rdam:P30139
rdf:resource="http://example.com/expression-1"/>
  <rdam:P30135 rdf:resource="http://example.com/work-1"/>
</rdf:Description>
<rdf:Description rdf:about="http://example.com/item-1">
  <rdf:type
rdf:resource="http://rdaregistry.info/Elements/c/C10003"/
>
  <rdai:P40047>Available only for university
students</rdai:P40047>
  <rdai:P40049
rdf:resource="http://example.com/manifestation-1"/>
</rdf:Description>
</rdf:RDF>
```

There are no specific vocabularies for the classes Person, Family and Corporate Body. These classes use the properties defined for Agent since they are subclasses of Agent and then they inherit the relevant properties. However, in the vocabulary of properties for Agent, some properties can be used for all the subclasses, while some can be used only for one subclass. The property *is singer of* can be used for all Agent subclasses, but *has date of birth* can be used only for Person. In this sense, the class

Agent makes the use and maintenance of vocabularies easier since it is not necessary to define several domains for a property that can be used for persons, families, and corporate bodies.

The domains and ranges defined in these five vocabularies make the properties useful only in the context in which FRBR conceptual model is implemented to some degree. Thus, the properties of these vocabularies are considered to be restricted to FRBR. However, as we describe in the next section, the Bibliographic Metadata Task Group also considered the need for vocabularies from RDA that can be used independent of the FRBR.

5.3   Unconstrained Properties

The FRBR conceptual model was developed in the library community and has not been broadly used for system design in this community. Outside the library community, there is little discussion about this model. Considering that, the development of vocabularies for exclusive use with FRBR would be a disadvantage, since they would not promote RDA use in the library community or outside that community.

To overcome the restriction imposed by FRBR and to make RDA vocabularies useful for any Semantic Web application, a vocabulary of FRBR unconstrained properties was created, published in namespace http://www.rdaregistry.info/Elements/u/ [14].

Similar to properties presented in section 5.2, the unconstrained properties were also created from RDA attributes and relationships. The difference, however, is that the domains and ranges of the unconstrained properties are undefined, thus the use of these properties does not require the use the classes Work, Expression, Manifestation, Item, Agent, Person, Family and Corporate Body. The property *has publisher's name* (Fig. 3) is an example of an unconstrained property created from the attribute *Publisher's name* defined in RDA, rule 2.8.4 [17].

#	⌃	Curies	⇕	Label/Definition	⇕	SubpropertyOf	⇕	Unconstrained ⇕
#		"has publisher's name" rdau:publishersName.en rdau:P60547		has publisher's name Relates a resource to the name of an agent responsible for publishing, releasing, or issuing a resource.		undefined		undefined
Domain:		undefined						
Range:		undefined						
SubProperties:		"has publisher's name" rdam:publishersName.en rdam:P30176						
Scope Notes:		undefined						
Status:		"Published" http://metadataregistry.org/uri/RegStatus/Published.en http://metadataregistry.org/uri/RegStatus/1001						

The RDA Registry navigation bar reads: RDA Registry   Elements ▾   Values ▾   Data ▾   Tools ▾   About ▾   FAQ   Guide   Project   RDA Toolkit

Fig. 3. The unconstrained property *has publisher's name* in RDA Registry

Despite their independence from FRBR, the unconstrained properties are associated with the restricted ones. In this relationship, unconstrained properties are considered broader than the restricted ones, and then the restricted properties are declared to be sub-properties of the unconstrained properties.

6   RDA Value Vocabularies

In addition to the vocabularies of classes and properties, there are vocabularies of values created from RDA. Some RDA attributes have their values defined by a list of terms, for example, *Carrier type* (RDA 3.3), *Content type* (RDA 6.9) and *Illustrative content* (RDA 7.15) [17]. These lists of terms were used to create the vocabularies for values. Certain vocabularies are already published in RDA Registry and in Open Metadata Registry, while others remain under development. Fig. 4 shows the term *text* that is part of the Content type vocabulary.

Although the vocabularies of values have been created from RDA attributes and RDA attributes have been used also for creating the vocabularies of properties, these two kinds of vocabularies may be used in an independent form. For example, it is not mandatory that the value of the property *has content type* to be a term from Content type vocabulary.

Vocabulary: RDA Content Type
Concepts: text

| Detail | Properties | History |

Detail

Preferred Label:	text
Language:	English
URI:	http://rdaregistry.info/termList/RDAContentType/1020 (RDF)
Top Concept?:	
Status:	Published

Properties

scope note	Dazu gehören alle Formen von Notationen für Sprache, die nicht über den Tastsinn wahrgenommen werden sollen.	German	Published
scope note	Includes all forms of language notation other than those intended to be perceived through touch.	English	Published
scope note	Incluye todas las formas de lenguaje de notación diferente de aquellos pensados para ser percibidos mediante el tacto.	Spanish	Published
scope note	Comprend toutes les formes de notation du langage différentes de celles devant être perçues au toucher.	French	Published
related to	computer dataset		Published
related to	tactile text		Published
preferred label	Text	German	Published
preferred label	text	English	Published
preferred label	texto	Spanish	Published
preferred label	texte	French	Published
definition	Content expressed through a form of notation for language intended to be perceived visually.	English	Published

Fig. 4. The term *text* from the Content Type vocabulary

7   Conclusions

After the brief explanation provided in this paper, we may remark on some conclusions regarding the RDA Element Sets and the RDA Value Vocabularies.

The decision to make the vocabularies of values independent of the vocabularies of properties allows the vocabularies to be opened in a way such that they can better meet the needs arising in different contexts. We can say the same for properties that usually have date or language codes as values but are presented in RDA Element Sets without ranges.

Since the unconstrained properties can be used in systems that are not FRBR-based, the unconstrained vocabulary may be used in the library community and beyond, for example, in museums, archives, publishers, and e-commerce.

We also think that an unconstrained vocabulary is very similar to metadata standards already used for data interchange in cataloging. One of these standards is MARC 21 Format for Bibliographic Data that, like an unconstrained vocabulary, does not separate bibliographic data into work, expression, manifestation, and item entities. This similarity may promote the use of RDA unconstrained vocabularies for the publication of current bibliographic data as RDF triples.

Although the RDA standard is independent of any metadata standard and RDA vocabulary developers aim to make the use of these vocabularies independent of RDA [9], we highlight that the close relationship between RDA and RDA vocabularies has benefits and costs. On the positive side, we think that the high level of compatibility between them may encourage institutions that use RDA to use RDA vocabularies for publishing their data in RDF. On the other hand, the fact that RDA is a closed standard – with access only by subscription or purchase – may discourage the use of the RDA vocabularies by institutions that do not use RDA, since using open standards is a key feature for Semantic Web projects.

References

1. Alves, R.C.V.: Metadados como elementos do processo de catalogação. Ph.D. thesis, Ciência da Informação, Univ Estadual Paulista, Marília, Brazil (2010). http://hdl.handle.net/11449/103361
2. Catarino, M.E., Souza, T.B.: A representação descritiva no contexto da web semântica. Transinformação 24(2), 78–90 (2012)
3. Coyle, K.: Understanding the Semantic Web: Bibliographic Data and Metadata. ALA Library Technology Reports 46(1), 5–32 (2010)
4. Data Model Meeting. http://www.bl.uk/bibliographic/meeting.html
5. DCMI/RDA Task Group Repurposing Proposal. http://wiki.dublincore.org/index.php? title=DCMI/RDA_Task_Group_Repurposing_Proposal&oldid=1724
6. Dunsire, G., Hillmann, D., Phipps, J.: Reconsidering Universal Bibliographic Control in Light of the Semantic Web. Journal of Library Metadata 12(2–3), 164–176 (2012)
7. Dunsire, G., Willer, M.: Standard library metadata models and structures for the Semantic Web. Library Hi Tech News 28(3), 1–12 (2011)

8. Ferreira, J.A., Santos, P.L.V.A.C.: O modelo de dados Resource Description Framework (RDF) e o seu papel na descrição de recursos. Informação & Sociedade estudos **23**(2), 13–23 (2013)
9. Hillmann, D., Coyle, K., Phipps, J., Dunsire, G.: RDA Vocabularies: Process, Outcome, Use. D-Lib Magazine **16**(1–2) (2010)
10. Open Metadata Registry. http://metadataregistry.org
11. OWL Web Ontology Language: Reference. http://www.w3.org/TR/2004/REC-owl-ref-20040210
12. Publication of RDA Content, Carrier, and Media Type Vocabularies. http://www.rda-jsc.org/rdatypespublish.html
13. Publication of the RDA Element Vocabularies. http://www.rda-jsc.org/RDAelementvocabs.html
14. RDA Registry Website. http://www.rda-jsc.org/RDAregistrywebsite.html
15. RDA Registry. http://www.rdaregistry.info
16. RDF 1.1 Primer. http://www.w3.org/TR/2014/NOTE-rdf11-primer-20140624
17. Resource Description and Access. http://access.rdatoolkit.org

Metadata for Scientific Audiovisual Media: Current Practices and Perspectives of the TIB|AV-Portal

Sven Strobel[(✉)] and Paloma Marín-Arraiza

Competence Centre for Non-textual Materials, German National Library of Science and Technology, Welfengarten 1B 30167, Hannover, Germany
{sven.strobel,paloma.marin}@tib.uni-hannover.de

Abstract. Descriptive metadata play a key role in finding relevant search results in large amounts of unstructured data. However, current scientific audiovisual media are provided with little metadata, which makes them hard to find, let alone individual sequences. In this paper, the TIB|AV-Portal is presented as a use case where methods concerning the automatic generation of metadata, a semantic search and cross-lingual retrieval (German/English) have already been applied. These methods result in a better discoverability of the scientific audiovisual media hosted in the portal. Text, speech, and image content of the video are automatically indexed by specialised GND (Gemeinsame Normdatei) subject headings. A semantic search is established based on properties of the GND ontology. The cross-lingual retrieval uses English 'translations' that were derived by an ontology mapping (DBpedia i. a.). Further ways of increasing the discoverability and reuse of the metadata are publishing them as Linked Open Data and interlinking them with other data sets.

Keywords: Video retrieval · Automatic indexing · Semantic search · Linked data

1 Introduction

Metadata are structured information about resources. Following [9], there are three main types of metadata: *descriptive metadata* describe a resource for purposes such as discovery and identification, *structural metadata* indicate how compound objects are put together, and *administrative metadata* provide technical information to help manage a resource. We focus exclusively on descriptive metadata in this paper.

Given the huge amount of unstructured data in databases, there must be structured descriptions of the data to find relevant search results efficiently [6]. There are different approaches for describing large amounts of data in a structured way: (i) the data are automatically indexed. A manual description of the content is often considered as too expensive and time-consuming [11]; (ii) the data are described at a fine-grained level, which enables a search for deeper structured information; (iii) different features and contents of the information resources are described, providing more opportunities for access [4]; (iv) written and spoken language of the information resources is indexed to allow for a full-text search [5],[7]; (v) the data are indexed with metadata of

© Springer International Publishing Switzerland 2015
E. Garoufallou et al. (Eds.): MTSR 2015, CCIS 544, pp. 159–170, 2015.
DOI: 10.1007/978-3-319-24129-6_14

an ontology, enabling a semantic search, which produces more relevant search results [3],[13],[15].

Methods to annotate content automatically have evolved a lot in the last decades. [5] presents technologies based on spoken text and segmentation to index documents automatically. [7] combines spoken words and images. The authors carry out a survey to evaluate whether automatically generated descriptions could reach the effectiveness of manual descriptions. The use of concept vocabularies to improve the recognition of video events is addressed by [3]. [15] handles the exploratory search and serendipitous discoveries combining Linked Data Vocabularies. [10], [13] and [15] show how to use this kind of vocabularies to perform a semantic search. Important projects such as the Open Video Digital Library[1] [8] or the Informedia Project[2] have stressed the importance of automatic indexing in video material – in and outside the library world.

In this context, this paper deals with the generation and retrieval of descriptive metadata of the TIB|AV-Portal, the scientific video portal of the German National Library of Science and Technology (TIB). The portal applies all of the approaches mentioned above. It is an example of how a research library can implement new information systems including media resources as it has been demanded by the Association of College and Research Libraries [2]. Other contributions are: automatic indexing, assignment of digital object identifiers plus long-term archiving from a single source; use of subject-specific automatic indexing of scientific videos based on the GND in combination with the implementation of a semantic and cross-lingual retrieval.

The structure of the paper is as follows: section 2 introduces the TIB|AV-Portal. Section 3 presents the process chain of its automatic video analysis. The process chain incorporates existing (manual) metadata into the system and generates new metadata. Section 4 discusses how the metadata are used in the video retrieval. In section 5, the different ontologies exploited in the knowledge base of the TIB|AV-Portal are illustrated. A semantic search and cross-lingual retrieval can be established based on the metadata of these ontologies. Section 6 summarizes the essential results. Finally, section 7 provides an outlook on future work by outlining concepts about publishing the metadata as Linked Open Data.

2   TIB|AV-Portal

The TIB|AV-Portal[3] is a web-based platform for quality-tested scientific videos from the fields of architecture, chemistry, engineering, information technology, mathematics and physics. Amongst other things, the videos portray computer visualisations, learning material, simulations, experiments, interviews, and recordings of lectures and conferences. The portal currently contains around 2900 videos and some 1900 film credits with external links. Most videos have been published under an open access licence. TIB[4] is planning long-term archiving of the collected videos.

---

[1]   http://www.open-video.org
[2]   http://www.informedia.cs.cmu.edu
[3]   http://av.getinfo.de
[4]   http://www.tib-hannover.de/en/the-tib

The Competence Centre for Non-Textual Materials[5] at TIB developed the TIB|AV-Portal in cooperation with the Hasso Plattner Institute for Software Systems Engineering[6] between 2011 and 2014. It went online in spring 2014. A key feature of the portal is the use of different kinds of automatic video analysis, which is illustrated in the next section.

3   Automatic Video Analysis of the TIB|AV-Portal

The process chain of the automatic video analysis starts with the ingest of the audiovisual media and manual metadata (cf. figure 1). A digital object identifier (DOI) is assigned to each video by the DOI Service of TIB[7]. There is a structural analysis as well as a text, speech, and image analysis of the video. First, shot boundary detection splits up the video into segments based on low-level image features. For every video segment, a number of keyframes that represent its relevant content is selected. Video optical character recognition (video OCR) localizes texts in keyframes, pre-processes and eventually extracts them as textual metadata (OCR transcript). Speech to text notes down spoken language in the video in the form of a speech transcript. Visual concept detection classifies keyframes according to pre-defined visual concepts. Finally, named-entity recognition maps the analysed textual metadata (OCR and speech transcripts) onto semantically associated terms. These terms are subject headings of the Gemeinsame Normdatei[8] (GND, Integrated Authority File).

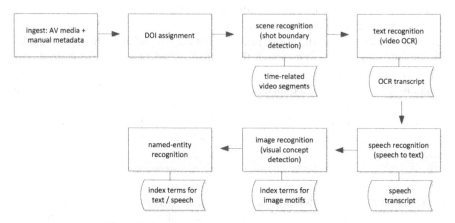

Fig. 1. Process chain of the automatic video analysis

The description above points out that numerous metadata are generated at different stages of the process chain. The following section considers the main characteristics of these metadata and their respective value for the retrieval.

---

[5] http://www.tib-hannover.de/en/services/competence-centre-for-non-textual-materials
[6] http://hpi.de/en.html
[7] http://www.tib-hannover.de/en/services/doi-service
[8] http://www.dnb.de/gnd

4   Metadata and Retrieval of the TIB|AV-Portal

4.1   Manual Metadata

Manual metadata are supplied by the video providers via an XML file and describe formal, technical and content-related features of the video. Formal metadata of the video are, for example, title, author, publisher, licence and DOI. Technical metadata are, for example, file size and duration. Content-related metadata are subject area, abstract and keywords.

The manual metadata represent coarse-grained descriptions referring to the whole video document. Their major advantage is their high reliability. They are created by a person and are therefore less error-prone than the automatic metadata. Consequently, the manual metadata enable the retrieval of highly relevant search results. However, it is a drawback that they only provide access to the whole video document and not to smaller parts of it.

4.2   Automatic Metadata

The automatic metadata are generated by means of several automatic video analyses, which produce either transcripts or index terms. They describe text, speech or image content of the video and represent fine-grained descriptions referring to the individual segments. The automatic metadata are less reliable than the manual ones since they are computed by algorithms. Their significant advantage is that they enable a pinpoint segment-based search within the video content.

It can be deduced from the above remarks that the manual and automatic metadata complement each other. Even though the manual metadata are coarse-grained, they are highly reliable. The automatic metadata, on the other hand, are less reliable but fine-grained. Consequently, the manual metadata provide very reliable search results, whereas the automatic metadata allow for a search for deeper structured information [13]. Different features (formal, technical and content-related ones) as well as contents (text, speech and image) of the video are described, ensuring various opportunities for access.

OCR Transcript

Video OCR converts written language of text overlays or slides into machine-encoded text, i.e. into the OCR transcript. A keyword-based full-text search can be performed in the OCR transcript. Video segments containing hits in the transcript are highlighted so that the user can navigate straight to these parts of the video. Moreover, the OCR transcript serves as the basis for the automatic indexing of written text in the video. Much of the metadata that can be extracted by video OCR has a high quality because text overlays and lecture slides condense the thematic content and mainly include nouns, which are essential for the query.

Speech Transcript
Speech to text converts spoken language in the video into a speech transcript, which allows a keyword-based full-text search. In figure 2, one finds the speech transcript to the right of the video player. Hits in the speech transcript are highlighted, as well as video segments that contain these hits. The speech transcript has timestamps, which allow accurate searches within the video content. Speech to text produces essential metadata because the spoken language conveys much of what is happening in the video. The speech transcript serves as the basis for the automatic indexing of spoken text in the video.

Fig. 2. Speech transcript with highlighted search results

Automatic Indexing
The automatic indexing of the TIB|AV-Portal can be classified into indexing of image motifs and indexing of written and spoken language.

Image Motifs
Visual concept detection classifies the moving image according to cross-subject concepts such as 'lecture' or 'computer animation' and subject-specific concepts such as 'microscopy' or 'façade detail'. Every classifier had to be trained with a set of at least 100 manually annotated keyframes. Based on the low-level image features of this training set, the classifier developed a model of the respective concept. In addition, every classifier received a label (GND subject heading) such as 'lecture' or 'experiment indoor'. Comparing its model with the image features of a representative

keyframe, the classifier determines whether its concept is present or not. Only in the first case, the video segment is indexed with the associated GND label [14]. Figure 3 shows a video segment, which depicts an indoor shot of an experimental set-up. Visual concept detection correctly classified this video segment as an 'experiment indoor'. Consequently, image motifs such as 'experiment indoor' can be searched directly or combined with other search terms.

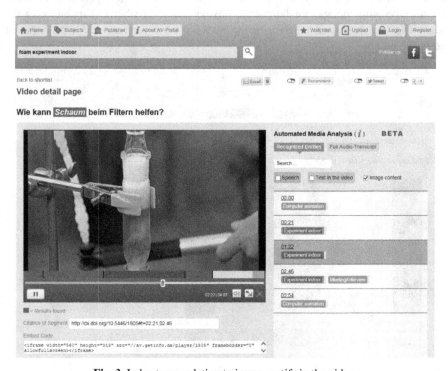

Fig. 3. Index terms relating to image motifs in the video

Named-Entity Recognition.
Named-entity recognition maps automatically extracted textual metadata from video analysis onto terms of a knowledge base. The extracted textual metadata are the OCR and speech transcripts, and the terms of the TIB|AV-Portal knowledge base are about 63 000 GND subject headings, which have been imported into the local RDF store. In the first step, the text component of the OCR or speech transcript is looked up in the TIB|AV-Portal knowledge base (cf. figure 4). Normally, there are several GND candidates, onto which the analysed text component could be mapped. The disambiguation algorithm then tries to find the right (or best) candidate by comparing the context information of the GND subject headings with the context of the text component. The context of a GND subject heading are its main and alternative labels, subject category, definition, related and broader terms from GND. The context of the text component are the other textual metadata, which are located in the same video segment, plus the manual metadata of the whole video. Broadly speaking, that GND candidate, the context information of which has the best match with the context of the text component,

wins the mapping and is finally assigned to the video segment [13]. In the example of figure 4, this is the GND term 'Thermodynamik' (thermodynamics).

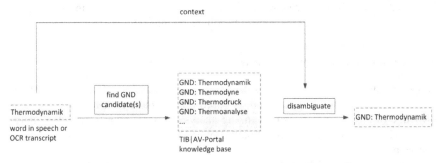

Fig. 4. Named-entity recognition of the TIB|AV-Portal[9]

As a result, written and spoken language in the video is indexed at segment level by GND subject headings. GND subject headings represent disambiguated terms that have a formally specified contextual meaning. A semantic search can be built upon that to either extend or narrow down search results. The next section explains in more detail which ontologies are used in the TIB|AV-Portal and how a semantic search as well as a cross-lingual retrieval can be established upon them.

5   Ontologies of the TIB|AV-Portal

5.1   Semantic Indexing Based on the GND

The Gemeinsame Normdatei serves as the ontology for the semantic indexing of the videos, meaning that textual metadata from text and audio analysis are linked to entities of this ontology (cf. section 4.2). In this paper, 'ontology' refers to an explicit formal specification of a set of terms in a particular domain and their interrelations [1]. The GND is managed by the German National Library in cooperation with the German-speaking library networks. The GND data[10] were published as Linked Data under Creative Commons Zero[11] (CC0).

The GND ontology includes the following features: synonyms are combined under a preferred term, homonyms are disambiguated by the assignment of distinct terms, hierarchical relations between terms (broader and narrower terms) and cross-references between related terms are listed. These properties can be exploited for a semantic search.

The videos of the TIB|AV-Portal are not indexed with the entire GND. Rather, each of the six TIB core subjects mentioned in section 2 has its own special GND vocabulary: the videos for physics, for example, are indexed by subject headings of the GND

---

[9]   Figure 4 is based on slide 37 from [10].
[10]   www.dnb.de/lds
[11]   https://creativecommons.org/publicdomain/zero/1.0

subject section for physics. This strategy warrants a higher precision of search results. The six GND subject sections used in the portal contain a total of 63 365 subject headings [14]. For these subject headings, main and alternative labels, subject category, definition, related and broader terms were extracted from GND and saved in the local RDF store. Only the main labels of the subject headings are indexed.

5.2   Ontology-Based Semantic Search of the TIB|AV-Portal

A keyword-based search searches for words in text, or more exactly: character strings. A semantic search, on the other hand, is based on an ontology, which represents the knowledge of a particular domain. Linking analysed textual data from video analysis with the GND allows the use of semantic properties and relations of that ontology when searching.

In the TIB|AV-Portal knowledge base, all synonyms of a GND term are listed. When the user enters one of these terms in the search field, all available synonyms are included in the query. When entering 'Thermodynamik' (thermodynamics), for example, the alternative expressions 'Wärmetheorie' and 'Wärmelehre' are searched as well. This functionality increases the completeness of relevant search results.

Since the GND terms are disambiguated in the automatic indexing, the accuracy of search results is improved when these terms are used in the retrieval. This applies to the semantic faceted search of the TIB|AV-Portal. There are facets for subject, language, author & contributors, publisher, licence, year of publication, person, organisation and image motif. The user can perform a query and then refine search results by means of these facets. The query of the faceted search is not comprised of keywords but of GND terms, which are identified by their uniform resource identifier (URI). By clicking on one of these faceted terms, the search for that entity is triggered. The search index stores the URI of the GND term, the ID of the video plus the corresponding position, which was assigned to that term [10]. The search returns those videos that contain the selected faceted terms; additionally, the terms and corresponding video segments are highlighted.

5.3   Ontology Mapping for the Establishment of a Cross-Lingual Retrieval

The TIB|AV-Portal contains German-language and English-language videos in its stock. The initial problem was that the indexing vocabulary used in the TIB|AV-Portal (63 356 GND subject headings from science and technology) possessed only very few English labels. In order to gain English labels for the automatic indexing of the English-language videos, the GND subject headings were mapped onto other knowledge bases that potentially provide an English translation of these terms. We used DBpedia[12], Library of Congress Subject Headings[13] (LCSH), results of the project 'Multi Lingual Access to Subjects[14] (MACS) and the WTI thesaurus 'Technology and Management'[15].

---

[12] http://de.dbpedia.org
[13] http://id.loc.gov/authorities/subjects.html
[14] http://www.dnb.de/DE/Wir/Kooperation/MACS/macs_node.html
[15] http://www.wti-frankfurt.de/index.php/produkte-thesaurus

The ontology mapping[16] uses an automated method similar to that applied by the named-entity recognition of the portal: first, main and alternative labels of the GND subject headings are looked up in the aforementioned knowledge bases to identify potential mapping candidates. Then, these mapping candidates are disambiguated by comparing context information of the GND subject headings with context information of the respective mapping candidates. Finally, the English label was extracted of those candidates which had the highest probability for a correct mapping. For 35.025 (55%) GND subject headings, at least one English label could be extracted and saved in the local RDF store [14]. These English labels are used for the automatic indexing of the English-language videos.

The cross-lingual retrieval of the portal works as follows: when the user enters a German search term, the English translation of this term is automatically included in the query, and vice versa. For example, when searching for 'Kernenergie' or 'Atomkraft', the search engine also retrieves hits for 'Nuclear Energy'. As with the inclusion of synonyms, this is likely to increase the completeness of relevant search results.

6   Conclusions

In the TIB|AV-Portal, different kinds of descriptive metadata are available, each with their own utility. It is certainly a great benefit for the retrieval when different kinds of metadata are used, metadata that complement each other and refer to various features, contents and granular levels of the information resources.

Video providers of the TIB|AV-Portal submit only a few manual metadata, which describe formal, technical and content-related features of the video. These are 'classical' metadata such as title, duration and keywords. The manual metadata are coarse-grained and highly reliable. However, most of the content is automatically analysed. The automatic metadata are transcripts and index terms (GND subject headings) describing text, speech or image content of the video. They represent fine-grained descriptions of the individual segments and are less reliable. The manual and automatic metadata complement each other: the manual metadata provide very reliable, albeit less detailed, search results, while the automatic metadata allow for a pinpoint search in the video content. By describing different features and contents of the video, many different opportunities for access emerge.

Written and spoken language in the video are converted to machine-encoded text: OCR and speech transcript. These transcripts permit a keyword-based full-text search. Image motifs as well as written and spoken language of the video are indexed at segment level by specialised GND subject headings from science and technology. Contextual meaning of these GND subject headings was extracted from GND and saved in the knowledge base of the TIB|AV-Portal. In addition, English translations of these GND terms were extracted from DBpedia, LCSH, MACS and WTI thesaurus and also stored in this knowledge base. The semantic search of the TIB|AV-Portal exploits the disambiguated terms and synonyms of the GND, while the cross-lingual retrieval

---

[16] The mapping was carried out by the Semantic Web research group of Hasso Plattner Institute on behalf of TIB.

exploits the English labels derived from the aforementioned ontologies. The semantic search and cross-lingual retrieval improve the traditional keyword-based search by both extending and specifying relevant search results.

7   Future Work: Publishing Metadata of the TIB|AV-Portal as Linked Open Data

Structured data are starting to be exposed and connected to other sources on the web. This initiative is known as Linked Data and mainly involves the identification, machine-readability and linking of data within and between data sets. Data items in these data sets are identified by a URI and are accessible via an HTTP URI. Interlinked data sets that are published under an open license such as CC0 are referred to as Linked Open Data (LOD) and together constitute the Linked Open Data Cloud[17].

Because of being structured, metadata present a huge potential to be used as LOD. As identified in [16], weaving metadata into the LOD Cloud makes them more accessible and facilitates their integration in different scenarios. The accessibility of metadata determines the visibility of both the described content and the institution that provides the data.

The fundamental question is how to publish metadata as LOD. In fact, there is no standardised way to do it [16]. However, there are some common requirements when facing a LOD project, namely: a local RDF store, an ontology that relates data items within the data set and with external data sets, capabilities to get data from other sources and republication of data.

The metadata of the TIB|AV-Portal are stored in RDF form in a local RDF store. RDF consists of subject, predicate and object, which are annotated as resources by using an internal ontology and URI scheme. Videos, films and collections are labelled as `<resource/video>`, `<resource/film>` and `<resource/collection>`, whereas manual metadata, automatic metadata and segment annotations are labelled as `<resource>`, `<resource/ocr>` (or asr or vcd) and `<resource/segment>`, respectively. Annotations related to OCR, automatic speech recognition (ASR) or visual concept detection (VCD) include the location of the recognized GND entity in the video frame.

In order to publish LOD, parts of the internal ontology and URI scheme need to become dereferenceable. We plan to map and merge the current ontology with existing LOD Vocabularies[18]. That is, our ontology will be compared and combined with external vocabularies to enrich and complement it. So far, DCMI Metadata Terms, Academic Institution Internal Structure Ontology, Ontology for Media Resources, Friend of a Friend, Simple Knowledge Organization System and Learning Object Metadata Ontology have been identified as the most adequate vocabularies for our purposes.

---

[17] http://lod-cloud.net/
[18] http://lov.okfn.org/dataset/lov/vocabs

Simultaneously, the internal URIs identifying films and authors will be interlinked with their corresponding external URIs by means of the property `owl:sameAs`[19]. This leads to an enrichment of the internal content, facilitating the future publishing in the LOD Cloud.

Further, the metadata can be embedded into the portal in form of RDFa. The last specification of RDFa 1.1[20] allows the use of RDF in HTML. RDFa defines attributes for the semantic markup such as `about`, `property` or `vocab` to identify the subject, relations between subject and object, and the vocabularies that are used.

Finally, the TIB|AV-Portal aims to promote the use and exposure of its metadata and facilitate the access to them. Users may want to access our data and reuse them. Therefore, all CC0 metadata will be offered as open data in standardised formats or encodings. Doing so, users will have a direct access to metadata and will not have to handle difficult structures that might be hard to understand or manage.

References

1. Gruber, T.R.: Toward Principles for the Design of Ontologies Used for Knowledge Sharing. International Journal of Human-Computer Studies **43**(5–6), 907–928 (1995)
2. Guidelines for Media Resources in Academic Libraries. ACRL Standards and Guidelines (2012)
3. Habibian, A., Snoek, C.G.M.: Recommendations for Recognizing Video Events by Concept Vocabularies. Computer Vision and Image Understanding **124**, 110–122 (2014). doi:10.1016/j.cviu.2014.02.003
4. Hentschel, C., Blümel, I., Sack, H.: Automatic annotation of scientific video material based on visual concept detection. In: Proc. 13th International Conference on Knowledge Management and Knowledge Technologies, 16 (2013). doi:10.1145/2494188.2494213
5. Kubala, F., Colbath, S., Liu, D., Srivastava, A., Markhoul, J.: Integrated Technologies for Indexing Spoken Language. Communications **42**(3), 48–56 (2000). doi:10.1145/328236.328146
6. Lichtenstein, A., Plank, M., Neumann, J.: TIB's Portal for Audiovisual Media: Combining Manual and Automatic Indexing. Cataloging & Classification Quarterly **52**(5), 562–577 (2014). doi:10.1080/01639374.2014.917135
7. Marchionini, G., Song, Y., Farell, R.: Multimedia Surrogates for Video Gisting: Towards Combining Spoken Words and Imagery. Information Processing and Management **15**, 615–630 (2009). doi:10.1016/j.ipm.2009.05.007
8. Marchionini, G., Geisler, G.: The Open Video Digital Library. D-Lib Magazine **8**(12) (2002)
9. National Information Standards Organization (NISO): Understanding Metadata. NISO Press, Bethesda (2004)
10. Sack, H., Waitelonis, J.: Linked Data als Grundlage der semantischen Videosuche mit Yovisto. In: Pellegrini, T., Sack, H., Auer, S. (eds.) Linked Enterprise Data. Management und Bewirtschaftung vernetzter Unternehmensdaten mit Semantic Web Technologien, pp. 21–62. Springer, Berlin (2014)

---

[19] http://www.w3.org/TR/2004/REC-owl-features-20040210/#sameAs
[20] www.w3.org/TR/html-rdfa/

11. Snoek, C.G.M., Huurnink, B., Hollink, L., de Rijke, M., Schreiber, G., Worring, M.: Adding Semantics to Detectors for Video Retrieval. IEEE Trans. Multimedia **9**(5), 975–986 (2007). doi:10.1109/TMM.2007.900156

12. Steinmetz, N., Sack, H.: Cross-Lingual Semantic Mapping of Authority Files. Presentation held at 'Semantic Web in Libraries 2013', Hamburg (2013)

13. Strobel, S., Plank, M.: Semantische Suche nach wissenschaftlichen Videos. Automatische Verschlagwortung durch Named Entity Recognition. Zeitschrift für Bibliothekswesen und Bibliographie **61**(4-5), 255–259 (2014). doi:10.3196/18642950146145154

14. Strobel, S.: Englischsprachige Erweiterung des TIB|AV-Portals. Ein GND/DBpedia-Mapping zur Gewinnung eines englischen Begriffssystems. In: obib. Das offene Bibliotheksjournal, vol. 1, pp. 197–204 (2014). doi:10.5282/o-bib/2014H1S197-204

15. Waitelonis, J., Sack, H.: Towards Exploratory Video Search Using Linked Data. Multimedia Tools and Applications **53**, 1–28 (2011). doi:10.1007/s11042-011-0733-1

16. Zuiderwijk, A., Jeffry, K., Janssen, M.: The Potential of Metadata for Linked Open Data and its Value for Users and Publishers. JeDEM **4**(2), 222–244 (2012)

Metadata Interoperability and Ingestion of Learning Resources into a Modern LMS

Aikaterini K. Kalou[1(✉)], Dimitrios A. Koutsomitropoulos[1],
Georgia D. Solomou[1], and Sotirios D. Botsios[2]

[1] High Performance Information Systems Laboratory (HPCLab),
Computer Engineering and Informatics Department, School of Engineering,
University of Patras, Building B 26500, Patras-Rio, Greece
{kaloukat,kotsomit,solomou}@hpclab.ceid.upatras.gr
[2] Dataverse Ltd, 98 G. Papandreou Street 54655, Kalamaria, Thessaloniki, Greece
sdm@dataverse.gr

Abstract. Over time, academic and research institutions worldwide have commenced the transformation of their digital libraries into a more structured concept, the Learning Object Repository (LOR) that enables the educators to share, manage and use educational resources much more effectively. The key point of LORs interoperability and scalability is without doubt the various standards and protocols such as LOM, SCORM etc. On the other hand, Learning Management Systems have boosted the expansion of the e-learning notion by providing the chance to follow remotely courses of the most well-known universities. However, there is no a uniform way to integrate these two achievements of e-learning and assure an effective collaboration between them. In this paper, we propose a solution on how we can ingest learning objects metadata into the Open eClass platform.

1 Introduction

Thousands of academic and research institutions worldwide implement Learning Object Repositories (LORs) [11,13] in order to maintain and manage their intellectual outcome, with several of them allowing open and free access to their content. A Learning Management System (LMS) on the other hand is a software package that can be used to administer one or more courses to one or more learners [1]. An LMS is typically a web-based system that delivers and manages instructional content, identifies and assesses individual and organizational learning or training goals, tracks the progress, and collects and presents data for supervising the learning process [16].

Modern LMSs offer an abundance of features for course design, creation, management and administration on-line. As a result they concentrate rich learning material or learning objects that can be reused and made available for other purposes. These learning objects most often originate from the instructor's manual labor and their curation level heavily depends on his personal authority. The availability of external learning resources managed and curated by LORs could considerably alleviate the burden of providing additional material to students.

© Springer International Publishing Switzerland 2015
E. Garoufallou et al. (Eds.): MTSR 2015, CCIS 544, pp. 171–182, 2015.
DOI: 10.1007/978-3-319-24129-6_15

Interoperability between educational systems has been investigated before, either by questing for a common unifying model, proposing metadata mappings [8] or even by specifying bridging languages [3]. Indexing of LMS material into a LOR has been also proposed [14]. However, most LMSs do not yet support automated ingestion of LOR material and when they do, the approach is mostly fragmented and oriented towards specific repositories only. Key reasons for this situation seem to include interoperability concerns and metadata schemas incompatibilities. For example, there exists a custom plugin for the Moodle LMS [10], which allows loading of objects from the MERLOT learning repository [12], through a proprietary process. Next, the EU-funded LUISA project [2] created an infrastructure that supports the integration of LOR with a Learning Content Management System (LCMS). It mainly addressed the key issue of Digital Rights Management (DRM) interoperability by exploiting semantic technologies.

Therefore, in this paper we propose a method that addresses the challenge of ingesting external educational resources into a modern LMS. Our proof-of-concept comes from a prototype implementation on top of Open eClass, a widely used LMS by higher education institutions worldwide. First, we consider the internal metadata schema imposed by eClass and examine how it maps to the well-known LOM standard (Section 2). This is necessary in order to assess the interoperability potential of the application and to identify possible points of alignment (mappings) with external collections' metadata. Then we present the design and implementation of our approach and specify a procedure that could automate the mapping process with external LORs (Section 3). Section 4 exemplifies our contribution through a possible usage scenario that involves the ingestion and manipulation of a thematic collection of learning material by the instructor, using the application's front-end. Finally, Section 5 summarizes our conclusions and future work.

2   Metadata Interoperability in Open eClass

Open eClass [4] is a free and flexible e-learning platform which can address the asynchronous distance learning demands of higher education institutions. In addition, it is the solution offered by the Greek Academic Network GUnet to support asynchronous e-learning services in universities. It is mainly designed, developed and supported by the GUnet Asynchronous eLearning Group.

However, it is not clear which of the standards and protocols the eClass platform embeds in its nature. In this section, we make an attempt to record the metadata schema of the eClass platform, map it to the LOM standard and identify which other specifications and standards are included in its infrastructure. We also explain our mapping strategy with external repositories.

2.1   Mapping to LOM and Other Standards

The IEEE Learning Object Metadata (LOM) [6] is a widely adopted standard aiming at the description of educational material (learning material) and training resources (learning resources). The LOM conceptual schema defines the structure of a metadata instance for a learning object (LO). Specifically, LOM contains over sixty elements which are further classified in nine categories (see Figure 1) and each one of them contains metadata about various aspects of a LO. The categories of LOM at the top of the data hierarchy are *General, Life-cycle, Meta-metadata, Technical, Educational, Rights, Relation, Annotation,* and *Classification.*

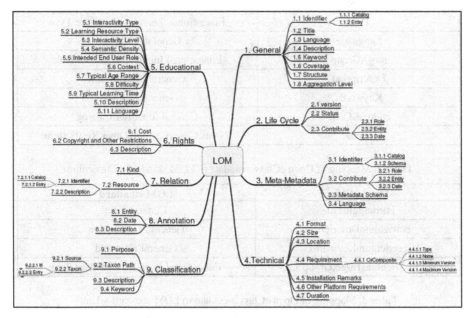

Fig. 1. LOM standard: The hierarchy of elements [7]

The LOM standard respects the general granularity hierarchy of LOs, containing the following six aggregation levels [15]. Similarly, the eClass platform seems to partially adopt these levels:

— *1st Level*: Curriculum
— *2nd Level*: Course
— *3rd Level*: Unit
— *4rth Level*: Topic
— *5th Level*: Lesson
— *6th Level*: Fragment

Based on the above aggregation levels and the set of available metadata, we made an attempt to find out intuitively the common elements between Open eClass and LOM. Our initiative is based on the native structure of Open eClass that appears to be compatible with the LOM specifications [5]. Tables 1-4 gather some of the metadata that can be defined for the wider notion of a course in the context of the Open eClass environment.

Table 1. Mapping of Open eClass metadata to LOM standard - Course

Open eClass	LOM standard
Title	General.Title
Code	General.Identifier.Entry
yearOfStudy	General.Coverage
Semester	
Type	Educational. Learning Resource Type
Language	General. Language
targetGroup	Educational.Intended End User Role
Description	General. Description
Keywords	General.Keyword
eudoxusCode	General.Identifier.Catalog
License	Rights.Copyright and Other Restrictions

Table 2. Mapping of Open eClass metadata to LOM standard - Curriculum

Open eClass	LOM standard
curriculumTitle	General.Title
curriculumDescription	General. Description
curriculumKeywords	General.Keyword
curriculumTargetGroup	Educational.Intended End User Role

Table 3. Mapping of Open eClass metadata to LOM standard – Unit

Open eClass	LOM standard
Title	General.Title
Description	General.Description
Keywords	General.Keyword

Note at this point that most of the metadata of the structural units *Course* and *Curriculum* should be completed during the creation of the Course by the head instructor. On the other hand, metadata related to *Units* and *Fragment-Material* can be filled out once the instructor enriches the *Course* with educational materials categorizing them in conceptual units.

Besides, the Open eClass qualifies to participate in popular international aggregators and directories, thus contributing to the increasing visibility of each educational repository to the broader public. The interconnection with other services is achieved by implementing the OAI-PMH protocol (Open Archives Initiative Protocol for Metadata Harvesting) [9] and the support for simple Dublin Core schema.

Table 4. Mapping of Open eClass metadata to LOM standard – Fragment/Material

Open eClass	LOM standard
Digital	
digital-url	General.Identifier
digital-library	General.Description
Multimedia	
multimedia-title	General.Title
multimedia-description	General.Description
multimedia-keywords	General.Keyword
Link	
link-title	General.Title
link-Category	Classification.Keyword
link-Description	General.Description
link-URL	General.Identifier

2.2   Mapping External Collections

In the context of Open eClass, a *course link* is considered a course fragment (Table 4) and can be specified by setting the following three metadata, a *URL*, a *URL Title* and a *URL Description*. *Category* is optional and can be used to provide an arbitrary header to group links, e.g. in a thematic manner. In our approach, we should extract all these useful and essential details from an incoming collection of external learning material and then map them to one unified metadata schema, which contains the above three fields at minimum. The rest of the metadata annotations are not lost. Rather, it would be easy to retrieve them from their sources directly using their unique URL or harvest them through an OAI service provider. The three metadata elements pertain to not the course itself but only to the external links a course may point to. Therefore, external learning material is mostly referenced, rather than replicated within the LMS. Such a strategy would only put unnecessary burden to the LMS database and would be hard to maintain or keep up-to-date.

In addition, incoming collections may contain metadata in proprietary structure. For example, in openarchives.gr, the main result node of the response is identified with the <entry> node and roughly follows RSS. For the Europe PubMed Central, each <result> node corresponds to a search result and so on. Therefore, in the next section, we also discuss a process for aligning external collections to our schema.

3   Importing Learning Objects

In this section, we present how we extend the Open eClass infrastructure and the overall design of our application and its interaction with learning object collections available within LORs. We also describe thoroughly the main features that have been implemented and advance the user experience in the Open eClass platform.

Finally, we illustrate the alignment procedure that may be followed so as to amalgamate external learning objects into the Open eClass metadata schema.

3.1   Design and Architecture

The modular philosophy of the Open eClass, as a typical and complete Learning Management System, allows us to extend its capabilities with ready-made modules and to reuse them in order to fulfill our new needs and purposes. To this end, we utilize the *Link module* that offers a front-end to enhance a course with useful resources and then group them together under categories, which the instructor can also define. The main obstacle of this module is that it allows instructors to add just one link each time.

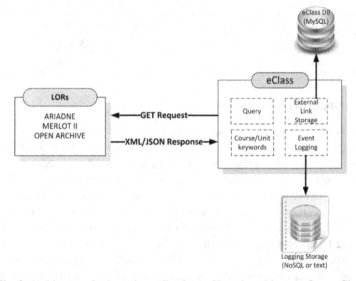

Fig. 2. Architecture for ingesting collections of learning objects in Open eClass

In order to overcome this limit, we have enhanced this module so as to support a more generic, batch way to add external links. In our case, the external links are not just links to web pages, but they are learning objects with high-value educational content. More precisely, the instructor can now add external links through the interface of the *Link* module by communicating with services that harvest LORs, such as Openarchives.gr, ARIADNE and MERLOT II. Additionally, the instructor can load directly a collection of learning object metadata, in XML format, available on the Web or using an appropriate service. The architecture of our re-engineered module is illustrated in Figure 2.

3.2   Implementation and Features

The modification of the *Link* module involves not only the front-end but also the back-end infrastructure. In order to assure asynchronous communication between the back-end and front-end, the capabilities of AJAX technology have been leveraged. All the new features are summarized below:

– *Front-end of the Link module*: The interface of the *Link* module is modified so as to display the learning objects metadata that are loaded from external collections. More precisely, after completion of the loading process, the web interface presents a table of learning object metadata organized into categories. These categories are in fact the keywords used in the query process (see function *Communicating with external web services* below). For each learning object, the URL, the title and the description are available to the end-user. All the front-end functionalities are implemented using the Javascript JQuery library, which is already exploited by the existing module.

– *Metadata retrieval for a course*: In order to discover new learning objects we are based on the existing metadata of the course. In particular, the keywords of the course, the course title and the title of each unit (in case the course includes those) should be recovered. The above function requires communication with the central database of the Open eClass (MySQL, PHP).

– *Link and category storage*: All the learning objects metadata and their corresponding categories, which the instructor has selected from the front-end, will be stored in the central database of Open eClass. This function is responsible for the storage of the title, the URL and the description that characterize a learning object, as well as the category into which the learning object is classified. The major contribution to the storage process is that we abolish the limitation of the storage of one link each time. The modified function supports a batch storage process of many links at once. In addition, this back-end modification makes feasible the automatic generation and storage of new categories for links classification. Until now, the insertion of links and categories were two discrete actions for the instructor. Before storing the learning objects metadata and categories, a check in order to avoid double-entries takes place, i.e. the same learning object of the same category will not be stored more than once. This operation requires communication with the central database of the Open eClass (MySQL, PHP).

– *Communication with external web services*: The *Link* module is modified appropriately to retrieve learning object metadata in XML format, either from XML sources or remote web services or from online repositories directly. In the first case, a simple function of XML file parsing has been developed (PHP). Each collection should always have a predefined, unique metadata schema (see Section 3.3). In the case of online retrieval, the module is capable of sending HTTP requests to external web services based on information that has been recovered as described in the function *Metadata retrieval for a course*, i.e. using course keywords as query terms. The external service to be queried can be configured within the main system configuration. The responses (XML and JSON format) are sorted and can be transformed in order to conform to the uniform metadata schema. The communication with the web services via the HTTP protocol is implemented using AJAX technology.

– *Logging instructors' actions*: Furthermore, we have implemented a logging process so as to gather data on i) how many learning objects are loaded from the external collections or how many results are retrieved for each keyword (especially when communicating with external services and/or LORs), ii) where the learning objects are coming from, iii) which instructor submits the load/search request (in the case of retrieval from external services we record also the specific set of keywords), iv) the date-time of each load/search request and v) how many of the results the instructor selects to save as links in his own course. We have adopted an external NoSQL-document database for the storage of all this information that is also configurable.

3.3   Alignment Procedure

When ingesting learning object metadata into the Open eClass platform, it is necessary to express them in compliance with the rules of the metadata schema that we propose in the context of this work. This schema consists of the five major elements as they are presented in the following table.

Table 5. Example instantiation of the metadata schema

```
<Results>
        <Category keyword="medicine">
            <Result>
                <URL>http://dx.doi.org/10.1097/JSM.0000000000000175</URL>
                <Title>American Medical Society for Sports Medicine position statement: inter-
                ventional   musculoskeletal ultrasound in sports medicine.</Title>
                <Description> (PUBMED) The use of diagnostic and interventional ultrasound
has significantly increased over the past decade. A majority of the increased utilization is by nonra-
diologists. In sports medicine, ultrasound is often used to guide interventions such as aspirations,
diagnostic or therapeutic injections, tenotomies, releases, and hydrodissections.
                </Description>
            </Result>
        </Category>
<Results>
```

As an initial step of the ingestion process, we need to configure not only which LORs we intend to utilize for the learning objects retrieval, but also how the responses will be efficiently transformed so as to manipulate them in one unified manner. It is necessary to create mapping rules in order to match the incoming results to the metadata of links (URL, URL title and URL description) according to the metadata schema. All the setting properties can be defined in a configuration file having JSON format. The following table shows through an example all the needed attributes that must be set so that the retrieved learning objects metadata from a new source would be consistent with the unified metadata schema.

In brief, the attributes repository_url and repository_extra_parameter are used in order to construct the HTTP GET requests. A typical URL in order to query the keyword 'semantic' in OpenSearch API is http://openarchives.gr/opensearch/semantic/page:1/ limit:25 and consists of the following parameters:

- http://openarchives.gr/opensearch/: the main url of the script that responds to HTTP GET request
- *query*: keyword with which you want to search, in our example is 'semantic'

- *page*: page number from which results start
- *limit*: the number of results per page

In our application, the parameter *query* should not be defined in the configuration file, since it is set ad lib from the end user at the front end. All the other attributes under the *metadata* attribute define how all the various responses can be translated in a uniform xml. The *result* attribute indicates how we can identify each result node in the xml response. Next, the *url*, *url_title* and *url_description* parameters allows us to distinguish the three elements from the rest of metadata that describe the result.

Table 6. An excerpt of the configuration file

```
{
        "repositoryA": {
            "repository_url":"http://www.ebi.ac.uk/europepmc/webservices/rest/search/query=",
            "repository_extra_parameter":"&resultType=core",
            "metadata": {
                    "result": "result",
                    "url": "url",
                    "url_title": "title",
                    "url_description": "abstractText"
            }
    },
        "repositoryB": {
        "repository_url":"http://openarchives.gr/opensearch/",
        "repository_extra_parameter":"/limit:25",
        "metadata": {
                "result": "entry",
                "url": "content",
                "url_title": "title",
                "url_description": "dc:identifier"
        }
    }
}
```

4   A Usage Scenario

After successful authorization, the logged instructor can select the *Link* module from the navigation menu of his course and then the *Add Learning Objects*. When an external harvesting service is to be used, a search form appears with a unique field that has a predefined set of keywords (see Figure 3).

These keywords, separated by a comma, include the keywords that the instructor has already set for his own course (section 3.2). However, the instructor is free to set a different set of keywords each time. The terms must always be separated by a comma so that they can be handled as distinct keywords by the recipient web service. In case the system is fed with a precompiled collection of metadata the keywords are simply ignored.

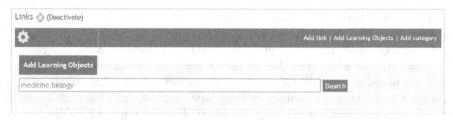

Fig. 3. Communicating search keywords to the recipient web service

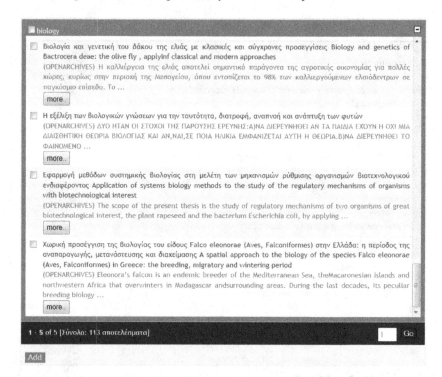

Fig. 4. List of learning objects – Front end

Once our application completes the loading process, the retrieved results, categorized based on each keyword, are presented in the form of a table (see Figure 4), under the search form. For clarity reasons, there is a pagination capability of the results' categories. Besides, the categories are shown by default collapsed and not the entire list of results is presented at once.

The instructor can traverse through the results' pages using the navigation buttons. The full list view of results for a particular category/keyword can be toggled by clicking on the plus/minus button or on the category title, which expands or collapses category results, respectively. Moreover, in order to pick a link for insertion, he can select the checkbox near the link title. In case he desires to select all the results for a category, he can do it at once by clicking the checkbox near the category title. Whenever he is ready to submit the selected links, he just pushes the button 'Add'.

5   Conclusions and Future Work

Achieving interoperability between repositories of learning resources and LMSs is a key challenge and critical for the efficient dissemination, sharing and reuse of the huge amount of knowledge they manage. In this paper we presented a method for bridging an LMS with external learning object collections. Going beyond batch importing, we have built on top of a modular architecture and we have additionally designed and implemented a workflow for presentation, traversal and selection of external resources to be followed by instructors.

While different metadata schemata may pose barriers for direct integration, it is possible to identify a least common set of elements by referencing well known educational metadata standards such as LOM. We have shown that this set can form the basis for a common schema to be used for immediate ingestion of learning objects into eClass.

Although we specify a procedure for aligning LORs' schemata with our own, the ingestion process can be fully automated by delegating this task to a specialized web service. In this sense, the eClass service we have developed is extensible, in that it is already capable of communicating with external services through requests and responses. Future work would consider the development of such a service, which would perform federated search across repositories and then feed the metadata ingestion subsystem of the LMS, thus aiming at the development of improved knowledge retrieval services that make educational material search and reuse more efficient and straightforward.

Acknowledgements. This work has been partially supported by the project "Information System Development for Library Functional Services" of the Democritus University of Thrace, co-financed by Greece and the European Union, in the context of Operational Programme "Digital Convergence" of the National Strategic Reference Framework (NSRF) 2007-2013.

References

1. Gallagher, P.S.: Assessing SCORM 2004 for its Affordances in Facilitating a Simulation as a Pedagogical Model. Doctoral Dissertation, George Mason University, Fairfax, VA (2007)
2. Garcia, R., Pariente, T.: Interoperability of Learning Objects Copyright in the LUISA Semantic Learning Management System. Journal Information Systems Management. **26**(3), 252–261 (2009)
3. Gavidia, A.R., Sicilia, M.A., Garcia-Barriocanal, E., Palazuelos, G.M.: Towards automated Specifications of Scenarios in Enhanced learning Technology. International Journal of Web-Based Learning and Teaching Technologies **3**(1), 68–77 (2008)
4. GUnet asynchronous eLearning group. Platform description (Open eClass 2.10). http://docs.openeclass.org/en:detail_descr (retrieved)
5. GUnet Open eClass Asynchronous eLearning Platform (Teacher Manual). http://www.ekpa-fa.gr/openeclass/manuals/mant/OpeneClass24_ManT_en.pdf (retrieved)

6. IEEE LTSC: Draft Standard for Learning Object Metadata (IEEE 1484.12.1-2002) (2002). http://grouper.ieee.org/groups/ltsc/wg12/files/LOM_1484_12_1_v1_Final_Draft.pdf
7. IMS: Metadata Best Practice Guide for IEEE 1484.12.1-2002 Standard for Learning Object Metadata. Version 1.3 Public Draft (2004)
8. Karampiperis, P., Kastradas, K., Sampson, D.: A schema-mapping algorithm for educational metadata interoperability. In: Edmedia-World Conference on Educational Multimedia, Hypermedia & Telecommunications (2003)
9. Lagoze, C., Van de Sompel, H., Nelson, M., Warner, S.: The Open Archive Initiative Protocol for Metadata Harvesting (2002). http://www.openarchives.org/OAI/openarchivesprotocol. html (retrieved)
10. Leal, J.P., Queirós, R.: Integration of repositories in Moodle. In: 8th National Conference on XML, Associated Technologies and Applications (XATA 2010), pp. 57–68 (2010)
11. Eap, M., Hatala, M., Gasevic, D.: Technologies for enabling the sharing of Learning Objects. International Journal of Advanced Media and Communication 2(1) (2008)
12. MERLOT: Multimedia educational resource for learning and on-line teaching website (2012). http://www.merlot.org/
13. Namuth, D., Fritz, S., King, J., Boren, A.: Principles of sustainable learning object libraries. Interdisciplinary Journal of Knowledge and Learning Objects 1, 181–196 (2005)
14. Ochoa, X., Cardinaels, K., Meire, M., Duval, E.: Frameworks for the automatic indexation of learning management systems content into learning object repositories. In: Edmedia-World Conference on Educational Multimedia, Hypermedia & Telecommunications (2005)
15. Stratakis, M., Christophides, V., Keenoy, K., Magkanaraki, A.: E-Learning Standards - SeLeNe (Self E-Learning Networks IST-2001-39045), Project Deliverable 2.1, Greece (2003)
16. Szabo, M., Flesher, K.: CMI theory and practice: historical roots of learning management systems. In: World Conference on E-Learning in Corporate, Government, Healthcare and Higher Education, Montreal, Canada, AACE (2002)

Clustering Learning Objects for Improving Their Recommendation via Collaborative Filtering Algorithms

Henrique Lemos dos Santos[1(✉)], Cristian Cechinel[1],
Ricardo Matsumura Araujo[1], and Miguel-Ángel Sicilia[2]

[1] Federal University of Pelotas, Pelotas, RS 96016-080, Brazil
{hldsantos,ricardo}@inf.ufpel.edu.br, contato@cristiancechinel.pro.br
[2] Computer Science Department, University of Alcalá, Polytechnic Building,
Ctra. Barcelona, Km. 33.6, 28871 Madrid, Spain
msicilia@uah.es

Abstract. Collaborative Filtering can be used in the context of e-learning to recommend learning objects to students and teachers involved with the teaching and learning process. Although such technique presents a great potential for e-learning, studies related to this application in this field are still limited, mostly because the inexistence of available datasets for testing and evaluating. The present work evaluates a pre-processsing method through clustering for future use of collaborative filtering algorithms. For that we use a large data set collected from the MERLOT repository. The initial results point out that clustering learning objects before the use of collaborative filtering techniques can improve the recommendations performance.

Keywords: Collaborative filtering · Learning objects · Recommender systems · Clustering

1 Introduction

Learning objects are self-contained units of learning that are an important component of many distance education programs. By providing such objects, a program can allow students the freedom to build an unique learning path that suits the students' preferences, abilities and previous knowledge.

Collections of learning objects are often organized in Learning Object Repositories (LOR), digital libraries where communities submit objects for students, educators and other stakeholders to be consumed through different means (e.g. directly from the repository or in other platforms such as LMS). Existing LOR can differ in several ways (e.g. location of the LO, specificity of the area, type of materials, metadata standards adopted) [1] and cater to different communities, countries or level of education.

Large repositories can contain tens of thousands different learning objects, making potentially difficult for students and educators to find relevant materials

© Springer International Publishing Switzerland 2015
E. Garoufallou et al. (Eds.): MTSR 2015, CCIS 544, pp. 183–194, 2015.
DOI: 10.1007/978-3-319-24129-6_16

of interest. As LORs are naturally organized around communities of interest, such platforms normally rely on the members of these communities to rate and comment the resources so that the higher-rated ones are further surfaced ranked and more visible during the search and retrieval process [2].

To improve learning object discoverability, the use of recommender systems has been largely investigated [3]. These systems can provide recommendations of new objects based on one's history of objects consumed or rated (e.g. collaborative filtering approach) and are largely available in electronic commerce, most notably in sites such as Amazon, and in the distribution of digital goods such as movies, games and books. They can also recommend objects based on its contents, e. g., if the user views many Drama movies, then, an unseen Drama movie could be a good recommendation.

Despite the possible benefits that collaborative filtering algorithms (CF) adoption could provide for the field of recommender systems in TEL, there is still a lack of studies reporting results obtained specifically from the use of CF in large quality data samples. This has mainly to do with the major lack of sharable datasets that can be used for testing solutions in a way they can be generalized [4]. Existing experiments of CF in TEL are normally conducted on small-scale scenarios and/or in controlled environments [5] , and few researchers have attempted to test and validate their recommender systems on data captured from real-life data settings [6].

The present work extends a previous experiment conducted by [7] with a large data sample collected from Merlot repository[1] and shows how clustering learning objects can improve recommendations based on CF. This work shows that by clustering learning objects prior to recommending can reduce error rates when compared to the same technique applied to non-clustered objects and have the added benefit of making computation less demanding.

The paper is organized as follows. Section 2 describes previous related works. Section 3 depicts the goals and the methodology followed in this study together with some characteristics of the database collected. Section 4 presents the results and discussion, and section 5 concludes the paper and presents some possibilities of future work.

2   Related Work

2.1   Recommender Systems in TEL

The work presented here falls under the scope of the broad field of Technology Enhanced Learning (TEL), a domain concerned with how different technologies can support educational processes. This field has seen a growing interest in recent years (e.g. [8], [9], [10], [11]), especially with the rise and success of massive open online courses (MOOCs) and large educational resource repositories [12].

Related works can be grouped into three broad sections. First, studies on how useful recommender systems are to learning scenarios evaluate traditional

---

[1] http://www.merlot.org

recommender algorithms applied to a variety of data sets. Second, studies on improving recommender systems applied to learning try to find how to improve recommender algorithms given specific features that arise from learning processes. Third, studies focusing on clustering methods applied to recommender systems show the benefits of this technique in fields other than learning.

In [13], a user-based collaborative filtering algorithm was applied to an online forum for English learning, aiming at recommending forum posts to readers. It was found that adding the recommender improves engagement and performance in language ability tests. In [14], a user-based collaborative filtering algorithm is evaluated using the Merlot repository, focusing on the analysis of different parameters of the algorithm and the impact they have on recommendation performance. We adopt this algorithm with the best-performing parameters found in our study, along with the data set.

Several attempts have been made at improving recommendation in learning settings. In [15] it is proposed to measure semantic similarity between objects by analyzing usage context. This similarity measure is used to help populate a sparse rating matrix and it is shown to improve recommendations. In [16] a content-based recommender system is shown to benefit from the growing use of Linked-Data. Early work of [17] attempts to combine content-based filtering and fuzzy ontologies, analyzing three main characteristics of a learning object in order to determine its recommendation: completeness, adaptation to the user context (temporal) and adaptation to the user preferences. TF-IDF is used in [18] in order to compute similarity between learning items and rank them using only good learners' ratings. In this paper, the first phase is basically identical to that one, however, here a collaborative filtering algorithm is used in order to recommend objects to users with a predicted rating value. In [19] recommendations are improved by classifying students' according to their learning styles and using this classification along with a traditional ratings matrix. Another such hybrid proposal is shown in [20] where students ratings about a learning object are stored together with their knowledge and their current learning goals in order to improve the recommendation system. These two approaches can be seen as working on the user level, whereas our approach perform a different attempt that initially focuses on the content level. Collaborative filtering and content-based recommendation were evaluated in [21]. More recently, [22] notes that the same collaborative filtering algorithm can display very different performance when applied to different datasets and propose the use of multi-criteria algorithms. A discussion and proposal of a set of guidelines appear in [23], where it is argued that educational resources recommendations must be both based on educators' experience and fitted to the learner context .

Finally, [24] argues that contextual information can improve recommender systems, since an adaptive response becomes possible and an extreme personalized response can be built by the recommender for each user. In the same paper, this contextual information is defined and an analysis of existing TEL recommender systems, based on the usage of this information, is shown.

2.2   Recommender Systems and Clustering Methods

One of the main challenges of deploying recommender systems is to scale when there are a very large number of users and items to recommend [25]. Clustering is an often applied technique to improve scalability of recommender systems, where users or items are grouped according to some similarity metric and recommendation is applied on a per-group base instead of to the whole population. It is also used to reduce sparsity in user-ratings matrix.

For instance, [26] shows that clustering users by their ratings before applying an item-based collaborative filtering algorithm in a real-world e-commerce system can improve scalability with little loss in recommendation performance. A similar approach is presented in [27], where a k-means clustering algorithm is applied to the MovieLens database users and a neighborhood of users is created based on each *centroid* of each item's cluster. Aiming at reducing the sparsity of the initial user-ratings matrix, [28] uses both item and user clustering with an smoothed users ratings matrix as an input. Likewise, [29] shows a recommendation engine that uses products' review information in order to reveal categories of users and products, along with co-clustering techniques applied to traditional ratings matrix for better predictions. Similar approaches can be found on [30], [31], [32].

In a TEL environment, [33] identifies the differences between general recommenders and e-learning recommenders and also presents an e-learning system where users are clustered by their learning interests; each cluster then has its own recommendation process using collaborative filtering techniques. This is a similar approach to what is presented in the current paper, but we propose clustering learning objects instead of users.

3   Goals and Methodology

3.1   Goals

Our main goal in this paper is to improve the applicability of recommendation algorithms to learning objects in LORs. Our objective is to evaluate the impact in recommendation efficacy of applying clustering techniques to objects beforehand and providing recommendations within each cluster. Our hypothesis is that such clustering may not only improve the scalability of a system as a whole, but also improve accuracy as similar learning objects are often consumed together.

3.2   Data Description

In this paper we use an updated version of the data set presented in [14], containing a sample of users, learning objects and ratings available at the Merlot repository. This data set contains 9910 ratings (ranging from 1 to 5) over 4968 learning objects from 3659 users.

The data set contained several information and meta-information about the objects (e.g. description, categories, material type, reviews, language) and users (e.g. affiliations, categories, member type), along with their relationships (ratings, comments and personal collections). We restricted our use to the following information on learning objects: description, title and ratings. Description and title are textual fields, while a rating is a tuple $< user\_id, object\_id, rating >$ and establishes a weighted relation between users and objects.

3.3 Generating Clusters and Recommendations

Our general approach to recommendation is based on applying collaborative filtering to clusters of learning objects instead of recommending across all available objects. In order to do so, we first perform a content-based clusterization of objects and then generate recommenders within each cluster. We analyze the performance of these recommenders when changes to the number of clusters and parameters of the recommender algorithm are changed. The implementations used are those available in the Apache Mahout environment[2], version 0.7. The same environment was used to calculate the main metrics and evaluations.

In order to generate clusters of objects, we used their textual information (title and description). A bag-of-words approach was chosen, where each object is represented by a n-dimensional vector where each position represents a single word. We applied the TF-IDF algorithm [34] to generate the values. For each word, the weight output from the algorithm is stored in the respective position in the vector. This technique ideally discards stop-words by making their values closer to zero, whereas relevant words receive higher values.

The k-means algorithm [35, Chapter 9] was then applied to the TF-IDF sparse vectors to generate the clusters, using cosine similarity and random initialization. We tested different values for k, varying between 2 and 9. Larger values lead to very sparse data, making the collaborative filtering algorithm unable to provide recommendations.

After applying k-means, each learning object is now attributed to one of the k clusters. As an example, Table 1 shows the results of applying the algorithm using $k = 6$. This table shows the resulting number of objects in each cluster and the number of users and ratings associated to these objects. It must be noted that while each object and rating are uniquely associated to a single cluster, the same user may appear in multiple clusters as they are associated to multiple objects.

In order to perform the recommendations, we applied a user-based collaborative filtering algorithm, using Log-Likelihood Ratio [36] as the similarity measure. Along with k for the k-means, the two main parameters of the user-based collaborative filtering algorithm were systematically varied to observe the changes in prediction error. Neighborhood size N was varied between 2 and 20. Minimum similarity was varied between 0.1 and 0.9. For each set of parameters the algorithm was run 50 times and the average results are presented.

Two metrics were used to measure prediction errors, following [37]: Mean Average Error (MAE) and Root-Mean Squared Error (RMS).

---

[2] https://mahout.apache.org/

Table 1. An example of applying k-means to the dataset using $k = 6$

Cluster	Number of users	Number of LOs	Number of ratings
1	1344	1403	2852
2	638	543	960
3	142	269	329
4	1206	616	1658
5	1255	1228	2438
6	1039	909	1673

4 Results and Discussion

We start by showing how varying the neighborhood size (N) and number of clusters (k) affect MAE and RMS, comparing the results to those obtained without clustering. Figure 1 summarizes the results for the most relevant values of k. For each k, the clusters unable to receive recommendations were excluded from the computation of the average MAE and RMS. In order to improve visualization, we choose not to show all values of k in this figure.

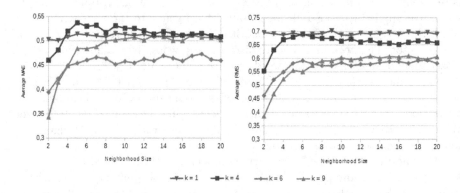

Fig. 1. Average of the MAE (left) and RMS (right) errors, for different values of k and on each tested value of neighborhood size. $k = 1$ represents the case where no clustering was performed.

An ANOVA test was ran to evaluate whether the means of the average MAE for the different k were significantly different, and a Kruskal-Wallis test was ran to evaluate differences among the medians. Both tests presented significant differences at the 95.0% confidence level. Figure 2 helps to better visualize these differences.

These figures show that introducing clusters can reduce MAE, but the performance is heavily dependent on the number of clusters and neighborhood sizes. In our results, setting $k = 9$ allowed for the lowest average error, using $N = 2$, with a median about 6% lower compared to the case without clustering. However, the resulting error was found to be too sensitive to N and, as it is increased, MAE quickly rises and becomes no different than for $k = 1$. For $k = 6$, on the other hand, MAE remain low for all tested values of neighborhood size.

For $k = 4$ errors are actually higher than having no clusters for a wide range of N, with the exception of very small N, where error is lower, and high N, where error converge to about the same level as $k = 9$ and $k = 1$.

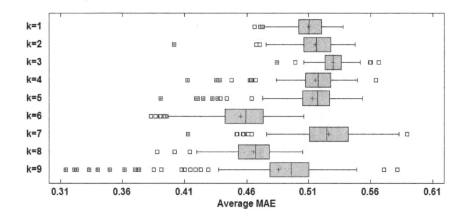

Fig. 2. Box-plots of Average MAE for each value of k

4.1 User-Space Coverage

We calculated the user-space coverage for the different values of k tested in the experiment. These values are show in Table 2.

Table 2. User-space Coverage

k	User-space Coverage (from total users)(%)
1	32,77
2	32,08
3	27,47
4	26,59
5	23,99
6	23,72
7	19,05
8	19,02
9	18,31

As it can be seen from the table, there is a clear trade-off between the number of clusters generated and the user-space coverage, i.e., as higher the value of k the lesser the user-space coverage. This can be happening because greater values of k reduce the average total of ratings (and learning objects, and users)

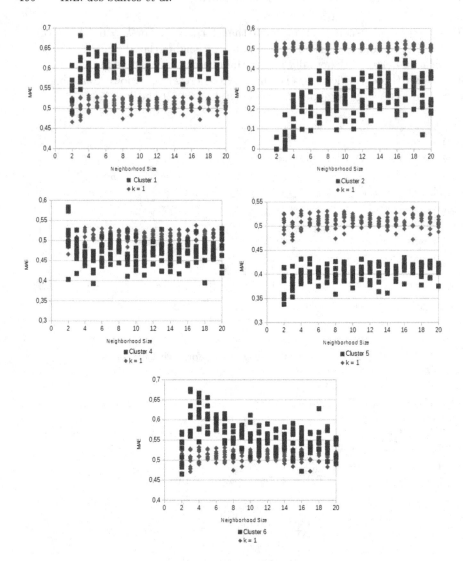

Fig. 3. Averages of the MAE error for five clusters of k=6 compared to total database, on each tested value of neighborhood size.

per cluster, which can increase the sparsity of the traditional user-item ratings matrix, thus deteriorating (or even forbidding) the recommendations for some resulting clusters. Therefore, the advantages of clustering learning objects to reduce errors in the recommendations have the drawback of diminishing the number of users that will benefit from the recommendations.

4.2   Inside the Clusters

We selected the clusters for k = 6 (which presented the best results) to take a closer look and compare their average MAE against the average MAE for k = 1 (the case without clustering). In Figure 3, each cluster for k = 6 is exposed in terms of neighborhood size and its respective average MAE, and compared to the same measures for the entire database (k = 1).

Clusters numbering are the same as those used in Table 1. Note that users on cluster 3 could not receive any recommendation, thus, MAE values for this cluster do not exist. Different scales were used in the Figure in order to improve visualization.

As it can be seen from the figure, different clusters presented different performances in terms of their average MAE. Recommendations for clusters 2, 4 and 5 presented lower MAE than recommendations for k=1 (no clustering), whereas clusters 1 and 6 presented higher MAE. An ANOVA and a Kruskal-wallis test confirmed that these differences were statistically significant at the 95.0% confidence level (means and medias significant different). This allow us to say that the gain obtained from clustering before applying a collaborative filtering algorithm is valid only for a certain number of clusters and therefore, a certain number of users.

5   Final Remarks

The work presented in this paper used an hybrid approach, in an attempt to group learning objects by their description and title similarity and then use collaborative filtering algorithms in more specific excerpts from the total ratings database. In order to compare with the traditional collaborative filtering approach, the entire ratings database had its recommendations also evaluated.

The obtained results have shown that even for small databases (with less than ten thousand ratings) clustering learning objects before applying collaborative filtering techniques can improve recommendation's quality. However, this gain is not universal and will depend on the cluster under evaluation. This proposal avoided to use explicit learning objects categories (also collected from the Merlot website) in order to be generic enough to be applied in any other learning object repository. Future work will focus on similiarities other than LLR, item-based collaborative filtering and another important measures of recommendation's evaluation [37]: item-space coverage and novelty.

Acknowledgments. This work has been funded by FAPERGS (Foundation for Research Support of the State of Rio Grande do Sul - Brazil) through its Pesquisador Gaúcho Program - PQG - Edital 02/2014, by CYTED (Ibero-American Programme for Science, Technology and Development) as part of project 'RIURE - Ibero-American Network for the Usability of Learning Repositories' (code 513RT0471), and by Federal University of Pelotas (UFPel - Brazil).

References

1. McGreal, R.: A typology of learning object repositories. In: Adelsberger, H., Kinshuk, Pawlowski, J., Sampson, D. (eds.) Handbook on Information Technologies for Education and Training. International Handbooks on Information Systems, pp. 5–28. Springer, Heidelberg (2008)

2. Cechinel, C., Sánchez-Alonso, S., García-Barriocanal, E.: Statistical profiles of highly-rated learning objects. Computers & and Education **57**(1), 1255–1269 (2011)
3. Manouselis, N., Drachsler, H., Verbert, K., Santos, O.C.: Recommender Systems for Technology Enhanced Learning: Research Trends and Applications. Springer Publishing Company, Incorporated (2014)
4. Drachsler, H., Bogers, T., Vuorikari, R., Verbert, K., Duval, E., Manouselis, N., Beham, G., Lindstaedt, S., Stern, H., Friedrich, M., Wolpers, M.: Issues and considerations regarding sharable data sets for recommender systems in technology enhanced learning. Procedia Computer Science **1**(2), 2849–2858 (2010). Proceedings of the 1st Workshop on Recommender Systems for Technology Enhanced Learning (RecSysTEL 2010)
5. Verbert, K., Drachsler, H., Manouselis, N., Wolpers, M., Vuorikari, R., Duval, E.: Dataset-driven research for improving recommender systems for learning. Proceedings of the 1st International Conference on Learning Analytics and Knowledge. LAK 2011, pp. 44–53. ACM, New York (2011)
6. Manouselis, N., Drachsler, H., Vuorikari, R., Hummel, H., Koper, R.: Recommender systems in technology enhanced learning. In: Ricci, F., Rokach, L., Shapira, B., Kantor, P.B. (eds.) Recommender Systems Handbook, US, pp. 387–415. Springer (2011)
7. Cechinel, C., Sicilia, M.Á., Sánchez-Alonso, S., García-Barriocanal, E.: Evaluating collaborative filtering recommendations inside large learning object repositories. Information Processing & Management **49**(1), 34–50 (2013)
8. Santos, O.C., Boticario, J.G., Prez-Marn, D.: Extending web-based educational systems with personalised support through user centred designed recommendations along the e-learning life cycle. Science of Computer Programming **88**, 92–109 (2014). Software Development Concerns in the e-Learning Domain
9. Mdritscher, F.: Towards a recommender strategy for personal learning environments. Procedia Computer Science 1(2), 2775–2782 (2010). Proceedings of the 1st Workshop on Recommender Systems for Technology Enhanced Learning (RecSysTEL 2010)
10. Schoefegger, K., Seitlinger, P., Ley, T.: Towards a user model for personalized recommendations in work-integrated learning: A report on an experimental study with a collaborative tagging system. Procedia Computer Science **1**(2), 2829–2838 (2010). Proceedings of the 1st Workshop on Recommender Systems for Technology Enhanced Learning (RecSysTEL 2010)
11. Grandbastien, M., Loskovska, S., Nowakowski, S., Jovanovic, J.: Using online presence data for recommending human resources in the op4l project. In: 2nd Workshop on Recommender Systems in Technology Enhanced Learning (RecSysTEL) - 7th European Conference on Technology Enhanced Learning (EC-TEL 2012), pp. 89–94 (2012)
12. Tzikopoulos, A., Manouselis, N., Vuorikari, R.: An overview of learning object repositories. Selected readings on database technologies and applications, pp. 44–64 (2009)
13. Wang, P.Y., Yang, H.C.: Using collaborative filtering to support college students use of online forum for english learning. Computers & Education **59**(2), 628–637 (2012)

14. Sicilia, M.Á., García-Barriocanal, E., Sánchez-Alonso, S., Cechinel, C.: Exploring user-based recommender results in large learning object repositories: the case of MERLOT. Procedia Computer Science **1**(2), 2859–2864 (2010). Proceedings of the 1st Workshop on Recommender Systems for Technology Enhanced Learning (RecSysTEL 2010)

15. Niemann, K., Wolpers, M.: Creating usage context-based object similarities to boost recommender systems in technology enhanced learning. IEEE Transactions on Learning Technologies PP(99), 1 (2014)

16. Dietze, S., Drachsler, H., Giordano, D.: A survey on linked data and the social web as facilitators for tel recommender systems. In: Manouselis, N., Drachsler, H., Verbert, K., Santos, O.C. (eds.) Recommender Systems for Technology Enhanced Learning, pp. 47–75. Springer, New York (2014)

17. Romero, F., Ferreira-Satler, M., Olivas, J., Prieto-Mendez, M., Menendez-Dominguez, V.: A fuzzy-based recommender approach for learning objects management systems. In: 2011 11th International Conference on Intelligent Systems Design and Applications (ISDA), pp. 984–989, November 2011

18. Ghauth, K., Abdullah, N.: Learning materials recommendation using good learners ratings and content-based filtering. Educational Technology Research and Development **58**(6), 711–727 (2010)

19. Klašnja-Milićević, A., Vesin, B., Ivanovi, M., Budimac, Z.: E-learning personalization based on hybrid recommendation strategy and learning style identification. Computers & Education 56(3), 885–899 (2011)

20. Gomez-Albarran, M., Jimenez-Diaz, G.: Recommendation and studentsáuthoring in repositories of learning objects: A case-based reasoning approach. International Journal of Emerging Technologies in Learning (iJET) 4(0) (2009)

21. Drachsler, H., Hummel, H.G.K., Koper, R.: Personal recommender systems for learners in lifelong learning networks: the requirements, techniques and model. Int. J. Learn. Technol. **3**(4), 404–423 (2008)

22. Manouselis, N., K.G.S.G.: Revisiting the multi-criteria recommender system of a learning portal. In: 2nd Workshop on Recommender Systems in Technology Enhanced Learning (RecSysTEL) - 7th European Conference on Technology Enhanced Learning (EC-TEL 2012), pp. 35–48 (2012)

23. Santos, O.C., Boticario, J.G.: Practical guidelines for designing and evaluating educationally oriented recommendations. Computers & Education **81**, 354–374 (2015)

24. Verbert, K., Manouselis, N., Ochoa, X., Wolpers, M., Drachsler, H., Bosnic, I., Duval, E.: Context-aware recommender systems for learning: A survey and future challenges. IEEE Transactions on Learning Technologies **5**(4), 318–335 (2012)

25. Ochoa, X., Carrillo, G.: Recomendación de objetos de aprendizaje basado en el perfil del usuario y la información de atención contextualizada. Conferencias LACLO **4**(1) (2013)

26. Gong, S., Ye, H.: Joining user clustering and item based collaborative filtering in personalized recommendation services. In: 2009 International Conference on Industrial and Information Systems, IIS 2009, pp. 149–151, April 2009

27. Huang, Y.: An item based collaborative filtering using item clustering prediction. In: 2009 ISECS International Colloquium on Computing, Communication, Control, and Management, CCCM 2009, vol. 4, pp. 54–56, August 2009

28. Mase, H., Ohwada, H.: A collaborative filtering incorporating hybrid-clustering technology. In: 2012 International Conference on Systems and Informatics (ICSAI), pp. 2342–2346, May 2012

29. Xu, Y., Lam, W., Lin, T.: Collaborative filtering incorporating review text and co-clusters of hidden user communities and item groups. Proceedings of the 23rd ACM International Conference on Information and Knowledge Management. CIKM 2014, pp. 251–260. ACM, New York (2014)
30. Sun, H., Wu, T., Yan, M., Wu, Y.: A new item clustering-based collaborative filtering approach. In: 2012 Ninth Web Information Systems and Applications Conference (WISA), pp. 91–94, November 2012
31. Rongfei, J., Maozhong, J., Chao, L.: A new clustering method for collaborative filtering. In: 2010 International Conference on Networking and Information Technology (ICNIT), pp. 488–492, June 2010
32. Li, X.: Collaborative filtering recommendation algorithm based on cluster. In: 2011 International Conference on Computer Science and Network Technology (ICC-SNT), vol. 4, pp. 2682–2685, December 2011
33. Tang, T., McCalla, G.: Smart recommendation for an evolving e-learning system: Architecture and experiment. International Journal on E-Learning **4**(1), 105–129 (2005)
34. Wartena, C., Brussee, R., Slakhorst, W.: Keyword extraction using word co-occurrence. In: 2010 Workshop on Database and Expert Systems Applications (DEXA), pp. 54–58, August 2010
35. Owen, S., Anil, R., Dunning, T., Friedman, E.: Mahout in action. Manning (2011)
36. Dunning, T.: Accurate methods for the statistics of surprise and coincidence. Comput. Linguist. **19**(1), 61–74 (1993)
37. Herlocker, J.L., Konstan, J.A., Terveen, L.G., Riedl, J.T.: Evaluating collaborative filtering recommender systems. ACM Trans. Inf. Syst. **22**(1), 5–53 (2004)

Conceptualization of Personalized Privacy Preserving Algorithms

Buket Usenmez and Ozgu Can[(✉)]

Department of Computer Engineering, Ege University, 35100 Bornova, Izmir, Turkey
usenmez.buket@gmail.com, ozgu.can@ege.edu.tr

Abstract. In recent years, personal data has been shared between organizations and researchers. While sharing information, individuals' sensitive data should be preserved. For this purpose, a number of algorithms for privacy-preserving publish data have been designed. These algorithms modify or transform data to protect privacy. While the anonymization algorithms such as k-anonymity, l-diversity and t-closeness focus on changing data to a protected form, the differential privacy model considers the results of queries posed on data. Therefore, these algorithms can be compared according to their performance or utility of the queries that have been applied on anonymized data or computed results with noise. In this work, we present a domain-independent semantic model of data anonymization techniques which also considers individuals' different privacy concerns. Thus, the proposed conceptualized model integrates the generic view of privacy preserving data anonymization algorithms with a personalized privacy approach.

Keywords: Data anonymization · Privacy · Semantic web · Personalization

1 Introduction

Several organizations publish personal data for research or statistical analyses. Shared data is beneficial for researchers, but it may cause a privacy problem for individuals whose data has been published. Besides, individuals have the right to demand the protection of their personal data. Governments and some organizations such as European Commission [1] are also enforcing corporations to protect individuals' personal data while sharing them. Therefore, data anonymization techniques are used to preserve the privacy of the published personal data. Anonymization methods, such as k-anonymity [2], l-diversity [3] and t-closeness [4], transform data to an anonymized form. The aim of anonymization is to protect person's sensitive information against data disclosure.

In order to protect individuals' privacy on statistical databases, differential privacy [5] has been described for privacy-preserving analysis of data. Differential privacy minimizes the increased risk to an individual incurred by joining the database and suggests the use of Laplace based noise addition [6]. The k-anonymity model provides the protection of individual's sensitive information

© Springer International Publishing Switzerland 2015
E. Garoufallou et al. (Eds.): MTSR 2015, CCIS 544, pp. 195–200, 2015.
DOI: 10.1007/978-3-319-24129-6_17

and guarantees that a record cannot be distinguishable from at least k-1 other records with respect to a set of attributes (such as zip code, birth date and gender) called *quasi-identifier*. A quasi-identifier is a set of attributes that can be joined with external information to re-identify individual records [2]. While l-diversity approach has been designed to overcome problems of k-anonymity, t-closeness approach has been designed to overcome problems of l-diversity. Therefore, as k-anonymity uses a k value, l-diversity and t-closeness methods use l and t values respectively to achieve data anonymization.

The proposed model aims to combine the main concepts of the existing anonymization methods at a higher level. Therefore, the existing anonymization approaches will be analyzed to deduce the basic concepts of each method and will be used to conceptualize a generic anonymization method. Hence, new anonymization methods could be easily integrated to the proposed model. As individuals may have different privacy concerns, the disclosure of personal data must consider personalized privacy needs. The differences in personal privacy concerns can also depend on the information type. For example, while age information is not a critical data for a person, her diagnose information may have a high importance. This difference in privacy concerns requires the personalization of privacy protection. The personalization of privacy preserving in the proposed model aims to ensure the individual's different privacy needs. For this purpose, the proposed semantic model is compromised of several data anonymization methods' components to conceptualize a semantic web based data anonymization. Also, the model provides a relation between the data anonymization methods and personalization concept to satisfy individuals' personal privacy needs. The proposed model is a conceptual data model aims to express both the common concepts of data anonymization methods and the released data. Also, the model uses privacy levels to satisfy individuals' different privacy needs. Therefore, new data anonymization methods could be easily integrated to the proposed semantic model, privacy-preserved query results is guaranteed and personalized privacy is ensured. The paper is organized as follows: Section 2 presents the related work. Section 3 explains the proposed model and its components. Finally, Section 4 concludes and summarizes the future work.

2   Related Work

An approach for preserving privacy is protecting original data and changing the result of query by adding a noise. In differential privacy, the researcher works on real data, however the result is not real. There is a query that is applied on data and results of this query are changed by adding noise. The problem of preserving privacy on statistical information has been worked on how to protect individual's privacy on statistical databases. Differential privacy technique guarantees individual's presence or absence can't be indistinguishable on statistical results [5]. The goal is to protect privacy while releasing data and to provide the optimum transformation on data or statistical result. The protected query results should be the nearest results of original data results.

In [6], an advanced approach for adding noise to statistical query result has been described with real life examples.

Privacy preserving in data mining is a critical issue to protect personal data. There is an enormous research to preserve privacy of statistical information and person-specific data. In [7], privacy preserving data mining models and algorithms are described according to different mining problems such as randomization method [8], k-anonymity [2], l-diversity [3], t-closeness [4]. The k-anonymity technique provides that for each information contained in the release cannot be distinguished from at least k-1 tuples that appears in the release [9]. Generalization and suppression are two approaches that are used to provide k-anonymity [2]. Also, the enhanced k-anonymity model protects both identifications and relationships on sensitive information [10]. While applying k-anonymity, weaknesses on the released data set have been realized. Therefore, l-diversity approach has been proposed to overcome the privacy problems of k-anonymity. In [3], two simple attacks on k-anonymized dataset are presented. In the first attack, an adversary may discover the values of sensitive attributes if there is no diversity in those values. In the second attack, adversaries may have a background knowledge that the k-anonymity approach could not guarantee privacy against the background knowledge attack. In l-diversity technique, an equivalence class which has same quasi-identifier values that must be have at least l different values for the sensitive attributes. On the other hand, l-diversity has also some limitations. Therefore, t-closeness approach is proposed in [4]. The t-closeness is the distance between the distribution of a sensitive attribute and the distribution of the attribute in the entire table that cannot be more than the threshold t for an equivalence class.

As health domain is one of the crucial concept in data mining. Many researches focus on privacy preserving on health data mining [11–14]. The report for Canadian Health Information Group includes tools and techniques for de-identification. In [13], privacy algorithms have been described against to different types of attacks on electronic health records. [14] presents a framework to protect privacy for medical document sharing with anonymization and clustering. Besides the general protection of privacy, patients may have different privacy concerns about their personal information. Therefore, personalized privacy is needed to preserve privacy in data anonymization. A personalized anonymity technique that all individuals can assign their sensitive information's privacy level from the generalization hierarchy is described in [15]. [16] presents a k-anonymity based semantic model. The model is developed for healthcare domain and an application is implemented to check quasi-identifier from text value. However, it is a domain-dependent approach and insufficient to define k-anonymity and its concepts in a semantical way. The main goal of our conceptualized model is to generate a generic semantic model based on differential privacy and k-anonymity, l-diversity and t-closeness. The conceptualized model combines these techniques to provide reasoning query results in order to evaluate privacy-preserving analysis of query results. Also, personalized privacy concepts are defined to meet individuals' different privacy preferences.

3   Personalized Privacy Preserving Algorithms Model

As the privacy preserving algorithms have different concepts in order to achieve data protection, the proposed model aims to combine the main concepts of anonymization methods at a higher level in order to conceptualize a generic personalized anonymization method. The proposed model is shown in Figure 1.

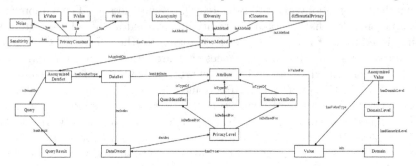

Fig. 1. Personalized Privacy Preserving Algorithms Model

The proposed personalized privacy preserving model has the following sets: DataOwner, DataSet, AnonymizedDataSet, Attribute, SensitiveAttribute, Identifier, QuasiIdentifier, PrivacyLevel, Value, AnonymizedValue, Domain, DomainLevel, Query, QueryResult, PrivacyMethod and PrivacyConstant.

- DataOwner defines the owner of data.
- DataSet is an entity that the researchers can perform queries on for statistical analysis. A DataSet represents a collection of DataOwner's data. For example, data such as zipcode, age or address.
- AnonymizedDataSet is an entity that presents a DataSet that has been applied to an anonymization method.
- Attribute represents information about DataOwner. Attribute may change depending on the currentDataSet which is going to be anonymized. For example, while a DataSet may have age, zipcode and diagnose attributes, the other may have birth date, location and treatment attributes.
- SensitiveAttribute is an entity that represents a critical data for DataOwner. SensitiveAttribute includes sensitive data that would lead to a privacy leakage when the data set is released. For example, in healthcare domain, diagnose information can be a SensiviteAttribute.
- QuasiIdentifier represents an attribute which is not an identifier by itself, but when it is used with other attributes it can expose the sensitive information.
- Identifier is used to identify data uniquely. It is a type of Attribute. Personal data would be accessible by knowing the Identifier value, For example, social security number which is unique to a person is an Identifier that can lead anyone to access her personal data.

– Value is DataOwner's value for an attribute like SensitiveAttribute, QuasiIdentifier or Identifier.

– AnonymizedValue defines the value of the new status that an anonymity method has been applied on.

– PrivacyMethod presents the method of the applied privacy preserving approach such as k-anonymization, l-diversity, t-Closeness and differential privacy.

– PrivacyConstant is the value of the applied PrivacyMethod. There are more than one PrivacyConstant in the proposed conceptualized model depending on the anonymization method.

  • If PrivacyMetod is k-anonymity or l-diversity or t-closeness, then a data type property kValue or lValue or tValue is used as PrivacyConstant, respectively. If PrivacyMetod is differential privacy, then a data type property Noise is used as a value that is going to be added to query results.

– Sensitivity is a data type property to show the sensitivity of the query result for differential privacy after noise addition.

– PrivacyLevel is used for all types of Attribute and is described as VeryLow, Low, Medium, High and VeryHigh. As VeryLow means that the value does not need to be protected, VeryHigh means that the value must be hidden.

– A Query is an entity that is posed on DataSet or AnonymizedDataSet for statistical results. A QueryResult is the result of the Query. QueryResult could be compared according to PrivacyLevel of DataOwner to analyze the quality of query results and to ensure personalized privacy requirements.

– In anonymization methods, hierarchical generalization tree is needed for DataSet attributes. The tree is created based on attributes of the related domain. Domain defines the concepts that are needed to generalize the hierarchy. A DomainLevel presents the level of the hierarchical tree for the Domain.

  • hasDomainLevel object property is used to define that the DomainLevel is the level of hierarchy tree for Domain.

  • hasHierarchyLevel object property is used to represent DomainLevel in which the AnonymizedValue is used.

4   Conclusion and Future Work

The proposed model provides to conceptualize data anonymization methods within a semantic model in order to ensure a privacy-preserved data set to maximize the quality of data analysis while preserving privacy. For this purpose, differential privacy method and data anonymization methods are integrated in a semantic based anonymization model. As users may have different privacy preferences, the proposed model is based on a personalized privacy concept. The proposed model is based on a generic data approach, therefore it is domain independent. The model can be applicable to different forms of data and also to different domains. Hence, the query results could be compared by performance and utility while applying different anonymization methods to the same data set. As a future work, a framework will be developed to implement the proposed conceptualized privacy preserving data anonymization model. The framework will be tested in healthcare domain for psychiatry data. As psychiatry domain is a very sensitive domain to share data, it would be efficient to examine the model for different personalized privacy levels and also to evaluate the quality of the query results based on the used anonymization method.

References

1. Boillat P., Kjaerum M.: Handbook on European data protection law (2014). http://www.echr.coe.int/Documents/Handbook_data_protection_ENG.pdf
2. Ciriani V., De Capitani di Vimercati S., Foresti S., Samarati P.: k-Anonymity. In: Advances in Information Security (2007)
3. Machanavajjhala, A., Kifer, D., Gehrke, J., Venkitasubramaniam, M.: L-Diversity: Privacy Beyond k-Anonymity. ACM Transactions on Knowledge Discovery from Data 1(1), Article 3 (2007)
4. Li N., Li T., Venkatasubramanian S: t-closeness: privacy beyond k-anonymity and l-diversity. In: ICDE Conference 2007 (2007)
5. Dwork, C.: Differential privacy: a survey of results. In: Agrawal, M., Du, D.-Z., Duan, Z., Li, A. (eds.) TAMC 2008. LNCS, vol. 4978, pp. 1–19. Springer, Heidelberg (2008)
6. Sarathy, R., Muralidhar, K.: Evaluating Laplace Noise Addition to Satisfy Differential Privacy for Numeric Data. Transactions on Data Privacy 4 (2011)
7. Aggarwal, C., Yu, P.: Privacy-Preserving Data Mining : Models and Algorithms. Springer Publishing (2008). ISBN:0387709916 9780387709918
8. Agrawal R., Srikant R.: Privacy preserving data mining. In: Proceedings of the ACM SIGMOID Conference (2000)
9. Sweeney, L.: k-Anonymity: A model for protecting privacy. Int. Journal on Uncertainty, Fuzziness and Knowledge-Based Systems 10(5), 557–570 (2002)
10. Wong, R., Li, J., Fu, A., Wang, K.: (α, k)-anonymity: an enhanced k-anonymity model for privacy-preserving data publishing. In: Proceedings of the 12th ACM SIGKDD Int. Conf. on Knowledge Discovery and Data Mining, pp. 754–759 (2006)
11. Fraser R., Willison D.: Tools for De-Identification of Personal Health Information. Pan Canadian Health Information (HIP) Group (2009)
12. Jin, H.W.: Practical issues on privacy-preserving health data mining. In: Washio, T., Zhou, Z.-H., Huang, J.Z., Hu, X., Li, J., Xie, C., He, J., Zou, D., Li, K.-C., Freire, M.M. (eds.) PAKDD 2007. LNCS (LNAI), vol. 4819, pp. 64–75. Springer, Heidelberg (2007)
13. Divanis, A., et al.: Publishing data from electronic health records while preserving privacy: A survey of algorithms. J. of Biomedical Informatics 50, 4–19 (2014)
14. Qin, J., Li, X.: A framework for privacy preserving medical document sharing. In: Thirty Fourth Int. Conf. on Information Systems (2013)
15. Xiao, X., Tao, Y.: Personalized privacy preservation. In: ACM SIGMOD Int. Conf. on Management of Data, pp. 229–240 (2006)
16. Omran, E., Bokma, A., Abu-Almaati, S.: A k-anonymity based semantic model for protecting personal information and privacy. In: IEEE Int. Advance Computing Conference (2009)

Data Quality and Evaluation Studies

Evaluation of Metadata in Research Data Repositories: The Case of the DC.Subject Element

Dimitris Rousidis[1,2(✉)], Emmanouel Garoufallou[1,2], Panos Balatsoukas[3], and Miguel-Angel Sicilia[1]

[1] University of Alcala, Madrid, Spain
`drousid@gmail.com, mgarou@libd.teithe.gr, msicilia@uah.es`
[2] Alexander Technological Educational Institute of Thessaloniki, Kentriki Makedonia, Greece
[3] University of Manchester, Manchester, UK
`panagiotis.balatsoukas@manchester.ac.uk`

Abstract. Research Data repositories are growing in terms of volume rapidly and exponentially. Their main goal is to provide scientists the essential mechanism to store, share, and re-use datasets generated at various stages of the research process. Despite the fact that metadata play an important role for research data management in the context of these repositories, several factors - such as the big volume of data and its complex lifecycles, as well as operational constraints related to financial resources and human factors - may impede the effectiveness of several metadata elements. The aim of the research reported in this paper was to perform a descriptive analysis of the DC.Subject metadata element and to identify its data quality problems in the context of the Dryad research data repository. In order to address this aim a total of 4.557 packages and 13.638 data files were analysed following a data-preprocessing method. The findings showed emerging trends about the subject coverage of the repository (e.g. the most popular subjects and the authors that contributed the most for these subjects). Also, quality problems related to the lack of controlled vocabulary and standardisation were very common. This study has implications for the evaluation of metadata and the improvement of the quality of the research data annotation process.

Keywords: Big data · DC.subject · Data quality · Descriptive analysis · Open access repositories · Metadata

1 Introduction

Modern e-Science and e-Research infrastructure has revolutionized the way scientists can store, retrieve, analyse, use, reuse and share data [4]. In this context, research data repositories have become an important predicate of the scientific workflow and a vital tool for research collaboration. To date, several studies have been conducted in order to examine the use, reuse, interoperability, sustainability, dissemination and long-term preservation of data repositories [3], [6], [7], [8]. Yet, there is little known about the use of metadata for research data repositories and in particular, the challenges and

© Springer International Publishing Switzerland 2015
E. Garoufallou et al. (Eds.): MTSR 2015, CCIS 544, pp. 203–213, 2015.
DOI: 10.1007/978-3-319-24129-6_18

problems associated with metadata application [11], [24]. Understanding the use of metadata in research data repositories is important for improving the quality of metadata for data re-use; and analyzing the growth and characteristics of this type of repositories for audit and policy making.

The aim of the research reported in this paper was to perform a descriptive analysis of the use of the DC.Subject metadata element and to identify the data quality issues associated with the specific element in the context of the Dryad repository. This work extends a previous study by [11] and [24] who performed a preliminary analysis of three metadata elements of the Dryad repository. These were: the DC.Creator, DC.Date and DC.Type metadata elements. The decision to focus our analysis on the DC.Subject was made for two reasons. First, there is a consensus among metadata specialist that subject metadata (e.g. keywords or controlled vocabularies) are frequently prone to bias and a lack of adherence to some form of standardization [5]; second, there is no previous work investigating the subject coverage of a mainstream research data repository, like the Dryad.

This paper is structured as follows: First, the Dryad repository is described and a review of previous work is discussed. Then the methodology and results of this study are presented. Finally, conclusions and suggestions for further research are reported.

2   Background

2.1   The DRYAD Repository

Dryad is an open-access international repository hosting peer-reviewed scientific, medical and evolutionary biology literature; and a membership organization administered by journals, publishers, scientific societies, and other interested parties [12], [14]. The repository's developers followed a two-pronged approach in order to create a long-term, sustainable system that will support academia's immediate needs. Dryad's metadata requirements are simplicity, interoperability and Semantic web compatibility [16]. Data are deposited as files with permanent identifiers (DOIs) and metadata.

The repository's development allows collections of related files and datasets to be grouped into data packages with metadata describing a combined set of files. By May 2015, the repository contained: approximately 8.700 data packages (an increase of 90% since the beginning of 2014 when the data used for the study was collected); 27.450 data files (100% increase) deposited by 21.360 authors (90% increase) associated with scholarly articles published in almost 410 international journals (42% increase) [11], [13], [24].

A selection of repository development oriented technologies have been used for the implementation and set up of Dryad like the Singapore framework metadata architecture (a framework created in order to maximize interoperability and reusability [15]) in a DSpace environment via an Extensible Markup Language (XML) schema [14, 15]. This infrastructure allows the automatically generated metadata to inherit characteristics from their original sources by harvesting keywords assigned by authors and controlled vocabularies – ontologies [16].

Finally, the metadata application profile of the Dryad repository is based on the DC Singapore Framework [15].

2.2   Previous Work

Several studies related to the technical and architectural components of Dryad have been published and the most notable papers and presentations can be found at Dryad's wiki [12]. Since the Dryad repository went live on January 2008 [12], the majority of the studies conducted e.g. [7], [15], [16], [18] were focused on the implementation and development of Dryad, its curation workflow, the metadata activities and the analysis of its technologies (mainly DSpace). Practical issues about the repository's further development were discussed in [14].

The phenomenon of metadata re-use and metadata quality in the context of Dryad has received less attention. In [8] the reusability of Dryad's metadata elements was examined and the main findings were that 8 out of the 12 metadata elements (contributor, corresponding author, identifier citation, subject, publication name, description, relation is referenced by and title) had a reuse level of 50% or greater. Also, the authors showed that the metadata reuse was more common for basic bibliographic elements like the author, title and subject. However, re-usability is still limited for more specific and complex scientific metadata elements (e.g. those related to spatial, taxonomic and temporal information).

Finally, [11] and [24] performed a statistical analysis of the Dryad repository and examined the quality issues associated with selected metadata elements of the Dryad's application profile. They found that 50% of the creators contributed two or three objects, 70% of which were datasets. The authors also examined the quality issues associated with selected metadata elements of the Dryad repository. Three metadata elements (Creator, Date and Resource Type) were analysed, quality issues associated with these elements were identified and recommendations for improving metadata quality were made. In particular it was shown that approximately 9% of the names of the Creators had various issues and the distribution of the problems was demonstrated. Problems were identified as well with the date as there were several different formats, while 2% of the dates were invalid. 21,4% of the quality problems associated with the DC.Type element consisted of non-standardised use jargon, blanks and non-relevant input. The work validated the results of a previous study by Sokvitne [19] regarding the DC.Creator element. Sokvitne questioned the suitability of Dublin Core for information retrieval by identifying serious issues with several bibliographic metadata, including the Title, Subject, Creator, Contributor and Publisher metadata elements.

2.3   DC.Subject

Since the research datasets deposited to the Dryad repository are linked to original journal papers published elsewhere, each dataset (data packages and data files) inherits the keywords assigned to the given publication [21]. However, other keywords may be manually applied to datasets. For this purpose additional descriptive attributes have been assigned to the DC.Subject metadata element in order to enhance its specificity. For example, the 'Field Label' is an attribute used to represent the Subject Keywords; the 'Formal Definition' is the general topic of the resource; and the 'User Definition' contains the specific Dataset keywords. The contents of Dryad can be searched using a SOLR[1] interface (a standalone enterprise search server with a REST-like API).

Despite the fact that this is the first study to examine the use of the DC.Subject metadata element in the context of research data repositories, findings from the institutional repository and learning object communities have shown that the subject metadata element was one of the most challenging areas for both metadata creation and resource discovery. In the majority of cases this happened because untrained in metadata authors failed to create proper and unproblematic subject metadata [3]. Evidence presented in several case studies showed that in order to achieve high quality subject metadata, both authors and metadata specialists should provide input collaboratively [5].

3   Methodology

A mechanism that involved the downloading of the metadata elements from the Dryad repository and their transformation to a proper format for analysis was employed. In particular, metadata was harvested in January 2014. At that point the Dryad repository contained 4.557 packages and 13.638 data files. The Open Archives Initiative Protocol for Metadata Harvesting (OAI-PMH) Validator and data extraction tool was used for the metadata harvesting[2]. A total of 516 .xml files were downloaded (135MB). The XML files were merged into a single file using Mergex, a command line tool for merging xml files[3]. Finally, a method to use and analyze the data from the xml files had to be employed. Due to the descriptive nature of the statistical analysis performed it was decided to analyze the data using Microsoft Access (as opposed to the use of more advanced analytics tools, like R). The .xml to .csv Conversion Tool[4] was used to transform the .xml files into .csv and import these in Access. The converter provided 19 .csv files, each corresponding to a metadata element of the Dryad. These are shown in Table 1:

Table 1. CSV files extracted from Dryad Repository

contributor	Format	Record	setSpec
coverage	Header	Relation	Subject
creator	identifier	Request	Title
date	listRecords	responseDate	Type
dc	Metadata	resumptionToken	

---

[1] http://lucene.apache.org/solr/
[2] http://validator.oaipmh.com/
[3] https://code.google.com/p/mergex/
[4] http://xmltocsv.codeplex.com/

The .csv files contained the metadata downloaded from the Dryad. In the above table the .csv files in bold are the ones containing data suitable for statistical analysis, whereas the remaining are used as interconnection points between .csv files as they contain tokens, specifications and resumption or response dates. In order to demonstrate the relationship between the different .csv files, a mapping of these files was performed using MS Access (Figure 1).

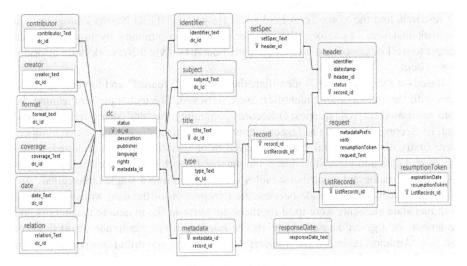

Fig. 1. The Dryad Mapping

3.1   Pre-processing: Preparing the DC.Subject for Analysis

Since the purpose of the paper is to present the results of the analysis of the DC.Subject metadata element, this section summarises the actions made to prepare this metadata element for descriptive analysis. Because we were interested in stratifying the analysis by author (in order to identify the top authors per subject) the analysis involved also the analysis of all author-related metadata elements. These were the Creator and Contributor elements. The workflow used to complete the analysis was split into two phases. Phase 1 involved the downloading of the repository's metadata, while Phase 2 initiated a set of steps needed for preparing metadata for analysis.

Specifically, the Identifier, Creator, Contributor and Subject CSV files were imported in MS Access to create the corresponding tables. These four tables had only two fields: a textual one (i.e. the actual values for the identifier, author, contributor and subject fields) and a numerical one (i.e. the dc identifier, a unique number for each dataset).

The DC.Identifier element was used to identify Dryad's packages and files. Most types of files can be uploaded (e.g., text, spreadsheets, video, photographs, software code) including compressed archives of multiple files. In order to distinguish the package from its files a '/number' suffix is added to the package's identifier in order to denote the file (i.e. doi:10.5061/dryad.20 is the package identifier and doi:10.5061/dryad.20/2 is the identifier of the second file of the package).

The Identifier .csv file had a series of issues and irrelevant data. In particular, there was no clear distinction made between packages and files as information about these was contained in the same metadata element and not in different elements as one would expect. Also, data from other repositories was found within the downloaded metadata files that actually contaminated Dryad's metadata. The repositories that are obviously collaborating with Dryad are the Knowledge Network for Biocomplexity (KNB)[5] - an international repository intended to facilitate ecological and environmental research, and the Long-Term Ecological Research (LTER) Network program[6] - a network that seeks to inform the broader scientific community by providing open access to well designed and well documented databases via a Network-wide information system.

Based on the Dryad's DOI identifier, the data was "cleaned" and the correct packages with the corresponding identifiers were retrieved. The technique for cleaning the data was based on SQL queries: i) Records containing the 'doi' string were retrieved and, ii) Records containing as last characters a forward slash and one or two numbers were firstly identified, catalogued and saved in new tables and then removed. Using the correct data and via a SQL query, the number of each unique Keyword was calculated. The Creator and Contributor tables were merged into a single table called 'Author'. This decision was made because after inspection of the data we observed that both metadata elements were used for the same purpose (i.e to denote the authors and co-authors of a given dataset). Then via the relationship (the common dc_id field) of the new 'Authors' table and the 'Subject' table the total   contributions per subject for each author was calculated.

4   Results

4.1   General Results for Packages and Files

The initial dc.identifier file was consisted of 127.853 records which as mentioned earlier included the identifiers for packages and files from Dryad along with data from the KNB and LTER repositories. With a series of queries the identifiers for the 4.557 packages (a 100% success) were retrieved. The number of files per packages was calculated and Figure 2 provides a depiction of the findings.

As it is shown in Figure 2, approximately half of the packages contained one file (49%), while two files were included in 810 packages (17,7%). By multiplying the number of packages by the number of files per package we managed to calculate the total of the files that were uploaded to Dryad. According to our calculations the total number of files in the repository was 13.633 - just five less than the ones referred to the Dryad's site. This means that each package contained on average three files.

---

[5] https://knb.ecoinformatics.org/
[6] http://www.lternet.edu/

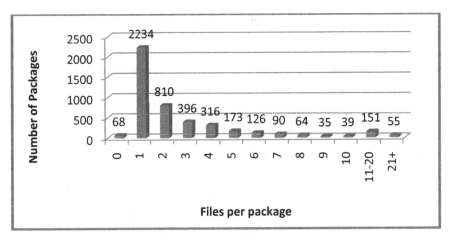

Fig. 2. Files per package diagram

4.2   Subject

The DC.Subject provides the keywords of each object of the repository. According to [21], initially only-explicitly stated keywords were meant to be catalogued and the final goal of Dryad's developers was to perform an automatic keyword insertion.

Table 2. Subject Top-25

Subject	Count	Percentage (%)	Subject	Count	Percentage (%)
Adaptation	366	1,68	Quantitative Genetics	115	0,53
Population Genetics – Empirical	304	1,39	Molecular Evolution	110	0,50
Speciation	258	1,18	Biogeography	104	0,48
Phylogeography	235	1,08	Microsatellites	98	0,45
Ecological Genetics	197	0,90	Birds	96	0,44
Hybridization	184	0,84	Phylogenetics	95	0,44
Conservation Genetics	177	0,81	climate change	93	0,43
Insects	143	0,66	Life History Evolution	90	0,41
Population Genetics	141	0,65	Mammals	90	0,41
Phenotypic Plasticity	132	0,61	Sexual Selection	87	0,40
Phylogeny	129	0,59	Invasive Species	85	0,39
Fish	123	0,56	natural selection	84	0.39
Gene Flow	119	0,55			

In total, 21.809 subjects were identified as keywords for the packages and the unique ones were 8.149. Therefore, approximately five keywords (4,79) were used on average per package. Table 2 shows Dryad's 25 most popular subjects. The most popular keywords were in accordance with the Dryad's subject coverage, i.e. focused on medical and evolutionary biology topics.

4.3   Subject distribution by author

The most frequent authors per subject area were also identified. With the aid of a query that used the *Authors* Table (which was created by merging the creator and the contributor tables) and the Subject Table, the count of subjects per author was requested. The query provided data for a new table with 3 fields: Subject, Author, and Author's Number of Contributions per Subject. Table 3 shows the top 10 of the subjects that were most frequently used from a unique author.

Table 3. Most frequent keyword from a unique author

Subject	Author	# of Contributions
Phylogeny	Douzery, Emmanuel J. P.	10
Fish	Bernatchez, Louis	10
Speciation	Bernatchez, Louis	8
Molecular dating	Douzery, Emmanuel J. P.	8
Supermatrix	Douzery, Emmanuel J. P.	7
Speciation	Rieseberg, Loren H.	7
Phylogeny	Delsuc, Frédéric	6
Conservation Genetics	Narum, Shawn R.	6
DNA metabarcoding	Taberlet, Pierre	6
sexual selection	Rundle, Howard D.	6

The analysis can identify also if an Author has contributed heavily to a specific subject. For instance 10 out of the 129 contributions (7,75%) and 10 out of the 123 contributions (8,13%) of the 'Phylogeny' and the 'Fish' subject respectively, come from specific authors.

For the top 25 most popular subjects we managed to identify the most contributive authors per subject. In table 4 only the top 10 subjects are shown along with the authors with more than 3 contributions per subject. For the 'speciation' subject there are 5 additional Authors with 4 contributions. An additional analysis of this table can provide associations between Authors and also between group of Authors and subjects.

Table 4. Most contributive Authors for the Top-10 Subjects

Subject	Author	# of Con.	Author	# of Con.	Author	# of Con.
Adaptation	Laurila, Anssi	4	Seehausen, Ole	4	Butlin, Roger K.	4
	Sota, Teiji	4	Merilä, Juha	4		
Population Genetics	Bernatchez, Louis	4				
Speciation*	Bernatchez, Louis	8	Rieseberg, Loren H.	7	Rieseberg, Loren H.	5
Phylogeography	Moritz, Craig	5	Schönswetter, Peter	4	Searle, Jeremy B	4
Ecological Genetics	Narum, Shawn R.	4	Bernatchez, Louis	4	Gagnaire, Pierre-Alexandre	4
	Kempenaers, Bart	4				
Hybridization	Moritz, Craig	4	Rieseberg, Loren H	4	Bernatchez, Louis	4
Conservation Genetics	Narum, Shawn R.	6	Campbell, Nathan R	4		
Insects	Foitzik, Susanne	4	Traugott, Michael	4		
Population Genetics	Bernatchez, Louis	4				
Phenotypic plasticity	Simmons, Leigh W.	4				

* there are five additional authors with four contributions

4.4   Data Quality Issues

Identifier
The main issues with the Identifier metadata are the repetitive data and most important of all the irrelevant to Dryad data. As it was mentioned in the methodology section, data from other repositories were included in the downloaded xml files. The main repercussion of such unwanted data is that researchers are led to biased and erroneous results. The downloaded data need first to be cleaned and corrected, via the procedure described in the methodology section. It seems that no data quality mechanisms are in place in the case of the metadata annotation process of the Dryad repository. An obvious solution that could lead to error-free data is the blocking of data that do not contain a DOI. Finally, an implementation of separate metadata identifiers for the packages and the files would aid the analysis of the repository.

Subject
Several quality issues are met in this element. First of all, the manual cataloguing of data entails typos and the input of irrelevant information. This can lead to multiple records for the same subject. Another serious problem was the extreme diversity of similar notions (synonyms). It is apparent that the subjects were not entered through the use of a controlled vocabulary that would obviously restrict and minimize mistakes. For instance, the 'Fertilization' subject has 21 similar entries: fertilization, fertilized, fertilizer, fertilizers and various forms of fertilization such as bias, success, plot, plots, Fertilization nitrogen and Fertilization phosphorus are a few examples that confirm the lack of standardisation.Similar problems were encountered in the case of

the 'Population' subject where 144 similar/diverse entries were recorded. The inconsistent use of singular and plural, adjectives, synonym terms and misspelled words failed the quality criteria check during the data pre-processing phase and made difficult the analysis of the subject metadata element.

5   Conclusions

The goal of this research was to perform a descriptive analysis of the DC.Subject metadata element used in the Dryad repository. Following this analysis a series of quality problems associated to the specific metadata element and the process implemented to analyse it were identified.

Despite the fact that several metadata quality issues have been documented in the literature during the past few years e.g. [5], [6], [10], [11], [19], yet many of these issues are still present in the case of the Dryad repository. It appears that there is a need for more manual control over the metadata input, since the automatic or semi-automatic method of populating the DC.Subject element with values is prone to quality errors. Improving the quality of the subject metadata in Dryad could also streamline the process of analyzing its contents. Therefore, establishing a coherent pre-processing method for cleaning the metadata is important for strengthening the validity of the analysis process. In this present paper we demonstrated a method for pre-processing specifically for the DC.Subject metadata element. This involved the mapping of the different metadata elements and their relationship (Figure 1); and the use of the DC.Identifier element as a means of identifying unique instances of packages and files for subject analysis.

Future work will be focused on applying data mining and text mining techniques to the DC.Subject metadata element in order to provide a better understanding of the repository's data; to identify associations, clusters or hidden patterns for this data; and to develop novel visualisations for displaying the contents of the Dryad repository [22].

References

1. Gargouri, Y., Hajjem, C., Lariviere, V., Gingras, Y., Brody, T., Carr, L., Harnad, S.: Self-Selected or Mandated, Open Access Increases Citation Impact for Higher Quality Research. PLOS ONE 5(10) (2010). http://www.plosone.org/article/info:doi/10.1371/journal.pone.0013636 (July 13, 2014)
2. Mabe, M., Amin, M.: Growth dynamics of scholarly and scientific journals. Scientometrics 51, 147–162 (2001). doi:10.1023/A:1010520913124
3. Hess, C., Ostrom, E.: A Framework for Analyzing the Knowledge Commons : A Chapter from Understanding Knowledge as a Commons: from Theory to Practice (2005). http://surface.syr.edu/cgi/viewcontent.cgi?article=1020&context=sul
4. Garoufallou, E., Papatheodorou, C.: A critical introduction to metadata for e science and e-research, special issue on metadata for e-science and e-research. International Journal of Metadata Semantics and Ontologies (IJMSO) 9(1), 1–4 (2014)
5. Currier, S., Barton, J., O'Beirne, R., Ryan, B.: Quality assurance for digital learning object repositories: issues for the metadata creation process. ALT-J, Research in Learning Technology 12(1), 5–20 (2004)

6. Heery, R., Anderson, S.: Digital repositories review. Other. Joint Information Systems Committee (2005). http://www.jisc.ac.uk/uploaded_documents/digital-repositories-review-2005.pdf

7. Greenberg, J., Vision, T.: The Dryad Repository: A New Path for Data Publication in Scholarly Communication. OCLC, Dublin, Ohio (2011). https://www.oclc.org/content/dam/oclc/community/presentations/guests/greenberg-20110425.pdf (January 22, 2015)

8. Greenberg, J, Swauger, S, Feinstein, E.M.: Metadata capital in a data repository. In: Proceedings of the International Conference on Dublin Core and Metadata Applications, pp. 140–150 (2013)

9. Beagrie, N., Eakin-Richards, L., Vision, T.: Business Models and Cost Estimation: Dryad Repository Case Study, iPRES2010 Vienna (2010)

10. Palavitsinis, N., Manouselis, N., Sanchez-Alonso, S.: Metadata quality in digital repositories: empirical results from the cross-domain transfer of a quality assurance process. Journal of the Association of Information Science and Technology **65**(6), 1202–1216 (2014)

11. Rousidis, D., Garoufallou, E., Balatsoukas, P., Sicilia, M.A.: Data Quality Issues and Content Analysis for Research Data Repositories: The Case of Dryad, ELPUB2014. Let's put data to use: digital scholarship for the next generation. In: 18th International Conference on Electronic Publishing, June 19–20, 2014, Thessaloniki, Greece (2014). http://elpub.scix.net/data/works/att/106_elpub2014.content.pdf

12. Dryad Digital Repository Wiki. Main Page, April 29, 2015. http://wiki.datadryad.org/Main_Page

13. Dryad Digital Repository. Frequently Asked Questions, April 29, 2015. http://datadryad.org/pages/faq

14. White, H., Carrier, S., Thompson, A., Greenberg, J., Scherle, R.: The Dryad data repository: a Singapore framework metadata architecture in a DSpace environment. In: The 2008 International Conference on Dublin Core and Metadata Applications, Berlin (2008)

15. Greenberg, J., White, H.C., Carrier, S., Scherle, R.: A metadata best practice for a scientific data repository. Journal of Library Metadata **9**(3), 194–212 (2009). http://dx.doi.org/10.1080/19386380903405090 (February 15, 2014)

16. Greenberg, J.: Theoretical considerations of lifecycle modeling: an analysis of the Dryad repository demonstrating automatic metadata propagation, inheritance, and value system adoption. Cataloguing & Classification Quarterly **47**(3/4), 380–402 (2009)

17. Peer, L.: The Role of Data Repositories in Reproducible Research. Yale (2013). http://isps.yale.edu/news/blog/2013/07/the-role-of-data-repositories-in-reproducible-research#.UzINafmSxyM

18. Greenberg, J.: Linking and Hiving Data in the Dryad Repository. The Semantic Web: Fact or Myth. CENDI, FLICC, and NFAIS Workshop. National Archives, Washington, DC, November 17, 2009 (2009b)

19. Sokvitne, L.: An Evaluation of the Effectiveness of current Dublin Core Metadata for Retrieval. Proceedings of VALA 2000. Victorian Association for Library Automation: Melbourne (2000)

20. Beagrie, N., Eakin-Richards, L., Vision, T.: Business Models and Cost Estimation: Dryad Repository Case Study, iPRES2010 Vienna (2010)

21. Dryad Digital Repository Wiki. Cataloging Guidelines (2009). http://wiki.datadryad.org/Cataloging_Guidelines_2009 (April 12, 2015)

22. Greenberg, J., Garoufallou, E.: Change and a future for metadata. In: Garoufallou, E., Greenberg, J. (eds.) MTSR 2013. CCIS, vol. 390, pp. 1–5. Springer, Heidelberg (2013)

23. Integrating Manuscript Processing with the Dryad Digital Repository, April 10, 2015. http://wiki.datadryad.org/images/c/c6/DryadIntegrationOverview.pdf

24. Rousidis, D., Garoufallou, E., Balatsoukas, P., Sicilia, M.A.: Metadata for big data: a preliminary investigation of metadata quality issues in research data repositories. Information Services and Use **34**(3), 279–286 (2014)

Software Applications Ecosystem for Authority Control

Leandro Tabares Martín[1][(✉)], Félix Oscar Fernández Peña[3],
Amed Abel Leiva Mederos[2], Marc Goovaerts[4], Dailién Calzadilla Reyes[1],
and Wilbert Alberto Ruano Álvarez[1]

[1] Universidad de Las Ciencias Informáticas, Havana, Cuba
ltmartin@uci.cu, waruano@estudiantes.uci.cu
[2] Universidad Central "Marta Abreu" de Las Villas, Santa Clara, Cuba
amed@uclv.edu.cu
[3] Instituto Superior Politécnico "José Antonio Echeverría", Havana, Cuba
felix@ceis.cujae.edu.cu
[4] Universiteit Hasselt, Hasselt, Belgium

Abstract. Authority control is recognized as an expensive task in the cataloging process. This is actually an active research field in libraries and related research institutions even when several approaches have been proposed in this research area. In this paper, we propose AUCTORITAS, a tool for exposing high value services on the web for the authority control in a generic institution environment. This paper describes the application ecosystem behind AUCTORITAS and how the semantic web languages make possible the semantic integration of heterogeneous applications. Likewise we evaluate the applicability of the proposal for academic libraries.

Keywords: Authority control · Linked open data · Semantic web

1 Introduction

Authority Control is the most expensive part of the cataloging process [7,20,21], it is a global problem, affecting not only libraries but organizations of all kinds [16]. Authority Control is necessary for meeting the catalog's objectives of enabling users to find the works of an author and to collocate all works of a person or corporate body. Authority control virtues have been debated and restated for decades. Catalogers for at least a century and a half have documented their decisions on how the single, authorized form of name for each entity should be represented in their catalog [20]. Several efforts has been made by library institutions in order to share their authority records [10,20] but, the publication of authority data on the Web in an heterogeneous or arbitrary way produces inefficiency in information retrieval and creates complications when attributing authority to a given work. The need to improve the interoperability within the world Wide Web gave rise to the development of the Semantic Web [2].

© Springer International Publishing Switzerland 2015
E. Garoufallou et al. (Eds.): MTSR 2015, CCIS 544, pp. 214–224, 2015.
DOI: 10.1007/978-3-319-24129-6_19

The Semantic Web is not a separate Web but an extension of the current one, in which information is given well-defined meaning, better enabling computers and people to work in cooperation [2]. The current work aims to create an applications ecosystem enabling authority control capacities for external applications, by reusing semantically structured data shared by different institutions. This work is structured as follows: a section exposing related work where authority control state of the art and specifically AUTHORIS, semantic web, linked open data, Openlink Virtuoso and VIVO are addressed. After that the applications ecosystem is explained in detail, evaluated and we conclude with future steps to follow in order to improve our proposal.

2   Related Work

2.1   Authority Control

Authority control is a matter that has exacted the efforts of generations of librarians and catalogers. The need to uniformly record information on each author included in a catalog is addressed in work and research stemming from several international organizations. Libraries and organizations of international prestige such as the United States Library of Congress (LOC), the Bibliothèque Nationale de France and International Federation of Library Associations (IFLA) acknowledge the fact that the information exchange protocols on the Web are insufficient means of controlling authority in the catalogs and systems of library management [16].

A brief outline of authority control would include the following landmarks:

- The need for authority control is made explicit, and the Name Authority Cooperative (NACO) comes to light with the US Library of Congress [16]. In Asia, the Hong Kong Chinese Authority Name (HKCAN) is established. This meant recognition of the issue in just two organizations worldwide - far [16], however, from the syndetic goals set forth by Charles Cutter in the nineteenth century [6].
- Lubetzky [17] improves the search and retrieval of authored works in bibliographic records, eliminating the deficiencies that interfered with the retrieval and location of authors in a catalog.
- Bregzis [4] creates the ISADN (International Standard Authority Data Number) to overcome difficulties when retrieving bibliographic records with works relative to a given author and with works recorded under a uniform title.

The Online Computer Library Center (OCLC), IFLA and LOC have fueled initiatives for authority control by sharing the records of various cataloguing agencies [16]. Fruit of this work is the Virtual International Authority File (VIAF), which has meant advances in the construction and generation of authority entries, though it has no reached all the major information institutions at the international level [3].

2.2   AUTHORIS

The need of creating high quality authority records has led the creation of tools like AUTHORIS [16]. AUTHORIS aspires to facilitate the processing of author- ity data in a standardized fashion, following the principles of Linked Data [1]. AUTHORIS allows the automatic generation of authority records by using learn- ing rules [16], however AUTHORIS does not takes advantage the high quality authority records shared by library institutions. Further AUTHORIS does not implement an interface for providing data services for other software applica- tions.

2.3   Semantic Web

Since Resource Description Framework (RDF) made it possible to define the meaning of data in a machine readable form [19], it seems that the semantic web technologies could be helpful in the integration of data managed between heterogeneous software applications. The evolution of RDF into Web Ontol- ogy Language (OWL) allows a richer semantic description based on Description Logic [12]. OWL is a formal language for representing ontologies in the Semantic Web [12]. This language has been used in many specific scenarios for the con- struction of flexible data semantic models [9,13,14]. Several knowledge organiza- tion systems takes advantage of semantic web technologies [8,11,18], SKOS [18] is one of them. In this proposal we reuse SKOS structured information sources provided by institutions and reuse their data.

2.4   Linked Open Data

The concept of Linked Open Data (LOD) is based on the idea of linking pub- licly available data "silos" on the internet. By linking data, all of the data objects become related to each other. By determining a number of rules about these relationships, such inter-linked data can be "understood" by machines and algorithms, which enables global data mining approaches and the discovery of truly new associations, patterns and knowledge. LOD is based on the Resource Description Framework (RDF) data model, which formulates syntax and rules about data and resources as well as their location on the internet [15].

Implementation of LOD approaches requires adherence to the four basic com- ponents as formulated by Berners-Lee [1]:

- Use Uniform Resource Identifiers to uniquely identify data.
- Use the Hypertext Transfer Protocol (HTTP) so that people, web agents and data mining tools can access and refer to data.
- A URI has to refer to usable information that can be provided with the RDF and queried with the Simple Protocol and RDF Query Language (SPARQL).
- Links to other RDF resources should be established in support of growing a world wide network of publically available and allowing for truly inter- disciplinary data mining.

There is a tremendous potential for the library community to play a significant role in realizing Berners-Lee's vision, the idea of moving thesauri, controlled vocabularies, and related services into formats that are better able to work with other Web Services and software applications is particularly significant. Converting these tools and vocabularies to Semantic Web standards will provide limitless potential for putting them in a myriad new ways [10].

2.5   OpenLink Virtuoso

OpenLink Virtuoso[1] is an innovative enterprise grade multi-model data server for agile enterprises and individuals. The hybrid server architecture of Virtuoso enables it to offer traditionally distinct server functionality within a single product that covers the following areas:

- SQL Relational Tables Data Management.
- RDF Relational Property Graphs Data Management.
- Content Management.
- Web and other Document File Services.
- Linked Open Data Deployment.
- Web Application Server.

Virtuoso capabilities managing Linked Open Data allow us to expose vocabularies such as AGROVOC[2] through its SPARQL endpoint and make them query available for other applications such as AUCTORITAS. AGROVOC is a controlled vocabulary covering all areas of interest of the Food and Agriculture Organization of the United Nations with over 32000 concepts. CCS vocabulary for Computer Sciences and MESH for Medicine and Life Sciences can be managed by Virtuoso also.

2.6   VIVO

VIVO[3] is an open source semantic web application originally implemented at Cornell University that enables the discovery of research and scholarship across disciplines, it supports browsing and search function which returns faceted results for rapid retrieval of desired information. VIVO allows also to manage authors and institution profiles and generates a Uniform Resource Identifier for each one of them.

All the information managed by VIVO is structured as Linked Open Data, this structure improves information discovery [15] and also facilitates the generation of authorship relations graphs. Information inside VIVO is SPARQL queriable and new ontologies can be added in order to expand VIVO's capabilities of semantically manage data. VIVO and AUCTORITAS integration is intended to use the information coming from institutions with intellectual production, so integrated library systems and digital repositories can use VIVO's data for uniquely identifying its authors.

---

[1] http://virtuoso.openlinksw.com/
[2] http://aims.fao.org/es/agrovoc
[3] http://vivoweb.org/

3 Applications Ecosystem

3.1 Preprocessing Tool

The Library of Congress of United States of USA has shared their authority graph[4] to the international community with the aim their data can be reused. In that graph information like author names and authoritative labels can be found in several different languages. AUCTORITAS is intended to initially use data expressed as Latin characters, so with the goal of extracting relevant information for AUCTORITAS coming from the LOC's graph, we created a preprocessing tool[5] that populates a relational database. The database structure is represented on figure 1.

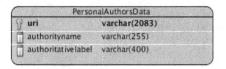 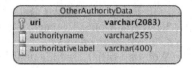

Fig. 1. Physical model of the preprocessing tool relational database

For improving the graph processing we have divided the original LOC's authority graph into one hundred and ninety-five RDF files containing around four million triples each one. The preprocessing tool uses parallel processing to optimize the processing of the graph by splitting the load in multiple threads. A regular expression is used for matching patterns contained in the graph, determining which information is about a personal author. After a preprocessing with testing purposes for six files of the LOC's we get 18592 personal authorities records stored in our database, ready to be exposed through AUCTORITAS services. Other 13215 records were identified as non-personal authority records or non-latin characters personal authority records, so they were stored into another table for further processing. This preprocessing phase allows us to reduce the significant-data table size in a 41.5% by eliminating non-relevant information for the tool.

3.2 AUCTORITAS Interface

AUCTORITAS interface is the main entry point for our applications ecosystem, it can be seen as a three dimensional vector A(v,p,w) where:

- v is a linked data datasource stored at Virtuoso.
- p is the relational database stored at PostgreSQL.
- w is the data managed by VIVO.

---

[4] http://id.loc.gov/static/data/authoritiesnames.rdfxml.madsrdf.gz
[5] https://drive.google.com/file/d/0B-Pkaic4zIO8T2FnQVIxdWR5WFU/view?usp=sharing

AUCTORITAS interface has four main functionalities exposed as REST web services:

- Search for personal authors information.
- Search for corporate authors information.
- Retrieve registered controlled vocabularies list.
- Search for an authorized term on a specified controlled vocabulary.

All these functionalities are explained in figures from 2 to 5.

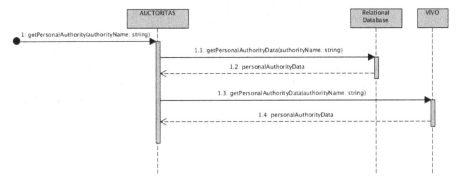

Fig. 2. Sequence diagram for a request about personal authors

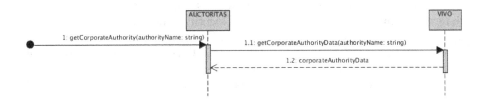

Fig. 3. Sequence diagram for a request about corporate authors

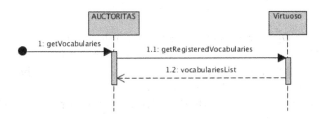

Fig. 4. Sequence diagram for a request about the registered vocabularies list

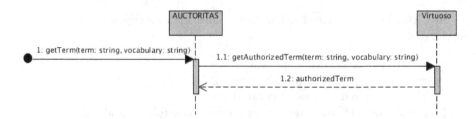

Fig. 5. Sequence diagram for a request about a term from a registered vocabulary

External applications like integrated library systems (ILS) and digital repositories send requests to AUCTORITAS with the objective of uniquely identify their authority entries, then AUCTORITAS queries its available information sources and retrieves the requested information structured as a XML.
Figure 6 shows AUCTORITAS answer to an external system after searching
for "database" term on the ACM Controlled Vocabulary.

```
<?xml version="1.0"?>
<vocabularyEntry>
<identifier>http://totem.semedica.com/taxonomy/The ACM Computing Classification System (CCS)#10002952</identifier>
<authorizedTerm>Data management systems</authorizedTerm>
</vocabularyEntry>
```

Fig. 6. AUCTORITAS answer to a query over ACM controlled vocabulary

Two main elements are sent as answer in this case, the identifier of the term
in the requested vocabulary and the authorized term by itself. The identifier of
the term is computer oriented for uniquely identify it by using an URI and the
authorized term is what the person using the system sees.

Also external applications may query AUCTORITAS services for personal
author entries. Figure 7 shows AUCTORITAS answer to a query about Jorge
Israel Rivera Zamora over LOC's graph processed information.

```
<?xml version="1.0"?>
<authorityEntry>
<identifier>http://id.loc.gov/authorities/names/no2010096115</identifier>
<name>Jorge Israel Rivera Zamora</name>
<label>Rivera Zamora, Jorge Israel</label>
</authorityEntry>
```

Fig. 7. AUCTORITAS answer to a query about Jorge Israel Rivera Zamora

In our proposal four applications are integrated to conform what will call the
Applications Ecosystem[6] as shown in the figure 8.

The ILS is represented by ABCD, which is a system that allows librarians
to manage their library data in a digital way. For managing Digital Repositories a customization of DSpace was developed by the University of Computer
Sciences of Cuba and that customization was integrated with AUCTORITAS.

---

[6] This proposal has been developed thanks to the Flemish Project VLIR-UOS.

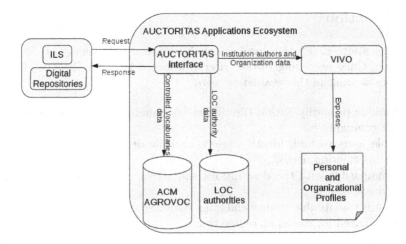

Fig. 8. Applications ecosystem overview

By exposing AUCTORITAS features as Web Services other software developers are allowed to consume AUCTORITAS services. Also AUCTORITAS provides a mechanism to reuse SKOS-structured controlled vocabularies, so it is not limited only to use the presented vocabularies. This mechanism is to add the string "vocab" before the last section of the URI that identifies the vocabulary to register it in Virtuoso, for example: *http : //ccs.vocab.cu*. AUCTORITAS uses a regular expression to identify this URI structure and use it as a controlled vocabulary.

3.3   Querying VIVO

AUCTORITAS queries to VIVO are done through VIVO's SPARQL endpoint, which is deployed in the URL [*vivoAddress*]/*api*/*sparqlQuery*, for example: http://localhost:8080/vivo/api/sparqlQuery. Queries to this endpoint must contain the parameters specified in Table 1:

Table 1. VIVO's SPARQL endpoint parameters

Parameter name	Parameter value
email	The email address of a VIVO administrative account
password	The password of the VIVO administrative account
query	The SPARQL query

VIVO 1.7 was used in order to manage personal and organizational data as LOD. Besides the main authority control that we achieve with the integration of this tools, VIVO also allows our institutions to make scientometric studies like the generation of science maps and the creation of graphics illustrating the authorship relations. At the same time the information managed by VIVO can be browsed, so the user can discover new related information and access to the full institutional scientific production.

4   Evaluation

The Applications Ecosystem has been evaluated in the University of Computer Sciences of Cuba according to the criteria proposed by RDA [5]. The elements taken into account in this evaluation were:

- Be usable primarily within the library community, but able to be used by other communities.
- Enable users to find, identify, select, and obtain resources appropriate to their information needs.
- Be compatible with the descriptions and access points in existing catalogs and databases.
- Be readily adaptable to new emerging database structures.
- Be optimized for use as an online tool.
- Be easy and efficient to use, both as a working tool and for training purposes.

A total 14 of users participated, divided into the following categories:

- Twelve Library and Information Science specialists with more than ten years of experience in cataloging.
- Two Computer Software Engineering specialists with more than five years of experience in programming.

All of these users interacted with the ILS and the Digital Repository System introducing new records into them. A total of one hundred new records were created in both systems. Figure 9 shows the amount of errors detected during the evaluation.

The evaluation concluded that the Applications Ecosystem is usable by library institutions and extensible to other institutions that needs it. The retrieval of information appropriate to users needs is partially met because there were problems about the precision in retrieving personal authority entries.

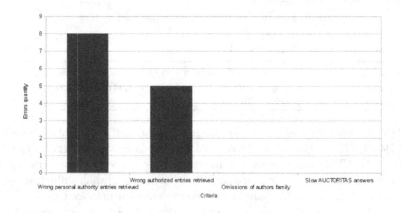

Fig. 9. Errors detected during the evaluation

The solution is compatible with existing catalogs and databases structured as SKOS and is easily adaptable to new databases structures. The Applications Ecosystem is designed to be used as an online tool and is easy and efficient to use in production or in training environments.

5 Conclusions and Future Work

The development of authority control faces new challenges in the Semantic Web. The need to facilitate interoperability and connection among non-bibliographic and bibliographic entities is one promising area to be implemented by the designers and developers of future cataloguing and authority control systems.

The tools presented in this paper are one step further in the development of new authority control systems. Still there is a lot of work to do in order to fully reuse available authority data shared by institutions. In new versions of AUCTORITAS similarity measures will be incorporated in order to create a better information retrieval mechanism. Also the incorporation of corporate authors coming from available authorities data sources has to be added to the preprocessing tool.

Multilinguality in non-latin characters is one aspect that has to be incorporated, for the purpose of allowing to other countries the usage of AUCTORITAS benefits. AUCTORITAS still has some limitations to be solved, but it provides a flexible mechanism to be extended in order to support the different authority control scenarios needed by Cuban institutions.

References

1. Berners-Lee, T.: Linked Data (2006). http://www.w3.org/DesignIssues/LinkedData.html
2. Berners-Lee, T., Hendler, J., Lassila, O.: The semantic web. Scientific American magazine **284**(5), 34–43 (2001)
3. Bourdon, F., Zillhardt, S.: Author: Vers une base européenne de notices d'autorité auteurs. International cataloguing and bibliographic control **26**(2), 34–37 (1997)
4. Bregzis, R.: The syndetic structure of the catalog. Authority control: the key to tomorrows catalog. In: Ghikas, M.W. (ed.) Proceedings of the 1979 Library and Information Technology Association Institute, Phoenix, AZ (1982)
5. Committee, U.R.T.C., et al.: Report and recommendations of the US RDA test coordinating committee (2011). Executive Summary. Online unter: http://www.nlm.nih.gov/tsd/cataloging/RDA_report_executive_summary.pdf (letzter Zugriff: 10 September 2011)
6. Cutter, C.A.: Rules for a printed dictionary catalogue. US Government Printing Office (1889)
7. Diaz-Valenzuela, I., Martin-Bautista, M.J., Vila, M.A., Campaña, J.R.: An automatic system for identifying authorities in digital libraries. Expert Systems with Applications **40**(10), 3994–4002 (2013)
8. Dunsire, G., Willer, M.: Standard library metadata models and structures for the semantic web. Library hi tech news **28**(3), 1–12 (2011)

9. Agus-Santoso, H., Haw, S.C., Abdul-Mehdi, Z.: Ontology extraction from relational database: Concept hierarchy as background knowledge. Knowledge-based Systems **24**(3), 457–464 (2011)
10. Harper, C.A., Tillett, B.B.: Library of Congress controlled vocabularies and their application to the Semantic Web. Cataloging & Classification Quarterly **43**(3–4), 47–68 (2007)
11. Hodge, G.: Systems of Knowledge Organization for Digital Libraries: Beyond Traditional Authority Files. ERIC (2000)
12. Horrocks, I., Patel-Schneider, P.F., van Harmelen, F.: From SHIQ and RDF to OWL: The Making of a Web Ontology Language. Web Semantics **1**(1), 7–26 (2003)
13. Čerāns, K., Būmans G.: RDB2OWL: a RDB-to-RDF/OWL Mapping Specification Language. In: Proceeding of the 2011 Conference on Databases and Information Systems, pp. 139–152. IOS Press, Amsterdam, The Netherlands (2010)
14. Munir, K., Odeh, M., McClatchey, R.: Ontology-driven relational query formulation using the semantic and assertional capabilities of OWL-DL. Knowledge-based Systems **35**, 144–159 (2012)
15. Lausch, A., Schmidt, A., Tischendorf, L.: Data mining and linked open data New perspectives for data analysis in environmental research. Ecological Modelling **295**, 5–17 (2015). http://dx.doi.org/10.1016/j.ecolmodel.2014.09.018
16. Leiva-Mederos, A., Senso, J.A., Domínguez-Velasco, S., Hípola, P.: AUTHORIS: a tool for authority control in the Semantic Web. Library Hi Tech **31**(3), 536–553 (2013). http://softwaredocumental.org/repositorio/Texto-completo/2013 - Leiva-Mederos et al. - AUTHORIS a tool for authority control in the Semantic Web.pdf
17. Lubetzky, S., Hayes, R.M.: The Principles of Cataloging: Report. University of California, Institute of Library Research (1969)
18. Miles, A., Bechhofer, S.: Skos simple knowledge organization system reference. W3C recommendation 18, W3C (2009)
19. Motik, B., Horrocks, I., Sattler, U.: Bridging the gap between owl and relational databases. Web Semantics: Science, Services and Agents on the World Wide Web **7**(2), 74–89 (2009)
20. Tillet, B.B.: Authority Control: State of the Art and New Perspectives. Cataloging & Classification Quarterly **38**(3–4), 23–41 (2004). http://www.tandfonline.com/doi/abs/10.1300/J104v38n03_04
21. West, W.L., Miller, H.S., Wilson, K.: Electronic journals: Cataloging and management practices in academic libraries. Serials Review **37**(4), 267–274 (2011)

Digital Libraries Evaluation: Measuring Europeana's Usability

Anxhela Dani[1], Chrysanthi Chatzopoulou[1], Rania Siatri[1], Fotis Mystakopoulos[2],
Stavroula Antonopoulou[3,4], Evangelia Katrinaki[5], and Emmanouel Garoufallou[1,4(✉)]

[1] Department of Library Science and Information Systems,
Alexander Technological Educational Institute (ATEI) of Thessaloniki, Thessaloniki, Greece
{antzelant,chatzopoulou.c,rsiatri}@gmail.com,
mgarou@libd.teithe.gr
[2] Southampton Solent University, East Park Terrace, Hampshire SO14 0YN, UK
fotis.mystakopoulos@solent.ac.uk
[3] American Farm School, Thessaloniki, Greece
santon@afs.edu.gr
[4] University of Alcala, Madrid, Spain
[5] M.A Digital Library Learning (DILL), Tallinn University, Tallinn, Estonia
evangeliakatrinaki@yahoo.com

Abstract. Europeana is an international trusted digital initiative providing access, from a single entry point, to prized collections from a number of European cultural institutions. Advanced Internet and digital technologies present new ways to connect with users; and there is a need continued evaluation of digital libraries. This paper reports on a task oriented, usability study exploring a number of aspects including user satisfaction specific to the Europeana Digital Library. Participants were students from Library Science and Information Systems department, who had some basic experience searching digital collections for information. Participants performed 13 tasks, and focused on the Hellenistic collection. Methodologically, the test was consisted of a list of tasks that among others aimed to assess user satisfaction and interest while performing them. The method applied was measuring Effectiveness, Efficiency, Learnability and Satisfaction. Despite the fact that it was not the first time that they came in contact with a digital library, several participants had difficulties while performing selected tasks, especially when they involved a variety of search types. In general, all of the participants seemed to comprehend how Europeana is organized, although the results also indicate that participants had feelings that expectations were not met when performing more complex tasks.

Keywords: Accessibility · Evaluation · Usability · User testing · Digital library · Europeana · Metadata · Organization · Information science · Information systems

© Springer International Publishing Switzerland 2015
E. Garoufallou et al. (Eds.): MTSR 2015, CCIS 544, pp. 225–236, 2015.
DOI: 10.1007/978-3-319-24129-6_20

1   Introduction

The availability of information and the constant changes occurring over the provided services on the Internet, have affected immensely the way in which people collect, organise, disseminate, access and use information [1]. Evaluating digital libraries serves users in satisfying their constant need and evolving demands, concerning both improvements relating to content and interface. One can pose many questions relating to DL evaluation, as there has been a plethora of issues identified as to what needs to be evaluated in a digital environment. DLs are not a single entity; they require advanced technology to link with the original included sources, leading to the necessity of assessing their usability and evaluating their full potential [2].

What can be said so far is that there are generic approaches that are very similar to each other, but what is unavoidable is that researchers, depending on their backgrounds and their research targets, differ from each other on the details. That creates confusion in the effort to establish particular practices or a single widely accepted approach towards evaluating digital libraries. Nevertheless, as physical libraries demonstrate a remarkable diversity, so are digital libraries, thus the approaches to evaluate them should be more versatile whilst focusing on foundation principles that bring together the common features.

The purpose of this research was to ensure that Europeana fulfils its aim and scope with success, to highlight any problems or weaknesses it might have that prevent users from feeling content when searching for information and last but not least, to provide this information for further research and development. The paper is structured in the following order. Introduction is followed by a literature review, where digital libraries ontology and usability studies are discussed. In the third section, Europeana is presented, the digital library in question. Methodology is discussed in the next section. Fifth section discusses the research results. Finally in the last chapter records conclusions drawn from the completion of the research.

2   Literature Review

Evaluation of digital libraries remains a complex endeavor. Several research works were undertaken by various researchers over the years, due to the unprecedented pace of changes and the evolving nature of the digital information landscape. On a more general note digital library evaluation, should be looked at from at least two different angles: 1) an evaluation can be done either internally (in-house by system developers and system users) or; 2) externally (end users of services). Researchers with enough professional expertise but not-associated with a particular digital library can only produce an external evaluation of a system carrying out a usability evaluation, a model that has been widely and successful used [22]. In this study, the research is conducted based on a usability evaluation model designed by Judy Jeng [3].

Digital libraries constitute an alternative reality, in the way information is being disseminated in the digital world. In a broader sense, they are cultural institutions playing a significant role in maintaining the momentum of the idea that information should be freely available to everyone, just like traditional libraries do. By definition *"Digital Libraries are organizations that provide resources, including the specialized staff, to select, to select, structure, offer intellectual access to, interpret, distribute, preserve the integrity of, and ensure the persistence over time of collections of digital works so that they are readily and economically available for use by a defined community or set of communities"* [4].

Effectively the definition leaves a lot of room for interpretation as to what a digital library evaluation process should involve. Marchionini [5] argues that "metrics such as response time, storage capacity, transfer rate, user satisfaction, and cost per operation may be useful in assessing technological components but may not be sufficient to characterize DL performance, let alone impact. As extensions of physical libraries and digital technologies, these metrics are good starting points, but we must look further to consider the effects of DLs".

While examining the landscape on digital libraries in India Mittal and Mahesh [6] noticed that "researchers are still investigating the who, what, when, how and why" of evaluating digital libraries, an opinion previously stated by Saracevic in 2004. Sandusky [7] ascribed six attributes that could define how digital libraries are represented and these include its Audience, Institution, Access, Content, Services Design and Development.

Blandford [8] identified two approaches to DLs evaluation, the first being the use of a checklist against a set of predefined criteria and the second being empirical studies with an implemented system.

The focus of this study however is on usability evaluation which has a very specific meaning. According to ISO usability is understood "as the extent to which a product can be used by specified users to achieve specified goals with effectiveness, efficiency and satisfaction in a specified context of use.

Saracevic [9] in 2004 proposed an analytical and structured approach to evaluate digital libraries: 1) content, and the quality of information offered by a website or a portal, 2) *process*, which relates to actually performing tasks on the source, 3) *format*, also known as design which includes the feel, look and how well information is presented and 4) *overall assessment*, which is the outcome of the combined use of the three previous sections and should answer whether users are satisfied by the content, processes and format that a digital library offers.

Bertot et al. [10] explain that "usability testing determines the extent to which a digital library, in whole or in part, enables users to intuitively use a digital library's various features". Intuition and ease of use appears also in Xie's [1] research, when analysing problems with existing digital libraries. A subject very specifically mentioned that "Project Gutenberg's interface was not as intuitive to navigate and use as it should be". At this point it should be mentioned that there is no actual benchmarking on what is the appropriate percentage for effectiveness, efficiency or ease of use [11]. However, that same year Chowdhury, Landoni & Gibb [12] suggest in their study that one of the reasons to perform evaluation on digital libraries should be to determine benchmarking, an issue not yet addressed.

Usability evaluation requires attributes to turn them into metrics [22]. In order for this to be more comprehensive, usability is measured against those attributes. Jakob Nielsen's [13] usability technique is the most widely used. He narrowed usability down to five attributes: learnability, efficiency, memorability, errors and satisfaction. Most recently, Jeng focused on digital libraries and developed a model for usability evaluation of such systems. What differentiates her model is that attributes are connected to each other and results are a consequence of cross-tabulation of data [14].

The notion of results being driven by a cross-tabulation of data is supported by Fuhr et al. [15] were an evaluation activity implemented by DELOS Network of Excellence resulted to the creation of the *Interaction Triptych Model*, which establishes connections among the system, content and the user. According to this model there should be correlations between the results provided by the system, content and user. Fuhr et al. [15] suggest usability, *usefulness* and *performance* as the axes of evaluation. Usability relates to user and system, usefulness tackles user and content relations and performance is about content and the system.

Nielsen [16] also concluded that fifteen users are enough to identify one hundred percent of the problems during a usability study. To be accurate with more participants same problems are being repeated. Since this assumption is confirmed also by other studies [22], the research was limited to twenty subjects. To signify the complexity of DLs evaluation, Ferreira and Pithan [16] conducted a somewhat different research by adding the use of Kuhlthau's Information Search Process theory to Nielsen's existing attributes or "variables". This study exemplifies the need to understand the fact that in order to carry out a usability study for digital libraries we need to consider both the human aspect as well as the system.

3   Europeana

Europeana was founded in 2008, aiming to make available to the public worldwide, European cultural material lying dormant in a plethora of cultural institutions. Its development was exceptionally rapid and today one hundred and fifty three cultural institutions have joined, in order to offer original source material to the DL's visitors. Currently its content comprises of almost forty million items including:

- Images: paintings, drawings, maps, photos and pictures of museum objects
- Texts: books, newspapers, letters, diaries and archival papers
- Sounds: music, spoken word from cylinders, tapes, discs and radio broadcasts
- Videos: films, newsreels and TV broadcasts

The main objective of Europeana was to bring into the light Europe's vast wealth of cultural heritage. In any occasion, for each search that a visitor performs, it connects you to the original source of the material, thus assuring quality of content. It provides a platform that allows users to explore its content in a variety of ways: one can browse the collection by title, creator, subject, time period, places or providers. Also, users have the ability to browse the featured items collection, find the latest added material or explore what is promoted through social media.

Fig. 1. Europeana's home page

4   Methodology

In order to collect the data required to perform the usability evaluation, a question-naire survey was employed. The model selected has been previously used in other usability evaluation testing performed by Garoufallou et al. [18, 19] measuring the usability of the Hellenic Broadcasting Corporation (ERT) and World Digital Library.

Data collection lasted two months and was carried out during May and June of 2014, at the Alexander Technological Educational Institute of Thessaloniki. Twenty students of Library Science and Information Systems Department participated in the study. Purposeful random sampling was employed aiming to gather information rich data and to maximize credibility. All data collected were analysed using the 19th version of SPSS software. A three-part questionnaire was designed to accommodate the four attributes necessary to evaluate usability according to Jeng's model. The four attributes were:

- Effectiveness, which is measured by the number of correctly accomplished tasks.
- Efficiency, where the researcher was recording the steps that each user needed to perform the tasks correctly, combined with the time needed to complete the search process for each task.

• Learnability is defined as the ability of the user to learn to navigate and locate information easily in the DL's environment. Learnability is calculated according to the response time (the time interceded between the first contact of the user with the task, until he starts performing the task).

• Satisfaction, that consists of other characteristics such as ease of use of the DL, information organising and labeling, interface attractiveness, error recovery and feeling of lostness.

In the first part, users had to answer some questions that helped us acquire some basic information on demographics (such as gender and age) and their level of experience on information retrieval. The second part involved a scavenger hunt style set of 13 tasks, with varying roles within the DL. For instance, some questions aimed at locating information, others suggested using features of Europeana e.g. create your own account on the website, whereas in the final 3 questions, participants were asked to interact with a particular digital library from Greece in order to test the possibilities of Europeana and how users respond to more complex enquiries (Table 1).

Table 1. List of tasks

Task 1	Where can you locate information regarding Advanced Search?
Task 2	Please locate information on World War I.
Task 3	Europeana's collection is divided into how many sections?
Task 4	Please identify the number of photographs related to Thessaloniki and World War I.
Task 4.1	Can you share, save or adjust any of the photographs retrieved?
Task 4.2	Can you cite on Wikipedia any of the photographs retrieved?
Task 5	Locate a video of Kaiser Franz Josef in 1910 from the European Film Gateway.
Task 6	Please locate a memorial ribbon of Emily Boddington for her two dead sons (1919), using Australian sources.
Task 7	What is My Europeana Service?
Task 7.1	Can you create an account in My Europeana?
Task 8	Can you locate information on which Greek Institutes or libraries provide material to Europeana and mention five of them?
Task 8.1	How many items are provided through the Public Library of Veria?
Task 8.2	Perform a search in the Public Library of Veria collection and find an item entitled Mount Athos.

Each task was accompanied by five questions before and after performing it. These questions aimed at describing their feelings of certainty, interest or satisfaction for each research. Finally, subjects had to answer a third set of questions regarding the overall level of satisfaction after interacting with Europeana.

The research process followed for this usability testing was combining questionnaires with participant observation. The researcher was pointing out to users each task after they had finished the previous one, in order to achieve task randomisation. This method was chosen to address the effect of learning while performing them, as there was not a dependency relationship among tasks. To achieve the estimation of all four attributes, researchers were also recording the steps required for the completion of each task. Furthermore, time recording for each task included not only the time needed to complete it, but also the time that intervened between the user reading the task and starting to perform it.

5   Results

Analysis of the questionnaire's first part, gave demographic indications regarding the participants. Most of them were women, aged between twenty and twenty five years old, while only 15% of the participants were men, aged between twenty two and twenty four years old. Table 2 presents detailed information on the population sample. This is in line with the demographics of the school, where female students far exceed their male counterparts.

Table 2. Age

Age	Percentage
20-21	50
22	10
23	15
24	10
25	15
Total	100

Furthermore, all the students that participated in the research were on the sixth or the eighth semester of their studies. The research was announced to students of all semesters, however, mostly final-year students responded. This could be attributed to the fact that students in these semesters have many courses that include information retrieval on a variety of digital environments and were intrigued by the research topic. Apart from that, all participants appeared to spend a lot of time on using databases or digital libraries for studying, which helped them relate to the subject of the research thus proving quite helpful to them.

The *effectiveness* of the DL is measured by analysing the number of correct answers and as previously stated, there was only one correct answer for each task. Participants were asked to evaluate the scale of difficulty of each performed task. The scale was on 1 to 7, where 1 being the easiest. Curiously enough, although participants, in some cases, described the tasks as being very difficult, as they felt that they would not be able to locate the correct answer, the level of success rose at 100%.

As described in Table 3, the average percentage for correct answers was 88%, which is a high rated percentage. To illustrate to point made earlier, the second task which involved locating information regarding the World War I was described as quite easy (two to four in the difficulty scale), but 40% of the users were unable to find the correct answer. In stark contrast to the second task was the fourth task. It required subjects to locate information about World War I and Thessaloniki and although all participants managed to accomplish d the task, they rated its accomplishment as very difficult. (six in the difficulty scale). The ratings were also high for the sixth task, which in fact proved to be more difficult than the rest, as only 65% of the participants managed to complete it successfully. It's worth noting that in some cases participants were confronted with functionality problems, such as in the completion of tasks 8 and 8.1, in which although they managed to locate the appropriate material, they couldn't access it.

Table 3. Effectiveness

	Correct answers
Task 1	95
Task 2	60
Task 3	75
Task 4	100
Task 4.1	100
Task 4.2	100
Task 5	100
Task 6	65
Task 7	100
Task 7.1	100
Task 8	95
Task 8.1	95
Task 8.2	70
Total Average	88%

As mentioned before, *efficiency* was measured by examining the average time and steps needed for the completion of each task. In order to achieve this, user moves and time were recorded, during each task performance for every user. As presented in the table below, the average time required to perform a complete research was 1 minute and 12 seconds, while the average number of steps needed was four.

Table 4. Efficiency

	Average time to complete a task	Average steps to complete a task
Task 1	0m 45sec.	3
Task 2	2m 04sec	6
Task 3	1m 28sec.	4
Task 4	1m 38sec.	5
Task 4.1	0m 41sec.	3
Task 4.2	0m 21sec.	2
Task 5	1m 33sec.	5
Task 6	3m 45sec.	12
Task 7	0m 15sec.	2
Task 7.1	0m 22sec.	2
Task 8	1m 12sec.	4
Task 8.1	0m 10sec.	1
Task 8.2	1m 35sec.	5
Total Average	1m 12sec.	4

It is worth mentioning that almost 50% of the tasks were completed successfully in less than a minute. For instance, in tasks 4.1 and 4.2, users were asked to download, or, share in social media information already retrieved from a previous task. The sixth task proved to be more time consuming, given the complexity of its design

Recording of steps also yielded some interesting results. Most of the tasks required three to five steps in order to be completed, but in some cases users seemed uncertain about the result they would find, resulting in further browsing within the collection and use of filters. This technique required more steps than using the search option. In some instances they even performed a search, raising the number of steps to fifteen, while the correct answer could be found in two or three. However in needs to be noted that although some of the tasks were time consuming and took more steps in order to be completed, participants indicated that the labeling was very clear and it assisted them in locating the required information.

Concerning *learnability*, one should take under consideration three factors. First and foremost is the elapsed time that each user requires until the first contact with the task. It is proven that the more confident a user feels in the environment of a DL, the quicker he/she starts performing the search. Secondly, effectiveness, which is the ability to actually locate the correct information, also plays an important role to measuring learnability. Finally response time represents the ability of user to get accustomed to the digital environment and perform a search in it. , One can form a full opinion on whether a participant tested, demonstrates a capacity for learnability, when effectiveness is paired with response time (Table 5).

Table 5. Learnability

	Response time	Average time to task completion	Effectiveness
Task 1	0m 02sec.	0m 45sec.	95%
Task 2	0m 01sec.	2m 04sec	60%
Task 3	0m 02sec.	1m 28sec.	75%
Task 4	0m 02sec.	1m 38sec.	100%
Task 4.1	0m 02sec.	0m 41sec.	100%
Task 4.2	0m 02sec.	0m 21sec.	100%
Task 5	0m 02sec.	1m 33sec.	100%
Task 6	0m 01sec.	3m 45sec.	65%
Task 7	0m 01sec.	0m 15sec.	100%
Task 7.1	0m 01sec.	0m 22sec.	100%
Task 8	0m 01sec.	1m 12sec.	95%
Task 8.1	0m 02sec.	0m 10sec.	95%
Task 8.2	0m 01sec.	1m 35sec.	70%
Total Average	0m 1,5sec.	1m 12sec.	88%

As presented in the table above, the average response time was very low (1.5 sec) and there were no considerable variations from user to user. This combined with the fact that the percentage of the correct answers was satisfactory and the average time to perform a task is considered normal, is leading us to assumption that Europeana holds a quite pleasant environment for its users.

In order to examine the last attribute of usability testing, *satisfaction*, users were given an extra set of questions to answer after performing all the tasks at Europeana. At this stage the questionnaire was designed to measure user opinion on how they perceived ease of navigation, content organisation, use of terminology, the labeling, feelings of being lost in the digital environment, ease of mistake recovery, as well as rating the rating the experience in using Europeana, as a whole in terms of satisfaction.

In this part of the research most of the participants appeared to rigorously judge the aforementioned elements and the results were slightly controversial. The perceived ease of use reached only 42.2%. Information organisation was considered clear by 55% of the participants, but only 25% of them noted that terminology used in the DL was easily understandable. Despite that fact, its interface was found very attractive because of the considerable number of audiovisual material. In contrary to these results, error correction and general satisfaction of users rose to 60%, mostly because users recognized that the provision of services on offer could prove to be very useful for their future searches. Having said that the recordings of users feeling lost were quite high, but most of the users commended that this was probably due to the fact that they felt overwhelmed with the amount of information available to them and that this feeling could easily diminish if they were to spend more e time in Europeana's environment. A more detailed description is presented in Table 6.

Table 6. Individual satisfaction characteristics

	Level of satisfaction
Ease of use	42,2%
Information organisation	55%
Terminology	25%
Interface	67,8%
Error correction	60%
Lostness	78%
Browsing	80%
General Satisfaction	60%

6   Conclusion

Europeana has been developed to a fully operational service containing remarkable and numerous collections. This research was conducted using four usability measurements: effectiveness, efficiency, learnability and satisfaction.

This study found that Europeana is based on a most promising environment and its users are most content by its use. Despite the fact that it was not characterised as an easy to use DL, all participants were left with a positive feeling from their first contact. Additionally, a user positive perception of the DL was not altered despite facing difficulties. Furthermore, the functionality problems mentioned above were located in tasks that required users to access specific material which was accessible by its providers. However, users were able to locate it easily, which confirms once more that the labeling was clear, but the links to the material were not accessible causing the average time for these tasks to rise.

Moreover, in some cases Europeana caused users feelings of uncertainty. However, the fact that it provides access to a significant number of items held by a number of organizations   through a single interface was more than enough to please them. The digital environment becomes more pleasant and attractive by the extensive audiovisual content and users are also helped by the fact that they can access any material by performing different types of search (for instance by browsing the collection, searching by title, author, dates, place, etc.). It is intelligible that different users with different needs can lead to produce controversial results.

However, all of these results could prove to be useful for enhancing the DL's usability, as it contains cultural material. Nonetheless, any problems that occurred during this research were offset by users themselves because of the positive feelings that were developed while discovering Europeana's treasures. At this point it should be noted that as mentioned in the literature review there is lack of benchmarking that sets a limit to usability. This fact prevents us from defining a percentage that would conclude to whether a DL is effective, efficient or easy to learn.

To conclude with, Europeana has its own working group that among others is responsible for conducting evaluation researches internally, aiming to its constant updating and enhancement. Nevertheless, this research provides feedback from an external view, as the evaluation testing was conducted independently and managed to capture the information retrieval habits from users that belong in a different working environment.

References

1. Xie, H.: Evaluation of digital libraries: Criteria and problems from users' perspectives. Library and Information Science Research **28**(3), 433–452 (2006)
2. Blandford, A., Buchanan, G.: Usability of digital libraries: a source of creative tensions with technical developments. IEEE Technical Committee on Digital Libraries Bulletin **1**(1) (2003)
3. Jeng, J.: Usability assessment of academic digital libraries: Effectiveness, efficiency, satisfaction, and learnability. Libri **55**(2–3), 96–121 (2005)
4. Borgman, C.L.: What are digital libraries? Competing Visions. Inf. Process. Manage. **35**(3), 227–243 (1999)
5. Marchionini, G.: Evaluating digital libraries: A longitudinal and multifaceted view. Library Trends **49**(2), 304–333 (2000)
6. Mittal, R., Mahesh, G.: Digital libraries and repositories in India: an evaluative study. Program **42**(3), 286–302 (2008)
7. Sandusky, R.J.: Digital library attributes: framing usability research. In: Proc. Workshop on Usability of Digital Libraries at JCDL, vol. 2, pp. 35–38, July 2002

8. Blandford, A., Keith, S., Connell, I., Edwards, H.: Analytical usability evaluation for digital libraries: a case study. In: Proceedings of the 2004 Joint ACM/IEEE Conference on Digital Libraries, pp. 27–36. IEEE, June 2004

9. Saracevic, T.: Evaluation of digital libraries: an overview. In: Notes of the DELOS WP7 Workshop on the Evaluation of Digital Libraries, Padua, Italy, Sutherland, L.A., September 2004

10. Bertot, J.C., Snead, J.T., Jaeger, P.T., McClure, C.R.: Functionality, usability, and accessibility: Iterative user-centered evaluation strategies for digital libraries. Performance Measurement and Metrics 7(1), 17–28 (2006)

11. Jeng, J.: Usability of the digital library: An evaluation model. College and Research Libraries News 78 (2006)

12. Chowdhury, S., Landoni, M., Gibb, F.: Usability and impact of digital libraries: a review. Online Information Review 30(6), 656–680 (2006)

13. Nielsen, J.: Usability metrics: Tracking interface improvements. Ieee Software 13(6), 12–13 (1996)

14. Jeng, J.: What is usability in the context of the digital library and how can it be measured? Information Technology and Libraries 3 (2005b)

15. Fuhr, N., Tsakonas, G., Aalberg, T., Agosti, M., Hansen, P., Kapidakis, S., Sølvberg, I.: Evaluation of digital libraries. International Journal on Digital Libraries 8(1), 21–38 (2007)

16. Nielsen, J.: Why you only need to test with 5 users, 2000. Jakob Nielsen's Alertbox (2012). http://www.useit.com/alertbox/20000319.html

17. Ferreira, S.M., Pithan, D.N.: Usability of digital libraries: A study based on the areas of information science and human-computer-interaction. OCLC Systems & Services 21(4), 311–323 (2005)

18. Garoufallou, E., Mystakopoulos, F., Siatri, R., Balatsoukas, P., Zafeiriou, G.: Usability evaluation of the digital archive of the Hellenic Broadcasting Corporation (ERT). QQML Journal (Qualitative and Quantitative Methods in Libraries): an International Journal of Library and Information Science, ISAST 1, 17–26 (2013)

19. Garoufallou, E., Dani, A., Siatri, R., Chatzopoulou, C., Virkus, S., Mystakopoulos, F., Katrinaki, E.: Usability evaluation of world digital library: estimating the utility of service platform. In: 7th International Conference on Qualitative and Quantitative Methods in Libraries (QQML), May 26–29, 2015, Paris, France (2015)

20. Nielsen, J.: Usability inspection methods. In: Conference Companion on Human Factors In Computing Systems, pp. 413–414. ACM, April 1994

21. Saracevic, T.: Digital library evaluation: Toward evolution of concepts. Library Trends 49(2), 350–369 (2000)

22. Garoufallou, E., Siatri, R., Balatsoukas, P.: Virtual maps virtual worlds: Testing the usability of a Greek virtual cultural map. Journal of the American Society for Information Science and Technology (JASIST) 59(4), 591–601 (2008)

Usability Testing of an Annotation Tool in a Cultural Heritage Context

Karoline Hoff and Michael Preminger[✉]

Oslo and Akershus University College of Applied Science, Oslo, Norway
karoline.hoff@outlook.com, michaelp@hioa.no

Abstract. This paper presents the result of a usability test of an annotation tool. The annotation tool is implemented, used and tested in a cultural heritage context (CH), the TORCH project at the Oslo and Akershus University College of Applied Science. The experiments employed non-experts with the intention of facilitating for crowd-sourcing of annotations. Interesting problems and usability patterns from the literature manifest in our experiments. Despite some weaknesses in the interface of the tool version used for the experiments, the annotators show a reasonable rate of success.

1 Introduction

The proliferation of semantic web application in recent years, has been followed by development of and research into automatic conversion of legacy data into semantic-aware formats, identifying entities and roles in those data. In order to make advances here, ground truths are needed, and in order to establish those, we need to have large samples of those data annotated.

Such annotation is performed intellectually and is facilitated by annotation tools. The best annotation results (e.g. ground truth) would be expected if the annotators were both domain experts and technically proficient. In most cases, alas, such annotators are scarce and expensive. For very specialized knowledge domains, such as agriculture, spacecraft and the like, domain experts would be needed, although leniency could be shown with regards to the requirement of technical proficiency. In domains like cultural heritage, which is the domain of our project, leniency could be shown with regards to both requirement, and crowd-sourcing could be used, given that the annotation tool facilitates non-experts input, and the usability is good. Moreover, particularly for cases that need great amounts of data, crowd-sourcing would be the only viable alternative, which challenges the design of the annotation tool.

The TORCH project at our institute is a conversion endeavour, attempting to convert programme description from the archives of the Norwegian national broadcaster (NRK) into Semantic aware formats. As described in [1], we have developed our own annotation tool, which we, in the long run, would like to adapt to a wider context and make hospitable to crowd sourcing. Successful crowdsourcing demands that the tool has as few usability issues as possible, which is the main objective of this endeavour.

© Springer International Publishing Switzerland 2015
E. Garoufallou et al. (Eds.): MTSR 2015, CCIS 544, pp. 237–248, 2015.
DOI: 10.1007/978-3-319-24129-6_21

In this article we report a study into the process of manual annotation by end-users using our annotation tool. For this, both information expert and non-expert users were observed in a usability study. Our goal is to gain insight into the end-users understanding of the tool, and to develop an adequate design for the annotation tool, making it usable for non-experts. This paper reports on the results of this user study.

The remainder of this paper is structured as follows: in section 2 we explore related work in evaluating the usability of manual annotation tools. Section 3 introduces our annotation tool, while section 4 explains the methodology and setup of our study. Section 5 contains the results of the study, and discusses the implications of the results.

We start by presenting the current state of the art of user testing in annotation.

2   Background

2.1   Usability Fundamentals

[2] claims that "usability is not some vague postulation, but actually a criterion that can be measured and systematically engineered".

Burghardt further explores this in his doctoral dissertation ([3]). Here Burghardt emphasizes the importance of an interface that makes the annotation process as convenient and efficient as possible, as manual annotation is typically a laborious task. To investigate the usability of the annotation tool, we conducted a study with participants who could be typical users of these systems.

Usability can be described as how well a system can be used, or the users' ability to carry out the task successfully. Nielsen ([4]) states that usability cannot be described as a one-dimensional criterion, but must be seen as a concept defined by five quality components: *learnability, efficiency, memorability, error rate* and *satisfaction*.

Each of these usability components can be measured individually. Learnability tells us something about how easy it is for users to accomplish basic tasks when they encounter the design. Efficiency is how quickly a user familiar with the design can perform tasks. Memorability is about how easily a user returning to the product after a period of not using it can re-establish proficiency. The error rate tells us how many errors the users make, how severe these errors are, and how easily a user can recover from these errors. Satisfaction is the users own experience and perception of the design.

A more formal definition, like the ISO 9241-11 standard from The International Organization for Standardization ([5]), states that the usability of a product is "the extent to which a product can be used by specified users to achieve specified goals with effectiveness, efficiency, and satisfaction in a specified context of use".

2.2   Usability Testing

There are several ways to evaluate the usability of a product, depending on factors like available resources, evaluator experience, ability and preference, and the stage of development of the product under review. Scholtz ([6]) states that the three most discussed evaluation methods are user-based, expert-based and model-based. In user-based evaluation methods individuals from a sample of the intended users try to use the application. Expert-based methods makes a usability expert do an assessment of the application. In model-based methods an expert employs formal methods to predict one or more criteria of user performance. In their user study, Hinze et.al. ([7]) state that usability typically is a factor in the interface development of manual annotation tools, and that end-user evaluations of interface and user interaction are very rare. Hinze et. al. also state that typical evaluation strategies of Semantic Web technologies seldom contain complex user aspect, despite aspects of Humancomputer interaction and user involvement being identified as important aspects.

> Few studies involving end-users have been executed in the context of semantic annotations. In particular, manual annotation tools have so far not been systematically evaluated for appropriate interaction design and semantic understanding. System evaluations that incorporated human participants did not seek their feedback on interaction issues nor did they evaluate the participants' mental models of the system interaction. So far, issues of understanding of semantic annotations by (non-expert) users have not been studied in a systematic manner. [7]

Like Barnum ([8]), when we talk about usability testing we are referring to the activity that focuses on observing users working with a product, performing tasks that are real and meaningful to them.

For usability testing to be an effective tool for understanding user interface design strengths and weaknesses, it needs to engage actual users in performing real work. Conducting formative usability testing as part of an iterative design strategy is the most reliable way to develop a truly usable product ([9], s. 7).

2.3   Usability Testing of Annotation Tools

If crowdsourcing is to become the reality, one of our goals has to be to create an environment where non-expert users are able to create meaningful and consistent annotations. Hinze et.al. identified following key requirements for non-expert users of manual annotation tools: *established interaction patterns, simple vocabularies, contextual semantic identity* and *focus on the user's task* ([7]).

"Established interaction patterns" entails making semantic web applications look like traditional applications and to use familiar interaction paradigms. Simple vocabularies is pretty self-explanatory, it is important because research indicates that complex category structures are disadvantageous for quality annotations. Contextual semantic identity means bridging the gap between objective knowledge (as encoded in the RDF data model) and subjective knowledge of human cognition, e.g. computers identifying resources by URIs in RDF, versus humans identifying entities with labels and disambiguate meaning using context. "Focus on the user's task" entails that semantic authoring and semantic annotations is integrated in a good way. This is not applicable to us, as the TORCH annotation tool is a pure annotation tool ([7]).

Burghardt describes 17 unique requirements for annotation tools, whereas two requirements are categorized as pure usability requirements, and eight requirements are categorized as mixed functional and usability requirements. Five of these requirements are relevant to us, as they describe usability aspects, and are categorized as relevant for the core group Burghardt calls "Annotators" i.e. our tool's user group. We have also left out the mixed requirements for functions our tool does not possess ([3, p. 77-81]). The two pure usability requirements are *documentation*, i.e. the availability of a user manual, which is important for the learnability of a system, and the general purpose requirement of an *easy-to-use interface*. The three mixed requirements relevant to us are *visualization of primary data*, meaning the original text should be displayed correctly in the annotation tool, and the tool should clearly differentiate between original and annotated text. *Visualization of annotation*, closely tied with the previous requirement. *Marking of anchors*, i.e. providing an interface making for an intuitive and effective selection of different anchor scopes ([3, p. 77-81]). The documentation and the three relevant mixed requirements are fulfilled as described in 3, and while our study is designed with these requirements in mind, the requirement of an easy-to-use interface is our main focus ([3, p. 77-81]). Within the mentioned usability requirements, Burghardt also identified twenty-six usability patterns for the domain of manual annotation tools. These are divided into the categories *general UI, installation, primary data, annotation scheme, annotation process* and *annotation visualization* ([3, p. 143]). We will use these patterns to identify potential problems with our tool later.

3   The Annotation Tool

Our annotation tool (first described in [1]) is developed in order to provide ground truth-data for the TORCH project[1]. In order to allow the collection of enough data, we believe that crowd-sourcing with the emphasis of non-experts, is mandatory. Our tool is developed for use in the context of Cultural Heritage (broadcasted material), where the term non-experts refers to quite a wide public. We believe nonetheless, that also other contexts to which annotating textual materials is relevant could gain a larger number of annotators, and more annotated material of high quality, if the annotation process is made more accessible.

To this end, we seek to provide simplicity in use. Moreover, our assumption is that annotators, be it domain experts or non-experts, do not read guidelines very thoroughly, which means that heavily basing correct annotations on

---

[1] The TORCH project is an activity of the research group Information systems based on metadata: http://tinyurl.com/k8gf7dr

detailed guidelines is hazardous. Therefore the usage of the tool should be as self-explanatory as possible, the approach to the annotated material should be gradual in the process, and learning while annotating possible without compromising the results.

The thought behind the design is that named entities are annotated first, with as few as possible classes to choose from. The classes are ordered in hierarchies, the annotation done with as specific as possible classes (closest to the leaves), with the provision to fall back to more general (closer to the root) classes. This means that RealPerson is available as a class, but not Actor (role). Here the user is prompted to choose a Wikipedia URI (from a list constructed on the fly for each mention), to provide the mention with a unique, global URI. The second phase in the annotation is assignment of relations between already annotated entities. The current experiments do not test the assignment of other than co-references, which have a specially designed short-cut.

Fig. 1. The annotation tool screen with the class selector activated.

4   Usability Testing of the TORCH Annotation Tool

Our goal is to develop an adequate design for the annotation tool, making it usable for non-experts, and to gain insight into the end-users understanding of the tool. We wanted to know what usability issues could be identified, what problems users experienced during the annotation process, how satisfied the users were with the tool, and how the tool could be redesigned to minimize above issues.

We studied the usability of the annotation tool in an end-user study. We performed the usability tests and interviews with real users. Even though the annotation tool is fully operational, this user study made only use of the functions relevant for phase one of the annotation process, and the making of co-references. This was decided at an early stage, to make the design manageable in terms of variables and causality. Moreover, this is the phase that will most probably be exposed to crowd-sourcing, as we are still considering annotating relations by the TORCH staff.

Data was collected in two ways: through observation and through questionnaires. The facilitator sat with each participant throughout the session, recording observations, noting any difficulties, any comments made by the participant, and whether they successfully completed the task. Participants were asked at the beginning of the session to "think-aloud" ([4, p. 195-198]).

Besides the standard instructions given to all participants, no further explanations or assistance were given. In cases where the participant forgot to think-aloud, the facilitator would ask "what did you expect to happen there?". If the participant asked for more instructions, the facilitator would remind the participant that we were testing the usability of the tool and needed to see if people could use it without further explanations.

The participants were given realistic tasks to perform by interacting directly with the tool. The tool does not explain how the interface is supposed to work, making it possible to identify which parts of the interface are self-explanatory and which parts are confusing.

Before starting the actual interaction with the tool, each participant was asked to read the guidelines. The facilitator clarified the nature of the task, and explained how the initial interface worked. Each task began with a brief scenario explaining the goal of the task from a user's perspective, followed by task instructions, and instructions on how to report the task as completed. A short summary of the user tasks is presented below.

- Task 1 Annotate two personal names of your choice
- Task 2 Annotate two creative works of your choice
- Task 3 Annotate a geographical place of your choice
- Task 4 Create an equivalence-relation between two annotations of your choice (in our own terminology called co-reference).
- Task 5 Correct the errors in the pre-existing annotation
- Task 6 Delete an annotation of your choice

We used a text that contained only general knowledge concepts for the annotation. With the exception of one incorrectly annotated entity, the experimental text was plain and free of annotations. The error was annotated by the facilitator beforehand, making it possible to ask the participants to find and correct it during the test.

The participants had a pen and a printout of the tasks available during the whole session. During the sessions, the participants were asked to evaluate every feature of the interface design that they thought should be changed in looks or functionality based on their expectations of the tool. They were not obliged to follow the guidelines, but they were asked to think aloud and justify the decisions they made.

The participants were requested to notify the facilitator when they assumed they had finished the task, or gave up trying.

5   Results

Here we report the results of our study, and describe our observations of how participants interacted with the annotation tool. We differentiate between observations about the participants' interaction with the tool and the creation of annotations, quality of annotations and participant feedback. We have categorized our findings based on [3].

5.1   The Data Collected

We collected data as follows

- Participant demographics (collected pr. questionnaire before the test itself)
- Think aloud recording summaries
- Pre-task expectations per task (collected pr. questionnaire at the beginning of each task, not reported here)
- Feedback: post-task experience with reference to pre-task expectations (collected pr. questionnaire at the end of each task)
- System usability scale (not reported here)
- The annotation results

5.2   Participant Demographics

As we aspire to make the tool usable for non-experts, we selected seven participants with varied backgrounds and varied levels of technical knowledge. The participants were asked to rate their knowledge on a 5-point scale, with 1 being "no knowledge" and 5 being "very knowledgeable". We surveyed their familiarity with word processing as a measure of computer literacy, tagging as an annotation task, familiarity with usability and semantic web as technical expertise, respectively. Fig. 2 shows the distribution of expertise for the 7 participants. All participants are computer literate. Four participants were familiar with tagging and semantic web, while three participants knew little of it. Based on their self-assessment, we identified participants U1-U4 as technical experts, and U5-U7 as non-experts.

5.3   Observed Usability Problems

Here we report the usability problems described in [3] that we could identify by observing the participants' interactions with the tool.

Within the mentioned usability requirements, Burghardt also identified twenty-six usability patterns for the domain of manual annotation tools. These are divided into the categories *general UI, installation, primary data, annotation scheme, annotation process* and *annotation visualization*. We will use these patterns to identify potential problems with our tool.

The main bulk of the problems found belong in the "General UI" part of Burghardts listing of usability patterns.

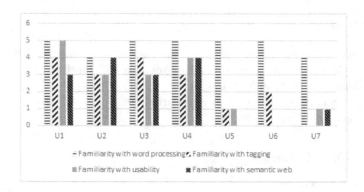

Fig. 2. The distribution of expertise for the 7 participants.

In "General IU", Burghardt has identified some problems that influence the overall user experience with the tool, with no explicit reference to any particular stage in the annotation work-flow. There are no generic solutions for these issues, but of the patterns Burghardt mentions, we could identify the following in our own study: Safe exploration, some users reported feeling afraid they would "break something". One user said "I feel like the developer is trusting me as a userperhaps a bit too much". We obviously have something to gain by making the tool seem less menacing, and ensure the users know that no mistake are unfixable.

We also identified the pattern Burghardt calls "Help for domain-specific functions" ("domain" here, unlike elsewhere in the paper, referring to semantic annotation as an activity.). Several users reported being unsure of exactly what a co-reference was, and thus being unsure if they had annotated it correctly. As seen in Figure 3, creating co-references was the task with the greatest number of semantically meaningless results, despite the participants having read the section on co-references in the guidelines before starting the task. Burghardt proposes several solutions, one of which being a brief explanation inside the tool. Providing help for the unintuitive, domain-specific functions, increases the learnability of the tool. This is especially important for non-expert users, and a thing we will have to consider within the TORCH project if we are to crowd-source.

Burghardt lists "Redundant controls" as a problem, and two participants were unsure of what "set" of buttons they were to use. Burghardt also mentions "no explicit save action" as a problem, and one participant in our study (an expert as it happens) exclaimed "I do not want to *update* anything, I want to *save*". However, he was the only one commenting on the wording of the button. In line with Burghardts "General UI" item, one other participant commented on the colour, saying yellow made him think of danger. Three participants commented on the amount of primary data, feeling a bit overwhelmed. Burghardt describes "tailored display of data", and recommends the possibility of customizing things like font-size, font-family and line spacing. This is to give the user control and freedom, and ultimately increase the annotation speed, or *efficiency*. In the category *annotation process*, Burghardt identifies the steps in the annotation

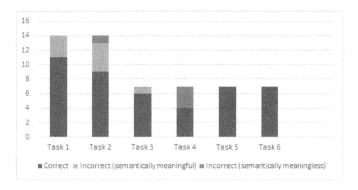

Fig. 3. Success rate by task.

process, and to us these are the important ones: *create anchor*[2], *select annotation*, *apply annotation*, *edit annotation* and *delete annotation*. All participants had some trouble with highlighting the anchor. Having to start the marking in the middle of the word they wished to select seemed foreign to them, but having done it once, all but one found it relatively easy. One participant wanted to find and select all instances of an entity with the ctrl+f-function. Another participant wanted to mark several instances of the same entity and annotate them at the same time to gain efficiency. Selecting annotations did not emerge as a problem, and as seen in Figure 3, each participant was able to successfully edit and delete annotations.

5.4   Quality of Annotations

Figure 2 shows a summary of the quality of the annotations created by the participants. The outcome of each task was recorded by the facilitator according to the following possible outcomes:

- an annotated entity which corresponds with the ground truth established by the facilitator is considered correct
- an annotated entity is considered incorrect, but semantically meaningful if it refers to a named entity (e.g., if participants annotated "filmen Øyenstikkeren"[3])
- The annotations are considered semantically meaningless if they do not refer to a named entity, (e.g., "innspillingen"[4])

All seven participants created at least one correct annotation, and three participants created nothing but correct annotations. There were two kinds of incorrect, but semantically meaningful annotations: Some were assigned the wrong Wikipedia URI, e.g. assigning the *movie* Øyenstikkeren [5] the article about the

---

[2] anchor being the highlighted text to be annotated
[3] The movie "Øyenstikkeren"
[4] The shooting (of a movie)
[5] dragonfly in Norwegian

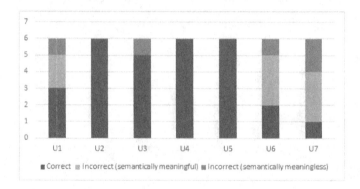

Fig. 4. Quality of annotations per participant

insect. The other kind had in common that participants included the determiner e.g. "the movie Øyenstikker" or "the host Mikal Olsen Lerøen". No one annotated wrong parts of the texts, however, this is most likely a consequence of the way we designed the tasks.

There were two kinds of incorrect annotations: some were faulty equivalence-relations between a referrer and the entity it was referring to, e.g. "the movie" referring to "Øyenstikker". The remaining were stand-alone nouns the participants wrongly interpreted as work-titles. It is clearly explained in the guidelines how to handle both of these occurrences, and none of them are to be annotated. Despite having access to the guidelines during the testing, and having to read through them in advance, only a single participant actually consulted them when in doubt. This indicates that our assumption about annotators not reading guidelines thoroughly is correct.

No participants gave up on a task without completing it, but some were unsure if they were done and if their annotation had been saved. Several participants reported that they had perceived little feedback from the tool, and were looking for some cue that they had been successful. They often commented "I *think* it did it" or "I guess I am done with that". Some participants perceived the tool as frozen when the tool was processing their request.

Like in [7] several participants switched from being an information provider to an information consumer in the course of the study. Four participants wanted to open the Wikipedia URI to read more about something, or making sure they had chosen the correct URI. Two participants showed interest in the ontology beyond what was described in the guidelines, e.g. "what if I found a pseudonym?".

5.5 Participant Feedback

Using a questionnaire as a guide while talking to the participants, we post-interviewed them about their experience in using the TORCH annotation tool. Figure 5 shows the participants' self-assessment regarding how difficult they found using the tool, with 1 being "very easy" and 5 being "very hard". We asked the participants for feedback on their experience of the different tasks:

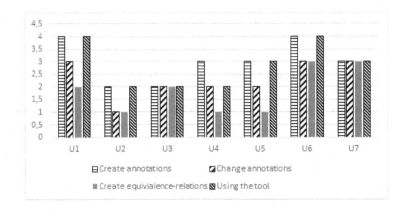

Fig. 5. How difficult the participants percieved the different tasks to be.

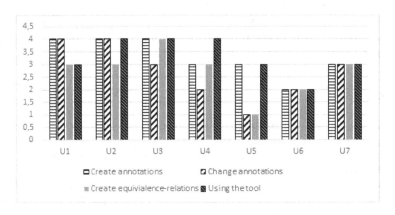

Fig. 6. The degree of interest participants were expressing.

create annotations (left), change annotation (second left), create co-references (second right), and their general experience of using the tool as a whole (right).

Five of the seven participants felt editing annotations and creating co-references was easier than creating new annotations and using the tool in general. The two others felt all activities were equally difficult. These results are also interesting in light of the quality of the created annotations (see Figure 2). U5 rated the tool fairly difficult to use (3), but all her annotations were correct. She was also the only non-expert participant with a 100 % success rate. Changing annotations was rated remarkably difficult, considering all participants successfully completed that task. We think this is because the participants were unsure whether they had indeed successfully completed the task, it being a tool-feedback issue. Figure 6 shows the participants' self-assessment regarding how interesting they found using the tool after completing the tasks, with 1 being "not interested" and 5 being "very interested". Like in Figure 5 we asked for feedback on their experience of the different tasks: create annotations (left), change annotation (second left), create co-references (second right), and their general experience of using the tool as a whole (right).

6   Summary and Concluding Remarks

We have performed a usability test of the TORCH annotation tool, with emphasis on functions that we would like to expose to crowd-sourcing. The results show that annotators with reasonable computer literacy, not being domain experts, have a high success rate performing the tasks. In line with the existing literature we find that designing the interface as similar as possible to traditional applications increases annotators' confidence. We also found no clear connection between annotators' perceived difficulty and interest in participating in further activity of the kind, which is encouraging in the context of crowd-sourcing. As further research we see the need to go deeper into users' attitudes towards annotating (performing in depth interviews with few participants) on the one hand, as well as exposing more of the functionality of our tool (and changes to the tool owing to the presented experiments) to further usability testing.

References

1. Tallerås, K., Massey, D., Husevåg, A.-S.R., Preminger, M., Pharo, N.: Evaluating (linked) metadata transformations across cultural heritage domains. In: Closs, S., Studer, R., Garoufallou, E., Sicilia, M.-A. (eds.) MTSR 2014. CCIS, vol. 478, pp. 250–261. Springer, Heidelberg (2014)
2. Burghardt, M.: Usability recommendations for annotation tools. In: Proceedings of the Sixth Linguistic Annotation Workshop, LAW VI 2012, pp. 104–112. Association for Computational Linguistics, Stroudsburg (2012)
3. Burghardt, M.: Engineering annotation usability - toward usability patterns for linguistic annotation tools, September 2014. http://www.annotation-usability.net
4. Nielsen, J.: Usability Engineering. Morgan Kaufmann Publishers Inc., San Francisco (1993)
5. International Organization for Standardization: ISO 9241–210:2010 Ergonomics of human-system interaction - Part 210: human-centred design process for interactive systems (2010)
6. Scholtz, J.: Usability Evaluation (2004)
7. Hinze, A., Heese, R., Luczak-Rösch, M., Paschke, A.: Semantic enrichment by non-experts: usability of manual annotation tools. In: Cudré-Mauroux, P., Heflin, J., Sirin, E., Tudorache, T., Euzenat, J., Hauswirth, M., Parreira, J.X., Hendler, J., et al. (eds.) ISWC 2012, Part I. LNCS, vol. 7649, pp. 165–181. Springer, Heidelberg (2012)
8. Barnum, C.M.: Usability testing essentials: ready, set– test. Morgan Kaufmann, Burlington (2011)
9. Norlin, E., Winters, C.: Usability testing for library websites: a hands-on guide. American Library Association, Chicago (2002)

An Exploration of Users' Needs for Multilingual Information Retrieval and Access

Evgenia Vassilakaki[1]([✉]), Emmanouel Garoufallou[2], Frances Johnson[3], and R.J. Hartley[3]

[1] Department of Library Science and Information Systems,
Technological Educational Institute of Athens, Egaleo, Athens, Greece
evevasilak@gmail.com

[2] Department of Library Science and Information Systems, Alexander Technological
Educational Institute of Thessaloniki, Sindos, Thessaloniki, Greece
mgarou@lib.teithe.gr

[3] Department Languages, Information and Communications,
Manchester Metropolitan University, Manchester, UK
{f.johnson,r.j.hartley}@mmu.ac.uk

Abstract. The need for promoting Multilingual Information Retrieval (MLIR) and Access (MLIA) has become evident, now more than ever, given the increase of the online information produced daily in languages other than English. This study aims to explore users' information needs when searching for information across languages. Specifically, the method of questionnaire was employed to shed light on the Library and Information Science (LIS) undergraduate students' use of search engines, databases, digital libraries when searching as well as their needs for multilingual access. This study contributes in informing the design of MLIR systems by focusing on the reasons and situations under which users would search and use information in multiple languages.

1 Introduction

The available information on the Web is increasing exponentially. Information is produced in different types (i.e. images, videos, text) but most importantly in different languages. Although English is still the predominant language used on the Internet, there is a steady increase of the amount of content available in other languages namely Russian, German, Chinese, Japanese, Spanish, French [1]. Therefore, it becomes now, more than ever, apparent the need to develop systems that will support multilingual information retrieval (MLIR) and access (MLIA).

MLIS is defined as the task of searching for relevant information by using criteria in a chosen language (preferable in mother tongue) and retrieve all documents which match all the search criteria, regardless of the language of the documents or the indexed language and present them in a unified list [2,3]. There is an ongoing discussion regarding the reason why would anyone wish to find information that he/she would not be able to read. However, development and use of translation tools has offered an adequate way of accessing the content of the desirable information.

© Springer International Publishing Switzerland 2015
E. Garoufallou et al. (Eds.): MTSR 2015, CCIS 544, pp. 249–258, 2015.
DOI: 10.1007/978-3-319-24129-6_22

This study aims to investigate users' needs for multilingual information. Specifically, it has the following objectives:

- to identify users' preferences in databases, digital libraries and search engines while searching for information;
- to explore whether knowledge of foreign languages affects users' search behaviours while searching across languages;
- to explore the type of multilingual information users search;
- to investigate the situations under which users search across languages;

It should be noted that here only preliminary results of an overall study conducted regarding users' information seeking behaviour in multilingual digital libraries are presented. This study contributes in providing an insight into the situations under which users would search across languages, the search engines, databases and digital libraries they would employ and their needs for multilingual information. This in turn, will assist in informing the design of the multilingual information systems and interfaces developed. This research addresses the developments in Digital Libraries and the needs of multilingual users for searching searching information in different languages.

This paper is structured as follows. A review of the literature on users' information seeking behaviour when searching across languages is critically presented. Details on the methodological approach adopted in this study are illustrated. Preliminary findings of this study are presented and critically discussed with the relevant literature.

2   Literature Review

Research on MLIR and MLIA is vast [4]. However, this research mainly focuses on developing MLIR systems [5,6], evaluating translation techniques [7,8], testing approaches and models [9]. Only a few studies investigated users' information seeking behaviour in multilingual environments.

These studies explored mainly four different aspects of user behaviour when searching for information across languages [4]. Wu, Ge and He [10], Wu, Luo and He [12] and Wu, He and Luo [11] focused on exploring users' expectations and needs for multilingual information. Wu, Ge and He [10] and Wu, Luo and He [12] argued that translations are essential in order to improve MLIA for the end users. Wu, He and Luo [11] found that users have many multilingual needs, especially when searching across databases for academic purposes.

Bilal and Bachir [13], Ghorab et al. [14], Takaku et al [15], Petrelli and Clough [16] and Vassilakaki [25], Vassilakaki, Johnson and Hartley [17] and Vassilakaki et al. [18,19] explored users' information seeking behaviour in multilingual environments. Users indicated a preference to the basic interface, searching in just one language [17–19,25] and using the browsing feature [13,17–19,25]. Ghorab et al. [14] found that users from different linguistic or cultural backgrounds demonstrate different search behaviours whereas Takaku et al. [15]

argued that novice users will perform a small number of actions and would need a longer time in searching.

Users' knowledge of foreigh languages as a factor affecting their multilingual searches was considered by Clough and Eleta [20] and Vassilakaki [25], Vassilakaki, Johnson and Hartley [17] and Vassilakaki et al. [18,19]. Knowledge of other languages proved to be a significant factor affecting users' search behaviour namely in terms of judging and/or relying on translations to retrieve the needed information. Vassilakaki [25], Vassilakaki, Johnson and Hartley [17] and Vassilakaki et al. [18,19] also found that knowledge of languages was also a factor affecting users' levels of trust in the system and confidence in their skills in searching.

Finally, Stafford et al. [21], Shiri et al. [22] and Shiri et al. [23] and Sastry, Manjunath and Reddy [24] evaluated different MLDL interfaces. Stafford et al. [21], Shiri et al. [22] and Shiri et al. [23] found that users would use the thesaurus-enhanced feature and language options, browsing and visualization provided. Sastry, Manjunath and Reddy [24] suggested that when developing MLDL interface different challenges should be considered namely user, search, content and network oriented challenges.

Overall, it could be argued that the number of studies exploring users' information needs in multilingual environments is still limited. However, different factors affecting users' information seeking behaviour across languages were identified namely system's interface, users' knowledge of foreign languages. The importance of these studies is evident when designing and offering multilingual information retrieval interfaces and systems to users.

3   Methodology

A questionnaire was designed based on the relevant literature [11,25]. Lime survey, an open source survey software was used to distribute the questionnaire to users. The questionnaire consisted of 15 closed type questions and relevant subquestions and was divided in three parts (see table 1). The first part inquired on users personal information (i.e. age, gender, level of comprehension with foreign languages) to define user characteristics and knowledge of languages. The second part referred to the frequency of use of specific Databases, Digital Libraries, Search Engines and online OPACs. Finally, the third part addressed the types of information users search across languages, and the means they employ. Only closed type questions were used in order to minimize the time participants had to spend in completing the questionnaire and also as a way to increase users' engagement.

The questionnaire was distributed to the first and fourth year undergraduate students of the Departments of Library Science and Information Systems in both Athens and Thessaloniki. Moodle was used to email the questionnaire to students of both departments and was available throughout May 2015. In total, 219 students participated from both Departments. Lime was also used to analyse the data and excel for creating the necessary graphs. This study collected 219,

Table 1. List of Questions

No	Question
01	Gender
02	Age
03	Degree obtained
04	Please tick the following according to your level of comprehension for each language. For languages not stated here, please fill in the table accordingly
05	How often do you search for information on the following Databases?
06	How often do you search for information on the following Digital libraries?
07	How often do you use the following Search engines to search for information (multiple choices)?
08	How often do you search for information on the following Library OPACs?
09	Besides documents in your native language, do you read any of the following?
10	Under which situations do you search for information in other languages?
11	When searching information for your research/teaching/work, do you feel that it is hindered by not having access to material in other languages?
12	What means do you employ for searching information across languages?
13	Translation tools used before
14	Overall, how do you feel about the effectiveness of the translation tools?
15	For the following sentences please indicate your degree of agreement choosing from 1= agree to 5 disagree

from which 40 (18.3%) were not completed. The data was analysed collectively to shed light on users' behaviour while searching for information across languages.

4   Findings

The majority of the users were female (64%) of age between 18 to 21 years old (64.4%). In terms of users knowledge of foreign languages, the majority of participants (70.8%) are Greek native speakers while they speak English "very good" to "excellent" and have a basic knowledge of French, German, Italian and Spanish.

In terms of the databases users most often use for searching, it was found that the majority of users use "always" Google scholar and then ERIC, Emerald, Web of Science and Elsevier Science Direct. They "sometimes" to "almost never" use PubMed, EBSCO, JSTOR, SpringerLink.

The majority of users use Google Book and Library of Congress World Digital Library to search when it comes to searching in digital libraries. They "very often" search to Europeanna whereas "almost never" to Perseus Digital Library, IEEE Xplore, IEEE Computer Science DL, ACM DL and Alexandria DL.

Google is the most used search engine followed by Yahoo, Bing, ASK and finally Excite. In terms of the OPACs used, the majority of the users search on the Union Catalog of Hellenic Academic Libraries and ATEI Thessaloniki's OPAC followed by the TEI of Athens and Library of Congress OPAC.

Users were asked to define the type of information they read in a language other than their native. The majority of users (44.3%) reads electronic articles followed by e-books (35.2%), electronic periodicals (30.1%) and electronic newspapers (20.1%). A 16% of the users stated that they only search in their mother tongue (see Appendix, Figure 1).

The main reasons users reported for searching for information across languages were for "completing course assignments" (48%), "shopping online" (44.3%), "going abroad" (36.1%), "interested in international news/affairs" (35.6%), "getting film reviews" (34.7%) and "socializing with friends" (29.7%) among others. It worth noted that only 1.8% of the users stated that do not search across languages (see Appendix, Figure 2).

When users were asked if their search for information is hindered by not having access to material in other languages, users were divided between hindered (33%) and not hindered (30%). Finally, users rely mainly on their own languages skills, online translators and dictionaries when searching across languages (see Appendix, Figure 3).

5 Discussion and Conclusions

This study reported on preliminary results on users' multilingual information needs and behaviours. Specifically, users would continue searching in their mother tongue (Greek), although they do know that the available information in this language is limited. This finding is inline with Bilal and Bachir [13], Vassilakaki [25], Vassilakaki et al. [18, 19] and Vassilakaki, Johnson and Hartley [17]. This could be attributed to users' limited knowledge of foreign languages and/or even low confidence in their languages and searching skills as suggested in Vassilakaki [25], Vassilakaki et al. [18, 19] and Vassilakaki, Johnson and Hartley [17]. However, further research with more qualitative methods is needed to shed light on users' thoughts and explanations of their preference of a single language for searching.

In terms of the reasons why users would search for multilingual information, it was found that multilingual information was sought both for educational purposes as well as for pleasure and fun. It was also interesting to find that the number of users stating whether finding the needed information is hindered or not by not showing information in different languages was equal. Further analysis revealed that both groups of users have the same level of knowledge of foreign languages, use the same databases, digital libraries and search engines. Therefore, there is no apparent explanation of this finding. Further research is needed to explore the reasons why both groups feel the way they feel about language barriers in information.

This research has also some implications. MLIR systems have to consider users' knowledge and experience in searching across languages; users' familiarity and use of translation tools as well as users' tendency to use just one interface (the basic one) and just one language (their mother tongue) to search for multilingual information.

This study had also some limitations. A quantitative method was used informing our knowledge on users' tendencies and preferences but not on the reasons why they would search for multilingual information in a specific way. This study employed students in LIS that could be considered experts in searching for information, therefore future research should explore also novice users' needs for searching across languages.

Acknowledgments. Acknowledgement is attributed to the Postdoctoral research on Users information seeking behaviour in Multilingual Digital Libraries carried out at University of Alcala, Spain in collaboration with the Alexander Technological Educational Institute of Thessaloniki, Thessaloniki, Greece.

References

1. W3Techs: Usage of content languages on websites, March 2015. http://w3techs. com/technologies/overview/content_language/all (accessed May 24, 2015)
2. Jorna, K., Davies, S.: Multilingual thesauri for the modern world: no ideal solution. Journal of Documentation **57**(2), 284–295 (2001)
3. Chen, A., Gey, F.C.: Multilingual Information Retrieval using Machine Translation, relevance feedback and decompounding. Information Retrieval **7**(1–2), 149–182 (2004)
4. Vassilakaki, E., Garoufallou, E.: Multilingual Digital Libraries: A review of issues in system-centered and user-centered studies, information retrieval and user behavior. The International Information & Library Review **45**(1–2), 3–19 (2013)
5. Pavlov, P., Nisheva-Pavlova, M., Lliev, A., Rousseva, K., Apostolova, N.: Authoeing tools for an academic digital library. Pregled Nacionalnog Centra Za Digitalizaciju, **17**, 9–16 (2010). http://elib.mi.sanu.ac.rs/files/journals/ncd/17/ncd17009. pdf (accessed May 24, 2015)
6. PROMISE: Deliverable 4.1 first report on alternative evaluation methodology (2011). http://www.promise-noe.eu/documents/10156/a0d664fe-16e4-4df6-bcf9-1dc3e5e8c18e (accessed May 24, 2015)
7. Stiller, J.: Leveraging user interaction and collaboration for improving multilingual information access in digital libraries. In: Proceeding of the 33rd International ACM SIGIR Conference on Research and Development in Information Retrieval e SIGIR 2010 (2010). doi:10.1145/1835449.1835689 (accessed May 24, 2015)
8. Mahajan, P., Singh, N.K.: Online guides to Indian languages with particular reference to Hindi, Punjabi, and Sanskrit. Library Philosophy and Practice1e (2012). http://digitalcommons.unl.edu/libphilprac/749 (accessed May 24, 2015)
9. Budzise-Weaver, T., Chen, J., Mitchell, M.: Collaboration and crowdsourcing: the cases of multilingual digital libraries. The Electronic Library **30**(2), 220–232 (2012). doi:10.1108/02640471211221340 (accessed May 24, 2015)
10. Wu, D., Gu, N., He, D.: The usages and expectations of multilingual information access in Chinese academic digital libraries. In: The Fifth Annual iConference, Champaign, IL, February 2010, pp. 317–322. https://www.ideals.illinois.edu/ bitstream/handle/2142/14933/541_camera_ready.pdf?sequenceZ2 (accessed May 24, 2015)
11. Wu, D., He, D., Luo, B.: Multilingual needs and expectations in digital libraries: a survey of academic users with different languages. The Electronic Library **30**(2), 182–197 (2012). doi:10.1108/02640471211221322 (accessed May 24, 2015)

12. Wu, D., Luo, B., He, D.: How multilingual digital information is used: a study in Chinese academic libraries. In: 2010 International Conference on Management and Service Science (MASS), pp. 1–4. doi:10.1109/ICMSS.2010.5576827 (accessed May 24, 2015)
13. Bilal, D., Bachir, I.: Childrens interaction with cross- cultural and multilingual digital libraries. II. Information seeking, success, and affective experience. Information Processing & Management **43**(1), 65–80 (2007)
14. Ghorab, M.R., Leveling, J., Zhou, D., Jones, G.J.F., Wade, V.: Identifying common user behaviour in multilingual search logs. In: Peters, C., Di Nunzio, G.M., Kurimo, M., Mandl, T., Mostefa, D., Peñas, A., Roda, G. (eds.) CLEF 2009. LNCS, vol. 6241, pp. 518–525. Springer, Heidelberg (2010). http://doras.dcu.ie/16037/1/Identifying_Common_User_Behaviour_in.pdf
15. Takaku, M., Egusa, Y., Saito, H., Ishikawa, D., Kando, N., Terai, H., et al.: CRES at LogCLEF 2010: toward understanding user behaviors through analysis of search sessions, search units and click ranks. In: CLEF2010 Workshop, pp. 1–11. http://clef2010.org/resources/proceedings/clef2010labs_submission_120.pdf (accessed May 24, 2015)
16. Petrelli, D., Clough, P.: Analysing users queries for cross-language image retrieval from digital library collections. The Electronic Library **30**(2), 197–219 (2012)
17. Vassilakaki, E., Johnson, F., Hartley, R.J.: Image seeking in Multilingual Environments: a study of the user experience. Information Research **17**(4), 1–12 (2012)
18. Vassilakaki, E., Johnson, F., Hartley, R.J., Randall, D.: A study of users' image seeking behaviour in flickling. In: Peters, C., et al. (eds.) CLEF 2008. LNCS, vol. 5706, pp. 251–259. Springer, Heidelberg (2009)
19. Vassilakaki, E., Johnson, F., Hartley, R.J., Randall, D.: Users' perceptions of searching in flickling. In: ECDL CLEF2009 Workshop, Greece, Corfu, October 01–03, 2009
20. Clough, P., Eleta, I.: Investigating language skills and field of knowledge on multilingual information access in digital li- braries. International Journal of Digital Libraries Systems **1**(1), 89–103 (2010)
21. Stafford, A., Shiri, A., Ruecker, S., Bouchard, M., Mehta, P., Anvik, K., Rossello, X.: Searchling: user-centered evaluation of a visual thesaurus-enhanced interface for bilingual digital libraries. In: Christensen-Dalsgaard, B., Castelli, D., Ammitzbøll Jurik, B., Lippincott, J. (eds.) ECDL 2008. LNCS, vol. 5173, pp. 117–121. Springer, Heidelberg (2008)
22. Shiri, A., Ruecker, S., Doll, L., Bouchard, M., Fiorentino, C.: An evaluation of thesaurus-enhanced visual interfaces for multilingual digital libraries. In: Gradmann, S., Borri, F., Meghini, C., Schuldt, H. (eds.) TPDL 2011. LNCS, vol. 6966, pp. 236–243. Springer, Heidelberg (2011)
23. Shiri, A., Ruecker, S., Bouchard, M., Stafford, A., Mehta, P., Anvik, K., et al.: User evaluation of searchling: a visual interface for bilingual digital libraries. The Electronic Library **29**(1), 71–89 (2011)
24. Sastry, H., Manjunath, G., Reddy, L.C.: User interface design challenges for digital libraries. International Journal of Computer Applications **15**(6), 7–13 (2011)
25. Vassilakaki, E.: Users' image seeking behaviour in a multilingual environments: a grounded theoretical approach. Manchester Metropolitan University, Faculty of Humanities, Law & Social Sciences, Department of Information & Communications, Doctoral Thesis (2012)
26. Wu, D., He, D., Luo, B.: Multilingual needs and expectations in digital libraries. The Electronic Library **30**(2), 182–197 (2012)

6   Appendix

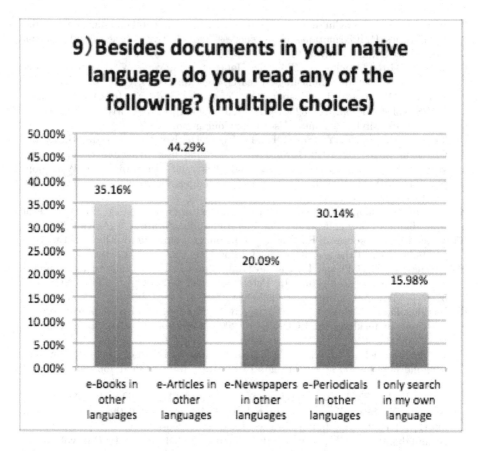

Fig. 1. Type of documents users read in foreign languages

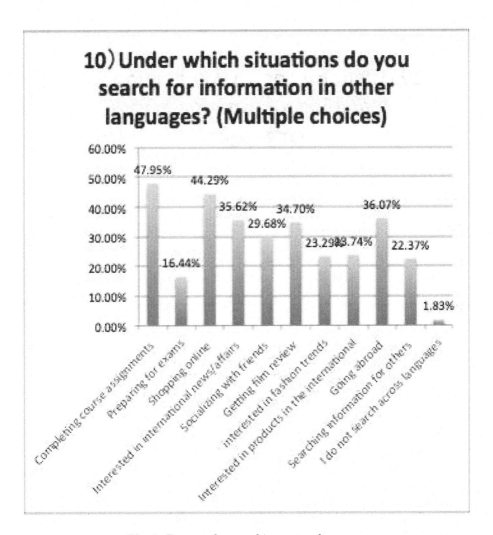

Fig. 2. Reasons for searching across languages

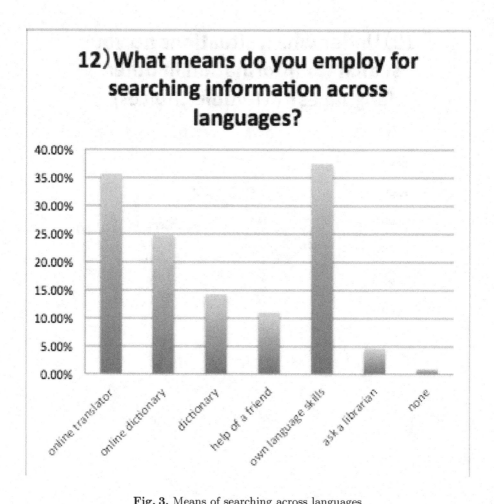

Fig. 3. Means of searching across languages

Track on Metadata and Semantics for Open Repositories, Research Information Systems and Data Infrastructure

Mapping Large Scale Research Metadata to Linked Data: A Performance Comparison of HBase, CSV and XML

Sahar Vahdati[1]([✉]), Farah Karim[1], Jyun-Yao Huang[2], and Christoph Lange[1,3]

[1] University of Bonn, Bonn, Germany
vahdati@uni-bonn.de, Karim@iai.uni-bonn.de
[2] National Chung Hsing University, Taichung, Taiwan
allen501pc@gmail.com
[3] Fraunhofer IAIS, Sankt Augustin, Germany
math.semantic.web@gmail.com

Abstract. OpenAIRE, the Open Access Infrastructure for Research in Europe, comprises a database of all EC FP7 and H2020 funded research projects, including metadata of their results (publications and datasets). These data are stored in an HBase NoSQL database, post-processed, and exposed as HTML for human consumption, and as XML through a web service interface. As an intermediate format to facilitate statistical computations, CSV is generated internally. To interlink the OpenAIRE data with related data on the Web, we aim at exporting them as Linked Open Data (LOD). The LOD export is required to integrate into the overall data processing workflow, where derived data are regenerated from the base data every day. We thus faced the challenge of identifying the best-performing conversion approach. We evaluated the performances of creating LOD by a MapReduce job on top of HBase, by mapping the intermediate CSV files, and by mapping the XML output.

1 Introduction

The European Commission emphasizes open access as a key tool to bring together people and ideas in a way that catalyses science and innovation. More than ever before, there is a recognized need for digital research infrastructures for all kinds of research outputs, across disciplines and countries. OpenAIRE, the Open Access Infrastructure for Research in Europe (http://www.openaire.eu), (1) manages scientific publications and associated scientific material via repository networks, (2) aggregates Open Access publications and links them to research data and funding bodies, and (3) supports the Open Access principles via national helpdesks and comprehensive guidelines.

Data related to those in the OpenAIRE information space exist in different places on the Web. Combining them with OpenAIRE will enable new use cases. For example, understanding changes of research communities or the emergence of scientific topics not only requires metadata about publications and projects,

© Springer International Publishing Switzerland 2015
E. Garoufallou et al. (Eds.): MTSR 2015, CCIS 544, pp. 261–273, 2015.
DOI: 10.1007/978-3-319-24129-6_23

as provided by OpenAIRE, but also data about events such as conferences as well as a knowledge model of research topics and subjects (cf. [15]).

The availability of data that is free to use, reuse and redistribute (i.e. *open data*) is the first prerequisite for analysing such information networks. However, the diverse data formats and means to access or query data, the use of duplicate identifiers, and the heterogeneity of metadata schemas pose practical limitations on reuse. Linked Data, based on the RDF graph data model, is now increasingly accepted as a lingua franca to overcome such barriers [19].

The University of Bonn is coordinating the effort of publishing the OpenAIRE data as Linked Open Data (LOD) and linking it to related datasets in the rapidly growing LOD Cloud[1]. This effort is further supported by the Athena Research and Innovation Center and CNR-ISTI. Besides data about scientific events and subject classification schemes, relevant data sources include public sector information (e.g., to find research results based on the latest employment statistics, or to answer questions such as 'how do the EU member states' expenses for health research compare to their health care spendings?') and open educational resources ('how soon do emergent research topics gain wide coverage in higher education?').

Concrete steps towards this vision are (1) mapping the OpenAIRE data model to suitable standard LOD vocabularies, (2) exporting the objects in the OpenAIRE information space as a LOD graph and (3) facilitating integration with related LOD graphs. Expected benefits include

- enabling semantic search over the outputs of European research projects,
- simplifying the way the OpenAIRE data can be enriched by third-party services, and consumed by interested data or service providers,
- facilitated outreach to related open content and open data initiatives, and
- enriching the OpenAIRE information space itself by exploiting how third parties will use its LOD graph.

The specifically tailored nature of the OpenAIRE infrastructure, its large amount of data (covering more than 11 million publications) and the frequent updates of the more than 5000 repositories from which the data is harvested pose high requirements on the technology chosen for mapping the OpenAIRE data to LOD. We therefore compared in depth three alternative mapping methods, one for each source format in which the data are available: HBase, CSV and XML.

Section 2 introduces the OpenAIRE data model and the three existing data sources. Section 3 presents our specification of the OpenAIRE data model as an RDF vocabulary. Section 4 establishes requirements for the mapping. Section 5 presents the state of the art for each of the three mapping approaches. Section 6 explains our three implementations. In section 7 we evaluate them in comparison, with regard to different metrics induced by the requirements. Section 8 reviews work related to our overall approach (comparing mappings and producing research LOD). Section 9 concludes and outlines future work.

---

[1] http://lod-cloud.net

2   Input Data

The data model of OpenAIRE infrastructure is specified as an entity relationship model (ERM) [12,13] with the following entity categories:

- **Main entities** (cf. figure 1)[2]: Result (Publication or Dataset), Person, Organization, Projects, and DataSource (e.g. Repository, Dataset Archive or CRIS[3]). Instances of these are continuously harvested from data providers.
- **Structural entities** representing complex information about main entities: Instances (of a Result in different DataSources), WebResources, Titles, Dates, Identities, and Subjects.
- **Static entities**, whose metadata do not change over time: Funding. E.g., once a funding agency has opened a funding stream, it remains static.
- **Linking entities** represent relationships between entities that carry further metadata; e.g., an entity of type Person_Result whose property *ranking* has the value 1 indicates the first author.

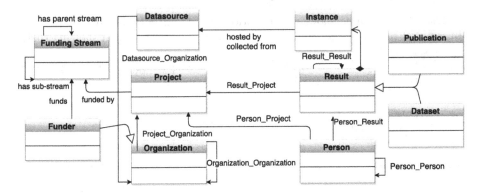

Fig. 1. OpenAIRE Data Model: core entities and relationships

So far, the OpenAIRE data have been available in three formats: HBase, CSV and XML.

2.1   HBase

Currently, the master source of all OpenAIRE data is kept in HBase, a column store based on HDFS (Hadoop Distributed File System). HBase was introduced in 2012 when data integration efforts pushed the original PostgreSQL database

---

[2] https://issue.openaire.research-infrastructures.eu/projects/openaire2020-wiki/ wiki/Core_Data_Model

[3] Current research information system, a system to manage information about the research activity of an institution.

to its limits: joins became inefficient and parallel processing, as required for deduplication, was not supported. Each row of the HBase table has a unique row key and stores a main entity and a number of related linked entities. The attribute values of the main entities are stored in the ¡family¿:body column, where the ¡family¿ is named after the type of the main entity, e.g., *result, person, project, organization* or *datasource*. The attribute values of linked entities, indicating the relationship between main entities, are stored in dedicated column families ¡family¿:¡column¿, where ¡family¿ is the class of the linked entity and ¡column¿ is the row key of the target entity. Both directions of a link are represented. Cell values are serialized as byte arrays according to the Protocol Buffers [17] specification; for example:

```
message Person {
    optional Metadata metadata = 2;
    message Metadata {
        optional StringField firstname = 1;
        repeated StringField secondnames = 2;
        optional Qualifier nationality = 9; ... }
    repeated Person coauthors = 4; }
```

The following table shows a publication and its authors. For readability, we abbreviated row keys and spelled out key-value pairs rather than showing their binary serialization.

RowKey	result: body	person: body	...hasAuthor: 30¡...001::9897...	...hasAuthor: 30¡...001::ef29...	...isAuthorOf: 50¡...001::39b9...
50¡...0 01::39 b9...	resulttype= "publication"; title="The Data Model of ..."; dateofacceptance= "2012-01-01"; language="en"; publicationDate= "2012"; publisher= "Springer";		ranking=1;	ranking=2;	
30¡...0 01::98 97...		firstname="Paolo"; lastname="Manghi";			ranking=1;
30¡...0 01::ef 29...		firstname="Nikos"; lastname="Houssos";			ranking=2;

2.2   CSV

CSV files aid the computation of statistics on the OpenAIRE information space. HBase is a sparse key value-store designed for data with little or no internal relations. Therefore, it is impossible to run complex queries directly on top of HBase, for example a query to find all results of a given project. It is thus necessary to transform the data to a relational representation, which is comprehensible for statistics tools and enables effective querying. Via an intermediate CSV representation, the data is imported into a relational database, which is queried for computing the statistics.

In this generation process, each main entity type (result, project, person, organization, datasource) is mapped to a CSV file of the same name, which is later imported into a relational database table. Each single-valued attribute of an entity (id, title, publication year, etc.) becomes a field in the entity's table. Multi-valued attributes, such as the publication languages of a result, are mapped to relation tables (e.g. `result_languages`) that represent a one-to-many relation between entity and attributes. Linked entities, e.g. the authors of a *result*, are represented similarly. As the data itself includes many special characters, for example commas in publication titles, the OpenAIRE CSV files use ! as a delimiter and wrap cell values into leading and trailing hashes:

```
#dedup_wf_001::39b91277f9a2c25b1655436ab996a76b#!#The Data Model of the OpenAIRE
Scientific Communication e-Infrastructure#!#null#!#null#!#Springer#!#null#!#null
#!#null#!#null#!#2012#!#2012-01-01#!#Open Access#!#Open Access#!#Access#!#null#!#
0#!#null#!#nulloai:http://helios-eie.ekt.gr:!#publication#10442/13187oai:pumaoai.
isti.cnr.it:cnr.isti/cnr.isti/2012-A2-040#!#1#!
```

Finally, using CSV has the advantage that existing tools such as Sqoop can be used, thus reducing the need to develop and maintain customly implemented components on the OpenAIRE production system.

2.3   XML

OpenAIRE features a set of HTTP APIs[4] for exporting metadata as XML for easy reuse by web services. These APIs use an XML Schema implementation of the OpenAIRE data model called OAF (OpenAIRE Format)[5], where each record represents one entity. There is one API for searching, and one for bulk access. For example, the listing below comes from http://api.openaire.eu/search/publications?openairePublicationID=dedup_wf_001::39b91277f9a2c25b165543 6ab996a76b and shows an excerpt of the metadata of a publication that has been searched for.

```
<oaf:result>
  <title schemename="dnet:dataCite_title" classname="main title"
   schemeid="dnet:dataCite_title" classid="main title">The Data Model of the
   OpenAIRE Scientific Communication e-Infrastructure</title>
  <dateofacceptance>2012-01-01</dateofacceptance>
  <publisher>Springer</publisher>
  <resulttype schemename="dnet:result_typologies" classname="publication"
   schemeid="dnet:result_typologies" classid="publication"/>
  <language schemename="dnet:languages" classname="English"
   schemeid="dnet:languages" classid="eng"/>
  <format>application/pdf</format>
  ...
</oaf:result>
```

The API for bulk access uses OAI-PMH (The **O**pen **A**rchives **I**nitiative **P**rotocol for **M**etadata **H**arvesting)[6] to publish metadata and its corresponding endpoint is at http://api.openaire.eu/oai_pmh. The bulk access API lets developers fetch the whole XML files step by step. For our experiments, we obtained the XML

---

[4] http://api.openaire.eu/

[5] https://www.openaire.eu/schema/0.2/doc/oaf-0.2.html

[6] http://www.openarchives.org/OAI/openarchivesprotocol.html

data directly from the OpenAIRE server, as an uncompressed Hadoop Sequence-File[7] comprising 500 splits of ~300 MB each.

3   Implementing the OpenAIRE Data Model in RDF

As the schema of the OpenAIRE LOD we specified an RDF vocabulary by mapping the entities of the ER data model to RDF classes and its attributes and relationships to RDF properties. We reused suitable existing RDF vocabularies identified by consulting the Linked Open Vocabularies search service[8] and studying their specifications. Reused vocabularies include Dublin Core for general metadata, SKOS[9] for classification schemes and CERIF[10] for research organizations and activities. We linked new, OpenAIRE-specific terms to reused ones, e.g., by declaring *Result* a superclass of http://purl.org/ontology/bibo/Publication and http://www.w3.org/ns/dcat#Dataset.

We keep the URIs of the LOD resources (i.e. entities) in the http://lod.openaire.eu/data/ namespace. We modelled them after the HBase row keys. In OpenAIRE, these are fixed length identifiers of the form $\{typePrefix\}|\{namespacePrefix\}::md5hash.$ $typePrefix$ is a two digit code, 10, 20, 30, 40 or 50, corresponding to the main entity types datasource, organization, person, project and result. The $namespacePrefix$ is a unique 12-character identifier of the data source of the entity. For each row, $md5hash$ is computed from the entity attributes. The resulting URIs look like http://lod.openaire.eu/data/result/dedup_wf_001::39b91277f9a2c25b1655436ab996a76b.

The following listing shows our running example in RDF/Turtle syntax.

```
@prefix oad: <http://lod.openaire.eu/data/> .
@prefix oav: <http://lod.openaire.eu/vocab#> .
# further prefixes omitted; see !\url{http://prefix.cc}! for their standard bindings.

oad:result/...001::39b9... rdf:type oav:Result, bibo:Publication;
    dcterms:title "The Data Model of the OpenAIRE Scientific Communication
        e-Infrastructure"@en ;
    dcterms:dateAccepted "2012-01-01"^^xsd:date ;
    dcterms:language "en";
    oav:publicationYear 2012 ;
    dcterms:publisher "Springer";
    dcterms:creator oad:person/...001::9897..., oad:person/...001::ef29... .
oad:person/...001::9897... rdf:type foaf:Person;
    foaf:firstName "Paolo"; foaf:lastName "Manghi";
    oav:isAuthorOf oad:result/...001::39b9... .
oad:person/...001::ef29... rdf:type foaf:Person;
    foaf:firstname "Nikos"; foaf:lastName "Houssos";
    oav:isAuthorOf oad:result/...001::39b9... .
```

---

[7] http://wiki.apache.org/hadoop/SequenceFile

[8] http://lov.okfn.org

[9] http://www.w3.org/2004/02/skos/

[10] Common European Research Information Format; see http://www.eurocris.org/cerif/main-features-cerif

4 Requirements

In cooperation with the other technical partners in the OpenAIRE2020 consortium, most of whom had been working on the infrastructure in previous projects for years, we established the following requirements for the LOD export:

R1 The LOD output must follow the vocabulary specified in section 3.
R2 The LOD must be generated from one of the three existing data sources, to avoid extra pre-processing costs.
R3 The mapping to LOD should be maintainable w.r.t. planned extensions of the OpenAIRE data model (such as linking publications and data to software) and the evolution of linked data vocabularies.
R4 The mapping to LOD should be orchestrable together with the other existing OpenAIRE data provision workflows, always exposing a consistent view on the information space, regardless of the format.
R5 To enable automatic and manual checks of the consistency and correctness of the LOD before its actual publication, it should be made available in reasonable time in a private space.

To prepare an informed decision on the preferred input format to use for the LOD export, we realised one implementation for each of HBase, CSV and XML.

5 Technical State of the Art

For each possible approach, i.e. mapping HBase, CSV or XML to RDF, we briefly review the state of the art to give an overview of technology we could potentially reuse or build on, whereas section 8 reviews work related to our overall approach. We assess reusability w.r.t. the OpenAIRE-specific requirements stated above.

HBase, being a sparse, distributed and multidimensional persistent sorted map, provides dynamic control over the data format and layout. Several works have therefore explored the suitability of HBase as a triple store for semi-structured and sparse RDF data. Sun et al. adopted the idea of the Hexastore indexing technique for storing RDF in HBase [20]. Khadilkar et al. focused on a distributed RDF storage framework based on HBase and Jena to gain scalability[9]. Others have provided MapReduce implementations to process SPARQL queries over RDF stored in HBase [16,6].

We are only aware of one work on exposing data from column-oriented stores as RDF. Kiran et al. provide a method for generating a SPARQL endpoint, i.e. a standardized RDF query interface, on top of HBase [8]. They map tables to classes, rows to resources, and columns to properties. Their approach do not scale well with increasing numbers of HBase entries, as the results show that the time taken to map HBase data to RDF is in hours for a few million rows [8].

CSV is widely used for publishing tabular data [11]. The CSV on the Web W3C Working Group[11] provides technologies for data dependent applications

---

[11] http://www.w3.org/2013/05/lcsv-charter.html

on the Web working with CSV. Several existing implementations, including that of Anything To Triples (any23)[12], map CSV to a generic RDF representation. Customizable mappings are more suitable for our purpose. In Tarql (Transformation SPARQL)[13], one can define such mappings in SPARQL; Tabels (Tabular Cells)[14] and Sparqlify[15] use domain-specific languages similar to SPARQL. Tabels provides auxiliary machinery to filter and compare data values during the transformation process. Sparqlify is mainly designed to map relational databases to RDF but also features the sparqlify-csv module.

XML is used for various data and document exchange purposes. Like for CSV→RDF, there are generic and domain-specific XML→RDF approaches. Breitling implemented a direct, schema-independent transformation, which retains the XML structure [3]. Turning this generic RDF representation into a domain-specific one requires post-processing on the RDF side, e.g., transformations using SPARQL CONSTRUCT queries. On the other hand, the current version of Breitling's approach is implemented in XSLT 1.0, which does not support streaming and is therefore not suitable for the very large inputs of the OpenAIRE setting. Klein uses RDF Schema to map XML elements and attributes to RDF classes and properties [10]. It does not automatically interpret the parent-child relation between two XML elements as a property between two resources, but a lot of such relationships exist in the OpenAIRE XML. XSPARQL can transform XML to RDF and back by combining the XQuery and SPARQL query languages to [1]; authoring mappings requires good knowledge of both. By supporting XQuery's expressive mapping constructs, XSPARQL requires access to the whole XML input via its DOM (Document Object Model), which results in heavy memory consumption. A subset of XQuery[16] is suitable for streaming but neither supported by the XSPARQL implementation nor by the free version of the Saxon XQuery processor required to run XSPARQL.

6   Implementation

As the only existing **HBase→RDF** implementation does not scale well (cf. section 5), we decided to follow the MapReduce paradigm for processing massive amounts of data in parallel over multiple nodes. We implemented a single MapReduce job. Its mapper reads the attributes and values of the OpenAIRE entities from their protocol buffer serialization and thus obtains all information required for the mapping to RDF. Hence no reducer is required. The map-only approach performs well thanks to avoiding the computationally intensive shuffling. RDF subjects are generated from row keys, predicates and objects from

---

[12] http://any23.apache.org
[13] https://tarql.github.io
[14] http://idi.fundacionctic.org/tabels
[15] https://github.com/AKSW/Sparqlify [5]
[16] cf. 'Streaming in XQuery', http://www.saxonica.com/html/documentation/sourcedocs/streaming/streamed-query.html

attribute names and cell values or, for linked entities, from column families/qualifiers.

Mapping the OpenAIRE **CSV→RDF** is straightforward: files correspond to classes, columns to properties, and each row is mapped to a resource. We initially implemented mappings in Tarql, Sparqlify and Tabels (cf. section 5) and ended up preferring Tarql because of its good performance[17] and the most flexible mapping language – standard SPARQL[18] with a few extensions. As we *map* CSV→RDF, as opposed to *querying* CSV like RDF, we implemented *CONSTRUCT* queries, which specify an RDF template in which, for each row of the CSV, variables are instantiated with the cell values of given columns.

To enable easy maintenance of **XML→RDF** mappings by domain experts, and efficient mapping of large XML inputs, we implemented our own approach[19]. It employs a SAX parser and thus supports streaming. Our mapping language is based on RDF triple templates and on the XPath[20] language for addressing content in XML. XPath expressions in the subjects or objects of RDF triple templates indicate where in the XML they obtain their values from. To keep XPath expressions simple and intuitive, we allow them to be ambiguous, e.g., by saying that *oaf:result/publisher/text()* (referring to the text content of the *publisher* element of a result) maps to the *dcterms:publisher* property of an *oav:Result*, and that *oaf:result/dateofacceptance/text()* maps to *dcterms:dateAccepted*. In theory, any combination of *publisher* and *dateofacceptance* elements would match such a pattern; however in reality only those nodes that have the shortest distance in the XML document tree represent attributes of the *same* OpenAIRE entity. XML Filters [4] efficiently restrict the XPath expressions to such combinations.

7 Evaluation

7.1 Comparison Metrics

The **time** it takes to transform the complete OpenAIRE input data to RDF is the most important performance metric (requirement R4). The **main memory usage** of the transformation process is important because OpenAIRE2020 envisages the development of further services sharing the same infrastructure, including deduplication, data mining to measure research impact, classification of publications by machine learning, etc. One objective metric for **maintainability** is the size of the mapping's source code – after stripping comments and compression, which makes the comparison 'independent of arbitrary factors like lengths of identifiers and amount of whitespace' [22].[21] The 'cognitive

---

[17] Tabels failed to handle large CSV files because it loads all the data from the CSV into main memory; Sparqlify works similar to Tarql but with almost doubled execution time (7,659 s) and more than doubled memory usage.

[18] http://www.w3.org/TR/sparql11-query/

[19] See source code and documentation at https://github.com/allen501pc/XML2RDF.

[20] http://www.w3.org/TR/xpath20/

[21] We used `tar cf - <input files> | xz -9`. For HBase, we considered the part of the Java source code that is concerned with declaring the mapping, whereas our CSV and XML mappings are natively defined in high-level mapping languages.

dimensions of notation' (CD) evaluation framework provides further criteria for systematically assessing the 'usability of information artefacts' [2]. The following dimensions are straightforward to observe here: *closeness* of the notation to the problem (here: mapping HBase/CSV/XML to RDF), *terseness* (here measured by code size; see above), *error-proneness, progressive evaluation* (i.e. whether one can start with an incomplete mapping rule and evolve it to further complete-ness), and *secondary notation and escape from formalism* (e.g. whether reading cues can be given by non-syntactic means such as indentation or comments).

7.2   Evaluation Setup

The **HBase→RDF** evaluation ran on a Hadoop cluster of 12 worker nodes operated by CNR.[22] As our **CSV→RDF** and **XML→RDF** implementations required dependencies not yet installed there, we evaluated them locally: on a virtual machine on a server with an Intel Xeon E5-2690 CPU, having 3.7 GB memory and 250 GB disk space assigned and running Linux 3.11 and JDK 1.7. As we did not have a cluster available, and as the tools employed did not natively support parallelization, we ran the mappings from CSV and XML sequentially.

7.3   Measurements and Observations

The following table lists our measurements; further observations follow below.

Objective Comparison Metrics	HBase	CSV	XML
Mapping Time(s)	1,043	4,895	45,362
Memory (MB)	68,000	103	130
Compressed Mapping Source Code (KB)	4.9	2.86	1.67
Number of Input rows/records	20,985,097	203,615,518	25,182,730
Number of Generated RDF Triples	655,328,355	654,193,273	788,953,122

For **HBase→RDF**, the peak memory usage of the cluster was 68 GB, i.e. ~5.5 GB per worker node. No other MapReduce job was running on the cluster at the same time; however, the usage figure includes the memory used by the Hadoop framework, which schedules and monitors job execution.

The 20 **CSV** input files correspond to different entities but also to relation-ships. This, plus the way multi-valued attributes are represented (cf. section 2.2), causes the high number of input rows. The size of all files is 33.8 GB. The **XML→RDF** memory consumption is low because of stream processing. The time complexity of our mapping approach depends on the number of rules (here: 118) and the size of the input (here: 144 GB). With the complexity of the XML representation, this results in an execution time of more than 12 hours. The size of the single RDF output file is ~91 GB. Regarding *cognitive dimen-sions*, the different notations expose the following characteristics; for lack of

---

[22] https://issue.openaire.research-infrastructures.eu/projects/openaire/wiki/ Hadoop_Clusters#section-3

space we focus on selected highlights. *Terseness*: the high-level CSV→RDF and XML→RDF languages fare better than the Java code required for HBase→RDF. Also, w.r.t. *closeness*, they enable more intuitive descriptions of mappings. As the CSV→RDF mappings are based on SPARQL, which uses the same syntax for RDF triples than the Turtle RDF serialization, they look closest to RDF. *Error-proneness*: Syntactically correct HBase→RDF Java code may still define a semantically wrong mapping. In Tarql's CSV→RDF mappings, many types of syntax and semantics errors can be detected easily. *Progressive evaluation*: one can start with an incomplete Tarql mapping rule CSV→RDF mapping rule and evolve it towards completeness. *Secondary notation*: Tarql and Java support flexible line breaks, indentation and comments, whereas our current XML→RDF mapping implementation requires one (possibly long) line per mapping rule. Overall, this strongly suggests that CSV→RDF is the most maintainable approach.

8 Related Work

Comparisons of different approaches of mapping data to RDF have mainly been carried out for relational databases as a source [21,14]. Similarly to our evaluation criteria, the reference comparison framework of the W3C RDB2RDF Incubator Group covers mapping creation, representation and accessibility, and support for data integration [18]. Hert et al. compared different RDB2RDF mapping languages w.r.t. syntactic features and semantic expressiveness [7].

For other linked datasets about research, we refer to the 'publication' and 'government' sectors of the LOD Cloud, which comprises, e.g., publication databases such as DBLP, as well as snapshots of funding databases such as CORDIS. From this it can be seen that OpenAIRE is a more comprehensive data source than those published as LOD before.

9 Conclusion and Future Work

We have mapped a recent snapshot of the OpenAIRE data to RDF. A preliminary dump as well as the definitions of the mappings are available online at http://tinyurl.com/OALOD. Mapping from HBase is fastest, whereas mapping from CSV promises to be most maintainable. Its slower execution time is partly due to the less powerful hardware on which we ran it; comparing multiple CSV→RDF processes running in parallel to the HBase→RDF implementation on the CNR Hadoop cluster seems promising. Based on these findings the OpenAIRE2020 LOD team will decide on the preferred approach for providing the OpenAIRE data as LOD; we will then make the data available for browsing from their OpenAIRE entity URIs, and for querying via a SPARQL endpoint.

Having implemented almost the whole OpenAIRE data model, future steps include interlinking the output with other existing datasets. E.g., we so far output countries and languages as strings, whereas DBpedia and Lexvo.org are suitable linked open datasets for such terms. Link discovery tools will further enable large-scale linking against existing 'publication' and 'government' datasets.

Acknowledgments. We would like to thank the partners in the OpenAIRE2020 project, in particular Claudio Atzori, Alessia Bardi, Glykeria Katsari and Paolo Manghi, for their help with accessing the OpenAIRE data. This work has been partially funded by the European Commission under grant agreement no. 643410.

References

1. Bischof, S., et al.: Mapping between RDF and XML with XSPARQL. English. Journal on Data Semantics **1**(3) (2012)
2. Blackwell, A., Green, T.: Cognitive Dimensions of Notations Resource Site (2010) http://www.cl.cam.ac.uk/afb21/CognitiveDimensions/
3. Breitling, F.: A standard transformation from XML to RDF via XSLT. Astronomische Nachrichten **330**(7) (2009)
4. Diao, Y., et al.: Yfilter: Efficient and scalable filtering of XML documents. In: Data Engineering. IEEE (2002)
5. Ermilov, I., Auer, S., Stadler, C.: CSV2RDF: User-Driven CSV to RDF Mass Conversion Framework. In: I-Semantics (2013)
6. Haque, A., Perkins, L. Distributed RDF Triple Store Using HBase and Hive. In: University of Texas at Austin (2012)
7. Hert, M., Reif, G., Gall, H.C.: A comparison of RDB-to-RDF mapping languages. In: I-Semantics. ACM (2011)
8. Kiran, K.V., Sadasivam, D.G.S.: A Novel Method For Dynamic SPARQL Endpoint Generation In NoSQL Databases. Australian Journal of Basic and Applied Sciences **9**(6) (2015)
9. Khadilkar, V., et al.: Jena-HBase: A distributed, scalable and efficient RDF triple store. In: ISWC Posters & Demonstrations (2012)
10. Klein, M.: Interpreting XML documents via an RDF schema ontology. In: DEXA (2002)
11. Lebo, T., Williams, G.T.: Converting governmental datasets into linked data. In: I-Semantics. ACM (2010)
12. Manghi, P., Mikulicic, M., Atzori, C.: OpenAIRE Data Model Specification. Deliverable
13. Manghi, P., Houssos, N., Mikulicic, M., Jörg, B.: The data model of the OpenAIRE scientific communication e-infrastructure. In: Dodero, J.M., Palomo-Duarte, M., Karampiperis, P. (eds.) MTSR 2012. CCIS, vol. 343, pp. 168–180. Springer, Heidelberg (2012)
14. Michel, F., Montagnat, J., Faron-Zucker, C.: A survey of RDB to RDF translation approaches and tools. Research report. **I3S** (2014)
15. Osborne, F., Motta, E.: Understanding research dynamics. In: Presutti, V., Stankovic, M., Cambria, E., Cantador, I., Di Iorio, A., Di Noia, T., Lange, C., Reforgiato Recupero, D., Tordai, A. (eds.) SemWebEval 2014. CCIS, vol. 475, pp. 101–107. Springer, Heidelberg (2014)
16. Papailiou, N., et al.: H2RDF: adaptive query processing on RDF data in the cloud. In: International conference on World Wide Web. ACM (2012)
17. Protocol Buffers (2015). https://developers.google.com/protocol-buffers/
18. Sahoo, S.S., et al.: A survey of current approaches for mapping of relational databases to RDF. W3C RDB2RDF Incubator Group Report (2009)
19. Scharffe, F., et al.: Enabling linked data publication with the Datalift platform. In: Proc. AAAI workshop on semantic cities (2012)

20. Sun, J., Jin, Q.: Scalable RDF store based on HBase and MapReduce. In: Advanced Computer Theory and Engineering (ICACTE), Vol. 1. IEEE (2010)

21. Svihla, M., Jelinek, I.: Benchmarking RDF production tools. In: Wagner, R., Revell, N., Pernul, G. (eds.) DEXA 2007. LNCS, vol. 4653, pp. 700–709. Springer, Heidelberg (2007)

22. Wiedijk, F.: The de Bruijn factor (2012). http://cs.ru.nl/freek/factor/

Contextual and Provenance Metadata in the Oxford University Research Archive (ORA)

Tanya Gray Jones[✉], Lucie Burgess, Neil Jefferies,
Anusha Ranganathan, and Sally Rumsey

Bodleian Digital Library Systems and Services, Bodleian Libraries,
Osney Mead, Oxford OX2 0EW, UK
{tanya.gray,lucie.burgess,neil.jefferies,
anusha.ranganathan,sally.rumsey}@bodleian.ox.ac.uk

Abstract. Context and provenance are essential for understanding the meaning and significance of an artefact. In this paper we describe how scholarly outputs deposited in a long-term data repository, the Oxford University Research Archive (ORA), are described with contextual information and provenance. In addition, the digital objects in ORA that act as proxies to the scholarly outputs are also described with contextual information and provenance. The ORA data model is presented together with a description of the relationships in context.

Keywords: RDF · Metadata · Provenance · Context · Open access repository

1   Introduction

An artefact such as a research output derives much of its meaning from attributes that are not intrinsic to the artefact itself. A description of the circumstances in which an artefact was created, and the route by which it came to be from where it is now, are prerequisites to an understanding of the artefact and its significance. For example, the date of creation of the research output, or the circumstances under which it was created, such as the technical details of the instrument through which it was created in an experiment, can be vital to understanding the importance and reliability of the research output.

This requirement for contextual information and provenance to fully understand an artefact is especially true for digital materials. A file on its own is a meaningless string of bytes, with a file name that can provide a description of or context about the file, but can readily be changed. The metadata describing an artefact can have more meaning that the artefact itself. This contextual metadata or provenance can have important applications in areas as varied as digital preservation or the reproducibility of scientific research.

In this work we describe how scholarly outputs and their digital proxies in a long-term data repository, the Oxford University Research Archive[1], are described with

---

[1]   Oxford University Research Archive (ORA), http://ora.ox.ac.uk/

© Springer International Publishing Switzerland 2015
E. Garoufallou et al. (Eds.): MTSR 2015, CCIS 544, pp. 274–285, 2015.
DOI: 10.1007/978-3-319-24129-6_24

context and provenance. This contextual and provenance information enables the digital objects within ORA to be searched and retrieved more effectively, and also plays a role in understanding the reliability, authenticity, trust, credit, licensing and rights to benefit from exploitation of the research outputs. Such provenance and contextual information for digital objects is increasingly important in open research environments, wherein organizations create and publish sets of open research outputs that are generated and transformed through multiple autonomous information systems, and used, mixed and re-used by others.

2   Open Access and the Oxford University Research Archive

Open Access refers to the free and unrestricted online access to and use of outputs of scholarly research such as journal articles[2]. Restrictions may be imposed in terms of i) the ability to access or read and ii) use, for example re-use in a derivative work. An example of a restrictive practice is the imposition of a journal paywall, where access to a journal is restricted to individuals that pay to view a specific article, or who have access to the journal via an organisational subscription.

In the UK, the desire to enable Open Access to the publicly-funded outputs of scholarly research funded by government-backed UK research councils, HEFCE[3] or major funders such as the Wellcome Trust has inspired much debate in recent years and consequent activity to enable much wider and unrestricted access to these outputs.

In addition to modifying the publishing model for journal articles, research organisations such as the University of Oxford have introduced Open Access repositories that act as long-term stores of scholarly research outputs. The type of scholarly outputs stored in an Open Access repository may include, *inter alia,* journal articles, conference papers, pre-publication versions of journal articles, book chapters, theses, presentations, datasets, software and research objects.

2.1   Open Access at Oxford

In March 2013, the University Council approved a statement[4] on Open Access at the University of Oxford. It recognized the importance of ensuring the widest possible access to research outputs of the University of Oxford.

The University Council recommended that researchers provide Open Access to published research outputs, making them available online with as few restrictions as possible. Copyright and licensing agreements were to be adhered to, and proper attribution given to items.

The University Council also recommended compliance with UK research funder mandates on Open Access, by means of self-archiving a copy of the item in a

[2]   Budapest Open Access Initiative statement, http://www.budapestopenaccessinitiative.org/read

[3]   Higher Education Funding Council for England

[4]   Statement on Open Access at the University of Oxford, http://openaccess.ox.ac.uk, http://bit.ly/1Dwu1La

repository for free public use, subject to an appropriate embargo period – commonly called the 'Green Route' to Open Access.

2.2   Oxford University Research Archive (ORA)

The Bodleian Libraries' Oxford University Research Archive (ORA) is a repository of research materials produced by members of the University of Oxford, and was established in 2007. The home page of ORA is shown in Figure 1.

Further to the University Council's statement on Open Access at the University of Oxford, ORA was enhanced, to become a single point of access and preservation for Open Access research outputs produced by members of the University of Oxford.

Metadata is harvested from other subject-based and publisher repositories such as PubMed Central and arXiv, Web of Knowledge and Scopus, the University's instance of the Symplectic current research system, and other publication and access management systems within the University. A dedicated team at the Bodleian Libraries supports the addition of items to the repository by members of the university, verifying metadata such as the licence conditions agreed with publishers.

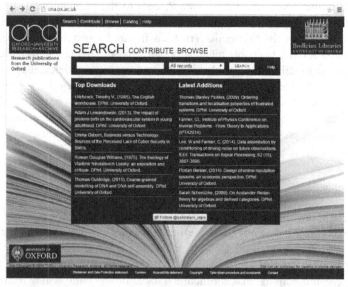

Fig. 1. Screenshot of the Oxford University Research Archive search interface

The technical platform for ORA is Fedora[5], a modular open-source repository system. Fedora is geared towards applications in digital libraries such as making digital collections available online. One feature of Fedora that is of interest here is that it exposes metadata about an object in the form of an RDF manifest, a text document that describes an item in an RDF syntax. Fedora3 is integrated with a triple store and uses

---

[5]   Fedora repository software, http://fedorarepository.org/software

Dublin Core to describe the object. The Dublin Core file along with the relationships metadata in Fedora are indexed in the triple store, enabling it to be queried using SPARQL[6].

3   Context and Provenance of Research Materials

The storage of research outputs in an open repository such as ORA requires that the research materials be described with contextual information such as authorship and publication. This drives faceted search and retrieval and is also important for applications such as digital preservation, citation and reproducibility of research, for example in the case of datasets. For compliance with the Research Councils UK mandate on Open Access[7], the copyright status of research materials, and the research grant(s) that funded the production of research materials also need to be recorded, and items published with a an open licence, which allows an item to be shared, copied, redistributed or adapted with appropriate attribution under certain circumstances. The CC-BY license allows an item to be shared, copied and redistributed and adapted for any purpose, with appropriate attribution.

The Bodleian Libraries has devised a data model for the representation of contextual information describing research materials contained in ORA. The data model has been devised within the broader context of a data modelling initiative called CAMELOT[8] that has as its aim the integration of data across multiple digital resources owned or managed by the Bodleian Digital Library. This integration, in turn, has been designed to allow cross-search and retrieval across multiple, seemingly unrelated silos of data, important in the context of multi- and inter-disciplinary research.

CAMELOT has at its core the notion of relationships in context, where a relationship between two entities is described in terms of an activity, to which information can be associated such as time and location, as well as agents and related entities. The role of an agent in an activity can explicitly be defined, rather than be implicit in the relationship type. A more detailed description of relationships in context is described in section 5.

Activity-based descriptions of relationships have been incorporated into the data model for the description of items in ORA.

4   Oxford University Research Archive Data Model

The Oxford University Research Archive (ORA) data model is a representation of various scholarly outputs e.g. journal articles, conference submissions, electronic thesis dissertations and research data associated with the scholarly outputs. As well as the properties of the scholarly outputs, the data model also includes a representation of

---

[6]   http://www.w3.org/TR/rdf-sparql-query/

[7]   Research Councils UK Policy on Open Access and Supporting Guidance, http://www.rcuk.ac.uk/RCUK-prod/assets/documents/documents/RCUKOpenAccessPolicy.pdf (2013)

[8]   CAMELOT contextual data model for the Bodleian Digital Library, http://camelot-dev.bodleian.ox.ac.uk

contexts with which the scholarly outputs are associated, and by which they can be comprehensively described and understood.

In order for ORA to satisfy its duties as described above, it is essential that the scholarly output is associated with the people and organizations that were involved in the creation of the scholarly output along with contextual information such as time and location.

As a value-added service, for deposits of datasets made in ORA, a DOI is minted and registered, and the deposit reviewed before being published online. This process necessitates the introduction of workflows to manage mediated deposits.

The relationships between a scholarly output such as a thesis, and the data objects that together form an ORA record are illustrated in Figure 2. Also shown are the relationship between data objects and the types of metadata that they contain.

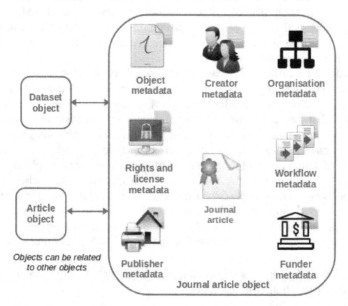

Fig. 2. Illustration of the relationships between a scholarly output (e.g. journal article) and its digital proxy (e.g. journal article object) in ORA. The types of metadata used to describe a scholarly output and its digital proxies include workflow metadata, systems rights metadata, publisher metadata, and funder metadata. Also shown are the relationships to other digital proxies of scholarly outputs described in ORA (e.g. dataset object and article object).

A record in ORA describing a scholarly output contains three different types of metadata:

1. Description of the scholarly output (described in section 4.1)
2. Rights and relationships of the data objects (described in section 4.2)
3. ORA system workflow description for the data objects (described in section 4.3)

4.1   Description of the Scholarly Output

The descriptive metadata for a scholarly output includes three types of assertions:

— Simple properties, e.g. title, subtitle, abstract
— Properties that link to external authorities and standards, e.g. subject, language and location
— Contextual information, e.g. authorship, funding, publishing, as well as the rights and licenses. Contextual information describe an activity including its time and location, as well as the associations between an activity, a scholarly output, and other entities, people and organizations, along with their respective roles.

Contextual Narrative

When representing a journal article, the narrative we would like to achieve in ORA for the different activities is exemplified below.

Creation Activity.
The journal article is associated with John Smith, who had the role of author and is affiliated with the Bodleian Libraries. His contact email is 'john.smith@example. com' and John Smith refers to the data object 'johnSmith'.

Funding Activity.
The journal article is associated with 'Organization B' that has the role of funder and funds John Smith with a funding award that has the grant number 'G0001'.

Publication Activity.
The journal article is associated with a publication activity. This activity has the status 'published' and has been 'peer-reviewed'. The activity generated a document 'journal article A' that was accepted on 01-Jan-2015 and published on 12-May-2015 in London. It has the DOI "10.n.n.n" and is published in the journal "Journal B". The document was associated with the organization "Organization A" who played the role of publisher and has the website 'https://www.example.org/'.

4.2   Rights and Relationships of the Data Objects

This metadata describes access rights to the data objects that together form the ORA data record, as well the relationships between the ORA data record and the scholarly output.

Scenario 1. The journal article has a content file that is the author-accepted version. The file has the access rights with embargo status 'embargoed' with an embargo duration that starts from today, 10-May-2015 and has a duration of 3 years and 4 months and a calculated end date 10-Sep-2018 and the reason for the embargo is copyright requirements. The embargo can be lifted automatically.

Scenario 2. The journal article has a content file that is the publisher version. The file has the access rights with embargo status 'embargoed' with an embargo duration that starts from the publication date and has a duration of 3 years and 4 months and an earliest possible end date of 10-Sep-2018 and the reason for the embargo is publisher requirements. Consult me before lifting the embargo.

Scenario 3. The journal article was influenced by 'journal article 2'. The journal article 'replaces' 'journal article 2' reference 'http://example.com/article' that has an identifier 'jA24523', is titled 'ABCD' and is of type 'Journal article'.

Scenario 4. The journal article was influenced by 'journal article 2'. The journal article 'replaces' 'journal article 2' reference 'http://dx.doi.org/10.n.n.n' whose bibliographic citation is '----'.

It should be noted that there are some subtle differences between scenarios 1 and 2. In scenario 1 the journal article is represented by the author-accepted version. This is a pre-publication version of the journal article that will most likely differ from the publisher version of the journal article described in scenario 2. Scenario 1 can arise when an author is required to meet HEFCE rules for the post-2014 Research Excellence Framework mandate, and the author-accepted version must be placed in an institutional repository within three months of acceptance.

Another difference to note is if the embargo can be lifted automatically or if the author should be consulted. Finally, DOIs for publications are only provided on publication, and so the author-accepted version of the journal article will not have a DOI associated with it.

4.3   ORA System Workflow Description

This metadata describes ORA system workflows and other tasks involved in publishing a record in ORA. Besides using each workflow to record a history of system activity, it is also used as a trigger by the ORA system, to perform actions based on states. This helps with tying to together the various aspects involved in publishing an item record in ORA.

5   Contextual and Provenance Metadata in RDF

5.1   Relationships in Context

In bibliographic metadata it is common to describe a relationship as a property with an implicit role. Dublin Core Metadata Initiative[9] [1] that have this characteristic include Contributor, Publisher and Creator. Using one of these properties results in a three-part assertion, with the property relating one entity to another, e.g. WorkA has creator PersonA. A three-part assertion is a syntax that is common to RDF triples. Besides the type of role that relates two things, a three-part assertion lacks information describing the context of the relationship. For this, a more detailed representation is needed. Additional assertions can describe the context of the relationship. An example narrative would be:

---

[9]   Dublin Core Metadata Initiative, http://dublincore.org

```
John Smith is author of the journal article ref 123
that was published on 12 January 2012. John Smith co-
authored the article with David Jones. The article
was funded by research grant ABC23 provided by the UK
research council BBSRC.
```

In RDF, assertions need to be expressed as triples or three-part statements, such as the following:

— John Smith author Of JournalArticle123
— JournalArticle123 publication date 12January2012
— John Smith co-author David Jones
— JournalArticle123 funded By ResearchGrantABC23
— ResearchGrant123 issued By BBSRC

A graphical representation of these assertions, Figure 3, shows that some contextual information is missing. The publisher of the journal article, the publication that the journal article was published in, and the date that the research grant was issued are not described.

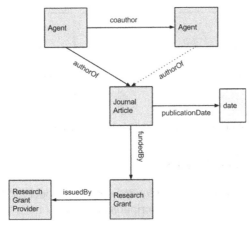

Fig. 3. Graphical representation of relationships and properties for a journal article. Dotted line indicates an inferred relationship.

Also, some of the information could be better represented. The research grant funds an individual or a project that the individual is associated with, rather than a specific journal article. The publication date would be better associated with a publication activity, than with the journal article, as it is the activity that is a temporal entity. By introducing an activity into the representation, it is possible to have a more comprehensive description of the relationships.

To continue with the example, two activities can be introduced into the representation, namely publication, and funding. An activity-based representation is shown in Figure 4. The publication date is now associated with an activity, rather than with the journal article. The agents are associated with the activity, and their roles in relation to the activity are explicitly defined, rather than being implicit in a relationship.

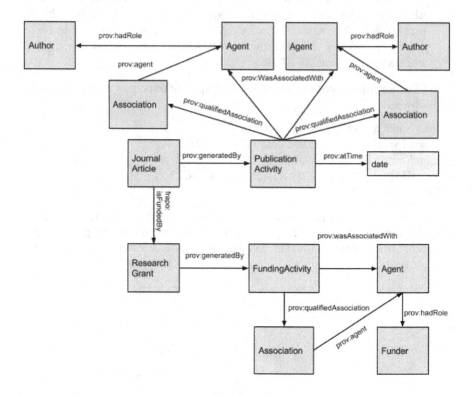

Fig. 4. An activity-based description of relationships for a journal article, using PROV-O[10]

5.2   Activity-Based Data Model

The CAMELOT data model, and consequently the data model for items in ORA, uses a general pattern of activity-based descriptions repeatedly for a broad range of relationships and activity types.

The introduction of an activity in to the description of a relationship adds a necessary complexity, allowing additional information to be associated with the relationship so that it may be properly understood.

A repeatable activity-based design pattern that includes entities such as role, activity, and agent for the representation of a wide variety of relationships and activities also introduces a simplification to the data model. This simplification is important for the goal of a shared data model, across many different types of digital library projects, that requires many different entities and relationships to be defined. The repeatable design pattern also helps with the development of a shared code library based on the data model that can be re-used in future projects.

---

[10] http://www.w3.org/TR/prov-o/

5.3   PROV Provenance Data Model

To describe a relationship in context, the W3C's PROV data model[11] [2] that became a W3C Recommendation in April 2013, has been incorporated into the ORA data model. The PROV data model includes a core model, illustrated in Figure 5 that describes the relationships between an entity, agent and activity. The PROV data model also includes the property 'hadRole' that allows the role of an agent or entity in an activity to be described.

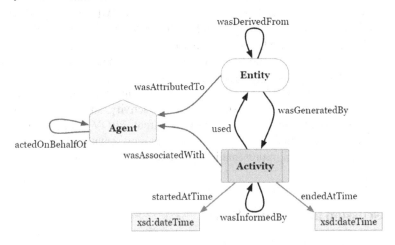

Fig. 5. A graphical representation of the basic PROV data model[12]

A number of data models have representations for context and provenance including CIDOC-CRM and PREMIS.

CIDOC Conceptual Reference Model (CIDOC-CRM)[13] is an ISO standard that is an output of the International Council of Museums. CIDOC-CRM provides definitions and a formal structure for describing the implicit and explicit concepts and relationships used in cultural heritage documentation. CIDOC CRM is intended to promote a shared understanding of cultural heritage information by providing a common and extensible semantic framework that any cultural heritage information can be mapped to. It employs some concepts that are similar to the PROV ontology and can be expressed in RDF. It has been utilized mainly in the museums and cultural heritage sector[14], for example, underpinning the British Museum's ResearchSpace service, rather than in digital libraries managing contemporary research outputs and we felt its complexity was such that it would not provide an appropriate data model for ORA.

---

[11] Moreau, Luc and Paolo Missier. "The prov data model" (2013), http://www.w3.org/TR/2013/REC-prov-dm-20130430/

[12] Image sourced from http://www.w3.org/TR/prov-o/

[13] The CIDOC Conceptual Reference Model, http://www.cidoc-crm.org/

[14] CIDOC-CRM applications http://cidoc-crm.org/uses_applications.html

The Library of Congress published v3.0 of PREMIS in June 2015. The PREMIS Data Dictionary is a comprehensive, practical resource for implementing preservation metadata in digital preservation systems[15]. PREMIS is based on a data model that defines five entities: Intellectual Entities, Objects, Events, Rights, and Agents. PREMIS is an XML schema which is focused on preservation metadata to support the viability, renderability, understandability, authenticity, and identity of digital objects in a preservation context. PREMIS represents the information most preservation repositories need to know to preserve digital materials over the long term, is implementable and embodies technical neutrality. As well as an XML schema, PREMIS is available as an OWL ontology. Again, while it bears some similarity to the PROV data model, PREMIS is focused on digital preservation whereas PROV is focused on the application of provenance and therefore has a much broader context and set of potential applications.

PROV was used in the ORA data model due to its simple activity representation that could be used repeatedly to describe any type of activity, and therefore any type of context that was needed to describe a scholarly output. PROV has previously been used to describe the provenance of data [3], but our representation is an innovative application of PROV for the representation of context underpinning a digital library repository.

6   Discussion and Future Work

The Oxford University Research Archive (ORA) data model uses an activity-based approach to represent many different types of context that relate to a scholarly output. The nature of scholarship entails that the intellectual content of objects including research materials derive their meaning from the circumstances in which they were created, modified, used, and referred to. By incorporating a detailed activity-based description of the context and provenance of scholarly items, ORA is supporting the activity of scholarship. For instance, thinking in terms of Research Objects[16] and the R dimensions described by Prof. David De Roure[17], describing the relationships between
journal articles and the datasets on which their conclusions are based, and their relationships to the article authors and dataset creators including their researcher identities such as provided by ORCID, addresses concerns such as reproducibility, reusability, and reliability.

An activity-based approach is also used to describe the context and provenance of digital objects in ORA that together act as a digital proxy for the scholarly output. For the long-term preservation of research materials, as happens in the ORA data repository, a description of the provenance of the digital proxies is essential for the long-term viability of digital objects stored in the repository. The provenance metadata can

---

[15] PREMIS version 3.0 http://www.loc.gov/standards/premis/v3/premis-3-0-final.pdf

[16] Research Objects http://www.researchobject.org

[17] E-Research and the Demise of the Scholarly Article, David De Roure http://www.stm-assoc.org/2013_12_04_Innovation_DeRoure_Scholarly_Demise.pdf

act as a safeguard against the potential negative impact of obsolescence and change in the technical platform of the data repository. The provenance of the digital proxies is also necessary for the publication of the metadata about the research items, and will help resolve potential issues with transmission errors, data loss, and data integration.

Since December 2014, each new item deposited in ORA has an RDF manifest associated with it that describes the item using the ORA contextual data model described here.

For scholarly items deposited in the ORA data repository, publishing contextual and provenance information as RDF opens up opportunities for resource discovery and data integration using Semantic Web technologies. For example, DataCite[18] provides a linked data service with access to RDF metadata about a dataset, and this metadata could be integrated with metadata contained in ORA about a given dataset using the dataset's DOI. RDF description of people in ORA could be integrated with metadata from the ORCID[19] project and also ISNI[20] linked data[21].

The contextual and provenance metadata contained in ORA will also aid the analysis of scholarly outputs at the University of Oxford enabling, for example with methods used in social network analysis to measure the relationships among people and organizations. Contextual and provenance information contained in ORA will also be used in the creation of reports summarizing various facets of the scholarly outputs of the university.

Finally, we continue to investigate the application of a simple activity-based data model, as utilized in the ORA data model, for the representation of contextual information of many different types of material and digital objects that are relevant to the Bodleian Digital Library.

References

1. Hakala, J.: Dublin core metadata initiative. CRIS 2000-Current Research Information Systems (2000)
2. Missier, P., Belhajjame, K., Cheney, J.: The W3C PROV family of specifications for modelling provenance metadata. In: Proceedings of the 16th International Conference on Extending Database Technology. ACM (2013)
3. Lagoze, C., Williams, J., Vilhuber, L., Block, W.: 2014 Encoding Provenance of Social Science Data: Integrating PROV with DDI

---

[18] DataCite https://www.datacite.org
[19] ORCID http://orcid.org/
[20] ISNI International Standard Name Identifier http://www.isni.org/
[21] ISNI and linked data http://www.isni.org/filedepot_download/143/429

Labman: A Research Information System to Foster Insight Discovery Through Visualizations

Oscar Peña[✉], Unai Aguilera, Aitor Almeida, and Diego López-de-Ipiña

Deusto Institute of Technology - DeustoTech, University of Deusto,
Avda. Universidades 24, 48007 Bilbao, Spain
oscar.pena@deusto.es

Abstract. Effective handling of research related data is an ambitious goal, as many data entities need to be suitably designed in order to model the distinctive features of different knowledge areas: publications, projects, people, events and so on. A well designed information architecture prevents errors due to data redundancy, outdated records or poor provenance, allowing both internal staff and third parties reuse the information produced by the research centre. Moreover, making the data available through a public, Internet accessible portal increases the visibility of the institution, fostering new collaborations with external centres.However, the lack of a common structure when describing research data might prevent non-expert users from using these data. Thus we present *labman*, a web-based information research system that connects all the actors in the research landscape in an interoperable manner, using metadata and semantic descriptions to enrich the stored data.

Labman presents different visualizations to allow data exploration and discovery in an interactive fashion, relying on humans' visual capacity rather than an extensive knowledge on the research field itself. Thanks to the visual representations, visitors can quickly understand the performance of experts, project outcomes, publication trajectory and so forth.

1 Introduction

Open Data principles are crawling their path through different actors present in our daily lives: governments publishing data about their members and hierarchical structures, councils providing open access to local data (i.e., energy consumption rates, air and water quality, cartography of the surrounding areas, etc.), prosumers uploading data captured by diverse sensors to allow third-parties benefit for it and so on. The academic world is not an exception.

Many universities are providing machine-readable data about their institutions on dedicated portals, in order to foster service discovery and data reusability. Topics covered span from map layouts of the different buildings and rooms of the faculties, to statistics about the number of enrolments for the new academic year, going through the courses offered, staff resumes, etc. *Linked Universities*, as stated in their official website[1], "*is an alliance of european universities engaged*

---

[1] http://linkeduniversities.org/

© Springer International Publishing Switzerland 2015
E. Garoufallou et al. (Eds.): MTSR 2015, CCIS 544, pp. 286–297, 2015.
DOI: 10.1007/978-3-319-24129-6_25

into exposing their public data as linked data". Whereas focused on educational data, they promote the use of shared vocabularies to describe resources, encouraging universities to publish data in an interoperable manner.

Regarding research centres, many of them expose official websites showing their scientific contributions (either publications, events or projects), contact and organizational information about their researchers, etc. Despite the similarity between research units worldwide, these websites lack a common structure, making it difficult to compare the success of various units between them. Furthermore, the possibility to automatically download data stored in the research information system is restricted to the implementation of a customized HTML parser for the portal's layout.

In this paper, we present our approach to harmonise how research information is collected, stored, linked and presented by developing **Labman** (Laboratory Management), a research-themed information management system which makes use of Semantic Web Standards and best practices to share data over the Internet.

This paper is structured as follows: section 2 presents similar works on research information visualization. Section 3 describes the system we have developed, and some of its most relevant highlights. Section 4 addresses some of the visualizations generated from the data within the system. Finally, section 5 summarises the conclusions drawn from the development and drafts some future work lines.

2   Related Work

There are some information systems and plugins which provide visual representations over research data.

The Semantic Web Journal (SWJ) published by IOS Press provides a Scientometrics portal[2] which gathers data from its SPARQL endpoint, generating publication and author related visualizations. Its goal is to make all submitted manuscripts, solicited reviews, status updates and comments available for everybody. This SWJ Portal [4] presents different visualizations about the data stored in SWJ, allowing visitors to consult an author's citation or co-authorship networks, the geospatial distribution of its articles' citations, or the usage of selected keywords. Similar results but based on the LAK (Learning Analytics and Knowledge) are reached in [5].

AMiner[3] [9] focuses its metrics on researchers, providing a set of statistics, metadata and visualizations for individuals in order to understand their contributions through time.

[2] used the *LOD Visualization Suite* on top of the RILOD (Research Information Linked Open Data) dataset to visualize the Flemish research landscape. With more than 400 million triples, it shows how visualizations can represent the

---

[2] http://semantic-web-journal.com/SWJPortal/
[3] http://aminer.org/

research status of a whole country. In their demo[4], users can navigate through publications, projects, topics and research centres, discovering the connections that link them.

The university of Indiana, with works such as [6,8], visualized the research status of the US and major international conference through topic, keyword and trend analysis.

Finally, the EU-funded CODE project[5] aims to collect publication data and metadata from different sources, extract scientific facts from them and publish everything to the LOD Cloud. Its Visualization Wizard [7] allows to analyse linked open datasets visually, offering a visualization recommender based on the data the user is interested in.

3 Labman

The need for updated, high-quality, non-redundant data is a must for any information architect, data analyst or management enthusiast. A centralised data storage helps in minimising data redundancy, avoiding common errors produced by keeping different versions of data resources in a variety of locations (i.e., when applying for a new fund, is usual to send a complete version of the participants CV. If some researchers keep their own updated CVs elsewhere, the provenance of the presented data will be damaged).

3.1 Modelling a Research Centre

Every research information system manages information about different resources of interest. Actually, *labman* stores information about nearly 100 entities, being the most important ones:

- **Publications:** Scientific articles are one of the main research items. Publications comprise a relevant contribution to a given field, which is presented to the community in order to gain knowledge about that particular field. Publications are related to their authors/editors, related publications within the system, projects where the presented contributions are applied, etc.
- **Projects:** Comprehended to be the application of gained knowledge to *real* scenarios, research projects can either test a scientific contribution in a controlled environment, or serve as the starting point to generate new knowledge. *Labman* also allows to manage "internal" projects, those initiatives born within the unit as pet projects in order to test new technologies, innovative approaches, etc. As an example, *labman* is considered an internal project, as we wanted a system to help research centres homogenise and share their data. Projects are linked with the people working in them, the funding calls that finance development, the organizations which collaborate towards its success, and the publications that expose the outcomes to the community.

---

[4] http://ewi.mmlab.be/academic/
[5] http://code-research.eu/

- **People:** Considered to be the most important asset in any organization, people are in charge of developing the projects, writing the articles, contributing to knowledge areas with new ideas, etc. Thus, *labman* categorises individuals under different roles: researchers, developers, administrative staff, PhD students, and so on. People are connected to the rest of primary entities in the system.
- **Events:** Any gathering of people with similar interests and a specific goal. With this definition, an event could be of academic nature (i.e., an international conference), a project meeting or a hackathon to develop new applications over Open Data repositories, among others.
- **News:** Brief reports of the latests actions carried out by the research unit, news establish an updated communication channel with interested individuals. As a mean to highlight the most important milestones reached by the research centre, they are connected with people, project, publication and event entities.
- **Doctoral Dissertations:** Research centres have a deep commitment towards training future researcher generations, often supporting young undergrads in exchanging programs. Doctoral dissertations are the realization of a long-term investigation in a specialised area under the direction of one (or more) supervisors, supported by a doctoral program and usually presented in *viva voce* in front of an experts panel.
- **Funding Programs:** Research needs money to endow its maintenance in the long run. As researchers, we are well-aware of the key value solid R&D programmes mean to a country's development, making it competitive in a global economy. *Labman* records information about the funding calls supporting the projects developed within the research centre, detailing the organization that promotes the call, the financed period and the geographical scope of the funding.
- **Organizations:** Given the significance of individuals promoting science, the organizations and institutions they represent are also considered an essential entity within *labman*. The type of organization determines its goal in the research landscape: companies searching for a commercial product, academic institutions pursuing scientific breakthroughs, public administrations transferring knowledge to society, etc.

3.2   Publishing as Linked Open Data

Labman is programmed in Django[6], a robust web framework implemented in Python. Django is database-agnostic, so new deployments of *labman* can select their database management system without further hassle. To make *labman* the dynamic, data-driven research information system it is, queries are written using Django's ORM (Object-Relational Mapping) language, decoupling data retrieval from specific SQL sentences.

---

[6] https://djangoproject.com/

Initially, *labman* published its contents as Linked Open Data using D2RQ [1], a system to access relational databases as virtual, read-only RDF graphs. Whilst it allowed resources to be publicly available using shared vocabularies in a machine-readable manner, we discovered the limits of this approach when we required conditional structures to control how resources were described when certain conditions were met (i.e., publishing the resource as a specific type based on the value adopted by a certain attribute).

The solution was to initially establish a direct mapping between each entity's model (classes with defined attributes, as in any object-oriented environment), and the ontology resource which defined it: for example, people in the system would be published as *foaf:Person* instances, and project titles would be mapped to *dc:title* values. After describing the correspondence between all the models in *labman*, we extended each model's *save()* method, thus getting full control each time an object's instance is created or updated. In that moment, we generate/update all the triples linked to the instance, publishing them to the specified RDF store in *labman's* configuration files. By modifying the *delete()* method in a similar fashion we are able to control data removals in the triple-store also.

The publication of *labman's* data as RDF is completely optional, although we encourage its adoption for all deployments. Once active, the Linked Open Data (LOD) life-cycle is automatically managed by *labman*, providing all the resources semantically annotated through a dedicated SPARQL endpoint and allowing third parties and interested users to consult all the information within a research centre directly. As of May 2015, our research unit's SPARQL endpoint[7] contains more than 20K triples.

To describe the resources within *labman*, we use some well known vocabularies, such as:

- **SWRC:** The Semantic Web for Research Communities ontology describes projects and derivatives.
- **SWRC-FE:** We extended SWRC's ontology with a *Funding Extension* (FE), in order to gather data about the financial aspect of projects.
- **FOAF:** The Friend-Of-A-Friend vocabulary is used to describe researchers and collaborators.
- **MUTO:** The Modular Unified Tagging Ontology is used to characterise the topics of both publications and projects.
- **BIBO:** Used to express publication-related facts.

Actually, *labman* publishes mostly 4-star LOD (according to Tim Berners-Lee 5 star deployment scheme[8]), with the possibility to generate manually created *rdfs:seeAlso* links to external resources for most of the primary entities in the data model.

---

[7] http://apps.morelab.deusto.es/labman/sparql
[8] http://5stardata.info/

3.3   Management Tasks

Labman provides a full-featured administration panel, in which all the entity models can be created, modified or removed from the system. Access to this administration panel is controlled by permission groups, controlling which user has access to each action. For example, a "Journalist" group can be defined who is only able to edit *News* related instances.

Apart from the administration panel, a management view is provided to deal with data quality related tasks. The most relevant one, being an automated tool to retrieve publications data, avoiding to feed all the information to the system from scratch. In order to achieve this automatic retrieval, we have implemented a *zotero* connector, responsible for the automatic gathering of publication-related metadata.

Zotero[9] is a free, open-sourced reference/bibliographic management tool which integrates with a huge variety of publication indexing databases and office software suits. With just a unique identifier for a publication (e.g., a DOI number, ISSN/ISBN, unique title, etc.), Zotero searches the Internet in order to gather as much available metadata as possible about it, taking the burden of filling all the fields from *labman*'s administrators.

Labman allows to collect publications from a library within zotero. By providing the API key and unique identifier for the repository, *labman* connects periodically to Zotero to retrieve updates. When new items are found, a publication instance is generated in the research information system, together with the available document if it is provided as an attachment.

However, when automatically retrieving data from the Internet, some conflicts may appear. The most usual one is the author-name redundancy, as the same researches might get different naming in diverse indexing databases. In order to disambiguate them, we apply a string-similarity algorithm which calculates the likeness between all the researcher names in the system. Those matches are presented to *labman*'s administrators in order to decide which action to take: *a)* merging both names (e.g., one of them is selected as the correct one, and all the instances linked to the other name are assigned to the correct match), or *b)* mark the match as a mistake, so both names are distinguished and the algorithm does not detect collisions from then on.

Finally, users can tag items in zotero. We use those tags with different purposes. Some *reserved* tags are searched for, so when a user tags an item with them, different actions are triggered. For example, the impact factor of a journal article can be made explicit through tags, as well as the quartile where it was published. By using a project's name within *labman* as a tag, a direct relationship is established between the project and the publication. If the tag does not match any of the special regular expressions, its considered a topic label and used for that end.

---

[9] https://zotero.org/

4   Visualising Research Data

All entity views in *labman* try to display at once all the available information about the items of interest and the resources connected with them. Presenting data and linked items in a clean and ordered way, we encourage website visitors to navigate through the system in an exploratory process, discovering new knowledge on the way.

Apart from textual information and links to related instances, *labman* provides different visualizations that summarise diverse aspects of the research centre's performance. Most visual representations can be found under the **Charts** menu, or from each researcher's personal view.

As our research information system is web-based, most of the visualizations are dynamic and interactive, to foster a serendipitous behaviour. The visualizations generated within *labman* are implemented using JavaScript graphing libraries, such as *d3.js*[10], *Google Charts*[11] and *sigma.js*[12].

Some of the most interesting charts are explained next, using as example our unit's deployment of *labman*[13]:

4.1   Historical Role Distribution

The visualization in Figure 1 helps understanding the organizational structure over time. By stacking the roles count by year, the total number of people working in the centre is displayed, and each colour-coded area shows how many people has been involved in different tasks.

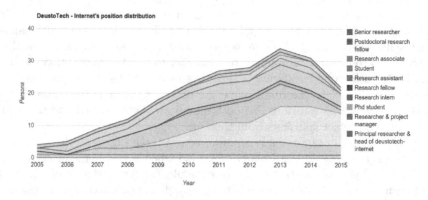

Fig. 1. Timeline with MORElab's role distribution since its creation a decade ago

---

[10] http://d3js.org/
[11] https://developers.google.com/chart/
[12] http://sigmajs.org/
[13] http://morelab.deusto.es/

This chart could exhibit interesting patterns in human-resource management: the growth/downturn of the group in a specific period, promotions (PhD student → Post-doctoral researcher), unification of *role labels*, etc.

4.2   Projects Timeline

Researchers usually test and apply their research innovations in controlled environments, in order to collect new evidences to support their work, or to transfer knowledge to society. People can play different roles in those projects, and when drafting new proposals, knowing the workload of each employee in the group is an important metric to have accessible (see Figure 2).

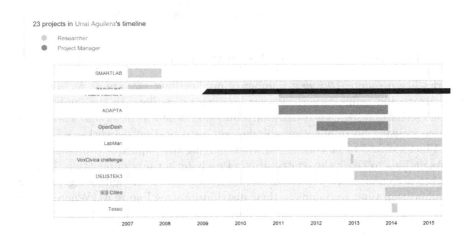

Fig. 2. Reduced version of the projects timeline for a selected person. The colour legend signals the role played during its execution

4.3   Research Topics

Finally, *labman* makes use of weighted word lists (also known as "word clouds") to depict the topics covered by the carried out works. Keywords for the resources of interest are weighted so the bigger the word is displayed, the more resources that have use it to define themselves, as displayed in Figure 3. Clicking on any keyword would filter the instances in the system which belong to the topic.

Topics are assigned to instances using Dublin Core's *subject* attribute, and published as LOD using the *muto:Tag* ontology. Topics in labman can be hierarchically organised, thus tagging a resource with a "child" class would result in assigning the "parent" tags to the object also. Through this technique, *parent topics* represent well-defined, independent knowledge areas; whereas *child topics* are used to mark specialised, deepen knowledge.

Fig. 3. Topic relevance of projects carried out within the group

4.4   Place Distribution in Authored Publications

Metrics like *h-index*, *i10-index*, number of publications, etc. are *de facto* means to evaluate and compare performance between researchers. In the "publish-or-perish" scenario research is usually surrounded in, where authors can "cheat" the metrics focusing on publication volume and auto-citation networks, a broader set of factors need to be considered when judging the impact of contributions.

As an idea to check the contribution of each author in a publication, *labman* presents a combo chart per researcher that aggregates the authoring position by publication type, and depicts their distribution (see Figure 4). Whereas this metric could not be relevant for all knowledge areas, in some fields such as *Computer Science*, usually place is proportionally related to the contributions made by each author.

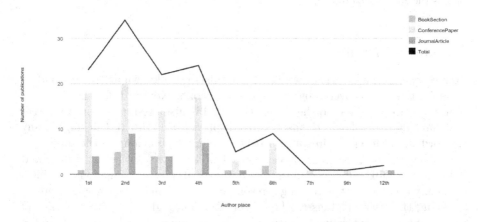

Fig. 4. Place distribution for a researcher of our group, aggregated by publication type

When a publication type is selected, the chart is re-arranged in a time-based series fashion. Both visuals can help detecting common patterns, i.e., PhD students starting from low-level places (collaborators in an existing research when they entered the lab) and climbing positions as their works produce significant results; well-positioned researchers with a successful trajectory co-authoring several articles in the same conferences/journals yearly, etc.

4.5   People Collaboration Networks

Science advances *"On the shoulders of giants"*, meaning that research is often made in collaboration with other researchers, both from the same organization or external institutions. When developing a project or working on a new publication, people establish ties between them which highlight common interests. Figure 5 depicts how active members of our group have related with each other carrying out the same projects. Similar graphs are calculated for co-authoring networks, egonetworks [3], etc.

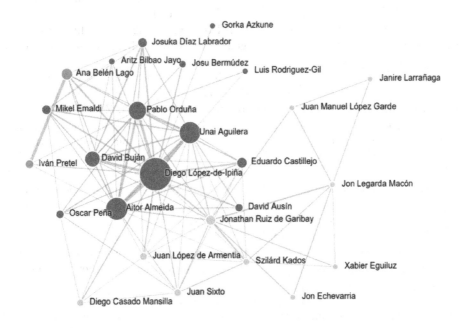

Fig. 5. Active members collaboration graph in projects

The stronger the connection (more projects/publications in common), the thicker the edge that connects two persons. Node size is calculated through Eigenvector centrality, a value that portrays the relevance of that particular item within the whole network. The colour indicates the community the node belongs to. Communities do not symbolise the organization a person works for, but the sub-group it belongs to due to certain particularities. For example, communities of practice, similar research topics, specialised knowledge areas, etc. Hovering over a node, only that person's connections are coloured, to avoid visual overloading.

5   Conclusions and Future Work

Labman summarises our efforts towards managing all the information within a research centre, with the possibility of publishing it as LOD, and presenting dynamic visualizations in order to get the full picture about the unit's status and performance in different scenarios. These charts and graphs also allow unit leaders plan strategic goals for the next years, empowering strong knowledge areas, promoting promising new research topics, presenting innovative project proposals to first-level funding calls, etc.

Actually, our research information system is deployed in three different research groups within the university: two from DeustoTech - Deusto Institute of Technology (Mobility[14] and MORElab's official websites), and one from the Transnational Law Research Unit[15]. These knowledge-areas diversity has improved *labman* by making it more generalist, without being closely-coupled with our unit's needs.

Labman has proven to be practical by its users, which was one of the main reasons to avoid standard CMSs and develop a generic system from the ground. The ease of importing all publication-related data thanks to Zotero is a really appreciated feature, and users have repeatedly pledged for a similar approach to import project-related data. However, as for the best of our knowledge there are no similar tools for project data, the need to input the data manually is still required. Nevertheless, the benefits still exceed the system's lacks.

The software is open-sourced under a GPL v3 license[16], and its code can be browsed, downloaded and contributed to in its GitHub repository[17]. The project is continuously improved by adding new features, solving bugs and including pull requests from different contributors.

As listed in the *issues* section of the code base, our focus is set on providing more insightful visualizations to foster information discovery when visiting a *labman*-powered website.

We are also considering the possibility to offer a JSON-LD[18] based API in order to allow both programmers and Semantic Web practitioners access the data stored within *labman* in a more traditional way, without the required knowledge about the SPARQL language and related technologies. Individual web views will

---

[14] http://research.mobility.deustotech.eu/
[15] http://research.transnational.deusto.es/
[16] http://www.gnu.org/copyleft/gpl.html
[17] https://github.com/OscarPDR/labman_ud
[18] http://json-ld.org/

also be extended with *schema.org*[19] metadata definitions for promoting resource discovery and interoperability.

Finally, we are completing the implementation of OAI-PMH[20] (Open Archives Initiative Protocol for Metadata Harvesting) to make all the metadata about publications discoverable by clients supporting these conventions. Many digital libraries, institutional repositories and digital archives have already adopted OAI-PMH in their systems.

Acknowledgments. The research activities described in this paper are funded by the Basque Government's Universities and Research department, under grant *PRE_2014_2_298*.

References

1. Bizer, C., Cyganiak, R.: D2r server-publishing relational databases on the semantic web. In: Poster at the 5th International Semantic Web Conference (2006)
2. Dimou, A., De Vocht, L., Van Grootel, G., Van Campe, L., Latour, J., Mannens, E., Van de Walle, R.: Visualizing the information of a Linked Open Data enabled Research Information System. Procedia Computer Science **33**, 245–252 (2014)
3. Everett, M., Borgatti, S.P.: Ego network betweenness. Social Networks **27**(1), 31–38 (2005)
4. Hu, Y., Janowicz, K., McKenzie, G., Sengupta, K., Hitzler, P.: A linked-data-driven and semantically-enabled journal portal for scientometrics. In: Alani, H., Kagal, L., Fokoue, A., Groth, P., Biemann, C., Parreira, J.X., Aroyo, L., Noy, N., Welty, C., Janowicz, K. (eds.) ISWC 2013, Part II. LNCS, vol. 8219, pp. 114–129. Springer, Heidelberg (2013)
5. Hu, Y., McKenzie, G., Yang, J.A., Gao, S., Abdalla, A., Janowicz, K.: A linked-data-driven web portal for learning analytics: data enrichment, interactive visualization, and knowledge discovery. In: LAK Workshops (2014)
6. Ke, W., Borner, K., Viswanath, L.: Major information visualization authors, papers and topics in the ACM library. In: Proceedings of the IEEE Symposium on Information Visualization, INFOVIS 2004, pp. 216.1–216.9. IEEE Computer Society, Washington, DC (2004)
7. Mutlu, B., Hoefler, P., Sabol, V., Tschinkel, G., Granitzer, M.: Automated Visualization Support for Linked Research Data. I-SEMANTICS (Posters & Demos) **1026**, 40–44 (2013)
8. Skupin, A., Biberstine, J.R., Brner, K.: Visualizing the Topical Structure of the Medical Sciences: A Self-Organizing Map Approach. PLoS ONE **8**(3) (2013)
9. Tang, J., Zhang, J., Yao, L., Li, J., Zhang, L., Su, Z.: ArnetMiner: extraction and mining of academic social networks. In: Proceedings of the 14th ACM SIGKDD International Conference on Knowledge Discovery and Data Mining, KDD 2008, pp. 990–998. ACM, New York (2008)

---

[19] http://schema.org/

[20] https://www.openarchives.org/pmh/

Repositories for Open Science: The SciRepo Reference Model

Massimiliano Assante(✉), Leonardo Candela, Donatella Castelli,
Paolo Manghi, and Pasquale Pagano

Istituto di Scienza e Tecnologie dell'Informazione "A. Faedo" – CNR, Pisa, Italy
{assante,candela,castelli,manghi,pagano}@isti.cnr.it

Abstract. Open Science calls for innovative approaches and solutions embracing the entire research lifecycle. From the research publishing perspective, the aim is to pursue an holistic approach where publishing includes any product (e.g. articles, datasets, experiments, notebooks, websites) resulting from a research activity and relevant to the interpretation, evaluation, and reuse of the activity or part of it. In this paper, we present the foundational concepts and relationships characterising SciRepo, i.e. an innovative class of scientific repositories that (*a*) promotes a publishing mechanism blurring the distinction between research lifecycle and its scholarly communication; (*b*) simplifies the "publishing" of an entire research activity allowing to seamlessly exploit and reuse every research product; and (*c*) is conceived to be nicely integrated on top of existing research infrastructures.

1 Introduction

Research today is based on digital research products, such as papers, datasets, software, and services, and the access and sharing of such products has mutated in order to adapt the underlying business models and mission to such new scenarios. Within this context, Research Infrastructures[1] (RIs) enabled a remarkable increase of scientific production by (*i*) *data intensive science* [13], i.e. the availability of datasets at petabyte level, processed through simulation software and empowered by high performance computing, (*ii*) *open science* [5], i.e. transparent access to scientific data as well as reliability of scientific discovery, and (*iii*) *collaboration science* [12], i.e. a changing paradigm towards large-scale research collaborations involving professional and nonprofessional scientists with the use of internet-based tools.

Despite that, *research publishing* is still adopting the traditional article paradigm, which separate *the place where research is conducted,* i.e. RIs, from *the place where research is published and shared,* i.e. third-party marketplace services. Specifically, research products are published "elsewhere" and "on date",

---

[1] A Research Infrastructure is intended as the compound of elements regarding the organisation (roles, procedures, etc.), the structure (buildings, laboratories, etc.), and the technology (microscopes, telescopes, sensors, computers, internet, applications, etc.) underpinning the implementation of scientific research.

E. Garoufallou et al. (Eds.): MTSR 2015, CCIS 544, pp. 298–311, 2015.
DOI: 10.1007/978-3-319-24129-6_26

i.e. when the scientists feel the products obtained so far are sufficiently mature. Although articles are evolving towards enhanced forms, e.g. [4,9,14], and repositories, publisher services and infrastructures are enlarging the array of supported research products it remains a divide between the wealth of artefacts daily managed by scientists and what is crystallised and released by an article (including its "supplementary" material). Scientists, funders, and organisations are therefore pushing for innovative scientific communication workflows (deposition, quality assessment and dissemination), marrying an holistic approach where publishing includes in principle any product (e.g. publications, datasets, experiments, software, web sites, blogs) resulting from a research activity, that is relevant to the interpretation, evaluation, and reuse of the activity or part of it.

There are several discussions and initiatives seeking consensus on solutions for effective research publishing, e.g. [7,8,15,16]. We introduced the notion of Science 2.0 Repositories (SciRepos) [1,2] and explained how they enable effective scientific communication workflows, by allowing research product *creation* and *publishing* to both occur "within" the RI (as opposed to "elsewhere") and "during" the research activities (as opposed to "on date"). Thus, by living in synergy with RIs, SciRepos meet research publishing requirements arising in open science by blurring the distinction between research life-cycle and research publishing as they interface with the ICT services of RIs to intercept and publish research products.

In this paper, we present a Reference Model for a SciRepo, an abstract work intended for understanding significant concepts and relationships among its components. The Reference Model is not directly coupled to any standard, technology or other concrete implementation detail. Its purpose is to provide a common semantic that can be used unambiguously across and between different implementations, in order to realise a general purpose platform facilitating the realisation of a SciRepo over any ICT-based research infrastructure environment with limited costs and efforts if compared with from-scratch approaches.

2 Science 2.0 Repositories in a Nutshell

In the following, a *Research Activity* (RA) is intended as the course of actions that leads to prove an initial thesis whose results bring novelty to a research field. Within a *Research Infrastructure* (RI) and relying on its ICT services (i.e. e-infrastructure), RAs build upon and create a wide array of *Research Products* (RPs), intended as digital objects ranging from documents, datasets, software, and services, to web sites, blogs, posts, etc. SciRepos [2] are repositories conceived to "hook" to the ICT Services of a given RI in order to keep track of the yield of RPs generated by RI's RAs and offer discovery, reuse, and Web 2.0 functionalities over both. As exemplified in Figure 1, SciRepos can adapt to a given RI scenario by adapting their *Information Space* to represent the typologies of RPs handled by the RI ICT services in a given RA (e.g. workflows W, executing processes P over datasets D) and how these are interconnected by semantic relationships (e.g. citedBy, versionOf, inputDataset). Relying on SciRepo APIs, RI developers must write code that "hook" their ICT Services to feed the SciRepo Information Space with RPs metadata descriptions (e.g. notify the end of a process P, the generation of a dataset D). Developers can personalise Web 2.0 end-user interfaces and APIs to offer *Functionalities* for managing (e.g. add, remove) and consuming (e.g. discover, access, assess, comment, share, post, enrich, execute) RAs and relative RPs. Typically, SciRepo end-users (e.g. researchers) can (*i*) be notified of new RP of interest, can exchange posts or assessments about RPs (e.g. enabling alternative forms of peer-review), (*ii*) perform RI ICT Service-enabled operations over RPs (e.g. execution of an experiment, quality evaluation), and (*iii*) rely on public or admin-moderated discovery facilities (access rights, e.g. group, laboratory, community, public) to the graph of RPs. Such features make it possible for researchers to carry out their RAs while delegating "publishing" of the RPs the created to the SciRepo. More generally, RPs are shared in their context of creation (RI and RA), thereby maximising chances of high-quality assessment and re-use.

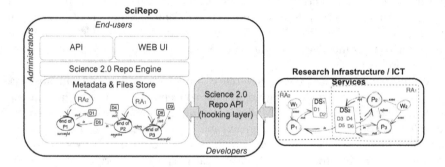

Fig. 1. The SciRepo High-Level Architecture

Worth highlighting that SciRepo is conceived to only supplement the tools daily used by scientists by inducing cutting-edge solutions to publishing practices. It will neither replace RI services and eventual Virtual Research Environments [10] nor research information management systems [11].

3   Reference Model

In the following we present the core concepts of the model. As Fig. 2 shows, a SciRepo supports Users by providing them with a set of Functionalities for managing its Information Space. Like any other system, all of this is regulated by Policies, e.g. who can do what, and it is characterised by an Architecture.

Information Space models the content managed by the SciRepo, described by an entity-relationship diagram. The diagram describes the entities and relationships representing the interconnections between Research Products in any Research Activity domain. *Functionality* represents the operations supported

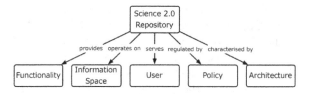

Fig. 2. The SciRepo Main Concepts

by SciRepo, which are oriented to open science settings and to the scholarly communication. *User* models the actors using a SciRepo, intended as consumers and/or providers of SciRepo content. SciRepo connects its users and support them in performing their research activities by consuming already available RPs to produce new knowledge. Besides, it provides its users with a clear view on what is happening in their Research Activities. *Policy* regulates the approval to use a functionality on one or more Research Activities in accordance with the role-based access control model explained in the following. Usage rights are modelled as associations between roles, functionality and Research Activities. *Architecture* models the mapping of functionality onto hardware and software components, the mapping of the software architecture onto the hardware architecture, and human interactions with these components. Unlike the other main four SciRepo concepts, the architecture becomes meaningful and of pertinence of the SciRepo Administrators and RI Application Developers only. SciRepo End-users are not associated to this characteristic because they perceive the SciRepo by interacting with a graphical user interface provided in a web browser [2].

In order to appropriately characterise a SciRepo, we decided to look at it from the perspectives of the actors that operate with it. These perspectives highlight the needs of the different actors, use the appropriate terms and definitions, and give the perception of the required relationships. The roles taken into account are three, namely *SciRepo End-users*, *SciRepo Administrators*, and *RI Application Developers*.

The *SciRepo End-users* are the actors that exploit the SciRepo functionality for providing, consuming and managing its content. They perceive the SciRepo as a stateful entity which serves their functional needs through the interaction with it.

The *SciRepo Administrators* are the actors selecting which RI services a SciRepo should support and decide where and how to deploy the SciRepo. They interact on top of the SciRepo hooking layer [2] by enabling specific operations and configuration parameters, i.e. configure the SciRepo by enriching the data model specification with directives regarding how the different functionalities should be instantiated with respect to it. For example, directives may (*i*) specify how end-user interfaces should enable discover and browse of the information space, e.g. which product typology and metadata fields should be displayed, browsable, post-able, assessable, or (*ii*) be used to configure export APIs, e.g. protocol, subset of information graph to be exported.

The *RI Application Developers* are the actors in charge of extending the RI ICT services and applications to exploit the SciRepo API. They interact symmetrically to the SciRepo Administrators, on the bottom of the SciRepo hooking layer through its APIs. Their role is to embed small programs, namely hooks, into existing RI services which react to RI events (e.g. dataset creation, experiment execution) by calling the hooking layer APIs, that in turn, transform these events in meaningful information.

For the sake of simplicity, the concepts and relationships of the model are graphically represented through concepts maps [17]. In the rest of this section we shall present conceptual maps for each of the above identified perspectives.

3.1   The SciRepo End-Users Perspective

The SciRepo End-users perspective is centred around the actions performed by three main actors: the *content consumers* that access and use the SciRepo content; the *content providers* that can provide content both manually (e.g. by ingesting it) or automatically (e.g. by using the RI's ICT services and applications to trigger the creation of new RPs); and the *RA managers*, whose tasks include describing the RAs in which they are involved, with management of users and policies.

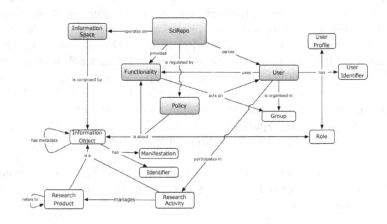

Fig. 3. The SciRepo End-user Domains Perspective

Figure 3 shows the main concepts and relationships of the model that represents how users perceive a SciRepo.

The *Information Space* perceived by SciRepo End-users is composed by *Information Objects* and, in turn, *Research Activities* and their related products *Research Products*. Each Information Object has an unique *Identifier*, associated *Metadata* and a *Manifestation*. The *Metadata* follows the "classic" definition of metadata, as is "data about data"; it can be used in different contexts with different purposes and is an Information Objects itself; our model captures the needs to have metadata associated to an information object as a mean for enhancing the functionality and in general the management of the object. *Manifestation*[2] is the physical representation of an Information Object; it is worth noting that we are dealing with digital objects and thus the manifestation is itself a digital object.

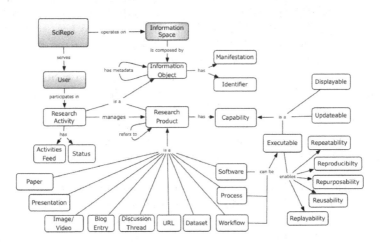

Fig. 4. The SciRepo End-user Information Space Perspective

Fig. 4 further defines the constituents and relationships of an Information Object. According to it, each *Research Activity* has a *Status*, an *Activities Feed* and manages *Research Products*. *Status* represents the current status of the *Research Activity*, for instance if is completed or ongoing. *User* participates in Research Activities and their interactions and actions are gathered into an *Activities Feed*; an aggregated collection of activities streamed in a chronological reverse order reflecting users' interactions. *Research Activity* manages *Research Product*; any output of the research process is potentially a relevant RP, as such it may be subject of publishing and be related to other products and Research Activities in time and semantics. We classify these outputs into separate sub-classes ranging from outcomes like a *Paper*, a *Presentation* or an *Image* to *Dataset*, *Workflow* (experiment) and its instantiation into a *Process*, but also *Blog Entry*, *Discussion Thread*, *URL*, and *Software*. According to Fig. 4, each *Research Product* can refer to other Research Products that may, or may not, belong to the same *Research Activity*. Further, a RP has *Capabilities*. The capabilities strongly depend on (*i*) the features supported by the underlying ICT RI Services, and on (*ii*) the subclass/type of a RP, which impacts on them. We identified three kinds of capabilities describing what users can expect from RPs. A RP could be *Displayable*: suppose researchers run experiments by executing a workflow collecting input data eventually creating a map, whose high-resolution

---

[2] This concept is borrowed from the well known IFLA FRBR model.

representation is stored as RP in SciRepo. Then this RP may have the capability to display the map in a RI ICT Service. A RP could be *Updatable*: in the case of automatic deposition RPs may have the updatable capability, meaning that RI ICT Services can update it by generating new versions of the same RP. A RP could be *Executable*: being executable is certainly key for the validation of research result, however, is apt only for three specific types of RPs, namely *Software*, *Process*, and *Workflow* and fits particularly well when we talk about experiments, i.e. workflows and processes. It is important to note that SciRepo is not meant to execute these RPs by itself, rather it delegates such feature to the ICT services of the underlying RI providing them with the necessary information they need; As Figure 4 shows, we distinguished five subclasses within the executable capability domain, namely *Repeatability*, *Reproducibility*, *Reporpusability*, *Reusability*, and *Replayability* [6].

Each RA has its group of users associated. As Fig. 5 shows, RA users can be logically divided in three categories: content consumers, content providers and RA managers. In the rest we further describe these roles and the associated functionalities.

All the tasks carried out by the SciRepo users are performed by invoking the available *Functionality*. As Fig. 5 shows, the SciRepo End-user functionalities can be classified in five categories: Personalisation, Collaboration, Access & Discovery, RPs Management and RA Management.

The *Personalisation* class models the functionality for the *Subscription* to existing Information Objects and for the request of new RA creations. *Subscription* is about enabling users to be notified about events related to Information Objects. Users can subscribe to events explicitly, i.e. by activating the subscribe function, or implicitly, i.e. by liking or commenting on an existing RA or RP. Subscribing implies *Notification* of events. End-users can subscribe to different type of events occurring in SciRepo, e.g. new product creation, new version products, comments on products. Once subscribed they can decide how to be notified about a given RA or RP by accessing the *Notification Settings*, i.e. a list of all the RPs and RAs they have subscribed where is possible to select the "channels" through which they should be notified (e.g. SciRepo, email, social platforms) or even decide not to be notified. Finally, any user can exploit the *Request RA* function to request creation of new SciRepo Research Activities. This request is sent to SciRepo Administrators that, if approved, assign the requesting user the role of *RA Manager* for the newly created RA.

The *Collaboration* class relies on social tools (e.g. likes, discussion threads, tags) and allows alternative forms of Quality Assessment. *Share* enables user to make RPs noticeable by others outside the SciRepo via standard protocols and APIs (RDF, OAI-ORE), towards third-party systems e.g. marketplace repositories, and scientific social networks e.g. ResearchGate [18], Academia.edu. *Messaging* provide means for the user to participate, interact and contact the other users (email-like or instant messaging). *Tag* enables to provide labelling to existing RA or RPs but also to end-users involving them in the Research Activity with the possibility to give personal contributes. Finally, the *Feedback* function

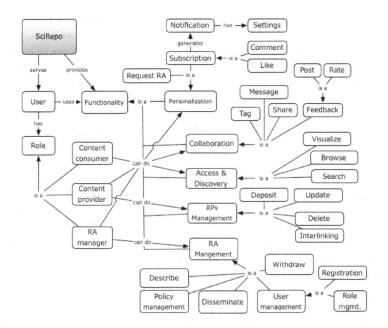

Fig. 5. The SciRepo End-user Functional Perspective

is composed by two important functions. The *Rate* function permits end-users to express their position with respect to the ongoing activities, just like the *post* function that permits end-users to add comments, thus both functions allow alternative form of quality assessment to existing RAs or RPs. Posts are themselves a special typology of RPs of the RA and are indeed searchable and browsable as explained in the following.

The *Access & Discovery* enables to consume the RAs and their RPs. It comprises the functionality allowing the discovery of and the access to, on these objects. The *Search* and *Browse* functions allow, respectively, to search and list existing RAs or RPs, enabling users to discover them. Once discovered, products are consumed by means of a *Visualise* function that produces human understandable visualisations.

The *RPs Management* class serves to populate the SciRepo information space, allowing the deposit, the update and the deletion of RPs. SciRepo offers both automatic deposit, i.e. in the style of RI services usage, and manual deposit, i.e. in the style of marketplace repositories. The *update* function allows to modify an existing RP. It is associated with accessibility policies that regulate who and under which condition can update them. It can produce a novel product that may be a newer version of an existing one. The *delete* function allows to delete an already existing RP.

The *RA Management* class regulates the "RA life" through the administration of its products and its users, it allows to *Describe* a RA so as to enhance its understandings, to *Disseminate* it, and to *Withdraw* it, by explicitly removing it. These functions can be performed only by users associated with the RA manager role. RA Managers also exploit the *User Management* function to perform the *Registration* of new users and their *Role Management*. They are also entitled to exploit Policy Management functions to define the rules governing the RA.

The *User* dimension identify the actors entitled to interact with SciRepo. In fact, SciRepo connects scientists with information during their research activities by supporting the production of new knowledge and the consumption of the already available RPs. Fig. 3 shows the SciRepo part involving the user concept map. According to the map each User (*i*) has a *User Profile*, i.e. the descriptive information SciRepo maintains about a single user, (*ii*) uses the *Functionality* as described in Fig. 5, and (*iii*) is organised in *Group*, i.e. a number of users that are considered or classed together. In addition, each User has (*iv*) an *Identifier* and (*v*) a *Role*, e.g. a job function within the context of the RI. In the context of the SciRepo end-user perspective, we identified three roles that any SciRepo should support, namely content consumer, content provider and RA manager.

The *content consumer* role is limited to the use of the access functions previously described. As a consequence, can search, browse and visualise RPs within the RA but also Tag and provide feedback on existing RPs by using Rate and Post functions. The *content provider* is an active participant of the RI. She performs experiments within the RI that yield to the automatic deposition of new RPs or can deposit them manually. It is envisaged that the update and delete functions belong to this role too. The *RA manager* is a key role in any SciRepo instance, she manages the RA and coordinates other users by registering them and assigning roles. This manager has also the possibility to withdraw his RAs.

Policies are the mechanism used to regulate and restrict the SciRepo access and usage to authorised users. In modelling the access control we used the Role-based access control (RBAC) approach. According to the Policy concept map depicted in Fig. 3 a *Policy* is a triple (role, functionality, information object). A policy can be indeed associated to a RA of any of its RP and is used to moderate the usage of the single functionality to an established role.

3.2 The SciRepo Administrator Perspective

The SciRepo Administrator perspective is focused on the *SciRepo Management Functionality* concept. The *User* dimension in this case is represented by SciRepo Administrators only, which exploit this set of functionalities to set up and maintain a SciRepo. The result of this activity is the definition of the most appropriate SciRepo architecture. To perform this task the SciRepo Administrator selects the appropriate components, assigns components to hosting nodes, configures each component including the *Hooking Layer* one and monitors the resulting SciRepo deployment. Figure 6 shows the concepts and relationships of the model that represent the SciRepo Platform from the SciRepo administrator perspective.

From the SciRepo Administrator perspective the *SciRepo Management Functionality* provided by the SciRepo Platform is entirely related with the set up of the architecture for a SciRepo by means of the configuration, deployment, and management of its constituent parts. Specifically, the *Configure* function allows

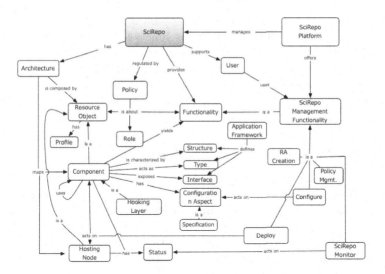

Fig. 6. The SciRepo Administrator Perspective

a SciRepo Administrator to act on the configuration aspects of a component in order to modify/customise its behaviour and thus the provided functionality. This task prepares a component (*i*) to be activated on a specific hosting node; and (*ii*) to be aware of the characteristics of the RPs it has to manage. The *Deploy* function enables the SciRepo Administrator to enact a function by assigning a component to a hosting node and make it capable to operate, i.e. to provide the functionality the component is implemented for. The *RA Creation* function enables the SciRepo Administrator to stage new Research Activities in SciRepo. The creation of new RAs can be also based on requests performed by end-users. In this case Administrators create the RA and successively assign the RA Manager role to the requesting user throughout the *Policy Management* function. Finally, the *SciRepo Monitor* function allows the SciRepo Administrator to monitor the deployed component status. It allows supervising the average number of requests managed by the component, the average load of the hosting node, the average number of queued requests, the latency, the throughput.

The *Architecture* is a representation of the system dealing with mapping functionality onto hardware and software components. Our model is based on the understanding that *Components* and *Hosting Nodes* are the building blocks of the SciRepo Platform and, that, in order to allow them to operate as an application, an *Application Framework* is needed. Each *Component* (CO) and *Hosting Node* (HN) has an unique Identifier, a Profile and associated Metadata. Specifically, HN identifies the hardware devices providing computational and storage capabilities while CO identifies the software package delivering a set of related functionalities. Both have a *Profile*. The HN profile is tailored to report the hardware architecture, the operating system, the environment, the available storage, and the installed software packages. The CO Profile contains a description tailored to simplify a correct and appropriate use of it. A CO can interact with other COs to deliver its functionality, either hosted on the same HN or not. In addition, when deployed a component may have a *Status* that expresses set of values of all the parameters that define its condition. The Application Framework models the environment each CO is conceived to work in. It defines CO *Structure*, *Type* and *Interface* to which other COs have to conform to interact.

3.3   The RI Application Developer Perspective

The RI Application Developer perspective concerns the actors in charge of extending the RI ICT services and applications implementing the hooks to connect a RI. This activity is performed by exploiting the APIs. The RI Application Developers do not know the SciRepo internals, rather they perceive it throughout its lower layered component: the *Hooking Layer* component. This component is the enabling core component of the SciRepo Platform, it is the bridge connecting any RI service to SciRepo capabilities and it is in charge of populating the SciRepo content automatically during the research life-cycle (without scientists being directly involved in the actual action of publishing). The RI developer interacts with the Hooking Layer by implementing specific RI programs/scripts, namely hooks. An *Hook* reacts to RI events (e.g. dataset creation) by calling the Hooking Layer API to transform these events in meaningful information (e.g. dataset deposition in SciRepo). Figure 7 shows the concepts and relationships of the model that represent the SciRepo from the RI Application Developer perspective. The Hooking Layer provides *functionality* acting on the *Information Space*, which is modelled by a graph (similarly to a classic entity relationship diagram) and all of this is regulated by policies. In the following we present the concepts and relationships of the model starting from the and Information Space, Functionality, User and Policy main concepts.

The *Information Space* within this perspective is modelled as a *Graph* similarly to a classic entity relationship diagram. The Hooking Layer API eventually acts on the SciRepo *Information Space*, for this reason the RI Application Developer needs to have a proper knowledge of the concepts behind this graph, which is certainly one of SciRepo main features. Information Objects can be tagged with labels, for contextualising them in the RA domain. In fact, a *Label* is an optional addition to the graph that allows to group Information Objects into sets. All Information Objects labeled with the same label belongs to the same set. An Information Object node may be labeled with one or more labels. *The Relationship* concept models directed and, semantically qualified connections between two or more Information Objects. A relationship always has a direction, a type, a start and and end Information Object.

The RI Application Developer invokes the Hooking Layer functionalities by exploiting the API exposed by them. As Fig 7 shows the RI Application Developer functionality can be classified in two categories: *Access & Discovery* and *RPs Management*. The *Access* class enables the identification of RAs and their RPs. It comprises the functionality allowing the "programmatic" discovery of

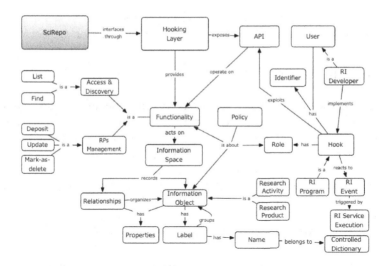

Fig. 7. The RI Application Developer perspective

and the access to of these objects. The *Find* function allows to look for existing Information Objects and obtain relevant information about them, i.e. RA/RP object instances containing properties characterising them. The *List* function provides access to a listing of existing Information Objects the hook is entitled to operate with. The *RPs Management* enables to populate the SciRepo content. It comprises the functionality allowing the deposit, the update and the deletion of RPs. The *deposit* function implements the automatic deposition of RPs and can be implemented either as a copy of the object generated in the RI or a registration of the object that links the SciRepo virtual object to the physical object at access time. The *update* function allows to modify an already existing RP and is associated with accessibility policies that regulate who and under which condition can update them. The *mark-as-delete* function allows to mark an existing RP for deletion. This is needed to handle cases where, for some reason, a deposit operation went wrong.

The *User* dimension within the Hooking Layer is represented by the actors entitled to implement programs interacting with it. Fig 7 shows the part involving the user concept map. Each User (*i*) is a RI developer who implements hooks (these exploits the API to enact the exposed functionalities), (*ii*) must be an identified user of the SciRepo and must possess the required credentials to access it, and (*iii*) has a *Role* that defines on which functionality and research activity he/she can operates on.

Policies are the mechanism used to regulate and restrict the Hooking Layer, and consequently the SciRepo, access and usage to authorised developers. Even in this case, for modelling the access control we used the RBAC approach. It is important to notice that within this perspective Roles are associated to hooks and not to users (since they are the entities using the functionalities). Therefore, each hook has an identifier in a SciRepo, and is associated to a Policy which defines what functionality it can use and on what Information Object.

4   Conclusions and Future Works

Science is in continuous evolution, so are the practices and approaches characterising it. This evolution is stimulated by new opportunities offered by technology development, e.g. the Web, the social networking, and cloud services are having impact on the daily activity of anyone. In this paper we described SciRepo, an innovative platform that is conceived to promote scholarly communication practices compliant with *open science* settings and expectations. SciRepo is designed to be easily integrated on top of existing ICT infrastructures and services to provide its community with a rich array of facilities enabling an holistic, comprehensive and "real" access to a research activity. In particular, we have presented the set of unifying principles, concepts and relations among concepts characterising this typology of platform, i.e. a *Reference Model*. According to this model, every SciRepo is described by the "content" it manages (Research Activities and Products), the "functionalities" it enables, the "users" it serves, the "policies" governing access rights, and the "architecture" of its software system. The model is described by using three complementary perspectives: the end-user, the administrator and the developer one. This model build upon previous experiences and its effectiveness is demonstrated by exploiting a system compliant with it in multiple contexts [3].

By design, a Reference Model is "just" the first step of a process leading to one or more concrete implementations of software systems realising it. Next steps will be to formalise a Reference Architecture describing an abstract solution for implementing the Reference Model, to instantiate this architecture by selecting concrete standards and technologies, and, finally, to produce a software system actually implementing it. This process will not start from scratch. It will be implemented by re-engineering, consolidating and extending the homologous facilities offered by gCube [3].

References

1. Assante, M.: Science 2.0 Repositories. PhD thesis, Doctoral School of Engineering, University of Pisa, June 2015
2. Assante, M., Candela, L., Castelli, D., Manghi, P., Pagano, P.: Science 2.0 Repositories: Time for a Change in Scholarly Communication. D-Lib Magazine **21**(1/2), January 2015
3. Assante, M., Candela, L., Castelli, D., Pagano, P.: Social Networking Research Environment for Scientific Data Sharing: The D4Science Offering. The Grey Journal **10**(2), 65–71 (2014)
4. Bardi, A., Manghi, P.: Enhanced publications: Data models and information systems. LIBER Quarterly **23**(4) (2014)
5. Bartling, S., Friesike, S.: Towards another scientific revolution. In: Opening Science, pp. 3–15. Springer International Publishing (2014)

6. Bechhofer, S., De Roure, D., Gamble, M., Goble, C., Buchan, I.: Research objects: Towards exchange and reuse of digital knowledge. Nature Precedings (2010)

7. Berman, F., Wilkinson, R., Wood, J.: Building global infrastructure for data sharing and exchange through the research data alliance. D-Lib Magazine **20**(1/2) (2014)

8. Bourne, P.E., Clark, T., Dale, R., de Waard, A., Herman, I., Hovy, E.H., Shotton, D.: Improving the future of research communication and e-scholarship. Force11 white paper, Force11 (2012)

9. Candela, L., Castelli, D., Manghi, P., Tani, A.: Data journals: A survey. Journal of the Association for Information Science and Technology (2015)

10. Candela, L., Castelli, D., Pagano, P.: Virtual Research Environments: an Overview and a Research Agenda. Data Science Journal **12** (2013)

11. de Castro, P., Shearer, K., Summann, F.: The Gradual Merging of Repository and CRIS Solutions to Meet Institutional Research Information Management Requirements. Procedia Computer Science **33** (2014)

12. Hand, E.: Citizen science: People power. Nature **466**, 685–687 (2010)

13. Hey, T., Tansley, S., Tolle, K.: The Fourth Paradigm: Data-Intensive Scientific Discovery. Microsoft Research (2009)

14. Hinsen, K.: Activepapers: a platform for publishing and archiving computer-aided research. F1000Research **3**(289) (2015)

15. Lagoze, C., Edwards, P., Sandvig, C., Plantin, J.-C.: Should i stay or should i go? alternative infrastructures in scholarly publishing. International Journal of Communication **9** (2015)

16. Manghi, P., Bolikowski, L., Manola, N., Schirrwagen, J., Smith, T.: OpenAIRE-plus: the european scholarly communication data infrastructure. D-Lib Magazine **18**(9/10) (2012)

17. Novak, J.D., Gowin, D.B.: Learning How to Learn. Cambridge University Press (1984)

18. Thelwall, M., Kousha, K.: ResearchGate: Disseminating, communicating, and measuring scholarship? Journal of the Association for Information Science and Technology **66**(5), 876–889 (2015)

On-Demand Integration and Linking of Open Data Information

Nuno Lopes[(✉)], Martin Stephenson, Vanessa Lopez, Pierpaolo Tommasi,
and Pól Mac Aonghusa

IBM Research, Smarter Cities Technology Centre, Dublin, Ireland
{nuno.lopes,martin_stephenson,vanlopez,ptommasi,aonghusa}@ie.ibm.com

Abstract. This paper introduces an extension of DALI, a framework for
data integration and visualisation. When integrating new data, DALI
automatically tries to recognise the schema and contents of the file,
semantically lift them, and annotate them with existing ontologies. The
extension presented in this paper allows users to import data from external data portals, namely portals using CKAN or Socrata, based on the
results of a search query or by selecting individual datasets. Furthermore, we perform a semantic expansion of the search terms provided by
the user in order to identify datasets that might still be relevant while
not containing the exact search terms.

1 Introduction

The amount of data being shared as Open Data is increasing everyday, from
high-level governmental data to very detailed city management activities [1].
Most governments now follow an open data policy and share their data using *portals* [2], for example the United States of America shares its data in the Data.gov
portal,[1] while other cities use similar approaches, e.g. New York[2] and Dublin.
Commonly used frameworks for these data portals include CKAN,[3] Socrata,[4]
and Dublinked.[5] An overview and statistics of CKAN and Socrata repositories
across North America is presented in [1]. With this abundance of Open Data
there have been several proposals to automatically integrate it, possibly with
other enterprise data, however the task of finding relevant datasets from the
different data portals is, so far, mostly overlooked.

In this paper we rely on our previous system: DALI [3]. DALI is a platform to
semantically lift, annotate, catalogue and query highly heterogeneous datasets
stored in tabular files, such as those published by cities, or in their original
enterprise relational systems. In DALI, a user is capable of integrating, lifting
and visualising the different datasets that are available. However, in its current

---

[1] http://www.data.gov/
[2] https://nycopendata.socrata.com/
[3] http://ckan.org/
[4] http://www.socrata.com/
[5] http://www.dublinked.ie/

© Springer International Publishing Switzerland 2015
E. Garoufallou et al. (Eds.): MTSR 2015, CCIS 544, pp. 312–323, 2015.
DOI: 10.1007/978-3-319-24129-6_27

version, adding datasets to DALI is only possible if the users already know the location of these new datasets. This approach leaves the burden of finding relevant portals and datasets to the user, requiring them to perform these operations externally to DALI, in each of the portals that may contain relevant information.

The contribution of this paper is two-fold: (i) discovering relevant datasets from different open data portals; and (ii) attempting to overcome differences between the metadata terms and the provided search terms. Regarding (i) we present an extension of DALI that allows users to search across different portals and portal solutions (CKAN, Socrata, and Dublinked) for relevant datasets and automatically integrate them in DALI. The objective is to allow users to add open data portals and allow them to search across these registered portals for any datasets that are relevant for their use case, without requiring importing all of the contents of the external repositories. For (ii) we also perform a semantic expansion of the query provided by the user, thus extending the search terms and attempting to find other relevant (semantically related) datasets.

Throughout this paper we will use the example of building a network of care coordination, called a *Safety Net*, and further introduced in Section 4. Once a portal (or some of its contents) are registered in the system, they are also *monitored*: if there is any change in the dataset in the remote portal, the respective stored metadata is updated to the new version and DALI (or any other user of the system) will be notified of this change.

The remainder of this paper is structured as follows: Section 2 presents the related work and Section 3 describes the necessary background information (namely the different data portals and DALI). Section 4 presents our specific use cases and Section 5 describes our approach for monitoring the different data portals. Some conclusions and possible future work are presented in Section 6.

2   Related Work

To the best of our knowledge, no other work tackles the problem of searching data across different portals. This discovery phase is commonly assumed on top of exactly one existing data portal with proper metadata available e.g. by directly exploiting CKAN capabilities [4]. Our own previous work, DALI [3,5] allows users to work with datasets that they know beforehand but does not tackle the problem of searching data portals.

Other available tools are UrbanProfiler and Data Near Here. UrbanProfiler [6] is a tool capable of extracting information about the content of the datasets, and creating a catalogue that can be used to support rich discovery queries over the data. Data Near Here [7] is a discovery tool initially designed for oceanographic data which applies Infrared spectroscopy to provide ranked search of (mostly) numeric data. Both UrbanProfiler and Data Near Here rely on the assumption that datasets of interest are already well-known and made available to the tool. In our work, we aim to discover datasets not yet known to the system, and then exploit the semantic capabilities of DALI to explore them.

3 Preliminaries

In this section we will briefly introduce the underlying data portals that are most commonly used and present DALI, our approach for integrating and linking the different datasets.

3.1 Data Portals

As briefly mentioned before the most relevant data portals are CKAN and Socrata. We also describe Dublinked, a data portal initiative for Dublin.

CKAN. CKAN is an open-source data management portal that allows to publish and share data. Data publishers can upload their data for sharing in a variety of formats, specify the respective metadata information, and CKAN will act as storage for this data while also providing versioning support. It includes a default user interface for browsing the data (faceted search), including different types of visualisation (search, geospatial, etc) for its contents. For the most part, CKAN relies on the specified metadata however, for certain types of structured information (e.g. CSV or spreadsheets), it will provide forms of querying the contents of the data in order to allow users to more efficiently locate and retrieve the relevant data. CKAN also exposes the data via a RESTful JSON API that allows to query and search the data, including possible download links for its contents, usage statistics, and list of recent changes.[6]

Data uploaded into CKAN is logically organised as *datasets* and *resources*. Datasets usually correspond a specific topic, for instance "Hospitals in Dublin", and contain the respective metadata describing its contents and a set of resources. Resources contain the actual data: the documents that are uploaded into the system for storage and sharing.

Socrata. Socrata is a commercially supported solution for storing and publishing data. Following a similar approach to CKAN, data managers can upload their datasets, specify the respective metadata and Socrata automatically provides the data exploration interfaces. Furthermore, Socrata provides real-time usage statistics and aims at leveraging social aspects to promote civic engagement with the published data.

In Socrata each uploaded data file corresponds to a different dataset and it focuses mostly on structured (tabular) data. Although Socrata supports other formats, its more advanced search and query features are only available for tabular data.

Socrata also exposes its data via a set of RESTful APIs, named SODA (Socrata Open Data API), and provides bindings for several programming languages.[7] Each *dataset* in Socrata is made available via a unique endpoint API,

---

[6] For this work we are relying heavily on the CKAN API and further information can be found at http://docs.ckan.org/.

[7] Further information can be found at http://dev.socrata.com/.

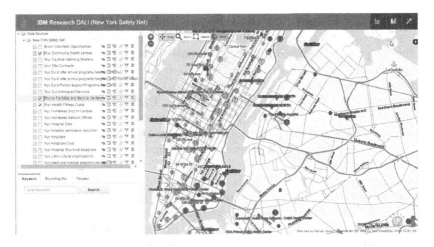

Fig. 1. DALI user interface

and each *row* in the dataset can also be accessed via an API endpoint. Simple searches over the datasets can be performed via the SODA API, while more advanced queries over the data can be specified in the Socrata Query Language (SoQL), an SQL-like query language. For this paper we are not considering querying specific rows of Socrata datasets and thus we rely only on the dataset metadata.

Dublinked. Dublinked is a data portal with special focus on the city of Dublin, enabling collaboration between industry, public sector, and academia to address data-driven challenges and promote economic activity.

Since the initiative was launched in 2011, the range and number of datasets published has increased to over 300 datasets and data providers have expanded beyond the Local Authorities to also include national bodies and datasets from private sector e.g. Dublin City Business Improvement Districts pedestrian footfall data.

Dublinked follows a similar approach to CKAN, where datasets group information regarding a common topic, and may contain several resources (the files containing the data). The data is freely available via an XML-based API.

3.2 DALI

DALI (Data Access Linking & Integration) is a system that exploits Linked Open Data (LOD) to provide federated entity search and spatial exploration across different information sources containing Open and Enterprise, including data pertaining to cities, stored in tabular files or in their original enterprise database systems. DALI exposes all of its functionality as RESTful APIs, and it also has a web based UI that exercises these APIs (shown in Figure 1). Using DALI's interface, users can select from the list of previously imported datasets, the ones that they want to visualise in the map. Users can also filter the existing datasets (e.g., using a faceted filtering) and, once a dataset is displayed on the map, they can select a bounding box to show only relevant entities. Figure 3a (on page 321) shows the previously available interface that allows users to integrate new datasets into DALI. This required users to know the URL of the dataset to be imported into DALI and include it in the "Dataset Integration" dialog. To realise the described functionalities, DALI performs two main tasks: (i) raw tabular data is ingested and lifted into a semantic layer; (ii) entities and relations from the semantic layer are automatically annotated and aligned to LOD vocabularies and resources.

The main architecture of DALI is described in [3] and is composed of (i) a list of available *input datasets*; (ii) a *semantic layer* that provides a virtualised view of the datasets in the relational databases; (iii) a centralised triple store (*context store*) ; and (iv) the *application server* that semantically uplifts entities from open and enterprise data to specified ontologies.

Each *input dataset* is represented and stored in a relational database, while the *semantic layer* enables de-coupling from this underlying representation of each source by using virtual RDF. There is added value in having a semantic representation on top of a relational one, in terms of improving data quality without adding too much overhead when converting CSV to a simple database schema. The datatypes in the input datasets are determined by examining the data: numbers, booleans, date values are converted into the correct format. We use -ontop- Quest [8] as a virtualisation technology, although, due to our flexible architecture, we can use many different types of SPARQL endpoints (e.g., interfacing directly to other triple stores, or other virtualised Enterprise DBs).

For each dataset in the virtualised RDF repositories, we extract schema information and store it in the centralised *context store* to create a richer representation: types, datatypes and object properties, and their set of possible instances, domains and ranges. For indexing purposes, we also include the labels of the instances in case they are known. Whenever possible, we reuse popular vocabularies, such as W3C Dublin core, and external sources to annotate the data, providing global meaning and common anchors across otherwise isolated data sources, without requiring the creation of a common model. We use the Integrated Public Service Vocabulary (IPSV) used by UK public sector organisations, schema.org, the general-purpose WordNet dictionary and DBpedia, which provides a wide domain coverage and geographical information. Specialist domain-knowledge models can also be used according to the use case.

For each dataset class in the context store, we use index searches and string similarity metrics [9] on the local name or label to annotate classes and properties with URIs found in the external sources used as annotators, as well as to find owl:sameAs links across instances. Annotations capture the meaning of entities across datasets and make explicit how entities are connected. Therefore they are used to improve dataset and entity search by: (i) improving user keyword searches by extending the keywords to also using the semantic annotations, thus finding entities that match the keywords both syntactically or semantically;

(ii) thematic cataloguing of the datasets based on a user selected model (e.g., IPSV), the datasets are automatically organised into a hierarchical view of sub-categories in the reference model when the entity representing the dataset type (topic) is annotated with the model; and (iii) identifying other datasets closely related to given one, based on finding datasets with annotations in common or semantically linked to the annotations of the given one.

4 Use Case Description

As a use case for this paper we will rely on the use of available open data about a city in order to build a *Safety Net*: a knowledge graph that supports care for seniors, homeless, and their families in New York City. A Safety Net aims to include a list of all known care services, their characteristics and connections for a target vulnerable population and area. This concept is highly relevant to the area of Integrated Care [10].

In order to build a Safety Net we can connect several sources for social and health related services but, for this paper, we focus on the data available in two data portals: the New York City Open Data Portal, which is using Socrata as their backend, and the Data.gov portal that publishes data from the United States federal government and is using CKAN as a backend.

Consider a version of the Safety Net that is available in DALI,[8] in which care workers can locate and explore facilities that their patients require. For a specific case, for instance when searching for treatment facilities for a home-less person with Post-traumatic stress disorder (PTSD), relevant data may not be available in DALI beforehand. Currently, in order to use DALI to explore data, the care worker must first find the relevant datasets in either the NYC or Data.gov open data portals and then specify the location of the data for integration. Furthermore, the care worker would possibly have to try different search strings (e.g. "ptsd", "post traumatic stress disorder", etc) in both data portals to find all the relevant data. By using our proposed extension to DALI, the care worker can conveniently search (from the DALI interface) the different data portals that are configured in the system. Additionally our semantic search terms expansion enables a more efficient search experience for the care worker by avoiding the need to perform multiple searches.

5 Monitoring Open Data Portals

The main objective of this work is to provide capabilities to monitor changes (uploads of new datasets or update of existing ones with new information) in existing data portals, in way that is transparent to the user and also indepen-dent of the different underlying data portal used. Furthermore, to overcome possible mismatches of search terms, we introduce a step of expansion of the search terms, where we not only search for the terms provided by the user but

---

[8] a video can be seen in: https://www.youtube.com/watch?v=FxpOq-Sr3Zs

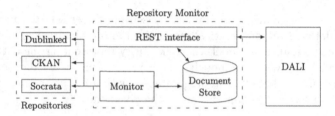

Fig. 2. Simplified architecture

also for other related terms. At this stage we are performing this searching and monitoring using a centralised store that is periodically updated. This approach also improves the runtime performance by avoiding to search directly over the different repositories but possibly introducing slightly outdated results.

5.1   Architecture

A simplified architecture for the system we are describing is included in Figure 2, including the different components of the system. In order to store the retrieved metadata we are relying on a *document store*, which provides us with the flexibility to represent the metadata of the different portals considered (while catering for their differences in the concept of dataset, c.f. Section 3.1). For our specific case we are using Elasticsearch[9] but any document store can be used.

The *Monitor* is responsible for updating the data in the document store by periodically retrieving the metadata from the external portal and determining if any of the datasets was updated. The *REST interface* is how we expose the functionalities of our system to users and allow them to manage the portals that are registered and specify what datasets and searches should be monitored. The connection to DALI relies mostly on performing searches and marking which datasets DALI is indexing and integrating. When a change is detected in the external dataset, DALI is notified in order to update its indexed version.

Stored Information. For the information retrieved from the external portals we are interested in the following:[10]

$$portal(id,\ location,\ type,\ should\_index,$$
$$updating,\ last\_updated, searches),$$

where *id* is an automatically generated (internal) identifier for the portal, *location* and *type* are the URL and the type (CKAN, Socrata, Dublinked) of the portal, respectively. Other stored information includes if the full metadata of the portal should be indexed and other internal information to determine if the portal is currently being indexed and the date of its last update. Finally, *searches* contains

---

[9] https://www.elastic.co/products/elasticsearch
[10] For simplicity we are representing "schema" information as tuples.

a list of search terms that are monitored for this portal (further detailed in the following section).

In order to abstract from the different data representations of portals (as mentioned in Section 3.1), we chose to define *items* of portals (which in the case of CKAN or Dublinked can be datasets or resources, while for Socrata these will be only datasets). As such, the items we store contain the following information:

$$item(item\_id, dataset\_id, external\_id, type, is\_monitored,$$
$$title, descripton, timestamp, created, notes, license),$$

where *item_id* is an internal identifier for the item, *external_id* is the identifier of the item (dataset or resource) in the remote portal, and *type* is the dataset's type: dataset or resource for CKAN and Dublinked and dataset for Socrata. In case the item represents a resource, the *dataset_id* field will contain the (external) identifier of the dataset it belongs to. For each item, we store its metadata, as provided by the external APIs, including *title, description, timestamp* of the last update and the timestamp it was *created,* and also the *license* text if present.

Types of Monitoring. In order to monitor a data portal, they must first be configured into the system. This is also performed via a REST API, which creates the respective *portal* record in the document store. The information necessary to register a portal consists only of the URL of the data portal and its type (CKAN, Socrata, or Dublinked) and an indication if the metadata of all the resources of the portal should be indexed.

We consider different types of monitoring of the external data portals: *full, search* based, and *fine-grained.* In the full monitoring case, all the metadata of the external portal is retrieved and stored in the local document store, creating a different record for each dataset (and possibly resource) in the data portal. Using this type of indexing, one clear advantage to the users is the ability to perform searches over the metadata of different portals from a centralised location.

In the case of fine-grained monitoring, the full contents of the data portal are not indexed but the users can specify what datasets and/or resources they are interested in monitoring and be notified of any changes.

The final type of monitoring a portal is by monitoring the results of a search (either across all the registered portals or a subset of these). For each result of the search query, a specific *item* record is created and marked for future monitoring. Furthermore, during the periodic update of the contents of the document store, the registered searches are also refreshed. As such, any new dataset that may have been added to the portal since the initial search was performed and matches the registered query or any existing dataset that a change in its metadata caused it to match the query, is also stored as a monitored dataset.

5.2   Semantic Search Terms Expansion

Full-text Elasticsearch is used to discover datasets matching the users keyword searches over some of the metadata fields. To bridge the gap between the vocabulary used by the user and the datasets titles and descriptions, the general purpose Linked Data ontologies (DBpedia, schema.org), dictionaries (WordNet) and domain models (IPSV) used to annotate the data in DALI, as explained in Section 3.2, are also used to expand the user query with lexically and semantically related words.

Following our use case example, the care worker may be concerned about the safety in the area where her homeless patient sleeps at night and searches for data using the keywords "antisocial behaviour". Public Safety datasets were not included in DALI Safety Net, thus the user needs to find relevant open datasets to be integrated. To discover them, the search query is annotated with terms URIs in the selected target models. In this case the query will be annotated with the DBpedia URI http://dbpedia.org/resource/Anti-social_behaviour and the IPSV term for "Antisocial behaviours and disorders" (http://id.esd.org.uk/subject/568). These set of Linked Data URIs enables us to uniquely identify topics and to access more information about them, fully reusing the Web-wide wealth of resources, rich in meaning and structure. The query terms are then semantically expanded by inferring new related terms along meaningful relations for the annotations, such as taxonomical relations *skos:broader/narrower* (e.g., for IPSV), *hypernyms* and *hyponyms* (e.g. for WordNet), and other type of semantic properties denoting alternative words, such as DBpedia *redirects*, *dcterms:subject*, *owl:sameAs*, etc. For each selected model, the set of relevant properties can be easily configured. In our example, the related terms are: "vandalism", "drug use and abuse", "young offending", "litter", "antisocial tendencies", "public order crime", among others.

While semantic expansion improves recall by retrieving good semantic matches, even if they are syntactically dissimilar, the results are often affected by the quality of the annotations, noisy mappings and ambiguous lexically related words. It may also produce too many results for the users to practically explore all of them. Therefore, the datasets with the best results (i.e., the more accurate semantic matches) should be ranked first, enhancing the precision of the results the user is likely to check. Datasets are ranked using a weighted sum of their matches, where the weight function is composed of (i) a syntactic average score that is given to each match (annotation), and (ii) a semantic score obtained for the dataset:

$$S_{c\_dataset} = \sum_i avg(W_{matches}) \times \frac{common\_annotations}{total\_annotations} \ ,$$

where *common_annotations* is number of annotations in common between the user query and the dataset description and *total_annotations* is the total number of annotations in the dataset description.

Syntactically, DALI assigns a confidence score to each annotation based on string distance metrics between the query term and the localname or label of URIs found in the external sources used to annotate the term (e.g., Jaccard, Jaro, Levenshtein [9]), assigning higher scores to exact matches over partial or approximate matches. When using the annotations to semantically expand the query, a higher weight is given to alternative terms (synonyms) vs. other taxonomical relations (e.g., hypernyms/ hyponyms).

(a) Integration of a dataset in DALI   (b) Data portal searching in DALI

Besides string similarity, the structure of the external ontologies and models can be used to disambiguate and assign a semantic confidence score to a candidate dataset. As part of the metadata most datasets contain small text descriptions, off-the-shelf named entity extractors, such as the DBpedia Spotlight service [11] or Alchemy API,[11] are used at indexing time to extract further metadata about the datasets by extracting entities from the unstructured text. At execution time, the system checks if the entities extracted from the dataset descriptions and the annotations for the user query terms are semantically close in the original graph. Using the given example, for a candidate dataset with the description "The number of incidents involving a stabbing and/or slashing and the associated DBpedia entities "stabbing" and "cutting", the entity "stabbing" is connected to the lexically related term "vandalism" in DBpedia (through the dcterms:subject and skos:broader relations to the parent DBpedia term "Category:Violence").[12] Like that, for each dataset a semantic score can be assigned considering the number of dataset annotations in common (or linked) with the query term annotations out of the total annotations for the datasets.

In DALI new models can be added at any time. In a domain specific scenario, a further mechanism to improve precision is to experiment assigning more relevance to annotations obtained from particular models. For instance, in the Safety Net scenario a higher weight could be assigned to a social care model, such as the 211 taxonomy.[13] As a future work, the metadata indexed for each dataset can be extended with part of its content (for example, annotations on the column headers), to improve both recall and precision (ranking).

---

[11] http://www.alchemyapi.com/

[12] This linkage is explored to a maximum depth of 2, to obtain real time performance and also the correlation between resources quickly decreases after two connections.

[13] https://211taxonomy.org/

5.3   Connection to DALI

The integration of our proposed approach for searching data portals in DALI is done via a new option in the "Settings" menu (shown in Figure 3b). By using this option, users can search the previously stored datasets (from the different data portals), visualise the results from the different portals as a list, and select the ones they want to integrate into DALI.

The users can also choose to expand the provided search string (using the method described in the previous section) and, in this case, the search performed over the data portals will include all the strings that were expanded. In our use case example, if the care worker is searching for "ptsd" and selects the "Expand Term" option, the complete list of search terms will be: "post traumatic stress", "post traumatic stress reaction", "posttraumatic stress disorder", "post traumatic stress syndrome", "posttraumatic stress", and "ptsd".

If desired, the users also have the option of restricting their search to a subset of the available data portals by selecting them from the drop-down list shown in Figure 3b. By selecting a search result, the user is presented with more information about that dataset (title, description, data portal that contains it) and also has the option of importing it into DALI for semantic annotation (as briefly described in Section 3.2). When users select a dataset for importing, they are presented with the "Dataset Integration" dialog (from Figure 3a) with the respective URL location automatically inserted.

By using this option of searching for datasets the users also have the possibility of saving the search terms as a monitored query and, in case new results that match the query become available, they will be notified that the search has produced new results. Since the original datasets are monitored for changes, in case any dataset that has been integrated into DALI has changed, the users are also notified of this and offered the possibility of integrating the new changes. At this time, the update of datasets that have already been loaded will cause a deletion of the existing annotations and a complete reintegration.

6   Conclusion

This paper briefly described the DALI system for semantic lifting, annotation, and visualisation of datasets and presented an extension of DALI that simplifies the task of locating new datasets to be included in DALI. This extension allows users to transparently search across different open data portals (namely portals using CKAN, Socrata, or Dublinked backends) and directly integrate selected search results into DALI.

Using semantic search expansion also reduces the number of searches the users need to perform, attempting to avoid common misspellings of words or simply the use of different terms in different data portals. Focusing on the use case of a care worker attempting to locate PTSD treatment facilities we have described the simplified workflow of ingesting new datasets into DALI, highlighting the searches across different data portals. Furthermore, we presented a possible architecture of a system that monitors the data portals for new data or changes to existing data in order to keep DALI updated with its source data.

Future Work. As for future work for this extension, we intend to provide a complex searching to the users. Currently the users can search the data portals for datasets that contain the (possibly expanded) search terms, however more advanced search mechanisms would be useful, e.g. datasets not containing certain terms or a fuzzy search of the provided terms. An evaluation on the semantic ranking is also planned in comparison to the ranking provided by the external data portals, however, when searching across different portals, this ranking is no longer valid. Another possible future work is to reuse approaches that determine the percentages of datasets that are updated in a portal [12] in order to optimise the number of visits to each individual data portal or adapting a more fine-grained approach that achieves this at the dataset level.

References

1. Barbosa, L., Pham, K., Silva, C., Vieira, M.R., Freire, J.: Structured open urban data: understanding the landscape. Big Data **2**(3) (2014)
2. Kučera, J., Chlapek, D., Nečaský, M.: Open government data catalogs: current approaches and quality perspective. In: Kő, A., Leitner, C., Leitold, H., Prosser, A. (eds.) EGOVIS/EDEM 2013. LNCS, vol. 8061, pp. 152–166. Springer, Heidelberg (2013)
3. Lopez, V., Stephenson, M., Kotoulas, S., Tommasi, P.: Finding Mr and Mrs entity in the city of knowledge. In: Hypertext and Social Media (2014)
4. Kučera, J., Chlapek, D., Mynarz, J.: Czech ckan repository as case study in public sector data cataloging. Systémová Integrace **19**(2) (2012)
5. Lopez, V., Kotoulas, S., Sbodio, M.L., Stephenson, M., Gkoulalas-Divanis, A., Aonghusa, P.M.: QuerioCity: a linked data platform for urban information management. In: Cudré-Mauroux, P., Heflin, J., Sirin, E., Tudorache, T., Euzenat, J., Hauswirth, M., Parreira, J.X., Hendler, J., Schreiber, G., Bernstein, A., Blomqvist, E. (eds.) ISWC 2012, Part II. LNCS, vol. 7650, pp. 148–163. Springer, Heidelberg (2012)
6. Castellani Ribeiro, D., Vo, H.T., Freire, J., Silva, C.T.: An urban data profiler. In: 24th International Conference on World Wide Web Companion (2015)
7. Megler, V.M., Maier, D.: Data near here: Bringing relevant data closer to scientists. Computing in Science and Engineering **15**(3) (2013)
8. Rodriguez-Muro, M., Hardi, J., Calvanese, D.: Quest: effcient SPARQL-to-SQL for RDF and OWL. In: ISWC 2012 Posters & Demonstrations Track (2012)
9. Cohen, W.W., Ravikumar, P.D., Fienberg, S.E.: A comparison of string distance metrics for name-matching tasks. In: Information Integration on the Web (2003)
10. Kotoulas, S., Sedlazek, W., Lopez, V., Sbodio, M.L., Stephenson, M., Tommasi, P., Aonghusa, P.M.: Enabling person-centric care using linked data technologies. In: e-Health - For Continuity of Care - Proceedings of MIE2014 (2014)
11. Mendes, P.N., Jakob, M., García-Silva, A., Bizer, C.: Dbpedia spotlight: shedding light on the web of documents. In: I-Semantics 2011. ACM (2011)
12. Atz, U.: The tau of data: A new metric to assess the timeliness of data in catalogues. In: Conference for E-Democracy and Open Governement (2014)

On Bridging Data Centers and Publishers:
The Data-Literature Interlinking Service

Adrian Burton[1], Hylke Koers[2], Paolo Manghi[3]($\boxtimes$), Sandro La Bruzzo[3],
Amir Aryani[1], Michael Diepenbroek[4], and Uwe Schindler[4]

[1] Australian National Data Service, Melbourne, Australia
{adrian.burton,amir.aryani}@ands.org.au
[2] Elsevier, Amsterdam, The Netherlands
h.koers@elsevier.com
[3] Institute of Information Science and Technologies "A. Faedo" - CNR, Pisa, Italy
{paolo.manghi,sandro.labruzzo}@isti.cnr.it
[4] PANGAEA, Bremen, Germany
{mdiepenbroek,uschindler}@pangaea.de

Abstract. Although research data publishing is today widely regarded as crucial for reproducibility and proper assessment of scientific results, several challenges still need to be solved to fully realize its potential. Developing links between the published literature and datasets is one of them. Current solutions are mostly based on bilateral, ad-hoc agreements between publishers and data centers, operating in silos whose content cannot be readily combined to deliver a network connecting research data and literature. The RDA Publishing Data Services Working Group (PDS-WG) aims to address this issue by bringing together different stakeholders to agree on common standards, combine links from disparate sources, and create a universal, open service for collecting and sharing such links: the Data-Literature Interlinking Service. This paper presents the synergic effort of the PDS-WG and the OpenAIRE infrastructure to realize and operate such a service. The Service populates and provides access to a graph of dataset-literature links collected from a variety of major data centers, publishers, and research organizations. At the time of writing, the Service has close to one million links with further contributions expected. Based on feedback from content providers and consumers, PDS-WG will continue to refine the Service data model and exchange format to make it a universal, cross-platform, cross-discipline solution for collecting and sharing dataset-literature links.

1 Introduction

Driven by innovations in digital technology and off-the-shelf availability of cheap storage solutions, research data is becoming ever more prominent in the way that research is performed and in the way research findings are communicated. Research data holds a big promise, and improving the storing, sharing, and usage of data is seen by many as a powerful way to accelerate the pace of science, even fuel economic growth. As Neelie Kroes, then Vice-President of the European Commission responsible for the Digital Agenda put it: "Knowledge is the engine of our economy. And data is its fuel."

© Springer International Publishing Switzerland 2015
E. Garoufallou et al. (Eds.): MTSR 2015, CCIS 544, pp. 324–335, 2015.
DOI: 10.1007/978-3-319-24129-6_28

Challenges to realize the full potential of research data exist at different levels - from cultural aspects, such as proper rewards and incentives, to policy and funding, and to technology. The challenges are interconnected and impact a diversity of stakeholders - including researchers, research organizations, funding bodies, data centers, and publishers. It is essential that these stakeholders work together to address common issues and push the envelope. ICSU World Data Systems (ICSU-WDS) and the Research Data Alliance (RDA) provide useful forums for such collaborations, such as the Publishing Data Interest Group (IG). This IG addresses a range of issues in data publication from a holistic and cross-stakeholder perspective, acting as the umbrella of Working Groups (WGs) that deal with data bibliometrics, data publication workflows, cost recovery, and services. Among these WGs, the Publishing Data Services WG (PDS-WG) brings together different parties in the research data landscape (e.g. data centers and publishers) with the objective of creating "an open, freely accessible, web based service that enables its users to identify datasets that are associated with a given article, and vice versa" [1]. The vision is that of moving away from the large set of bilateral arrangements that characterizes the research eco-system today, towards establishing common standards and tools that sit in the middle and interact with all parties. Such a transition would facilitate interoperability between platforms and systems operated by the different parties, reduce systemic inefficiencies in the ecosystem, and ultimately enable new tools and functionalities to the benefit of researchers.

This paper presents the work carried out by PDS-WG in the realization of a Data-Literature Interlinking Service (referred to as "the Service" in the following) capable of supporting such a shift. In this process, the WG has joined forces with the OpenAIRE project[1] and infrastructure [10] in order to design, develop and deploy an operative and sustainable prototype of the Service. The Service has been conceived in such a way that its common data model and exchange format can be refined over time to become community-driven standards, balancing between the information that can be shared across data providers and the information that is needed by consumers of the Service.

2   The Need for a Data-Literature Interlinking Service

The most immediate benefit in establishing links between articles and data is to increase visibility and discoverability, thus bringing data (and articles) more to the forefront and stimulating re-use. In addition, by providing links to the scholarly literature, data can be put in the right context that is often necessary to reproduce findings or re-use data properly (see also [5]). Researchers across disciplines strongly support the notion that there is value is creating links between data and the literature, as testified by results from the PARSE.Insight study[2], which was carried out with the help of EU funding in 2008—2010 : 85% respond *"yes"* to the question *"Do you think it is useful to link underlying research data with formal literature"* [5]. However, what is also

---

[1] OpenAIRE, http://www.openaire.eu

[2] *PARSE.Insight project*, http://www.parse-insight.eu/

clear is that in order to be fruitful, such linking needs to be done properly, by means of infrastructural solutions, delivering agreed-on policies, formats, and tools [3]. For example, a recent study in the astronomical literature showed that more than 50% of links from articles to data using a hard-coded HTTP web address were broken after 15 years [6]. Many parties, in fact, are taking efforts to link up articles and data in a robust and future-proof way: A number of data repositories keep track of articles that cite, or refer to, their data; several publishers have some form of data-linking program to connect the articles they publish with relevant data hosted externally (see e.g. [7]); providers of bibliographic information are increasingly looking at data alongside the traditional article output; and organizations such as CrossRef, DataCite and OpenAIRE are developing systems to track or infer relationships between data and the literature (see also [8] for some examples of how data and literature publications are currently interlinked).

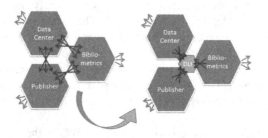

Fig. 1. Moving towards common standards and one-for-all services.

However, these initiatives typically live in isolation, and there is no common framework for inter-linking datasets and published articles. As a consequence, although different parties have a "piece of the puzzle", those pieces cannot be readily combined to exploit at best the potential of a rich and comprehensive network of published literature and data sets. The work of PDS-WG is seeking to tackle the comprehensiveness and interoperability challenges underlying this scenario by realizing an open and one-for-all Data-Literature Interlinking Service (Figure 1). The Service will serve as a flexible sandbox where major scholarly communication stakeholders interested in sharing or consuming dataset-literature links will be able to do so while reporting their requirements, preferences, recommendations, obstacles to the PDS-WG. Such an incremental approach will enable the refinement of exchange formats, data model, and aggregation workflows implemented by the Service and, in the long run, to agree on common practices for sharing dataset-publication links. The operation of the Service will bring the following benefits (adapted from [1]):

1. *For data repositories and journal publishers: it will make the process of linking data sets and research literature more scalable and with less overhead, ensuring more visibility for data sources (and their "customers") as well as publication platforms.*

2. *For research institutes, bibliographic service providers, and funding bodies: it will enable advanced bibliographic services and productivity assessment tools that track datasets and journal publications within a common framework;*

3. *For researchers: it will make the processes of sharing and accessing relevant articles and data easier, more efficient, and more accurate, thereby increasing scientific reward and enhancing its practices.*

2.1 Modus Operandi

Four key principles underpin the thinking and the work carried out in the PDS-WG. First, the challenge of developing an open, universal interlinking system is as much of a "soft" (social) problem as it is a "hard" (technical) problem. The WG has therefore invested a considerable amount of time and effort in building a broad base of support through communication and outreach activities. Today all of the groups that were identified as key stakeholders - including data centers, publishers, providers of bibliographical information, funding bodies, etc. - are supporting the initiative, be it through WG membership, contributing a corpus of article/data links, participating in the technical work, or a combination thereof. The initiative is open and inclusive[3] and additional participation by other groups or individuals will be welcomed.

Second, the WG is prioritizing its efforts towards building, a working prototype of the Service that can be used to demonstrate value to the intended users and stakeholder groups. This work is carried out in synergy with the OpenAIRE project and infrastructure, PANGAEA, and ANDS. As with any demonstrator system, coverage and functional scope are initially limited but the ambition is to develop a service that will be of direct value in real-world situations. The admittedly important set of questions around longer-term sustainability and governance of the Service is deferred to a later stage of the WG's lifetime. Specifically, a pragmatic, ground-up approach was followed: aggregate as many corpora of literature-data links as possible, harmonizing them into a common data model, and making them available online through an openly accessible Service.. That means that in the initial stage of operation the WG admits a considerable effort to ingest heterogeneous information from contributors. In the long run, the expectation is that the Service will help at establishing exchange standards that will reduce conversion costs and lead to a more scalable approach. To this aim the Service will enable a "test & learn" approach, by facilitating the extension of the common data model and schema over time.

Third, the WG takes a generic, one-size-fits-all (as opposed to e.g. domain-specific) approach as much as possible to avoid fragmentation and preserve the value that lies in developing a comprehensive solution for all articles and all datasets. This approach necessarily means that the Service common data model is relatively discipline-agnostic, leaving domain-specific metadata a responsibility of the data repositories.

Finally, the WG places significant emphasis on provenance, reliability, quality of data-literature links and the associated metadata, considered of great importance for most key use cases (e.g. linking from online publishing or data platforms, bibliometrical analyses). This principle is reflected in the Service operation, which ensures

---

[3] A set of "guiding principles" that includes statements on the open character of the project can be accessed through the WG's RDA website: https://www.rd-alliance.org/groups/rdawds-publishing-data-services-wg.html

that: (i) links are contributed by trusted sources, rather than inferred by the system, and (ii) the origin and completeness of links and metadata is tracked at a high level of detail and granularity.

2.2   Related Work

The ambition to develop a Data-Literature Interlinking Service is not unique, and there are a number of related initiatives. In particular, CrossRef and DataCite have announced they will be working on increasing interoperability between their systems to more easily expose article/data links in cases where both can be identified through DOI's. Other initiatives – though often broader in scope than "just" linking literature and data, for example including funder or researcher ID's – include the RMap project [11], the National Data Service[4], bioCADDIE[5], the Open Science Framework[6], and THOR[7]. In addition, there are several RDA WGs and IGs for which data-literature linking is also an important topic, most notably the Data Description Registry Interoperability (DDRI)[8] WG, which has developed RD-Switchboard.org[9]. Apart from its own development agenda, the PDS-WG aims to provide a forum for such initiatives to share and discuss their ideas, so as to avoid duplication, learn from each other, and cooperate.

3   The Data-Literature Interlinking Service

The Data Literature Interlinking (DLI) service ("the Service") aims to populate and provide access to the *DLI information space*, a graph of relationships between datasets and the literature, and between datasets and datasets. Objects and relationships are provided by data sources managed by publishers (e.g. Elsevier, Thomson Reuters), data centers (e.g. PANGAEA, CCDC), or other organizations providing services to manage links between datasets and publications (e.g. DataCite, OpenAIRE). The Service aggregates content and implements programmatic access (APIs) to the resulting information space. Such APIs offer full-text search by field or free keywords and bulk access to the collection (e.g. OAI-PMH protocol). They enable the construction of services on top of the Service (e.g. end-user search and statistics portal) and serve content to third-party community services (e.g. RD-Switchboard).

The Service is also intended as a flexible playground where data curator users can monitor the aggregation outputs, collect feedback from data providers and service consumers, and refine ingestion workflows and common data model accordingly. The expectation is that such incremental and agile methodology will converge to an ideal data model and exchange metadata format for description and exchange of links

---

[4] National Data Service, http://www.nationaldataservice.org/
[5] BioCADDIE, https://biocaddie.org/
[6] https://osf.io/
[7] THOR EC project, http://cordis.europa.eu/project/rcn/194927_en.html
[8] *DDRI*, https://www.rd-alliance.org/group/data-description-registry-interoperability.html
[9] See http://www.rd-switchboard.org/

between datasets and publications. The following sections present the functional requirements of the Service and the initial DLI information space data model.

3.1   Functional Requirements

Users of the Service. The Service will support four categories of users. *Data source managers*, serving content to the Service and willing to gain visibility and serve their user communities; *Portal end users* (e.g. researchers, funders, publishers, data centres), searching for datasets or publications via their relationships or for statistics regarding the provenance of objects and relationships; *Service data curators*, needing tools to monitor and orchestrate their data aggregation activities in order to guarantee an expected QoS; and *Third-party service developers*, willing to (bulk) collect the DLI information space to process and offer it to their users.

Aggregating Content from Data Sources. Data sources are intended as providers interested in feeding object-to-object relationships to the Service. Data sources deliver to the service so-called *metadata packages* (records) that encode the description of how a *source object* is interlinked via relationships to a set of *target objects*; objects are uniquely identified by a PID together with its namespace (e.g. DOI, PMCID, URL). Data sources can provide metadata packages according to three modalities: *pull*, i.e. the Service bulk-collects relationships via data source APIs; *push*, i.e. the data source sends relationships into the Service; or *resolution*, i.e. the Service collects content about one object and its relationships sending a PID to a data source resolver service. Data source resolvers (e.g. DataCite, CrossRef, PDB) are used to complete object metadata when this was not fully included in its original metadata package.

In the future, data sources should deliver metadata packages that conform to an exchange format and data model recommended by the DLI information space, the exchange format being entitled to become a standard for sharing dataset-literature links. In the initial stage of operation, the Service cannot expect data source to conform to such format. It must therefore provide mechanisms to map metadata packages, whatever native data model and format they conform to, onto objects and relationships conforming to the DLI information space data model.

De-duplication. Different data sources may provide duplicate information about the same objects and relationships: objects with the same PID-namespace from different sources or objects with different PID-namespaces (e.g. DOIs and PMCIDs) but corresponding to the same dataset or publication. The service will deliver de-duplication tools, capable of identifying groups of duplicates and merging them into one "representative" object. Representative objects will keep the PID-namespaces of the objects they merge and maintain a reference to their original data sources.

Publishing the Information Space Graph. The Service provides a web portal for end users to (full-text) search and browse relationships between datasets and publications and to visualize statistics on the distribution of such relationships (e.g. per data source, per type, etc.). Moreover, it supports OAI-PMH APIs to export the DLI information space towards interested third-party services. Looking ahead, the PDS-WG is working to connect the Service with a data-linking provision platform developed by

PANGAEA, and with an interactive network visualization tool developing in the context of RD-Switchboard (this will be discussed in more detail in section 4.3).

3.2   Data Model

The conceptual data model of the DLI information space is depicted in Figure 2. The model (as well as the corresponding exchange format defined in the following section) is intended as an initial starting point, but is bound to be refined, as new requirements from service stakeholders and consumers will surface. Objects can be of two types, *publications* (intended as scientific literature) or *datasets*.[10] Relationships between them are directed and bidirectional; e.g. if an object A has a relationship "isCitedBy" to an object B then also the inverse relationship "cites" will be found in the information space. Relationships bear semantics, expressed by a label that belongs to a given ontology (e.g. DataCite vocabulary), and may contain a *description* in order to encode and represent dataset annotations.

Items (i.e. objects and relationships) are into the system because either (*i*) they have been pulled from external providers, (*ii*) pushed by third-party services, or (*iii*) obtained by resolving a PID using a resolver service. In order to keep track of their provenance, items are equipped with *provenance information* that consists of a reference to the originating data source, the time of ingestion of the item into the system, and the modality of bringing the item into the system ("pull", "push", "resolved"). The field *completion_status* in object provenance tracks down whether the data source has contributed full object metadata description or only a PID-namespace. This way the Service can identify which objects are "incomplete" and should be subject to subsequent resolution attempts. When the same items are provided by different data sources (duplicates) and are merged together into one representative item to disambiguate the information space, then the resulting "representative" item keeps provenance information about all the items it merges.

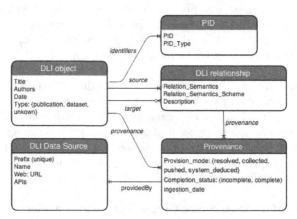

Fig. 2. Conceptual Data Model

---

[10] Currently, only title, authors and publication date fields are kept, but this choice may change in the future based on user or third-party service needs.

4   The Prototype

The Service prototype is powered by the D-NET Software Toolkit ([2]). D-NET is today the platform of production systems of several aggregation infrastructures (e.g. OpenAIRE, EFG/EFG1914, HOPE, EAGLE) and repository federations (e.g. CEON Poland, MINCYT Argentina, FECYT Spain). The software is devised to enable the construction and monitoring of aggregative data infrastructures, by orchestrating a set of highly configurable D-NET data aggregation services (and/or third-party web services) into autonomic workflows. For example, data storage is possible via relational databases (Postgres), XML databases (Exist), column stores (MongoDB, HBASE), full-text indices (Apache Solr) and remote file systems (GridFS); while data processing is available via general purpose services, such as XSLT engines, Groovy Engines, Hadoop MapReduce, which are highly configurable and already embed customizable algorithms for metadata transformation, de-duplication, and inference by (text)mining collected files or metadata.

The Service prototype implements an *aggregation system* and a *provision system* as described in the following sections. The prototype meets all requirements described in the previous sections, except for the following: (*i*) data sources are only of type "pull" and "resolution"; (*ii*) de-duplication is implemented only at the level of PID-namespace (i.e. provenance information does not include original PIDs), and (*iii*) the semantics of relationships is limited to the subset of DataCite (i.e. no support for multiple vocabularies): *references, cites, isSupplementTo, isReferredBy, isCitedBy, isSupplementedBy* and otherwise mapped onto the *unknown* value.

4.1   Content Aggregation System

The system handles (de)registration of data sources and aggregation of their content. Data sources register to the Service by submitting a profile describing their general properties (e.g. name, location, etc.) and technical interoperability properties (e.g. data collection APIs, data collection modality). Each registered data source is associated with an autonomic workflow (see Figure 3) that collects its metadata packages and processes them to populate the DLI information space.

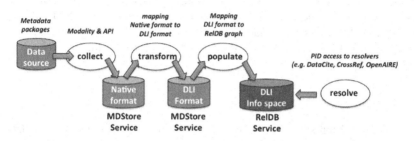

Fig. 3. Data source aggregation workflow.

To achieve this, the workflow makes use of D-NET's MetadataStore Service, Transformation Service, and RelationalDB Service. Initially, metadata packages are cached in their native format (e.g. XML, CSV, TXT), then transformed, given a set of mapping scripts, from such format onto an internal XML format called "DLI" (**Table 1**).

Table 1. DLI record structure

```
DLI_ID: % obtained as <PID_type>::<PID>
PID
PIDType: % from a vocabulary doi, PMCID, ncbin, pdb, etc.
authors
title
date
type: {publication, datasets, unknown}
provenance*
    providedBy_datasource
    provision_mode: {resolved, collected, pushed, system_deduced}
    ingestion_date
    completion_status: {incomplete, complete, failed_to_resolve}
        % incomplete => type, authors, title, and date fields
        % are empty
relationship*
    target_object_type: {publication, dataset, unknown}
    target_object_title  % to be used as anchor label
    target_object_PID:
    target_object_PIDType % doi, PMCID, others
    target_object_DLI_ID
    provenance*
        providedBy_datasource
        provision_mode: {resolved, collected, pushed,system_deduced}
        completion_status: {incomplete, complete, failed_to_resolve}
        ingestion_date
        relationship_completion_status: {incomplete, complete}
            % incomplete => type and title fields are empty
        semantics
            % from DataCite relationships vocabulary or "unknown"
```

The DLI exchange format includes all information described in the data model, but also introduces some redundancy in order to become self-explanatory (e.g. enabling interpretation of target objects without necessarily accessing them). A conclusive step will transform DLI records into objects and relationships of the graph, which are encoded as records of a relational database. The graph thus built may feature objects whose *completion_status* is *"incomplete"*. Accordingly, whenever an ingestion workflow terminates, the Service fires a resolution workflow, which finds such objects, identifies the respective resolver service based on the object PID namespace, and tries to fetch the missing metadata fields. The result of such operation, be it successful or not, is tracked by the system and ends up enriching the provenance information of the given objects.

4.2   Content Provision System

The content provision system consists of a workflow that is fired whenever data ingestion and resolution workflows are terminated. The workflow collects the information space graph from the RelationalDB Service, converts its objects onto DLI exchange format records (post duplicate identification and object resolution), and delivers them (in parallel) to a Full-text Index Service and an OAI-PMH Publisher Service. Users can search and browse the index from a portal available at http://dliservice.research-infrastructures.eu, while OAI-PMH APIs are available from http://dliservice.prototype.research-infrastructures.eu/oai. Currently, the prototype includes relationships and objects from the data sources reported in **Table 2**.

Table 2. Objects and relationships contributed by data source at the moment of writing. At the time of writing, the service holds 890273 dataset-literature links; further contributions from these and other sources to the PDS-WG are expected.

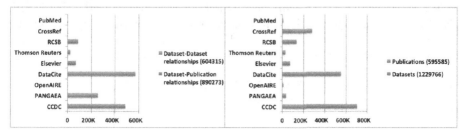

4.3   Forthcoming Actions

The prototype will be completed to allow "push" modality for data sources, introduce de-duplication across different PID-namespaces (using D-NET de-duplication Services [4]), modify the model in order to introduce relationships of type "annotations", and support more advanced access modalities to the Information Space. On this last matter, the PDS-WG is working to connect the Service to a linking service backbone under development by PANGAEA and to leverage network visualization tools developed in the context of the RD-Switchboard platform for a front-end demonstrator tool that allows users to explore the literature-data network. Finally, we expect additional contributions from organizations represented in the PDS-WG to substantially increase the number of literature-data links.

Upgrading to PANGAEA Provision System. The PANGAEA data center team is working to extrapolate the current PANGAEA linking service[11] into a generally usable linking service that will enhance the current Service content provision system. The service will offer PID-resolution APIs and be optimized for high-volume read access by science publishers and bibliometrics service providers. It will be based on Elasticsearch[12], hosted in the Amazon EC2 cloud, and will provide linking information and render metadata badges that can be embedded into article publisher's web pages to show linked data sets (see [7]). Based on this service, a new section of the portal will

---

[11] *Elsevier and PANGAEA Take Next Step in Connecting Research Articles to Data,* http://www.prnewswire.com/news-releases/elsevier-and-pangaea-take-next-step-in-connecting-research-articles-to-data-99533624.html. See also [7].

[12] Elasticsearch, https://www.elastic.co/products/elasticsearch

display linking statistics based on Elasticsearch aggregations using visualization features of Kibana[13].

Integration with RD-Swichboard. RD-Switchboard is an interoperability platform developed by ANDS in the context of DDRI-WG of RDA (Data Description Registry Interoperability), whose aim is to offer cross-platform discovery of related research datasets. The platform aggregates links between publications, datasets and research grants from national and international data services/centers (members of the DDRI-WG); then, it adopts graph-modeling techniques (e.g. exploiting co-authorship or related research projects) to identify missing links between related works. For example, RD-Switchboard has identified the datasets co-authored by Australian researchers in Dryad and CERN data repositories, and linked them to datasets in the Research Data Australia repository.

Fig. 4. Screenshot of the RD-Switchboard browser

As a result of the integration, the Service will benefit from RD-Switchboard's graph navigation and visualization tools (Force Directed Graph Drawing Algorithm [9], see Figure 4), while RD-Switchboard will profit from the rich set of literature-data links.

5   Conclusions

This paper described the work carried out in the context of the joint ICSU-WDS and RDA Working Group "Publishing Data Services" (PDS-WG) with the support of OpenAIRE. This WG has set out to create an open, universal Data-Literature Interlinking Service that aggregates, harmonizes, completes, and offers access to links between the scholarly literature and research data. The technical development reflects the WG's principles of openness, inclusivity, quality, provenance, domain-agnosticism – and, finally, a pragmatic, "ground-up" approach to develop software in a test-and-learn approach that allows for continuous refinement of the system and the underlying data model. By establishing this service, the PDS-WG aims to progress the field from the current situation of many ad-hoc, bilateral agreements (between e.g. a data center and a publisher) to realize a one-for-all service architecture with common standards to the benefit of all stakeholders in the research data landscape.

---

[13] Kibana, https://www.elastic.co/products/kibana

Acknowledgements. The authors would like to thank the PDS-WG members and representatives from CrossRef, DataCite, The National Data Service, ORCID, The Research Data Alliance, ICSU World Data Systems, and the RMap project for many valuable discussions and constructive interactions. This work is partially funded by the EU projects RDA Europe (FP7-INFRASTRUCTURES-2013-2, grant agreement: 632756) and OpenAIRE2020 (H2020-EIN FRA-2014-1, grant agreement: 643410).

References

1. Publishing Data Services Working Group Case Statement. https://www.rd-alliance.org/filedepot/folder/114?fid=239
2. Manghi, P., Artini, M., Atzori, C., Bardi, A., Mannocci, A., La Bruzzo, S., Candela, L., Castelli, D., Pagano, P.: The D-NET software toolkit: A framework for the realization, maintenance, and operation of aggregative infrastructures. Program: Electronic Library and Information Systems **48**(4), 322–354 (2014)
3. Castelli, D., Manghi, P., Thanos, C.: A vision towards scientific communication infrastructures. International Journal on Digital Libraries **13**(3–4), 155–169 (2013)
4. Manghi, P., Mikulicic, M., Atzori, C.: De-duplication of aggregation authority files. International Journal of Metadata, Semantics and Ontologies **7**(2), 114–130 (2012)
5. Smit, E.: Abelard and Héloïse: Why Data and Publications Belong Together. D-Lib Magazine **17** (2011). doi:10.1045/january2011-smit
6. Pepe, A., Goodman, A., Muench, A., Crosas, M., Erdmann, E.: How Do Astronomers Share Data? Reliability and Persistence of Datasets Linked in AAS Publications and a Qualitative Study of Data Practices among US Astronomers. PLOS One (2014). doi:10.1371/journal.pone.0104798
7. Aalbersberg, I.J., Dunham, J., Koers, H.: Connecting Scientific Articles with Research Data: New Directions in Online Scholarly Publishing. In: Proceedings of the 1st ICSU World Data Systems Conference (2011)
8. Callaghan, S., Tedds, J., Lawrence, R., Murphy, F., Roberts, T., Wilcox, W.: Cross-Linking Between Journal Publications and Data Repositories: A Selection of Examples. International Journal of Digital Curation (2014). doi:10.2218/ijdc.v9i1.310
9. Kobourov, S.G.: Spring embedders and force directed graph drawing algorithms. arXiv preprint arXiv:1201.3011 (2012)
10. Manghi, P., Bolikowski, L., Manold, N., Schirrwagen, J., Smith, T.: Openaireplus: the european scholarly communication data infrastructure. D-Lib Magazine **18**(9), 1 (2012)
11. The RMAP project, white paper. http://rmap-project.info/rmap/wp-content/uploads/RMap_Project_Overview_Revised_Final.pdf

Historical Records and Digitization Factors in Biodiversity Communities of Practice

Michael Khoo[1(✉)] and Gary Rosenberg[2]

[1] College of Computing & Informatics, Philadelphia, USA
khoo@drexel.edu
[2] Academy of Natural Sciences of Philadelphia, Drexel University, Philadelphia, PA, USA
rosenberg.ansp@drexel.edu

Abstract. A central aim of biodiversity informatics initiatives is the global aggregation of biodiversity data. This work depends significantly on the translation of local data and metadata into wider global standards. While this is often considered to be primarily a technical task, there are also organizational factors to consider. In this paper, we use a Communities of Practice approach to argue that data and metadata in individual departments and institutions has often adapted over time to meet local organizational contexts, and that digitization workflows need to account for and capture the historical dimensions of collections, to support productive data migration. As part of this work, the central role of curators' and managers' practical and everyday knowledge of their collections is emphasized.

Keywords: Biodiversity · Communities of practice · Data · Digitization · Metadata · Organizational knowledge

1 Introduction

The creation of centralized information infrastructures and repositories for biodiversity is an important task. Standardized descriptions of specimens, collections, environments and ecologies, etc., support activities such as global repositories [12], data-intensive ('big data') research [15], and the stewarding of global biodiversity resources [e.g. 6, 14, 22, 25]. The endeavor is large-scale. Worldwide, biodiversity institutions hold 2.5-3.0 billion specimens representing 1.75 million species [10], with 1 billion specimens in over 1,000 collections (natural history museums, universities, botanical gardens) in the United States alone [7]. Currently, it is estimated that only about 10 per cent of collection holdings are described online, and this includes online access at the institutional level rather than at a central facility [7, 10].

The work required to digitize existing collections, including imaging and metadata generation, is detailed and resource intensive, and the timelines for digitization initiatives stretch into the future. An ongoing concern is therefore with improving digitization workflows. This often focuses on technical issues, but in this paper we argue that organizational factors are also important, and contribute an organizational perspective

© Springer International Publishing Switzerland 2015
E. Garoufallou et al. (Eds.): MTSR 2015, CCIS 544, pp. 336–347, 2015.
DOI: 10.1007/978-3-319-24129-6_29

on digitization workflows that draws on theories of Communities of Practice (CoPs) [20, 33]. The framework helps to explain how biodiversity digitization involves not just technical but organizational and sociotechnical factors. There will always be significant aspects of digitization work that require human understanding and intervention, and workflows need to account for and develop tools that leverage this knowledge. To illustrate our argument, in this paper we review some digitization issues associated with historical labels. Through a case study, it is argued that old labels are not simply prior or simpler versions of current electronic database records, but different types of information artifacts, with characteristics specific to particular times and places. It requires higher-order knowledge of their history not contained in the labels themselves – that is, knowledge *of* the labels, as well as of the knowledge in the labels – to understand how to migrate them to new standards.

1.1   Biodiversity Informatics

Biodiversity research addresses the history and variety of forms of life on earth, for instance through taxonomics (the identification of organisms and their classification according to evolutionary relationships), nomenclature (the systematic naming of groups of organisms (taxa) according to established conventions), and ecology (the complex interactions of organisms with their environment, including other organisms, at particular times and places) [10]. Biodiversity research is increasingly data-intensive, and supported by biodiversity informatics, it aims to integrate, analyze, and visualize global biodiversity information [14]. An underlying component of biodiversity informatics is interoperable metadata such as Darwin Core [29].

The usefulness of biodiversity informatics systems is determined by their comprehensiveness, for instance in terms of temporal, geographical, and species coverage, and biodiversity informaticians seek to aggregate as many sources of data as possible, often from historical collections. This includes the digital imaging of objects such as specimens, and capturing existing metadata and/or creating new metadata in standards such as Darwin Core. Given the number of specimens requiring digitization it would be useful, for reasons of efficiency, scalability, and cost, to build reliable automated digitization workflows. This is seen as one of the 'grand challenges' of biodiversity informatics [10]. One important factor here is the widely heterogeneous nature of biodiversity collections. Globally, billions of specimens have been collected by thousands of researchers over several centuries, and there is a vast diversity in specimen types, preservation techniques, mounts and labels, descriptions, data and metadata formats, and other phenomena. Channeling this vast and unruly diversity into the relatively strict confines of standard metadata formats is not an easy task; however, digitization workflows have to be able to address this task at a very large scale.

Many biodiversity digitization issues are technical in nature. Imaging targets include a wide variety of specimen types, labels, and containers (boxes, vials, jars, etc.); there are OCR issues with labels, specimen sheets, and other documents, including handwriting in different languages dating back several centuries; it is difficult to parse and interpret the components of the OCR and map these to new metadata formats; and digitization tools need to be user friendly [e.g. 7, 9, 21, 24, 31]. We argue that in addition, the practical and organizational knowledge of biodiversity researchers (curators, collection managers, and others) also plays a crucial part in digitization (c.f. [16] on ontology building in archaeology). This includes not just the explicit and documented knowledge of physical collections such as scope, holdings, and data and metadata formats, but also unwritten tacit knowledge, such as the personalities of earlier collectors and organizational histories. To understand better this organizational knowledge, the rest of this paper focuses on a case study of factors associated with the digitization of historical specimens in a malacology collection.

1.2 Communities of Practice

To examine the role of organizational knowledge in biodiversity informatics, this study uses the theoretical perspective of Communities of Practice (CoPs) [20, 33]. CoPs are frequently glossed along the lines of 'groups of people engaged in a common task,' however the concept has considerable theoretical depth, particularly in relation to knowledge sharing. Knowledge in CoPs resides with more experienced members, who share their knowledge with novices when inducting them into the community. While knowledge sharing can take place through the medium of documents, it frequently occurs in and through practice, with experienced members showing new members what to do. The practical knowledge involved in 'showing' is often not formally or precisely documented, and thus when community members acquire organizational knowledge over time, this is often undocumented, practice-based, taken-for-granted, and hard to articulate. Even when documentation exists, practice can deviate from it. Wenger [33] discusses this in terms of a duality of participation and reification: participation is shaped by documentary artifacts that reify organizational procedures, and as practices evolve, procedures (and the documents that describe them) change, leading in turn to modified modes of participation, then modified documents, and so on. Knowledge in CoPs is therefore susceptible to change over time. In considering biodiversity institutions as CoPs, it can be seen how these processes can lead to the emergence of 'local' institutional practices that are customized local forms of wider biodiversity practices.

2   Setting and Methods

This study is part of research being conducted at the Academy of Natural Sciences of Philadelphia (ANSP) [3]. The 200 year-old ANSP collection of 18 million biological specimens is of global significance. Founded in 1812 in Philadelphia, the story of the Academy is in many ways the story of natural history in the United States, beginning with early independent collectors, followed by the emergence of natural history as a formal discipline in the nineteenth century, the adoption by natural history museums of public education missions, innovation in computing and database technologies in the 1970s and 1980s, and the adoption of the World Wide Web in the 1990s [26]. Currently, making ANSP collections accessible online requires the standardization of data fields at the institutional level, and the creation of Darwin Core metadata. ANSP data includes descriptions of specimens (mollusks, birds, moths, plants, fossils, etc.)

in terms of taxonomy and date and place of collection, and metadata includes descriptions of who collected, donated and identified the specimen, and when these actions occurred. In order to design institutional data management tools that usefully integrate these heterogeneous sources, it is necessary to understand how they can be standardized; and a CoP analysis can support this analysis by providing showing how historical and contemporary data is formatted. The research questions that are being addressed include:

- What evidence is there for historical and current CoPs at ANSP?
- What are their characteristics?
- What are the implications for metadata work?

The study reported in this paper looks at these questions in the context of an historical sequence of labels and catalog records in the Department of Malacology. It might be expected that each new record was an incremental improvement on the previous one, with earlier labels being simpler versions of later labels. However, as this study shows, this is not necessarily the case. Not only do the types of information being recorded on different labels vary, but there is no direct linear sequence, with some information not being migrated between labels. This information would be lost if not for the efforts of the current department staff.

2.1   Ethnographic Action Research

This study is part of an ethnographic action research project being carried out with the Malacology Department at ANSP [4, 5, 28]. Action research studies and shapes change in organizations through longitudinal theory building, practical intervention, and action-taking. Investigations and outcomes are mutually constituted over time in interactions between researchers and research subjects, and both contribute to the research outcomes. This study looks at the role of CoPs in biodiversity institutions, with practical interventions focused on how historical records might add new data and metadata to the Department's databases, and to Darwin Core. Activities include interviews with ANSP staff, observations of workplace practices, and observations in the collections and archives. The history of ANSP and natural history in the United States is also being studied. The data are being analyzed using a grounded theoretical approach, to identify CoPs and associated data practices. The results are being used to build CoP-informed models of organizational knowledge that can support data tool design. The results are being presented back to ANSP, for instance in 'brown bag' lunchtime discussions.

2.2   Data

The data includes detailed descriptions of labels from the Malacology Department's collection, which is the oldest and second largest in the United States [1]. The focus is on specimen 4295, *Pleurodonte lucerna sublucerna*, a Jamaican land snail (for a more detailed account of this specimen and associated labels, see [18]). The intent here is to show that these labels not successive versions of each other, but different types of artifacts, which require mediation, translation, and integration.

Fig. 1. 1860s. A. D. Brown's label - written in the 1870s?

Fig. 2. 1880s. Examples of historical labels from the malacology collection.

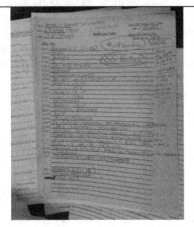

Fig. 3. EDP data entry sheets, c. 1970s.

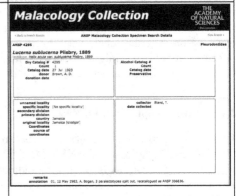

Fig. 4. Public front end for malacology department database.

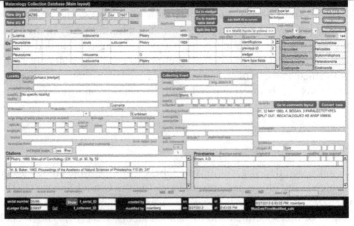

Fig. 5. Malacology department database. (This is intended to show some of the overall complexity of the database and not the details of the individual fields)

The oldest label (Fig. 1) was created in the mid-nineteenth century, perhaps the 1870s or 1880s, although when is not precisely known. This small label was handwritten not by an Academy staff member but by Albert Dod Brown (1841-1886), who donated his shell collection to ANSP in the 1880s (the label thus predates the donation). The label reflects the practices of independent natural historians of the time. There is no date of collection, and the location is simply 'Jamaica.' Brown supplied his own item number, 4295, which was subsequently adopted by the Department and ANSP. Two small initials written in the top left corner of the label – "T. B." – show that Brown acquired the shell from Thomas Bland (1809-1885), who collected in Jamaica in the 1860s. There are no details of any data that Bland might have provided to Brown when Brown acquired Bland's collection, although Brown may have transcribed some or all of Bland's data onto his own labels; and so there are opportunities here for archival work, to try and trace any evidence of Bland's collection materials. The species identifications on the label include crossings out and questions marks, suggesting uncertainty on Brown's part. It is possible that Brown may have recorded further information in other places, such as display cabinets, but this is not known. (It is worth remarking that labels have not always been seen as the primary descriptions for specimens; Linnaeus for example often did not use labels, or abbreviated labels, relying on drawer locations and catalogs to provide the necessary information [32]).

The next two labels in the box are similar; one of them is shown in Figure 2. These are the first labels actually created in the Department. The writing on the labels is that of Henry Pilsbry (1862-1957), who was appointed Conservator of the Conchology Section at the Academy in 1888. At this point the roles of individual collectors were diminishing, and ways were being found to share data with researchers at other nascent institutions. The Pilsbry labels are attempts to systematize existing labels in the Department's collections for internal and external use. They were also used for public display, and include a blank patch of card where the specimen would have been glued. This format is related to the growth of museums as public institutions, along with innovations in engineering and architecture that permitted the construction of multi-story atrium-lit halls which could be filled with display cases, which (in this case) carried specimens on labeled cards. At one point these labels consisted of one piece of card, but as display practices changed, they were cut into pieces and stored in the specimen box. In terms of the information on the labels, there is still some uncertainty in terms of identification. Further, while the specimen is marked as being from the 'A. D. Brown Collection,' and 'Jamaica' is retained as the location, any reference to Thomas Bland as Brown's source (and perhaps original collector) has disappeared. This change is not unique to this label; the original source was omitted from the ledger records and ANSP labels of thousands of lots in A.D. Brown collection. With the Paul Hesse collection, for example, the source and date received on original labels were often misinterpreted as the collector and date-collected on subsequent labels [8].

The next item represents some of the Department's first moves to computer-based database systems in the 1970s and 1980s (Fig. 3). This included the Electronic Data Processing program (EDP), which created computer records and a unique database serial number for each sample. The early EDP work followed a manual data entry workflow, which involved copying data from various labels into standardized fields on photocopied data entry sheets. The handwritten data-entry sheets were then sent to the Smithsonian for actual data entry into a SELGEM-based system. The format of these fields was developed by the Smithsonian Institute at the time, and represented an attempt to set a wider standard for specimen description. There are a number of issues to be explored further here, including the decision-making behind the fields adopted by the Smithsonian, and technical restrictions with these early databases such as character limits in individual fields. Other issues include transcription errors (for instance with transcribing handwritten labels) and handwriting issues on the part of the transcriber, which could cause issues with data entry at the Smithsonian. Most of these data sheets are no longer available, having been discarded by the department.

Subsequently, the Department began to develop in-house information systems, and Department records were migrated across increasingly powerful systems. Currently, there are two primary repositories for the Department's data. First, there is a MySQL database with a limited dataset, a back end for the Department's web site, which allows public queries of the Department's collections; Figure 4 shows the current record and description of ANSP 4295 that researchers see via the Web interface [2]. Second, there is a more comprehensive FileMaker Pro (FMP) database maintained within the department; a screenshot of interface for this database is shown in Figure 5. This database has two main purposes: (1) to aggregate all known data in the Department, from labels, documents, and other sources; and (2) to provide a platform for selective exporting and crosswalking of records for use outside the Department, including to the ANSP Web back end, and also to Darwin Core. The FMP database has a number of customized fields, where heterogeneous data from multiple sources can be recorded (for instance, chain of owners from original collector to donor to ANSP).

3   Discussion

One ongoing aim of the research is to analyze the different ways in which historical data and metadata at ANSP are structured, in order to understand how these might then be converted into interoperable forms. Perhaps the most desirable situation would be one in which historical descriptions are structurally similar over time, with equivalences in what are now called (in database terms) attributes and values. In this case, some kind of semi-automatic solution – for instance in terms of mapping data in fields in older labels to similar fields in newer labels – might at least be considered. However, as the preceding section suggests, the history of descriptions in the Department is one of heterogeneity and discontinuous change, and this has implications for digitization workflows.

3.1   Changes Over Time

One example of discontinuity is when a new collector or curator takes charge of an existing collection, and decides to create new types of description; for example, Brown relabeled Bland's specimens, and Pilsbry then relabeled Brown's specimens.

A century later, Pilsbry's data, along with new data, was digitized. In these cases the mappings are not simple, and the successive descriptions are not straightforward versions of each other, but include also new forms of description. It seems to be both a case of updating, but also of re-inventing to a certain degree, which data is reported and in what manner. It will be interesting to see how the data from the labels made it into (or did not make it into) the EDP sheets, and then into subsequent database formats. A related discontinuity concerns the ways in which some data is not carried forward over time. Examples here include Brown's identification of Bland as the original source of 4295, as well as some of the prior identifications of 4295, all of which are sources of useful information. For instance, with the right kind of historical research, it might be possible to identify more of the links between Bland and Brown, for example, and then use these to add additional metadata, for instance by researching further exactly where Bland may have collected the original specimens.

These observations are more productive when situated within a Communities of Practice perspective. It has just been noted that the evolution of labeling and other descriptive practices in the Department did not follow a linear and teleological path from proto-labels to the current versions; rather, there were distinct styles of labels in different eras. These differences can be related to wider historical contexts, and correlate broadly with historical accounts of the stages of growth of natural as a history as a science over time in the USA [11, 13, 26]. Three of these stages are described here.

Pre-1850s/1860s. Natural history as a science is founded and shaped by individual collectors (such as Bland and Brown) who develop their collections in relative isolation. While collectors are increasingly in touch with each other, for instance through personal correspondence, they are also developing their own research methods. These early collectors can be seen as increasingly sharing similar ideas and moving towards at least general standards of description.

Post-1850s. ANSP, established in 1812, was already growing quickly as an institution. By the 1840s and 1850s, members were being recruited, education missions articulated, and (partly as a consequence of new printing technologies) proceedings and other forms of scientific communication were gaining ground. The forebears of the modern departments emerged at this time: the Conchological Section was formed, with its own external membership, and began publishing the American Journal of Conchology (http://www.biodiversitylibrary.org/item/30579#page/245/mode/1up). There was also a trend towards more standardized descriptions within departments and display cases (see for example Pilsbry's display cards).

1970s-present. This period saw the adoption of computing technologies from pre-networked mainframe computers, through the invention of electronic databases, and the development of the Internet and World Wide Web. There is a constant increase in technological capacity, and the cycles between different versions of databases in the Department are short compared to the intervals between different labels. This period saw the first moves towards wider standardization, although there was little realization at the time of the need to document the assumptions made in moving data into standard forms, such as adding coordinates without stating the source, or adding locality levels without capturing the verbatim locality. Nevertheless, the Department continues to recognize that one of the most powerful things it can do is to provide users access to primary data – images of specimens and documents – so that it is possible to see what assumptions were made in capturing the data and metadata that made discovery of the primary objects possible. This is part of the continuing evolution of reproducibility in science.

From the perspective of this paper, each stage demonstrates longitudinal iterations between participation and reification [33]. The practices of early collectors shaped their correspondence and early publications, which further shaped collectors' practices; and when research became concentrated in early museums, these institutions produced increasingly large amounts of formal publications which guided the activities of their members, in turn generating new research and specimens which created new data for further publications. In the twentieth century, the creation of EDP sheets provided an initial data standard for researchers to orient to, while at the same time initiating a centralized repository from which data could be shared. In each case, iteration did not proceed at the same pace. Descriptive practices in the Department consist often of longer periods of relative stability (especially in the nineteenth and earlier twentieth century), interspersed with short periods of change and revision that then give rise to new standards. The shift to digital technologies and documents facilitated more rapid cycles of creation and dissemination, but these still occurred at irregular intervals, rather than gradually and constantly. To borrow a term from evolutionary biology, practices display a form of punctuated equilibrium, in which the punctuations can be correlated with external organizational drivers, such as new personalities, organizational changes, and new technologies.

3.2   The Human Element: Implications for Biodiversity Infrastructure

The narrative accompanying the labels and documents in Figures 1-5 contains much additional information not shown in these pictures. This latter information is part of the local knowledge of the Department. Examples include recognition of the handwriting of Brown, Pilsbry, and others; biographical details of various personalities connected with the Department; the wider history of the Academy; the interpretation of various initials written in various documents (e.g. the 'T.B.' on the label in Figure 1); the format and cardstock of cards on which specimens were glued in the late nineteenth century; and so on. This knowledge is often not formally documented, and it has only been articulated in this paper in narrative form as part of the ethnographic action research work in this project. One place where some of this knowledge *is* documented to an extent is the FMP database maintained in the Department (see above). At the same time, however, this is not a public document, and while specific organizational knowledge may be captured in tables, records, and fields, it often requires background knowledge (or asking someone with background knowledge) to navigate. This points again to the existence of complex and nuanced forms of organizational knowledge that are not codified, yet deeply intertwined with and manifested in departmental practices.

Some implications are as follows. First, it is debatable to what extent this complex knowledge is fully codifiable, at least for the foreseeable future; there therefore has to be a sustainable way to integrate this local knowledge into biodiversity informatics infrastructures, without relying on formal descriptions in rule-based ontologies and metadata schemas. Second, the research so far has thrown into relief the central knowledge role of biodiversity researchers and their professional knowledge, and questions the extent to which digitization initiatives can ever really fully automatically capture this knowledge. Rather, the study suggests that curators, collection managers, and others, should play increasingly central human roles in digitization workflows and programs. This echoes previous research that has looked at the role of reference librarians as information managers who map and translate clients' reference questions into formal database queries. [23] describes such roles as 'keystone species' in information ecologies, and a similar function is played by biodiversity researchers who translate local department knowledge into wider formats such as Darwin Core.

Several design implications are as follows. First, resources need to be invested in the design of digitization workflows to include support for ongoing elicitation of expert knowledge from biodiversity researchers, and for these researchers to provide input into the design of wider metadata schemas and tools. Second, new ways need to be found to think about creating metadata that can capture this expert knowledge. If this knowledge is complex, then one option to consider here is the creation of substantive unstructured narrative/discursive fields, which can provide background to particular specimens or collections, perhaps fashioned after the finding aid approach common in archival work.

3.3   Summary and Future Work

Over time, the temporal and spatial scope of collections at ANSP has increased. In the past, individual collectors aggregated specimens into collections, departments aggregated individual collections into departmental collections, and institutions sought to aggregate across individual departments. Before the development of networked communication and information technologies, this aggregation often proceeded at the local level. With the development of the Internet, however, and the potential to bring together data from multiple local institutions into global facilities, institutional data now has to be translated from the local formats in which it has been shaped (sometimes for 200 years) into new global standards. As has just been described, it is not always easy to unbundle knowledge that has been created in local CoPs and then map it to wider standards. Related findings of the research so far therefore include: (1) significant heterogeneity in data sources and formats over time; (2) a non-linear evolution of data and metadata practices over time; (3) the central role of curatorial staff and collection managers; and (4) a need for unstructured narrative metadata fields.

Research at ANSP is continuing to explore these themes, as well as other historical and current data practices, with a focus on comparative studies in different departments, with the aim of understanding further the relationships between local and historical data practices, and current standard models. An interesting challenge here is to document initial EDP efforts and subsequent database migrations; no such history currently exists. Another is to develop a set of metadata elements (based on existing gazetteers of biographies of malacologists) that will provide the elements of a collective biography, in order to tease out possible co-locational and co-temporal relationships, especially amongst early researchers in the nineteenth century. From a theoretical perspective, the research is exploring further ways to theorize and understand data and metadata work in biodiversity CoPs, and how these are constituted at local levels in iterative cycles of participation and reification. The focus will be on understanding better the local production of data and metadata, and the balance between explicit documentation on the one had, and local knowledge on the other, and the ways in which this balance affects data sharing in wider contexts.

4   Conclusion

The development of global biodiversity standards depends significantly on translating local collections of data and metadata into common formats. While this is often seen as primarily a technical task, we have argued that organizational knowledge factors are also important. As members of Communities of Practice, curators, collection managers, and others acquire over time tacit practice-based knowledge of their collections, which can be crucial to successful collection digitization. One important recommendation is therefore that attention needs to be paid to eliciting and modeling this knowledge, in order to support the design of biodiversity digitization workflows, and to create metadata that can provide enhanced overviews of collection histories.

References

1. ANSP: Malacology (2015). http://www.ansp.org/research/systematics-evolution/collections/malacology/ (retrieved June 1, 2015)
2. ANSP. Malacology Collection (2015). http://clade.ansp.org/malacology/collections/ (retrieved June 1, 2015)
3. ANSP: Research (2015). http://ansp.org/research/ (retrieved June 1, 2015)
4. Baskerville, R.: Investigating Information Systems with Action Research. Communications of the Association for Information Systems **2** (1999)
5. Baskerville, R., Pries-Heje, J.: Grounded action research: a method for understanding IT in practice. Accounting Management and Information Technologies **9**, 1–23 (1999)
6. Beach, J.A., Ibarra, J.E.: Cyberinfrastructure for International, Collaborative Biodiversity and Ecological Informatics. Report of the Pan-American Advanced Institute (PASI) held at the Organization of Tropical Studies, Costa Rica, May 31–June 12, 2008 (2009)
7. Beyond The Box: Digitization Competition (2015). https://beyondthebox.aibs.org/ (retrieved June 1, 2015)
8. Borrero, F., Rosenberg, G.: The Paul Hesse collection at the academy of natural sciences of Philadelphia, with a review of names for Mollusca introduced by Hesse. In: Proceedings of the Academy of Natural Sciences of Philadelphia, vol. 164 (2015, accepted)
9. Bromley, J., King, D., Morse, D.R.: Finding agriculture among biodiversity: metadata in practice. In: Closs, S., Studer, R., Garoufallou, E., Sicilia, M.-A. (eds.) MTSR 2014. CCIS, vol. 478, pp. 185–192. Springer, Heidelberg (2014)
10. Canhos, V., de Souza, S., De Giovanni, R., Canhos, D.: Global Biodiversity Informatics: Setting the Scene for a 'New World' of Ecological Modeling. Biodiversity Informatics **1**(2004), 1–13 (2004)
11. Farber, P.: Finding Order in Nature. The Naturalist Tradition from Linnaeus to E. O. Wilson. The Johns Hopkins University Press, Baltimore (2000)

12. GBIF: Global Biodiversity Information Facility (2015). http://www.gbif.org/ (retrieved June 1, 2015)
13. Gerstner, P.: The academy of natural of sciences of Philadelphia, 1812–1850. In: Oleson, A., Brown, S.S. (eds.) The Pursuit of Knowledge in the Early American Republic. American Scientific and Learned Societies from Colonial Times to the Civil War, pp. 174–193. The Johns Hopkins University Press, Baltimore (1976)
14. Heidorn, P.B.: Biodiversity Informatics. Bulletin of the American Society for Information Science and Technology 37(6), 38–44 (2011)
15. Hey, T., Tansley, S., Tolle, K. (eds.): The Fourth Paradigm. Data-Intensive Scientific Discovery. Microsoft Research, Redmond (2009)
16. Khazraee, E., Khoo, M.: Practice-based ontologies: a new approach to address the challenges of ontology and knowledge representation in history and archaeology. In: García-Barriocanal, E., Cebeci, Z., Okur, M.C., Öztürk, A. (eds.) MTSR 2011. CCIS, vol. 240, pp. 375–386. Springer, Heidelberg (2011)
17. Khoo, M., Hall, C.: Managing metadata: Networks of practice, technological frames, and metadata work in a digital library. Information & Organization 23, 81–106 (2013)
18. Khoo, M., Rosenberg, G.: Historical Considerations in Biodiversity Informatics. Paper presented at the The iConference, Newport Beach, CA (2015)
19. King, D., Morse, D.R.: Document mark-up for different users and purposes. In: Garoufallou, E., Greenberg, J. (eds.) MTSR 2013. CCIS, vol. 390, pp. 355–360. Springer, Heidelberg (2013)
20. Lave, J., Wenger, E.: Situated Learning. Cambridge University Press (1991)
21. Makris, K., Skevakis, G., Kalokyri, V., Arapi, P., Christodoulakis, S., Stoitsis, J., Manolis, N., Rojas, S.L.: Federating Natural History Museums in Natural Europe. In: Garoufallou, E., Greenberg, J. (eds.) MTSR 2013. CCIS, vol. 390, pp. 361–372. Springer, Heidelberg (2013)
22. Moritz, T.: Building the Biodiversity Commons. D-Lib Magazine, 8(6) (2002)
23. Nardi, B., O'Day, V.: Intelligent Agents: What We Learned at the Library. Libri 46, 59–88 (1996)
24. NSF. (2015). Advancing Digitization of Biodiversity Collections (ADBC). http://www.nsf.gov/funding/pgm_summ.jsp?pims_id=503559 (retrieved June 1, 2015)
25. PCAST: Sustaining Environmental Capital: Protecting Society and the Economy. President's Council of Advisors on Science and Technology, Washington, D.C. (2011)
26. Peck, R.M., Stroud, P.T.: A Glorious Enterprise. The Academy of Natural Sciences of Philadelphia and the Making of American Science. University of Pennsylvania Press, Philadelphia, PA (2012)
27. Steinke, K-H., Gehrke, M., Dzido, R.: Recognition of Humboldt's Handwriting in Complex Surroundings. Frontiers in Handwriting Recognition (ICFHR), Kolkata, India (2010)
28. Tacchi, J., Slater, D., Hearn, G.: Ethnographic Action Research: A User's Handbook. UNESCO, New Delhi, India (2003)
29. TDWG. (2015). Darwin Core. http://rs.tdwg.org/dwc/ (retrieved June 1, 2015)
30. Tsiflidou, E., Dimitropoulos, A., Makrodimitri, Z.A., Palavitsinis, N.: Intellectual property rights in environmental and natural history collections: a preliminary discussion. In: García-Barriocanal, E., Cebeci, Z., Okur, M.C., Öztürk, A. (eds.) MTSR 2011. CCIS, vol. 240, pp. 445–452. Springer, Heidelberg (2011)
31. Tzitzikas, Y., Allocca, C., Bekiari, C., Marketakis, Y., Fafalios, P., Doerr, M., Minadakis, N., Patkos, T., Candela, L.: Integrating Heterogeneous and Distributed Information about Marine Species through a Top Level Ontology. In: Garoufallou, E., Greenberg, J. (eds.) MTSR 2013. CCIS, vol. 390, pp. 289–301. Springer, Heidelberg (2013)
32. UUZM: Catalogue of type specimens. 4. Linnaean specimens. Uppsala University Museum of Evolution, Zoology section (2014)
33. Wenger, E.: Communities of Practice. Cambridge University Press (1998)

Ontologies for Research Data Description: A Design Process Applied to Vehicle Simulation

João Aguiar Castro[1]([⊠]), Deborah Perrotta[2], Ricardo Carvalho Amorim[1], João Rocha da Silva[1], and Cristina Ribeiro[3]

[1] Faculdade de Engenharia da, Universidade do Porto/INESC TEC, Porto, Portugal
{joaoaguiarcastro,ricardo.amorim3,joaorosilva}@gmail.com
[2] Faculdade de Engenharia da, Universidade do Porto/LIACC, Porto, Portugal
deborahperrotta@gmail.com
[3] DEI—Faculdade de Engenharia da, Universidade do Porto/INESC TEC,
Porto, Portugal
mcr@fe.up.pt

Abstract. Data description is an essential part of research data management, and it is easy to argue for the importance of describing data early in the research workflow. Specific metadata schemas are often proposed to support description. Given the diversity of research domains, such schemas are often missing, and when available they may be too generic, too complex or hard to incorporate in a description platform. In this paper we present a method used to design metadata models for research data description as ontologies. Ontologies are gaining acceptance as knowledge representation structures, and we use them here in the scope of the Dendro platform. The ontology design process is illustrated with a case study from Vehicle Simulation. According to the design process, the resulting model was validated by a domain specialist.

Keywords: Metadata models · Research data management · Ontologies · Vehicle simulation

1 Introduction

As research environments are capturing more and more diverse data, the management of such data becomes more challenging. In the long tail of science [4] where a large number of small research groups are producing a large quantity of heterogeneous data, management structures are more fragile and the problem is aggravated.

Recognizing that the value of research data goes way beyond the purpose of their creation, funding agencies are now issuing mandates that establish data deposit and publication as a requirement for project funding.

However, the support for data curation is not a common practice in most institutions, and researchers tend to store undocumented versions of their data in common storage devices. Research data is thus frequently at risk of being lost, sometimes permanently [10]. Sooner or later researchers have to deal with

E. Garoufallou et al. (Eds.): MTSR 2015, CCIS 544, pp. 348–354, 2015.
DOI: 10.1007/978-3-319-24129-6_30

problems of data integrity, accuracy and accessibility, and therefore the creation of detailed metadata records is highly advisable, namely in the early stages of a project.

In this paper we deal with the problem of data description in small research groups. This is part of an ongoing effort to engage researchers in the management of their data, supporting it on Dendro, a prototype ontology-based data management platform, that offers researchers an environment to organize and document their data right from the beginning of a research project [9]. We elaborate here on the process of modelling domain-specific lightweight ontologies, to be loaded into Dendro as a source of descriptors. This process is instantiated with a case study from the Vehicle Simulation domain.

2   Data Management Workflow

Research data management is no more of a technological issue as it is a conceptual one. Sophisticated technological infrastructures are proposed every day [1] but the success of data management ultimately depends on the efforts of researchers.

Unlike publications, research data is not self-expressive about their content, thus requiring relevant contextual information in order to be accessed and fully interpreted, making metadata essential for its reuse [11]. However, data description needs are not the same for every scientific domain—datasets are heterogeneous and belong to different research cultures and interests [2]. Therefore, to obtain comprehensive and accurate metadata may prove hard. Our assumption is that research data reuse strongly depends on detailed descriptions that only their creators can provide.

In this context our research data platform, Dendro, aims to address both technical and conceptual data management issues. In Dendro we provide researchers with a collaborative environment to systematically capture timely metadata about the datasets they are creating [9]. Datasets together with metadata records can then be submitted to an external data repository for long-time preservation. We have a strong focus on the definition of domain-specific metadata models, formalized as ontologies, for research groups in the long tail of science, and our recent work includes the definition of those models for the fracture mechanics, analytical chemistry and the biodiversity domain [3,9]. These ontologies add new descriptors to be combined with those proposed by generic ontologies, or standards, that are already loaded in Dendro, such as **Dublin Core**[1], **Friend of a friend**[2] or **CERIF**[3]. Our process depends on the interaction between the data curator and the researchers who are the domain experts. Figure 1 depicts our vision for the process of combining generic and specific metadata models in a research data workflow.

---

[1] available at http://bloody-byte.net/rdf/dc_owl/

[2] http://www.foaf-project.org/

[3] http://eurocris.org/cerif/main-features-cerif

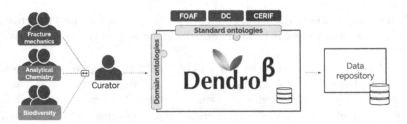

Fig. 1. Ontologies in the research data workflow

The benefits of adopting metadata schemas for data description are obvious, but their use by researchers with no metadata skills can be a problem [8]. Vocabularies that capture common concepts in the researchers domain will most likely encourage them to document their data, but these are typically not available.

Ontologies are intrinsically incremental semantic representations, and this is their main advantage for supporting metadata records. Furthermore, in a landscape of vocabularies and metadata schemas, ontologies are being largely adopted for the sake of interoperability. They can be developed and refined with the collaboration of specific communities, and are therefore flexible enough to face the challenges of a fast-paced research data production system. They combine expressiveness, accuracy and non-ambiguous syntax, for both humans and machines, and these are essential in research data description.

3   The Modelling Process

In this paper we are proposing an agile ontology design process to face the challenge of data description in a multi-domain research environment. Being aware that every research domain, or experiment configuration, has different data description requirements, we are collaborating with a panel of researchers from several domains at the University of Porto. Our goal is to provide researchers with metadata models suited to their domains, with familiar terminology that mitigates their entry barriers to data description.

The interaction between data curators and researchers is crucial for metadata model design. Data curators acknowledge the value of metadata best practices, and can make good use of their data skills. However, their contribution in the long run can have less impact if researchers are not motivated to collaborate in the overall process. Data curators are not domain experts, or at least not in a wide variety of fields, and have limited know-how in experimental set-ups. On the other hand, researchers are domain experts and, as data creators, they are most apt to produce accurate metadata. Moreover, ideally metadata should be registered as soon as possible in the research workflow, where it is more likely that researchers hold full knowledge of the research context, otherwise the result can be lackluster descriptions [6].

A first moment in our process is a meeting between the data curators and the domain experts. This meeting consists in a preliminary interview supported by a script, adapted from the Data Curation Toolkit[4]. The interview provides insight of the current data management practices at the research team, as it informs on the way the research group organizes and shares their data, whether they are following standards to document the data, among other data management activities. This is also the opportunity to introduce them to research data management concepts, since in many cases researchers are not familiar with concepts like metadata or descriptor.

A second moment includes a content analysis based on researchers' publications, to manually extract the main operational domain concepts. The criteria for selecting these concepts is based on the many parameters at the core of a given research configuration, for instance collected materials, spatial and temporal variables.

After a selection of possible descriptors we take another session to propose a set of domain-specific descriptors, and we also ask researchers to think about what contextual information must be provided to help retrieve and interpret their datasets. Finally the researchers are invited to validate the metadata model. Our interaction with the researchers takes a total of three sessions, with durations ranging between one and two hours.

The metadata model is then formalized as a lightweight ontology, that uses properties from standard vocabularies, if available, and otherwise purpose-built ones. To link together the domain-specific ontologies, we have defined a generic *Research* ontology, that models broad multi-domain concepts. This ontology comprises few classes that represent research types (such as Experiment, Simulation), and generic scientific properties like the instrumentation, software or method applied to data capture.

When creating a lightweight ontology for a concrete scenario, one can subclass Experiment with a specific type of experiment, using it as an extension point from which domain-specific properties can be devised. Our lightweight ontologies are then loaded into Dendro. Our process was already fully explored in two research domains–fracture materials and analytical chemistry experiments [3]. The next section presents a case study, in the Vehicle Simulation domain, to illustrate the use of the proposed process in a systematic way.

4   The Vehicle Simulation Case Study

At the time of the interview the Vehicle Simulation research group was dealing with data concerning the performance of electric buses in an urban context. In order to evaluate this performance the research group uses datasets containing the bus routes, files containing technical vehicle properties provided by the manufacturer and specific environmental information such as the air coefficient or the surface roughness. In the laboratorial context the data are loaded to run a simulation as close as possible to reality. As a consequence of this simulation new datasets are created, and those are liable to different interpretations and can be

---

[4] available at http://datacurationprofiles.org/

analyzed, or reused, according to any particular research goals. According to the researchers, data is mainly organized as Excel spreadsheets. When new external data arrives it is stored via Dropbox and personal e-mail to keep track of the new entries, while regular backups are maintained. The research group does not describe their data, although the simulation variables are part of a "ReadMe" file.

A mathematical model is in place to calculate specific electric bus performance parameters [7]. This model includes several subsystems; one computes the required energy for a vehicle to complete a driving cycle, another uses the kinetic energy of the vehicle to calculate the possible amount of energy that can be recovered from the regenerative braking. Other subsystems are related to the batteries and supercapacitors and evaluate if these are capable of absorbing the energy from the braking.

There are high-level entities that are essential to contextualize the electrical bus simulation set-up, like the vehicle itself, and the driving cycle from which all the vehicle calculations are based [5]. Both the tractive force, that compels the vehicle forward, and the kinetic energy have a great influence on the way the vehicle behaves.

Figure 2 shows the Vehicle Simulation lightweight ontology that domain experts can use to create their metadata records. This ontology uses properties related to the high-level entities. For instance we create the properties `vehicle` (corresponding to a vehicle category, like "electric bus", or other depending on the study) and `vehicleModel`, so researchers can record the vehicle used in the simulation. Since there are available driving cycles, produced by different organizations, ready to be used in vehicle simulations, the `drivingCycle` property was also defined. These are properties with the potential to create access points to the dataset, as they can yield information that distinguishes a dataset from the rest. All the other properties deal with a set of variables that constrain the entire simulation and are tied to the calculation of the tractive force

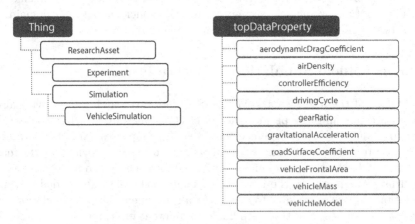

Fig. 2. Vehicle Simulation lightweight ontology

and of the kinetic energy. Values concerning the `aerodynamicDragCoefficient`, the `roadSurfaceCoefficient` or other variables are associated to many performance parameters, and therefore must be annotated to help one interpret, or reproduce, the output from a vehicle simulation.

This ontology is not intended to fully represent the vehicle simulation domain, instead it captures the description needs of a group of researchers that run simulations to evaluate specific parameters on electrical bus performance. However, most of the properties defined are generic and can be widely applied to other vehicle simulation scenarios. If the researchers need to provide extra contextual information, namely the description of batteries and supercapacitors, the corresponding properties can easily be added to the ontology. By supporting our process in ontologies we are making sure that our approach is incremental and can easily account for any description needs.

5 Conclusions

In this paper we have presented a systematic process to design lightweight ontologies for the description of research data. We consider that metadata models must result from the collaboration of data curators and domain experts. The Vehicle Simulation ontology presented here served as an instantiation of our process, and was loaded to Dendro, together with those for other 10 domains. The experience of researchers describing their data with Dendro is currently running, as a part of an ongoing research on descriptor recommendation. We expect to show that the timely documentation of datasets will result in more data reaching the final stages of the research workflow and being reused by a broader community.

Acknowledgments. Project SIBILA-Towards Smart Interacting Blocks that Improve Learned Advice, reference NORTE-07-0124-FEDER000059, funded by the North Portugal Regional Operational Programme (ON.2O Novo Norte), under the National Strategic Reference Framework (NSRF), through the European Regional Development Fund (ERDF), and by national funds, through the Portuguese funding agency, Fundao para a Cincia e a Tecnologia (FCT). Deborah Perrotta is supported by FCT through PhD scholarship grant SFRH/BD/51256/2010, within the MIT-Portugal Program in Engineering Design and Advanced Manufacturing Leaders for Technical Industries focus area. João Rocha da Silva is supported by research grant SFRH/BD/77092/2011,provided by the Portuguese funding agency, Fundao para a Cincia e a Tecnologia (FCT).

References

1. Amorim, R.C., Castro, J.A., da Silva, J.R., Ribeiro, C.: A comparative study of platforms for research data management: interoperability, metadata capabilities and integration potential. In: Rocha, A., Correia, A.M., Costanzo, S., Reis, L.P. (eds.) New Contributions in Information Systems and Technologies. AISC, vol. 353, pp. 101–111. Springer, Heidelberg (2015)

2. Borgman, C.L.: The conundrum of sharing research data. Journal of the American Society for Information Science and Technology **63**(6) (2012)

3. Castro, J.A., Ribeiro, C., da Silva, J.R.: Creating lightweight ontologies for dataset description. Practical applications in a cross-domain research data management workflow. In: IEEE/ACM Joint Conference on Digital Libraries (JCDL), pp. 0–3 (2014)

4. Heidorn, P.B.: Shedding Light on the Dark Data in the Long Tail of Science. Library Trends **57**(2), 280–299 (2008)

5. Weiss, M.A., Heywood, J.B., Andreas Schafer, E.M.D., Au Yeung, F.F.: On the road in 2020 - A life-cycle analysis of new automobile technologies. Energy Laboratory Report EL 00–003, 3–6 to 3–14 (October 2000)

6. Martinez-Uribe, L., Macdonald, S.: User engagement in research data curation. In: Agosti, M., Borbinha, J., Kapidakis, S., Papatheodorou, C., Tsakonas, G. (eds.) ECDL 2009. LNCS, vol. 5714, pp. 309–314. Springer, Heidelberg (2009)

7. Perrotta, D., Macedo, J.L., Rossetti, R.J., Sousa, J.F.D., Kokkinogenis, Z., Ribeiro, B., Afonso, J.: Route Planning for Electric Buses: A Case Study in Oporto. Procedia - Social and Behavioral Sciences **111**, 1004–1014 (2014)

8. Qin, J., LI, K.: How portable are the metadata standards for scientific data? a proposal for a metadata infrastructure. In: Proceedings of the Internacional Conference on Dublin Core and Metadata Applications, pp. 25–34 (2013)

9. da Silva, J.R., Castro, J.A., Ribeiro, C., Lopes, J.C.: The Dendro research data management platform: applying ontologies to long-term preservation in a collaborative environment. In: Proceedings of the iPres 2014 Conference (2014)

10. Smit, E., Van Der Hoeven, J., Giaretta, D.: Avoiding a Digital Dark Age for data: why publishers should care about digital preservation. Learned Publishing **24**(1), 35–49 (2011)

11. Treloar, A., Wilkinson, R.: Rethinking metadata creation and management in a data-driven research world. In: 2008 IEEE Fourth International Conference on eScience, pp. 782–789 (2008)

Track on Metadata and Semantics
for Agriculture, Food and Environment

Setting up a Global Linked Data Catalog
of Datasets for Agriculture

Valeria Pesce[1(✉)], Ajit Maru[1], Phil Archer[2], Thembani Malapela[3],
and Johannes Keizer[3]

[1] Global Forum on Agricultural Research, Rome, Italy
{valeria.pesce,ajit.maru}@fao.org
[2] ERCIM, Sophia-Antipolis, France
phila@w3.org
[3] Food and Agriculture Organization of the United Nations, Rome, Italy
{thembani.malapela,johannes.keizer}@fao.org

Abstract. The movement to share data has been on the rise in the last decade and lately in the agricultural domain. Similarly platforms for publishing scientific and statistical datasets have sprouted and have improved visibility and availability of datasets. Yet there are still constraints in making datasets discoverable and re-usable. Commonly agreed semantics, authority lists to index datasets and standard formats and protocols to expose data are now essential. This paper explains how the CIARD RING provides a global linked data catalog of datasets for agriculture. The first part of this paper will describe the Linked Data layer of the CIARD RING focusing on the data model, semantics used and the CIARD RING LOD publication. The second part will provide examples of re-use of data from the RING. The paper concludes by describing the future steps in the development of the CIARD RING.

Keywords: Datasets · Data catalogs · Directories · Linked data · Interoperability · Semantic Web · Vocabularies

1   Introduction

The need for better sharing and easier discovery of data has become more evident in the past few years with increasing calls and trends in open government data. In agriculture, the commitment was reinforced in 2013 by leaders at the G-8 International Conference on Open Data for Agriculture.[1] Repetition of research and difficulty in building upon other experts' findings in a timely manner hinders research uptake and innovation. This situation can be significantly improved if data and datasets used and produced in research are easily shared and found. "Sharing other products of research on the Web, including raw datasets and other re-usable results, is seen as essential for enabling innovation on important topics of agricultural research for development and food security" [1]. This can only be achieved if the process of managing and sharing datasets is made easier and global registries of these datasets exist.

---

[1] https://sites.google.com/site/g8opendataconference/home

© Food and Agriculture Organization of the United Nations 2015
E. Garoufallou et al. (Eds.): MTSR 2015, CCIS 544, pp. 357–368, 2015.
DOI: 10.1007/978-3-319-24129-6_31

In addition, the need for integrated information systems in the agricultural domain is widely acknowledged (cf. [1, 2]). Integrated information systems should provide information gathered from as many relevant sources as possible and re-purposed for the specific needs of the prospected audiences. The main difficulty in building such integrated information systems is the little awareness of what information sources exist, how interoperable they are, how to tap into them and how to exploit their semantics. There is no comprehensive list or directory of agricultural information sources and technical details about these sources are often not documented and known only to the developers.

This is why the CIARD[2] movement set up the CIARD RING[3], managed by the Global Forum on Agricultural Research (GFAR).

The CIARD RING (henceforth shortened as the RING) is a global directory of web-based information services and datasets for agriculture such as search engines, databases, repositories, Open Archives, feeds, data sheets etc., associated with software tools that can process them. The services are described in details and categorized according to both content criteria such as thematic coverage, geographic coverage, content type, target audience; and technical criteria such as metadata sets adopted, vocabularies used, technologies used, protocols implemented. A new feature of the RING is the addition of a directory of dataset processing software tools and web services: datasets can be associated with software tools and APIs that can process them in different ways (convert, analyse, combine with other data etc.).

Our intent was that this information, besides being manually browsed by data and service managers, should be directly usable by the applications that needed it to build value integrated services on top of the data exposed by the datasets registered in the RING.

This paper will focus on how we used Linked Data technologies and semantics to make the RING a machine-readable hub / switchboard to datasets.

Our objectives in doing this were:

- Datasets registered in the catalog have to be found by applications
- Applications have to be able to read all the metadata about datasets and filter datasets according to their needs
- Applications have to find enough technical metadata in the catalog to:

  — Identify datasets with a specific coverage (type of data, thematic coverage, geographic coverage)
  — Identify datasets that comply with certain technical specifications (format, protocol etc.)
  — Access the dataset and get the data
  — Possibly identify APIs and software tools that can process the identified datasets

To achieve this, we needed agreed semantics and authority lists to index datasets and standard formats and protocols to expose the data. This led us to the choice of

---

[2] CIARD is a global movement dedicated to open agricultural knowledge: http://www.ciard.info

[3] http://ring.ciard.info

creating an RDF store[4] using existing metadata vocabularies and Knowledge Organization Systems (KOS) and exposing all data using Linked Data[5] technologies.

This paper will initially give a brief overview of some related work that has already been carried out and explain why we think the RING fills a gap. The we will describe the Linked Data layer of the RING, focusing first on the data model and semantics used and then on the implementation of the Linked Data good practices.

1.1   Related Work

Recently, thanks to the open government and open data movements, dataset publishing platforms have become popular. Harvard University has made available the DataVerse[6] platform for publishing scientific and statistical datasets. Another popular publishing platform is CKAN[7], maintained by the Open Knowledge Foundation, which also provides a global dataset hub called the Datahub[8].

Some important agriculture-related datasets have been published using similar platforms. Government agricultural datasets are available on *data.gov* public platforms for some developed countries (US[9], UK[10], some statistics from European countries) and BRICS countries (India in particular has started a data.gov project that includes agricultural data; Brazil has an open data portal). Very little within the agricultural domain is available from developing countries (Kenya has started an open data portal including data on agriculture, while for Africa there is the Open Data for Africa portal[11]). Some agricultural research centers (IFPRI, Bioversity International, ICRAF) have started publishing their datasets on their own DataVerse instance and sharing them through the DataVerse Network.

At the regional and global level, OpenAIRE[12] and the European Union Open Data Portal[13] include agricultural datasets from Europe; the World Bank has been publishing datasets for a while; the Food and Agriculture Organization of the United Nations

---

[4] The Resource Description Framework (RDF, http://www.w3.org/standards/semanticweb/) is a family of specifications that has come to be used as a general method for conceptual description or modeling of information that is implemented in web resources (http://en.wikipedia.org/wiki/Resource_Description_Framework). An RDF store is a way of storing data using a machine-readable "grammar" (RDF) and documented semantics (RDF vocabularies).

[5] Linked Data is a "recommended best practice for exposing, sharing, and connecting pieces of data, information, and knowledge on the Semantic Web using URIs and RDF." (Wikipedia). See http://www.w3.org/DesignIssues/LinkedData

[6] http://dataverse.org/

[7] http://ckan.org/

[8] http://datahub.io/

[9] http://catalog.data.gov/dataset?groups=agriculture8571

[10] http://data.gov.uk/data/search?q=&publisher=department-for-environment-food-and-rural-affairs

[11] http://opendataforafrica.org/

[12] https://www.openaire.eu/

[13] Currently at http://publicdata.eu/ but expected to move to data.europa.eu in October 2015

(FAO) started working on *data.fao.org* a few years ago and some interesting general dataset catalogs and / or repositories that include agricultural data exist, like Data-Cite[14] (using re3data[15] to search repositories) and Dryad[16], a curated general-purpose repository that makes the data underlying scientific publications discoverable, freely reusable, and citable.

The current situation seems to be that datasets for agriculture are gradually being made available (especially from developed countries) but are not easily discovered and not easily accessible (remotely searchable, re-usable). The existing platforms and catalogs have of course improved the situation and help in finding relevant datasets for agriculture. However, there are still tough challenges in making datasets really discoverable and re-usable.

1.2   Challenges

An overview of the existing platforms showed that there were still gaps in the provided solutions in terms of general interoperability and our specific thematic interest.

- None of the existing catalogs and repositories has a coverage that is at once global and specific to agriculture; agricultural datasets can be identified in some catalogs using keywords, but with no further thematic specialization.
- Each platform uses different categorizations for datasets and metadata are usually not detailed enough to allow for federated searches or selective harvesting from these systems. Overall, the existing platforms do not seem to have very rich metadata or to follow common standards for describing dataset nor common authority reference data.
- No platform exposes machine-readable metadata about semantic and technical aspects of the datasets (dimensions / vocabularies, reference authority data, formats, protocols…), making it difficult for applications to automatically re-use the data.

Regarding the second point, many dataset publishing platforms have their own data model and their own metadata vocabulary (Dataverse [3], OpenAIRE (Datacite) [4], re3data [5], Dryad [6]), while very few[17] adopt for instance standard vocabularies like the W3C DCAT vocabulary[18] or the dataset properties recommended by CRIS standards like VIVO (Datastar[19]) [7] or CERIF[20] [8]. And very few adopt a Linked Data approach.

Therefore, our effort with the RING was towards filling these gaps: we wanted to create a global dataset hub for agriculture which is fully machine-readable, provides

---

[14] http://search.datacite.org/ui?q=subject%3Aagriculture
[15] http://www.re3data.org
[16] http://datadryad.org/
[17] http://www.w3.org/2011/gld/wiki/DCAT_Implementations
[18] http://www.w3.org/TR/vocab-dcat/
[19] http://sourceforge.net/projects/vivo/files/Datastar%20ontology/
[20] See https://cerif4datasets.wordpress.com/c4d-deliverables/

very rich metadata and uses standard vocabularies (integrating them when necessary) and concepts so that applications can automatically re-use the data.

2   Semantics for the RING Linked Data

We decided to use the Linked Data approach [9] and to aim for Tim Berners Lee's 5th star[21] because we wanted to achieve the maximum level of interoperability possible.

The first step was the definition of our semantics.

Semantics in Linked Data are defined by "vocabularies": this term is often used to indicate two types of vocabularies that are both needed for describing and indexing any resource: 1) the metadata elements used to describe a resource defining its characteristics: these are usually defined in what we call metadata vocabularies, metadata element sets, or simply vocabularies; 2) the controlled vocabularies allowed for any of the metadata elements: these are normally defined in "concept schemes" or "value vocabularies" and can be of different types: thesauri, authority lists, classifications, or more in general Knowledge Organization Systems (KOSs). We maintain this distinction [cf. 10] in this paper using the terms "metadata vocabulary" and "value vocabulary".

2.1   Data Model and Metadata Vocabularies

We needed to identify a data model and related metadata vocabulary that was suitable for the catalog. The main type of resources that we wanted to cover in the RING is datasets and the definition of datasets that we adopted is the definition proposed by the W3C Government Linked Data Working Group: "A collection of data, published or curated by a single source, and available for access or download in one or more formats."[22]

Around this definition, the W3C Working Group created the Data Catalog Vocabulary[23]. There are several reasons why we chose this vocabulary as our core vocabulary:

- We limited our survey to RDF vocabularies. There are good vocabularies for datasets that have not been formalized as RDF (like the re3data metadata set), but we wanted to make our dataset "linked" and wanted to adopt vocabularies that are formalized as RDF and use URIs.
- We wanted to adopt a vocabulary that was widely endorsed and we thought having the W3C behind it made DCAT a good candidate. Besides, the EC has since made available the DCAT Application Profile – a set of recommendations for how to use DCAT in European data portals (see main text below).
- We needed a model that could represent the reality of the datasets we already had in our system, which in many cases had two or three "forms" of the same dataset.

---

[21] See http://www.w3.org/DesignIssues/LinkedData (bottom of page) and http://5stardata.info/. The 5th star is about "linking your data to other data to provide context"

[22] http://www.w3.org/TR/vocab-dcat/#class--dataset

[23] http://www.w3.org/ns/dcat#

DCAT is designed around the relation between the dataset (the collection of data) and the "instances" of the dataset "available for access or download in one or more formats", called "distributions". This model suited our situation perfectly.

- We needed something sophisticated enough to distinguish between the dataset and its "distributions" but not so much specialized to be suitable only for very advanced cases (like VOID). We looked also at DataCite but the RDF version is still not official and the data model did not clearly distinguish between dataset and distributions.

In practice, since DCAT defines only new classes and properties for datasets while assuming the use of other existing vocabularies for the generic properties of any resource (like title, description etc.), we adopted an Application Profile that uses DCAT and formalizes also the re-use of other existing classes and properties from other vocabularies: the DCAT Application Profile for Data Portals in Europe (DCAT-AP)[24]. The figure below[25] shows the core entities of the DCAT-AP RDF model.

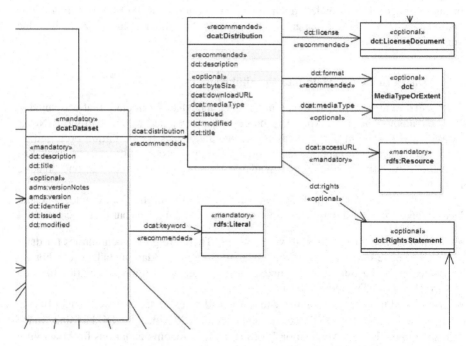

Fig. 1. Detail of the DCAT Application Profile RDF model

Besides the vocabularies already included in the DCAT-AP (Dublin Core[26], DCAT, FoaF[27], Vcard[28], SKOS[29]), in order to be interoperable with as many other systems as possible we also use other existing RDF vocabularies (VOID[30], DOAP[31], schema.org[32]) for additional (partial) descriptions of the datasets.

Furthermore, in order for the database to be fully interoperable by applications that needed more technical information on how to access the datasets, we needed a few additional properties that we published in a small extension to the DCAT vocabulary: the RING DCAT Extension.[33]

This small extension adds properties that support applications in accessing the datasets: for instance, the OAI-PMH[34] metadata prefix to specify the identifier of the metadata prefixes supported by the OAI-PMH target; or the subset ID to specify the name of the set or the URI of the graph that identifies the sub-set if a dataset is accessible through an API that supports the identification of a subset by limiting to a set (like OAI-PMH) or a graph (like SPARQL). This vocabulary also provides properties to link a dataset to a software tool or to an API method that can process it.

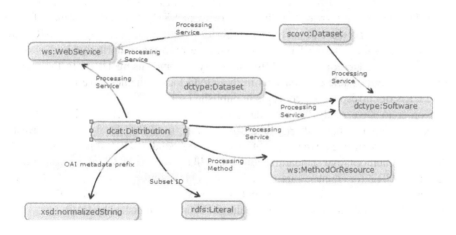

Fig. 2. A graph view of the small RING DCAT extension vocabulary

---

[26] http://purl.org/dc/terms/
[27] http://xmlns.com/foaf/spec/
[28] http://www.w3.org/TR/vcard-rdf/
[29] http://www.w3.org/TR/skos-reference/
[30] http://www.w3.org/TR/void/
[31] https://github.com/edumbill/doap/wiki
[32] http://schema.org
[33] http://vocabularies.aginfra.eu/dcatext#
[34] OAI—PMH is an exchange protocol for exposing metadata: https://www.openarchives.org/pmh/

2.2   Value Vocabularies

This LOD layer, besides the RDF metadata vocabularies mentioned before, needs an infrastructure of LOD Knowledge Organization Systems (KOSs) or "value vocabularies" to univocally identify certain concepts that constitute the "values" for many of the dimensions that are essential to describe a dataset. Examples are: topics, geographic scope, data exchange protocols, metadata standards, file formats, data types etc.

Particular importance is given to the use of standards in the management of information: datasets are also linked to the vocabularies that they use. In order to provide comprehensive "authority" lists of existing information management standards that can be linked to the datasets, the RING harvests information from the registries available in the Agricultural Information Management Standards (AIMS)[35] website: the registry of metadata sets and the registry of Knowledge Organization Systems (KOS).

As regards other technical standards that are relevant to interoperability (protocol, notation), no comprehensive authority lists have been found, so the system provides either free-tagging lists that users can extend or local controlled lists. Such lists of controlled values are provided in the form of local SKOS Concept Schemes. These schemes have no pretense of becoming authority lists: they are used by the RING and by applications that use the RING until some the relevant authoritative bodies (e.g. IANA[36], W3C[37], Dublin Core) publish authority schemes using URIs. In the meantime, whenever possible the concepts in the RING local schemes have been mapped to the URIs of corresponding concepts in published schemes.

In order to have really "linked" data, whenever possible URIs in the RING are mapped to URIs in other authority data: for example, the RING local URIs of formats and notations are mapped, when possible, to the corresponding URIs (and in some cases URLs) from authoritative standardization bodies like IANA or W3C, as we said above; while local URIs for countries are mapped to the corresponding URIs in the FAO Geopolitical Ontology[38] and URIs of agriculture-related topics are mapped to the corresponding URIs in AGROVOC[39], the agricultural thesaurus published by FAO.

3   LOD Publication Approach for the RING Linked Data

Beyond the semantic aspects and the serialization of data as RDF, the actual publication of Linked Open Data (LOD) requires some additional steps and design work (cf. [12, 13]).

---

[35] http://aims.fao.org

[36] The Internet Assigned Numbers Authority (IANA) is responsible for the global coordination of the DNS Root, IP addressing, and other Internet protocol resources.

[37] The World Wide Web Consortium (W3C) is an international community where Member organizations, a full-time staff, and the public work together to develop Web standards.

[38] http://www.fao.org/countryprofiles/geoinfo/en/

[39] http://aims.fao.org/vest-registry/vocabularies/agrovoc-multilingual-agricultural-thesaurus

The first thing to consider for the actual publication of linked data is URI design and persistence [13, 14].

As for URI design, we initially decided to go for a simple URI pattern including the original RING domain name, a string identifier for the type of resource, and an ID for the resource. The URI for each resource in the RING is built as follows: {RING-domain}/node/{resource-ID}, e.g. http://ring.ciard.net/node/2417. The URI of each "concept" is built as follows: {RING-domain}/taxonomy_term/{concept-ID}, e.g. http://ring.ciard.net/taxonomy_term/108

This satisfied the requirements of having short unique and "opaque"[40] URIs for all entities. However, we have recently realized that URIs containing the domain name of an initiative or an institution are not ideal for persistence (see more on URI persistence in [14]): we are in the process of moving from the ring.ciard.net domain to the ring.ciard.info domain and we may lose control of the ciard.net domain in one year. So we decided to gradually move to PURL URIs: PURLs (Persistent Uniform Resource Locators) are Web addresses that act as permanent identifiers, allowing the underlying Web addresses of resources to change over time without negatively affecting systems that depend on them. RING URIs will become http://purl.org/net/ciardring/{resource type}/{resource-ID} and will resolve to the RDF and HTML versions of the resource at the URL where they are available at that moment.

The second thing is to provide machine access to the RDF data: the recommendations for Linked Data are to make them accessible through a) an RDF description at the resource URI; b) a SPARQL endpoint for querying the whole RDF store.

The RING was built with the Drupal[41] Content Management System, which provides modules that enable both the serialization of the metadata for each resource as RDF under a specific path and a SPARQL endpoint (for the RING: http://ring.ciard.info/sparql1). The RING also implements content negotiation[42] through Apache rewrite rules.[43]

In the end, the resulting LOD store publishes 74951 triples, 1186 concepts (around 500 of which mapped to external URIs), 1067 entities of type dcat:Dataset and 300 of type dcat:Distribution.

4   Examples of Data Re-use

Other applications can re-use data from the RING by sending SPARQL queries [15]. SPARQL queries are conceptually similar to SQL queries but rely on the published

---

[40] Not meaningful: humans or machines should not infer anything about the resource from the resource URI.

[41] http://drupal.org

[42] When an HTTP client attempts to dereference a URI, it can specify which type (or types) of content it would prefer to receive in response: if the client specifies HTML (like a normal browser), the system has to serve an HTML page; if the client specifies RDF, the system has to serve an RDF version of the resource.

[43] See http://www.w3.org/TR/swbp-vocab-pub/#recipe6

semantics of RDF vocabularies. These published semantics allow the application to write a query without the need to look at the internal structure of the database.

By just looking up the URIs of the entities and concepts in the RING[44], developers can send a query for instance to get all datasets available through the OAI-PMH protocol (the URI of the concept "OAI-PMH protocol" is http://ring.ciard.net/taxonomy_term/108): see an example of such a query at http://ring.ciard.info/get-all-datasets-available-through-oai-pmh.

The following examples illustrate how two types of applications (data aggregators and data processing tools) can leverage the RING to broaden the range of data sources they rely on. Using the RING instead of a local database of data sources a) allows data owners to update information on their datasets without the need of informing all the service / application providers that are using them (all applications using them will get the updated information in the query results from the RING); b) allows applications to dynamically find new suitable datasets without the need of constantly searching the web and updating their local lists, also exploiting work done by others; and therefore c) minimizes the duplication of effort and the creation of new silos.

4.1   Example 1: Data Aggregators Using the RING as Their Collection Database

Applications like data aggregators can register their data providers in the RING and then use it as a collection / dataset store to send queries and execute part of their workflows on them. An example of such usage of the RING data is AGRIS[45], a database of more than 7 million bibliographic references on agricultural research and technology and links to related data resources on the Web. AGRIS retrieves information on AGRIS data providers through a SPARQL query run against the RING looking for datasets that "belong to" (dc:partOf) the AGRIS network (http://ring.ciard.net/node/10687 is the URI of the AGRIS network in the RING):

```
... WHERE { ?dataset rdf:type dcat:Dataset . ?dataset
dc:partOf <http://ring.ciard.net/node/10687> ...
```

A similar use of the RING is made by AgriFeeds[46], an aggregator of news and events in agriculture that retrieves from the RING technical metadata about datasets available as RSS feeds. AgriFeeds makes a more dynamic use of the RING compared to AGRIS as it doesn't limit the query to datasets belonging to the AgriFeeds network but retrieves any dataset that is of type RSS and uses the "RSS metadata set", thus automatically increasing the number of feeds behind the service as new feeds are registered in the RING.

---

[44] http://ring.ciard.info/concept-uris and http://ring.ciard.info/entity-uris
[45] http://agris.fao.org
[46] http://www.agrifeeds.org

4.2   Example 2: Data Processing Applications Retrieving Suitable Datasets from the RING

Another example of data re-use is the iPython Notebook for estimating temperatures developed in the agINFRA project[47]. There are datasets, like the "European daily mean temperature series" maintained by the European Climate Assessment and Dataset project, that can be processed by this application. Since datasets in the RING are linked to software tools that can process them, the iPython Notebook can run regular queries to the RING to always retrieve the new datasets that might become available that are processable by the tool. The URI of the iPython Notebook in the RING is http://ring.ciard.net/node/19483, so the following fragment would filter all datasets that can be processed by the Notebook:

```
. ?distro dcat-ext:processingService
<http://ring.ciard.net/node/19483> .
```

5   Discussion and Further Work

Building the RING was partly a good generic exercise in creating a Linked Data dataset catalog and partly a practical community-specific implementation.

As concerns the exercise of building a Linked Data dataset catalog, what we think the Linked Data community may have to consider for the future is that existing dataset catalogs do not seem to be fully ready for data exchange, in either direction: a) aggregating data from them is in some cases possible but not to a high degree of granularity and not using shared semantics; b) most of these platforms, even the few that work as global directories (like CKAN), don't implement harvesting or aggregation: they require manual submission of datasets, thus implementing a centralized model and in the end building new silos.

As for the semantic aspects, what we have learnt is that there is a need on the one hand for extensions to the existing metadata vocabularies in order to better describe certain technical aspects of datasets (dimensions, syntax, reference standards...) and on the other hand for more authoritative reference lists exposed as Linked Data, possibly published by the relevant authorities, e.g. a comprehensive LOD reference list of serialization formats by IANA or an extension of the DCMI Type vocabulary.

Regarding the specific real case of the RING, our practical goal is to make it the reference dataset hub for agricultural information services: to get there, the RING has to reach a critical mass of registered datasets and a high level of metadata quality in order to become comprehensive and reliable enough for external services. To reach a critical mass of datasets registered, a move towards a federated approach is necessary. Past experiences show that centralizing the management of datasets is not a sustainable solution. Also forcing all providers to use the same platform will not work.

Therefore, there is a need for a global directory of datasets in agriculture adopting a two-pronged approach: preferably, manual submission for higher quality of metadata

---

[47] agINFRA is an EC FP7 project completed in 2015 whose products are still accessible through the new website: http://aginfra.eu

and categorizations that are customized to agriculture and optimized for interoperability (this approach would also suit organizations that do not use any local platform and would provide them with a publishing platform); alternatively, exchange of metadata with existing platforms, in order not to force institutions to have a duplicate dataset publishing workflow. The implementation of a federation mechanism is the next step for the RING.

The objective remains that of making data produced by agricultural organizations more visible, better shared, easier to re-use and therefore actually consumable by integrated end-user services.

References

1. Chinese Academy of Agricultural Sciences, Global Forum on Agricultural Research, Food and Agriculture Organization of the United Nations: Interim Proceedings of International Expert Consultation on "Building the CIARD Framework for Data and Information Sharing", CIARD (2011)
2. Ballantyne, P.: ICTs transforming agricultural science, research and technology generation. In: Summary of the ICT Workshop at the Science Forum. GFAR (2009)
3. Crosas, M.: The Dataverse Network: An Open-Source Application for Sharing, Discovering and Preserving Data. D-Lib. Magazine 17(1/2) (2011)
4. OpenAIRE Guidelines: For Data Archives. https://guidelines.openaire.eu/wiki/OpenAIRE_Guidelines:_For_Data_Archives
5. Vierkant, P., Spier, S., Rücknagel, J., Gundlach, J., Fichtmüller, D., Pampel, H., Kindling, M., Kirchhoff, A., Göbelbecker, H., Klump, J., Bertelmann, R., Schirmbacher, P., Scholze, F.: Vocabulary for the Registration and Description of Research Data Repositories Version 2.0, re3data (2012)
6. Dryad Development Team: Dryad Metadata Application Profile, Version 3.0 (2010). http://wiki.datadryad.org/wg/dryad/images/8/8b/Dryad3.0.pdf
7. Ginty, K., Kerridge, S., Fairley, P., Henderson, R., Cranner, P., Bokma, A., Garfield, S.: CERIF for Datasets (C4D) – An Overview, C4D (2012)
8. Khan, H., Caruso, B., Corson-Rikert, J., Dietrich, D., Lowe, B., Steinhart, G.: DataStaR: Using the Semantic Web approach for Data Curation. The International Journal of Digital Curation 6(2) (2011)
9. Berners-Lee, T.: Linked Data. http://www.w3.org/DesignIssues/LinkedData
10. Isaac, A., Waites, W., Young, J., Zeng, M.: Library Linked Data Incubator Group: Datasets, Value Vocabularies, and Metadata Element Sets. W3C (2011)
11. DCAT Application Profile for Data Portals in Europe – Final, ISA Programme (2013)
12. Heath, T., Bizer, C.: Linked data: evolving the web into a global data space. In: Synthesis Lectures on the Semantic Web. Theory and Technology, 1:1, pp. 1–136. Morgan & Claypool (2011)
13. Best Practices for Publishing Linked Data, W3C (2014). http://www.w3.org/TR/ld-bp/
14. Archer, P., Goedertier, S., Loutas, N.: Study on persistent URIs, with identification of best practices and recommendations on the topic for the MSs and the EC. ISA Programme (2012). http://philarcher.org/diary/2013/uripersistence/
15. SPARQL Query Language for RDF, W3C (2007). http://www.w3.org/TR/rdf-sparql-query/

Improving Access to Big Data in Agriculture and Forestry Using Semantic Technologies

Rob Lokers[1(✉)], Yke van Randen[1], Rob Knapen[1], Stephan Gaubitzer[2], Sergey Zudin[3], and Sander Janssen[1]

[1] Alterra Wageningen UR, Wageningen, The Netherlands
{rob.lokers,yke.vanranden,rob.knapen,sander.janssen}@wur.nl
[2] Austrian Institute of Technology, Vienna, Austria
stephan.gaubitzer@ait.ac.at
[3] European Forest Institute, Joensuu, Finland
sergey.zudin@efi.int

Abstract. To better understand and manage the interactions of agriculture and natural resources, for example under current increasing societal demands and climate changes, agro-environmental research must bring together an ever growing amount of data and information from multiple science domains. Data that is inherently large, multi-dimensional and heterogeneous, and requires computational intensive processing. Thus, agro-environmental researchers must deal with specific Big Data challenges in efficiently acquiring the data fit to their job while limiting the amount of computational, network and storage resources needed to practical levels. Automated procedures for collection, selection, annotation and indexing of data and metadata are indispensable in order to be able to effectively exploit the global network of available scientific information. This paper describes work performed in the EU FP7 Trees4Future and SemaGrow projects that contributes to development and evaluation of an infrastructure that allows efficient discovery and unified querying of agricultural and forestry resources using Linked Data and semantic technologies.

Keywords: Semantic technologies · Metadata · Big data · Forestry · Agriculture

1   Problem Statement

The amount of data available for science has grown enormously in the past years, driven by technological developments that allow larger, faster and more complex data collection, data-intensive processing and analysis. This enhanced complexity and the huge growth rates make it hard to oversee the evolving global data ecosystem and effectively exploit and reuse available data. A major cause are structural insufficiencies due to the networked nature of our society, where the specialist nature of many enterprises and experts is not yet mirrored well enough in the way we manage information and communicate [1]. Data is produced at ever increasing rates making it impossible for humans to manually validate and document it. This is also expressed by the "metadata generation bottleneck" [2], describing the fact that we are producing

© Springer International Publishing Switzerland 2015
E. Garoufallou et al. (Eds.): MTSR 2015, CCIS 544, pp. 369–380, 2015.
DOI: 10.1007/978-3-319-24129-6_32

more data than we can analyze and document ourselves. Moreover, the more the data becomes interconnected, using ever more elaborate information models, the harder this will be for humans to oversee. Hence part of this work will have to be done by computers, and teaching them how to classify and enrich available metadata as best as possible is a necessary part of it.

Obviously these phenomena also pose barriers for agro-environmental researchers to efficiently collect and use data relevant for their scientific work and in return provide the data they produce to other scientists in their own and other domains. It is often claimed that improving interoperability, and specifically closing the gap regarding semantic interoperability is key for more effective integration and automation of key processes in agro-environmental research [3] [4] [5]. Realistic use cases show a variety of challenges associated for instance with environmental modelling ranging from metadata oriented information retrieval issues to heavily data-oriented problems related to Big Data mining and data integration [6]. These concern first of all the effective discovery of the appropriate data for a specific research task. Many disciplines still lack the technical, institutional and cultural frameworks required for efficient data sharing, leading to a "scandalous shortfall" in the sharing of data by researchers [7]. Besides, reuse of data created by others requires assessment of the data's relevance, and seeking confidence that the data can be understood and trusted [8], requiring more contextual information than usually available in metadata. In practice, researchers tend to be traditionally quite dependent on their own peers and scientific networks when accessing data required for their work. However, agro-environmental research has become more and more interdisciplinary through the years and the amounts of data potentially available for science are growing enormously. At the same time this data is often not harmonized nor reusing existing data schemas, making the total of data more heterogeneous. Consequently, in data-intensive research areas like agro-environmental modelling we have reached the point where automated procedures for selection, collection and indexing that are able to handle big, distributed, heterogeneous data are becoming indispensable to effectively exploit the global network of data.

To enable such processes to be able to find a way through available resources, a first requisite is that datasets are properly documented and that this metadata is accessible through standardized, machine-readable protocols and formats. One challenge here is that metadata has often been registered by humans for humans. Even though metadata standards force users to use (often XML based) machine readable formats, a great part of the contained metadata remains textual and unstructured. Insight in the semantics of this content is indispensable to be able to interpret specific data in the context of often very specialized science domains. Exploiting and efficiently combining semantic networks from domain specific vocabularies and ontologies relevant for agro-environmental research, like e.g. AGROVOC [9], Climate and Forecast (CF) metadata conventions (http://cfconventions.org/) or GEMET (General Multilingual Environmental Thesaurus: https://www.eionet.europa.eu/gemet/) in the case of agro-environmental research can support better rendering of data from multi-disciplinary domains to targeted application domains. Moreover, agro-environmental research often deals with data-intensive tasks, requiring analysis and processing of large and often multi-dimensional datasets. Thus, specific Big Data related challenges also play an important role. In essence it requires the implementation of innovative methods to efficiently acquire the data fit to the researcher's job that limit the amount of manual work as well as the amount of required computational, network and storage resources. This should at the very end lead to transparent and unified discovery and querying of distributed heterogeneous data for use in scientific studies.

This paper describes work performed in the EU FP7 Trees4Future and SemaGrow projects to setup an infrastructure that efficiently collects and makes available agricultural and forestry resources. It provides facilities for researchers to discover data resources relevant to their scientific work, combining common metadata standards and protocols with semantic technologies. The infrastructure also provides an implementation that allows querying the underlying ecosystem of distributed and heterogeneous data in a unified way. After finding the relevant datasets the infrastructure, based on available metadata and semantics, allows retrieval of pre-processed and integrated data coming from different sources which can be downloaded in a format of their choice, e.g. as a NetCDF (Network Common Data Form) formatted file.

2   The Trees4Future Project: Semantic Access to Agro-Forestry Data for Research

The EU FP7 Trees4Future project Trees4Future (www.trees4future.eu) is an Integrative European Research Infrastructure project that aims to integrate, develop and improve major forest genetics and forestry research infrastructures. Its aim is to provide the wider European forestry research community with easy and comprehensive access to currently scattered sources of information (including for instance genetic databanks, forest modelling tools and wood technology labs) and expertise. One of the objectives of the project is to set up a "Clearinghouse", acting as an operational forestry metadata repository that makes European datasets discoverable and accessible for the whole community. This repository exploits open standards to register and harvest metadata, and to access the associated data and data services. To improve semantic interoperability and thus increase the discoverability of datasets, Linked Open Data (LOD) and semantic technologies are used.

The overall workflow of the Trees4Future metadata repository is straightforward and is depicted in Figure 1. Data providers from the forestry domain supply metadata for their datasets, using metadata schemas that adhere recognized standards like Dublin Core, ISO-19115 etc. Provided that their metadata repositories also support common protocols for harvesting (for instance OAI-PMH), these metadata are automatically collected, stored in the central linked data repository of the Clearinghouse and semantically tagged. Subsequently, the end users, notably researchers and decision makers in the forestry domain, can search and discover datasets over this distributed global network of data nodes.

Fig. 1. Trees4Future metadata processing workflow

2.1   Improving Metadata to Support Agro-Environmental Research

The promotion of data discoverability through a federated metadata query endpoint harvesting metadata from distributed sources is a quite commonly applied mechanism. However, many of these endpoints lack the semantic interoperability required to support agro-environmental research, with its aforementioned challenges. In many cases such mechanisms do not even cover the specific semantics of often relatively "small" specialized knowledge domains, let alone that they are meaningfully linking the contexts of the broad range of domains associated with multi-disciplinary research. An illustrative use case would be one where a researcher is searching for datasets including climate data using the term rainfall. In practice, many weather and climate change datasets will be annotated using the broader concept precipitation, referring to a more commonly measured and modelled parameter, covering rain but also other types of precipitation (e.g. snow, hail). These datasets will only be found using the term rainfall if there is an explicit semantic relationship defined between the terms rainfall and precipitation that can be used by a search algorithm. Although this example is over-simplified, we will use it here to explain how we have used semantic technologies to improve semantic interoperability and develop the federated search endpoint for forestry and related environmental data.

Agro-environmental research, and in particular the more data-intensive activities within this area, like modelling and data analysis, usually require very specialized datasets. In the provided example of precipitation data, a researcher could be interested in (combinations of) historical or forecasted data. This data could either be based on observations and measurements (historical) or on the output of meteorological and climate models (either historical, short term weather forecasts or long term climate projections based on climate scenarios). Besides, available data will usually not be the immediate sensor, satellite, or model output data, but will be post-processed. Such processing can concern for instance spatial or temporal up- or downscaling, corrections for elevation differences or bias corrections that can be implemented through a variety of methodologies and approaches. In practice, depending on the research application there will be a multitude of detailed requirements and boundary conditions for determining the best fitting datasets. A scientific model or data analysis methodology might pose conditions, but also the characteristics of other available datasets usually influence the final selection.

Commonly used metadata standards like Dublin Core, ISO-19115/ISO-19119 and others have proven to be valuable to the improvement of data discoverability in general. However, they tend to fall short when it comes to supporting researchers in finding the best applicable data for their complex research challenges. The design of these common metadata schemas is such that they do support e.g. structured topic searches or basic searches on keywords (sometimes standardized through controlled vocabularies), but most relevant information (e.g. the lineage of a dataset) is only available as unstructured text. Moreover, metadata is usually filled in by humans, with other humans in mind as its users. As a result it is not uncommon that it is sparse and ambiguous, and difficult to use for automated processing beyond automated harvesting and human interpreted searching. The metadata schemas and the way they are handled in general lack both the semantic richness that is required for automatic reasoning and to decide on its usability for specific jobs as well as the depth that is required to describe the characteristics and detailed specification of the dataset's contained data.

The idea adopted by Trees4Future is that from the technical perspective there are various methods to improve the way metadata can be (automatically) exploited. Nevertheless, we also state that a first requisite to improve on this situation is that data providers and researchers need to become more aware that good metadata increases the value of their datasets and the chances of reuse and that vice versa datasets of other scientists can be more efficiently used. To motivate data providers to adopt good metadata practice, the project provides through its infrastructure a set of working examples. This is done first of all by improving the capabilities of the metadata to be self-describing and semantically richer. Secondly, the project has developed a simple ontology to structure and annotate metadata of scientific datasets. Finally, an infrastructure was developed, implementing this ontology and using the available (improved) metadata services and automatic procedures to process and structure metadata in such a way that users can more efficiently query it.

2.2 Improving Metadata Capabilities of Forestry Resources

To improve on the current situation, data and metadata needs to be harmonized where possible. This typically is a complex and time consuming activity, in particular when considering large amounts of legacy data that have never been properly documented. We have therefore implemented some relatively simple concepts to improve the semantic richness of metadata, thus facilitating more efficient processing and use of metadata. In parallel we have promoted some practices for generating and editing metadata that build on these improvements.

Within the Trees4Future project, several concepts were elaborated to improve the semantic richness of metadata for forestry related purposes. First of all, we have exploited the self-describing capabilities of specific dataset that are already used in forestry research. The NetCDF format, often used in the agro-environmental domain as the format for large multidimensional gridded datasets, metadata can inherently be included as part of the dataset, so the dataset becomes self-describing. Besides using some of the standard metadata fields available in NetCDF, we have used the extensibility of NetCDF with additional metadata fields. Publishing these metadata in harvestable way through the OAI-PMH protocol, allows to automatically harvest these metadata from registered sources.

Table 1. Dublin Core metadata extensions for forestry genetics.

T4F Elements	Element description
T4F.Species	This element contains just the species names as list elements because the family and genus of this type can be derived. A population contains one or more Species.
T4F.Populationtype	There are 6 types of populations which describe the main purpose of the research area.
T4F.Size	Represents the size (number of individuals) of the population.
T4F.Traits	If there are phenotypic or genotypic traits measured within the population the name of the trait is given. When there are more than one trait available they are provided as a list.
T4F.Samples	Some experiments require storing material of the samples in a resource centre. If this is the case we provide the amount and tissue type of the collected samples.

A lot of scientific data providers in the agro-forestry domain use the Dublin Core (DC) schema to describe datasets. Its relative simplicity compared to other available metadata schemas makes it easy-to-use, even for non-experts. On the other hand, it also turned out that this simplicity limited the options to document forestry specific details of datasets. For example the specific domain characteristics of the forestry genetics domain cannot very well be described within the limits of the DC format. Thus, we decided for the purpose of this project to extend the DC schema with a set of additional forestry genetics specific metadata fields (Table 1). The addition of these fields allows to enrich the metadata of the associated datasets with the most essential characteristics relevant for its users. Moreover, since many forestry genetic data providers already have integrated the information to be included in these fields in some way in their systems, it is easy to automatically generate this additional metadata thus avoiding manual editing. Finally, we promoted that metadata of newly developed and where possible also of existing datasets are annotated using commonly referred domain specific vocabularies and ontologies. In this way the process of automatic annotation of the harvested metadata that has been developed can be applied in a less erroneous and more effective manner.

2.3   An Ontology for Structuring and Annotation of Scientific Metadata

An inventory of use cases in forestry research showed that there are basic requirements regarding the metadata of involved datasets that are currently still lacking. First
of all, references to harmonized vocabularies are required to be able to consistently
assess the value of datasets from multiple sources for research purposes. Moreover, it
appears that there is a need for more depth and detail than commonly available in
current metadata. Evident use cases in this respect are the ones that include the use of
data-intensive agricultural and forestry models. These models require data that generally follows strict and precise definitions, not only on the dataset level (e.g. temporal
and spatial resolution) but also on the attribute and data level. Referring again to the
precipitation example, a typical model could require an input parameter specifically
defined as the projected daily sum of precipitation in millimeters.

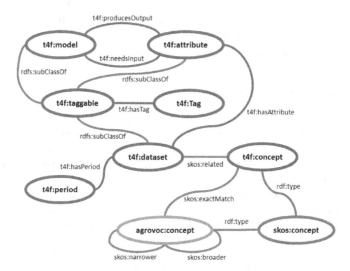

Fig. 2. Trees4Future metadata ontology

Based on these conclusions, and aiming to be able to automatically link datasets to
scientific models, the base ontology shown in Figure 2 was developed. This framework takes into account the requirements derived from use cases, and additionally
provides the functionality to be able to conceptually link datasets and models via a
description of the characteristics of both the dataset content and the input/output
attributes of models. The Trees4Future metadata ontology is composed of five basic
concepts, describing datasets and models and their relations:

- *Dataset* – a collection of data (e.g. climate projections for 2015-2050 with model X
  for climate scenario Y etc.), usually including multiple *attributes*
- *Model* – a computer model that requires one or multiple input *attributes* in order to
  be executed and produces one or multiple output *attributes*.

- *Attribute* – a characteristic of the content of a *dataset*, and/or the input and/or outputs from a *model* (e.g. '*projected precipitation*', or '*texture*').
- *Taggable* – an abstraction of *dataset*, *model* and *attribute* that can have multiple *tags* of the form name-value. E.g. an *attribute* can have a *tag* 'name=thickness' and another *tag* 'unit=mm'
- *Tag*– a name-value pair (e.g. '*unit*' = '*mm*')

At a conceptual level there is a high similarity between model and dataset. In this ontology models, datasets and attributes are considered a specialisation of the taggable concept. Taggables can have any number of tags. Each tag describes one aspect of the concept it is assigned to. One tag can be assigned to multiple concepts. Tags can contain simple values (numbers, dates, strings) or can contain a link to an external ontology or vocabulary. Because tags can be used in queries their use enables a powerful mechanism for complex searches which is extensible to other types of concepts (e.g. maps, documents, projects). The model allows establishing and determining the interrelationships between datasets and dataset attributes and models and model input and output parameters.

2.4   Exploiting Metadata Semantics to Improve Discoverability

As a basis for the semantic network required to support the Trees4Future concept, we have investigated the availability of forestry specific vocabularies or ontologies that could be used for our objectives. Earlier research [10] has called for a "Multilingual Forestry Ontology Project" with strategic links to ongoing ontology framework projects and encourages the use of the Global Forest Decimal Classification (GFDC). However, up till now no forestry specific ontology has been published from such initiatives, while GFDC itself is a plain classification which does not provide the semantic richness we consider necessary for our purposes. Nevertheless, several useful unpublished taxonomies exist in the forestry domain, which are used in smaller scientific networks to support research. Examples are tree species and wood product taxonomies. Most of these fairly scattered semantic resources are however also covered by AGROVOC, a multilingual controlled vocabulary covering all areas of interest to the Food and Agriculture Organization of the United Nations (FAO), including food, nutrition, agriculture, fisheries, forestry and the environment. AGROVOC is made available by FAO as an RDF/SKOS-XL concept scheme and published as a linked data set aligned to 16 other vocabularies (http://en.wikipedia.org/wiki/AGROVOC). As such it does not only cover the core agricultural domain, but is also fit for broader agro-environmental applications, with even some links to related domains like biotechnology, economics, geopolitical and geographical entities, thus providing a multidisciplinary view required to cover the domain. To also be able to coop with the semantics associated with specialized subdomains of the forestry domain, we support inclusion and alignment of additional semantics. Developing the semantic network of the Trees4Future Clearinghouse we have for instance integrated a forestry genetics traits taxonomy which was specifically developed in the Trees4Future project to support the structuring and annotation of such resources in specialized databases.

The core semantic framework for the developed system is set up in an OpenRDF Sesame triple store (http://rdf4j.org). The before mentioned base ontologies were locally imported into this framework. This is mainly to prevent querying over several distributed ontologies and thus evade associated issues of performance and multiple points of failure. Besides, it allows to strategically import parts of the larger ontologies like AGROVOC, allowing the elimination of non-relevant sections from the rather broadly oriented AGROVOC domain or concept translations in languages that are incomplete or non-relevant for the application. In order to enable the integration of collected datasets into this semantic framework, the datasets and their metadata are stored as RDF (http://www.w3.org/RDF/) in the triple store and subsequently automatically linked to the broader semantic network. To accomplish this, as a first step the harvested metadata records are analyzed. Individual metadata fields and their values are explicitly stored as tags (*t4f.tag*) so the original metadata can be reproduced. Subsequently the metadata is further processed using NLP techniques. In Trees4Future, such techniques for extracting meaning from natural language are used to automatically identify forestry domain specific terms, with the aim to automatically generate RDF/SKOS (Simple Knowledge Organisation System: http://www.w3.org/TR/skos-reference/) concepts linked to the analyzed dataset. In principle, advanced NLP algorithms are able to "learn" the language and semantics of the forestry domain by using a domain specific corpus. Machine learning could then be used to exploit that knowledge for automated classifying and tagging of datasets based on metadata contents. Unfortunately, a domain specific corpus was not available and limited project resources have up till now withhold us from building this corpus and setting up the required algorithms. However, less advanced use of NLP was possible and the approach was taken to use its syntactical ability to do a text analysis over the harvested metadata. This syntactical analysis determines the type of each word (e.g. noun, noun plural, or verb) in a dataset's metadata elements. Because in practice searches mainly consist of nouns it was decided to only use nouns, combinations of nouns (e.g. "leaf area") and multi-word expressions containing nouns (e.g. "organic matter") from this analysis. The dataset itself as well as the terms detected from the metadata in the syntactical analysis are added to the triple store as subclasses of SKOS concepts. The final step in this process is the linkage of the analyzed dataset with the external ontologies. This is performed by an automated enrichment process, which creates a link (*skos:exactMatch*) between the concepts derived from the metadata and corresponding concepts from the external ontologies. Links are created only if the concepts values are identical and are defined in the same language.

In the before mentioned "rainfall example", one would expect datasets containing measurements or modelling values to refer to the term precipitation in their metadata elements. Figure 3 gives a schematic representation of such a dataset. The NLP analysis would extract from the harvested metadata content the term precipitation, resulting in a RDF triple connecting the dataset with the generated concept "precipitation". In the available semantic network, the AGROVOC ontology also contains the concept precipitation. Moreover, AGROVOC relates this concept to other concepts, using SKOS predicates to determine broader, narrower and synonym relationships between its concepts. Thus, an explicit relationship exists between "precipitation" and a concept which has "rainfall" as one of its synonyms. Combined with the automatically generated skos:exactMatch relationship between the Trees4Future and AGROVOC concept of precipitation this allows automated reasoning over the semantic network and thus (among others) resolving a user query including the term rainfall.

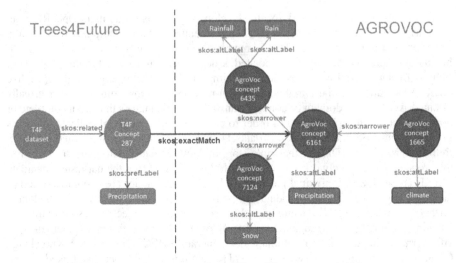

Fig. 3. Schematic representation of Trees4Future semantic linkage.

Based on the described methodology to enrich metadata with semantics, a semantic search query engine was developed. The engine allows search interfaces to perform semantic queries on the developed triple store using a SOAP (Simple Object Access Protocol) interface. The query engine dynamically transforms the SOAP request parameters into SPARQL queries that exploit the defined semantic relationships to return a broader result set of matching datasets. It includes algorithms to weigh the individual datasets in the returned result set based on proximity criteria, thus being able to valuating for instance results based on exact matches or synonyms with higher scores than results based on broader or narrower relationships.

3   Future Extensions Towards Semantic Reasoning Over Data

The Trees4Future project has mainly focused on the semantic access to datasets through its associated metadata. More enhanced applications could also utilize the semantics of the data itself, thus revealing even more of the specifics of the contained data. Applications vary from fairly straightforward sub selections along the dimensions of datasets (like spatial or temporal subsets) to applications to complement missing data by looking for data using similarity criteria (e.g. finding crop trial data from locations with similar soil and climate conditions as the study location). The ongoing EU FP7 SemaGrow project develops an infrastructure that allows transparent access to distributed heterogeneous and constantly updated large datasets. It aims to tackle this challenge by developing novel algorithms and methods for querying distributed triple stores, scalable and robust semantic indexing algorithms and effective ontology alignment. These innovations will be tested by applying them to data and knowledge intensive use cases from the agro-environmental domain, where aspects like the large heterogeneity of datasets, their often explicit spatial and temporal dimensions resulting in relatively large volumes and their inherent nature of uncertainty provide additional challenges which are not usually dealt with till so far [6]. Through one of its use cases, the SemaGrow project seeks to broaden the scope and applicability of the previously described semantic concepts developed in the Trees4Future project. This concerns first of all the technical scope. Underlying data of resources are triplified and its semantics are explicitly defined and exploited. Moreover, the available infrastructure provides a unified entry point to query the data of distributed data sources, without users having to know the specifics of the schemas associated with every individual resource and its physical location. The use case also broadens the application domain from the forestry and environmental domain towards the more general domains of agriculture, forestry and environment, thus providing its services to a potentially much broader user community.

The SemaGrow project is currently producing its first results, as selected scientific use cases from the agro-environmental domain are being implemented and evaluated. This includes a demonstrator that extends the described Trees4Future semantic search interface with the functionality to query sub selections of discovered dataset. It builds on the improvements accomplished in the Trees4Future project, exploiting among others the concepts developed to extend metadata and to semantically link with agro-environmental ontologies.

4   Discussion and Conclusions

Given the growth of the available amount of data and its complexity, researchers will be no longer able to fully oversee and handle the network of data required for their work. Automated procedures for collection, selection, annotation and indexing of data and metadata are becoming indispensable in order to be able to effectively exploit the global network of available scientific information. The Trees4Future project has developed metadata concepts and automated procedures to provide semantic access to agro-forestry data resources. The work included i) improving the capabilities of the metadata to be self-describing and semantically richer; ii) development of a simple ontology to structure and annotate metadata of scientific datasets and iii) development of an infrastructure to process, structure and semantically query metadata. The developed infrastructure serves as a crucial component of a European research Infrastructure for forestry providing transparent discovery of forestry data. It also serves as an illustrative showcase of potential for agro-environmental research, provided that good quality metadata is available, thus creating awareness and motivating researchers to document their data in a better way. To that respect future integration with broader European infrastructure for agriculture and forestry, e.g. agINFRA (http://aginfra.eu), could benefit both the currently targeted community of forestry research and the broader agro-environmental research and modelling community.

The first experiences demonstrating to groups of forestry researchers in the Trees4Future community have been positive and also indicate that showing the potential of exploiting semantically rich metadata can motivate researchers to improve their efforts to document datasets. This can be seen as a positive signal towards research and the development of more sophisticated ways to (automatically) generate, process and utilize metadata. Another possible way to motivate scientific data providers could be the promotion of "(open) data journals", that allow high quality and well documented scientific data to be published through a peer-reviewed process and cited by others. An example is the Open Data Journal for Agricultural Research (www.odjar.org) which has been recently set up for agro-environmental researchers to be able to publish their work.

Acknowledgements. The research leading to these results has received funding from the European Union's Seventh Framework Programme (FP7/2007-2013) under grant agreement No. 284181 (Trees4Future) and 318497 (SemaGrow).

References

1. Bauer, F., Kaltenböck, M.: Linked Open Data: The Essentials A Quick Start Guide for Decision Makers. Abu Dhabi: The Semantic Web Company; Renewable Energy and Energy Efficiency Partnership
2. Liddy, E.D., et al.: Breaking the metadata generation bottleneck: preliminary findings. In: Proceedings of the 1st ACM/IEEE-CS Joint Conference on Digital Libraries. ACM, Roanoke, Virginia, USA (2001)
3. Laniak, G.F., et al.: Integrated environmental modeling: A vision and roadmap for the future. Environmental Modelling & Software **39**, 3–23 (2013)
4. Macario, C.G.N., Medeiros, C.B.: A framework for semantic annotation of geospatial data for agriculture. International Journal of Metadata, Semantics and Ontologies **4**(1–2), 118–132 (2009)
5. Harvey, F., et al.: Semantic interoperability: A central issue for sharing geographic information. The Annals of Regional Science **33**(2), 213–232 (1999)
6. Lokers, R., Konstantopoulos, S., Stellato, A., Knapen, R., Janssen, S.: Designing innovative linked open data and semantic technologies for agro-environmental modelling. In: 7th Intl. Congress on Env. Modelling and Software, International Environmental Modelling and Software Society (iEMSs), San Diego, CA, USA (2014)
7. Data's shameful neglect **461**(7261), 145–145 (2009)
8. Faniel, I.M., Jacobsen, T.E.: Reusing Scientific Data: How Earthquake Engineering Researchers Assess the Reusability of Colleagues' Data. Comput. Supported Coop. Work **19**(3–4), 355–375 (2010)
9. Caracciolo, C., Stellato, A., Morshed, A., Johannsen, G., Rajbhandari, S., Jaques, Y., Keizer, J.: The AGROVOC Linked Dataset. Semantic Web **4**, 341–348 (2013)
10. Schuck, A.: Towards a European forest information system. Brill, Leiden (2007)

A Semantic Mediator for Handling Heterogeneity of Spatio-Temporal Environment Data

Ba-Huy Tran[1]([✉]), Christine Plumejeaud-Perreau[2], Alain Bouju[1], and Vincent Bretagnolle[3]

[1] L3i, Université de La Rochelle, La Rochelle, France
ba-huy.tran@univ-lr.fr
[2] LIENSs, U.M.R. CNRS 7266, Université de La Rochelle, La Rochelle, France
[3] CEBC, U.M.R CNRS 7372, Université de La Rochelle, La Rochelle, France

Abstract. This paper presents the "Environment and landscape geo-knowledge" project which aims to exploit heterogeneous data sources recorded at the Chizé environmental observatory since 1994. From a case study, we summarize the difficulties encountered by biologists and ecologists experts when maintaining and analyzing collected environmental data, essentially the spatial organization of landscape, crop rotation and wildlife data. We show how a framework which use a spatio-temporal ontology as a semantic mediator can solve challenges related to the analysis and maintenance of these heterogeneous data.

Keywords: Data integration · Ecology · Environment · Spatio-temporal ontology

1 Introduction

In rural areas with a predominance of agricultural activities, the study of environmental issues such as biodiversity preservation, soil erosion by water and tillage, erosive runoff, water pollution and gene fluxes may benefit from the long-term analysis of the crop mosaic resulting from farming practices. In fact, agricultural landscapes are primarily designed by farmer decisions dealing with crop choices and crop allocation at the farm scale. The arrangement, the shape and the nature of crops compose the spatial organization of a landscape which impacts ecological processes at various scales. This information can be relevant when studying links between socio-economic environment and agricultural practices and subsequent spatial organization of landscapes.

Recognizing the benefits of the long-term observation of agricultural practices for research on environmental issues, the UMR Chizé has established an observatory for crop rotations on the Plaine & Val de Sevre workshop area. Since 1994, a Geographic Information System for the Environment (GIS-E) has been deployed in order to monitor the crop rotation of agricultural parcels.

© Springer International Publishing Switzerland 2015
E. Garoufallou et al. (Eds.): MTSR 2015, CCIS 544, pp. 381–392, 2015.
DOI: 10.1007/978-3-319-24129-6_33

This paper presents first the context of this interdisciplinary research around the GIS-E. In the next sections, a spatio-temporal ontology as well as a new framework are proposed in order to improve the performance of the previous one and to solve the challenge in spatio-temporal data analysis. Finally, the conclusion summarizes the progress achieved with the system while highlighting our future work.

1.1   Spatio-Temporal Environment Data

For over twenty years, several databases have been collected by AGRIPOP teams (CNRS Chizé). These data can be categorized as follows.

Land-Uses Database. This spatial organization evolves throughout time, because farmers occasionally change the land-use and boundaries of their parcels. Since 1994, land-uses and spatial organization of 19,000 agricultural parcels are recorded from the field each year and centralized in a database that is initially modeled based on the Space-Time Composite paradigm[17]. This paradigm introduced a small geometry, here called *microparcel*, which is obtained by the intersection of all the parcels during the observation period. The geometry of any parcel can be rebuilt on the fly by unionizing all microparcels belonging to it. The database contains over 600,000 records managed by the PostgreSQL DBMS extended with the PostGIS plug-in.

Biology Database. Meanwhile, wildlife data are collected in the field for several years by another AGRIPOP team of Chizé and centralized in another database. These data, timely and dated, come from researchers who report their observations on over 600 species, mostly birds and plants, through their mobile devices. For birds, the base is a collection of observations describing the behavior of the observed species, their nests, and their context such as vegetation height, date, time, location, and weather condition. Over 26,000 observations are also managed by the PostgreSQL DBMS with its PostGIS extension.

There also exist numerous sets of structured data about different species, often in spreadsheets or in Microsoft Access databases. These data concern the observation of ground beetles and small beetles which are auxiliaries of the fields and very sensitive to the quality of the environment. These insects have been monitored for over 9 years.

1.2   The Need of Spatio-Temporal Analysis

With these available data, a significant number of analyses can be conducted. These analyses, described as follows, require queries accomplished with spatio-temporal reasoning.

1. The analysis can be used first to verify the collected data sets. On crop rotation, the experts can describe a certain number of successions rules in order to

eliminate or to correct questionable values. For example, the unlikely crop succession like "Sunflower-Sunflower" or "Sunflower-Rapeseed" as well as the disappearance of wood in the workshop area can be detected and examined. Primarily, this type of analysis needs temporal relationships reasoning between interval of recorded land-uses statements.

2. On another hand, territorial events, such as fusion, integration, scission, extraction, reallocation and rectification[18], are desired to be pointed out. Analyzing these events allows to discover the correlation between land-use decision and land fragmentation or aggregation in farm practice. These events can be detected through spatio-temporal reasoning based queries.

3. Finally, experts also want to seek the correlation between species observations and land-uses of parcels. They could concern such preferences animals by type and form of crop rotation. Cross database queries with spatio-temporal relationships reasoning are required to select observations that occur in interval of recorded land-uses statements.

2   Spatio-Temporal Ontology

We wish to develop an ontology which acts as a mediator to resolve the heterogeneities between these different data sources. Ontologies help to structure the knowledge and to improve the understanding of concepts through making clear how entities are linked to each other[11]. By defining entities and their relations, ontologies are considered as a feasible solution of the semantic heterogeneity problem[22], thus become the heart of semantic data integration systems[5]. The ontology of time and ontology of fluent are considered for this development.

2.1   Ontology of Time and Ontology of Fluent

OWL-Time[1] [14], dedicated to the concepts and temporal relationships as defined in the theory of Allen[2] and formalized in OWL, is certainly the best candidate. This ontology is used first to describe the temporal content of Web pages and the temporal properties of web services. This ontology is recommended by the W3C for modeling temporal concepts due to its vocabulary for expressing topological relations between instants and intervals. However, the ontology of time alone is not sufficient to represent the evolution of an object. Therefore, an upper-level ontology, such as the ontology of fluent which is based on ontologies of time is strictly necessary.

Traditional ontologies are synchronic, i.e. they refer to a single point in time, thus the temporal dimension must be incorporated in order to monitor the spatial and semantic evolution of objects. Indeed, philosophers have distinguished between two paradigms: endurantism and perdurantism to represent diachronic identities. Endurantism assumes that objects (referred to *enduring* or *continuant*) have three dimensions and are available in full at every moment of their

---

[1] http://www.w3.org/2006/time

lives. Thus, these objects do not have temporal dimension. In contrast, the perdurantist approach considers objects (called *occurrent* or *perdurant*) to have four dimensions. These objects have several time slices in their lives constituting the temporal dimension. This approach represents the various properties of an entity over time as fluents that are validated only during certain intervals or instants. Therefore, the perdurantiste approach enables richer representations of real-world phenomena through its flexibility and expressiveness[1].

The two main languages of the Semantic Web, RDFS and OWL, allow only binary relations between individuals, as a result, the temporal relationships between object are neglected. The *4D-fluent*[23] approaches have been proposed to overcome this limitation. The authors introduced the *TimeSlice* class to represent temporal parts of the entity which is linked to the *TimeInterval* class, a class of the time domain. Each entity is associated with an instance of the *TimeSlice* by the *tsTimeSliceOf* object property. This latter is connected to an instance of the *TimeInterval* by the *tsTimeInterval* property.

Several approaches based on the *4D-fluent* have been introduced. Towl[6] extends OWL with a temporal dimension in order to allows for the representation of complex temporal aspects, such as process state transitions. SOWL[3] extends OWL-Time by enabling representation of static as well as of dynamic information. Recently, the *Continuum* model[12] allows tracking the identity of spatio-temporal entities through time. This model has been successfully applied in studies of the urban evolution[12] or decolonization process[13].

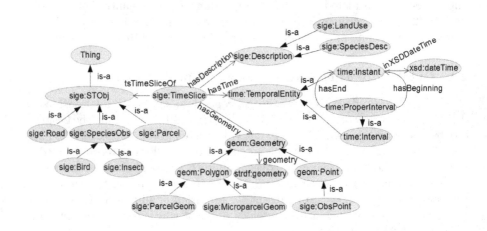

Fig. 1. A spatio-temporal ontology for environment

2.2   A Spatio-Temporal Ontology for Environment

We propose a spatio-temporal ontology (Fig.2) based on the *4-D fluent* approach that serves as a semantic mediator to integrate the presented data sets. This ontology is inspired by the *Continuum* model that examines the evolution of objects in both the temporal and spatial dimension. The main entities in our research, primarily parcels, roads and fauna and flora, have several time slices that match their different characteristics and spatial occupancy through their lives. In this way, crop rotations, boundary changes of each parcel or information of species observations can be represented and analyzed.

While crop rotation or boundary changes of the parcels are periodically archived by predetermined intervals of temporal validity, the position and behavior of species are collected at will. For this reason, the *4D-fluent* model is extended by generalizing the *Interval* class to the *TemporalEntity* class of OWL-Time that has two sub-classes, *Interval* and *Instant*.

As presented, the land-uses database is built based on the *Space-Time Composite* paradigm which uses microparcel as the management unit. In consequence, we introduce the *MicroparcelGeometry* class as a subclass of the *Polygon* class that specializes the *Geometry* class. The difference in the spatial reference system used in these databases is an additional heterogeneity problem. Indeed, while land-uses database uses the *NTF (Paris) / Lambert zone II* reference system for parcels geometry, observations point in the two other databases are recorded on the *WGS 84* one. This problem is handled in the mapping process which transforms these geometry data into virtual RDF triples and converts them into the same spatial reference system as well.

The following prefixes and associated namespaces URIs are used in the spatio-temporal ontology:

Prefix	URI	Description
sige	http://gemina.univ-lr.fr/owlSigE#	The spatio-temporal ontology for environment
geo	http://geovocab.org/spatial#	NeoGeo Spatial Ontology, a vocabulary for describing topological relations between features
strdf	http://strdf.di.uoa.gr/ontology#	The data model stRDF defining spatial datatype used in the Strabon triplestore
xsd	http://www.w3.org/2001/XMLSchema#	The W3C XML Schema Definition Language
time	http://www.w3.org/2006/time#	OWL-Time, an ontology for describing temporal concepts

2.3   Spatio-Temporal Reasoning

Qualitative relationships in the time domain is based on binary relationships which are mutually exclusive. The work of Allen[2] introduced a temporal algebra to define topological relationships between dated objects. For two temporal intervals defined by their start and end date, there are the following relationships *before, meets, overlaps, during, starts, finishes* and their reverse, respectively *after, met-by, overlapped-by, contains, started by, finished-by*, and *equals* which does not have an inverse. These intervals can be viewed as instances of the *ProperInterval* class of OWL-Time. An interval is linked to two instants by the *hasBeginning* and *hasEnd* attribute that determine their boundaries. Besides these 13 relations, the *inside* relationship between an instant and an interval must be also considered in order to link between databases.

To discover new temporal relationships between objects, these above relations must be expressed by a set of rules. The *Semantic Web Rule Language* (SWRL[2]) is chosen due to its available libraries, called *built-ins*, that provide several predicates, mostly for date, time and duration processing. In this way, qualitative temporal relationships between spatial objects are derived by the Pellet[3] engine through a set of SWRL rules. This reasoning mechanism was applied in the SOWL[3] ontology which was afterwards improved by the CHRONOS[8] system. The SWRL rule corresponding to the *inside* relationship between an instant and an interval can be represented as follows:

```
Instant(?x),ProperInterval(?a), hasBeginning(?a,?b),hasEnd(?a,?c),
inXSDDateTime(?b,?d),inXSDDateTime(?c,?e), inXSDDateTime(?x,?y),
lessThanOrEqual(?y,?e), greaterThanOrEqual(?y,?d)->inside(?x,?a)
```

The spatial dimension of objects in our databases are represented by points and polygons which are defined by coordinates of points. In order to discover their spatial relations, qualitative relationship must be deducted from these quantitative information. In the literature, the topological analysis between spatial objects is often performed by the Nine Intersection Model[7] or the RCC8 model[19]. In both cases, we obtain an equivalent set of eight basic pairwise disjoint topological relations which are mutually exhaustive: *equals, disjoint, intersects, touches, within, contains* and *overlaps*.

Unfortunately, these relations cannot be inferred with simple SWRL rules. Several studies[15,21] have introduced the SWRL built-ins for spatial processing and spatial relationships representation, but there are still limitations with regard mainly to the performance and reuse capability. Therefore, in our project, reasoning on complex spatial information is realized by the geospatial triplestore and thus, the spatio-temporal reasoning is accomplished through combining temporal SWRL rules and spatial functions of the triplestore.

With the deducted spatio-temporal relations, the three major needs of data analysis can be fulfilled. Let's examine three simple corresponding cases below:

1. Species observation and land-uses data can be linked by combining the *inside* temporal relation between an instant of observation and an interval of land-uses statement and the *within* spatial relation between observations point and parcels polygon (Fig. 2).
2. Crop rotation can be verified by the *meets* temporal relation between two intervals of land-uses statement of the same parcel (Fig. 3).
3. Territorial events can be detected by incorporating the *meets* temporal relation between interval of different timeslices and the *within* spatial relation between parcels geometry(Fig. 4).

---

[2] http://www.w3.org/Submission/SWRL/
[3] http://clarkparsia.com/pellet/

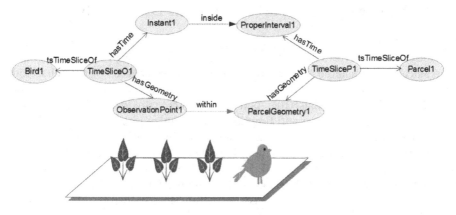

Fig. 2. Integration of species observations and land-uses data

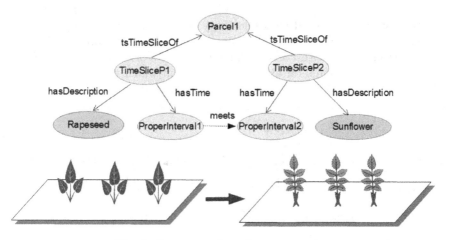

Fig. 3. Representation of a crop rotation

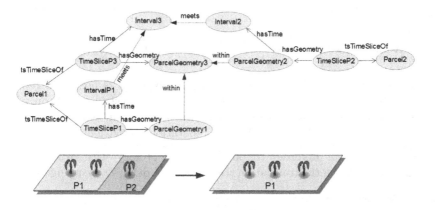

Fig. 4. Representation of the integration event

3   A Framework for Spatio-Temporal Data Analysis

In our previous work[20], a system architecture based on translation technique was introduced. Nevertheless, the system cannot provide a promising response time since the translated queries do not exploit the strengths of the relational model nor the query optimizer. Furthermore, the selection conditions are not pushed down to the database[10]. As a consequence, triplestores are considered to improve the performance and functionality of the system.

Triplestores are DBMS for data modeled in RDF. Currently, several triplestores support storing and querying spatial data using GeoSPARQL or stSPARQL, extensions of SPARQL language. Those open-source that manage the best are uSeekM[4], Parliament[5] and Strabon[6]. Other triplestores support only a few type of geometries and geospatial functions[9]. Strabon[16] is chosen since this open-source triplestore has a very good overall performance comparing to uSeekM and Parliament. This advantage can be explained by the push of the evaluation of SPARQL queries to the underlying spatially-enabled DBMS which has recently been enhanced with selectivity estimation capabilities[9]. Strabon extends the Sesame triplestore, allowing spatial RDF data stored in the Postgres DBMS enhanced with PostGIS. The triplestore works over the stRDF data model[16], a spatio-temporal extension of RDF in which the OGC standards, WKT and GML, are adopted to represent geospatial data.

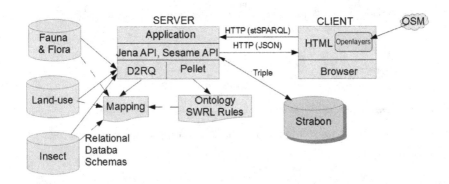

Fig. 5. A framework based on a semantic mediator for environmental data analysis

A framework (Fig.5) is developed, where a web server is hosted to receive the stSPARQL queries from a user in the form of a request in a Web browser. This framework consists of four parts: the data translation, temporal relation inference, triplestore bulk load, and data preparation and visualization.

1. Data translation: In order to populate the ontology with existing data sources, we rely on the translation technique that defines a mapping between

---

[4] http://dev.opensahara.com/projects/useekm/
[5] http://parliament.semwebcentral.org/
[6] http://strabon.di.uoa.gr/

databases and ontology. The D2RQ[7] [4] framework is chosen due to its support of different DBMS. The latter transforms relational data into virtual read-only RDF graph through a mapping file which describes how to connect to databases and to match our ontology to the databases schema. This RDF graph is then managed by the *Jena*[8] framework.

2. Temporal relation inference: The Pellet reasoner is used to deduce relationships between temporal entities through a SWRL rules set defined in a OWL file.

3. Triplestore bulk load: RDF triples are then imported to the Strabon triplestore that also host a SPARQL Endpoint.

4. Data preparation and visualization: RDF triples returned from Strabon are then prepared by *Jena* for visualization. The returned result is visualized through the *OpenLayers*[9] library with geographical data from *OpenStreetMap*[10]. The results are stored in several different layers to facilitate the presentation and analysis.

Fig. 6. A search for correlation between the positions of Montagu's Harrier and different types of grassland parcels in 2009

Fig. 7. A search for integration events of parcels in 2009

```
select ?ts1 ?ts2 ?geom1 ?geom2
where
{
?p1 rdf:type sige:Parcel.
?p2 rdf:type sige:Parcel.
?ts1 sige:tsTimeSliceOf ?p1.
?ts2 sige:tsTimeSliceOf ?p2.
?ts1 sige:hasGeometry ?geom1.
?ts2 sige:hasGeometry ?geom2.
?ts1 sige:hasTime ?t1.
```

```
?ts2 sige:hasTime ?t2.
?t1 time:intervalMeets ?t2.
?ts1 sige:hasLandUse ?lu1.
?ts2 sige:hasLandUse ?lu2.
?lu1 sige:name "Rapeseed".
?lu2 sige:name "Sunflower".
}
```

Query 1: A query for the "Rapeseed-Sunflower" succession

---

[7] http://d2rq.org/
[8] http://jena.apache.org/
[9] http://openlayers.org/
[10] http://www.openstreetmap.org

4   Data Analysis

The proposed framework along with the use of a spatio-temporal ontology as a semantic mediator can fulfill the three major needs of spatio-temporal analysis. Indeed, the data model in the form of subjacent RDF graph facilitates integration of different databases lying in the same or in different triplestores. In addition, thank to the Strabon triplestore and the Pellet engine, spatio-temporal relationships between objects can be deducted. At the first time, only the land-uses and wildlife database are selected for experiments.

1. To analyze the correlations between crop rotations and biodiversity, experts can visualize the references of animals by type and form of crop rotation. For example, they can check out the correlation between the positions of Montagu's harrier (Circus pygargus) and different type of grassland parcels (Fig.6).
2. Through qualitative temporal relationships inferred by the Pellet engine, researchers can also verify the quality of their recorded data. Indeed, domain rules or expert knowledge on crop rotation, appearance or disappearance of certain crop plants can be represented by stSPARQL queries to detect anomalies in collected data. For example, parcels having a hardly occurred succession "Rapeseed-Sunflower" can be located by the (Query 1).
3. Territorial events applied on farmland can be discovered by combining qualitative spatio-temporal relationships. For example, integration events, in which a parcel has been absorbed by another, in 2009, can be retrieved and displayed in the map like (Fig.7). Since real parcels geometry can not be recorded with an absolute precision, the spatial relationships between them can be converted to a more complex combination of others spatial relations and functions. In the latter example, the *within* relation is replaced by the *intersects* relation and the *area* and the *intersection* function.

These experiments are carried out on a 4 cores personal machines running at 2.8GHz with 8GB RAM. The performance of the new system is noticeably improved compared to the previous one[20]. The response time of a query for crop rotation decreases from 25 minutes to 5 seconds, thank to the Strabon triplestore. Furthermore, the system supports now spatial reasoning through the stSPARQL language.

5   Conclusion

The presented work are part of the "Environment and landscape geo-knowledge" interdisciplinary project which sets out to improve the use of collected environment datasets on the "Plaine & Val de Sevre" workshop observatory since 1994. We seek to develop a open-source framework to exploit environmental data through semantic web technologies. We present an ontology and a framework that can fulfill the need of spatio-temporal analysis of these heterogeneous data.

The proposed approach could be reused to perform management and analysis of long-term environmental data for other observatory.

In our perspectives, we consider to integrate other datasets of the workshop area, such as insects and botanical data, or the satellite data. It will be then possible to use the system to enrich and qualify our data sources. We also plan to publish a portion of these data over the web as linked data in order to facilitate interchanges with other available datasets, especially weather and infrastructure data concerning the workshop area.

References

1. Al-Debei, M.M., Al Asswad, M.M., de Cesare, S., Lycett M.: Conceptual modelling and the quality of ontologies: Endurantism vs. perdurantism. CoRR (2012)
2. Allen, J.F.: Maintaining knowledge about temporal intervals. Commun. ACM **26**(11), 832–843 (1983)
3. Batsakis, S., Petrakis, E.G.M.: SOWL: a framework for handling spatio-temporal information in OWL 2.0. In: Proceedings of the 5th International Conference on Rule-based Reasoning, Programming, and Applications, RuleML 2011 (2011)
4. Bizer, C.: D2rq - treating non-rdf databases as virtual rdf graphs. In: Proceedings of the 3rd International Semantic Web Conference (iswc 2004) (2004)
5. Cruz, I.F., Xiao, H.: The Role of Ontologies in Data Integration. Journal of Engineering Intelligent Systems **13**, 245–252 (2005)
6. Frasincar, F., Milea, V., Kaymak, U.: towl: Integrating time in owl. In: de Virgilio, R., Giunchiglia, F., Tanca, L. (eds.) Semantic Web Information Management, pp. 225–246. Springer, Heidelberg (2010)
7. Egenhofer, M.J., Herring, J.R.: Categorizing binary topological relations between regions, lines, and points in geographic databases. Technical report, Department of Surveying Engineering, University of Maine (1990)
8. Anagnostopoulos, E., Batsakis, S., Petrakis, E.G.M.: CHRONOS: A Reasoning Engine for Qualitative Temporal Information in OWL. Procedia Computer Science **22**, 70–77 (2013); ISSN 1877–0509
9. Garbis, G., Kyzirakos, K., Koubarakis, M.: Geographica: A benchmark for geospatial rdf stores. CoRR, abs/1305.5653 (2013)
10. Gray, A.J.G., Gray, N., Ounis, I.: Can RDB2RDF tools feasibily expose large science archives for data integration? In: Aroyo, L., Traverso, P., Ciravegna, F., Cimiano, P., Heath, T., Hyvönen, E., Mizoguchi, R., Oren, E., Sabou, M., Simperl, E. (eds.) ESWC 2009. LNCS, vol. 5554, pp. 491–505. Springer, Heidelberg (2009)
11. Gruber, T.R.: A translation approach to portable ontology specifications. Knowledge Acquisition **5**(2), 199–220 (1993)
12. Harbelot, B., Arenas, H., Cruz, C.: Continuum: A spatio-temporal data model to represent and qualify filiation relationships. In: Proceedings of the 4th ACM Sigspatial International Workshop on Geostreaming, pp. 76–85. ACM (2013)
13. Harbelot, B., Arenas, H., Cruz, C.: Un modle smantique spatio-temporel pour capturer la dynamique des environnements. In: 14 me conference Extraction et Gestion des Connaissances, Rennes, France (2014)
14. Hobbs, J.R., Pan, F.: An ontology of time for the semantic web. ACM Transactions on Asian Language Information Processing **3**, 66–85 (2004)

15. Karmacharya, A., Cruz, C., Boochs, F., Marzani, F.: Use of geospatial analyses for semantic reasoning. In: Setchi, R., Jordanov, I., Howlett, R.J., Jain, L.C. (eds.) KES 2010, Part I. LNCS, vol. 6276, pp. 576–586. Springer, Heidelberg (2010)

16. Kyzirakos, K., Karpathiotakis, M., Koubarakis, M.: Strabon: a semantic geospatial DBMS. In: Cudré-Mauroux, P., Heflin, J., Sirin, E., Tudorache, T., Euzenat, J., Hauswirth, M., Parreira, J.X., Hendler, J., Schreiber, G., Bernstein, A., Blomqvist, E. (eds.) ISWC 2012, Part I. LNCS, vol. 7649, pp. 295–311. Springer, Heidelberg (2012)

17. Langran, G.E., Chrisman, N.R.: A framework for temporal geographic information. Cartographica: The International Journal for Geographic Information and Geovisualization 25(3), 1–14 (1998)

18. Plumejeaud, C., Mathian, H., Gensel, J., Grasland, C.: Spatio-temporal analysis of territorial changes from a multi-scale perspective. International Journal of Geographical Information Science 25(10), 1597–1612 (2011)

19. Randell, D.A., Cui, Z., Cohn, A.G.: A spatial logic based on regions and connection. In: KR (1992)

20. Tran, B.H., Plumejeaud, C.P., Bouju, A., Bretagnolle, V.: Conception d'un système d'information géographique résilient pour l'environnement. In: Conférence Internationale de Géomatique et Analyse Spatiale SAGEO 2014 (2014)

21. Vandecasteele, A.: Spatial ontologies for detecting abnormal maritime behaviour. In: OCEANS 2012 MTS/IEEE Yeosu Conference: The Living Ocean and Coast - Diversity of Resources and Sustainable Activities, Yeosu, South Korea (2012)

22. Wache, H., et al.: Ontology-Based integration of information - a survey of existing approaches. In: IJCAI 2001 Workshop: Ontologies and Information, pp. 108–117 (2001)

23. Welty, C., Fikes, R.: A reusable ontology for fluents in owl. In: Proceedings of the Conference on Formal Ontology in Information Systems, pp. 226–236. IOS Press (2006)

Ontology Evolution for Experimental Data in Food

Rim Touhami[1,2]([⊠]), Patrice Buche[2], Juliette Dibie[1], and Liliana Ibanescu[1]

[1] INRA and AgroParisTech, 16, rue Claude Bernard, 75231 Paris Cedex 5, France
rim.touhami@gmail.com, {juliette.dibie,liliana.ibanescu}@agroparistech.fr
[2] INRA and LIRMM, 2, Place Viala, 34060 Montpellier, France
buche@supagro.inra.fr

Abstract. Throughout its life cycle, an ontology may change in order to reflect domain changes or new usages. This paper presents an ontology evolution activity applied to an ontology dedicated to the annotation of experimental data in food, and a plug-in, DynarOnto, which assists ontology engineers for carrying out the ontology changes. Our evolution method is an *a priori* method which takes as input an ontology in a consistent state, implements the changes selected to be applied and manages all the consequences of those changes by producing an ontology in a consistent state.

Keywords: Ontology evolution · Web semantic language

1 Introduction

Ontologies are one of the fundamental layer of the Semantic Web and are designed to represent the knowledge from a domain in terms of concepts (or classes), relations between these concepts and instances of these concepts [1]. An ontology, defined as a formal, explicit specification of a shared conceptualisation [2] may change whenever the domain changes or when domain experts need to add or to restructure the knowledge. When an ontology is used as a system component (the knowledge backbone) of an advanced information system its evolution is a complex process and raise many challenges as, for example, the formal representation of ontology changes, the verification of ontology consistency after applying the ontology changes, and the propagation of those changes to the ontology related entities (e.g. underlying data sets) (see [3] for a complete and detailed overview of the current research activities in ontology evolution).

In [4] a complete system, called ONDINE (ONtology-based Data INtEgration) is predented. It is designed to extract experimental data from tables and to store them into a data warehouse with the purpose of enriching local data sources and to allow afterword a flexible querying of the knowledge base. The backbone of the ONDINE system is an ontology which was first designed for predictive microbiology in food [5]. Later a new version of the ontology was designed for the assessment of chemical risk in food. Experimental results of the

© Springer International Publishing Switzerland 2015
E. Garoufallou et al. (Eds.): MTSR 2015, CCIS 544, pp. 393–404, 2015.
DOI: 10.1007/978-3-319-24129-6_34

ONDINE system in those two domains were presented in [4]. When ONDINE system was used for the MAP'OPT project in the domain of food packaging, its ontology had to be adapted to this new domain, and we defined in [6] an Ontological and Terminological Resource (OTR), called naRyQ, dedicated to represent an experiment involving a studied object, some control parameters and a result. During this project, ontology engineers had to manage naRyQ changes. Based on the methodological guidelines given in [7,8], we propose the workflow given in Figure 1 for carrying out the ontology evolution activity, then we combined, adapted and extended existing approaches in ontology evolution [8–13], and finally we implement a plug-in, called DynarOnto, to fit naRyQ evolution needs.

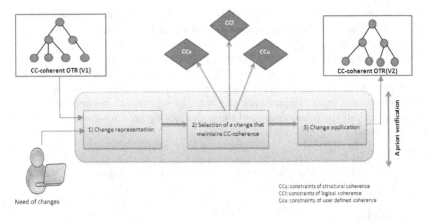

Fig. 1. The ontology evolution activity.

Our paper is organized as follows. Section 2 shows some related works. In Section 3 we first briefly recall the structure of the OTR dedicated to the annotation of experimental data in food and present our definition of its coherence. In Section 4, its evolution process is detailed, and we present in Section 5 the implementation and evaluation of our plug-in designed to assist ontology engineers in the evolution activity.

2   Related Work

In [3], a recent overview of the current research activities in ontology evolution, authors give first the different definitions of ontology evolution, then they present and discuss the various process models that were proposed for the ontology evolution tasks and afterword they propose a unified ontology evolution cycle thus providing a unique overview over several research fields. Our evolution method is defined as in the NeOn Glossary of ontology engineering tasks [7] which states that ontology evolution is "the activity of facilitating the modification of an ontology by preserving its consistency" and this is a narrower view than in [3].

To maintain the coherence of an ontology during its evolution, the authors of [8,10,13] proposed *a posteriori* approaches. This type of approach allows the application of changes in order to evaluate the evolution impact on the ontology, then suggests how to repair inconsistencies in case of problems. To avoid backtracking after modification, resulting in a loss of time and resources, *a priori* approaches, where the coherence checking is made before the application of changes, were proposed in the literature [11,12,14]. The work of Stojanovic [9] is the first to propose an ontology evolution process defined for KAON ontologies and using strategies for the task of managing changes. In [11] authors define kits of changes in order to manages the inconsistencies generated by each change. The authors of [12] propose a system of evolution of an OTR dedicated to the semantic annotation of text documents. [14] propose a framework based on graph rewriting rules that maintains a set of constraints. To the best of our knowledge, our preventive approach is the first one which is based on a definition of ontology coherence and manage quantitative data. In this paper we combine, adapt and extend existing approaches to fit naRyQ evolution needs.

3 naRyQ Model and Its Coherence

In this section, we first recall the naRyQ model presented in [6] then we define the coherence constraints it must respect.

3.1 naRyQ Model

naRyQ (*n-ary Relations between Quantitative experimental data*) is designed to model experiments in order to annotate data tables representing scientific experiments results in a given domain (see [6] for more details). Experiments which involve a studied object, several experimental parameters and a result are represented using n-ary relations without distinguished arguments as recommended by the W3C (World Wide Web Consortium) in [15]. More precisely "pattern 1" is used and it consists in representing a n-ary relation thanks to a concept associated with its arguments via properties.

Example 1. Let us consider the experiment where the permeability, which is the experiment's result, of a given packaging, which is the studied object, is studied in a set of control parameters specified by the packaging thickness, the temperature and the differential partial pressure. This experiment with 6 arguments can be represented by a n-ary relation *Permeability_Relation* as given in Figure 2.

The conceptual component of naRyQ is composed of a *core ontology* to represent n-ary relations between experimental data and a *domain ontology* to represent specific concepts of a given application domain. Figure 3 gives an excerpt of naRyQ in the food packaging domain. The representation of n-ary relations between experimental data requires a particular focus on the management of quantities. In the up core ontology, generic concepts *Relation_Concept* and *Argument* represent respectively n-ary relations and their arguments. In the down core

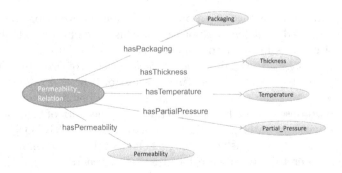

Fig. 2. n-ary relation Permeability_Relation.

ontology, generic concepts *Dimension*, *UM_Concept*, *Unit_Concept* and *Quantity* allows the management of quantities and their associated units of measure. The sub-concepts of the generic concept *Symbolic_Concept* represent the non numerical arguments of n-ary relations between experimental data. The domain ontology contains specific concepts of a given application domain. They appear in naRyQ as sub concepts of the generic concepts of the core ontology. All concepts are represented as OWL classes[1], hierarchically organized by the subsumption relation *subClassOf* and pairwise disjoints.

The terminological component of naRyQ contains the set of terms describing the studied domain and are used to annotate data tables. Sub concepts of the generic concepts *Relation_Concept*, *Symbolic_Concept* and *Quantity*, as well as instances of the generic concept *Unit_Concept*, are all denoted by at least one term of the terminological component. Each of those sub concepts or instances are, in a given language, denoted by a preferred label and optionally by a set of alternative labels, which correspond to synonyms or abbreviations. Labels are associated with a concept or an instance thanks to SKOS labeling properties[2] recommended by W3C. For instance, in Figure 3, English terms *Ethylene vinyl alcohol* and *EVOH* denote the symbolic concept *Ethylene_Vinyl_Alcohol*.

3.2   naRyQ *CC*-Coherence

In [8] the coherence of an ontology is classified in three categories: i) structural coherence which is related to constraints of the ontology's representation languages, ii) logical coherence where the semantic correctness of the ontology's entities are checked and iii) user-defined coherence which refers to specific user requirements and constraints related to the ontology's context of use. Inspired by [9] we define a set of conditions that the ontology must respect for each category of coherence. These conditions are called Coherence Constraints, denoted by *CC*-constraints. An ontology is *CC*-coherent if it respects a set of defined *CC*-constraints. We briefly present below the *CC*-constraints defined for naRyQ.

---

[1] http://www.w3.org/TR/owl-ref
[2] http://www.w3.org/TR/skos-reference

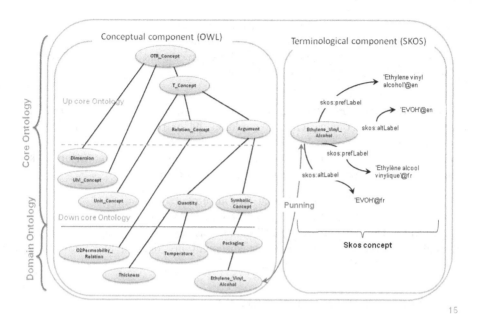

Fig. 3. An excerpt of naRyQ in the domain of risk in food packaging.

Structural Constraints. We have modeled naRyQ using a subset of OWL2-DL entities (i.e. classes, properties, constructors of classes, etc.) and axioms (see the technical report [16] for more details).

To define structural coherence associated with the conceptual part of naRyQ, the constraint defined by the W3C group, which says that every OWL axiom must be well defined[3] was extended to associate it with each axiom and constructor used in the modeling of naRyQ: if an entity refers to an other entity, this latest must be defined in the OTR. 15 structural $\mathcal{CC}$-constraints were defined, denoted by $\mathcal{CC}$s. We present below two examples of $\mathcal{CC}$s.

- CS1- Each anonymous class defined by a value restriction, owl:allValues-From or owl:someValueFrom links a pair property-class or property-data type. The property and the class used in the definition of the anonymous class must be defined in the OTR.
- CS2- Each instance of skos:concept must have at least a preferred label.

Logical Constraints. We defined 6 logical $\mathcal{CC}$-constraints, denoted by $\mathcal{CC}l$, which take into account the subset of OWL constructors and axioms used to

---

[3] http://www.w3.org/TR/owl-ref/#OWLDL

model naRyQ. Those constraints are taken from the literature [10]. We present below two examples of $\mathcal{CC}$l.

- CL1- A class can not be disjoint with its superclass.
- CL2- If two values restrictions `owl:allValuesFrom` which connect a pair property-concept are associated with the same concept c, then the concepts defining the restrictions cannot be disjoint.

User-Defined Constraints. The user-defined $\mathcal{CC}$-constraints, denoted by $\mathcal{CC}$u, correspond either to quality criteria modeling [9] or to specific criteria corresponding to the modeled task. We defined 9 generic $\mathcal{CC}$u which refer to quality criteria modeling and 20 new $\mathcal{CC}$u which are specific to the annotation task, detailed in [16]. We present below two examples of $\mathcal{CC}$u.

- CU1- A n-ary relation has at least two arguments.
- CU2- Each quantity must be associated with its units of measurement (at least one) through the `owl:allValuesFrom` restriction and the property `hasUnitConcept`. The units of measurement are defined by enumeration using the `owl:oneOf` constructor.

4   Coherent Evolution of naRyQ

As suggested in [7, 8] our ontology evolution activity consists in applying changes to an ontology while preserving its $\mathcal{CC}$-coherence, i.e. respecting all its $\mathcal{CC}$-constraints presented in the previous section (i.e. structural, logical and user-defined constraints). Figure 1 presents the evolution process composed of three main steps. The first step consists in presenting all the possible changes for naRyQ evolution to the ontology engineer. From this list of changes, the ontology engineer chooses the ones to be applied. The second step consists in preserving the $\mathcal{CC}$-coherence of naRyQ during its evolution. To do this, an additional set of changes is added automatically to the requested changes in order to maintain *a priori* (i.e. before the application of the requested changes) the $\mathcal{CC}$-coherence of the OTR. In the third and last step, requested and additional changes are applied to the OTR. In the following, we present the two first steps.

4.1   Change Representation

This first step consists in presenting to the ontology engineer all the possible changes for naRyQ. In order to generate all possible changes we first identified all entities and axioms used to model naRyQ in OWL2-DL and SKOS. We selected 55 changes from the literature and defined 26 new changes to take into account the specificity of naRyQ. The complete list is available in [16]. Among these changes, some changes are not accessible to ontology engineer but are rather used in the kits of changes, presented in the following section. Table 1 contains a subset of changes required for the evolution of naRyQ, where changes in bold are new ones compared to the literature.

Table 1. A subset of changes for naRyQ.

Change	Element	Role
addClass	NamedClass	add an OWL class to an ontology
addSubClassOf	SubClass	add a subsumption link
updateDomain	Domain	update the domain of a relation
updateSomeValuesFromRestriction	SomeValuesFrom	update an existential restriction
addDataTypeRestriction	DataTypeRestriction	add a value range
deleteFromAllDisjointClasse	DisjointClasses	delete a class of a set of disjoint classes
updatePrefLabel	SkosPrefLabelAssertion	update a preferred label of a SKOS concept

4.2   Selection of a Change That Maintains $\mathcal{CC}$-Coherence

After applying a change, one or more $\mathcal{CC}$-constraint may be violated (e.g. adding a new concept which represents a n-ary relation violates CU1 constraint presented in Section 3.2). Hence, a second step is necessary to restore the $\mathcal{CC}$-coherence of the OTR while applying a change. To achieve this goal, we adapted the notions of kit of changes [11] and of strategy [9] to our needs.

Kit of Changes. To maintain a priori the $\mathcal{CC}$-coherence of naRyQ during its evolution, we associated a kit of changes with each change that violates one or more $\mathcal{CC}$-constraints and wich is accessible to ontology engineer. Its definition takes into account all the $\mathcal{CC}$-constraints which can be violated by the requested changes.

Definition 1 ([11]). Given a $\mathcal{CC}$-coherent ontology O and a change c. If the application of c to O doesn't maintain the $\mathcal{CC}$-coherence of O, then **a kit of changes** is associated with c. It is composed of:

- preconditions: a set of assertions which must be true in order to apply c to O;
- the change c;
- mandatory additional changes: a set of changes which are attached to c in order to correct the inconsistencies that may occur in O when c is applied to it;
- optional additional changes: a set of changes which can be applied in addition to mandatory additional changes.
- post-conditions: a set of assertions which must be true after the application of c to O.

Two examples of kits of changes are presented in [16] and 15 kits from 63 were implemented.

Example 2. The *addClass* change allows a new class to be added to the OTR. The kit of changes associated with the *addClass* change is defined in the following.

Because of the constraint *"An ontology should not contain two concepts with the same URI"*, the **precondition** states that a new class *newc* can be added to the set of concepts C of naRyQ if its URI doesn't already exist in C. The requested change, which is the creation of the new class *newc*, is then applied to naRyQ. Unfortunatly, the application of this change violates several CC-constraints of the OTR. The application of a set of **mandatory additional changes** is then required:

1. The additional changes `addSkosConcept` and `addPrefLabel` are triggered to resolve the CC-incoherence linked to the terminological part of naRyQ due to the constraint *"Each n-ary relation and each argument is associated with a terminological part"*.

2. The creation of a disjunction relationship between the new class and all its sibling classes resolves a second CC-incoherence due to the contraint which requires that *"n-ary relations and their arguments should be mutually disjoint"*.

3. If the new class *newc* is a n-ary relation, then at least two arguments must be associated with *newc*. Additional changes `addAllValuesFromRestrictionToClass`, `addSomeValuesFromRestrictionToClass` or `addHasValueRestrictionToClass` are applied.

4. If the new class *newc* is a n-ary relation, then exact (greater than or equal to 1) cardinality restrictions must be associated with the mandatory arguments of *newc* to ensure their existence at the instance level.

5. If the new class *newc* is a quantity, then a dimension and a unit of measurement must be associated with it.

6. Adding a specialization relationship between *newc* and its superclass c resolves the CC-incoherence due to the constraint *"Each concept must be connected by a relation of specialization to at least one other named concept.*

Besides these mandatory additional changes, it is possible to apply other optional additional changes which are not necessary to maintain the CC-coherence of naRyQ but which may be requested by the ontology engineer. These optional additional changes may be for instance: adding other prefered and alternative labels to the new class, adding other arguments to the new class if it is a n-ary relation or other units of measurement if it is a quantity.

It is important to notice that each mandatory or optional additional change can in turn cause other CC-incoherences which can be resolved by triggering the required kits of changes. So each additional change can also call a kit of changes.

Evolution Strategies. The kit of changes defined in Definition 2 can be used when there is only one possible solution to solve an incoherence. But sometimes there can be several possible solutions to correct violated constraints. In this case, we have to use evolution strategies [9] in order to represent the different alternatives.

Definition 2. Given a CC-coherent ontology O and a change c, if the application of c to O leads to several possible alternatives to maintain the CC-coherence of O, then we call **evolution strategy** the choice made between these alternatives.

There exist two types of kits of changes: those with evolution strategies and those without. The kit of changes associated with the change *addClass*, presented above, is an example of a kit without evolution strategies. Kits with evolution strategies can be considered as a variant of the first type since they need to fix the strategy (i.e. the choice) before applying the kit.

Example 3. In order to delete a concept, there are several solutions to deal with its sub concepts and there are also several solutions to deal with its terms:

- To deal with orphaned concepts (sub concepts of deleted concept), the possible solutions are i) delete them, 2) reconnect them to super concepts or 3) reconnect them to the root.
- To deal with terms of deleted concept, the possible solutions are: 1) delete them or 2) reconnect them to super concepts.

5 Implementation and Evaluation

5.1 Implementation

We implemented the ontology evolution activity presented above as a Protégé plug-in called DynarOnto. Figure 4 shows the different designed menus:

- The *Relation Changes* menu presents the changes that can be applied to a n-ary relation (e.g. add a n-ary relation, delete a n-ary relation, update the arguments of a n-ary relation).
- The *Argument Changes* menu presents the changes that can be applied on arguments of a n-ary relation (i.e. Quantity and Symbolic_Concept).
- *Evolution Parameters* menu helps the ontology engineer to define its evolution strategy that will be taken into account during the OTR evolution.

The screen shot presented in Figure 4 is the interface for the kit of changes associated with the change *addClass* presented in Example 2. Let us consider that we want to add the new n-ary relation *CO2Permeability_Relation*, which is a sub relation of the existing n-ary relation *Permeability_Relation*. *CO2Permeability_Relation* is defined by the following arguments: Packaging, Thickness, Temperature, Partial_pressure_difference, **Relative_humidity** and **CO2_permeability**. Arguments presented in bold are specific to the sub n-ary relations. The other arguments are inherited from its super n-ary relation *Permeability_Relation* (see Figure 2). To add this new n-ary relation, ontology engineer starts by clicking on *Add relation* of the *Relation changes* menu. Using the panel of the displayed interface, the ontology engineer enters the name of the new n-ary relation, *CO2_permeability_Relation*. Then, he chooses *Permeability_Relation* as its parent class in the hierarchy of n-ay relations of the OTR displayed by clicking on "Choose" button. By confirming the choose of the n-ary relation's parent, inherited arguments appears in panel 3 of the displayed interface. The ontology engineer can both specialize inherited arguments and add new ones by indicating their numbers in panel 2. To define the new n-ary relation $CO2\_permeability\_Relation$, ontology engineer should add the new argument $Relative\_humidity$ and specialize the inherited argument $Permeability$ in $CO2\_permeability$, using the panel 2. To associate terminology to the new n-ary relation, ontology engineer uses panel 4. Finally, when the ontology engineer clicks on "OK" button to validate the add of $CO2\_permeability\_Relation$, DynarOnto plugin checks that the associated preconditions are verified (e.g. $CO2\_permeability\_Relation$ does not exist in the OTR). The interface facilitates the verification of some preconditions. For instance, when the ontology engineer decides to specialize an argument, the plugin displays only the hierarchy of more specific concepts. Once the preconditions are checked, the plugin applies the requested change and the set of additional mandatory changes, allowing violated CC-constraints to be resolved.

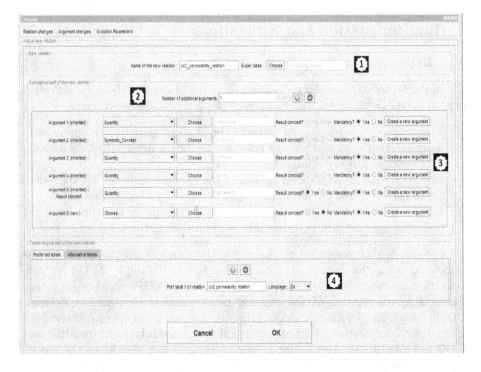

Fig. 4. Screen shot of the interface to add a new n-ary relation.

5.2   Evaluation of DynArOnto Plugin

DynArOnto was evaluated in an incremental way by ten users, with different backgrounds. Three evaluation sessions were organized, DynArOnto interface being improved after each session. Users were asked to apply three changes (add n-ary relations, update n-ary relations and delete arguments). A questionnaire was created to collect their evaluations. Most participants affirm that using DynArOnto to manage the evolution is easier than using Protégé. It is also reflected in the time spent by users to apply the changes: the add relation change (resp. update/suppress change) was done with Protégé in an average of 42 minutes (resp. 11 minutes). Using DynArOnto, user time was reduced by 20% (resp. 27%). Finally, DynArOnto helped the users to manage the evolution of an OTR dedicated to the annotation of experimental data while guaranteeing its CC-coherence, which was not the case in Protégé where the users were not guided and make some errors (e.g. incorrect use of OWL restrictions used to link arguments to n-ary relations, forgetting to associate terms to concepts).

6 Conclusion

We have proposed in this paper an ontology evolution activity for an OTR dedicated to the annotation of experimental data which preserves its CC-coherence. To do this, we first identified all the necessary constraints (i.e CCs, CCl and CCu) to be checked in order to avoid possible inconsistencies. Secondly, we identified all the required changes for the evolution of naRyQ. Then, we identified all the CC-incoherences which can occur after the application of each change. In order to solve these CC-incoherences, we defined a kit of changes for each change which violates one or more CCs-constraints. A kit of changes allows the CC-coherence of naRyQ to be preserved *a priori* by checking a set of preconditions, by applying a set of additional changes and/or by using evolution strategies. The originality of our method is to propose an evolution activity of an OTR containing inter dependent concepts to manage quantitative data. Further work is to explore how to propagate changes to all the ontology related artifacts: individuals, mapping, applications, metadata.

Acknowledgments. This work has been supported by the French Research Agency (ANR) in the framework of ALIA/MAP'OPT project, by the Carnot Institute 3BCAR in the framework of the IC2ACV project and by the Labex NUMEV.

References

1. Guarino, N., Oberle, D., Staab, S.: What is an ontology? In: Staab, S., Studer, R. (eds.) Handbook on Ontologies. International Handbooks on Information Systems, pp. 1–17. Springer, Heidelberg (2009)
2. Studer, R., Benjamins, V.R., Fensel, D.: Knowledge engineering: Principles and methods. Data and Knowledge Engineering **25**(1–2), 161–197 (1998)
3. Zablith, F., Antoniou, G., d'Aquin, M., Flouris, G., Kondylakis, H., Motta, E., Plexousakis, D., Sabou, M.: Ontology evolution: a process-centric survey. Knowledge Eng. Review **30**(1), 45–75 (2015)
4. Buche, P., Dibie-Barthélemy, J., Ibanescu, L., Soler, L.: Fuzzy web data tables integration guided by an ontological and terminological resource. IEEE Trans. Knowl. Data Eng. **25**(4), 805–819 (2013)

5. Buche, P., Couvert, O., Dibie-Barthélemy, J., Hignette, G., Mettler, E., Soler, L.: Flexible querying of web data to simulate bacterial growth in food. Food Microbiology **28**(4), 685–693 (2011)

6. Touhami, R., Buche, P., Dibie-Barthélemy, J., Ibǎnescu, L.: An ontological and terminological resource for n-ary relation annotation in web data tables. In: Meersman, R., et al. (eds.) OTM 2011, Part II. LNCS, vol. 7045, pp. 662–679. Springer, Heidelberg (2011)

7. Palma, R., Zablith, F., Haase, P., Corcho, Ó.: Ontology evolution. In: del Carmen Suárez-Figueroa, M., Gómez-Pérez, A., Motta, E., Gangemi, A. (eds.): Ontology Engineering in a Networked World, pp. 235–255. Springer (2012)

8. Haase, P., Stojanovic, L.: Consistent evolution of OWL ontologies. In: Gómez-Pérez, A., Euzenat, J. (eds.) ESWC 2005. LNCS, vol. 3532, pp. 182–197. Springer, Heidelberg (2005)

9. Stojanovic, L.: Methods and Tools for Ontology Evolution. PhD thesis, University of Karlsruhe, Germany (2004)

10. Djedidi, R.: Approche d'évolution d'ontologie guidée par des patrons de gestion de changement, Thèse de doctorat, Université Paris-Sud XI, November 2009

11. Jaziri, W., Sassi, N., Gargouri, F.: Approach and tool to evolve ontology and maintain its coherence. Int. J. Metadata Semant. Ontologies **5**(2), 151–166 (2010)

12. Tissaoui, A., Aussenac-Gilles, N., Hernandez, N., Laublet, P.: EvOnto - joint evolution of ontologies and semantic annotations. In: KEOD 2011, pp. 226–231 (2011)

13. Khattak, A.M., Latif, K., Lee, S.: Change management in evolving web ontologies. Knowledge-Based Systems **37**, 1–18 (2013)

14. Mahfoudh, M., Forestier, G., Thiry, L., Hassenforder, M.: Algebraic graph transformations for formalizing ontology changes and evolving ontologies. Knowl.-Based Syst. **73**, 212–226 (2015)

15. Noy, N., Rector, A., Hayes, P., Welty, C.: Defining n-ary relations on the semantic web. W3C working group note. http://www.w3.org/TR/swbp-n-aryRelations

16. Touhami, R.: Definition of naRyQ OTR CC-Constraints and kits of changes. Technical report, INRA , April 2015. http://umr-iate.cirad.fr/content/download/4847/36913/version/1/file/TechnicalReport.pdf

Graph Patterns as Representation of Rules Extracted from Decision Trees for Coffee Rust Detection

Emmanuel Lasso[1]([✉]), Thiago Toshiyuki Thamada[2],
Carlos Alberto Alves Meira[3], and Juan Carlos Corrales[1]

[1] Telematics Engineering Group, University of Cauca, Popayán, Colombia
{eglasso,jcorral}@unicauca.edu.co
[2] University of Campinas, Campinas, São Paulo, Brazil
ic.tiba@gmail.com
[3] Embrapa Agricultural Informatics, Campinas, São Paulo, Brazil
carlos.meira@embrapa.br

Abstract. Diseases in Agricultural Production Systems represent one of the biggest drivers of losses and poor quality products. In the case of coffee production, experts in this area believe that weather conditions, along with physical properties of the crop are the main variables that determine the development of a disease known as Coffee Rust. On the other hand, several Artificial Intelligence techniques allow the analysis of agricultural environment variables in order to obtain their relationship with specific problems, such as diseases in crops. In this paper an extraction of rules to detect rust in coffee from induction of decision trees and expert knowledge is addressed. Finally, a graph-based representation of these rules is submitted, in order to obtain a model with greater expressiveness and interpretability.

Keywords: Graph · Coffee rust · Rules · Decision tree · Disease · Agriculture · Semantics

1 Introduction

For coffee production, coffee rust is a disease that has greater negative impact on crops. In order to minimize the risks on this problem, many experts have studied the coffee rust development process and have obtained a number of variables that influence it.

On the other hand, one of the areas within computer science more used to address problems in agricultural environments is data mining. Decision Tree Induction is a technique corresponding to this area that aims to generate models (classifiers) that relate the different variables and classes contained in a dataset, using symbolic and interpretable representations for understanding decision limits and implicit logic in existing data[1]. Furthermore, it is possible to re-express complex decision trees as small sets of rules that outperform the original trees when is required to classify a new dataset[2].

© Springer International Publishing Switzerland 2015
E. Garoufallou et al. (Eds.): MTSR 2015, CCIS 544, pp. 405–414, 2015.
DOI: 10.1007/978-3-319-24129-6_35

Some research has proposed the use of decision trees in agricultural environments. Wu et al.[3]propose an improvement to C4.5 algorithm for decision trees induction [4], in order to classify agricultural data related to several issues. In research conducted by Mahmoud Omid [5], it is presented the design of an expert system for sorting pistachio nuts through decision trees and a fuzzy logic-based classifier. In this case, the discovery of relevant fuzzy rules was achieved also using the decision tree algorithm. In the case of the study presented by Molineros et al. [6], the objective was to relate weather data with the percentage of severity of wheat scab from the decision tree induction. Finally, some approaches have been used to generate decision trees for coffee rust detection [7][8]. These investigations are based on expert knowledge to identify the variables most associated with the emergence of conditions conducive to the development of coffee rust.

Additionally, it is necessary to consider a structure that represents the diversity of information in complex environments, such as the case of agriculture. Indeed, graphs are presented as a data structure well structured, which is defined as $G = (V, E)$, where V denotes a finite set of nodes that represent entities within an environment, connected by direct links or vertices E, such that $E \subseteq VxV$ correspond to the relationships between nodes of the graph [9].

Knowledge representation as graphs enables greater expressiveness through specification of attributes in nodes and edges, keeps essential properties of modeled objects and reasoning can be graphically represented in a natural manner using the graphs themselves [10]. Also, there are some problems in large rulesets (integrity, conflicting rules, missing rules, duplication, subsumption) that can be addressed through its representation based on graphs [11]. Therefore, this data structure is exploited in many areas of knowledge, since they can be used to model dynamic processes within each area. In order to include the variety of semantics contained in real life problems, a *Data Graph* is defined as $G(V, E, L)$ [12], where V and $E \subseteq VxV$ keep the same general definition for a graph and L is a function defined in V so that for each v in V, $L(v)$ is the label of v. Indeed, $L(v)$ may indicate semantic variety mentioned as types of relationships, properties of nodes, etc. Furthermore, research carried out by Lasso et al. [13], Baget and Mugnier [10] and Buche et al.[14] have made use of labeled graphs and semantic concepts in order to improve reasoning and modeling tasks in different areas of knowledge.

This paper presents, initially, the extraction of rules to detect coffee rust from decision tree induction and expert knowledge. Finally, a graph-based representation of these rules in order to obtain a model with greater expressiveness and interpretability is presented. The remainder of this paper is organized as follows: Section 2 describes rules extraction; Section 3 refers to rules as graph patterns; and Section 4 relates the discussion and conclusions.

2   Rules Extraction

Coffee rust epidemic is closely linked to the physiological development of the crop, production level of the plant, crop management and distribution of some climatic variables such as rainfall, temperature and relative humidity [15][16]. Given that the objective was to extract rules that correlate these factors with the development of rust in a specific period, the analysis of data was taken as a process of knowledge discovery in databases [17], modeled on data mining process CRISP-DM [18]. The stages of data preparation, modeling and evaluation for this process are described below.

2.1   Data Preparation

The dataset used was obtained by Corrales et al. [8] at the experimental farm Los Naranjos, belonging to the company Supracafé which is located in Cajibío (Cauca), Colombia. This dataset contains information from different lots of the farm, such as weather data, state of cultivation, crop properties and coffee rust incidence measures for several months between 2011 and 2013. The dependent variable was obtained from the disease behavior analysis, according to the impact value of coffee rust existing in the dataset between consecutive months. Thus, the infection rate is calculated by evaluating the increase or decrease in the incidence among the analyzed month and next month, getting three classes or categories: **TI1** ($<= 0$): reduction or latency, to negative or none rates of infection; **TI2** ($> 0 <= 2$): moderate growth, to positive infection rates greater or equal to 2 percentage points (pp); and **TI3** (> 2): accelerated growth, infection rates higher than 2 pp.

In addition, predictive attributes (independent variables) were built from expert knowledge that allows the identification of the variables most related to disease development. Crop **Density** determines the competition between plants for nutrients, spore interception and coverage of fungicides on the foliage [15]; While excessive **Shade** increases the infection intensity [19]. At the same time, the fungus requires splatter rain to begin the process of dispersion, as well as the presence of a layer of water on the underside of leaves to germinate [15], whereby the number of rainy days (accumulated rainfall $>= 1$mm [20]) (**DLLUV**), average daily rainfall (**PRE-MED**) and average daily accumulated rainfall are taken into account (**PRE-ACUM**). To estimate the period of leaf wetness, is measured the number of hours with relative air humidity above a specific limit, usually 90% or 95% [21]. Moreover, 6 hours of leaf wetness was established as the minimum time required for an infection occurs [20].

In the same way, we define **HORHR90** and **HORHRN90** attributes (average number of daily and night hours respectively, with relative humidity $>= 90\%$); **SUMHR90** and **SUMHRN90** (sum of number of daily and evening hours respectively, with relative humidity $>= 90\%$); and **RH** (mean daily average relative humidity). Similarly, once the leaf surface is wet, the temperature is the main factor that determines the percentage of spore germination and penetration [20], resulting in **T-HR90** and **T-HRN90** attributes (mean average temperature during day and night hours respectively, with relative humidity $>= 90\%$). Temperatures between 16 and 28 °C directly influence the development of coffee rust [15], leaving as attributes to consider the mean maximum, average and minimum daily temperature (**TMAX, TMED, TMIN**).

Finally, it is defined **WSPEED** attribute, representing mean daily average wind speed as the wind is a required element of the fungus dispersion [22].

Therefore, a dataset with 124 instances was built, to which is applied the SMOTE algorithm [23] (available in Weka Software [24]) in order to balance the classes. As a result, 161 instances were obtained and the number of records for each class was 63 for TI1, 50 for TI2 and 48 for TI3.

2.2   Modeling and Evaluation

The decision tree induction was made using the C4.5 algorithm [4] available in Weka as J48 implementation, with a minimum of instances per leaf 2 and a confidence factor of 0.25. This algorithm constructs the decision tree with a *divide and conquer* strategy. Each node in a tree is associated with a set of cases and a path from the root to a leaf of the decision tree can be followed based on the attribute values of the case. The class specified at the leaf is the class predicted by the decision tree.

As a result, the decision tree generated is presented in Figure 1, where circles represent nodes that evaluate the predictive attributes and gray boxes represent the predicted classes. In this way, from the 16 predictive attributes found in the dataset, the algorithm used relates only 8 of these in the resulting model.

Additionally, measures of performance of classification algorithm, after being applied cross-validation of order 10, left as result a total of 131 instances correctly classified (81.4%) and 30 instances incorrectly classified (18.6%). The confusion matrix, where diagonal represents the correct classifications made by the model

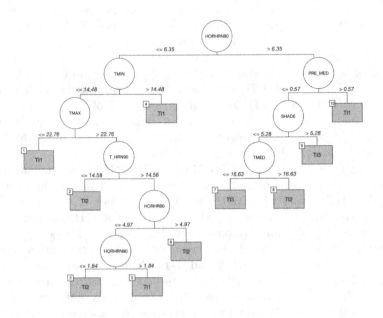

Fig. 1. Decision Tree generated

Table 1. Confusion Matrix of model generated

Classes	Classified as		
	TI1	TI2	TI3
TI1 (63 instances)	53	6	4
TI2 (50 instances)	3	33	14
TI3 (48 instances)	1	2	45

while the other elements represent errors related to each class, can be seen in Table 1. In the case of TI1 class (63 instances), 53 instances were classified as TI1, 6 as TI2 and 4 as TI3. For TI2 class (50 instances), 3 instances were classified as TI1, 33 as TI2 and 14 as TI3. Finally, for TI3 class (48 instances), 1 instance was classified as TI1, 2 as TI2 and 45 as TI3. From this matrix can be calculated precision and recall measures of the model, obtaining a precision of 93%, 80.5% and 71.4%; and recall of 84.1%, 66% and 93.8%; for TI1, TI2 and TI3 respectively.

To analyze the model generated (Figure 1), we start from the root node, where it is evaluated HORHRN90. In this case, the model sets two ranges: average number of night hours with leaf wetness (HORHRN90) greater than 6.35 hours and smaller or equal than 6.35 hours; which is related to the number of hours with minimum leaf wetness necessary for an infection [20]. For the case where HORHRN90 is below or equal to 6.35 hours, the next variable to be analyzed is TMIN (average minimum temperatures), for which, if it is above 14.48 °C, the predicted class is TI1; and, on the other hand, if it is less than or equal to 14.48 °C, should be followed with the evaluation of TMAX (average maximum temperatures). If TMAX is less than or equal to 22.76 °C, the predicted class is TI1, and if it is greater than this value, T-HRN90 (mean temperature in night hours with relative humidity greater than 90%) is analyzed. The T-HRN90 variable leading to the prediction of TI2 class when it is equal to or less than 14.58 °C and, alternatively, when it is greater than this value should be passed to an analysis of HORHR90 (average daily hours of relative humidity greater than 90%). When HORHR90 is evaluated, if the value is above 4.97 hours, the predicted class is TI2; and if it is less than or equal to 4.97 hours, root node variable HORHRN90 must be reassessed. In this case, if it is greater than 1.84 hours, the predicted class is TI1, which could be expressed as TI1 greater than 1.84 hours and less than or equal to 6.35 hours (recalling the evaluation of the root node). In contrast, if it is less than or equal to 1.84 hours, the predicted class is TI2.

Meanwhile, back to the root node, if HORHRN90 is greater than 6.35 hours, the next variable to be evaluated is PRE-MED (mean daily average rainfall). If PRE-MED is greater than 0.57 mm, the predicted class is TI1, otherwise, if it is less than or equal to 0.57 mm, SHADE variable must be analyzed. If the crop has a shade percentage greater than 5.28%, the predicted class is TI3 and for crops with lower shade, TMED variable should be evaluated (mean of daily average temperatures). For TMED greater than 16.63 °C, the predicted class is TI2 and for TMED equal to or less than this value, the predicted class is TI3.

In this regard, the path from the root node to each of the predicted classes may be taken as a set of conditions or rules to be met by variables analyzed, in order to predict a particular situation.

3   Rules as Graph Patterns

The rules obtained from expert knowledge and through decision tree induction can be expressed using graph patterns. Thus, generated patterns should be modeled according to the variables related to coffee rust (predictive attributes). Accordingly, some of relevant entities corresponding to nodes of a graph pattern are:

- **Instance:** Entity related to predictive attributes registration for a timescale, which in this case is monthly.
- **Crop Property:** Entity that contains information of crop properties as shade and density, related to a particular instance.
- **Weather parameter:** Entity that contains information of weather monitoring, expressed as predictive attributes.

Besides, based on Fan et al. [25], we define a graph pattern as $Q = (V_p, E_p, f_v, f_e)$, where:

- V_p is a set of nodes and E_p is a set of directed edges, as they were defined for a *Data Graph*.
- $f_v()$ is a function defined in V_p, so for each node u, $f_v(u)$ is a label of u.
- $f_e()$ is a function defined in E_p, so for each edge (u, u') in E_p, $f_e(u, u')$ is a label of the relationship between nodes (u, u').

Thereby, these functions can be used to specify semantic search conditions or variables ranges, defined by labels in terms of Boolean predicates.

Taking into account the foregoing considerations, 10 graph patterns, corresponding to each decision tree leaf obtained above, were generated . If the tree is taken from the root node (HORHRN90), there are several possible routes to reach one of the classes (gray frames), which are conditioned by variables evaluation in other nodes. Each class at the end of leaf is related to a predicted infection rate and, therefore, generated graph patterns are divided into three groups: 4 patterns for TI1 (infection rate less than or equal to 0pp), 4 patterns for TI2 (infection rate between 0 and 2pp) and 2 patterns for TI3 (infection rate greater than 2pp).

As an example, for leaf labeled as "7" in Figure 1, the path to reach TI3 begins when HORHRN90 is greater than 6.35 hours. In this case, the next variable to be evaluated is PRE-MED (mean daily average rainfall). If PRE-MED is is less than or equal to 0.57 mm, SHADE variable must be analyzed. If the crop has a shade percentage less than 5.28%, TMED variable should be evaluated (mean of daily average temperatures). Finally, for TMED evaluation equal to or less than 16.63 °C, the predicted class is TI3. As a result, in Figure 2 can be seen

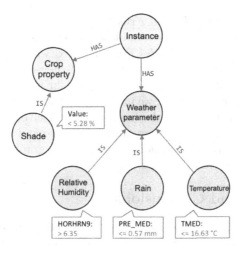

Fig. 2. Graph pattern for TI3

one of the graph patterns generated for TI3, obtained from the rule described by decision tree leaf mentioned above.

In the graph pattern presented, each node is associated with a unit of classification (Instance, Crop Property, etc), indicating their role in a graph repository containing coffee crops information. Furthermore, this classification allows

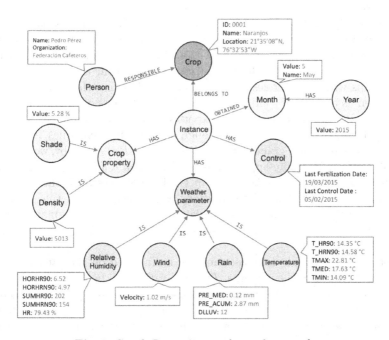

Fig. 3. Graph Respository sub-graph example

grouping predictive variables for coffee rust appearance, according to their nature (crop physical property or weather variables) and representing evaluation ranges of their values as node labels. Nodes are connected with labeled edges, which helps to further establish the semantic context of their environment. Additionally, a graph-based representation has advantages for management information systems, considering that, as users, we infer semantic dependencies between entities, but the data models (even the databases themselves) are blind to these connections and the ability to add properties to nodes and relationships is particularly useful for providing additional metadata for graph algorithms, adding additional semantics to this elements [26].

4   Discussion and Conclusions

In the previous sections, the extraction of rules for coffee rust detection from the application of a decision tree induction algorithm was presented. The dataset used contains crop information (agronomic and weather) for a specific timescale, according to the recommendations of coffee rust experts. Although algorithm performance measures are of high grade, it is ideal to have a training set larger so that the result can be more reliable. From rules obtained, we have proposed their representation as graph patterns, in order to model them with greater expressiveness and considering the semantic context of the problem. These graph patterns contain in their structure, conditions that must be presented in a crop for the occurrence of three coffee rust incidence rates and allow easy interpretability of these rules.

Additionally, there is a technique of data mining in graphs called *Graph Pattern Matching*, which is defined as: *given a data graph G, and a pattern of graph Q, find all matches of Q in G* [25]. These types of search are usually aimed at finding entities with specific characteristics in their attributes and relationships with other nodes in the graph. In this sense, the searched pattern can be seen as a series of conditions within the attributes of the graph.

Considering the use of rulesets in expert systems, drawn from the knowledge produced by experts and extracted through data mining techniques, each ruleset can be defined as a set of graph patterns $R = (R1, ..., Rn)$. Thereby, we can define a *Graph Pattern Matching* approach as follows: *given a data graph G, and a set of patterns R, find all matches of R in G*. This process finds the sub-graphs $M(R, G)$ that comply with the conditions established in each rule. This way, it is possible to find, within a graph database, the subgraphs matching each pattern, which in this case, correspond to crop registers where there is a risk of coffee rust infection.

From this, the graph database must be built based on the same criteria of predictive variables in the patterns. This generation can be addressed through a *Graph Parser* that takes weather monitoring data and crop properties to relate them with other relevant entities within the coffee production and create a graph repository. An example of a sub-graph of this repository can be seen in Figure 3.

In the example shown, the sub-graph contains interconnected nodes in a similar way to the pattern of Figure 2. In addition, there is a principal entity called *Crop* corresponding to monitored crop, an entity *Person*, and entities of timeline type that facilitate the search of a instance based on a specific date.

As future work, it is intended to implement a Graph Pattern Matching technique from the generated patterns in order to identify favorable conditions for coffee rust in Colombian coffee crops. Under this approach, crops conditions can be analyzed regularly, so that coffee rust early warnings can be generated to farmers. These alerts allow timely decision-making in the crop chemical control, improve product quality and avoid large losses in production.

Acknowledgments. The authors are grateful to the Telematics Engineering Group (GIT) of the University of Cauca, AgroCloud project of The Interinstitutional Network of Climate Change and Food Security of Colombia (RICCLISA) and Embrapa Agricultural Informatics for supporting this research.

References

1. Apté, C., Weiss, S.: Data mining with decision trees and decision rules. Future generation computer systems **13**(2), 197–210 (1997)
2. Quinlan, J.R.: Generating production rules from decision trees. In: IJCAI, vol. 87, pp. 304–307. Citeseer (1987)
3. Wu, J., Olesnikova, A., Song, C.H., Lee, W.D.: The development and application of decision tree for agriculture data. In: Second International Symposium on Intelligent Information Technology and Security Informatics, IITSI 2009, pp. 16–20. IEEE (2009)
4. Quinlan, J.R.: C4. 5: programs for machine learning. Elsevier (2014)
5. Omid, M.: Design of an expert system for sorting pistachio nuts through decision tree and fuzzy logic classifier. Expert Systems with Applications **38**(4), 4339–4347 (2011)
6. Molineros, J., De Wolf, E., Francl, L., Madden, L., Lipps, P.: Modeling epidemics of fusarium head blight: trials and tribulations. Phytopathology **95**(6) (2005)
7. Meira, C.A.A., Rodrigues, L.H.A., Moraes, S.A.: Análise da epidemia da ferrugem do cafeeiro com árvore de decisão. Tropical Plant Pathology **33**, 114–124 (2008)
8. Corrales, D.C., Ledezma, A., Peña, A.J., Hoyos, J., Figueroa, A., Corrales, J.C.: Un nuevo conjunto de datos para la detección de roya en cultivos de café colombianos basado en clasificadores. Sistemas & Telemática **12**(29), 9–23 (2014)
9. Bondy, J.A., Murty, U.S.R.: Graph theory with applications, vol. 290. Macmillan, London (1976)
10. Baget, J.F., Mugnier, M.L.: Extensions of simple conceptual graphs: the complexity of rules and constraints. Journal of Artificial Intelligence Research, 425–465 (2002)
11. Higa, K., Lee, H.G.: A graph-based approach for rule integrity and maintainability in expert system maintenance. Information & management **33**(6), 273–285 (1998)
12. Fan, W.: Graph pattern matching revised for social network analysis. In: Proceedings of the 15th International Conference on Database Theory, pp. 8–21. ACM (2012)
13. Lasso-Sambony, E.G., Ortega-Ponce, S.M., Corrales, J.C.: Semantic enrichment and inference of relationships in an online social network. Ingeniería y Universidad **17**(2), 355–373 (2013)

14. Buche, P., Cucheval, V., Diattara, A., Fortin, J., Gutierrez, A.: Implementation of a knowledge representation and reasoning tool using default rules for a decision support system in agronomy applications. In: Croitoru, M., Rudolph, S., Woltran, S., Gonzales, C. (eds.) GKR 2013. LNCS, vol. 8323, pp. 1–12. Springer, Heidelberg (2014)
15. Rivillas, C., Serna, C., Cristancho, M., Gaitán, A.: Roya del cafeto en colombia: Impacto, manejo y costos del control. Chinchiná: Boletín Técnico (36) (2011)
16. Waller, J.M., Bigger, M., Hillocks, R.J.: Coffee pests, diseases and their management. CABI (2007)
17. Fayyad, U., Piatetsky-Shapiro, G., Smyth, P.: From data mining to knowledge discovery in databases. AI magazine **17**(3), 37 (1996)
18. Chapman, P., Clinton, J., Kerber, R., Khabaza, T., Reinartz, T., Shearer, C., Wirth, R.: Crisp-dm 1.0 step-by-step data mining guide 2000. SPSS Inc. (2013)
19. Nutman, F., Roberts, F., Clarke, R.: Studies on the biology of hemileia vastatrix berk. & br. Transactions of the British Mycological Society **46**(1), 27–44 (1963)
20. Kushalappa, A., Akutsu, M., Ludwig, A.: Application of survival ratio for monocyclic process of hemileia vastatrix in predicting coffee rust infection rates. Phytopathology **73**(1), 96–103 (1983)
21. Sutton, J., Gillespie, T., Hildebrand, P.: Monitoring weather factors in relation to plant disease. Plant disease **68**(1), 78–84 (1984)
22. Becker, S.: Diurnal periodicity in spore dispersal of hemileia vastatrix in relation to weather factors [coffee, kenya]. Zeitschrift fuer Pflanzenkrankheiten und Pflanzenschutz (Germany, FR) (1977)
23. Chawla, N.V., Bowyer, K.W., Hall, L.O., Kegelmeyer, W.P.: Smote: synthetic minority over-sampling technique. Journal of artificial intelligence research **16**(1), 321–357 (2002)
24. Hall, M., Frank, E., Holmes, G., Pfahringer, B., Reutemann, P., Witten, I.H.: The weka data mining software: an update. ACM SIGKDD explorations newsletter **11**(1), 10–18 (2009)
25. Fan, W., Li, J., Ma, S., Tang, N., Wu, Y., Wu, Y.: Graph pattern matching: from intractable to polynomial time. Proceedings of the VLDB Endowment **3**(1–2), 264–275 (2010)
26. Robinson, I., Webber, J., Eifrem, E.: Graph databases. O'Reilly Media, Inc. (2013)

Track on Metadata and Semantics for Cultural Collections and Applications

Aggregating Cultural Heritage Data for Research Use: The Humanities Networked Infrastructure (HuNI)

Deb Verhoeven[1] and Toby Burrows[2,3(✉)]

[1] School of Communication and Creative Arts, Deakin University, Melbourne, Australia
deb.verhoeven@deakin.edu.au
[2] Department of Digital Humanities, King's College London, London, UK
toby.burrows@kcl.ac.uk
[3] School of Humanities, University of Western Australia, Nedlands, Australia
toby.burrows@uwa.edu.au

Abstract. This paper looks at the Humanities Networked Infrastructure (HuNI), a service which aggregates data from thirty Australian data sources and makes them available for use by researchers across the humanities and creative arts. We discuss the methods used by HuNI to aggregate data, as well as the conceptual framework which has shaped the design of HuNI's Data Model around six core entity types. Two of the key functions available to users of HuNI – building collections and creating links – are discussed, together with their design rationale.

Keywords: Data aggregation · Humanities · Creative arts · Social linking

1 Introduction

The Humanities Networked Infrastructure (HuNI) [1] is one of the Virtual Laboratories developed with funding from the Australian Government's NeCTAR (National e-Research Collaboration Tools and Resources) programme. [2] The general parameters for these Virtual Laboratories, as defined by NeCTAR, focused on integrating existing e-research capabilities (tools, data and resources), supporting data-centred research workflows, and building virtual research communities to address existing well-defined research problems. Most of the other Virtual Laboratories were funded in big data areas of science, including climate science, geophysics, astronomy, genomics, characterisation and marine science.

The "data-centred" nature of the framework presented a challenge for the humanities research community. It was clear that NeCTAR expected something other than a service built around a collection of digital images or digital texts; a digital library or a *Europeana*-type service was not what was envisaged. To address this, the HuNI consortium had to develop and apply a definition of "data" which would be relevant to humanities researchers but would also meet NeCTAR's expectations.

In the humanities, "data" is a term that is not always well understood or agreed upon. [3] Collections of source material, whether physical or digital, are often described as "humanities data", usually accompanied by "metadata" descriptions of

© Springer International Publishing Switzerland 2015
E. Garoufallou et al. (Eds.): MTSR 2015, CCIS 544, pp. 417–423, 2015.
DOI: 10.1007/978-3-319-24129-6_36

these sources. [4] HuNI has taken a different approach. For HuNI, "humanities data" consists primarily of the *semantic entities* referenced by the products of the humanities research process, whether these be books, articles, artworks, annotations, tags, reviews, ratings or other types of content. HuNI is not a collection of digital texts or images, nor is it built around catalogue records for these kinds of resources. Instead, HuNI focuses on the people, places, events and concepts referenced and discussed by humanities researchers.

This means that HuNI does not contain catalogue-style records for books like Richard Flanagan's *The Narrow Road to the Deep North* or for movies like Baz Luhrmann's *Australia*. Instead of combining information into one record about the people involved with these works (authors, directors, actors, producers), the titles of the works, their themes, and their locations, HuNI separates these out into individual entity records. There are individual entities for Flanagan, Luhrmann, Hugh Jackman, Nicole Kidman, *Australia*, *The Narrow Road to the Deep North*, and so on. This approach was taken because it is these entities – and the relationships between them – which are the fundamental focus for the discussions, analyses and conversations of humanities researchers.

The user community for HuNI is, effectively, the entire range of humanities and creative arts researchers in Australia and beyond. This was reflected in the composition of the various project teams and working groups, as well as in the disparate sources of data. Thirteen different institutions actively contributed to the project – including universities, government institutes, and e-research service providers. HuNI is designed to bridge the gap between cultural heritage institutions, academic researchers, and the wider community. The design and testing groups during the project included people from all of these sectors.

2   Data Aggregation

Thirty different humanities datasets have been incorporated into HuNI. The data in some of these services conform to standard schemas, but many use their own customized format. A wide range of disciplines within the humanities and creative arts are covered, including history, literature, performing arts, art and design, biography, and media studies. The datasets, for the most part, have been developed as ongoing services by consortia involving researchers and cultural institutions, usually with government funding.

HuNI harvests records from these datasets in both XML and non-XML formats. But HuNI does not aggregate the incoming records by normalizing or mapping them to a uniform schema, as services like *Europeana* do. HuNI is not a "union catalogue" of humanities database records. Instead, the incoming harvested records are parsed to identify their primary entity type. They are then mapped to one of the six core entities in the HuNI Data Model: Person, Organization, Event, Work, Place, and Concept.

This approach positions HuNI somewhere between a "data warehouse" in which the incoming data are first cleaned and organised into a consistent schema and a "data lake" in which the incoming data are ingested in their raw form and the responsibility for making sense of the data lies entirely with the end user.

The initial plan for HuNI envisaged that all the incoming data would be mapped to a detailed and sophisticated ontology – assembled from such sources as CIDOC-CRM (Comité International pour la Documentation – Conceptual Reference Model), FOAF (Friend of a Friend) and FRBR-$_{oo}$ (Functional Requirements for Bibliographic Records – Object Oriented). This approach was abandoned after fundamental conceptual and ethical difficulties were identified with it. [5] The HuNI team felt that it was inappropriate to attempt to impose a single, unified, complete ontological perspective across disciplines which have very different (and yet overlapping) approaches to categorization and knowledge representation.

HuNI was not intended to replace the underlying datasets, which continue to exist and develop within their disciplinary context. As a result, any modelling of the data in HuNI did not need to cover comprehensively everything represented in the contributing services. And finally, as one of HuNI's key rationales was to encourage interdisciplinary understanding in humanities research, a Domain-Driven Design (DDD) process based on the recognitition and preservation of "bounded contexts" (in this case scholarly disciplines) was also deemed unsuitable. [6]

Instead, the HuNI team implemented a very generic framework for categorization, with the aim of acknowledging disciplinary perspectives while providing a level of interoperability between them. Because of this, the HuNI Data Model is deliberately restricted to six core entities: concept, event, organization, person, place, and work. This Data Model was derived from a thorough analysis of the types of entities present in the source datasets, in order to identify the generic common ground between them. As of May 2015, HuNI contained more than 750,000 entities, categorized as follows:

- Concept (5,970)
- Event (76,015)
- Organization (45,276)
- Person (289,458)
- Place (10,828)
- Work (322,818)

No relationships between entities are imported or inferred as part of the HuNI ingest process. Initially, this was partly the result of constraints imposed by the project's timelines and resources. But there was also a conceptual reason behind this decision: inferring and creating relationships in HuNI between entities from different data sources would again be imposing an unwarranted "supra-disciplinary" perspective on disparate data. Relationships recorded in a single incoming record from a single data source can still be replicated between the resulting HuNI entities without distorting the disciplinary perspective inherent in the original data.

A deliberate decision was also made not to merge entities from different data sources into a single "authoritative" entity. The intention was to ensure that the different disciplinary contexts for these apparently duplicated entities were preserved. This also indicates that HuNI does not intend to replace the underlying datasets by imposing its own version of the original information or its meaning. Records are ingested on the HuNI side and displayed in the HuNI service with pointers back to the original source records.

Typically a limited range of record types and entity fields are mapped from the source datasets to HuNI. This is done by harvesting only those source records which can be matched to one of HuNI's six basic categories. In some cases, this is straightforward; "Person" records in the AustLit database, for example, map to the HuNI "Person" category. In other cases, the mapping is more indirect; "Venue", "Company", and "Film" records in the CAARP database map to the HuNI categories "Event", "Organisation", and "Work" respectively. These mappings are hard-coded into the harvest and ingest process, and are based on a thorough comparison between the data models of the source datasets and the HuNI data model.

Currently the HuNI ingest process only picks out one entity from each incoming record from each of the source datasets. This means that there is a simple one to one relationship between an incoming record and the HuNI record produced. Future iterations of HuNI will provide the ability to extract more than one HuNI entity from each incoming source record.

The HuNI entities have not yet been mapped to a normative vocabulary, though exposing HuNI entities to the Linked Data cloud will be tackled as part of the next stage of HuNI's development, during 2015/16. Also currently under development is a data ingest pipeline for entity references identified in the text of the Australian digitized newspapers hosted by the National Library of Australia's Trove service. [7]

3   Technologies

The HuNI Virtual Laboratory is built with Open Source technologies, and consists of four main components:

- The Solr Document Index contains the harvested and indexed partner documents. [8] It exposes a search API, allowing matching documents to be returned. It is a read-only resource.
- The Database stores user profile information, links between documents, collection lists, and associated metadata. It is a read-write resource, allowing users to manipulate HuNI information.
- The Virtual Laboratory functionality is delivered through an Nginx HTTP server and a RESTful API service. The Nginx server sends the application's JavaScript, HTML components, stylesheets, and images to the user's browser client. [9] The RESTful API allows the client application to query and manage the user profile information, links, and collections. [10] It also enforces access restrictions.
- The Nginx proxy server accepts all Internet-facing requests and delegates them to the appropriate backend service. All access to the HuNI Virtual Laboratory is via the HTTPS protocol.

Data is imported into the Solr Document Index through a four-step pipeline. Each partner site makes a feed available to HuNI for harvesting on a publicly accessible location via the Internet. Each step in the pipeline results in a file on disk in the raw, clean, and final Solr format for every document ingested into HuNI. The four steps in the pipeline are as follows:

1. Harvesting: partner sites are polled daily for updates using either HuNI's custom "Simple XML" format or the Open Archives Initiative's Protocol for Metadata Harvesting (OAI-PMH). [11] The harvest code uses custom Python and bash scripts.
2. Pre-processing: where necessary, the harvested data are pre-processed to ensure they can be properly transformed.
3. Transforming: custom Python code and XSLT templates are deployed to transform the harvested data into the standard HuNI Data Model, ready for indexing by Solr.
4. Indexing: Documents created by the transformation process are submitted to a Solr instance for indexing. The result is a body of indexed documents made up of the most recently harvested versions. This can be quickly searched through an HTTP interface.

4   Using the Data

As well as searching the aggregated data and browsing the entities attached to each of the six core entity types, registered users of HuNI can carry out two key functions: creating collections of entities, and creating links between individual entities. User collections bring together selected entities under a heading assigned by the user. These collections can be public or private, and users can add or delete entities from their own HuNI collections at any time. User-created collections in HuNI can be exported for reuse in other software environments. The HuNI record for each entity in a user-created public collection includes the information that they are part of that collection.

Users cannot create entity records directly in HuNI; new entity records can only be added to the HuNI aggregate by the ingestion of datasets through the HuNI pipeline. But there is a way in which individual users can contribute entity records to HuNI through that pipeline. The Heurist humanities e-research tool (developed to manage individual researchers' data collections) has been modified to export its datasets to HuNI. [12] The first major dataset loaded through the Heurist tool was *TUGG: The Ultimate Gig Guide*. This dataset contains 624 records related to live music venues in Melbourne. [13]

The next stage in developing upload functionality for HuNI is being explored in the context of Omeka, the Open Source collections and exhibitions publication platform. [14] As part of a national e-research project, a "publish to HuNI" plug-in will be developed for Omeka. This feature will be incorporated into a hosted version of Omeka, which will be available to all Australian university researchers.

Creating links between individual entities is central to HuNI's purpose and functionality. A user can select two entities to connect, can describe the nature of the relationship between the entities, and can annotate the link. This process has been dubbed "social linking", since the links are public by default. In the initial version of HuNI, there are no pre-set vocabularies or taxonomies for describing links, and users are free to choose their own form of words – though they are prompted with pre-existing matching strings to choose from when creating a link. Multiple links can be created in both directions between two entities, both by different users and by the same user. It is also possible to assert "is not" relationships, such as "is not the sister of".

No central editorial control is imposed by HuNI on the creation of links. Nor do the creators of links have to be recognized "experts" in a particular disciplinary area. Any registered user of HuNI is able to create links and publish them into the HuNI network graph. The creator of each link is recorded and publicly identified, enabling subsequent users to see the source of the link and assess its authoritativeness. This approach recognizes the critical importance of contestation and plurality in humanities-based frameworks for knowledge formation. [15]

The graph of links between entities can be browsed through a network visualization interface. Each different type of entity is identified with a distinct icon. These entities, in their turn, link outwards to other related HuNI entities, as well as to user-created collections. Selecting any of the icons representing entities in the initial network graph changes the focus of the graph. These newly-revealed entities can then be selected in their turn. The number of "degrees of separation" which can be displayed is only limited by the size and resolution of the user's screen.

The two functions discussed in this section are intended to allow researchers to add their own meaning and structure to the aggregated HuNI data. The "collections" functionality allows users to create their own categories and groupings for entities. The "social linking" function allows them to create their own graph of relationships and to contribute to the growing HuNI network graph. Researchers can trace routes along these interconnected networks, as an alternative discovery process to a keyword search.

Researchers who tested the initial version of the HuNI prototype commented on the benefits of this approach in enabling them to make "serendipitous discoveries through identifying points of commonality between data" and to "cross-search a significant amount of data in a single software environment and see networks of relationships" (anonymous user feedback). This reinforces HuNI's role in contributing to the design of digital resources for the humanities which foster serendipity. [16]

5   Conclusion

Interpretation is at the heart of the humanities and creative arts. HuNI combines humanities data in a way which enables researchers to express, share and discuss their differing interpretations of the data. The different perspectives between (and within) disciplines are preserved and foregrounded, instead of being hidden behind a normalized, "authoritative" framework. HuNI has kept categorization and taxonomical structures to a minimum, and has provided the tools for researchers to create their own semantic frameworks for the data.

Cultural data are not economically, culturally, or socially insular. Researchers need to collaborate across disciplines, institutions, and social locations, in order to explore data fully. [17] If we understand humanities research problems as comprising interdependent networks of institutional, social, and commercial practices, then it follows that new kinds of "evidence" and new ways of organizing, accessing, and presenting this evidence are critical for our enquiries. HuNI is designed to address this need.

References

1. http://huni.net.au
2. http://nectar.org.au
3. Burrows, T.: Sharing humanities data for e-research: conceptual and technical issues. In: Thieberger, N. (ed.) Sustainable Data from Digital Research, pp. 177–192. PARADISEC, Melbourne (2011)
4. Borgman, C.: Scholarship in the Digital Age, pp. 215–217. MIT Press, Cambridge (2007)
5. Burrows, T.: Ontologies and the humanities: some issues affecting the design of digital infrastructure, Digital Humanities Congress, Sheffield, UK, September 2014. http://www.slideshare.net/TobyBurrows/dhc2014-burrows-final
6. Evans, E.: Domain-Driven Design: Tackling Complexity in the Heart of Software. Addison-Wesley, Boston (2004)
7. http://trove.nla.gov.au/ndp/del/about/
8. http://lucene.apache.org/solr/
9. http://nginx.org/en/
10. Richardson, L., Ruby, S.: RESTful Web Services. O'Reilly Media, Farnham (2007)
11. https://www.openarchives.org/pmh/
12. https://code.google.com/p/heurist/
13. http://tugg.me
14. http://omeka.org
15. Rowland, S.: The Enquiring University. McGraw-Hill, Milton Keynes (2006)
16. Verhoeven, D., Burrows, T.: Crowdsourcing for serendipity. The Australian Higher Education Supplement, December 10, 2014
17. Verhoeven, D.: New cinema history and the computational turn. In: Beyond Art, Beyond Humanities, Beyond Technology: A New Creativity: World Congress of Communication and the Arts Conference Proceedings. University of Minho, Minho, Portugal (2012)

Historical Context Ontology (HiCO):
A Conceptual Model for Describing Context
Information of Cultural Heritage Objects

Marilena Daquino[1] and Francesca Tomasi[2(✉)]

[1] CRR-MM - Multimedia Research Resource Centre, University of Bologna, Bologna, Italy
marilena.daquino2@unibo.it
[2] Department of Classical Philology and Italian Studies, University of Bologna, Bologna, Italy
francesca.tomasi@unibo.it

Abstract. Communities addressing the problem of a shareable description of cultural heritage objects agree that a data-centric and context oriented approach should be reached in order to exchange and reuse heterogenous information. Here we present HiCO, an OWL 2 DL ontology aiming to outline relevant issues related to the workflow for stating, and formalizing, authoritative assertions about context information. The conceptual model outlines requirements for defining an authoritative statement and focuses on how a description of context information can be carried out when data are extracted from full-text of documents.

Keywords: FRBR · TEI · Linked Open Data · Scholarly editions · Authoritativeness

1   Introduction

The cultural heritage domain is a huge and challenging area of interest, also concerning approaches to formal and conceptual description. Commonly, documents, books and artifacts – i.e. objects cured by libraries, archives, museum and more recently galleries, in an open access dimension[1] – are the main focus of representation, dissemination and preservation activities.

Important topics are now emerging in approaches to conceptualization. First of all, the cultural heritage domain description is mostly related to well-known efforts in representation of meta-level information, while, when dealing with textual documents, description at full-text level represents a semantic issue, on which archives and libraries are now developing new interpretative models (e.g. with regard to scholarly editions). It surely is a shared idea that there is a common need to adhere to interoperability standards, preserving however the richness of data representation. The dominant technique in full-text documents digital representation, is currently document-centric

---

[1] GLAM, Galleries, Libraries, Archives, Museums. Open Knowledge Foundations, OpenGLAM, http://openglam.org/

E. Garoufallou et al. (Eds.): MTSR 2015, CCIS 544, pp. 424–436, 2015.
DOI: 10.1007/978-3-319-24129-6_37

[1], i.e. oriented to the embedded markup method. Here, a flexibility in descriptive facets prevents the loss of precious information. A real example can be found in Text Encoding Initiative (TEI) activities[2], where the scholarly community has defined a huge schema for encoding a large amount of humanistic/literary features. However, this approach entails to abstain from the creation of a real common vocabulary across communities. It is a well-known issue that each cultural institution (archive, library, museum, gallery) requires specific metadata sets and vocabularies, capable to reach different descriptive needs[3]. The most widely-used metadata sets – primarily, Dublin Core (DC) – demonstrate that while adoption of a shared vocabulary is encouraged, it's always necessary to enrich it in a domain-oriented way, both when dealing with high-level and content-level metadata. Therefore, there is a common interest to converge on a suitable data-centric approach[4] – as the Linked Open Data [2] movement is asking for – which should be capable to represent information regarding:

- content, maybe directly extracted from the full-text of documents;
- context, required to understand content, derived from documents themselves or from literature;
- provenance and authoritativeness of assertions (i.e. interpretations), both for content and context information.

In fact, another acknowledged topic of interest for cultural institutions is that a cultural object has to be managed in relation to its context. 'Context', meaning any information concerning the network of relations in which a cultural object is somehow involved, is a precious key for interpretation of its content and its identification. Nevertheless, which – and how – information should be formalized is the result of a choice, i.e. a hermeneutical activity made by one or more interpreters, representable as a complex assertion. Then, being information a result of an interpretative process, even such information about the process itself should be provided in order to formalize enriched, self-descriptive and understandable data.

Here we present and analyze a model aiming to correctly deal with above described issues, i.e. extraction of information about content and context of documents (mainly available as TEI/XML files) as RDF statements. In order to reuse data in a Linked Data context, an OWL 2 DL ontology has been defined, called HiCO ontology[5].

In order to describe the model the paper is organized as follows. A special attention is firstly given to the concept of cultural heritage object, involved in the interpretative process. A new object, describing the object of interest, is always created with the purpose of clearly distinguishing three phenomena as RDF assertions: original objects, objects born to explain assumptions, and interpretations (section 3). Then we explain how any information extracted by an agent from the 'content' of an object (i.e. the full-text encoded in a document-oriented perspective), or even from any other source

[2] Text Encoding Initiative: TEI P5: Guidelines for Electronic Text Encoding and Interchange, http://www.tei-c.org/release/doc/tei-p5-doc/en/html/

[3] Library Linked Data Incubator Group: Datasets, Value Vocabularies, and Metadata Element Sets. W3C Incubator Group Report, 25 October 2011, http://www.w3.org/2005/Incubator/lld/XGR-lld-vocabdataset-20111025/

[4] W3C Data Activity, Building the Web of Data, http://www.w3.org/2013/data/

[5] Daquino, M., Peroni, S., Tomasi, F., HiCO, Historical Context Ontology Documentation (2014), http://purl.org/emmedi/hico

regarding the object (i.e. any other document able to let the interpreter to assert something), can be considered as an entity bounded to the object through an interpretative act. Intuitive or arbitrary categories can be used to define which sphere the interpretation belongs to, and the criterion used to state it. The act of producing RDF statements about real interpretations is an interpretative process too, and should also be identified through a provenance attribution (section 4). After definition of meta-level required to state that information is extracted as an interpretation, content-level has to be modeled. Actually, in order to restrict the scope of the proposal, the model focuses on events, people and people's relation as subjects of interpretation, although it can be simply extended in order to describe any other relevant phenomenon (section 4.3). A particular focus is then devoted to information resulting from event-driven and interpretation-driven approaches, like the formalization of synchronous and diachronic relations among interpretations (section 5). Finally we propose criteria to state authoritativeness of assumptions (section 6).

The project aims then to define, thought the ontology, a methodology – i.e. a workflow – for describing context information of cultural objects as entities indirectly bounded to the objects themselves via an intermediate one (i.e. the interpretation act). This condition ensures authoritativeness of interpretations can be inferred, both in terms of quality (e.g. an interpretation gains authoritativeness through authoritative citations) and in terms of trust (i.e. with a clearly defined provenance of statements). Since Linked Data enable anyone to state assertions about everything (any URI) without owning it [2], an intermediate entity, with provenance statements, ensures a complete, self-descriptive representation. This modus operandi can be useful to communities which daily work with interpretations of literary works – like the TEI community – and need a means to extract information from the full-text of the sources, and then declare paternity of such assertions, without possible complexities generated by contradictory statements.

As use case, for the model and the data testing, an XML/TEI edition has been used, precisely the digital edition of *Vespasiano da Bisticci's Letters* [3], as the better suited example at the current state of the ontology. The edition is the representation (philological transcription with historical notes on people, events, place and dates) of a collection of manuscript letters (archival documents and miscellaneous codices) sent and received by Vespasiano, a Florentine copyist who lived during the XV century.

2   Related Works

To achieve the proposals here presented, and as a good practice, existing ontologies have been reused in HiCO, to solve specific issues: an OWL DL 2 formalization of the FRBR model[6] was considered for a clear definition of layers of cultural objects, and then to outline levels needed to correctly characterize interpretations; certain properties of PROV-O ontology[7] were used to declare provenance of interpretations and to describe some features of the interpretative process; CiTO[8] and PRO[9] ontologies (part

---

[6] Ciccarese, P., Peroni, S., Essential FRBR in OWL2 DL, http://www.essepuntato.it/lode/ http://purl.org/spar/frbr

[7] Lebo, T., Sahoo, S., McGuinnes, D.: PROV-O: the PROV Ontology. W3C Recommendation (2013), http://www.w3.org/TR/prov-o/

[8] CiTO, Citation Typing Ontology. Documentation, http://purl.org/spar/cito

of SPAR ontologies[10]) were imported to describe thoroughly relations among interpretations and involved agents; N-ary Participation pattern[11] and again PRO ontology were used to describe information extracted from texts in form of RDF triple.

This work also moves from studies on similar themes in research fields like prosopography, archival science and history: FACTOID ontology [4], which deals with prosopographic information, was the starting point for rethinking and enhancing the definition of an interpretation act; PRoles ontology [5] and EAC-CPF ontology [6] were considered as general models for issues in describing people, their relations and the importance of provenance assertions when extracting information from full-text of resources.

HiCO has been developed using SAMOD methodology[12], which consists of several small steps of an iterative workflow that focuses on creating well-developed and documented models.

Actually, the ontology can be considered ready for a first evaluation, while further analysis and implementations have to be done, e.g. a mapping to CIDOC-CRM[13] and FRBRoo model[14] to test interoperability and consistency of predicates in a wide conceptual model (see section 7 for further explanations). At the same time a possible interaction with EDM[15] will be useful in order to test the HiCO model on cultural heritage collections, i.e. in Europeana.

3   Identifying Cultural Heritage Objects and Interpretations

As we said, cultural heritage object is a wide concept: it includes any sort of representation of culture heritage embodied in a tangible form, like artifacts (books, documents, and works of art), but also any concept, assertion and interpretation somehow bounded to cultural objects. Furthermore, in a broader perspective, any object making explicitly or implicitly assertions about a cultural object – like a scholarly edition or an interpretative essay – could be considered as a cultural object itself, strictly related to the first one.

We can consider a real example on which, as we said before, we test the HiCO ontology: the digital edition of *Vespasiano da Bisticci's Letters*. This edition, embodied in an XML/TEI document, has to be considered as a second cultural heritage object, dealing with the original one, i.e. Vespasiano's original letters. In the edition, an editor states his/her ideas and assumptions, maintaining a direct relation with the subject of interest.

---

[9]   PRO, Publishing Role Ontology. Documentation, http://purl.org/spar/pro
[10] SPAR, Semantic Publishing and Referencing Ontologies. Documentation, http://sempublishing. sourceforge.net/ (in particular see CiTO and PRO, developed by University of Bologna research group)
[11] Gangemi, A., Presutti, V., Nary Participation pattern. OWL ontology, http://www.loa.istc.cnr.it/ ontologies/naryparticipation.owl
[12] Peroni, S.: SAMOD: an agile methodology for the development of ontologies, http://speroni.web. cs.unibo.it/publications/samod.pdf
[13] Crofts N., et al. (2011, Nov.). Definition of the CIDOC Conceptual Reference Model (version 5.0.4), http://www.cidoc-crm.org/docs/cidoc_crm_version_5.0.4.pdf
[14] FRBRoo Introduction. Documentation, http://www.cidoc-crm.org/frbr_inro.html
[15] Europeana Data Model. Documentation, http://pro.europeana.eu/page/edm-documentation

In order to formalize this situation, we have to consider two different *responsible entities* (i.e. the author and the editor of the cultural object), and two different *works*, (i.e. a new cultural object describing the first one); then we should consider the *expression* level of the first one as 'subject' of the new *work*. All these elements can fully be described within FRBR model (fig. 1).

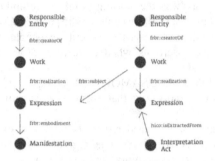

Fig. 1. FRBR representation of cultural heritage objects

Formalizing this scenario in Vespasiano's edition we say that: Vespasiano da Bisticci's first letter ("vdb-work-letter-1") is a work, edited by a person (the responsible entity Francesca Tomasi, "ft", i.e. the editor), by creating another work with an expression into which interpretation acts ("intact") are outlined. In Turtle syntax we could describe the scenario in this way:

```
:vdb-work-letter-1 a frbr:Work .
:vdb a foaf:Person ;
frbr:creatorOf :vdb-work-letter-1 .
:vdb-expr-letter-1 a frbr:Expression ;
frbr:realizationOf :vdb-work-letter-1 .

:ft-work-letter-1 a frbr:Work ;
frbr:subject :vdb-expr-letter-1 .
:ft a foaf:Person ;
frbr:creatorOf :ft-work-letter-1 .
:ft-expr-letter-1 a frbr:Expression; frbr:realizationOf :ft-work-letter-1
.

:intact-1-ft-transc-lett-1
a hico:InterpretationAct ;
hico:isExtractedFrom :ft-expr-lett-1 .
```

More precisely, we consider the original Vespasiano's letters as the object of interest (i.e. a *work*); the text of the work (i.e. one of the possible *expressions* of that work) as the subject of the scholarly edition (i.e. another *work*); in the text of the new work (i.e. in its *expression*), assumptions are made by an editor. Typically, this happens when an interpreter (the editor) is going to create a philological edition (transcription) or an historical essay talking about a source (comment). When it comes to paleographic studies (graphical signs interpretation), the subject of the new work will be the embodiment of the original letters (i.e. the *manifestation* of the work).

Now consider a statement about the object of interest an editor could assert, like "the letter 19 states that Pipo was the illuminator of the manuscript". It means that underlying data of the text have to be represented in a formal way: to represent information contained in the letter – that may be interpreted in different ways from different editors at different times and not as it is, like an indisputable fact – an intermediate stage is required in order to describe this situation. A correct formalization of the issue prevents contradictory statements about the same subject without a right provenance assertion. An interpretation cannot be just directly related to its subject of interest as a fact, but requires a new entity – physical or not – where the phase of conceptualization (deduction, assumption, transcription etc.) takes place (the new *work*), where the creation of the interpretation happens (the *expression* of the new *work*) and where the authorship of interpretation is clearly defined. Then, its formalization and embodiment (an interpretation act) can be correctly formalized in order to represent something that can change over time or can be questionable.

In fact, by representing such complex entities as a process, and not just through a single assertion, the model enables further possible relations among interpretations (diachronic versioning of an interpretation and synchronous citations between interpretations), between editors (disputes about a theme or else) and between interpretations and cultural objects (criteria for defining authoritativeness of interpretations).

4   Describing an Interpretation Act

As we said, stating something about an object (or extract something from its content) is a subjective 'reading' of an editor.

Following this idea, interpretations, strictly bounded to the expression of a work with a defined authorship, can be considered as facts: they've been chosen by the editor and – in that expression of that work – no other contradictory assertions can be stated. When interpretations are instead directly related to their subject of interest and no authorship is stated, they are represented as facts too, but without the possibility to make other assertions about them, unless invalidating consistency of the first statement.

So an interpretation act is a situation in which an agent can represent some useful information as RDF triples extracting them from the 'content' of an object. This action entails two moments, or better, two other situations as part of a process:

1.   The conceptualization of the interpretation and its classification, for enabling further relations among different kind of interpretations;

2.   The embodiment of the interpretation as RDF statements, for representing information extracted from the content of the object of interest.

These phases involve different agents and different layers of description, but as a complete process, they can be represented as a single entity, the `hico:InterpretationAct` class.

4.1   Conceptualizing an Interpretation

An interpretation act is related to the expression (an `frbr:Expression` individual) where it comes from through a specific object property, `hico:isExtractedFrom`, a subproperty of PROV-O `prov:wasInfluencedBy`, and therefore is indirectly related to the editor of the work in which it is conceptualized.

Individuals of `hico:InterpretationAct` class are also defined through two fundamental object properties: the `hico:hasInterpretationType` property and the `hico:hasInterpretationCriterion` property. The former states an arbitrary classification of the interpretation, which can be simply defined as philological, historical, semiotic, linguistic etc. The latter is a briefly explanation of the criterion used to state information extracted from a source, e.g. a literally transcription, a hypothesis, or the adoption of the literature about a specific argument (fig. 2).

These information are not strictly required, but they are meaningful when trying to explain why an interpretation is more authoritative than another one. Indeed, an interpretation act could be related to other acts through citations: more an act is related to other acts, probably more authoritativeness it gains in literature. Annotating these relations when describing the adopted criterion, could be an easier way to judge (and query) interpretations.

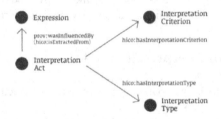

Fig. 2. Conceptualization of an interpretation act

We can continue with the first example. An editor's transcription of the first letter of *Vespasiano da Bisticci's Letters* is a philological interpretation of the text of the letter, obtained through a diplomatic-interpretative approach. In Turtle syntax, we can assert this as:

```
:intact-1-ft-transc-lett-1
a hico:InterpretationAct ;
hico:isExtractedFrom :ft-expr-lett-1 ;
hico:hasInterpretationCriterion
:diplomatic-interpretative-transcription ;
hico:hasInterpretationType :philological .
```

4.2   Representing Information as RDF Statements

Once the abstract phase of an interpretation act has been represented, also its embodiment as an RDF statement has to be formalized. This concept can be expressed through another object property, `prov:wasGeneratedBy`, which relates individuals of the class `hico:InterpretationAct` with any entity, representing exhaustively the information extracted by the editor.

Here, a distinction has to be made when talking about the editor of interpretations and the agent responsible for its RDF embodiment. Each individual of `hico:InterpretationAct` has to be related with the agent who materially transforms an assertion into a RDF statement. This one shall be the same editor, but could also be a software agent or another human agent who materially creates the RDF statements. To fix this issue, another PROV-O object property has been reused, `prov:wasAssociatedWith`, which relates the interpretation act with the creator of its RDF statements (fig. 3).

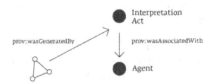

Fig. 3. Embodiment of an interpretation act

To continue with the previous example, we can assert that Marilena Daquino ("md") has extracted the RDF statement about Francesca Tomasi interpretation of the first letter (further explained below, section 4.3):

```
:intact-1-ft-transc-lett-1 a hico:InterpretationAct .
:da-sender-1-1-28-9-1446 prov-o:wasGeneratedBy :ia-1-ft-transc-lett-1 ;
prov-o:wasAssociatedWith :md .
:md a frbr:ResponsibleEntity .
```

4.3   A Focus on Historical Context

Historical context is another wide concept that cannot be uniquely defined. Here it's intended as any information explicitly described in an object of interest (like a description of an event in a document), but also recognized as implicit (like a citation of art styles in a paint), or even any information coming from other objects dealing with the object of interest (parallel or secondary source), which are all useful elements to clearly understand the content of the object and then to identify it as a hub of a network of relations.

All these sort of information are meaningfully part of the context of a cultural object. Trying to define the nature of historical context, different kinds of information can be represented (linguistic, philologic, semiotic, prosopographic, etc.) as information useful to define relevant issues related to the object of interest. In order to simplify possible scenarios, at the current state of HiCO ontology, only information dealing with people, people's relations and participation in events can be represented as extracted statements from the content of an object, in so far as these information represent, in a traditional meaning of historical context, evenemential narratives.

Indeed, a particular focus is given to information about people and events in an event-driven approach, assuming that these relationships can cover a wide range of information about the context, needed by communities to identify, clearly and unambiguously, their subject of interest, i.e. the cultural object. In spite of this, other types of information can be represented simply importing suitable models for the specific issue, without modifying the TBox of HiCO ontology. Precisely, HiCO imports PRO and N-ary Participation pattern as the simplest and the most comprehensive ontologies that, merged, can represent a wide range of scenarios described in (or dealing with) a document, with a special regard to historical events. In fact, through them it's possible to represent:

- relationships between people;
- relations between people and cultural objects;
- people's time-indexed roles on objects or other people;
- people's participation in events with a time-indexed characterized role;
- objects involved in a space/time-indexed situation.

We can analyze, again, an example from *Vespasiano da Bisticci's Letters*. "Donato Acciaioli ("da") sends the first letter ("item-lett-1") to Vespasiano da Bisticci in 28 september 1446". This is an information extracted from the transcription of the first letter itself which can be represented in Turtle syntax as:

```
:da-sender-1-1-28-9-1446 a pro:RoleInTime ;
tvc:atTime :28-9-1446 ;
pro:isHeldBy :da ;
pro:relatesToDocument :item-lett-1 ;
pro:withRole pro:sender ;
prov-o:wasGeneratedBy :intact-1-ft-transc-lett-1 .
```

5   Diachronic and Synchronous Relations Among Interpretations

Once defined, interpretations can be related each other. As above said, an interpretation with a correct provenance assertion shall be considered as a 'fact' in the expression of the work whence it comes, just because that expression represents the realization of the work at a given time and with specific features at that time. So there cannot be contradictory statements in the same expression.

When it happens, or better when a contradictory statement is needed, an editor has to create a new expression of its work which revises the previous one. As FRBR cataloging rules state about revisability of expressions, it "(...) reflects the expectation that the intellectual or artistic content of the expression will be revised" [7]. This means that conceptual revisions happen at the level of the expression of a work. So, in a new expression, new interpretations may revise a previous one, and such relation can be formally represented directly. For this purpose specific properties of CiTO ontology can be re-used, like cito:refutes, for revising statements, i.e. interpretations, rather than revising simply expressions (fig. 4).

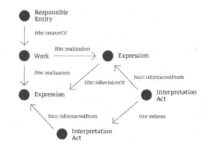

Fig. 4. Diachronic relations among interpretations

Then, through a mechanism of 'versioning', the agent responsible of an interpretation can keep track of the phases of its conceptualization from a diachronic point of view. This approach is useful when different factors can affect the validity of an assertion over time: e.g. an editor may retract his/her interpretation after he/she reads an essay demonstrating that his/her interpretation is wrong.

Although, when an editor follows a theory, he/she should include references to similar studies and other authors' points of view. To achieve this level of description, synchronous citations among interpretations have to be represented too, as well as diachronic ones, through CiTO properties, which offers a detailed range of possible connections between citing and cited entities.

Citations and versioning will establish then a network of relations among interpretations – a literature, with a defined authorship and qualification for each interpretation – that allows further possibilities in querying data and, as below explained, permit to enable inferences about authoritativeness of interpretations.

6   Defining Rules for Authoritative Interpretations

Defining criteria to state authoritativeness of assumptions is an open question, that cannot be solved in an unanimous way. Each community, field of research, school of thought applies different methodologies for defining authorities. Here, we assume as example, without claim of completeness, a common methodology used in philological editions. The aim is to demonstrate how authoritative interpretations can be stated as deduced information, inferred from the network of the aforementioned relations. To reach this goal, a simple SWRL rule[16] is used to formalize requirements that an historical authoritative interpretation must satisfy.

When seeking for historical interpretations, users expect a proof to validate such assertions. Modeling these evidences could be rather arbitrary, but some issues can be formally stated in order to define rules for establishing historical authoritative interpretations.

First of all, an interpretation shall be supported by other editors' similar statements: indeed, agreement with scholarship is considered a shared criterion to state authoritative

---

[16] SWRL: A Semantic Web Rule Language. Combining OWL and RuleML. W3C Member Submission (21 May 2004), http://www.w3.org/Submission/2004/SUBM-SWRL-20040521/

assertions. Through the CiTO object property `cito:agreesWith` we can represent such relation between an historical interpretation and any type of other interpretations.

Secondly an interpretation can also be defined with a 'type' declaration, to qualify it in a specific class of assertions (e.g. philological assumptions rather than linguistic ones). So, an historical assumption shall be based on available material evidences, possibly from a different sphere of assumptions, i.e. an historical interpretation shall be supported by a philological interpretation act (the transcription of the text), wherefrom the historical interpretation has been extracted and deduced. Reusing another CiTO object property, `cito:obtainsBackgroundFrom`, to relate interpretations each other, we can meet this condition. We could at the same time specify the nature of the related interpretation through a value qualification of the HiCO object property `hico:hasInterpretationType` (in this case, is `hico:philological`).

At last, an historical interpretation shall be related to an authoritative source for the transcription of the text wherefrom it belongs. Here authoritative means both a source published by an authoritative editor (person or cultural institution), or a source identified by a shareable authority file which defines the object univocally, assuring trust in its description. Likewise other citations, CiTO object property `cito:cites AsAuthority` has been reused.

No one cardinality restriction has been considered, as quantifying citations appears too questionable. In a human-readable syntax the SWRL rule stating these three requirements can be explained as:

```
hico:InterpretationAct(?a)
^ cito:citesAsAuthority(?a, ?b)
^ cito:agreesWith(?a, ?c)
^ cito:obtainsBackgroundFrom(?a, ?d)
^ hasInterpretationType(?d, hico:philological)
    → hico:hasInterpretationCriterion
       (?a, hico:authoritatively-based)
```

These basic requirements improve trust in assertions about historical events, which earn authoritativeness. So, asking for an historical authoritative interpretation in philological editions, an inferred 'criterion' attribution will be bounded to the historical interpretation (the individual `hico:authoritatively-based` as value of the `hico:hasInterpretationCriterion` object property). This approach does not entail that retrieved interpretations are surely true, i.e. facts, but – in a dialectical approach – restrictions on so qualified interpretations, limit the scope, and in terms of query of data, it reduce efforts. E.g. an historical interpretation of Vespasiano da Bisticci's first letter states that Donato Acciaioli wrote some letters in latin instead of Vespasiano (who asked Donato to help him). This assumption was deduced by the editor from his/her transcription of text, based on an authoritative source, and the editor cites other philological interpretations in support to the thesis. An example of first Vespasiano's letter query is, in SPARQL syntax (prefixes declaration is omitted):

```
SELECT ?authoritative-int ?text
WHERE { ?authoritative-int
                  hico:hasInterpretationCriterion
                  hico:authoritatively-based;
                  hico:hasInterpretationType :historical;
                  hico:isExtractedFrom ?expression .
                  ?expression c4o:hasContent ?text }
```

This query returns the URI of the interpretation act inferred as authoritative and its related text, i.e.: "NOTE 1.2 «Donato evidentemente prestava il suo latino a Vespasiano, quando questi doveva contrattare con i committenti delicate questioni relative alle dimensioni e al formato dei codici, alla tipologia dei caratteri da impiegare nella copia, ai costi delle trascrizioni e alle tariffe degli amanuensi. Puntuale e preciso il profilo dell'Acciaiuoli nelle Vite (p. 586 [II, 21]).»[17] "

7   Conclusions and Future Prospects

HiCO provides a complete scenario for describing the interpretative workflow need to represent cultural objects strictly related to their historical context.

Being a first step for defining a methodology, HiCO will have to be tested on other different use cases, in order to verify further implementations of the model. A particular attention will be given to the CIDOC-CRM model, and the FRBRoo extension. A future mapping between HiCO and these models will be provided, in order to guarantee the maximum dialogue and interoperability, under the work in progress Zeri e LODE project [8]. The aim is to create a broad network of assertions about cultural objects and to provide further connections among interpretations, ensuring their qualification and a correct provenance assertion as fundamentals steps for re-use such information in a wide Linked Data environment, allowing more defined and shareable inferences about them.

A future step will be in fact to enable more inferences, in order to establish authoritative interpretations with shareable criteria for other communities and providing thereby different use cases, also taking into account that logical inference cannot faithfully reproduce human's dialectical approach when choosing an assertion rather than another one, but can help in judgment through iterative qualification of interpretations.

References

1. Pitti, D.: Designing sustainable projects and publications. In: Schreibman, S., Siemens, R., Unsworth, J. (eds.) A Companion to Digital Humanities. Blackwell, Oxford (2004). http://www.digitalhumanities.org/companion/
2. Heath, T., Bizer, C.: Linked Data: Evolving the Web into a Global Data Space. Synthesis Lectures on the Semantic Web: Theory and Technology. Morgan & Claypool (2011)
3. Tomasi, F. (ed.): Vespasiano da Bisticci, Letters. CRR-MM, Bologna (2013). http://vespasianodabisticciletters.unibo.it

---

[17] http://vespasianodabisticciletters.unibo.it/lettere/lettera1.html

4. Pasin, M., Bradley, J.: Factoid-based prosopography and computer ontologies: Towards an integrated approach. Literary and Linguistic Computing (2013)
5. Daquino, M., Peroni, S., Tomasi, F., Vitali, F.: Political Roles Ontology (PRoles): Enhancing Archival Authority Records through Semantic Web Technologies. Procedia Computer Science **38**, 60–67 (2014)
6. Mazzini, S, Ricci, F.: EAC-CPF Ontology and Linked Archival Data. Semantic Digital Archives (SDA). In: Proc. of the 1st Int Workshop on Semantic Digital Archives (2011). http://ceur-ws.org/Vol-801/
7. IFLA Study Group on the Functional Requirements for Bibliographic Records: Functional Requirements for Bibliographic Records. In: IFLA Series on Bibliographic Control, 19. K.G. Saur Verlag, Munich (1998)
8. Gonano, C.M., Mambelli, F., Peroni, S., Tomasi, F., Vitali, F.: Zeri e LODE. Extracting the Zeri photo archive to Linked Open Data: formalizing the conceptual model, in: Digital Libraries (JCDL), IEEE, London (2014)

Track on European
and National Projects

Standardizing NDT& E Techniques and Conservation Metadata for Cultural Artifacts

Dimitris Kouis[1(✉)], Evgenia Vassilakaki[1], Eftichia Vraimaki[1],
Eleni Cheilakou[2], Amani Christiana Saint[2], Evangelos Sakkopoulos[3],
Emmanouil Viennas[3], Erion-Vasilis Pikoulis[3], Nikolaos Nodarakis[3],
Nick Achilleopoulos[3], Spiros Zervos[1], Giorgos Giannakopoulos[1],
Daphne Kyriaki-Manessi[1], Athanasios Tsakalidis[2], and Maria Koui[2]

[1] Department of Library Science and Information Systems,
Technological Educational Institute of Athens, Egaleo, Greece
{dkouis,evasilak,evraim,szervos,gian,dkmanessi}@teiath.gr
[2] Department of Materials Science and Engineering, NDT Lab, School of Chemical
Engineering, National Technical University of Athens, Athens, Greece
{elenheil,amani,markoue}@mail.ntua.gr, tsak@ceid.upatras.gr
[3] Graphics, Multimedia and GIS System Lab, Computer Engineering
and Informatics Department, University of Patras, 26504, Rio Patras, Greece
{sakkopul,biennas,pikoulis,achilleopoulos}@ceid.upatras.gr

Abstract. Conservation activities, before and after decay detection, are considered as a prerequisite for maintaining cultural artifacts in their initial/original form. Taking into account the strict regulations where sampling from art works of great historical value is restricted or in many cases prohibited, the application of Non-Destructive Testing techniques (NDTs) during the conservation or even decay detection is highly appreciated by conservators. Non-destructive examination include the employment of multiple analysis approaches and techniques namely Infrared Thermography (IRT), Ultrasonics (US), Ground Penetrating Radar (GPR), VIS–NIR Fiber Optics Diffuse Reflectance Spectroscopy (FORS), portable X-Ray Fluorescence (XRF), Environmental Scanning Electron Microscopy with Energy Dispersive X-Ray Analysis (ESEM-EDX), Attenuated Total Reflectance-Fourier Transform Infrared Spectroscopy (ATR-FTIR) and micro-Raman Spectroscopy. These produce a huge amount of data, in different formats, such as text, numerical sets and visual objects (i.e. images, thermograms, radargrams, spectral data, graphs, etc). Moreover, conservation documentation presents major drawbacks, as fragmentation and incomplete description of the related information is usually the case. Assigning conservation data to the objects' metadata collection is very rare and not yet standardized. The Doc-Culture Project aims to provide solutions for the NDT application methodologies, analysis and process along with their output data and all related conservation documentation. The preliminary results are discussed in this paper.

Keywords: Conservation · Cultural objects · Non-destructive testing techniques · CIDOC · Dublin core · Metadata · kNN classifier

© Springer International Publishing Switzerland 2015
E. Garoufallou et al. (Eds.): MTSR 2015, CCIS 544, pp. 439–450, 2015.
DOI: 10.1007/978-3-319-24129-6_38

1   Introduction

Conservation activities are considered as a prerequisite for maintaining cultural artifacts in their initial/original form [1]. On the other hand the use of NDT techniques is
highly appreciated by conservators for art works and monuments of great cultural
value, where strict regulations prohibit invasive testing during the conservation or
even decay detection [2, 3, 4]. Up to now, different teams of researchers, materials
and electronic engineers, conservators, etc, involved in the cultural heritage maintenance use NDT techniques in a non-standardized way, and consequently are unable to
exchange data and share knowledge. Also, these techniques usually produce a large
amount of data sets (typically a series of images, spectral data and graphs). Therefore,
it is imperative to work towards the management of the data output, in order to
achieve a comprehensive analysis from a single method and, if it is possible, to combine different sets of results from different methods. Finally, the output data (raw or
deriving from specific data process methods) should be integrated either with the
objects' metadata or incorporated in a decision support system.

This paper aims to present initial results on the research work done by the Doc-
Culture project[1]. Three research teams have collaborated, namely the NDT standardization team, the Computer Science and Image Processing research team and the
Information Science research team. Each research team focused on different aspects
of conserving museum artifacts, while the National Archeological Museum - NAM
(Athens, Greece) acted as the test-bed for the project's needs. This paper contributes
in providing a valuable insight into the way data derived from application of conservation techniques are handled along with cultural artifacts' basic documentation.

The paper is organized as follows. In section 2 an example of NDT standardization
process is depicted, using FORS & XRF methods. In section 3 an example of NDT
data output analysis is presented using the k-NN approach for FORS pattern recognition. In section 4, the metadata standards employed to host both the standardization
process and the output data are discussed whereas in section 5 an innovative Management Information System for NDTs is introduced, integrating all the components
(NDT standardization, output analysis tools and extended metadata schemes) occlu-
sions and future work are discussed. Final section presents conclusions and future
work to be done.

2   Non-destructive Testing Techniques Standardization

The overall objective of the NDT research team is the development and standardization of the appropriate NDT application methodologies on specific cultural objects
categories for the materials characterization/ evaluation, as well as the decay detection
and assessment of conservation-restoration interventions compatibility.

---

[1] Development of an integrated information environment for assessment and documentation
of conservation interventions to cultural works/objects with NDT&E techniques, for more
information see www.ndt-lab.gr/docculture

In this context, 82 cultural objects were selected from the NAM collection as well as from other archeological sites around Greece. These artifacts were classified into categories such as wall paintings, marble statues and figurines with or without existing traces of polychromy, copper based objects, golden objects and mosaics. Archeologists, conservators and material scientists collaborated in order to provide a complete metadata description with information like type, structural material, origin, dating, dimensions, preservation state, description / historical and archaeological data/ previous analyses / previous conservation-restoration interventions/ references etc..

For each one of the aforementioned object categories, an optimization and recording of the developed NDTs application methodologies was specified, taking into account certain restrictions. The example that follows describes the identification of coloring material (pigments) saved on marble statues using different NDT techniques.

Cultural Object under examination (GL-1827)

A. Type: Female statue, Structural material: Marble, **Origin:** Cyclades, Delos, House of the Lake**, Date:** Copy made in the 2nd c. BC of an original dating from about 300 BC, **Dimensions:** 1,75m height, **Preservation state:** Intact. Loses at the fingertips of the thumb and the index of the left arm. The tip of the nose... **Description / Historical and archaeological data:** ... (see Fig. 1)

Fig. 1. *In-situ* measurements on color traces saved on Object No GL 1827 (i.e. red color remains on the sandal)

B. NDT methods used

Portable X-Ray Fluorescence (XRF), **output**: X-Ray Fluorescence spectra (data file of energy data vs counts per second data) and Portable VIS-NIR Fiber Optics Diffuse Reflectance Spectroscopy (FORS), **output**: Diffuse reflectance spectra in the spectral range of 350-1000 nm (data file of wavelength (λ) data vs reflectance (R) data)

C. Restrictions

Micro-sampling was not allowed from the selected marble figurines and statues for a more detailed study by means of advanced laboratory methods (e.g. ESEM-EDX, ATR-FTIR, micro-Raman) and therefore, our optimized analytical methodology consists only of two steps (Steps 1 and 2) that combine the application of portable XRF and FORS techniques, as described below.

D. Standardization procedure: Following are the steps of the optimized NDTs application methodology for the identification of pigments saved on the selected marble figurines and statues category (with existing traces of polychromy).

- **Step 1 - XRF Analysis (method used for elemental analysis and chemical analysis, particularly in the investigation of metals, glass, ceramics and building materials):** XRF spectrum collected from a red spot saved on the sandal of the Object GL 1827 revealing high Ca and Fe contents. The identification of red ochre pigment in the form of Hematite (Fe_2O_3) and Calcite ($CaCO_3$) coming from the substrate (marble) is suggested. The high Pb content indicates the application of a white lead [$2PbCO_3.Pb(OH)_2$] surface preparation layer (substrate), in order to achieve a better adhesion to the upper color layers.
- **Step 2 - FORS Analysis (method used for the identification of pigments and for the analysis of color and its variation on paintings):** FORS spectra obtained from the red color traces saved on the sandal and hair of the statue (Object GL 1827) verifying the presence of red ochre in the form of Hematite (Fe_2O_3) as the main component of the pigment producing the red color.

3   NDT&E Techniques Output Data Analysis and Process

The overall objectives of the Computer Science and Image Processing research team are the development of a complete set of techniques and software tools for digital image analysis and processing of the NDT techniques output data, as well as the development of an Integrated Information Environment for the documentation of NDT processes and its implementation model. Digital image processing includes a variety of techniques, namely contrast increase/enhancement, histograms, re-coloring, advance annotation etc. On the other hand, the NDT output data processing includes mainly the implementation of algorithms for graphic pattern detection (detection of areas, patterns, colors etc.).

For example, a complete data management solution was developed, that combined a library of known reference pigments/colors of ancient objects, along with a proposed novel pattern matching technique. This technique allows for the automatic classification of any new pigment that is recovered from cultural objects based on FORS and/or XRF measurements, coupled possibly with input provided by the human analyst. To be more specific, the overall system consists of two standalone subsystems, whose goal is to estimate the correct label (class identifier) corresponding to a given feature vector or a template, based on prior knowledge obtained through training (supervised learning) [5, 6]. The aforementioned subsystems, namely the FORS-based and the XRF-based classifiers, work independently of each other and yield separate decisions. Then, in a second stage, the system combines one or both of the automatically generated recognitions, with possible input from the human analyst (that could be used to solidify or reject the automatic selection) and produces an overall decision (pigment).

3.1   The FORS-Based Classifier

The FORS-based subsystem constitutes basically a kNN classifier [7, 8] whose implementation can be divided into two major phases, namely the design phase, and the running phase. Although we initially experimented with various ML algorithms, the k-NN's performance is very satisfactory for the needs of the application at hand.

This fact, combined with the simplicity of k-NN, both in its design/ implementation phases, were the main reason for the aforementioned selections.

A brief description of the steps involved during the design phase, as well as an outline of the proposed algorithm that is executed during the running phase, is given in the following paragraphs.

Design Phase

The design phase of the system consists of the following steps:

— *Training & Validation data sets*: The training data set comprises the knowledge of the system regarding the different classes it is able of recognizing. For the specific system at hand, the training data set consists of 10 reference measurements from each of the pigments mentioned in Table1 (see below). The validation data set on the other hand, represents a sample of the future (unknown) measurements and can be used in order to estimate the system performance in real conditions. For this task, we selected measurements taken form from real cultural objects (with known pigment content) and we used them in the final design stage for the evaluation of system performance and the selection of its parameters.

— *Preprocessing*. We have designed a preprocessing procedure, tailored to the specific needs of the FORS measurements, with the goal of data enhancement. More specifically, in the preprocessing step the linear trends that are present in many FORS measurements and obscure their true class-dependent characteristics, are removed through linear regression, and the resulting measurements are then normalized.

- *Specification of system parameters*: We have conducted a series of experiments using the validation data set, with the goal of maximizing system performance, with respect to the following degrees of freedom: (i) Number of patterns per class (pigment), (ii) value of k and (iii) employed Distance Function.

Table 1. Pigment Library automatically detected using FORS method

Class ID	Pigment	Class ID	Pigment
Red Color			
1	Caput mortum	9	Malachite
2	Hematite	Brown Color	
3	Minium	10	Sienna Raw
4	Red ochre	11	Umber Burnt
Yellow Color		Blue Color	
5	Sienna Burnt	12	Azurite
6	Yellow Ochre	13	Egyptian Blue
7	Massicot	14	Ultramarine
Green Color		15	Indigo
8	Green Earth		

Algorithm.

Input: FORS measurement array of unknown class (pigment).

The steps that are executed during the running phase are the following:

1. *Preprocessing*: apply the same procedure used for training data.
2. *Calculate distances* of input template form the patterns of the training data set.

3. *Sort* the resulting array of distance values.
4. *Count* the memberships of each class in the first k labels of the sorted distance array.
5. *Assign* the class with the highest membership to the input template.

3.2   The XRF-Based Classifier

The automatic characterization of the XRF measurements constitutes a feature-based system, meaning that the classification procedure depends on the successful extraction and identification of class-specific features. Similarly to the FORS-based subsystem, the implementation of the XRF classifier is divided into the design phase, and the running phase.

- *Training & Validation*: For the collection of the training and validation data sets is a procedure identical to the one followed for the kNN classifier, was adopted. Contrary to the kNN classifier however, here the training measurements are used in order to guide the feature selection step in the system design phase, and the way they are used when the decision made, but the data themselves are not used in the latter phase.
- *Preprocessing*. The preprocessing was focused on the enhancement of the original measurements with respect to two aspects, namely, a)the smoothing (i.e. denoising of the curve) and b) the elimination of the baseline drift [9] that is present in many measurements.
- *Feature Selection*: As it is to be expected, in the case of XRF measurements, the aforementioned features are related to the element-indicative characteristic peaks of the XRF spectrum. More specifically, the feature set upon the classification is made consists of the most significant peaks of the spectrum, ordered with respect to the area below each peak (i.e. the integral of the spectrum in the interval occupied by the peak).
- *Specification of system parameters*: The impact of the following design aspects was examined, with the help of the validation data set:
  - o Peak identification procedure.
  - o Number of the significant peaks that the decision will be based on.
  - o Ordering and normalization of peaks.

Algorithm
1. *Peak Identification.* Every identified peak constitutes a quadruplet of values, namely the two endpoints of the interval it occupies in the spectrum, the position it attains its maximum, as well as the maximum value itself.
2. *Area Estimation.* For each of the identified peaks, we use a well-known method of numerical integration (namely the trapezoidal one) for the approximation of the measurements integral within the endpoints of the peak interval.
3. *Order* the identified peaks with respect to their estimated areas, excluding pigment-irrelevant elements such as Ca, which is mostly due to substrate materials and not due to the used pigment.

4. *Peak assignment (or labeling)*. With the help of a lookup table specifying the position of every known element in the XRF spectrum, label each identified peak, with respect to the position of its maximum, i.e. assign the peak to a chemical element.

5. *Selection* of the top K most significant elements, (where K equals usually 2-3), based on the ordered set of the significant peaks.

6. *Pigment recognition*. Decide on the used pigment by comparing the ordered set of elements provided in the previous step to the expected set of elements for each of the considered pigments (determined in the design phase). The latter sets are provided by the human analysts during the design phase. It is important to be stressed here that, since the chemical fingerprint (or at least its most significant elements) does not uniquely define a pigment, the reached decision is specific to the point that the identified allow for it (e.g. Fe is characteristic element of both red and yellow ochre). In many cases, the recognition provided by the XRF system specifies a whole family of pigments (e.g. the Fe-based ones) rather than a unique pigment.

The experimental evaluation results of the proposed techniques showed that data management is both effective and efficient. The obtained results are indeed very favorable, thus encouraging the exploration of other similar approaches within the NDT framework. Initial feedback from the proposed system is promising because it would allow automation and thus a radical decrease of time for pigment/color matching and provoke further critical restoration actions. In this direction a feedback step was incorporated in the implemented k-NN classifier, so that its training data set can be constantly updated with new measurements (entered by the user) so that it can best adapt to the nature of the encountered environment.

Finally, we are currently experimenting with a more elaborated, Bayesian-like classifier, where the decision for the correct label of the measurement is based on the likelihood of a pre-selected, class-dependent set of features being present. Such features include e.g. the maximum and minimum positions, the rate of steepest slope, the curvature in specific intervals, etc.

4   The Metadata Scheme Outline

The vast information produced during the conservation procedures is crucial for further documenting the cultural artifact and successfully applying any future conservation interventions. A domain model was developed to accommodate both information referring to the cultural artifact itself, as well as the various conservation related techniques employed (see Fig. 2). Specifically, five main entities were identified [7]:

1. Object defined as the cultural artifact and comprises a series of relevant properties that describe the object.

2. *Conservation* defined as an "event". It entails a series of relevant elements defining time, duration, type of event and description. Type of conservation comprises a property that is describing the technique used and it is perceived in the domain model as a property of conservation.

3. The entity **Measurement** is defined as an "event". It entails a series of relevant elements defining time, main body of responsibility, type of event and description. Type of measurement comprises a property that is describing "sampling" and it is perceived in the domain model as a "property" of measurements.

4. **Equipment**, defined as a physical object that comprises a number of properties describing the equipment utilized for conservation and measurement actions

5. **Digital documentation** is an entity linked to all the others, as it refers to depicting both any digital representation of the cultural object as well as any digital documentation, imagery or dataset produced throughout the course of conservation and measurement actions.

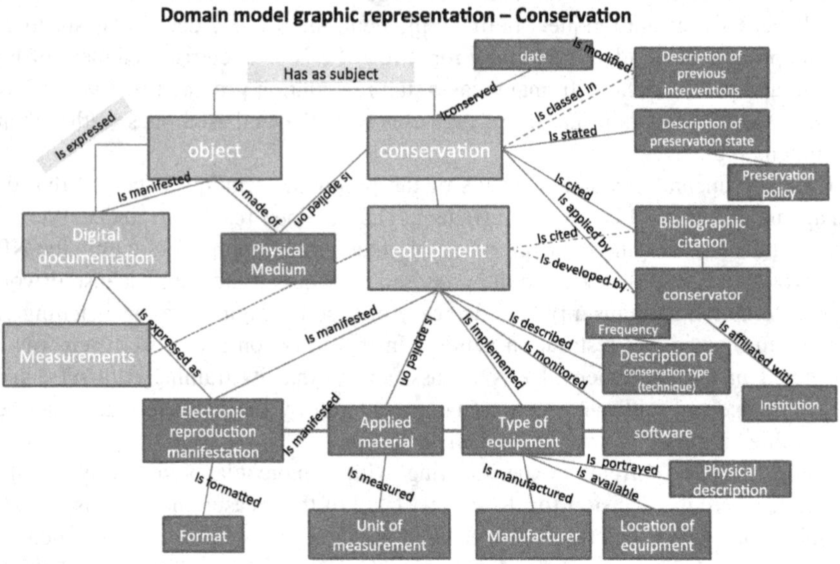

Fig. 2. Domain model graphic representation – conservation

Two well-known metadata standards were used to define the properties of the aforementioned entities. In particular, Dublin Core Metadata Initiate (DCMI) and CIDOC Conceptual Reference Model (CRM) were adopted. Both standards (CIDOC CRM and DCMI) are international, well-established and adopted from various Information Organizations for handling cultural information and allow either the incorporation of extensions on the basic structure of the model (i.e. CIDOC CRM) or provide the ability to employ elements from other standards, in order to address the specific information needs of both objects and processes (i.e. DCMI). However, the artifact collections of every museum are unique and thus require special treatment. The same applies for the conservation procedures these cultural artifacts undergo. CIDOC CRM and DCMI provide a variety of different elements and sub-elements and thus address the majority of the documentation needs of each cultural artifact and a large portion of the conservation process [10, 11].

Nonetheless, there was still information regarding both the cultural artifact and the conservation intervention that needed to be considered. Two new CIDOC-CRM extensions are identified under the sub-classes *E7: Activity* and *E4: Period* in terms of describing the conservation process performed on cultural artifacts. The proposed extensions are *E94: Conservation activity* is assigned to the *E7: Activity* to describe in detail the process of conservation and *E95: Frequency* is identified under the *E4: Period* to further describe the frequency of the time span [12, 13].

In the context of formulating "application profiles" and employing different specialized vocabularies, four additional to DC metadata standards namely Metadata Object Description Schema (MODS), Resource Description and Access (RDA), PREMIS and Muse Meta were adopted (see Table 2).

Table 2. Additional to DCMI standards adopted

Standard	Element	Scope Note
RDA	placeOfOriginOfTheResource	Relates a work to the country or other territorial jurisdiction from which a work originated
RDA	has affiliation	Relates a person to a group with which a person is affiliated or has been affiliated through employment, membership, cultural identity
RDA	appliedMaterial	Related a resource to a physical or chemical substance applied to a base material of a resource
RDA	productionStatement	A statement identifying the place or places of production, producer or producers, and date or dates of production of a resource in an unpublished form
MODS	location	Identifies the organization holding the resource or from which access is obtained
Meta Muse	unitMeasurement	A measurement standard; e.g., metric
PREMIS	fixity	Information used to verify whether an object has been altered in an undocumented or unauthorized way. Validates the authenticity or integrity of the Content Information: for example, a check sum, a digital signature, or a digital watermark. (Fixity Information)

5   Management Information System for NDTs

In this section, we present and describe an innovative information system for Cultural Heritage Management (CH), with support for NDTs output data. It is built upon open source technologies such as Apache, MySQL, JavaScript, PHP. The benefit in building upon such open platforms is their modular architecture and wide choices for extensions development and deployment for any data centric service that additional functional specifications are required or may be needed in the future by experts/archaeologists and conservators.

The User Interface has been designed with a responsive HTML template, such that its Graphical User Interface (GUI) is user-friendly and the functionality is efficiently adapted to the screen of the device each time (especially for small screens such as tablets and smartphones). In this point, we stress out that all data and metadata produced or stored in the management information system can be public or private.

The core subsystems are: Image Processing - Numerical Analysis - Metadata Management - Image Annotation - Documentation Management. Similar efforts that include all these functionalities and support NDTs output data process are limited [16].

The Image Processing Subsystem is used to allow the application of filters on images of cultural objects. Currently lots of types of filters are available and there can be added more if needed, e.g. the grayscale and the color analysis. For example a filter, when applied, produces a new image that displays the color composition of the original one and assists conservators to take the right decisions related to future conservations.

Numerical Analysis provides functions for the manipulation and final identification of previous conservation processes (such as FORS or XRF NDT techniques) that have been applied to a cultural object. Moreover, it can detect possible lesions on the surface of the cultural object and propose a suitable NDT method for its restoration. To achieve this, the conservator provides the measurement results that contain the output of an NDT method (e.g. Infrared Thermography, XRF, FORS, etc.). Next, the file is given as input to an algorithm that decides to which class of known colors the measurement belongs. The color class is decided/ chosen with a certainty percentage and then it is up to the conservator to make further decisions.

The numerical analysis service enables the researcher to analyze and visualize (see Fig. 3a) the measurement result into a diagram in order to further detect colors of pigment under review. The system keeps an archive record of all previous analyses that follow the particular cultural item under research for its lifetime within the system.

The metadata framework adopted is in essence an extension to the basic Dublin Core metadata standard. In other words, for each column of a content type in the database there exists a respective metadata element.

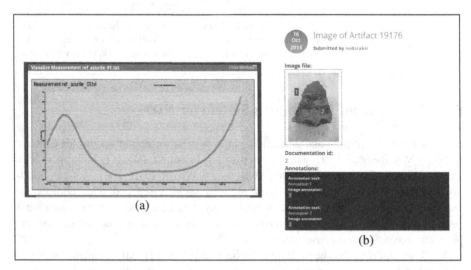

Fig. 3. (a) Visualization of measurement, (b) annotations of a cultural item image online

The Image Annotation subsystem (see Fig. 3b) enables an expert to add annotation marks or areas to an image together with respective information pertaining previous conservations. The conservator may add a marker with a number on an image via drag and drop and add clarifications, conditions and guidelines as well as description that are related to the position of the marker on the image.

Documentation Management functionality implements the metadata scheme as well as the documentation process for conservationists.

6   Conclusions – Future Work

Strict regulations when comes to cultural object conservation (and examination) makes the application of Non-Destructive Testing techniques (NDTs) very important. Non-destructive examination includes the employment of multiple analysis approaches and techniques with different methods of application for each category of object. The standardization of the followed process, when one method is applied or more than one are combined together, is absolutely necessary. Moreover the a huge amount of data, in different formats, produced during NDT&E application request both for advanced techniques of analysis and documentation. This paper aimed to provide initial results for the NDT application methodologies, analysis and process along with their output data and all related conservation documentation.

By the end of the project, all methodologies, tools, the management information system, as well as the metadata schemes extension will be available to the scientific community for use and further development.

Acknowledgements. Acknowledgements are attributed to the Doc-Culture research project entitled "Development of an Integrated Information Environment for assessment and documentation of conservation interventions to cultural works/objects with Non Destructive Techniques (NDTs)", which is coordinated and managed by NTUA. MIS: 379472. The 3-year project began in April 2012 and is co-financed by the European Union (European Social Fund – ESF) and Greek national funds through the Operational Program "Education and Lifelong Learning" of the National Strategic Reference Framework (NSRF) - Research Funding Program: THALES.

References

1. Walston, S.: The Preservation and Conservation of Aboriginal and Pacific Cultural Material in Australian Museums. ICCM Bulletin **4**(4), 9–21 (1978)
2. Arinat, M., Shiyyab, A., Abd-Allah, R.: Byzantine glass mosaics excavated from the Cross Church, Jerash, Jordan: an archaeometrical investigation. Mediterranean Archaeology and Archaeometry **14**(2), 43–53 (2014)
3. Del Federico, E., Blümich, B., Chiari, G., Kehlet, C., Haber, A., Zia, W., Quang, S., Manzano, C.G.: Non-destructive multi-analytical investigation of roman mosaics at herculaneum. In: 5th Int. Conference on Synchrotron Radiation in Art and Archaeology (SR2A), New York, Unites States (2012)

4. Cheilakou, E., Troullinos, M., Koui, M.: Identification of pigments on Byzantine wall paintings from Crete (14th century AD) using non-invasive Fiber Optics Diffuse Reflectance Spectroscopy (FORS). Journal of Archaeological Science **41**, 541–555 (2014)
5. Cheilakou, E., Dritsa, V., Saint, A., Theodorakeas, P., Koui, M., Kostanti, K., Christopoulou, A.: Non-invasive identification of pigments on mycenaean wallpaintings (14th -12th century BC) from the archaeological sites of mycenae and tiryns, peloponnese. In: Proc. the 9th International Symposium on the Conservation of Monuments in the Mediterranean Basin, Ankara, Turkey (2014). (in press)
6. Saint, A.C., Cheilakou, E., Dritsa, V., Koui, M., Kostanti, K., Christopoulou, A.: The combined use of XRF and VIS-NIR FORS spectroscopic techniques for the non-invasive identification of pigments on archaeological works of art. Technart 2015- No-destructive and microanalytical techniques in art and cultural heritage, Catania, Italy (in press, 2015)
7. Polikar, R.: Pattern Recognition, σε Wiley Encyclopedia of Biomedical Engineering. John Wiley & Sons (2006)
8. Jain, A.K., Duin, R.P.W., Mao, J.: Statistical Pattern Recognition: a review. IEEE Transactions on Pattern Analysis and Machine Intelligence **22**, 4–37 (2000)
9. Bishop, C.: Pattern Recognition and Machine Learning. Springer (2006)
10. Duda, R., Hart, P., Stork, D.: Pattern Classification, 2nd Edition. Wiley (2000)
11. Zhu, F., Qin, B., Feng, W., Wang, H., Huang, S., Lv, Y., Chen, Y.: Reducing Poisson noise and baseline drift in X-ray spectral images with bootstrap Poisson regression and robust nonparametric regression **58**, 1739-1758 (2013). doi:10.1088/0031-9155/58/6/1739
12. Kyriaki-Manessi, D., Zervos, S., Giannakopoulos, G.: D4.2.1. identification of extension points to CIDOC- CRM. In: DOC-CULTURE, Thalis- Development of an integrated information environment for assessment and documentation of conservaiton interventions to cultural works/ objects with non-destructive techniques, Athens (2013)
13. Kouis, D., Giannakopoulos, G.: Incorporate cultural artifacts conservation documentation to information exchange standards- the DOC-CULTURE case. In: Proceedings of the 3rd International Conference on Integrated Information, Prague, Czech Republic, September 5–9, 2013
14. Kouis, D., Kyriaki-Manesi, D., Zervos, S., Giannakopoulos, G., Cheilakou, E., Koui, M.: Integrating non destructive testing techniques data for cultural heritage monuments to cidoc conceptual reference model. In: The 9th International Symposium on the Conservation of Monuments in the Mediterranean Basin, Ankara, Turkey, June 3–5, 2014
15. Vassilakaki, E., Kyriaki-Manessi, D., Zervos, S., Giannakopoulos, G.: CIDOCCRM extensions for conservation processes: a methodological approach. In: Sakkas, D. (ed.) 4th international Conference on Integrated Information, Madrid, Spain, September 5–8, 2014
16. Amat, A., Miliani, C., Brunetti, B.G.: Non-invasive multi-technique investigation of artworks: A new tool for on-the-spot data documentation and analysis. Journal of Cultural Heritage **14**(1), 23–30 (2013)

Poster Papers

ALIADA, an Open Source Tool for Automatic Publication of Linked Data from Libraries and Museums

Cristina Gareta[✉]

ALIADA Project Consortium, Vitoria-Gasteiz, Spain
cgareta@scanbit.net
ALIADA Project Consortium, Rome, Italy
ALIADA Project Consortium, Budapest, Hungary

Abstract. ALIADA, Spanish word that means 'ally', is intended to be a tool to help librarians and curators from cultural heritage institutions to automatically publish their high quality data in the Linked Data Cloud. Traditionally, data from libraries and museums have been stored as 'silos' of information because their metadata are codified using their own schemes and formats, not accessible by machines and applications more general public-focused. In addition, these information professionals create rich data from their collections, but they are not expert enough to face the coming technologies required to take advantage of the opportunities that the information and open knowledge era provides. To overcome these limitations, ALIADA EC-funded Project has developed an open source tool compliant with libraries and museums standards that automatically converts library and museum metadata into structured data ready to be published in the Linked Data Cloud, according to the Linked Data paradigm. Thus, heritage and cultural data are also open and available to be queried and reused by machines, innovative applications, search engines and other cultural and research institutions to generate more open knowledge.

Keywords: Libraries · Museums · Linked data · Semantic web · Open data

1   Introduction

Memory institutions or GLAM (Galleries, Libraries, Archives and Museums) have to face the challenge of opening their data in the era of the open knowledge society. They preserve cultural heritage and provide universal access to information about it to people, communities and organizations. These institutions generate high quality local information particularly interesting to the web community because often it is not accessible by web search engines and, therefore, it is not open to the world. This is because institutions such as museums and libraries have their own data codification standards. As services of public bodies, they should publish their datasets as "linked data" to enrich the web and to be reused to create new knowledge, to help other cultural institutions to be more efficient or to contribute to innovative applications.

In this context, ALIADA Project is an European Commission-funded project that aims to develop an open source tool to be the "ally" (that is the translation in Spanish)

© Springer International Publishing Switzerland 2015
E. Garoufallou et al. (Eds.): MTSR 2015, CCIS 544, pp. 453–456, 2015.
DOI: 10.1007/978-3-319-24129-6_39

for non-expert users, such as librarians and museum curators, in the publication of their datasets in the Linked Open Data Cloud. This tool is intended to be multilingual and suitable to integrate in existing library and museum systems to overcome the limitations of those systems. ALIADA tool supports the current standards for cataloguing bibliographic and authority records in libraries (MARC, Dublin Core) and collections and objects in museums (LIDO). Also the standards for the Semantic web technologies are used in this tool: RDF, URI, OWL, HTTP or SPARQL.

The project was promoted by IT companies experts in library software (Scanbit, in Spain, and @Cult, in Italy), art museums (Artium, in Spain, and Museum of Fine Arts Budapest) and a research agency expert in Semantic web technologies (Tecnalia). ALIADA was born as a two-year project and it is expected to be finished in October 2015. After the first year of project, ALIADA Consortium has launched the first prototype which is available for downloading on GitHub and on ALIADA website [1].

2   Project Goal and Objectives

Linked data (often capitalized as Linked Data) is a method for exposing, sharing, and connecting pieces of data, information, and knowledge on the Semantic Web using URIs and RDF[2]. To help libraries and museums to publish their data as "linked open data" (linked data that is open content), ALIADA project[3] aims to provide an open source tool compliant with the library and museums' data management systems and with the Linked Data Cloud[4] rules and standards. According to that goal, the following are the main objectives that guided the development of this innovative tool:

- Automatic publication in the Linked Open Data Cloud (LODC) of data generated by libraries and museums. Input data are descriptions of cultural and heritage collections stored and maintained by public institutions. Metadata schemes used for cataloguing those documents and objects are specific for libraries and museums (MARC, LIDO)
- Development of a Java-based web application to integrate with library and museum management systems, as a plugin or as an external tool supporting their metadata schema and file formats
- ALIADA will be a non-expert user oriented application. Librarians and curators are experts in cultural information and heritage management, but they don't know about the Linked Open Data technology. Therefore, usability will be a key aspect.
- Open data requires open source code. It's expected the creation of a community of developers and users around the ALIADA open source tool. Target users are libraries, museums, research agencies, IT SMEs and developers.
- As European project, ALIADA will be multilingual. Initially, it will support English, Spanish, Italian and Hungarian languages.

---

[1] http://aliada-project.eu

[2] http://linkeddata.org/

[3] http://cordis.europa.eu/project/rcn/110907_en.html

3 ALIADA, a Linked Data Publisher for Libraries and Museums

ALIADA was designed following the requirements provided from every role represented in the project: cultural heritage institutions (art libraries and museums), library systems developers, consultants on library software and services and experts in Semantic Web technology. The primary motivation for the project was the similar challenge that libraries and museums have opening their collections as linked open data. Libraries and museums should walk together to integrate their data with the web. However, the implementation of linked data technology in these cultural heritage institutions according the W3C Semantic Web standards is not so easy because of the specific and complex standards used by these institutions for describing and cataloguing library and museums' collections.

ALIADA is a non-expert user oriented web application supporting the entire cycle of publication of library and museum metadata in the Linked Data Cloud (LDC). So, the main elements of ALIADA are:

- the user interface, to allow the selection and validation of input metadata files coming from the library or museum management system. ALIADA supports MARC21, Dublin Core and LIDO metadata schemes and XML as file type
- the metadata-to-RDF-Converter ('RDFizer') and the RDF triple store (SPARQL endpoint)
- the linking, to link the own data to external datasets (DBpedia, VIAF, Europeana, …), and the URI creation
- the CKAN publisher and the Linked Data Server

In addition to the application, ALIADA includes its own ontology that seeks to become an standard in the "GLAM"[5] industry. The ALIADA ontology is mainly based on the CIDOC-CRM and FRBR conceptual models for museums and libraries, but it also includes other ontologies and vocabularies in the same domain but more popular and used in the Semantic web, such as FoaF (Friend of a Friend, ontology describing persons, their activities and their relations to other people and objects), SKOS (Simple Knowledge Organization System, a W3C recommendation designed for representation of thesauri, classification schemes, taxonomies, subject-heading systems, or any other type of structured controlled vocabulary) or WGS84 (RDF vocabulary for describing the location of resources). The well-known consultant on library technologies Karen Koyle already wrote about the FRBRoo ontology in her blog[6]. The FRBRoo is a formal ontology intended to capture and represent the underlying semantics of bibliographic information and to facilitate the integration, mediation, and interchange of bibliographic and museum information. ALIADA is based on this ontology.

---

[5] Galleries, Libraries, Archives and Museums
[6] http://kcoyle.blogspot.com.es/2006/11/frbroo-object-oriented.html

4   Results

The second prototype of ALIADA is already finished and it's available for download-ing from the project website[7]. The final release is expected in October 2015. During the project development, the source code is maintained and updated on GitHub by the ALIADA Consortium, but then it's expected to create a developers community around the open source code.

The most important problems facing the project were related to the system require-ments, the performance, the conversion of the bibliographic entities and relationships to RDF according to the selected ontologies and the usability of the user interface.

After releasing the second prototype it has been possible to assess and measure the impact of the tool among not only the GLAM community, but also the Semantic Web community. The feedback from this assessment will be used to improve the tool to meet the needs of the target users and institutions.

The GLAM community fully understands the challenge of liberating cultural institutions from their current data silos and integrating library and museum data onto the Seman-tic Web. But they don't know how to do it and how to take advantage of it. In this context, the open source ALIADA for automatically publish library and museum linked data emerges as an alternative and simple open source solution for the cultural institutions that are looking for creating Linked Open Data themselves.

Now, next questions are what data should be published as linked data, what license will be used and how to exploit the exposed datasets.

References

1. Linked data. Wikipedia. http://en.wikipedia.org/wiki/Linked_data
2. GLAM (industry sector). Wikipedia. https://en.wikipedia.org/wiki/GLAM_%28industry_sector%29
3. International Federation of Library Associations and Institutions (IFLA): Functional requirements for bibliographic records (2008). http://www.ifla.org/files/assets/cataloguing/frbr/frbr_2008.pdf
4. International Council of Museums (ICOM): Definition of the CIDOC Conceptual Reference Model (2015). http://www.cidoc-crm.org/docs/cidoc_crm_version_6.0.pdf
5. Coyle, K.: FRBRoo (Object-Oriented). Coyle's Information Blog, November 05, 2006. http://kcoyle.blogspot.com.es/2006/11/frbroo-object-oriented.html
6. Schilling, V.: Transforming library metadata into linked library data. American Library Association (ALA) (2015). http://www.ala.org/alcts/resources/org/cat/research/linked-data

---

[7] http://aliada-project.eu

Resource Classification as the Basis for a Visualization Pipeline in LOD Scenarios

Oscar Peña[(✉)], Unai Aguilera, and Diego López-de-Ipiña

Deusto Institute of Technology - DeustoTech, University of Deusto,
Avda. Universidades 24, 48007 Bilbao, Spain
oscar.pena@deusto.es

Abstract. After more than a decade since the first steps on the Semantic Web were set, mass adoption of these technologies is still an utopic goal. Machine-readable data should leverage to provide smarter summarisations of any dataset, making them comprehensible for any user, without the need for specific knowledge. The automatic generation of coherent visual representations based on Linked Open Data could stand for mass adoption of the Semantic Web's vision.

Our effort towards this goal is to establish a visualization pipeline, from raw semantically annotated data as input, to insightful visualizations for data analysts as output. The first steps of this pipeline need to extract the nature of the data itself through generic SPARQL queries in order to draft the structure of the data for further stages.

1 Introduction

Open Data-friendly policies are encouraging different actors to make their data available under open licenses, allowing them to be processed, merged, mixed and analysed by third parties in innovative processes that lead to understanding and gaining knowledge of the surrounding area. The *Linked Data* (LD) principles introduced by Tim Berners-Lee [2] provide great opportunities for public publishing, especially when data is ranked as 4 or 5 stars[1].

However, reality hits hard to those still expectant to see a full-extended Web 3.0 usage. Works such as [3,5] address the status of LD adoption on different points in time, throwing out some ideas and desired features to eventually reach a widespread use from Internet users.

Our proposal for inverting this situation relies on the definition of a visualization pipeline, which eases the path of understanding new datasets with data analysis in mind. John W. Tukey proposed *Exploratory Data Analysis* (EDA) [10] as a way to deal with new information combining basic statistical analysis with graphical representations, taking the datasets as they are and not trying to fit them in a model. This *data-driven* approach lacks the rigour of more formal methodologies, but adopts a more natural, suggestive and insightful approach based on the discoveries about the data (fostering the *"follow your nose"* principles [11]), without pre-established assumptions and loss of information due to variable selection.

---

[1] http://www.w3.org/DesignIssues/LinkedData.html

© Springer International Publishing Switzerland 2015
E. Garoufallou et al. (Eds.): MTSR 2015, CCIS 544, pp. 457–460, 2015.
DOI: 10.1007/978-3-319-24129-6_40

2   Resource Classification

2.1   Metadata Based Statistics

As outlined by the *Visualization Mantra* [9], the **Overview** task is understood as a broad view of the data, a high-level zoom where little details are exposed.

Despite Shneiderman's intention with the first visualization task, different authors have adapted this stage to their purposes. [1, 7] implement the *Overview* stage as a collection of statistical metrics performed on top of a SPARQL endpoint, e.g., number of classes, properties, in/out-degree, instances, etc. [4, 6] take the same metrics, and generate simple graphics to display the values.

Our metadata extraction approach tries to infer how each resource is structured, performing generic queries against the available SPARQL endpoint. This inference is based on how each property is used within a dataset, measuring it as *property usage* $= \frac{cs}{ci}$, where cs is the number of unique class instances acting as subjects in those triples actually making use of the property, and ci being the total number of instance objects for that class. This metric shows a naïve assumption when evaluating relevant properties: the more instances making use of the property, the more important it is to define the class.

We also implement what we call as the *completeness ratio* (cr), calculated as $cr = \frac{pi}{ci}$, in which pi is the number of values assigned to the given property within the class. This ratio summarises the interpretation users make of the property from their values, e.g., if $cr = 1$ for *foaf:name* it means that each *Person* instance **should** have a defined name-value, but when $cr \neq 1$, it could indicate either that the property is not compulsory for every instance ($cr < 1$); or that multiple values are available ($cr > 1$), i.e., *foaf:nick* triples.

2.2   Primitive Datatype Inference

In order to apply any preprocessing, statistical or visualization technique, we need to know which is the nature or format of those data items. The term "*datatype*" could be misleading depending on the background of the reader. In computer science, a datatype outlines the manner a variable should be interpreted, how is implemented, encoded and stored in the system, what operations allows, its meaning and the value ranges for the observation [8].

For our datatype classification purposes, we will use the following categories, referring to them as "*primitive datatypes*" (note that this groups are intended to be conceptual and programming-language agnostic):

- **Integer:** Composed by the finite computer representable subset of whole numbers, such as the height of a person in centimetres, or the number of wheels in a given vehicle. Negative values are permitted.
- **Float:** The representation of any real number, as the height of a person in metres. Negative values are permitted.
- **Boolean:** A value meaning a logical truth, such as "*true/false*", "*0/1*", "*yes/no*" pairs of values.

- **IRI:** Internationalised Resource Identifiers are a standard defined upon the URI scheme, formed by any Unicode character sequence which uniquely identifies any resource over the Internet. IRIs are especially relevant in the SW, as they constitute one of its core components, making resources to be linkable and discoverable between them.
- **String:** Defined as any sequence of characters, they are understood as a superset covering the rest. In fact, many values in LD are typed as plain strings (*xsd:string*, *rdfs:Literal*, etc.), without any more concrete "^^*xsd:datatype*" defined for the object's values or the property's *rdfs:range*.
- **Datetime component:** A part of either a date, a time or both, expressed in any standardised format (preferably following ISO 8601's directives).
- **Geographical component:** Any geographical dimension which could help locating a resource in space, e.g., a pair of *latitude-longitude* coordinates and its projection system, a geographical feature or point, etc.
- **Categorical data:** Marking a property as *categorical* means that the range of used values is limited or within a certain range, which enables new visualizations to represent the property, e.g., histograms which display the instance count per occurrence, value distribution or usage.

3 Evaluation

In order to validate the first steps in our LOD visualization pipeline, we conducted an evaluation of the primitive datatype inference task. We run the inference algorithm on five datasets covering diverse topics and available through their respective SPARQL endpoints. In total, 190 ontology properties were evaluated (149 of them unique). For each property, the datatype was inferred from a randomised sample of actual values (the reason for the randomisation is to avoid always taking the first instances of a given property).

After running the algorithm through all the properties, we compared the results to those tagged by a group of 6 experts in computer science with knowledge in semantics and LOD. To reach a general consensus on the datatypes, they were presented about 10 random values extracted for each property, and an agreement of at least 80% was needed to relate the datatype to the property. The results of the algorithm's prediction against the expert-tagged corpus is shown in Table 1. We also include the number of detected categorical datatypes.

Table 1. Dataset primitive datatype inference results

Dataset	TP	TN	FP	FN	Categories	Correct	Incorrect
Air quality	17	160	2	10	5	93.65%	6.35%
Restaurants	17	201	3	17	5	91.6%	8.4%
Historical sites	14	165	4	13	3	91.33%	8.67%
MORElab	56	399	15	13	12	94.2%	5.8%
Teseo	22	162	4	1	3	97.35%	2.65%

4   Conclusions and Future Work

The presented results show a promising approach in the first steps towards visualising LOD, addressing some common pitfalls when datasets are automatically generated: missing property datatypes and ranges, data redundancy (same values encoded using different properties and ontologies) and the predominance of values typed as plain, literal strings.

The next stage in the pipeline is to generate *Entity Visualization Templates*, where all the metrics and structure extracted from the work presented in this paper is combined with visualization best practices and property relevance statistics in order to recommend the most fitting visualizations for the analysed resources, with no prior knowledge about the dataset required.

Acknowledgments. The research activities described in this paper are funded by the Basque Government's Universities and Research department, under grant *PRE_2014_2_298*.

References

1. Auer, S., Demter, J., Martin, M., Lehmann, J.: LODStats – an extensible framework for high-performance dataset analytics. In: ten Teije, A., Völker, J., Handschuh, S., Stuckenschmidt, H., d'Acquin, M., Nikolov, A., Aussenac-Gilles, N., Hernandez, N. (eds.) EKAW 2012. LNCS, vol. 7603, pp. 353–362. Springer, Heidelberg (2012)
2. Berners-Lee, T., Hendler, J., Lassila, O.: The semantic web. Scientific American **284**(5), 28–37 (2001)
3. Bizer, C., Heath, T., Berners-Lee, T.: Linked Data - The Story So Far. International Journal on Semantic Web and Information Systems **5**(3), 1–22 (2009)
4. Brunetti, J.M., Auer, S., García, R., Klímek, J., Nečaský, M.: Formal linked data visualization model. In: Proceedings of International Conference on Information Integration and Web-based Applications & Services, IIWAS 2013, pp. 309–318. ACM, New York (2013)
5. Heath, T.: How Will We Interact with the Web of Data? IEEE Internet Computing **12**(5), 88–91 (2008)
6. Klímek, J., Helmich, J., Neíaský, M.: Application of the Linked Data Visualization Model on Real World Data from the Czech LOD Cloud (2014)
7. Langegger, A., Woss, W.: RDFStats - an extensible RDF statistics generator and library. In: 20th International Workshop on Database and Expert Systems Application, DEXA 2009, pp. 79–83, August 2009
8. Parnas, D.L., Shore, J.E., Weiss, D.: Abstract types defined as classes of variables. In: Proceedings of the 1976 Conference on Data : Abstraction, Definition and Structure, pp. 149–154. ACM, New York (1976)
9. Shneiderman, B.: The eyes have it: a task by data type taxonomy for information visualizations. In: Proceedings of the IEEE Symposium on Visual Languages, 1996, pp. 336–343, September 1996
10. Tukey, J.W.: Exploratory Data Analysis. Pearson, Reading (1977)
11. Yu, L.: Follow your nose: a basic semantic web agent. In: A Developer's Guide to the Semantic Web, pp. 533–557. Springer, Heidelberg, January 2011

Author Index

Printed in the United States
By Bookmasters